THE
FINE ART
OF MURDER

THE
FINE ART
OF MURDER

The Mystery Reader's Indispensable Companion

Edited by

Ed Gorman

Martin H. Greenberg

Larry Segriff

with

Jon L. Breen

Galahad Books · New York

First Galahad Books edition published in 1995.

Galahad Books
A division of Budget Book Service, Inc.
386 Park Avenue South
New York, NY 10016

Galahad Books is a registered trademark of Budget Book Service, Inc.

Published by arrangement with Carroll & Graf Publishers, Inc.

Library of Congress Catalog Card Number: 95-79145

ISBN: 0-88365-910-7

Printed in the United States of America.

CONTENTS

THE BLACK DETECTIVE

RELIGIOUS MYSTERIES

PRIVATE EYE MYSTERIES

GAY MYSTERIES

BRITISH MYSTERIES

DARK SUSPENSE

PERMISSIONS

The majority of pieces in this book were written for *The Fine Art of Murder*. The Editors would like to acknowledge the following pieces, all copyright © 1993 by their respective authors:

Foreword by Ed Gorman and Introduction by Jon L. Breen.

American Mysteries

"Mysteries of New York" by William L. DeAndrea; "Los Angeles Mysteries" by Jon L. Breen; "Chicago as a Mystery Setting" by Barbara D'Amato; "Midwest Mysteries" by Mary Helen Becker; "Small-Town Mysteries" by Jon L. Breen; "Small Towns, Big Motives" by Nancy Pickard; "New England Mystery Authors" by Kate Mattes; "New England Blood" by Marilis Hornidge; "Southern Fried" by Joan Hess; "The Mystery of the Rocky Mountains" by Marvin Lachman; "Mysteries in the Southwest" by Anne Wingate; "Lone Star Crime" by Bill Crider; and "The Florida Mystery Scene" by Harrison Arnston.

Traditional Mysteries

Introduction by Jon L. Breen; "Why Cozies?" by Carolyn G. Hart; "The Topical Mystery" by Dorothy Salisbury Davis; "Searching for Agatha Christie" by Carolyn G. Hart; "Mistress of Mayhem: The Best of Agatha Christie on Film" by John McCarty; "Cats in Mysteries" by Ellen Nehr; "Dogs in Mysteries" by Ellen Nehr; "A Dogged Look at Lilian Jackson Braun" by Donna Huston Murray; "John Dickson Carr: The Magician of the Locked Room" by Douglas G. Greene; "The Doubleday Crime Club—1928-1991" by Ellen Nehr; "Traditionally Yours" by Marilis Hornidge; "Backgrounders" by Marilis Hornidge; "The Cornerstones of Crime" by Angela and Barry T. Zeman; "Sex and the Mystery" by Elaine Raco Chase; "It's Murder On Stage" by Barbara Paul; and "Does Anybody Love a Researcher?" by Walter Albert.

Religious Mysteries

Introduction by Jon L. Breen; "The Jewish Mystery" by Serita Stevens and Fanny Zindel; and "Saints Preserve Us: The Catholic Mystery" by Ralph McInerny.

Private Eye Mysteries

Introduction by Jon L. Breen.

Gay Mysteries

Introduction by Jon L. Breen and "The Gay and Lesbian Mystery" by Mark Richard Zubro.

British Mysteries

"Two or Three Things You Should Know About British Crime Fiction" by Maxim Jakubowski; "Some of My Characters Who Haunt Me" by Margaret Yorke; "The Transplanted Brit" by Dorothy Cannell; and "Humorous Crime, or Dead Funny" by Mike Ripley.

Dark Suspense

Introduction by Jon L. Breen and "Building the Bates Motel" by Robert Bloch.

Women's Suspense

Introduction by Jon L. Breen.

Police Procedurals

Introduction by Jon L. Breen and "A Cop's View of Cop Books" by Hugh Holton.

Hard-Boiled Mysteries

Introduction by Jon L. Breen; "Serial Killers: A Motive for Murder" by Brian Harper; and "Formula for the Past" by Harold Adams.

Thrillers and Other Mysteries

"How I Came to Write *The Skin of Rabinowitz* and Other Literary Milestones" by Warren Murphy.

Young Adult Mysteries

"Writing the Young Adult Mystery Novel" by Joan Lowery Nixon; "Much Ado about Nancy Drew" by Christina Mierau; and "Young Adult Mysteries: A Few 'Must Read' Winners" by Sharron McElmeel.

Short Stories

Introduction by Jon L. Breen; "*Ellery Queen's Mystery Magazine*" by Janet Hutchings; "*Alfred Hitchcock Mystery Magazine*" by Wendi Lee; and "Getting Started" by Edward D. Hoch.

True Crime Mysteries

"Interview: Anne Wingate" by Charles L. P. Silet and "True Crime: Stranger than Fiction" by Wendi Lee.

Fandom

"An Overview of Mystery Fandom" by Robert Napier; "Conventions: Malice and Mayhem in Numbers" by Janet A. Rudolph; "A Dinner to Die For" by Janet A. Rudolph; and "Interview: Allen J. Hubin" by Steven A. Stillwell.

Television Mysteries

"Solving the Mystery of *Murder, She Wrote*" by Marlys Millhiser; and "Jessica is Nancy Drew Grown Up" by Margaret C. Albert.

Comic Books

"Death of Autumn Mews" copyright © 1949 by Will Eisner, as published in *The Spirit Casebook* copyright © 1990 by Kitchen Sink Press. The name, "The Spirit," is registered by the U.S. Patent Office, Marc Registrada, Marquee Deposee. Art appears on page 326. "Johnny Dynamite" copyright © by Max Allan Collins and Terry Beatty. Art appears on page 328. The "Ms. Tree" drawing that appears on page 331 is unpublished. Copyright © 1993 by Max Allan Collins and Terry Beatty. "Ms. Tree" is a trademark of DC Comics. Used with permission. "Secret Agent X-9" cover from the first SECRET AGENT X-9 collection was published by the David McCay Company in 1934 and reprinted in *Secret Agent X-9*, copyright © 1990 by Kitchen Sink Press. The art appears on page 333.

"The Fine Comic Art of Murder" by Max Allan Collins.

Nostalgia

"The Golden Era of Gold Medal Books" by George Tuttle.

Organizations

"Mystery Writers of America, Inc. . . . a Historical Story" by Angela and Barry T. Zeman; "Who Are All of These Sisters in Crime?" by Elaine Raco Chase; "The Private Eye Writers of America" by Jan

FOREWORD

STAND IN A MYSTERY BOOKSTORE sometime and eavesdrop on the conversations. You'll find that there are nearly as many kinds of popular mystery novels as there are mystery fans.

We hope that *The Fine Art of Murder* will introduce you to virtually all types of mystery fiction and help you do a little "sampling"—I've actually met people who enjoy both Agatha Christie and Raymond Chandler, for instance. The two shouldn't be mutually exclusive.

But please understand one thing. This book is not meant as a definitive statement about the art of the mystery story. What you'll find here is opinion, artfully argued in most cases . . . but nothing more than personal opinion.

Some deserving writers have not been mentioned at all. There simply wasn't room to include every single worthy writer or novel.

But overall, we feel we've given you a good sense of the mystery novel as it's written and read today. And we've given you some revealing glimpses into the lives of writers and editors.

As for the facts and details of this book, there are bound to be errors. We've guarded against this as much as possible by having Professor Douglas Greene read the manuscript for mistakes. But even so, in a book this size, it's likely you'll find a few errors. We apologize in advance and will correct them in the next edition.

It's our belief that of all forms of commercial fiction, the mystery novel offers the writer the greatest freedom and the most intelligent audience. And by the time you finish this book, we hope you'll agree.

—the Editors

INTRODUCTION

Jon L. Breen

THE ORIGIN OF the detective story is usually traced to the three tales Edgar Allan Poe wrote about C. Auguste Dupin in the early 1840s: "The Murders in the Rue Morgue," "The Mystery of Marie Roget," and "The Purloined Letter." There are plenty of examples of "prehistoric" detective fiction, both European and Asian, but it has been handiest to start the detective story with Poe, since he created so many of the standard elements and devices of the form[1]: the eccentric amateur detective and his admiring friend and chronicler, the locked-room mystery, the accusation of an innocent suspect, and the trap laid for the real villain (in "Rue Morgue"); the fictionalization of a real case, the establishment of a series character, and the "armchair detective" solution (in "Marie Roget"); the solution that is so obvious it is overlooked (in "The Purloined Letter"); and, in a story outside the Dupin series, the least suspected person as culprit ("Thou Art the Man").

Not all contemporary crime fiction is descended directly from Poe, however. The private eyes and spies of our day are at least equally rooted in the dime novels of the nineteenth century. And the school of romantic suspense can be traced at least in part to the work of eighteenth-century gothic novelists like Ann Radcliffe (*The Mysteries of Udolpho,* 1794), Horace Walpole (*The Castle of Otranto,* 1765), and Matthew Gregory Lewis (*The Monk,* 1796), and to nineteenth-century novels like Charlotte Brontë's *Jane Eyre* (1847).

Elements of mystery and detection existed in many of the three-decker novels of the nineteenth century, and at least a handful, most notably Wilkie Collins's *The Moonstone* (1868), Charles Dickens's *Bleak House* (1853), and the works of Frenchman Émile Gaboriau are claimed as important milestones in the genre today. Anna Katharine Green's landmark novel, *The Leavenworth Case* (1878), launched a long career most notable for book-length stories. But most of the major early examples of pure detective fiction came in the short story form, starting with Poe, receiving new popularity with Arthur Conan Doyle's Sherlock Holmes, who debuted at novella length in *A Study in Scarlet* (1887) but achieved his greatest popularity with the short stories collected in *The Adventures of Sherlock Holmes* (1892) and later volumes, and continuing into the early part of this century with writer-character combinations like R. Austin Freeman and Dr. Thorndyke, Arthur Morrison and Martin Hewitt, G. K. Chesterton and Father Brown, and Jacques Futrelle and The Thinking Machine. While many detective novels were written in the period between 1880 and 1920—Fergus Hume's *The Mystery of a Hansom Cab* (1886) was an early best seller; Gaston Leroux's *The Mystery of the Yellow Room* (1908) achieved for some critics a classic status equal to or surpassing his more famous *The Phantom of the Opera* (1911); Conan Doyle (most notably in *The Hound of the Baskervilles,* 1902), Freeman, and Futrelle all produced occasional novels; and Americans like Burton E. Stevenson and Carolyn Wells made their pre–World War I contributions in the long form—the short story predominated.

E. C. Bentley's *Trent's Last Case* (1913), which ironically was intended at least in part as a parody of the genre, is now considered a milestone of the modern detective novel. With the 1920 debuts of Agatha Christie with *The Mysterious Affair at Styles* and Freeman Wills Crofts with *The Cask,* followed a scant three years later by Dorothy L. Sayers's first Lord Peter Wimsey novel, *Whose Body?,* the Golden Age of Detection began. Although short sto-

---

[1] One of the most exhaustive lists of Poe's innovations is found in Robert A. W. Lowndes's essay "The Contributions of Edgar Allan Poe," reprinted in Francis M. Nevins, Jr., ed., *The Mystery Writer's Art* (Bowling Green University Popular Press, 1970), pp. 1–18.

ries continued to be important and influential, the novel now became the form in which most major work was done.

The Golden Age twenties are usually ceded to the British. Apart from Christie, Sayers, and Crofts, such novelists as Philip MacDonald, Anthony Berkeley, H. C. Bailey, and John Rhode came into prominence. The only Americans to make a comparable impact were Earl Derr Biggers, who introduced the popular and later controversial Charlie Chan in *The House Without a Key* (1925), and S. S. Van Dine, who began the Philo Vance series with *The Benson Murder Case* (1926).

By the end of the decade, though, American writers were ready to mount a challenge. Ellery Queen (Frederic Dannay and Manfred B. Lee), who began a long and varied career with *The Roman Hat Mystery* in 1929, and John Dickson Carr, whose *It Walks by Night* appeared the following year, became two of the key figures of the pure, fair-play detective novel. *Black Mask* writers Dashiell Hammett and Carroll John Daly introduced a new kind of detective story, written in tough, terse style and drawing on dime-novel adventure as much as the intellectual detection invented by Poe.

In the thirties, the hard-boiled school continued to develop, while the Golden Age reached its fullest flower. New British writers like Nicholas Blake, Michael Innes, Margery Allingham, and Ngaio Marsh came into the field. American classicists, though somewhat overshadowed, included Clyde B. Clason, C. Daly King, Clayton Rawson, Stuart Palmer, and Clifford Knight. An American hybrid form that combined the hard-boiled style with Golden Age plotting began to develop, typified by Rex Stout, Erle Stanley Gardner, and George Harmon Coxe. Late in the decade, Raymond Chandler entered the private-eye field. In Britain, the pure crime novel, eschewing the whodunit element and concentrating on the psychology of the criminal, was pioneered by writers like Francis Iles (like Anthony Berkeley, a nom de plume of humorist A. B. Cox).

The 1940s saw several interesting developments as the pure crime novel and psychological suspense came to the fore, with the pure detection of the Golden Age still strong but its domination of the genre somewhat receding. As had occurred earlier in the century, the advent of war brought a new interest in espionage, some of it addressed in estab-

lished detective series. Dark suspense, sometimes called fiction *noir,* came into its own in the works of writers like Cornell Woolrich, Jim Thompson, and David Goodis, paralleling the onset of film noir in motion pictures. The first real police procedurals were published, with Lawrence Treat's *V as in Victim* (1945) a milestone. And the private eyes continued strong, bolstered by the overwhelming commercial success of Mickey Spillane and his novels about Mike Hammer.

The trends to psychological suspense, tough-guy private eyes, and police procedurals continued into the fifties, a decade also marked by the best effort to date to cross detective and science fiction, Isaac Asimov's two robot novels, *The Caves of Steel* (1954) and *The Naked Sun* (1957). As the pulp magazines disappeared, original softcover novels took their place. A new generation of crime writers, including such formidable figures as John D. MacDonald, Charles Williams, and Donald Hamilton, grew up in the paperbacks, which were hard and tough and sexy, if rarely as sexy as their covers suggested. Though paperbacks were primarily masculine in this period—the O'Hara-esque Vin Packer was a notable exception—in hardcover women were running with the leaders of the pack as such writers as Dorothy Salisbury Davis, Charlotte Armstrong, and Margaret Millar attracted both popular and critical acclaim.

The sixties, a time of turmoil and change in so many areas of human existence, were probably the most traumatic decade for the mystery genre. With the worldwide success of Ian Fleming and James Bond, plus the advent of more serious cold-war espionage specialists like John le Carré, Adam Hall (Elleston Trevor), and Len Deighton, the spies almost drove out the detectives. Romantic suspense also entered a period of unprecedented boom, led by hardcover writers like Mary Stewart, Victoria Holt, and Phyllis A. Whitney. For the first time, female bylines became a going commodity in paperback original crime fiction, as many women writers (and men writers using female pseudonyms) flooded the market with latter-day gothics, their covers usually featuring a big old house with a light in one window. Police procedurals continued strong in the sixties; classical detection was practiced primarily by old favorites (Queen, Carr, Marsh, and Christie were among the old-timers still going strong); and private eyes became an endangered species.

Though the seventies continued to be healthy for espionage and romantic suspense, the traditional and private-eye forms managed a mild comeback, sometimes in a nostalgic mode. Though there had been scattered examples of historical mystery fiction in past decades (notably some of the novels of John Dickson Carr, Lillian de la Torre's short stories about Dr. Samuel Johnson, and Robert van Gulik's modular novels about Chinese magistrate Judge Dee), mysteries had been contemporary almost by definition. Now mysteries set in other times became popular, including the works of such Victorian specialists as Peter Lovesey (the Sergeant Cribb series beginning with *Wobble to Death,* 1970), Elizabeth Peters (Barbara Mertz) (in *Crocodile on the Sandbank,* 1975, and other adventures of Amelia Peabody), and Francis Selwyn (in the Sergeant Verity series beginning with *Cracksman on Velvet,* 1974); and the medieval Brother Cadfael novels of Ellis Peters (Edith Pargeter), beginning with *A Morbid Taste for Bones* (1977). Along with this historical trend came a wave of nostalgic mysteries, including private eye novels (like Andrew Bergman's two books about forties shamus Jack LeVine) and classical detective novels (like Kingsley Amis's thirties-based *The Riverside Villas Murder,* 1973) set in the decades seen to represent the subgenres at their peak.

The eighties saw a period of unprecedented boom for the crime and mystery novel in all its forms, gradually building to the end of the decade and continuing into the early nineties. Both traditional detection and the private eye enjoyed major comebacks, with any number of talented new writers entering the field. Women, who had been prominent in detective and mystery fiction from the beginning but were comparatively neglected in the late seventies and early eighties due to a critical overemphasis on the hard-boiled and espionage schools dominated by men, entered a new period of ascendancy. With the recognition that most of the readers of mysteries are women, more and more writers (both male and female) sought to feature strong female characters in lead roles.

While there will never be agreement between those who believe the real Golden Age of mystery fiction is right now and those who look back with longing on the classics of earlier decades, several facts on the current market are unassailable. While writers of forty and fifty years ago were encumbered by any number of rules and conventions regarding their subject matter and how they could treat it, today's writers, aside from the somewhat exaggerated specter of "political correctness," can deal with just about any subject matter and any point of view in a mystery novel and can seriously explore social issues and subcultures that a writer of the thirties would never have dreamed of addressing. And regardless of what kind of crime or mystery fiction you favor, from the coziest to the toughest, the most realistic to the most artificial, someone is practicing it and practicing it well. If fiction generally is not enjoying robust health, that can only help genre fiction, where talents are operating that ordinarily might be drawn to the mainstream.

As these trends would suggest, there has also been a blurring of genre lines. Writers are more reluctant to be pigeonholed. As more and more mysteries have found a place on best seller lists, and as the length of mysteries has grown (not always beneficially), the line between "category" and mainstream fiction has become less and less distinct. Best-selling writers like Stephen King and Dean R. Koontz regularly draw on any number of popular categories in molding their entertaining novels, and more and more "literary" writers have used the accoutrements of the mystery in their works. The past couple of decades have seen Joyce Carol Oates, Don DeLillo, Walker Percy, Diane Johnson, Norman Mailer, Paul West, and any number of other mainstream authors appropriate elements of crime and mystery fiction, often (but not always) to subvert them. It sometimes seems in browsing among the new fiction—and certainly in perusing the best seller lists—that the presence of crime and mystery elements is the rule rather than the exception. In a parallel trend, some writers who have been associated with the crime and mystery genre from the beginning of their careers have tended to downplay those elements in their works, stinting on plot while using the mystery as an excuse for social observations, character analysis, or dramatic scenes. Prominent examples are Sharyn McCrumb and Robert B. Parker.

Another trend is the overwhelming amount of secondary material appearing in print: journals like *The Armchair Detective* and *Mystery Scene;* scholarly studies of major writers; and books like the one you hold in your hand. Should this proliferation, delightful as it is to fans and scholars, be a cause for alarm? When a category of literature gets this much critical scrutiny, does that suggest it is near the end of its useful existence?

A pessimist can always find justification for a dire outlook. After all, why does anybody bother to publish mystery novels, or books at all, for that matter? Don't we all know that nobody reads books anymore, that whole generations have been destroyed as readers by the pervasiveness of television? And yet the evidence of the marketplace is that enough people *must be* reading mysteries, and other kinds of books, for publishers who are in busi-

ness not for the good of humanity but for profit to turn them out in unprecedented numbers. And while the icons of the past—Hammett and Chandler, Christie and Sayers, Queen and Carr—deserve to retain their loyal fans, even many traditionalists admit that the general level of quality in crime fiction writing in the early 1990s is far above the general level of the thirties or the forties. Whatever future turns it may take, the contemporary mystery scene is a stimulating place for reader and writer alike, as the contents of *The Fine Art of Murder* will show.

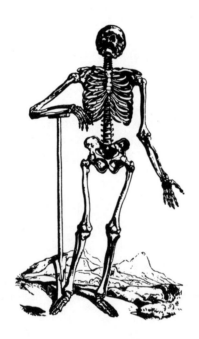

AMERICAN MYSTERIES

MY LIFE IN CRIME
A personal overview of American mystery fiction
Lawrence Block

Roger W. Vargo/Daily New LA

IT WAS IN THE eleventh grade that I knew I would be a writer. The conviction grew out of two awarenesses that dawned at about the same time. I became aware of the world of realistic adult fiction, with all its power to inform and enchant and absorb one utterly. I became aware, too, of my own talent with words. I seemed to be capable of doing with them what I had been unable to do with a baseball bat or a hammer or a monkey wrench or a slide rule.

And so I wrote—poems, sketches, stories, the usual juvenilia. Artistically, my childhood had been one of deprivation, in that I was not the product of a dysfunctional family. Accordingly, the things I wrote derived less from experience and inner turmoil than from other writings that I admired.

During my freshman year at Antioch I sent what I wrote to various magazines, and they sent it back. I was not greatly dismayed. I mounted the rejection slips on the wall, displaying them like campaign ribbons. I suppose I was proud of them, and perhaps I was right to be. I was, after all, actively engaged in the process of becoming a writer, and they were evidence of that engagement.

I read all the time, and one of the many things I read, the summer after my first year at college, was *The Jungle Kids,* a paperback collection of short stories by Evan Hunter. A couple of years previously Hunter had hit the best seller list with *The Blackboard Jungle,* and the stories were all about what were then called juvenile delinquents. (I don't know what you'd call them now. Kids, I guess.)

There were some fine stories in *The Jungle Kids,* including a positively Chekhovian tour de force called "The Last Spin," in which two rival gang leaders become friends in the course of a game of Russian roulette. There were other stories that were less remarkable, just good workmanlike efforts. But the book had a profound effect upon me because I found what Hunter had done at once estimable and attainable. I sensed that I could do what he had done here, and that it was worth the doing. I couldn't write these stories, but I could write stories that were good in the way in which these stories were good.

I sat down at once and tried writing a story about juvenile delinquents, and it was awful, and I left it unfinished. And then some months later I was living in New York and working in a publisher's mailroom, and one Sunday afternoon I wrote a short story about a young man in New York who lived by his wits, making ends meet through petty theft and mail fraud. I didn't send it anywhere because I couldn't think where to send it, but eventually I recalled that Evan Hunter had published in a magazine called *Manhunt,* so I mailed my story off to it. The editor asked for a rewrite, complaining that my ending was inconclusive. I rewrote it and it came right back again, and the following summer, the summer of '57, I actually bought a copy of *Manhunt* and read everything in it and saw how to fix my story. I sent it off again, and damned if the magazine didn't buy it. Paid me a hundred bucks for it too.

And so my fate was sealed. For the past thirty-some years I've been writing crime fiction.

Imagine if my first sale had been to "Heloise's Household Hints" . . .

Poe started it. "The Murders in the Rue Morgue" is the first detective story, C. Auguste Dupin fiction's first detective. (He is a series detective too, reappearing in "The Mystery of Marie Roget" and "The Purloined Letter.") The story is a curious one, beginning with a couple of pages arguing the natural superiority of checkers to chess as a game of pure ratiocination and ending with an orangutan unmasked as the murderer. In its course its author set several remarkable precedents. He employed a mere mortal as narrator, a counterwheel to the brilliant detective; Conan Doyle took this device and made it his own, and ever since we have called such narrators Watsons. At the same time, Poe pitted his hero against the bumbling and unimaginative police, and this pattern of antagonism has characterized much of mystery fiction down through the years.

Both Nero Wolfe and Philip Marlowe are descendants of Dupin, so it is only fitting that American mystery fiction's highest accolade should be named for his creator. The Edgar Allan Poe awards are presented annually by the Mystery Writers of America in the form of a rather woebegone porcelain bust of the great man.

But did it really start with Poe? Men have been writing about crime ever since Cain invented fratricide, and I don't know that there is any level of literary excellence that some sort of crime fiction has not attained. *Hamlet* is many things, but if it is not a detective story, what on earth is? It is, to be sure, a story as vague and uncertain as its hero. Hamlet's father may or may not have been murdered, and Hamlet's mother and stepfather may or may not have done it. The plot of *Hamlet* has turned up, by coincidence or by design, in a number of mystery novels, not the least of them Fredric Brown's Edgar-winning first novel, *The Fabulous Clipjoint.*

Murder is a plot element in most Shakespearean tragedy, and many of the plays have their echoes in what we recognize as crime and mystery fiction, even as they have their antecedents in the playwright's own resource material. *Othello, King Lear, Macbeth, Julius Caesar*—crime stories, every one of them, their pages fairly dripping blood.

What is *Les Misérables* but a crime story? What is *Crime and Punishment* but a story of, well, crime and punishment? Or Dreiser's *An American Tragedy?* Or Hemingway's "The Killers"?

Still, it would seem that crime fiction does constitute a category, and that not every book with a crime central to its plot perforce belongs in that category. Certain novels are automatically shelved by booksellers and librarians as mysteries. Others are not. The distinction is easier to make than to define; as someone said of pornography, one can't define it, but knows it when one sees it.

A few years ago the publishing industry had a very useful definition of a mystery. A mystery, everyone agreed, was any novel about a crime that was sure to sell between three and six thousand hardcover copies. As a result of this perception, publishers who had something they thought might sell respectably did what they could to hide the fact that the book was what most people would label a mystery.

All of this changed utterly, and a glance at the *New York Times* best seller list makes the reason clear. Week after week, books that are undeniably mysteries occupy a dominant position. Writers like Dick Francis and Tony Hillerman and Elmore Leonard and Sue Grafton and Martin Cruz Smith and Robert B. Parker hit the list with every book they write. Books about the detection of crime are selling as well as anything can without promising weight loss and personal growth.

Why?

The explanation that seems to me to make the most sense holds that readers have a hunger for more substance than much contemporary mainstream fiction provides. Minimalist novels, academic novels, novels that aren't about anything tend to garner M.F.A. degrees and National Endowment for the Arts grants without winning over the reading public. I read recently of a woman who has been secretly getting her reading matter from the young adult section because the books are about something. Much of crime fiction, too, is about something. There's a crime, and there's an attempt to do something about it. There are characters, and some of them live and some of them die, and the whole thing works out in the end. Or it doesn't, and *that's* how it works out. Either way there's a story, and you want to know what happens next.

What happened next in my own career is that I kept at it. I wrote more crime stories and sold some of them, to *Manhunt* and other magazines. I wrote other stuff too. Articles for the male adventure magazines. A couple of true confession stories. A slew of erotic paperback novels. The fabricated case histories of a nonexistent psychiatrist.

This and that.

The ideas that came to me and the stories that worked best for me tended to fit somewhere in the broad category of mystery and suspense. Even when they didn't start out that way, they tended to wind up there.

For example, in the late sixties I wrote a light-hearted little novel, a sort of *Lecher in the Rye* about a seventeen-year-old boy and his efforts to lose his virginity. Gold Medal published it as *No Score,* with the byline Chip Harrison, that being the name of the narrator. It sold particularly well, probably because it had a terrific cover, and I was moved to write a sequel, which the publisher imaginatively titled *Chip Harrison Scores Again.*

Well, I wanted to write more about Chip, but I sensed a problem. In the first book he'd been seventeen years old and innocent. In the second he was a year older and a good deal more experienced. At this rate he'd be a jaded roué in no time at all, and his charm was by no means the sort that age cannot wither, nor custom stale.

Inspiration struck. In the third book I put him to work for a private detective, a road-company Nero Wolfe, and knew he'd last like an insect in amber. "You were wise to take this job," his employer told him. "Now you'll never grow old. You'll be the same age forever, like all the private eyes in fiction." He never did grow old, but not because of the mystery's fountain-of-youth properties. Alas, after he'd appeared in two Nero Wolfe pastiches, I ran out of things for him to do and let him retire.

Some fictional detectives age. Some stay young (or middle-aged or old) forever. Some die. Agatha Christie left two manuscripts to be published posthumously; in them she killed off her two most enduring detectives, Hercule Poirot and Miss Marple. Nicholas Freeling did not wait for his own death to kill his Inspector Van der Valk. He bumped him off in midcareer in remarkably cavalier fashion, and alienated most of his readers in the process. Conan Doyle tried that, sending Sherlock Holmes over the Reichenbach Falls, but wound up bringing him back in response to popular demand.

At the other extreme some fictional detectives outlive their creators. A number of writers have kept Sherlock Holmes going, often matching him up with historical personages; in one of the more successful books, Holmes and Sigmund Freud wind up doing coke together. Robert Goldsborough wrote a Nero Wolfe novel after Rex Stout's death with the aim of amusing his mother. He has since written and published several more. A couple of years ago a dozen writers produced an anthology of new stories about Philip Marlowe, ostensibly to honor Raymond Chandler on his hundredth birthday. I suppose it's all right, so long as they do it only once every hundred years.

There are, as everyone knows, two kinds of people in the world: these who divide the world into two kinds of people and those who don't. The world of crime fiction gets similarly cleft in twain. Mysteries are divided into two categories: the tough, gritty, mean-streets, in-your-face kind, which is labeled hard-boiled, and the gentle, effete, British-country-house body-in-the-library sort, which is called cozy.

Stereotypically, the hard-boiled mystery is American. It features, and is very likely narrated by, a private detective, a hard-drinking soft-hearted cynic who looks a little like Humphrey Bogart when he's not looking like Robert Mitchum. The hard-boiled novel is written by a man and read by men. It is sour and downbeat and violent, and it means business.

In contrast, the cozy is English, written by women and for women. Its detective is apt to be an inspired amateur, male or female, and all its characters, except for the odd charming rustic, tend to be well spoken and courteous, decorous even in death. Its violence is offstage and unthreatening, leaning toward esoteric poisons and ingenious murder methods. The sleuth sets things right by working out an elaborate puzzle, and order is restored to a universe that is orderly at heart.

These stereotypes are undoubtedly useful, but they have their down side. Their rules are broken in book after book. British writers drag the reader through London's mean streets while Americans employ country-house settings. Women write hard-boiled private-eye novels about tough female detectives, and other women read them, while men turn out intricately plotted cozies.

More to the point, the stereotypes tend to trivialize books of either persuasion. The cozy would seem to be frivolous, a bit of fluff that diminishes murder, and some of its specimens may have that effect. Yet no one epitomizes the cozy writer more than Agatha Christie, with her brilliantly worked plots and her comforting village settings. Her finest creation, Miss Jane Marple of St. Mary Mead, is the ultimate amateur sleuth, a little old lady in plimsolls with a steel-trap mind. The books are entertainments, surely. And yet they are dead serious. Christie's concern in all her fiction, and especially in the Marple books, is the nature and origin of human evil. It is possible to read the novels attentively without becoming aware of it, but make no mistake about it, that is what they are about.

One of the abiding virtues of crime fiction, it seems to me, and one of the chief factors in its survival over the generations as a literary genre is the seemingly infinite variety of work that falls within its scope. The house of mystery has many mansions, and it is a rare reader who can't find something he or she likes in one chamber or another. Now and then I run into someone who professes never to read mysteries, and I find such specimens at least as curious as those who read nothing else. The majority seem to be people who never got the knack of reading for diversion; a few are of the sort who read one mystery once, didn't much like it, and assumed all others to be the same.

As a reader I have always been able to find crime novels to read even as my own taste has changed and evolved. As a writer I have found that the genre's wide-spaced boundaries have allowed me to write whatever it has occurred to me to write without placing myself beyond the pale. Over the years I have written novels about four different series characters. Evan Tanner, who has appeared in seven books, is a sort of freelance adventurer whose sleep center was destroyed by a stray shard of shrapnel. He speaks innumerable languages, supports no end of lost causes (among them the restoration of the House of Stuart to the British throne), and slips himself and others across international borders, all in the interest of peace and freedom.

Bernie Rhodenbarr is a bookseller by day, a burglar by night. Typically he has to solve an intricate murder puzzle in order to extricate himself from suspicion incurred in the commission of a burglary. He is an urbane and literate chap, a nice guy who lives on the West Side and steals on the East Side. Whoopi Goldberg played him in the movie. (Don't ask.) His best friend is a lesbian poodle groomer.

Matthew Scudder is an alcoholic ex-cop, divorced, living alone in a cheap hotel in the West Fifties, eking out a living as an unlicensed private eye. He hangs out in churches (and, recently, at AA meetings in church basements), leads an angst-ridden life, and walks down some very mean streets indeed.

And I've already mentioned Chip Harrison, playing a horny adolescent Archie Goodwin to Leo Haig's version of Nero Wolfe.

Here's the point. These series differ considerably one from another—in type, in tone, in purpose. And I've also written a dozen or so nonseries novels, and they don't run to type either. Yet all these books manage to be at home in the field of crime fiction. Not all my readers care for me in all my guises. One working private detective is a big Scudder fan but won't read my Bernie Rhodenbarr books because he disapproves of my glorifying a character who is, when all is said and done, a miscreant and a lawbreaker. Some of Bernie's fans find Scudder's world too relentlessly downbeat for them. Quite a few readers have found Tanner's exploits too far-fetched to be taken seriously, yet others keep turning up to ask me when I'm going to write another book about him.

I should say something about fans. Compared with science fiction, mysteries barely have a true fandom. Science-fiction fans hold dozens of conventions annually, read everything written in their chosen field and nothing outside it, publish innumerable amateur magazines and newsletters (''fanzines''), and, according to one of the field's leading editors, are all fifteen-year-old boys who aren't very well socialized.

Mystery fans assemble at a single annual convention, the Bouchercon, named for the late Anthony Boucher, a mystery writer himself who was even more renowned as the field's foremost critic. Held every year in a different city, Bouchercon brings together upward of five hundred crime-fiction devotees. One writer is chosen as the annual guest of honor, his expenses paid by the host committee, but fifty or more other writers pay full price for the chance to natter away on celebrity panels, inscribe books for fans, hang out with booksellers and editors, and play poker until daybreak.

Bouchercon is always a great success, and a big factor here, I'm convinced, is the estimable nature of the people involved. Mystery readers are an uncommonly literate lot, inclined to choose substance over pretense every time. (It is interesting to note what they read outside the genre. Several mystery bookstores carry the odd nonmystery now and then because the proprietor just knows it will appeal to the store's customers. Most but by no means all of these books are about cats. W. R. Kinsella's *Shoeless Joe* sold well in mystery bookshops, as did Walter Tevis's wonderful novel of a girl chess prodigy, *The Queen's Gambit*.)

The mystery bookstore is largely a phenomenon of the last decade. Booksellers in general are a dedicated bunch, and the proprietors of stores dealing exclusively in mysteries would not be in the field if they did not love it. Their shops often have the ambience of clubhouses, and many of their customers drop in as much to chat as to buy books. Murder Ink., Grounds for Murder, Sherlock's Home, Rue Morgue, Footprints of a Gigantic Hound, Booked for Murder, Foul Play, The Butler Did it, Murder Undercover, Once Upon a Crime, Murder for Pleasure, Scene of the Crime—the ingenuity displayed in the stores' names suggests the resourcefulness of the people who operate them.

Finally, mystery writers themselves tend to be an amiable sort. At a recent Bouchercon in Philadelphia, several of us were sitting around while one talked about his difficulties with an author. "What's remarkable about the guy," someone said, "is he's the only thoroughgoing SOB in the field. I can think of a few guys I'm not crazy about, but he's the only real bastard around."

I could, if pressed, name another, but given the traditional nature of auctorial ego and artistic temperament, it seems extraordinary that such a large barrel should have so few sour apples in it.

While I'll leave it to psychiatry to explain why men and women who spend their lives writing about bloody murder should be so affable on their own time, I can guess why we're so apt to relish one another's company. The great majority of us are enthusiastic readers of crime fiction. Most of us were fans before we were writers, and continue to read one another's work avidly.

Besides such domestic organizations as Mystery Writers of America and Private Eye Writers of America, I belong to a fairly new outfit called the International Association of Crime Writers, with members on both sides of what we used to call the Iron Curtain. In the summer of 1988 I attended an IACW convocation at Gijón, on Spain's northern coast. There were around sixty writers present from all over the world, and the majority of us were unfamiliar with one another's work. Most of our contingent spoke only English, and the group as a whole was a testament to the far-reaching effects of the Tower of Babel. There was one woman from Japan who came accompanied by an interpreter, and even he could barely understand her, as her first language was some outer-island dialect more exotic than Basque.

No matter. We all were crime writers. Everybody had a wonderful time.

Oh, all right. Enough stalling. A piece like this has to have a ten-best list, doesn't it?

People do keep coming up with lists. An English mystery writer published a book not long ago with two-page discourses on each of his hundred favorites. (I'd mention his name, but he didn't mention mine, so to hell with him.) My list has a couple of special characteristics that ought to be pointed out. First of all, it consists solely of American writers. I am writing, after all, for a magazine devoted to matters American, so I trust I am not being excessively parochial in keeping foreign writers off this particular list.

It is perhaps largely for this reason that most of the writers I've listed are of the hard-boiled school. Born in the detective pulps after the turn of the present century, hard-boiled crime fiction was very much an American invention.

After Poe, preeminence in the mystery field passed to the British. Wilkie Collins wrote *The Moonstone*, Sir Arthur Conan Doyle created Sherlock Holmes, R. Austin Freeman wrote about Dr. Thorndyke, and any number of British writers went on to develop the detective story as a suspenseful adventure, an intellectual exercise, and a look into the darker corners of the human psyche.

Some American writers followed in these British footsteps, with greater or lesser success. But in the pulp magazines another tradition was born. Crude, violent, rough-edged, cynical, often antiauthoritarian, pulp crime fiction spoke in a new voice that caught much of the spirit of post–World War I America.

A group of writers centered on *Black Mask*

magazine forged hard-boiled fiction into something honest and vigorous; of their number, Hammett and Chandler emerged to produce something that will pass for art. Years after their passing we still write this sort of book better than anyone else. The French have an insatiable appetite for the *roman noir* and accord the work considerable critical respect—rather more, I sometimes think, than it truly deserves. But very few of the hard-boiled crime novels published in France are homegrown.

The British can write hard-boiled books, but some of their best tough writers set their books in America, as if to say that a hard-boiled crime story demands an American setting. James Hadley Chase and Peter Chambers, the latter a devoted admirer of Raymond Chandler, are quite popular at home but have never traveled well, and few of their books are published here. Their American settings and dialogue may strike a British reader as perfectly authentic, but they clang horribly on an American ear. (This sort of thing works both ways. An American woman writes British cozies set in England, to the rich delight of an enormous American following. Most of her fans assume she's English, a mistake no English reader would be likely to make. "She gets everything all wrong," an English fan told me. "I can't believe your lot takes her seriously.")

At the same time, I have to admit that the preponderance of the hard-boiled on my list reflects a prejudice of the author. I tend to prefer hard-boiled (or, if you will, realistic) crime fiction and to see it as of more fundamental importance than softer, gentler books.

The reader will further note that my list has no women on it. This would certainly appear to be evidence of blatant sexism, and perhaps it is. In rebuttal I would argue that Agatha Christie and Dorothy Sayers would certainly be on my list but for the fact that they are British. And several American mystery writers would be on the list, too, but for the happy fact that they are alive.

Because, you see, I have listed only writers who have gone to that great Bouchercon in the sky. I have mentioned how generous and amiable mystery writers are, how much I enjoy their company, how well we all get along. If you think I am going to change all that by assembling a list of favorites and leaving some of them off it, you're out of your mind.

One last note. This is a list not of best books but of favorite writers, although I have occasionally mentioned a book or two that I remember with special fondness.

Here's the good news: Instead of ten favorites, I seem to have come up with sixteen. And it was easy to put them in order, I just used the alphabet.

Anthony Boucher (1911–68). Boucher's reputation rests largely upon his influence as a reviewer, which was monumental. From 1951 until his death he wrote the weekly Criminals at Large column for *The New York Times Book Review,* covering virtually everything of note published in the mystery field. He reviewed paperback originals at a time when no one else took much notice of them, discovered and encouraged promising new writers, and widened the tastes of his readers while sharpening their perceptions. During many of the same years he also reviewed plays and opera and science fiction, appeared on radio and television, edited a science fiction magazine and a number of anthologies, and died young after many years of intermittent ill health.

In addition, he wrote eight novels and a couple of dozen short stories. I think it is safe to say that he would have been more prominent as a writer of fiction if less of his energy had gone into other pursuits. His books are slight, but their charm and the skill with which they were written keep them sprightly and engaging. My own favorite, though but dimly recalled, is *Nine Times Nine,* a locked-room mystery investigated by Sister Ursula of the Order of Martha of Bethany. (As a reviewer and editor, Anthony Boucher was always an easy mark for a story with a nun or a cat in it.)

It was published under the name H. H. Holmes, an alias previously employed by a mass murderer of the nineteenth century. "Anthony Boucher" was itself a pen name; the author's actual name was William Anthony Parker White.

Fredric Brown (1906–72). I discovered Fredric Brown around the time I began selling stories to the crime pulps, and I read everything of his I could get my hands on. One time, after a hard week at a literary agency where I was gainlessly employed as a reader of unsolicited submissions, I read *Murder Can Be Fun,* in which a murder is committed early on in full view of dozens of bystanders—by a killer dressed up as Santa Claus. I had a bottle of bourbon on the table, and every time Brown's hero took a drink, I had a snort myself. This is a hazardous undertaking when in the company of Brown's characters and, I've been given to understand, would have been just as dangerous around the author himself. By the time the book was finished, so was I.

Brown was a playful, inventive, prolific writer who never wrote the same book twice. *The Fabulous Clipjoint,* his Edgar-winning first novel, is perhaps his best book. In it young Ed Hunter joins forces with his uncle Ambrose, a former carnival performer, to investigate the murder of Ed's father. The Chicago background is perfect, the carny lore a big plus. *The Screaming Mimi* and *Night of the Jabberwock* are also vintage Brown. My own favorite is *The Wench Is Dead,* about a sociology professor immersing himself in L.A.'s Skid Row in the name of research.

James M. Cain (1892–1977). While he is generally regarded as one of the seminal figures of hard-boiled crime fiction, Cain would have no part of it. "I belong to no school, hard-boiled or otherwise," he insisted.

Oh, well. The writer is always the last to know. On the basis of two books, *The Postman Always Rings Twice* and *Double Indemnity,* Cain's place in the field is assured. He wrote sparely and convincingly of ordinary and fundamentally decent human beings moved by sexual passion to commit murder for gain. A whole generation of strong American fiction, the archetypal gold-medal novels of Charles Williams and Gil Brewer and others, springs directly from these two books.

Not everyone admired him. "Everything he touches smells like a billy goat," Raymond Chandler complained. "He is every kind of writer I detest, a *faux naïf,* a Proust in greasy overalls, a dirty little boy with a piece of chalk and a board fence and nobody looking."

I always think of Cain when the subject of film adaptation comes up. Several of his novels were filmed, and he was often asked how he felt about what Hollywood had done to his books. "But they have done nothing to my books," he would reply. "They are right over there on the shelf, exactly as I wrote them."

Raymond Chandler (1888–1959). Chandler has long been the intellectual's darling, a mystery writer for people who don't like mysteries. On the one hand, he talked of taking murder out of the English

drawing room and putting it in the streets, where it belonged. At the same time, his characters spent a surprising amount of time in the homes and haunts of the California rich, a West Coast equivalent of the country house on the moors. His achievement, it seems to me, is less that he brought the traditional mystery into the alleys and gutters than that he put a novelist's spin on the pulp tradition of *Dime Detective* and *Black Mask.*

All the novels are first-rate, except for *Playback,* a tired and confused effort published a year before the author's death. I suppose my own favorite is *The Long Good-bye,* which shows rather more of Chandler's detective Philip Marlowe than did any of the previous books. In its exploration of Marlowe's friendship with Terry Lennox, the book is as much a novel of character as of plot. If ultimately flawed, *The Long Good-bye* thereby fits Randall Jarrell's definition of a novel—a lengthy prose narrative with something wrong with it.

Stanley Ellin (1916–86). Stanley Ellin was a perfectionist, working slowly and deliberately, producing a page of typescript on a good day. He admitted to having rewritten the opening paragraph of a short story as many as forty times before going on to the next paragraph and polishing each subsequent page in similar fashion before proceeding further.

It is possible to write short stories in this fashion, and Ellin consistently wrote the best mystery short stories of his time. His very first published story, "The Specialty of the House," endures as a classic, although it is probably less surprising to today's reader simply because so much fuss has been made about it. But all of Ellin's stories are wonderful. He managed only one a year, sent each in turn to *Ellery Queen's Mystery Magazine,* and never had one rejected.

He received more financial remuneration, if less critical acclaim, for his novels. (He did not write them as slowly and laboriously as the stories. You can't.) An early private eye novel, *The Eighth Circle,* impressed me when I read it years ago. His later novels never worked terribly well for me, but the short stories are timeless, and a national treasure.

Erle Stanley Gardner (1889–1970). Eighty-two novels about Perry Mason. Nine about D.A. Doug Selby. Twenty-nine (under the name A. A. Fair) about the private eye team of Donald Lam and Bertha Cool. If Stanley Ellin crept through his stories at a snail's pace, Erle Stanley Gardner wrote as if his hair were on fire.

I discovered Perry Mason when I was twelve, and I don't know how many of the books I read over the next three or four years. They were relentlessly formulaic, and, in a sense, if you'd read one, you'd read them all. On the other hand, if you enjoyed one, you would enjoy them all.

The prose narration was sloppy, the descriptions clichéd. Gardner hurried through those parts, and so does the reader. But the dialogue, effortless for the author, was absolutely masterly, and the courtroom scenes, however unrealistic they may have been, worked magically upon the page.

Mason himself changed over the years. In the earlier books he himself was a shady character willing to bend and even break the law in the service of a client. He grew respectable in his middle years, when most of his cases were serialized in *The Saturday Evening Post,* and he turned staid and dull later on.

After a period of neglect Perry Mason seems to be coming back into favor with readers. Try one of the prewar Masons—*The Case of the Sulky Girl* is a good one—or any of the A. A. Fair books. The latter are very different, breezily narrated by Donald Lam, and characterized by much better writing than the Masons.

Dashiell Hammett (1894–1961). Hammett's colossal reputation rests upon a very small body of work. After several years laboring for the pulps, he published five novels in as many years, then wrote virtually nothing for the remaining twenty-seven years of his life. And the last of the novels, *The Thin Man,* is really not much good.

No matter. The others are superb, as impressive now as when they were written more than a half century ago.

Hammett was a Pinkerton detective before he started writing, and his experience informs his work. But his greatness is far more than a matter of being able to write knowledgeably of crime and criminals. Both his literary style and his artistic vision cast an unsparing light on Prohibition-era America. In sentences that were flat and uninflected and remarkably nonjudgmental, he did much the same thing Hemingway did. I would argue that he did it better.

The Maltese Falcon is my own favorite, and the Bogart film won't spoil it for you; the book quite literally *is* the John Huston screenplay.

Chester Himes (1909–84). If Hammett brought the special perceptions of a detective to crime fiction, Chester Himes came at it from the other side. He began writing toward the end of a seven-year stretch in an Ohio state penitentiary. His first books were novels of the black experience, critically successful but not widely read. In 1957 he wrote his first crime novel and introduced his pair of Harlem detectives, Grave Digger Jones and Coffin Ed Johnson, who were to appear in eight more books.

Savage, violent, and wildly funny, Himes was never as successful in America as he was in France, where he lived from 1953 until his death. I don't know how well the books hold up, but I know they were terrific when I read them, especially *Cotton Comes to Harlem.*

John D. MacDonald (1916–86). The creator of Travis McGee, boat bum and self-styled salvage expert, had an M.B.A. degree from Harvard Business School. I don't suppose that's anywhere near as weird as Wallace Stevens working for an insurance company and writing *Peter Quince at the Clavier* in his spare time, but it's a far cry from the way Hammett and Himes prepped for their writing careers.

It seems likely that McGee, hero of twenty-two fast-paced novels, will stand as MacDonald's greatest creation. By the time McGee made his initial appearance in *The Deep Blue Goodby* in 1964, MacDonald had already published some forty books, all but a handful of them paperback originals. They're almost all crime novels, and they're almost all excellent.

The French, connoisseurs of our literary dark side, don't know from MacDonald, and on reflection I can understand why. For all the ecological foreboding of the McGee books, MacDonald's vision is not on the surface noir at all. His sensibilities were always Middle American, and his characters approached difficult situations with the problem-solver attitude of an engineer. But there is a darkness to MacDonald, evident in his unparalleled ability to limn a sociopath, present too in that neglected late work *One More Sunday.* But it is not the knee-jerk darkness of the noir world view but the somehow bleaker darkness of a light that has failed.

Some of the late McGees are weak books, but so what? Start with *The Deep Blue Goodby* and read them all in order. Of the non-McGees, I have especially fond recollections of *The End of the Night* and *One Monday We killed Them All*. Each in its own quiet way is dark enough to make noir look like a light show.

Ross Macdonald (1915–83). Ross Macdonald was born Kenneth Millar and wrote his first mystery novels under that name. Then he wrote one book as John Macdonald and five as John Ross Macdonald, finally dropping the "John" to avoid confusion with John D. MacDonald.

He began writing in frank imitation of Hammett and Chandler, and the early books in the Lew Archer series are markedly Chandleresque, with Archer wisecracking briskly in the Philip Marlowe mode.

With *The Doomsters* in 1958 and *The Galton Case* a year later, Macdonald came into his own and went on to write a series of books unlike anything before him. Against the background of the Southern California ecosystem in metastasis, Archer bears witness as the mills of God relentlessly exact retribution for long-past sins.

A few years ago my wife and I were in West Africa for three weeks. We had plenty of luxuries like food and water, but nothing to read, and the only books and magazines available were in French. Then, in our hotel in Lomé, the capital of Togo, I discovered five Lew Archers, second-hand paperbacks that had been badly printed in India. The newsdealer wanted an extortionately high ten dollars a piece for them, and I paid it willingly. They sustained us all the way back to JFK.

Of course we had read them all before, some of them two or three times. It didn't matter. It is one of the singular properties of Ross Macdonald's fiction that ten minutes after you have turned the last page, every detail of the plot vanishes forever from your mind. I'm sure I could reread those five books right now without much more than the faintest sense of déjà vu.

In a sense the plot of every book is much the same. A character did something reprehensible twenty or thirty or forty years ago—in the war, perhaps, or in Canada. Now things begin to fall apart,

and, even as Archer rushes around trying to forestall disaster, the guilty and innocent alike are sucked down into the primordial Freudian ooze.

Wonderful books. Read any of the post-1958 Archers for a start. And don't throw it away when you're done. In a few years you'll be able to read it again for the first time.

Ellery Queen (Frederic Dannay, 1905–82, and Manfred B. Lee, 1905–71). Prohibition must have been a time of great self-discovery. Even as Americans were discovering themselves as hard and tough and cynical, and confirming this discovery in the works of Hammett and Chandler, so were many of us waking up to find ourselves clever, and rejoicing in our mental agility by working crossword puzzles, playing contract bridge, and repeating the Round Table talk of the Algonquin crowd. And by reading intricate deductive mystery novels and trying to figure them out.

The books of Frederic Dannay and Manfred Lee, two cousins from Brooklyn, were bylined Ellery Queen and featured a detective of the same name. (They were not first-person narratives, however; Ellery Queen wrote about himself in the third person.) They took the intellectual puzzle of S. S. Van Dine's insufferable Philo Vance and elevated it to its highest level. Vintage Ellery Queen mysteries (*The Greek Coffin Mystery, The Chinese Orange Mystery*) feature a formal challenge to the reader at the point where all the clues needed to solve the puzzle have been furnished. The books were always fair, and diabolically clever.

During the forties Ellery Queen matured artistically, and the books became more than brainteasers, with a richness of character and setting and mood. *Calamity Town, Ten Days' Wonder,* and *Cat of Many Tails* are especially successful.

The books alone make up a towering body of work. Add in a slew of first-rate short stories, innumerable radio plays, and four decades at the editorship of the field's preeminent magazine, and the extent of Lee and Dannay's achievement begins to become clear.

Jack Ritchie (1922–83). For years I did the same thing whenever I got hold of a copy of *Ellery Queen's* or *Alfred Hitchcock's Mystery Magazine*. I looked to see if there was a story by Jack Ritchie. If there was, I read it right away.

Ritchie was a miniaturist in an age when writers are judged by the number of trees cut down to print their work. He wrote only short stories, and he tried to do so without wasting a word. His work was sprightly and surprising and always engaging, and he never wrote an awkward sentence or a lifeless line of dialogue.

Then one day he died, and his stories went on appearing for several months and then trickled out, and ever since I have picked up those magazines with diminishing anticipation. Nowadays I look to see if they've reprinted one of his stories. If they have, I read it right away.

Rex Stout (1886–1975). I know several men and women who are forever rereading the Nero Wolfe books. They read other things as well, of course, but every month or two they have another go at one of Stout's novels. Since there are forty books, it takes them four or five years to get through the cycle, at which time they can start in again at the beginning. They do this not for the plots, which are serviceable, or for the suspense, which is minimal even on first reading. Nor are they hoping for fresh insight into the human condition. No, they reread the books for the same reason so many of us do, for the joy of spending a few hours in the most congenial household in American letters, the brownstone on West Thirty-fifth Street that is home to Nero Wolfe and Archie Goodwin.

The relationship of these two, Wolfe the genius and Archie the man of action, is endlessly fascinating. Ultimately it is less Wolfe's eccentricities—the orchids, the agoraphobia, the food and drink, the yellow pajamas—than the nuances of character that keep us transfixed. Stout wrote these books almost effortlessly, in a matter of weeks, and his first drafts went to the printer with no need to change so much as a comma. They seem as flawless today, and utterly timeless.

Jim Thompson (1906–76). Thompson published twenty-nine books during his lifetime, all but one of them paperback originals. More than half of his output appeared in the fifties, with five books each published in 1953 and 1954. Most of them were published by Lion Books, a third-rate house. They were rarely reviewed and never commanded a wide readership. In the late sixties Thompson did a few novelizations of films and television shows to make

ends meet. By the time he died, all his books were long out of print.

Now, seventeen years after his death, Jim Thompson is the hottest writer around. His novels of doomed losers and flippant sociopaths are all back in print, and there are several films in production or recently released, among them the highly successful *The Grifters,* the screenplay of which earned the mystery writer Donald E. Westlake an Oscar nomination.

For years Thompson was unjustly neglected. Now I suspect he's getting rather more attention than he deserves. His books are intermittently wonderful, casting a cold eye indeed on life and death and providing an utterly unsparing view of the human condition. They are also intermittently awful, flawed by chapters of slapdash writing, adolescent character development, and mechanical plotting.

The Killer Inside Me, Pop. 1280, and *The Getaway* show Thompson at his best. He is surely an important writer and very much worth reading, but it helps to keep it in mind that the stuff ain't Shakespeare.

Charles Willeford (1919–88). In one of his Hoke Mosely mysteries, Charles Willeford supplied a character who had retired after a lifetime spent painting pinstripes on the sides of automobiles. He now lived in a development in South Florida, where he liked to walk through his neighborhood with a kind word and a cheerful smile for everyone he met. He carried a walking stick, its hollow interior stocked with poisoned meat pellets; the affable old boy delighted in poisoning every dog that crossed his path.

I can't think of anyone else who could have created that little man, let alone made him work. Willeford kept coming up with quirky characters and put them in wonderfully quirky books. A career soldier in the horse cavalry and a highly decorated tank commander in World War II, he wrote a variety of books over the years, all of them providing a skewed vision of the universe.

It was in the Hoke Mosely novels, starting with *Miami Blues,* that Willeford came into his full powers as a writer. He wrote four of them, each better than the last, and was just beginning to win the wide readership and critical recognition he deserved when he went and died. It was the sort of joke he would have appreciated.

I am told he left the rough first draft of a fifth Mosely novel, darker than dark, unpublishably dark, with Hoke rounding things out by murdering his own teenage daughters. If that manuscript's out there somewhere, I want to read it. Meanwhile, read the other four in order. Willeford wrote two volumes of autobiography, *I Was Looking for a Street* and *Something About a Soldier*. Both are a treat.

Cornell Woolrich (1903–68). A couple of years ago I read a Woolrich short story in which a pulp writer locks himself in a hotel room and works all night to meet a deadline. When he's done, he falls asleep, exhausted; when he wakes up, he's horrified to discover that the pages are blank. There was no ribbon in the typewriter. Presumably the hero took each page in turn from the typewriter without noting the absence of words on it.

Cornell Woolrich was capable of this sort of plotting. Loose ends and illogical twists and turns abound in his books, but they don't really matter. His great strength, it seems to me, lay in his unrivaled ability to make novels of the stuff of nightmares. Woolrich's characters prowl tacky dance halls and alleyways. They smoke dope in strange apartments, swallow spiked cocktails, and run hallucinating through unfamiliar streets. The suspense is relentless, the sense of impending doom ever present.

Woolrich wrote his best books early on, starting with *The Bride Wore Black* in 1940.

The most noteworthy aspect of my list, it seems to me, is the number of significant writers I've had to leave out. I could easily have included a dozen more. If I were fool enough to include living writers, I'd have had to write a book. Because, for all the talk one hears of the mystery's vintage years, I think it is abundantly clear that the very best crime fiction ever is being written today. These are the good old days, and a very real reason for the huge popularity of mysteries is that the genre is in its Golden Age. Many of the very best writers alive are writing crime novels, and they are doing extraordinary things within the genre, things no one has previously attempted.

If there's a lot of wheat, surely there's no end of chaff. I suppose ninety percent of what's being published today is nothing special, but when was it ever otherwise? The good stuff, I assure you, is very good indeed.

You'll excuse me, I hope, if I decline to point it out to you. But think of the fun you'll have digging it out for yourself!

MYSTERIES OF NEW YORK
William L. DeAndrea

THE NEW YORK MYSTERY.

It's a topic, like the city itself, that's almost too big to take in, largely because New York itself is a mystery, a collection of hopes, dreams (good ones and nightmares), and elbows that somehow sustains critical mass, and against all logic, keeps on going.

I like to tell people that everything, good and bad, that they've ever heard about New York is true. Because the truth is, there are *many* New Yorks.

To Washington Irving it was Gotham, after a legendary English village famous for the foolishness of its inhabitants. One-time jailbird and sometime crime writer O. Henry liked to describe it as Baghdad-on-the-Hudson, invoking Baghdad in the Arabian Nights sense of wonder and magic and endless possibilities (though a modern-day sense of a third-world city run by the corrupt and insane might not be too far off the mark either). Jazz musicians of the twenties dubbed it the Big Apple, and this is the image New Yorkers like the best—"if I can make it there, I'll make it anywhere''—the wise cracking-cabbie hard-driven-executive sarcastic-waiter New York, the city of people who've seen it all twice and can take anything in stride.

Ironically, it's the smallest slice of the Big Apple that's been the setting for the most mysteries—Society New York. Murder here is done in penthouse apartments and double-width brownstone mansions, among people who go to nightclubs and take taxis and limos everywhere.

It's a milieu that goes back at least as far as Peter Clancy, the society private eye (he even had a Jeeves-ish manservant), the creation of Lee Thayer. Thayer established a record in the mystery world by publishing well into her nineties, so Clancy, who debuted before Hercule Poirot, was solving the same kinds of crime among the same kinds of people from the days immediately post-World War II until the swinging sixties.

The apotheosis of Society New York detectives was, of course, S. S. Van Dine's Philo Vance. His first published detection, *The Benson Murder Case,* in 1926, is considered by most authorities to mark the start of the so-called Golden Age of the mystery in the United States. Vance, a Nietzschean aesthete who drops psychological pronunciamentos on crime and the *gs* from the ends of words with equal aplomb, investigates crimes not for a living, or for a love of justice, but for light entertainment, and to help his continually baffled friend, the district attorney. It was a conceit of the series, at least at first, that all of Vance's twelve investigations took place during his friend's one term as Manhattan D.A. Considering the slaughter that took place among the moneyed classes during that time, it's no wonder he wasn't reelected. The two most famous of Vance's investigations, *The Greene Murder Case* and *The Bishop Murder Case,* could have been detected by a trained chimpanzee, since both consist of a family of suspects being bumped off one after another until practically nobody is left but the killer. Vance, by the way, that irrepressible little *Übermensch,* is not above solving the case in the first half hour, then letting the police thrash around to his amusement for the rest of the book, or knocking off the killer in cold blood himself.

How very different from the first important Society New York detective. Anna Katharine Green's Ebenezer Gryce appeared for the first time in *The Leavenworth Case* in 1878 (some nine years before Sherlock Holmes). Though he's New York's most brilliant detective of the day, his wellborn author puts the conviction in his head that his profession disqualifies him as a gentleman. Gryce has to recruit a sympathetic member of the appropriate class to help him on those frequent occasions when he is called to investigate crime among the gentry.

The pull of the Society New York murder is a strong one for the mystery author. Even the master of the mean streets, Dashiell Hammett, sent his hard-boiled hero into the depths (as it were) of High Society in *The Thin Man* (1934), his only mystery to be set in New York. To be sure, the story takes us to the occasional speakeasy, where we rub elbows with the odd riff or raff, but the motive and the crime are solidly in the social register stratum.

There are others who moved primarily in these circles. As head of Manhattan Homicide, Helen Reilly's Inspector Christopher McKee must have investigated hundreds of knifings in barrooms, but virtually the only cases we are given to read about are the ones that take him to the penthouses and town houses. McKee, at least, doesn't have the class hangups that plagued Gryce—he mingles among the rich himself. With his books appearing between 1930 and 1962, McKee was sort of an unrumpled, East Coast predecessor of *Columbo.*

Stuart Palmer's old-fashioned schoolma'am spinster sleuth, Hildegarde Withers, who also detected from the thirties to the sixties, defied the laws of probability in stumbling over multitudinous corpses in her life. She absolutely antagonized them with the number of times the corpse led to a case involving big money. During the course of the series, Miss Withers retired from teaching. It's a good thing. The reader could accept the horse-faced lady in the eccentric hat finding bodies and even solving murders. The mind boggles at the thought of her in a New York City school today, frisking students for Uzis and passing out condoms.

The New York Society murder has faded to near extinction as a fictional form; perhaps because the members of this particular segment of society have been killed off so assiduously in the past that they've been declared an endangered species. Perhaps the closest thing to this these days are the novels about John Putnam Thatcher, vice president of the Wall Street giant the Sloan Guaranty Trust, whose cases always involve big money, but rarely

Society. New York yuppie murders, if you like. Since the series began in the early 1960s, the two ladies who write these books as Emma Lathen were writing about yuppies some twenty years or so before the term was invented. My own novels about TV network troubleshooter Matt Cobb explore similar territory.

Taking a step down the social pyramid, Frances and Richard Lockridge's stories of Mr. and Mrs. North plunk down solidly in the upper middle class of which they themselves were members. Jerry is a publisher, you see, and Pam easily outdistances Hildegarde Withers as a stumbler over bodies, discovering legions of them in a twenty-year detecting career that began in 1940.

Rex Stout's Nero Wolfe gets involved in murder for profit, not by accident, but his clientele comes by and large from the circles the Norths move in. He does have the odd old-money, Society client, but mostly he solves crimes for (and among) businessmen and their families. The Wolfe books rate special mention for two reasons. One, his narrator-assistant Archie Goodwin, in addition to his other talents, is virtually a walking map of Manhattan. Two, Wolfe living as he does on westernmost West Thirty-fifth Street (most of the addresses of the luxurious brownstone given in the novels would put it well out into the Hudson River, maybe even into New Jersey), he resides in what is now, and has been since the series started in 1934, a fairly crummy neighborhood. The neighbors must have been quite amused by the parade of topcoated lawyers and businessmen to the old brownstone.

There are no purely lower-class New York mysteries, although New York *is* the town for which the term *underclass* was first coined. The reason is simple. It's much more interesting (and commercial) to *contrast* the poverty, struggles, etc. of the poor (especially the noble, struggling working poor) at least occasionally, with those more fortunate (and frequently more villainous). Thus, even Mike Hammer, whose world seems to be stuck in perpetual dark and drizzle, has his encounters with the upper class. Hammer creator Mickey Spillane, in perhaps his best book, did set a mystery in one workingclass neighborhood—the non–Mike Hammer novel *The Deep*.

Michael Collins's one-armed private eye Dan Fortune began his adventures working out of Chelsea, which has been recently gentrified but was once

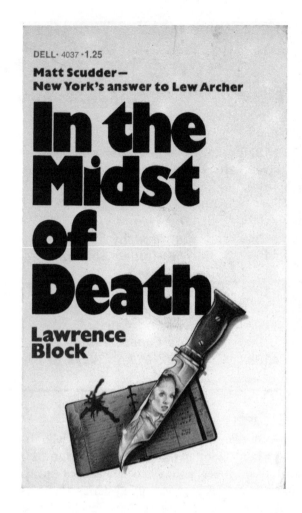

a fairly seedy neighborhood. His friends and clients tend to be local, the crimes themselves the results of the greed of the rich.

Evan Hunter produced a novel and a short-story collection ostensibly written by first-person narrator Curt Cannon. Cannon was a Bowery derelict who slept on park benches and solved crimes for drinking money. *All* his cases were social ascents.

The astute reader will have noticed by now that the books and characters we have discussed have been concerned solely with the borough of Manhattan. That is a reflection of the literature. In the 1980s, Robert J. Randisi gave us private eye Nick Delvecchio, who lives and works in Brooklyn, the most populous borough; a couple of Donald E. Westlake's comic capers make use of the outer boroughs—*The Fugitive Pigeon* actually gets to Brooklyn, Queens, and Staten Island before it's done. But Manhattan is the scene for most New York murders.

Some Notable New York Mysteries
Selected by William L. DeAndrea

1878	*The Leavenworth Case*	Anna Katharine Green
1926	*The Bishop Murder Case*	S. S. Van Dine
1932	*The Tragedy of X*	Ellery Queen (writing as Barnaby Ross)
1934	*The Thin Man*	Dashiell Hammett
1949	*Cat of Many Tails*	Ellery Queen
1953	*The Golden Spiders*	Rex Stout
1961	*The Deep*	Mickey Spillane
1971	*Hail, Hail the Gang's All Here*	Ed McBain
1975	*Night of the Juggler*	William P. McGivern
1976	*Dancing Aztecs*	Donald E. Westlake
1980	*The Lunatic Fringe*	William L. DeAndrea
1982	*Eight Million Ways to Die*	Lawrence Block

Australian-born William Marshall, who made his first reputation in the genre with his surreal Yellowthread Street police procedurals set in Hong Kong, later did a series of mysteries set in New York at the turn of the century, invoking a sense of both nostalgia and the extent to which things have (and have not) changed since the turn of the century.

Finally, I want to call to your attention to three very different authors, who, over the course of their careers, have taken the whole panorama of life in New York as the background of their mysteries.

The first is Ellery Queen, the joint pseudonym of cousins Frederic Dannay and Manfred B. Lee. Granted, a portrait of New York is not the first thing that springs to mind when Queen is mentioned. The things that do—a giant of the Golden Age, a master of the classic fair-play mystery puzzle—are all true. But during the course of their career, running from the twenties to the seventies, the cousins found time to touch on virtually every aspect of life in New York, from the Philo Vance-ish dallying among the upper crust in their early work, to late thirties-style screwball comedy, to socially conscious short stories of the late forties and early fifties, highlighting

the postwar housing shortage, or the burgeoning problem of juvenile delinquency, to one truly magnificent novel. *Cat of Many Tails* (1949) is not only a pioneering serial-murders novel melded with a fair-play puzzle and cognizant of the dawning of the age of the couch, it is a glorious snapshot of the city in a time of crisis.

Aaron Marc Stein, whose career stretched from the thirties to the eighties, early on adopted the technique of seizing on some aspect of life in New York to build a mystery around, especially in his Inspector Schmidt novels as George Bagby, and his novels about Assistant D.A.'s Gibby and Mac written as Hampton Stone. Over the years he treated topics as diverse as life in the shadow of the Third Avenue el and life in the city's specialized high schools. He explored the problems of welfare mothers, and murder in an unusual Manhattan enclave called Turtle Bay. His work was always brisk and eminently readable.

It is a paradox that the greatest writer of New York City in the mystery—for my money, the greatest writer of New York City, period—avowedly does not write about New York at all. The city he writes about, we are assured in every book, is fictitious. It is also nameless, consisting of the boroughs of Isola, Majesta, Riverhead, Calm's Point, and Bethtown.

We are not fooled. We know Manhattan, Queens, the Bronx, Brooklyn, and Staten Island when we see them. Especially when we see them as they really are. Since 1956, Ed McBain (another manifestation of Evan Hunter) has explored every facet of life in New York, from slums to mansions, from juvenile delinquents to professional gangsters, from all sorts of victims to all sorts of heroes. McBain's 87th Precinct is a microcosm of New York, as New York is a microcosm of the world.

As I have said in print before, if scholars of the future want to know the emotional reality of life in New York in the twentieth century, they should read the 87th Precinct novels of Ed McBain.

This has been by no means an exhaustive discussion of the subject. There are dozens more— hundreds. Space considerations force me to do you the disservice of failing to call them to your attention. And there are more to come, many more. I'll be writing some of them myself.

After all, there are eight million stories in the Naked City. And a lot of them are mysteries.

LOS ANGELES MYSTERIES
Jon L. Breen

THERE IS NO PARTICULAR reason that some major cities should be considered more desirable than others as mystery story locales—or even why urban stories have to take place in major cities at all. Still, certain metropolitan areas have been favored—the London of Sherlock Holmes, the Paris of Maigret, the New York of Philo Vance and Ellery Queen, the San Francisco of Dashiell Hammett, and the Los Angeles of Raymond Chandler.

Chandler was not the first mystery writer to use L.A. as a backdrop, but he is certainly the most closely associated with the city, putting his stamp on it with timeless, unforgettable passages of description. Chandler had a love-hate relationship with the city, a sprawling area lacking the compact center to be found in most other metropolises. While some of his descriptions still resonate with truth about present-day Los Angeles, others fall into the realm of nostalgia.

In an essay on Chandler's L.A. in *Ellery Queen's Mystery Magazine* (October 1963)[1], Philip Durham discusses the author's gradual disenchantment with the city (and incidentally his homo-

[1] It later became part of Durham's pioneering study *Down These Mean Streets a Man Must Go: Raymond Chandler's Knight* (U. of North Carolina Press, 1963).

phobia) as reflected in a passage from *The Little Sister* (1949):

> "I used to like this town. A long time ago. There were trees along Wilshire Boulevard. Beverly Hills was a country town. Westwood was bare hills and lots offering at eleven hundred dollars and no takers. Hollywood was a bunch of frame houses on the interurban line. Los Angeles was just a big dry sunny place with ugly homes and no style, but good-hearted and peaceful." But now all of the homey attractiveness had gone, having given way to pansy decorators, lesbian dress designers, riffraff of a "big hard-boiled city with no more personality than a paper cup"—a city without the "individual bony structure" a real city must have.
>
> In the old days, Marlowe had driven along that same Sunset Boulevard on a "crisp morning with just enough snap in the air to make life seem simple and sweet." On the way back down the coast from Malibu he had driven on a highway washed clean by the rain; on his left were low rolling hills of "yellow-white sand traced with pink moss"; on his right the gulls were wheeling and swooping over something in the surf. Marlowe was on his way into the city to do something for the betterment of society, and willingly. (Pages 60-61)

It needs to be noted that at the same time Marlowe and Chandler were becoming disillusioned, newcomers were still seeing L.A. as the promised land, and today more recent residents look back nostalgically on the early seventies before the city was ruined. (In a parallel situation, characters in Earl Derr Biggers's 1925 novel *The House Without a Key* decried the ruin through overdevelopment and commercialization of Honolulu, which had been a great place in the 1880s.)

While Chandler and his successor Ross Macdonald (Kenneth Millar) only occasionally involved the motion picture world in their complex plots, it is the part of L.A. called Hollywood that has attracted most mystery writers. An early example is Raoul Whitfield's *Death in a Bowl* (1931), in which private eye Ben Jardinn investigates the murder of the conductor during a Hollywood Bowl concert. Some of Whitfield's pulp stories also employed a filmland setting.

Two of the most prominent and long-running of the pulps' Hollywood sleuths were W. T. Ballard's studio troubleshooter Bill Lennox, who first appeared in the *Black Mask* short story "A Little Different" (September 1933) and was a character in several book-length cases beginning with *Say Yes to Murder* (1942); and Robert Leslie Bellem's Dan Turner, a Hollywood shamus who filled the pages of *Spicy Detective* and other pulps with sexy prose and crazy slang from 1934 to 1950.

Especially after the advent of sound, many stage, book, and magazine writers were lured to Hollywood from their safe and sane eastern and midwestern homes to accept screenwriting assignments. Unsurprisingly, many of them were attracted to the movie world for their plots. Thus, Richard Sale, a New Yorker who had begun a two-track writing career as the pulp chronicler of Daffy Dill and Candid Jones and a writer of "literary" fiction beginning with *Not Too Narrow, Not Too Deep*

(1936), used a Hollywood background for the novels *Lazarus No. 7* (1942), *Passing Strange* (1942), and *Benefit Performance* (1946). Sale subsequently became a screen director as well as a writer and produced a noncriminous Hollywood novel, *The Oscar* (1963).

When the Ellery Queen team was brought to Hollywood for a short stint as screenwriters in the thirties, they shifted their sleuth's base of operations west for a pair of books: *The Devil to Pay* (1938) and *The Four of Hearts* (1938). They returned to the setting one last time in *The Origin of Evil* (1951), the best of their Hollywood works. In fact, one writer of my acquaintance, caught up in the ghostwriter hunt occasioned by rumors (sometimes true) about the final Queen novels, swore the real author of *The Origin of Evil* had to be Ross Macdonald. Actually, there is no indication any Queen novel published in hardcover before *The Player on the Other Side* (1963, written by Theodore Sturgeon from an outline by Frederic Dannay) involved ghostwriters or third collaborators.

Another writer who began writing about New York backgrounds, Wisconsin native Stuart Palmer, brought his schoolteacher detective Hildegarde Withers to the West Coast for a Hollywood case in *The Puzzle of the Happy Hooligan* (1941). Palmer's sometime collaborator, Craig Rice, never brought her heavy-drinking Chicago lawyer John J. Malone to Hollywood, but she did ghostwrite (with Cleve Cartmill) a Hollywood case for George Sanders, *Crime on My Hands* (1944). Actor Sanders is his own first-person narrator of the comic mystery. Rice did transport her team of con men and street photographers, Bingo Riggs and Handsome Kusak, to the film capital in her final novel, *The April Robin Murders* (1958), completed after her death by Ed McBain. Another Chicago writer who was lured to Hollywood for a screen career and used the background for a novel was Jonathan Latimer with *Black Is the Fashion for Dying* (1959).

While Hollywood filmmaking from the thirties forward has been used—and maybe overused—as a background for mysteries, the silent era has been relatively neglected. It was left to an Englishman, Peter Lovesey, to exploit the criminous possibilities of Mack Sennett's comedy factory in *Keystone* (1983). More recently, L. J. Washburn has introduced a silent-picture-era private eye in cowboy Lucas Hallam, beginning with *Wild Nights* (1987).

The mysterious 1922 murder of director William Desmond Taylor has been fictionalized in Samuel A. Peeples's time-travel fantasy *The Man Who Died Twice* (1976), but most book-length treatments of the case have come in nonfiction studies. The same is true of the case of Fatty Arbuckle, the silent comic accused (probably wrongly) of rape in the death of an actress, though the case was fictionalized (with names changed) in Garet Rogers's trial novel *Scandal in Eden* (1963). Perhaps the most notable mystery novel about the silent film industry written at the time it was actually operating, Arthur B. Reeve's *The Film Mystery* (1921), was set not in Hollywood but in New York. Movie columnist Jimmy Starr, who would produce some novels in the forties and fifties beginning with *The Corpse Came C.O.D.* (1944), included a soundstage whodunit in his limited-edition collection *365 Nights in Hollywood* (1926).

With Jack Webb's *Dragnet* radio and television series achieving overwhelming popularity in the fifties, the Los Angeles Police Department became prominent in the development of the police procedural form. It may also be attributable to the presence of the Hollywood film industry that the department has probably produced more moonlighting writers than any other, beginning with the best-selling novelist Joseph Wambaugh and continuing with such formidable scribes as Dallas Barnes and Paul Bishop. Some writers, such as James Ellroy in his historical series beginning with *The Black Dahlia* (1987), give a somewhat less than flattering view of the L.A.P.D. The Dahlia case, an L.A. cause célèbre of the late forties, has also been fictionalized by John Gregory Dunne in *True Confessions* (1977), which in 1981 was made into one of the classic L.A. crime films by screenwriters Dunne and Joan Didion and director Ulu Grosbard.

Through the years Los Angeles has been home to a long string of prominent private eyes who follow, to a greater or lesser degree, in the tradition of Chandler's Marlowe and Macdonald's Lew Archer. One of the best, Jake Gittes, appeared not in print but in the classic film *Chinatown* (1974), directed by Roman Polanski from Robert Towne's original script. Some of the better-known print private eyes, in approximate chronological order, are Roy Huggins's Stu Bailey (later the main character of the TV series *77 Sunset Strip*), Richard S. Prather's Shell Scott, William Campbell Gault's Brock

Callahan and Joe Puma, William F. Nolan's Bart Challis, Joseph Hansen's Dave Brandstetter, Roger L. Simon's Moses Wine, Arthur Lyons's Jacob Asch, Dick Lochte's Leo Bloodworth, and Robert Crais's Elvis Cole. Of the principal "nostalgia 'tecs," Stuart Kaminsky's Toby Peters is, of course, centered in Los Angeles, and encounters real Hollywood celebrities of the forties in each of his cases, while Andrew Bergman's Jack LeVine visits in the course of his second case, *Hollywood and LeVine* (1975). Some of the foreign authors of American-style p.i. fiction, notably the Australian Carter Brown and the British Basil Copper, have used Los Angeles as their scene with varying degrees of credibility.

Why is Los Angeles such an attractive locale for fictional crime? Throughout the twentieth century, indeed until the combination of bad air, overpopulation, and civil unrest somewhat marred its reputation, it was the place people all over the country, even the world, wanted to come to, at least to visit and with luck to live. They looked longingly at its mild climate, and its glamorous associations with the entertainment industry didn't hurt. Viewers in the frozen Midwest and East would watch the annual Rose Parade on New Year's Day (not in L.A. proper, but in nearby Pasadena) and envy those who had the good fortune to live year-round with all that sun. But that same envy gave visiting writers the desire to tear the place down, expose the shallowness and enervating quality of living in such a perfect environment.

Nothing makes a better locale for crime fiction than a spoiled paradise: See, for example, the recent spate of crime novels set in Florida. Los Angeles has long had a well-earned reputation as a center for oddball political, social, and religious movements: Witness all those private eye novels centering on crazy cults. That most inhabitants of Southern California have survived over the years without much direct contact with the crime or the craziness doesn't matter. The combination of warm weather, loosening of social restraints, glamour, and all manner of corruption made L.A. the best of mystery backdrops.

CHICAGO AS A MYSTERY SETTING

Barbara D'Amato

CHICAGO IS A PLACE where blizzards bring down mayors, where streets are dry but floods go underground and creep into buildings from the tunnels, where bridges sometimes fall up and stick that way, where winters can go to twenty-six below, where it may snow in mid-April and hit ninety in mid-May. There are strong winds in Chicago, and not all of them are in the City Council meetings. You go abroad and tell somebody you're from Chicago and they say "Chicago? Rat-a-tat-tat-tat!"

If you can survive the winters and the politics, you can survive anything.

Is there any wonder Chicago writing is often called gritty? People usually mean gritty in the colloquial sense—plucky and full of character. But a bit of the meaning of grit in the formal sense has crept in. Like those small rough particles of stone called grit—you can't wear 'em down, can't get rid of 'em, can't entirely civilize 'em.

Whatever *gritty* means, there is implied a Chicago style of writing, straightforward, no-nonsense,

Miriam Berkley

the poorest neighborhoods in the nation, and they're all in one ward. There's the Art Institute, the Museum of Science and Industry, and the Chicago Symphony. Live theater. Comedy clubs. Jazz and blues. There are hundreds of ethnic neighborhoods. You want to send a detective to a Peruvian restaurant? Choice of several. Swedish? Sure. Ethiopian? No problem.

Many writers who live in Chicago and set their stories in other places still have elements of the Chicago straightforwardness. Robert Goldsborough, Ronald Levitsky, William Love, and Marion Markham are a few.

For a complete walking guide to the locations of fictional criminal doings in Chicago, with lots of extra insights about the area and historical notes on real Chicago crimes as well, see Alzina Stone Dale's, *A Mystery Reader's Walking Guide: Chicago,* to be published by Passport Books in spring 1994.

and aggressive. No fancy writin' and very little excess verbiage. Not much fantasy. Nothing very abstract and not much Utopia. Some anger but not much angst. Chicago is a city that works, in its own unabashed way, and Chicago writing is not much given to despair or existential gloom.

Because of Chicago's reputation as a crime capital, there is a general view that Chicago crime fiction all contains rampant mob-involvement. This is a lot less true than it used to be. Motives for murder in Chicago mysteries now also include Board of Trade scams, medical malpractice, insurance fraud, mental illness, child abuse, public aid scams, job competition, and such political motives as anti-fur, anti-abortion, pro-choice, anti-prostitution, and anti-lottery. Things have gone far beyond the recycling of the Al Capone story under different guises. On the other hand, some elements, such as dead people who vote, political payoffs and patronage, machine politics, ward heelers, corrupt judges, crooked prosecutors, and other staples of the crime story remain unfortunately very believable.

Chicago has a lot of advantages to offer authors as a setting: the world's tallest buildings, a lakefront that rivals Rio four months of the year (there's another four months when it's more like the waterfront in Anchorage). There's the el, and O'Hare, and the tunnels off Lower Wacker, where homeless live in winter. There are some of the richest and

Criminal Chicago by Current Writers
Selected by Barbara D'Amato

Eleanor Bland **Dead Time**

Martin Blank **Shadowchase**

Bill Brashler (as Crabbe Evers with Reinder VanTil) **Murder in Wrigley Field**

D. C. Brod **Murder in Store**

Howard Browne **Pork City**

Charles Cohen **Silver Linings**

Max Allan Collins **Dying in the Postwar World**

Robert Campbell **The Junkyard Dog**

Michael Cormany **Lost Daughter**

Barbara D'Amato **Hard Women**

Marc Davis **Dirty Money**

Gerald DiPego **Keeper of the City**

Michael A. Dymmoch **The Man Who Understood Cats**

Paul Engleman **The Man with My Name**

David Everson **Suicide Squeeze**

John Fink **The Leaf Boats**

Bill Granger **Public Murders**

Andrew Greeley **Happy Are the Meek**

Barbara Gregorich **Dirty Proof**

C. A. Haddad **Caught in the Shadows**

Richard Hyer **Riceburner**

Eugene Izzi **Tribal Secrets**

D.J.H. Jones **Murder at the MLA**

Michael Kahn **Grave Designs**

Stuart Kaminsky **Lieberman's Choice**

Michael J. Katz **Murder off the Glass**

Harold Klawans **Sins of Commission**

Arthur Maling **Lover and Thief**

Ralph McInerny **Seed of Doubt**

Jay Robert Nash **A Crime Story**

Catherine O'Connell **Skins**

Sara Paretsky **Guardian Angel**

Percy Parker **Good Girls Don't Get Murdered**

Monica Quill **Let Us Prey**

Michael Raleigh **Death in Uptown**

Sam Reaves **A Long Cold Fall**

Les Roberts **Seeing the Elephant**

Michael Sherer **Death Came Dressed in White**

Scott Turow **Burden of Proof**

R. D. Zimmerman **Blood Trance**

Mark Zubro **Sorry Now?**

MIDWEST MYSTERIES

Mary Helen Becker

THE MIDWEST, which, for our purposes, includes the vast area from Michigan to the Dakotas, Ohio to Kansas, and all the states north to the Canadian border, is home to some notable writers of mystery and crime fiction. While the majority of American crime fiction writers live on the coasts or in the Chicago area, no survey of the scene would be complete without a consideration of the authors in the heartland.

Detroit author Elmore Leonard is an incomparable storyteller noted for his brilliant dialogue, his intricate plots, and his humorous depiction of American culture. Leonard moves his plots forward by apparently authentic—but actually carefully stylized—conversation; he has said that his characters must ''audition'' for their roles. Elmore Leonard began writing westerns but changed his focus to crime novels featuring small-time crooks, gangsters, con-men, politicians, and punks. His use of topical situations is prophetic, as in the Nicaraguan connection in *Bandits* (written before the Iran-Contra scam began to unravel). Leonard's Detroit, Miami, and Hollywood are the real thing for his readers. More than thirty novels, among them *Stick, Glitz, Get Shorty,* and *Rum Punch,* have ensured a place for Leonard on any list of the best American crime novelists.

Loren D. Estleman, who also began as a writer of westerns, is the creator of Detroit private eye Amos Walker, whose cases reveal a gritty portrait of the Detroit underworld. In his trilogy of Detroit novels, *Whiskey River, Motown,* and *King of the Corner,* Estleman has chronicled crime and society from the days of Prohibition to the present, an ambitious and successful effort. Michael Thall, in his traditional mystery *Let Sleeping Afghans Lie,* has used his hometown of Ann Arbor, Michigan, as a setting.

Les Roberts, who lives in Cleveland Heights,

Ohio, writes two different series: the first set in California featuring actor-private eye Saxon; the second set in Cleveland, Ohio—*Deep Shaker, Pepper Pike, Full Cleveland,* etc.—starring private investigator Milan Jacovich, ethnic ex-cop. The two protagonists offer a good contrast in age and temperament, as do the locales: Hollywood and blue collar Cleveland.

Indiana's most famous mystery author is undoubtedly Ralph McInerny, creator of Father Roger Dowling, made famous on television but well worth meeting in the novels. Father Dowling is sometimes soft on crime, but he is very serious about sin. Under the name Monica Quill, McInerny has a second series of clerical mysteries featuring Sister Mary Teresa. Father Dowling and Sister Mary Teresa (aka Attila the Nun and Emtee Dempsey), serve the church first, and detection only as it enhances their religious vocation. The versatile story teller has written several novels with small-town lawyer Andrew Broom as protagonist; and nonseries books such as *The Search Committee,* set on the Fort Elbow campus of the University of Ohio, which recounts the comic hunt for a new chancellor after the incumbent was caught driving drunk—a must read for fans of academic mysteries, and for academics themselves.

Ronald Tierney, who lives in Indianapolis, sets his series in Cleveland, and features a sixty-nine-year-old part-time private eye and his forty-five-year-old girlfriend.

From Illinois, outside the Chicago area, are three very different—and excellent—mystery writers, all worth attention. Dorothy Cannell, English by birth and long a resident of Peoria, Illinois, has created a delightful series of lighthearted, comic mysteries featuring formerly fat Ellie Haskell, and her gourmet cook husband, Ben. Introduced in *The Thin Woman,* their adventures continue in *The Wid-*

ows Club, Mum's the Word, Femmes Fatal, and *How to Murder Your Mother-in-Law* coming soon from Bantam.

Wayne Dundee, of Rockford, Illinois, writes about good old boy Joe Hannibal, blue collar private eye. *Brutal Ballet* deals with professional wrestling, and *Burning Season* takes Hannibal to hillbilly country to track down a bail jumper.

David Everson, professor of political science in Springfield, Illinois, has developed a good series starring former baseball player (not successful) turned private eye, Robert Miles. Miles works for the speaker of the Illinois House of Representatives. In *Suicide Squeeze,* Miles is sent to Chicago to protect a former Cubs pitcher who is appearing at a baseball "fantasy camp," where a 1969 game between the Mets and the Cubs is to be replayed. Springfield is Lincoln country, and Abraham Lincoln and the Lincoln legend figure in *False Profits.*

John Lutz of Webster Groves, Missouri, author of more than a hundred short stories, won both an Edgar (Mystery Writers of America) and a Shamus (Private Eye Writers of America) award. He has created the memorably unlucky and unaggressive St. Louis private eye, Alo Nudger, loser. Lutz's other series, set in Florida, features ex-cop Fred Carver.

Eileen Dreyer, veteran romance writer who lives in St. Louis, Missouri, has written two successful mysteries—a humorous medical thriller, *A Man to Die For,* and a suspense tale about a writer, *If Looks Could Kill.* Suspense writer Joan Banks, also from Missouri, specializes in scary woman-in-jeopardy novels such as *Death Claim,* and *Gently Down the Stream.*

Robert Randisi, lifelong New Yorker, has recently moved to St. Louis, Missouri. Founder of the Private Eye Writers of America and co-founder of *Mystery Scene* magazine, Randisi has written extensively in the western (some of his westerns have a strong mystery element) and men's adventure genres, but is primarily interested in mystery. Miles Jacoby, protagonist of *Private Eye in the Ring,* leaves boxing to become a private eye. Ex-cop Nick Delvecchio is the investigator in *No Exit from Brooklyn.*

Kansas suburbs of Kansas City, Missouri, are home to several mystery writers. Nancy Pickard, winner of various awards in the field, is the best known. Her excellent series featuring Jenny Cain has drawn an ever-increasing number of readers. Nancy Pickard, who lives in Fairway, Kansas, located Jenny and her Port Frederick Civic Foundation in a mythical small town in Massachusetts. Nevertheless, the opening scene in *Generous Death,* the first book in the series, is set in an art museum which the author identifies as the actual Nelson-Atkins Museum of Art in Kansas City, Missouri. Jenny Cain, foundation director and amateur sleuth, gets involved in cases that deal with serious social issues: mental illness, domestic violence, the funeral industry, the homeless, etc. In *Bum Steer* Jenny travels to Kansas because of a bequest to the foundation. Nancy Pickard and her heroine share a keen sense of humor.

Jill Churchill (Janice Young Brooks), who lives in Shawnee Mission, Kansas, writes the comic adventures of Jane Jeffry, suburbia's finest, in *Grime and Punishment, A Farewell to Yarns,* and *A Quiche Before Dying.* Kevin Robinson, also of Shawnee Mission, has begun a witty, fast-paced series with an amateur sleuth who does his detecting from a wheelchair. Randy Russell of Kansas City, Kansas, has created Rooster Franklin, reformed car thief and ex-con, as the star of his series. *Caught Looking* is a complicated yarn involving the Kansas City Royals. Gaylord Dold, critically acclaimed author from Wichita, Kansas, has written several good novels, the most recent *A Penny for the Old Guy.* Dold practices criminal law.

M. K. Lorens (Margaret Keilstrup), who lives in Fremont, Nebraska, writes about Winston Marlowe Sherman, Shakespearean scholar and pseudonymous mystery writer Henrietta Slocum, who, of course, has "her" own sleuth, G. Winchester Hyde. If this seems Byzantine, so are the plots! The series begins with *Sweet Narcissus,* and continues with *Ropedancer's Fall, Deception Island, Dreamland,* and *Sorrowheart.* M. K. Lorens weaves academia, scholarly research, the theater, mystery writing, and intriguing characters into enjoyable tales. William J. Reynolds, who writes about an investigator named "Nebraska," lives in Sioux Falls, South Dakota.

Minnesota is home to a large number of fine mystery writers. The list is long—as are the winter nights, which can be whiled away plotting crime fiction! Most of the writers live in the Twin Cities—Minneapolis and St. Paul. An alphabetical listing of the dozen mentioned begins with Harold B. Adams of Minnetonka, who writes about Carl Wilcox, hard-boiled rustic who detects in Depression-era South Dakota. Marjorie Dorner, professor of Victorian literature, writes suspense stories set in Wisconsin. L. L. Enger, brothers Leif and Lin Enger, write tough, hard-boiled tales about Gun Pedersen, former Detroit Tigers star, who moved to Minnesota after the death of his wife. *Comeback*, first in the series, was nominated for an Edgar in 1990.

Kate Green, poet, teacher of creative writing, children's author, and mystery writer, has produced three critically acclaimed crime novels: *Shattered Moon, Night Angel,* and *Shooting Star.* Thriller writer David Hagberg of Duluth also uses the name Sean Flannery. Some of Hagberg's recent titles include *Counterstrike, Crossfire,* and *Countdown.*

Ellen Hart (the pen name of Pat Boehnhardt) is author of the fine series featuring lesbian detective Jane Lawless. Hart's first book, *Hallowed Murder,* is set in a sorority house on the University of Minnesota campus. The author, who formerly worked as a cook in a sorority house, uses both food and the Minnesota setting to good advantage. The series continues with *Vital Lies* and *Stage Fright.*

M. D. Lake is the pseudonym of Allen Simpson, former professor of Scandinavian languages at the University of Minnesota. His thorough knowledge of academia and the campus environment gives life to his engaging heroine, campus cop Peggy O'Neill. Peggy is introduced in *Amends for Murder,* and returns in *Cold Comfort, Poisoned Ivy,* and *A Gift for Murder.*

Mary Logue, journalist, children's author, and critic, is author of *Red Lake of the Heart.* Logue has begun a new series introducing journalist Laura Malloy in the beautifully written *Still Explosion,* about the consequences of a bombing at an abortion clinic.

Mary Monica Pulver has written a popular series featuring policeman Peter Brichter and his wife, Kori. The first to be published in the series is *Murder at the War* (*Knightfall* in paperback), set among the members of the Society for Creative Anachronism at their annual battle in medieval garb. *Unforgiving Minutes* takes place earlier in time. The series continues with *Ashes to Ashes, Original Sin,* and *Show Stopper.* With Gail Bacon, Pulver has begun a new series of medieval mysteries: *The Novice's Tale,* followed by *The Servant's Tale,* both by "Margaret Frazer."

Pulitzer Prize–winning journalist John Camp, who lives in Minnesota but was raised in Iowa, wrote *Fool's Run* under his own name, but writes most of his thrillers as John Sandford. His series featuring policeman Lucas Davenport began with *Rules of Prey,* and continues with *Shadow Prey, Eyes of Prey, Silent Prey,* and *Winter Prey.* Sandford has made *The New York Times* best seller list with these extremely tough, violent, sex-filled, and truly scary sagas. L. A. Taylor's detective is J. J. Jamison; her titles include *Deadly Objectives* and *Only Half a Hoax.*

One of the best of the Minnesota writers is surely R. D. Zimmerman, highly regarded by his fellow mystery novelists as well as by fans and readers. Zimmerman majored in Russian in college, studied in St. Petersburg, and does business in the former Soviet Union. *Blood Russian* and earlier novels were influenced by his experiences in Russia. *Deadfall in Berlin,* a brilliant book as well as a deeply personal one, was nominated for an Edgar. Hypnosis figures often in his work, and Zimmerman used it to great effect in *Deadfall.* His new series, which begins with *Death Trance: A Novel of Hypnotic Detection,* features severely handicapped Dr. Madeline Phillips, confined to a wheelchair, who helps her brother Alex solve a murder, continues with *Blood Trance,* in which Alex becomes her assistant. Forensic hypnosis is, of course, central to the plots. Zimmerman has written half a dozen books for children, as well as the stories for mystery puzzles from *BePuzzled.*

Cedar Rapids, Iowa, is both the birthplace and the home and headquarters of Ed Gorman, editor and publisher of *Mystery Scene* magazine. Before becoming a full-time writer, Gorman worked in advertising, a background used in *Night Kills.* Television and film—game shows, performers, critics—are the backdrop for *Murder Straight Up* and *Murder on the Aisle.* His detectives are Jack Dwyer, ex-cop and part-time actor; Tobin, a movie critic; and Jack Walsh, the protagonist of *The Night Remembers,* set in Cedar Rapids. Ed Gorman writes with wit and compassion about the outsiders who populate the mean streets of the Midwest. Gorman also writes historical western/crime novels.

Max Allan Collins, born in Muscatine, Iowa, continues to live in his hometown, and until recently wrote the comic strip "Dick Tracy," edits other comics, and writes crime novels with several series characters. Nate Heller, an ex-cop who quit the Chicago force, is a private investigator in 1930s Chicago, meeting up with Al Capone, Eliot Ness, and other famous figures. Some of Collins's darker books feature Quarry, a psychotic Vietnam vet and hired killer. Mallory, a mystery writer who lives in a small Iowa town, is a character Collins patterned on himself.

David Morrell, a former professor of American literature at the University of Iowa, writes popular thrillers such as *The Brotherhood of the Tomb, The Brotherhood of the Rose,* and *The Fraternity of The Stone.* Morrell created the character upon which Rambo was based.

Wisconsin mystery writers include anthologist and editor Martin H. Greenberg of Green Bay; Ellen Porath of Elkhorn; and English professor Thomas Bontly of Milwaukee, author of *Celestial Chess* and *The Giant's Shadow.* Thomas McCall, a physician practicing in Janesville, Wisconsin, has written a fine first mystery, *A Wide and Capable Revenge.* Noreen Gilpatrick, who lives in Fond du Lac, Wisconsin, is the author of the much-praised winner of the first traditional mystery competition held by St. Martin's Press, *The Piano Man.* Gunnard Landers

lives in northern Wisconsin; his environmental thrillers include *The Deer Killers* and *The Violators.*

Michael Bowen, Milwaukee trial lawyer and prolific mystery writer, has produced six novels since 1989. His first series features young attorney Thomas Curry and Algerian-French Sandrine, who becomes his wife after their debut in *Badger Game.* Bowen's second series stars Washington insider Richard Michaelson, introduced in *Washington Deceased. Fielder's Choice,* which combines baseball and the witty mystery duo Thomas and Sandrine, was enthusiastically reviewed by Bowen's peers who are members of the bar as well as by mystery publications.

This long ramble through the American Midwest is coming to an end without mentioning all who deserve to be—none of the wonderful children's authors are considered here, nor are the excellent critics and authors of nonfiction books and articles in the mystery genre. It should be apparent that there is great diversity in style, character, and setting, in the books written by crime novelists who live in America's heartland.

SMALL-TOWN MYSTERIES

Jon L. Breen

THERE IS A TENDENCY to think of the mystery as an urban genre. From Dupin's Paris to Holmes's London to Vance's New York to Spade's San Francisco to Marlowe's L.A., the great characters are identified with the major cities in which they operate. Yet, as Sherlock Holmes himself remarked to Watson in "The Adventure of the Copper Beeches," "the lowest and vilest alleys in London do not present a more dreadful record of sin than does the smiling and beautiful countryside." Some of the most memorable mysteries take place in English villages and small American towns.

The character most immediately identified with the English village mystery is, of course, Agatha Christie's Miss Jane Marple, whose home base of St. Mary Mead is revealed over a long series of novels and short stories as a hotbed of criminality. One of the drawbacks of a continuing village background is, of course, that a high murder rate in such a small and seemingly peaceful location strains reader credibility. Thus, Miss Marple frequently travels, as does her direct descendant Jessica Fletcher, resident of Cabot Cove, Maine, in the long-running TV series *Murder, She Wrote.*

Small-town detective characters fall into several

categories. The first and most prominent is the detecting amateur, often but not always an aged spinster in the Marple mode. Among the British examples are Heron Carvic's Miss Seeton (Plummergen) and Martha Grimes's Melrose Plant (Long Piddleton), while American equivalents include Phoebe Atwood Taylor's Asey Mayo (Wellfleet, Massachusetts), Hugh Pentecost's Uncle George Crowder (Lakeview, New England, state unspecified), and Nancy Pickard's Jenny Cain (Port Frederick, Massachusetts). Lately book dealers are frequently cast as sleuths, including M. K. Wren's Conan Flagg (Holliday Beach, Oregon), Carolyn G. Hart's Annie Laurence Darling (Rock Island, South Carolina), and Joan Hess's Claire Malloy (Faberville, Arkansas). Then there are small-town academics like Bill Crider's Carl Burns (Pecan City, Texas), clergy like Margaret Scherf's Reverence Martin Buell (Farrington, Montana), and mystery writers like Max Allan Collins's Mallory (Port City, Iowa).

Apart from the pure amateurs are various professionals who are not official police but whose work logically brings them in contact with crime. Small-town reporters and editors often figure as continuing sleuths, among them Lucille Kallen's C. B. Greenfield (Sloan's Ford, Connecticut) and Lilian Jackson Braun's cat-fancying Jim Qwilleran (Pickax City, state unspecified). Then there are the small-town doctors, like Jonathan Stagge's Dr. Hugh Westlake (Grovestown, Pennsylvania), and the small-town lawyers, like Joe L. Hensley's Donald Robak (Bington, Indiana) or August Derleth's Judge Ephraim Peck (Sac Prairie, Wisconsin).

Another category is the small-town law-enforcement officer, usually in this country a sheriff or police chief, or perhaps a district attorney like Erle Stanley Gardner's Doug Selby (Madison City, California). Even if the crime rate seems unacceptably high, at least the official police have an excuse for being there and are saved the contrivances necessary to involve an amateur. Prominent American examples include A. B. Cunningham's Jess Roden (Deer Lick, Kentucky), Hillary Waugh's Fred Fellows (Stockford, Connecticut), Joan Hess's Arley Hanks (Maggody, Arkansas), K. C. Constantine's Mario Balzic (Rocksburg, Pennsylvania), John Ball's Jack Tallon (Whitewater, Washington), A. B. Guthrie, Jr.'s, Chick Charleston (Midbury, Montana), Dorothy Gardiner's Moss Magill (Notlaw,

Fifteen Small-Town Mysteries
(all-time)
Selected by Jon L. Breen

Fredric Brown
Night of the Jabberwock

Agatha Christie
The Body in the Library

Dorothy Salisbury Davis
The Clay Hand

Michael T. Hinkemeyer
The Fields of Eden

Cleo Jones
Prophet Motive

Sharyn McCrumb
If Ever I Return, Pretty Peggy-O

Margaret Maron
Southern Discomfort

Ellis Peters
Fallen Into the Pit

Ellery Queen
Calamity Town

Dorothy L. Sayers
The Nine Tailors

David Stout
Carolina Skeletons

Phoebe Atwood Taylor
Banbury Bog

John Holbrook Vance
The Fox Valley Murders

Colin Watson
Lonelyheart 4122

Sara Woods
They Love Not Poison

Colorado), Michael T. Hinkemeyer's Emil Whipple-tree (Stearns County, Minnesota), Bill Crider's Dan Rhodes (Blackline County, Texas), and Sharyn McCrumb's Spencer Arrowood (Hamlin, Tennessee). Some British small-town cops include Colin Watson's Inspector Purbright (Blaxborough), Ellis Peters's George Felse (Comerford), Ruth Rendell's Inspector Wexford (Kingsmarkham, Sussex), and M. C. Beaton's Hamish Macbeth (Scottish villages).

The small-town private eye is a relatively rare bird. For, after all, how much work can a small community provide? The two principal examples of the comic correspondence-school sleuth, Ellis Parker Butler's Philo Gubb (of Riverbank, Iowa) in the 1918 volume bearing his name and Percival Wilde's Peter Moran (of Surrey, Connecticut) in the 1947 collection *P. Moran, Operative* both operated in short stories and out of small towns. One early example of the more serious small-town p.i. was Wilson Tucker's Charles Horne (Boone, Illinois), a more recent one Stephen Dobyns's Charlie Bradshaw (Saratoga Springs, New York). Harold Adams's Depression-era Carl Wilcox occasionally takes p.i. work in and around his home town of Corden, South Dakota.

Some detectives most connected with urban backgrounds have made occasional small-town forays. Ellery Queen first visited Wrightsville in the classic *Calamity Town* (1941) and returned there in a succession of later novels. Ellery the character was not involved in the Queen team's second most memorable small-town mystery, *The Glass Village* (1954), in which a McCarthyesque witch-hunt affects the citizens of Shinn's Corner. (The Queen team, by the way, never assigned their archetypal small towns to specific states.) Sara Woods's London barrister Antony Maitland had his own Wrightsville in the occasionally visited Yorkshire town of Arkenshaw. Arthur Train's long-running *Saturday Evening Post* lawyer Ephraim Tutt, though

based in New York City, had some of his most entertaining cases in the upstate town of Pottsville. Agatha Christie's Hercule Poirot, who did his detecting all over the map, often visited the villages most associated with Miss Marple, most memorably King's Abbot in the classic *The Murder of Roger Ackroyd* (1926), which included an earlier version of the Marple character in the doctor-narrator's busybody sister. Many of the other British detectives make the village scene from time to time, including Lord Peter Wimsey in Dorothy L. Sayers's *The Nine Tailors* (1934), set in Fenchurch St. Paul. Urban private eyes often visit corrupt small towns for the purpose of cleaning them up, most notably Dashiell Hammett's Continental Op in *Red Harvest* (1929), based in Personville (a.k.a. Poisonville, state unspecified but based on Butte, Montana). Michael Shayne goes to Centerville, Kentucky, in Brett Halliday's *A Taste for Violence* (1949), while the Chicagoan known only as Mac visits Wesley, Illinois, in Thomas B. Dewey's *Deadline* (1966). Though John Ball's Virgil Tibbs works for the police force of suburban Pasadena, California, he made his first bow in one of the most memorable small-town mysteries of them all, *In the Heat of the Night* (1965), set in the Carolina town of Wells.

Most of the small towns mentioned above are fictitious. For obvious reasons (the potential for lawsuits prominent among them), a mystery writer is far less likely to use a real small town as a setting—at least under its right name—than a more anonymous and thus safer big city. My own L.A.-based bookseller Rachel Hennings, though, goes to the California mountain town of Idyllwild, which really does exist and really is small, in *Touch of the Past* (1988). I have escaped the lawyer's summons so far, and using a real town (though none of its real people, I hasten to add) does provide a concentrated outlet for moving a few more copies.

SMALL TOWNS, BIG MOTIVES
Nancy Pickard

Roy Inman

I HAVE A FRIEND who lives in a small town, population approximately five thousand. She used to date a man who lives in the next town over. My friend lives about six blocks from his ex-wife, who lives about four blocks away from my friend's ex-husband. Just about five blocks away from him lives my friend's ex-boyfriend's ex-wife's first ex-husband and his new family. Those two ex-husbands used to be best friends, but they haven't spoken to each other for years because the first ex-husband believes his former best friend stole his wife. My friend carpools with the second wife of the ex-husband who used to be married to the woman who married my friend's ex-boyfriend. A good friend of hers, who lives about ten blocks away from her, used to know my friend's ex-boyfriend's ex-wife's sister, whom my friend's friend detests because, she says, the woman stole something from her years ago. All of these people, with the exception of my friend, are acquainted with the new girlfriend (and her ex-husband and his new wife) of my friend's ex-husband. Frankly, they think my friend's ex-husband's new girlfriend's ex-husband was a fool to get his girlfriend pregnant (at *his* age!) and marry her. My friend is now dating a new man. *He* used to date a woman who lives in the same town as my friend's ex-boyfriend, and *that* woman is in a book club with my friend's ex-boyfriend's ex-wife who . . .

And people ask me why I set mysteries in small towns!

NEW ENGLAND MYSTERY AUTHORS
Kate Mattes

IT'S HARD TO MENTION mysteries and Boston in the same sentence without thinking of Robert Parker and his alter ego, Spenser. But long before Spenser, New England was brimming with fictional murder. Several romantic suspense writers—Mary Roberts Rinehart and Mignon Eberhart, for example—included portrayals of the New England upper class and summer resorts. Phoebe

Atwood Taylor, writing in the lighthearted madcap tradition, had two wildly popular New England detectives. In eight of her books we see Boston through the eyes of Leonidas Witherall, Shakespeare's look-alike, who was forever finding himself in situations which, though improbable, take us on a hilarious romp before becoming perfectly clear. Her most famous series, however, was set on the Cape and featured that Cape Cod native and jack-of-all-trades, Asey Mayo. Mayo, who was related to everyone on the Cape, worked with his cousin, Jennie, and her husband, Syl, solving mysteries of all kinds while introducing people to, or reminding them of, their visits to picturesque Cape Cod. Asey knew all the dirt roads and shortcuts as well as the criminal inclinations of the natives. Through Mr. Porter, world-renowned financier, he had access to information on tourists which allowed him to mend broken hearts, find missing items, and bring the Cape back to normal (as normal as it could be with all those ———— tourists running amok). George Harmon Coxe had two photographer–reporters, Kent Murdoch and Flash–Gun Casey, working for the *Courier-Herald,* who marked the beginning of a long trail of reporters and ex-reporters who seek out crime in New England.

Fletch by Greg Mcdonald, who won Edgars in 1974 and 1976, continued the reporter–sleuth tradition. Fletch captured attention during the Watergate era by encapsulating both an irreverence for authority with the reporter's thirst for truth. Fletch eventually quit the paper and nosed around everywhere, ignoring all boundaries. In one of the genre's rare spinoffs, Mcdonald also penned separate books centering on Flynn, the Irish-Catholic policeman who often worked with Fletch. The sensitive portrait of Flynn with his family playing music on Sunday afternoons presented an interesting contrast to the violence he faced daily. After a long hiatus, Fletch and hopefully Flynn will soon be back.

While Mcdonald wrote of South Boston and the counterculture, Harry Kemelman was introducing us to the fictional North Shore community of Barnard's Crossing, with Rabbi Small ministering to his congregation, using and explaining Talmudic thought as he worked with an Irish-Catholic policeman in his town. Kemelman did much more than write mysteries as he explained religious holidays and customs to nonbelievers—Jewish and non-Jewish alike—and gave a sense of a Jewish community

to many Gentiles, including Chief Lanigan. Thank goodness, the Rabbi Small mysteries, which began on Friday, are continuing even though Kemelman ran out of days of the week. George Higgins's crime novels gained national acclaim with the publication of *The Friends of Eddie Coyle.* Higgins's ear for dialogue and knowledge of the mob show a Boston not known to many. I also think *The Rat on Fire* is a remarkable novel.

For our generation of mystery readers, Spenser put Boston on the map. Used to calling the shots, Spenser struggles to participate in an equal relationship with a confident psychotherapist, Susan Silverman. The villains in Parker's books are often obvious and many fans at my store are much more involved in the mystery of their relationship than the case at hand. (As is Spenser, if the truth be told.) Spenser, with his black friend, Hawk, often bullies his way to a successful case resolution. (As one customer said, "Who wouldn't like to have a friend like Hawk? He'll kill the people that cross you.") These tactics represent an extension of the belief that you can't trust the system. In the end, if justice is to prevail, you must use the system and sometimes operate outside it.

Boston has other full-time p.i.'s who have gained national attention, including a Shamus award in 1986 for Best Mystery. Jeremiah Healy has now written eight books in the J. F. Cuddy series. This p.i. was introduced in 1984 with *Blunt Darts*—named one of the notable mysteries of the year by *The New York Times.* Healy, who is a former litigator and presently teaches at the New England School of Law, provides the reader with more intricate plots than Parker, and many often revolve around legal issues and he *almost* always works within the system. For instance, the premise of one of Healy's books, *Yesterday's News,* begins with the question as to whether or not the notes of a dead journalist are protected by reporter confidentiality. In *Right to Die,* Healy explores legal and ethical issues of the patient's right to die. This is a series that definitely needs to be read from the beginning as Cuddy struggles with the loss of his wife to cancer through the first few books.

Speaking of cancer, Dick Cluster has created a detective/auto mechanic who *is* a cancer survivor. In the first of the series, *Return to Sender,* Alex Glauberman is getting chemotherapy and is dealing with it and how it effects both his daughter, whose custody he shares with his ex-wife, and also his own relationships. In the most recent—a real page-turner—Alex is trying to help a hospital recover some bone marrow, needed for a transplant, which is being held for ransom. Few people want to read about cancer, but this series offers tremendous insight into the ways people choose to cope with this diagnosis and treatment and what they need from their friends. I also think the way Alex handles the primary care of his daughter and works on maintaining a steady relationship makes him one of the most feminist men in mystery fiction.

Boston is such a large medical center, you would think we would have more medical thrillers than we do set there. What we have, though, is great. Robin Cook writes from here, as does Michael Palmer, who himself used to be an emergency room doctor and now writes full-time. Palmer's character are always well developed and his situations diabolical. *Sisterhood* addressed "caring" euthanasia and the pressures on nurses who work with dying patients devastatingly well—long before Dr. Kevorkian.

Matt Jacobs, Zachary Klein's reluctant detective self-medicates himself—mainly with cocaine and marijuana. His main goal is getting through each day, one day at a time, while coping with a well-deserved depression. He is philosophical and raises many provocative and interesting ideas for the reader as he tries to help out his friends. He has some growing to do in his romantic relationships with women, but in other ways demonstrates remarkable self-awareness and a sense of responsibility for his life.

I digressed a little from Boston private eyes. I wouldn't want to leave out Carlotta Carlyle, Linda Barnes's woman p.i. who drives cabs to pay the bills. Carlotta is tough and soft at the same time. She loves the blues, her cat, and women's volleyball. She takes her responsibility as Paolina's "Big Sister" very seriously. She lives in a run-down apartment and is surrounded by very typical Boston-type friends. She can hold her own in bars, dealing with the IRA, with rich people in the suburbs, and fellow cabbies—not to mention the passengers. She's quite happy-go-lucky, but you don't want to cross her. Her creator, Linda Barnes, has also penned another series featuring Michael Spraggue—an actor out of work enough to be pulled into crime-solving reluctantly. Usually by his Brahmin aunt

Mary—one of my favorite characters. Barnes writes with a tongue-in-cheek sense of humor and a walker's feel for the milieu and detail of a place. *Dead Heat,* in the Spraggue series, is a must read for any Boston marathoner.

Carlotta is one of two six-foot-tall, red-haired crime-solving women in the Boston area. The other, authored by Susan Kelly, is Liz Connors, an investigative reporter who lives with a Cambridge policeman, Jack Lingermann. (Kelly is also an investigative reporter who has worked with the Cambridge Police Department.) Connors gets so involved in a story, she often doesn't think about her own safety, which drives me a little nuts because I care about her. Kelly knows Cambridge well and has some delightful descriptions of restaurants and Harvard square that hard-core Cambridge liberals revel in.

Cambridge hosts three other detectives, all representative of the diversity of one of the country's most liberal, eccentric communities (it's not called the People's Republic of Cambridge for nothing). Susan Conant's main character, Holly Winter, is also a journalist. Her main interest, however, is dogs, not crime. As she researches her articles for a dog journal, she runs across crime at dog shows, on the street walking her dog, or at obedience school. You will learn a lot about the large world of dogs, specific breeds of dogs, and the care of dogs from her books. Serious information is couched in light, breezy writing. It is a pleasure to read stories told by an obsessed person who sees everything in terms of their obsession. And Conant has some of the best put-downs of Cambridge "types" I've ever read.

Katherine Lasky Knight has created a detective who *is* a Cambridge type. Calista Jacobs, a children's book illustrator, and her preteen son form a formidable duo. Her husband, who taught at Harvard, dies on the first page of the first book and his death then becomes the subject of *Trace Elements.* The politics of the university and faculty parties are done to perfection. Subsequent books take her out of Cambridge. Learning to live without a husband and a partner really gives this series a poignant edge. These people could be neighbors. (Katherine Lasky Knight has won many awards as a children's book author and has an excellent young adult mystery series.)

Jerome Doolittle's detective, Tom Bethany, has

New England Mysteries
Selected by Kate Mattes

Boston

Nathan Aldyne—All Valentine and Clarisse mysteries except *Canary*

Oliver Banks—*The Rembrandt Panel*

Sophie Belfort—Molly Raferty and Nick Hannibar series

Eliza Collins—*Going Going Gone*

Bill Eidson—both titles

Emma Lathen—*Pick Up Sticks Something in the Air*

Margaret Logan—*Killing in Venture Capital*

Charlotte MacLeod—Most Sarah Kelling/-Max Bittersohn mysteries

Dan Matheson—*Stray Cats*

Lynn Meyer—*Paperback Thriller*

George M. O'Har—*Psychic Fair*

Rod Philbrick—The Jack Hawkins series

Robert Reeves—The Thomas Theron series

John Lawrence Reynolds—The Joe McGuire series

Barbara Shapiro—*Shattered Echoes*

Richard Smith—The James Maxwell Mallory series

Winona Sullivan—*A Sudden Death at the Norfolk Cafe*

Ned White—*The Very Bad Thing*

Mary Wing—*She Came Too Late*

Cape Cod

Peter Abrahams—*Revolution #9*

Nathan Aldyne—*Canary*

Margot Arnold—*The Cape Cod Mystery*

Carole Berry—*Nightmare Point* George Foy—*Asia Rip*

Douglas Kiker—The Mac MacFarland series

Anne LeClaire—*Grace Point*

Barbara Paul—*In-laws and Out-laws*

Nancy Thayer—*Spirit Lost* (Nantucket)

Maine

Mary Ann Brahns—Most books Sarah Dreher—*Something Shady*

Timothy Findley—*The Telling of Lies*

Carolyn Hougan—*The Romeo Flag*

Phyllis Knight—*Switching the Odds*

Leslie Meier—*Mail Order Murder*

Patricia MacDonald—*The Unforgiven*

B. J. Morrison—The Elizabeth Lamb series

Katherine Hall Page—*Body in the Kelp*

William Tapply—*Dead Meat*

Janwillem van de Wetering—*The Maine Massacre*

New Hampshire

Robert J. Begiebing—*The Strange Death of Mistress Coffin*

North Shore

Andrew Coburn—Most mysteries

Margaret Press—The Detective Sergeant Gabriel Dunn series

William Story—All mysteries

Vermont

B. Comfort—All mysteries

Christopher A. Bohjalian—*Hangman*

Western Massachusetts

S.F.X. Deans—The Professor Neil Kelly series

Stephen Dobyns—The Charlie Bradshaw series *(Saratoga)*

Lucille Kallen—The C. B. Greenfield series

Lee Stansberg—*The Spoiler*

David Willis McCullough—The Ziza Todd series

Susanna Hofmann McShea—*Hometown Heroes*

Richard Stevenson—The Don Strachey series

Rhode Island

Raymond Paul—*Tragedy at Tiverton*

Geoffrey Wolff—*Providence*

an office in Harvard Square at the Tasty—a real place in Harvard Square. An ex-political operative (Doolittle himself worked for the McGovern campaign), Bethany begins his detective career by checking out the past of a potential nominee for Secretary of State for a Massachusetts politician who is considering a presidential run. The idea is very believable. He doesn't want to find any skeletons in the closet. I wonder where Doolittle, who now teaches at Harvard, got that idea?

Katherine Hall Page presents us with the delightful Faith Fairchild, caterer, who, in spite of her New York upbringing, finds herself in Boston's suburbs, happily married to a minister, living amid unfashionably dressed people who feed terrible food to their families. And she *is* happy—except she keeps stumbling across murders with her baby in tow. Written with a witty eye, the Fairchild books *are* more substantive than a cursory examination would lead you to expect.

Rick Boyer, winner of the 1982 Edgar for Best Novel, picked the suburb of Lincoln for Doc Adams's home. Adams is an oral surgeon who will drop anything to get involved with murder. Boyer's plots can *sometimes* be far-fetched (I don't think even the Kennedys could swing getting one of their own appointed medical examiner in a case where the murder happened in his house with the son as the chief suspect.) It is a tribute to his poetic descriptions and character development that you race through the pages anyway. *Penny Ferry* is particularly fascinating for the accurate historical research Boyer did on Boston during the Sacco-Vanzetti trials.

Speaking of research, we are also home to the queen of well-researched mysteries, Jane Langton, who also does the illustrations for all of her own books. Langton spends about a year researching each of her subjects: the Gardner Museum and its artwork, Memorial Hall at Harvard, the life and works of Emily Dickinson, Transcendentalism and Emerson. Her books are full of well-researched information, and are a treasure-trove for people wanting to learn more about the area. John McAleer, biographer of Rex Stout and Jane Austen, has penned a book in a similar vein on the Boston Athenaeum and the immediate vicinity. He doesn't illustrate his own books, but *The Coign of Vantage* is filled with interesting information on Revolutionary Boston and parts of the Athenaeum not open to the public. William Martin's *Back Bay* traces the history of Beacon Hill and is a delight to genealogists.

It wouldn't be fair to leave Boston without mentioning our only Brahmin lawyer who investigates for his rich clients. If someone mentions the blues to me, I think Muddy Waters. Not Coyne. It's bluefish and he's out the door. Brady Coyne would *always* rather be fishing and his books are full of his passion. Coyne is uneasily divorced, with two sons he wishes he were closer to, more women than is healthy in a time of AIDS, and a soft touch for people in need. William Tapply, Coyne's creator, used to teach high school and his portraits of adolescents are particularly poignant. Except for *The Spotted Cats,* Tapply also has very clever plots, reminiscent of Ross Macdonald at his best. Coyne is discreet as he explores the secrets of the rich, tiptoes through the political mine fields of Boston, and sneaks off with Doc Adams (Boyer's character) to fish whenever possible. (Tapply and Boyer used to be neighbors and their main characters always make at least an appearance in each other's books.)

Building on Phoebe Atwood Taylor's legacy, the Cape has become a hotbed for fictional crime. The only thing that remains the same is the year-round dislike of (and dependence on) tourists and the terrible traffic jams—now worse as the back ways have all been developed. Sally Gunning, with Peter Bartholomew, a kind of jack-of-all-trades, is most similar to the Taylor tradition.

Several firsthand reporters and policemen have retired to the Cape and tried to rid it of crime. Paul Kemprecos's detective is retired cop Aristotle Plato Socarides, whose Greek parents are very disappointed in him because he has not helped out with the successful family pizza business in Lowell. Instead, "Soc" gets by hiring out on fishing fleets and occasional security jobs. *Cold Blue Tomb,* the first in the series, won the Shamus for Best Original Paperback of 1991. It is full of information on sunken ships and the salvaging business. In *Death in Deep Water,* "Soc" is hired to prove a killer whale did *not* kill his trainer so the owner that runs the Oceanus Aquatic Park can sell it to the Japanese conglomerate eager to buy it.

Philip Craig's retired policeman lives on Martha's Vineyard, where he lives off bluefish pâté (which Craig has brought to the store and I can vouch for it) with his girlfriend, Zee. Off-islanders often come to him for help. Since Craig is a professor at Wheelock College, it is not surprising that the politics of academic life often play a large part in his cases—whether it be politics within departments or relationships between faculty and students.

Boston has a large gay population, and that is reflected in the number of gay detectives that live in the area. Probably the most famous is the team of Valentine, gay bartender, and his straight woman friend, Clarissa, created by Nathan Aldyne (Dennis Schuetz and Michael McDowell, who also writes under his own name). Four books were written in the eighties that were for the most part about a fun-loving gay community, pre-AIDS. With the death of Schuetz, the stories ended. Except for *Canary,* which takes place one summer in Provincetown, the books are set in Boston. Boston also boasts a lesbian who earns her living as a travel agent. Created by Sarah Dreher, Stoner MacTavish travels all over the country, solving crimes from her home base. *Something Shady* takes her to Maine and a private asylum, where she goes undercover as a patient. Working with an obsessive-compulsive patient, she finds out why her friend died there.

Phyllis Knight has also started a series with Lil Ritchie, a lesbian detective living in Maine. In her first impressive book, *Switching the Odds,* Lil is hired to find a runaway son who, father hopes, will try to connect with his grandfather in Maine. It's not hard for Lil to find the boy, but it takes a while for her to determine whether his father is involved in the murder he witnessed. Her ethical concerns and view of her charge offers a refreshing change from the normal ''case.''

Although most New England mysteries are farther south, the state of Maine, where George Bush owns a home but doesn't vote, is becoming a hotbed of crime. If mystery writers are to be believed, it's not safe to go to school in Maine. Susan Kenney, a professor at Colby College, and more well known for her nonmysteries, has penned an irreverent academic series at the small Canterbury College. J. S. Borthwick's Sarah Deane, an English fellow, also offers an often funny picture of academic life in a small Maine town. Nancy Pickard has the director of a small-town philanthropy working hard at preserving her agency's reputation and the lives of the townspeople in her Jenny Cain series. And we all know from Virginia Rich how deadly those baked bean suppers can be. I won't even mention what Stephen King's books say about Maine.

Vermont and New Hampshire are occasionally settings for murder or offer weekend escapes from the pressures of crime fighting. Archer Mayor, however, a Vermont native, has created Brattleboro Police Lieutenant Joe Gunther, who covers the state looking for criminals. His first book, based on a true incident, finds townspeople being arbitrarily shot by a sniper. His second, predating Waco, involves cultists who die in a fire.

Most of this essay is devoted to series characters, but I want to mention a couple of extremely fine writers who are personal favorites of mine and who meticulously represent parts of Boston even though they haven't developed a series character. Alexander Coburn used to be an investigative reporter and has written six books set in the Boston area. His eye for physical and psychological detail is exquisite. With incredible realism he has painted a picture of a small bedroom community's reaction to violent murder in *No Way Home.* In *Sweetheart,* Coburn's experience with the mob is evident as he presents the moral dilemmas of an undercover agent caught between the Mafia community he has infiltrated and the zealous boss he works for.

Most people don't think of Rhode Island as part of New England, but if you love baseball and hate the Red Sox, Pawtucket offers some pretty good baseball. That's where R. D. Rosen's detective, Harvey Blissberg, found himself in the later stages of his baseball career (or the beginning of his detective career, depending on how you look at it). *Strike 3 You're Dead,* which won Best First Mystery of 1984, finds Blissberg, a Cambridge resident, trying to figure out who killed his roommate. He soon retires from baseball and helps stop crime in other sports.

Walter Walker has also written a couple of books that probe the history and workings of small Boston suburbs, as only someone who was born and raised here could. *The Immediate Prospect of Being Hanged* is a real page-turner, exposing the complex political overtones even in the most proper of suburbs. (Told by a D.A.'s investigator who is looking into the murder of the wife of the man who wants to take on his boss, you know this could be true. Not as well written, but true.) *A Dime to Dance By* is based on a true incident in Walker's hometown as he was growing up.

If I had more space, I would love to tell you about other New England writers.

NEW ENGLAND BLOOD

Marilis Hornidge

IT'S ELEMENTALLY RAW. The coast is bleak in the winter, fogbound in the summer. Inland the trees and mountains brood. Most of the towns are small, shut in by the land or the sea, closed in against strangers, not always cherishing of their own. Its big town is Boston, suspicious, supercilious Boston, the center of its own universe. Never mind the eastern Big City Blues, forget the steamy earthy South and the varied violent West. *This* is mystery country USA.

This is New England.

Mysteries are our favorite reading. I asked librarians of the four small-to-midsize libraries I frequent to estimate the proportion of mysteries circulated over other fiction. The results astounded even me—twenty to thirty percent. "Look at the shelves of general fiction versus the mystery section," said one of them whose library segregates mysteries. "Look at the condition of the books," said one of her aides in an aside. The mysteries showed signs of much handling: many had been recovered in those distinctive library bindings, and even those looked worn.

New England takes its murders seriously. It isn't just that Legendary Lizzie, I know that for a fact. Researching a particularly intriguing un(or wrongly)-solved local tale in a neighboring town, I found people willing and eager to discuss it in tales and remembrances as clear as if it were yesterday—up to a point. The points of divergence have caused short-term feuds and occasioned great arguments and still are sore ones: the murder occurred one hundred years ago.

I would love to write a book on the subject, but I would probably have to move to Vermont.

If, like me, you read books *on* mysteries with pen in hand and a large piece of paper right there to jot down names and other data on authors of books of which you have never heard with the hopes of finding them yourself, you can relax. At

New England Top Twenty

A Personal View

Selected by Marilis Hornidge

Phoebe Atwood Taylor
Going, Going, Gone!

Kathleen Moore Knight
Death Blew Out the Match

Timothy Fuller
Harvard Has a Homicide

Herbert Brean
Wilders Walk Away

Margaret Page Hood
The Bell on Lonely

Jane Langton
The Transcendental Murder

J. S. Borthwick
The Down-East Murders
The Student Body

Charlotte MacLeod
The Palace Guard
Rest You Merry

Virginia Rich
The Nantucket Diet Murders

Rick Boyer
The Penny Ferry

Linda Barnes
Dead Heat

Nancy Pickard
Say No to Murder

Douglas Kiker
Murder on Clam Pond

B. J. Morrison
Champagne and a Gardener
The Martini Effect

Philip Craig
The Woman Who Walked into the Sea

Katherine Hall Page
The Body in the Kelp

Leslie Meier
Mail Order Murder

the end of this essay-into-the-northeastern-wilderness, I will give you a list in quasi-chronological order of my own favorites, most of which I will be mentioning en passant. The reason I will not be going into a lot of detail on each one is the same reason d'être for which I write my notorious book column "The Book Bag." I write for readers. I write so that they, bewildered by the numbers of books produced today, will at least have a knowledgeable if somewhat opinionated guide along the way. I may miss some, I may slight others, I will leave out those who I think aren't trying or are absolutely beyond the pale. But I would always rather have you reading the book than reading me sounding off about the book in a professorial manner—which I doubt I could pull off anyway.

Thus endeth the lesson.

In the beginning there was Nathaniel Hawthorne's *House of the Seven Gables* which certainly had the atmosphere. I'd call it a mystery even if that does mean squeezing the category a little. John Greenleaf Whittier's poetry, little read today but still evocative, sets an eerie scene, and there are even parts of *Moby Dick* that can give you that mystery feeling. New England has figured in more gothic novels than just about any other region, and we won't even mention Stephen King, many of whose books, shorn of their fantasy feel, would be routinely shelved under mysteries with a New England setting.

Early on in the mystery's past, New England (by which I mean Maine, Vermont, New Hampshire, and Massachusetts) was one of the few places in which a murder mystery could be recognizably set. Throw in a few pine trees, a crashing ocean wave or two, and natives whose speech could be approximated by lavish use of the apostrophe in order to distinguish them from non-natives, and readers would know where they were supposed to be. If the plot required a remote or cut-off setting, where would you find better islands, deeper snow, more awful roads, and casts of menacing locals than Cape Cod, inland New England, or the bays of Maine? If your mystery needed an academic setting vaguely reminiscent of England with donnish professors and erudite students, why, Boston was the perfect answer with the affluent prep schools of New England as alternatives.

Some writers transcended the trite even then. Phoebe Atwood Taylor's Asey Mayo series beginning in 1931 had a devoted audience and holds up well today even if the dialect gets under your skin after a while. Her background is always clear and present—and part of the story. Just compare one of these (or the series starring ex-professor Leonidas Witherall which she wrote pseud-anonymously as Alice Tilton) with one of similar vintage by the equally popular Mary Roberts Rinehart—for example, *The Yellow Room,* a mystery supposedly set in a Maine that could just as well be Connecticut. Kathleen Moore Knight's Elisha Macomber series, contemporaneous with Taylor's, had many of the same characteristics and an equally devoted audience. Timothy Fuller's *Harvard Has a Homicide,* if you are lucky enough to find a copy of the 1944 paperback with one of those marvelous, wonderful scene-of-the-crime maps on the back, is a terrific example of the Murder-Most-Ivy-League British-spinoff (even if the modern watchdogs of political correctness would howl in affront over some of its characters). It's a fly-in-amber of its type and era, but a lot of fun to read on a cold night with the fire going.

Between the earlier New England regionals and the explosion that occurred after 1980 is a writer from the 1950s whose books have been overlooked—I cannot understand how—Herbert Brean. *Wilders Walk Away,* a tale set in a very small Vermont town, has a well-paced plot, an interesting premise, enough background to satisfy even me, and the kind of writing that keeps you moving without running right up to the end. Brean wrote several books, including a wonderful island-bound mystery called *The Clock Strikes Thirteen,* but I reread *Wilders* every once in a while and it always holds up. I refuse to lend my copy anymore, however, because no matter how trustworthy the borrower, the book manages to disappear—quite a recommendation. If you're looking for atmosphere and a linear descendant of Taylor and Knight from this middle era, you couldn't do better than the books of Margaret Page Hood.

In the mid-1970s someone in publishing seemed to have discovered that readers *liked* mysteries in a definite setting. It always amazes me when publishers discover with great fanfare something that has been obvious to readers all along—but I digress. Suddenly a great many mystery writers found that they were a) regional mystery writers, and b) popular with their publishers as well as with their readers

(see note on publishers' habits above). Slightly ahead of the trend was Jane Langton, whose *The Transcendental Murder* mingled history, literature, and murder in a chocolate-chip cookie of a book, followed by other books with a signature New England Massachusetts background.

Boston has always considered itself New England's capital city and many of the new kids on the regional block come from "Our Fair City," as it is sometimes sarcastically known hereabouts. (I warn you, I am not counting private eye sagas or the novels of George Higgins in this group. P.I.'s, with a few exceptions, tend to set background simply by naming streets, restaurants, and bars: George Higgins is *sui generis*.) Linda Barnes, in *Dead Heat,* makes use of the Boston Marathon as the core of her murder and sets the city as part of the story. Charlotte MacLeod gives us a backstage look at the Gardner Museum (a rose by any other name) in *The Palace Guard,* just one of a truly clever series about a beautifully eccentric Boston family. Ever consider an oral surgeon as a detective/hero? Rick Boyer's *The Penny Ferry* stars one and you get the Sacco-Vanzetti case revisited and the Mafia and a marvelous finale to boot.

The New England academic mystery is still with us as well, although not quite so Ivy-hung. J. S. Borthwick's *The Student Body* takes place in a very-Maine college which is enough of a collage of the famous ones so that they can all claim it and its clever plot and personnel. B. J. Morrison's *The Martini Effect* uses the prep school experience at a mythic one on Mt. Desert Island and winds up with a cross between a younger (and mouthier) Nancy Drew and Josephine Tey's *Miss Pym Disposes.* And somewhere in the wilds of Massachusetts lies Balaclava College, home of Charlotte MacLeod's Peter Shandy and the most diverse faculty and students you will ever want to meet, starting with the wacky and wonderful *Rest You Merry.* I would accept a scholarship to any one of the three.

Irresistible murder locales seem to abound along the Massachusetts coast. Douglas Kiker set *Murder on Clam Pond* on Cape Cod in the bleak chill of winter, a very different Cape Cod from the one tourists know. The delicious Virginia Rich sent her Mrs. Potter to Nantucket for a reunion in *The Nantucket Diet Murders,* and Jane Langton staged a reunion of a rather different sort in *Dark Nantucket Noon,* complete with a solar eclipse and an impossible crime. Philip Craig's series set on Martha's Vineyard has the real feel of the place rather than the summer glitz as well as plots to give your brain a workout. Set in the imaginary town of Port Fredrick, Nancy Pickard's series gives the reader a totally modern small town with problems and people anyone can recognize, and at the same time manages to be fun rather than grit.

After which, alas, we leap straight to Maine . . . if you can find me some Vermont and/or New Hampshire murders, I promise to send you a surprise package from my extensive mystery library.

Where are we going in Maine? L. L. You-know-who, of course, and a murder in that venue (names changed to protect the innocent, of course), *Mail Order Murder* by Leslie Meier, set during the Christmas rush and starring exactly the kind of people you always *knew* worked there. Good Maine food and the inside/outside clashes between incomer and native are the focal point for both Katherine Pages's *The Body in the Kelp* and Virginia Rich's *The Baked Bean Supper Murders*, although *Kelp*

does take some side trips into the fascinating art of quilting. J. S. Borthwick's books are marvelous examples of integrating Maine setting, characters (and some of them *really* are), and plot which it doesn't pay to try to second-guess. There are two that aren't set in Maine, but they are all worth chasing down. All of B. J. Morrison's five "little Maine murders" are set on Mount Desert Island—an enclave of money, new and old, have and don't—sport dialogue that verges on the tongue-in-cheek, and feature plots that amble on top and run somewhere else underneath.

Carolyn Wells, in her classic book on the writing of the "detective" story, said that the setting must *seem* real to the reader in the same sense that fairy tales (and, one might add, the truly frightening ghost story) must *seem* real to work at all. Perhaps the ambience that stands for New England in the collective mind of the mystery reader (if there is such an entity) is more of a reality than that of anywhere else.

SOUTHERN FRIED

Joan Hess

NOW THAT I COME to think about it, murder is the crime of choice only in the South. Everybody with a lick of sense knows that Yankees steal expensive cars and burn down warehouses for the insurance money. Their notion of murder is a mob hit outside a restaurant. Pretentious Midwesterners are more likely to bore people to death talking on their cellular phones than to knock 'em upside the head with a pool cue. Californians risk their tans to shoplift designer water. Southwesterners rustle stock options and speed into the sunset in their fancy Cadillacs. Northwesterners don't do much of anything except fret about the influx of overly tanned Californians and the proper way to grill fresh salmon.

But way down here in the land of cotton, in the land of Tennessee Williams and Tennessee Ernie, of sweltering afternoons, of glistening pink gums and glittering rhinestone tiaras, of smoldering looks, of sweaty pitchers of iced tea, of gunracks and gunky-eyed dogs and six-packs, murder is always a feasible option. Until the Late Unpleasantness, the South thrived on the devaluation of human life; nowadays we've modified our approach to avoid indictments whenever possible. Maybe this is why we're a sight fonder of Mr. Matlock than of Mr. Mason. There's something innately comforting about an affable lawyer in a rumpled white suit, sitting on the bench outside the barbershop and swapping jokes with the likes of Atticus and Clarence.

Passion simmers in the south. A well-bred southern lady never raises her voice or expresses outrage with anything more confrontational than an arched eyebrow; she politely bides her time until she has a clear shot at her victim's back. She stalks pledges for Kappa Kappa Gamma with the same intensity her brother stalks the winners of the weekly wet T-shirt contests at the Dew Drop Inn. Good ol' boys with designs on a new divorcee slap each other on the back and suggest a hunting trip to a remote patch of woods. Military surplus stores are as common as drive-in movie theaters, country clubs, and trailer parks. Sure, making moonshine may land you in the prison farm, but it beats working at the body shop and you're liable to have more than a few kinfolk to keep you company. Southerners have kinfolk most everywhere, although in some families the consanguinity's awful hard to sort out. But no matter what, they gather for weddings, family reunions, baptisms, and burials. Why, I can't count the number of summer evenings we all sat on the porch beneath the fan, sipping dandelion wine and listening to the mournful baying of hounds as they chased an escapee from the chain gang across the swamp. "That's Ol' Yeller," Granddaddy would say as he passed the grits. "Helluva dawg."

This isn't to say that New York, Chicago, Detroit, and Los Angeles don't have their fair share of fatalities, but drive-by shootings and liquor store holdups lack the old-fashioned fervor that characterizes southern mayhem. Around these parts it's not polite to shoot strangers—unless, of course, they commence making lewd remarks to a lady or gibbering like a Republican, in which case they'll be invited to step outside to settle the matter. Bigotry's no longer an acceptable motive; we leave that kind

of tackiness to sanctimonious northerners and Hollywood producers. We're much more inclined to poison an eccentric old aunt for the family silver or take an ax to a spouse in order to avoid the social stigma of a divorce (not to mention the legal fees and the problematic issue of who gets the season football tickets).

In *Sanctuary* (1931), William Faulkner captures the essence of this brooding obsession with the turbid and sensual aspects of death in this description of a small town jail: "After supper a few Negroes gathered along the fence below—natty, shoddy suits and sweat-stained overalls shoulder to shoulder—and in chorus with the murderer, they sang spirituals while white people slowed down and stopped in the leafed darkness that was almost summer, to listen to those who were sure to die and him who was already dead singing about heaven and being tired; or perhaps in the interval between songs a rich, sourceless voice coming out of the high darkness where the ragged shadow of the heaven-tree which snooded the street lamp at the corner fretted and mourned: 'Fo days mo! Den dey ghy stroy de bes ba'ytone singer in nawth Mississippi!' "

Then along comes John D. MacDonald's Travis McGee, who muses and eschews bourbon and might have problems recognizing a snooded streetlamp if he was standing beside it. Carl Hiaasen's Florida has swamps and homecoming queens, but not once does he unveil the unspeakable family secrets that have tormented the children into bankruptcy and driven poor Mother to her bedroom, where she can perpetuate a nervous breakdown without unduly disrupting dinner. Granddaddy'd have rumbled like a rusty cotton gin if he'd lived to see the day when some upstart acted like there was something funny about the South.

Up the road in North Carolina, Margaret Maron writes about a woman judge (if you can imagine such a perversion of the natural order) named Deborah Knott who has the audacity to speak her mind, even to her own daddy. She went all the way through college and law school without joining a sorority, and doesn't fret about not being married to an insurance agent from a good family in Charlotte. Great-aunt Eulalie had a word for women like that, but it's not appropriate for mixed company.

Right next door in South Carolina, Carolyn G. Hart sets breezy books about a snippety young thing named Annie Laurance Darling, who owns a successful mystery bookstore. Just to flaunt tradition, she's happily married. We all know sure as God made little green apples that the rich couples live in houses on the National Historic Register, where they get drunk and scream insults at each other, while the poor ones live in shacks, where they have sex with every last relative who isn't unequivocally dead. What kind of true southern boy lets his wife run a business instead of keeping her barefoot and pregnant?

I'd like to think we could at least find tobacco-chawin' rednecks living in abject poverty in Johnson City, Tennessee, but Sharyn McCrumb keeps writing about these folks just like they're complex and intelligent and familiar with indoor plumbing. Some say her work is downright lyrical, but as far as I can tell, it doesn't rhyme. She can't even be bothered to portray Appalachian folklore as ignorant hillbilly superstition. Frankly, not one of her characters could hold his or her own with the Dukes of Hazzard, which we all know were the stars of a documentary series back in the seventies.

John Grisham also has some pretty peculiar ideas about the great state of Tennessee. Let's be honest—how many of us would as soon mix our bourbon with swamp water as consult an intrepid woman-lawyer like Diane Sway, who wears trousers instead of petticoats? And Steven Womack has no problem letting his brash p.i., Harry James Denton, make all kinds of wry and irreverent remarks about the Nashville yuppies, who, I happen to know, are all very nice when you get to know them.

Something's rotten in the state of Georgia too. At least Charlaine Harris's Aurora Teagarden is a small-town librarian, a suitable profession for a spinster of thirty-odd years. It seems to me that Aurora might better spend her energy shelving books rather than snooping. Sarah Shankman flat out encourages her impudent Atlanta heroine, Sam Adams, to earn her living as a free-lance writer and make fun of such cherished deities as the King hisself. Patricia Sprinkle's young widow, Sheila Travis, didn't even take to her bed for a decade after her husband passed on. She upped and got herself a public relations job in Atlanta, and keeps sashaying off to hunt for murderers. Even worse, Celestine Sibley writes about Kate Mulcay, a widow of significant years, who not only supports herself as a reporter but also had the temerity to learn how to pilot an airplane in an emergency. In Great-aunt

Eulalie's day, a widow found solace presiding over the punch bowl at weddings and locking herself in the parlor with a bottle of sherry. Neither Sheila nor Kate will ever be invited to join the better garden clubs or staff the gift shop for the hospital auxiliary.

Things are still steamy in New Orleans, thanks to James Lee Burke and Julie Smith. Steamy—but where are the knife fights outside the tatty bars on Bourbon Street? The indecipherable patois of the Cajuns? The streetcars named Desire? Dave Robicheaux might ought to concentrate on drinking beer and fishing instead of getting involved with hoodlums who're so nasty they'd suck the head off a crawdad. And as for Smith's Skip Langdon, it's not at all hard to understand why her distinguished family disapproves of her career as a police officer. Granddaddy would roll in his grave if any of his girls so much as hinted that she might miss her alumnae meeting to clean a nasty ol' gun. I'd hate to think what he'd say about how Skip insists on delving into respectable families' dirty linens. Didn't her mama teach her that the civilized place for that behavior is the bridge table?

All I'm gonna say about Deborah Adams's Jesus Creek, Tennessee (pop. 430), Taylor McCafferty's Pigeon Fork, Kentucky (pop. 1511) and a certain Maggody, Arkansas (pop. 755), is that you'd better observe the speed limit when you hit the edge of town—and you'd better not underestimate the locals. They may not go around quoting Mr. Shakespeare, or even Mr. Faulkner, but they attend funerals a sight more often than you'd think.

It's as plain as the nose on my face that someone is trying to kill the southern stereotype. It wouldn't be polite to go naming names, but there are a lot of folks who are feeling threatened these days. Bubba says him and his dawg are thinking about joining a twelve-step program, and Mary Margaret claims she hardly ever gets invited to a pink tea these days, even though she's the current president of Junior League. In fact, she says since her cleaning woman, Blanche, went on the lam, it's all she can do to pack Trip's lunch box and get him to preschool in time for his French lesson.

As for myself, I do believe I'll lie down with a cool compress until this trendy nonsense passes and we can get back to murder under the magnolias. In the meantime, y'all help yourselves to another grit.

THE MYSTERY OF THE ROCKY MOUNTAINS

Marvin Lachman

THOUGH THE SMALLEST REGION of Mystery Writers of America in terms of members (only about seventy-five), the five states comprising the Rocky Mountain region cover more area than any other. Mysteries set in New Mexico, Colorado, Utah, Wyoming, and Montana are part of the "regional revolution," in which almost every recent American mystery has a strong regional component. Yet, there is a long history of Rocky Mountain mysteries, including books like *Old Stonewall, Colorado Detective* (1888) by Judson Taylor and *The Female Barber Detective, or Joe Phoenix in Silver City* (1895) by Albert W. Aiken.

Part of an even older book, Sir Arthur Conan Doyle's *A Study in Scarlet* (1887), is set in Utah, on what he calls "the Great Alkali Plain." Thus, the creator of gaslit London's Sherlock Holmes also wrote one of the first American regional mysteries. In it, Brigham Young and the Mormon elders are depicted as willing to annihilate those who oppose their belief in polygamy.

The tradition of mysteries about Utah's dominant church, the Latter-Day Saints, continues, and Mormonism generally does not come off well. Most are told from a non-Mormon viewpoint, even Robert Irvine's series about Salt Lake City private eye Moroni Traveler who, though his first name is that of a Mormon angel, no longer practices the religion. In books like *Baptism for the Dead* (1988), Traveler's detective work places him in conflict with the church.

Author Cleo Jones is also an ex-Mormon, and her *Prophet Motive* (1984) has as detective the chief of police of Magpie, Utah, a fallen Mormon trying to solve the murder of a Mormon bishop. In Thomas H. Cook's *Tabernacle* (1983), not only is Tom Jackson a non-Mormon detective, but he is from New York, and Cook describes hostility on the part of church members toward outsiders. Jackson is investigating links between the murder of a church spokesman and a prostitute.

"Bodily Harm," a 1992 short story, provides balance. Ray Davidson creates a private eye, newly moved to Salt Lake City, who dislikes divorce cases. He thinks the Mormon lifestyle makes it unlikely he'll be offered many.

Dashiell Hammett, an early regional mystery writer, is associated with San Francisco. However, his first book, *Red Harvest* (1929), is set in Personville, a fictional Butte, Montana, better known as "Poisonville." It is "an ugly city . . . dirtied up by smelters, whose brick stacks had yellow-smoked everything into uniform dinginess." In this corpse-laden mystery, some of its killing stems from the battle between a company based on Anaconda Copper and a radical union like the IWW.

After Hammett, there was a period when Montana mysteries tended toward the comic. Elliot Paul's *Fracas in the Foothills* (1940) has his wacky characters flee wartime Paris for a Montana ranch. There is a memorable meeting between a tribe of Blackfoot Indians and Dr. Hyacinthe Toudoux. Many Margaret Scherf mysteries are set in Montana towns; her titles include *The Curious Custard Pie* (1950) and *The Corpse in the Flannel Nightgown* (1965).

Rex Stout's *Death of a Dude* (1969) improbably has Nero Wolfe come to Lame Horse, Montana, to help Archie Goodwin solve the case that is keeping him away from West Thirty-fifth Street. Wolfe fords a mountain stream and deals with clues like trampled brush and displaced rocks.

Recent Montana mysteries are prone to treat social issues. Clark Howard, the most socially conscious American mystery writer, describes injustices done to Native Americans in two short stories, "Custer's Ghost" (1983) and "The Wide Loop" (1986). A. B. Guthrie was a Pulitzer Prize–winning author of westerns like *The Big Sky* and *The Way West*. In 1973, at age seventy-two, Guthrie became a mystery writer, creating Montana Sheriff Chick Charleston. Though light reading, this series tackles issues like Indian rights and strip mining.

Missoula, the site of the University of Montana, is also the center of a mystery boom, with five writers connected to the city (John Hugo, James Crumley, James Lee Burke, Robert Sims Reid, and Steven M. Krauzer) having published mysteries.

Hugo, a talented poet, died after writing one mystery, *Death and the Good Life* (1981). Crumley has written only three mysteries but has gained great popularity with his counter-culture characters. Though most of his Dave Robicheaux books are set in Louisiana, Burke lives in Missoula. *Black Cherry Blues* (1989) brings Robicheaux to Montana, giving Burke an opportunity to wax lyrical regarding the state's trout fishing.

Montana is called the "Big Sky State"; Robert Sims Reid titled his first mystery *Big Sky Blues* (1988). Reid works for the police in Missoula, and his detectives in fictional Rozette, Montana, are policemen. Steven M. Krauzer is a mystery scholar who has edited anthologies and now writes fiction about Victor Rojak, a former Montana police detective.

The low population density of Montana and its neighbor Wyoming contributed to their selection as Cold War missile sites. In two Montana books, Walter Wager's *Viper Three* (1971) and James Gra-

dy's *Shadow of the Condor* (1975) and one set in Wyoming, Payne Harrison's *Storming Intrepid* (1989), there is danger of nuclear warheads falling into the wrong hands.

An atypical Mary Roberts Rinehart mystery, *The State vs. Elinor Norton* (1934), has a Wyoming cattle ranch setting and stresses its isolation. One of Stout's non-series books, *The Mountain Cat Murders* (1939), is set in Cody, Wyoming. There is a western character "whose lean old face and tough oil-bereft skin . . . make him look like the dry country around him."

Mysteries such as Francis Bonnamy's *Death on a Dude Ranch* (1937) and Maude Parker's *Murder in Jackson Hole* (1955) stress Wyoming's resorts. Richard Powell sets part of *Say It with Bullets* (1953) in Yellowstone Park, as did Leslie Ford, who places Grace Latham and Colonel Primrose on horseback, in *Old Lover's Ghost* (1940), for a trip that ends in murder. Mabel Seeley's *Eleven Came Back* (1943) is set beneath the peaks of the Grand Tetons. A dozen people go on a midnight horseback ride, and one is murdered.

In *Medicine Dog* (1989), Wyoming President Geoffrey Peterson created private eye Boyd Sherman, who has moved from Arizona and dislikes Wyoming winters: he even has to defrost his daily newspaper.

Twenty-two years before the Pilgrims landed at Plymouth Rock, Spain settled what is now New Mexico. Its long history has attracted short-story writer Edward D. Hoch. He used the Penitentes, a group of religious fanatics reputed still to live in isolated mountain areas and practice self-flagellation, in "Sword for a Sinner" (1959). In "The Trail of the Golden Cross" (1992), Hoch has Ben Snow (a cowboy often mistaken for New Mexico's most famous outlaw, Billy the Kid) solve a murder during a stagecoach ride in 1882.

Dorothy B. Hughes set two mysteries in Santa Fe, New Mexico's capital. In *The Blackbirder* (1943) she describes, without creating an oxymoron, the "scenic barrenness" of the starkly beautiful road from Albuquerque to Santa Fe. *Ride the Pink Horse* (1946) takes place during the annual fiesta celebrating the return to Santa Fe, in 1693, of the Spanish, who had been forced out by a Pueblo Indian revolt.

Taos is a popular tourist town of art galleries, museums, and a pueblo about sixty miles north of

Santa Fe. Frances Crane's Santa Maria, in two of her mysteries, seems based on Taos. Fredric Brown once lived in Taos, trying to find a climate that would bring him relief from a severe pulmonary condition. One of his best novels, *The Far Cry* (1951), is set there.

Ursula Curtiss was another mystery writer with health problems; her son's severe asthma forced her to move to Albuquerque in 1960. Her mother, Helen Reilly, also a mystery writer, spent her last years in New Mexico and even brought series detective Inspector McKee from Manhattan for two of his last three cases. In *Follow Me* (1960), another New Yorker notes, "The stars were bright in the clear New Mexican night, a sky you never saw in the East."

Stuart Woods left Georgia and became a part-time Santa Fe resident after the success of mysteries like *Chiefs*. His *Santa Fe Rules* (1992) provides a good picture of his new home, though not going beyond what tourists may find on a weekend visit. The best current writer regarding Santa Fe is Walter Satterthwait, whose Joshua Croft series captures the flavor of the city he calls "Greenwich Village in the desert," with its predilection for alternative lifestyles.

Tony Hillerman and Richard Martin Stern were among the first to create as protagonists people who traditionally have not played major roles in mysteries. To many readers, Hillerman, whose books about Navajo policemen Joe Leaphorn and Jim Chee began with *The Blessing Way* (1970), epitomizes the regional mystery. Never sacrificing narrative, he captures the flavor of the Navajo way of life. He respects Indian culture and religion, but realizes some Indians cannot follow the strict Navajo ways, yet have trouble adapting to Anglo culture. Hillerman shows the likely result of their unresolved conflicts: the high alcoholism rate near New Mexico's reservations.

Stern, in *Murder in the Walls* (1971), created Johnny Ortiz, a Santa Fe (his thinly disguised city is called Santo Cristo) detective whose background represents the three cultures in New Mexico: Indian, Latino, and Anglo.

New Mexico's recent history includes the atomic era, ushered in by World War II research at Los Alamos. James Kunnetka's *Shadow Man* (1988) combines nuclear energy with Indian culture when the body of a Los Alamos National Laboratory scientist is found in a cave on the San Ildefonso Reservation.

Judith Van Gieson knows that a major problem in the Rocky Mountain region is disposal of nuclear waste, the by-product of experiments at western laboratories. In *North of the Border* (1988) she uses a controversial political issue, the Waste Isolation Pilot Project (WIPP), a real plan to bury nuclear waste in the Carlsbad caves.

Colorado mysteries emphasize the state's mountains and its mines. In Clyde B. Clason's *Blind Drifts* (1937), Professor Theocritus Westborough acquires a share in a gold mine and solves a disappearance and a murder below ground. In a similar vein (pun intended) are Hugh Lawrence Nelson's *Gold in Every Grave* (1951) and Carolyn Thomas's *Narrow Gauge to Murder* (1953).

Some current mysteries focus on Colorado's new "industry," skiing resorts like Vail and Aspen. Norma Schier's detective, Kay Barth, is a district attorney in Aspen, and two Barth mysteries have a skiing background, including a harrowing description of a whiteout in *Death Goes Skiing* (1979). Jack Pearl's *A Time to Kill . . . a Time to Die* (1971) and Ron Faust's *The Wolf in the Clouds* (1977) present a "popular" Colorado villain, the killer on the ski slopes. Colorado writers Michael Allegretto and Yvonne Montgomery write of its frequent snow, with the latter employing an April storm in *Scavengers* (1987), what she ironically calls "springtime in the Rockies."

The police procedurals and private eye novels of Rex Burns provide the best picture of Denver of any books written about that city. His police detective, Gabe Wager, is a mix of Anglo and Latino, and his books reflect Denver's racial tensions and drug crimes. In a lighter moment Burns describes the impatience of Denver residents toward "flat-landers," visitors unfamiliar with driving in the mountains. Montgomery and John Dunning write well of Colfax Avenue, Denver's main thoroughfare, a crime-ridden street at night, after office workers go home.

The authors I mention are a small fraction of those who have written about the Rocky Mountain region. Their mysteries, to a greater degree than elsewhere in the United States, tend to be set outdoors. They provide fine indoor reading.

MYSTERIES
IN THE SOUTHWEST
Anne Wingate

Photo by GlamourShots of Salt Lake City

IN MYSTERY WRITING, as in almost everything else, the Southwest is a state of mind in
which things transform themselves so that they
no longer work quite the same way as they do in
the rest of the country. Definitely not a hybrid of
mysteries and westerns, the mystery in the Southwest nevertheless uses, and transforms, many of the
most important topics and themes of both.

Thus the detective is as likely to be a sheriff
(Bill Crider's Dan Rhodes, D. R. Meredith's
Charles Matthews) or a deputy (Susan Rogers Coo-
per's Milton Kovak) as a p.i. (Susan Baker's Mavis
Davis, Karen Kijewski's Kat Colorado, Bernard
Schopen's Jack Ross, Ken Grissom's John Rod-
rigue, Walter Satterthwait's Joshua Croft) or a po-
lice officer. Where police officers do occur, they
may be Navajo (Tony Hillerman's Jim Chee and
Joe Leaphorn), Apache (Richard Martin Stern's

Johnny Ortiz), Cherokee (Jean Hager's Mitch
Bushyhead), or even Japanese-American (Anne
Wingate's Mark Shigata). Or they're unusual in
other ways: Mary Morrell's lesbian detective in San
Antonio, Lucia Ramos; Lee Martin's happily mar-
ried grandmother detective in Fort Worth, Deb
Ralston.

The brilliant amateurs or people who work on
the fringes of law enforcement and suddenly find
themselves in the middle of it also tend to be
quirky: Austin Bay's antihero Bill Buchanan, an illegal helicopter pilot who succeeds in stealing two
million dollars from a drug cartel; Lee Head's delightful octogenarian Lexey Jane Pelazoni, who can
find murder in Dallas's most exclusive health spa
(Head calls it The Terrarium, but it's recognizably
The Greenhouse): children's artist Callista Jacobs,
who finds murder and mayhem in a religious cult
adjacent to her new lover's archaeological dig; B.
J. Oliphant's twice-widowed and highly opinionated
rancher Shirley McClintock; Aimee Thurlo's half-
Navajo botanist Belara Fuller; Mary Willis Walker's dog trainer Katherine Driscoll; and M. J. Rod-
gers's assorted women anthropologists and
pathologists. A particularly good new entry into the
brilliant amateur corner is Jake Page's blind Santa
Fe sculptor Mo Bowdre and his Anglo-Hopi girlfriend Connie Barnes, who may over several books
do for the Hopi what Tony Hillerman's characters
do for the Navajo. Ray Ring's assorted antiheroes
bring an unexpected bitter flavor to what often becomes a paean of praise for the region. Although
many of the mysteries will be of interest to younger
readers, Joan Lowery Nixon with her teenage Texas
heroes and heroines stands almost alone in writing
directly for the young adult audience.

Until the late 1980s mysteries in the Southwest
were almost exclusively male-dominated; the few

women who wrote them had male lead characters and often (like Doris Meredith) disguised themselves behind male initials. But with the late 1980s and the 1990s came a sudden burgeoning of female leads and female authors.

Historical mysteries, so popular in other areas, seem poorly represented in the Southwest as yet, although one is interesting: Walter Satterthwait's *The Wilde West,* in which Oscar Wilde, Baby Doc, and Doc Holliday trap Jack the Ripper near Denver, Colorado.

Quality, of course, varies widely. At the top of the scale are Tony Hillerman's books, but some winners emerge in unexpected places. M. J. Rogers's *Bone of Contention,* an unusually brilliant forensic mystery, is a Harlequin Intrigue. There are also some disappointments; despite Richard Martin Stern's excellent reputation, his Johnny Ortiz feels to the cognoscenti like a cross between Dell Shannon's Luis Mendoza without money and Arthur W. Upfield's Boney without charm. Some few feel like "Lincoln's doctor's dog" books; that is, mysteries that attempt to tap into an already existing market. Bernard Schopen's *The Big Silence* becomes so confusing that the fact that several important characters are Shoshone really is immaterial. The writer needs a chart to keep track of who is doing what with, to, for, and about whom.

Themes tend to be somewhat repetitive: in a fast survey of fifty southwestern mysteries, I found that twenty-nine concerned Native Americans and/or the environment. In this case, however, repetitive does not mean boring, as different writers approached Native Americans as individuals and environmental problems as specific problems, not as generic situations.

Interestingly, unusual problems also crop up: in Richard Martin Stern's *Murder in the Walls,* the story revolves around the city fathers' decision to raze the oldest house in Santo Cristo—for which read Santa Fe—because it is being used as a whorehouse, and the way Johnny Ortiz saves the day. Walter Satterthwait's *A Flower in the Desert* involves Joshua Croft's attempts to find the missing daughter-in-law of a Mafioso who is outraged at his son's habit of child abuse. Aimee Thurlo's Belara Fuller, in *Night Wind,* sets out to take his nitroglycerine tablets to her elderly uncle who has gone on foot to visit the old family home now on the White

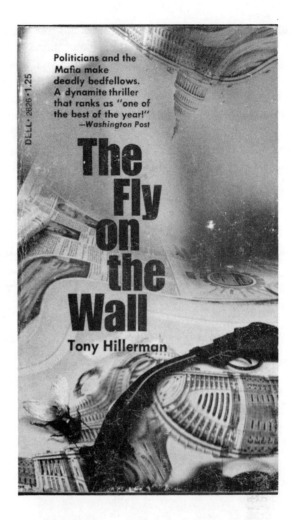

Sands Missile Range and winds up tangling with two separate sets of spies. Ray Ring's *Peregrine Dream*—not just another environmental novel—starts out with stolen falcons and leads into murder, incest, and endangered species of frogs and birds at a land development. (Really.)

As always in fiction, the romantic problems of the protagonists mount up. Susan Rogers Cooper's *The Man in the Green Chevy* is a particularly fine example of that: Deputy Milton Kovak definitely falls for the wrong woman when he falls for Laura Johnson. In Bill Crider's *Evil at the Root,* Sheriff Dan Rhodes starts out investigating stolen false teeth, winds up with two murders (one of them thirty years old), and nearly misses his own wedding after being beaten up twice.

The more common mystery problems—money, organized crime, family relationships—are encountered less frequently in the southwestern mystery than in novels set in other places, but they are not unheard of. In Ray Ring's *Arizona Kiss*, the lies of an obsessed girl lure a reporter into murdering a judge; Susan Baker's *My First Murder* and Susan Rogers Cooper's *Other People's Houses* both revolve around inadequately disguised and protected witnesses. Even motorcycle gangs (Bill Crider's *Shotgun Saturday Night*), pimps (Bill Crider's *Dead on the Island*), and Mafiosi (Ken Grissom's *Drowned Man's Key* and Lee Head's *The Crystal Clear Case*) turn up occasionally.

In general, the southwestern mystery has more relationship to the Australian mysteries of Arthur W. Upfield than it has with most regional mysteries in the United States. That is no accident; Upfield's Australia is the same type of country, substituting Aborigines for Native Americans and Australian slang for southwestern slang. In its native land, the southwestern mystery stands alone. And there is far more there than the casual reader, who thinks only of Tony Hillerman, ever imagined.

LONE STAR CRIME

Bill Crider

WHATEVER KIND OF CRIME or mystery story you're looking for, someone in Texas is writing it.

You want courtroom thrillers? Jay Brandon writes some of the best. He began his career with a couple of original paperback suspense novels, *Deadbolt* and *Tripwire,* then moved into hardcover with *Predator's Waltz,* and hit the big time with his fourth book, *Fade the Heat,* set in San Antonio and based in part on his experiences in the Bexar

County courthouse while working on the staff of the district attorney. The story of a prosecutor whose son is accused of rape, *Fade the Heat* was optioned for the movies by Steven Spielberg and nominated for an Edgar Award by the Mystery Writers of America. This novel was followed by *Rules of Evidence,* another strong effort that also takes place in the Alamo city.

Do you like a bit of social consciousness in your mysteries, with an emphasis on the psychology of the killer and the investigator? David Lindsey has written a series of critically acclaimed, best-selling police procedurals that range from Houston to Guatemala. Lindsey's novels are often violent in the extreme, but Lindsey says that he is presenting violence as it really is, in all its ugliness and horror, not the sanitized violence of television that tends to deaden us to the true nature of evil. He speaks from experience, having developed a relationship with the Houston Police Department that has allowed him to visit the scenes of homicides and see what the real thing is like. Most of his books feature a wealthy, psychologically troubled Houston cop named Stuart Haydon, who sometimes ventures out of Texas in books such as *In the Lake of the Moon* and *Body of Truth,* the latter a frightening investigation that involves the *desaperacidos* in Guatemala. *Mercy,* perhaps Lindsey's most successful novel to date, with its serial killer working the lesbian underground, has a female protagonist, Carmen Palma, also a Houston police officer.

The truth is, quite a few Texas authors have done books about serial killers. Maybe it's something in the water. At any rate, there are my own gory *Blood Marks* as well as three other books mentioned later, Ed Mathis's *Only When She Cries,* Joe Lansdale's *Act of Love,* and D. R. Meredith's *The Masquerade Murders.*

If you're looking for small-town crime, D. R. Meredith, Susan Rogers Cooper, and I all have rural lawmen working overtime. My own Sheriff Dan Rhodes is a laid-back guy who works in Blacklin County, somewhere in central Texas, and who has to deal with things ranging from stolen false teeth to unburied body parts in books like *Evil at the Root* and *Shotgun Saturday Night.* Meredith's Sheriff Charles Timothy Matthews operates in the Panhandle (indeed, the first novel in the series is *The Sheriff and the Panhandle Murders*), and several of her other novels, including *The Masquerade Murders,* feature an attorney, John Lloyd Branson, who works in the same area. Both series present a good picture of the country and the people, and they provide some engrossing plots as well. Susan Rogers Cooper's Milt Kovak, the chief deputy in Prophecy County, Oklahoma, spends most of his time outside Texas, though he made a trip to the Gulf Coast in *Houston in the Rearview Mirror.* Cooper's other series, with amateur sleuth Eloise Janine (E.J. for short) Pugh, is set in Codderville, Texas. The first book in the series, *One, Two, What Did Daddy Do?,* concerns an apparent homicide/suicide that of course is not exactly what it seems. Good writing, precisely rendered settings, and engaging characters highlight both series.

You're wondering about private eyes? Texas has those too. My contributions to the genre, *Dead on the Island* and *Gator Kill,* are set on Galveston Island, though in the latter, Truman Smith, the narrator of the series, ventures into the river bottoms of southeast Texas to solve the murder of an alligator. The late Ed Mathis was the creator of one of Texas's most popular private eyes, Dan Roman, and Ed left a number of unpublished manuscripts at his death, assuring that the series will continue for at least a few more years. Most of his books are set in the Dallas/Fort Worth area, and some of them, *From a High Place* being only one example, are very good indeed. Mathis also wrote some excellent

suspense novels, like *Only When She Cries.* Richard Abshire, a former Dallas policeman, knows the Dallas/Fort Worth region like Raymond Chandler knew Los Angeles, and Abshire's Marlowesque private eye, Jack Kyle, has appeared in several cleverly plotted novels, including *Turnaround Jack* and *Dallas Deception.* And of course there's James Reasoner's near-legendary *Texas Wind,* one of the earlier private eye novels to be set in Texas and now a hard-to-obtain collector's item. James's wife, L. J. Washburn, has a private eye of her own, Lucas Hallam, a former Texas Ranger who works as both a detective and a stuntman in the early days of Hollywood. His adventures both on and off movie sets provide exhilarating entertainment in such cleverly plotted books as the award-winning *Wild Night* and *Dead Stick.*

You want show biz? Since the glory days of the Armadillo World Headquarters, Texas has been home to its share of popular musicians, and the rock subculture is covered in absorbing fashion by Jesse

Sublett and his rock drummer/detective beginning in *The Rock Critic Murders*. Sublett's carefully crafted books show a side of the music business that most readers don't often get to see except through such examples of well-wrought fiction.

Suspense? Joe Lansdale is a writer who established his reputation in the field of dark fantasy, though his first novel, *Act of Love,* published near the beginning of his career, was a powerful suspense story about "the Houston Hacker." Lately he has turned more and more to suspense with such excellent work as *Savage Season* and *Cold in July,* both set in Texas. These books have credible protagonists, frightening villains, and plots that uncoil with the inevitability of fate.

Like Lansdale, Neal Barrett, Jr., established his reputation in another field, this time science fiction, before writing *Pink Vodka Blues,* a novel with a light touch and plenty of laughs and thrills. The book established Barrett as an "overnight success" in the mystery field and had mystery readers eagerly looking forward to his next mystery, *Dead Dog Blues.*

For straightforward suspense there are the novels of Deanie Francis (D. F.) Mills, books like *Free Fall* and *Spell Bound,* that catch the reader on the first page and don't let up until the final paragraph.

What about the classic tale of detection as practiced by Sir Arthur Conan Doyle? Carole Nelson Douglas gives a different twist to the idea of the Great Detective in her novels showcasing Irene Adler, the only woman ever to outsmart Sherlock Holmes. In *Good Night, Mr. Holmes* and *Good Morning, Irene,* Penelope Huxleigh serves as Adler's Watson, and the two prove to be as clever as any dedicated Holmesian could wish, while at the same time demonstrating some of the problems an intelligent, clever woman has to deal with in a male-dominated society. Douglas also has a treat for cat fans, of which there seem to be many among mystery readers, in her novels about Midnight Louie, the cat detective whose first-person narrative style resembles that of Damon Runyon.

And speaking of cats, there's one featured on the covers of both *Ashes to Ashes* and *Dust to Dust,* two of Lillian Stewart Carl's novels. The cat figures prominently in the plots of these uniquely entertaining stories too. The books are mysteries, true, with murder in the past and murder in the present, but they also combine mystery with romantic suspense,

archaeology, and a touch of the genteel gothic thriller.

A. W. Gray, on the other hand, isn't exactly genteel. His work has been compared to that of Elmore Leonard, and he began writing in a federal correctional institution. Gray has been very successful with a succession of crime novels that make use of his knowledge of the criminal justice system, some of it gained the hard way. One of a number of entertaining Gray characters is Bino Phillips (*Bino* and *In Defense of Judges*), who played basketball at SMU and who now works as a Dallas attorney. The narrator of the fast-paced *The Man Offside* is a former Dallas Cowboy football player who's not exactly on the right side of the law.

And then there's Kinky Friedman, leader of the musical group the Texas Jewboys and composer of such classic tunes as "Get Your Biscuits in the Oven and Your Buns in the Bed." Friedman has now turned his hand to mystery writing in a series of quirkily funny novels featuring a private eye named, of all things, Kinky Friedman. Plot is not necessarily the strong point of books like *A Case of Lone Star* and *Greenwich Killing Time,* but Friedman fans don't mind, as the Kinkster gets off a series of classic one-liners and works his way through the bodies to the conclusion.

As for major award winners, Texas has those too. Joan Lowery Nixon practically needs a separate house to store all her trophies, including three Edgars, not to mention awards from schools and state library associations all over the country. Nixon's mystery novels are aimed specifically at the school market, though her legions of devoted readers include quite a few adults who like thoughtful, well-plotted mysteries. Her work ranges from the grippingly suspenseful (*Whispers from the Dead, The Other Side of Dark*) to a very funny take on the classic form of the locked-room murder story in *The Weekend Was Murder.*

Houston's Mary Blount Christian writes for a somewhat younger audience than Nixon, but with equally impressive results. Her Determined Detectives solve such crimes as *The Mysterious Case Case* and perform admirably in a book with one of the great all-time groaner titles, *Merger on the Orient Expressway.* And for those who would rather read about dogs than cats, Sebastian (Super Sleuth) is Texas's (and the world's) leading canine detective. Not only is he clever at deduction, he can even make a call on a push-button phone if there's a pencil handy, though he's never properly appreciated by his human, Detective John Quincy Jones.

Politics and academics aren't neglected by Texans either. In my own *The Texas Capitol Murders,* two murders take place inside the state capitol. The governor fears for his life, and it takes a Texas Ranger and a resourceful capitol employee to figure things out. As for academics, my character Carl Burns, professor of English at Hartley Gorman University, gets mixed up in the murders of characters who richly deserve it in *One Dead Dean* and *Dying Voices.*

We've covered everything from crime-solving animals to private eyes who investigate the murder of alligators. Could there be anything missing? If there seems to be, check out the work of several up-and-coming writers, like Jan Grape, whose short stories, some of which feature a female private eye, have begun to appear in numerous collections, and for a new twist on blackmail, look for Marilyn Cooley and James Gunn's hard-boiled procedural *You'll Hear from Us,* and for an unusual backdrop read Mary Willis Walker's award-winning *Zero at the Bone,* which is set in an Austin zoo, or Susan Wittig Albert's *Thyme of Death,* whose main character owns an herb shop. Deborah Crombie, in *A Share in Death,* has even written a traditional (and quite good) fair-play mystery with a British setting, featuring Detective Superintendent Duncan Kinkaid and Sergeant Gemma Jones of Scotland Yard. And finally, for all-out suspense, don't miss Billie Sue Mosiman's Edgar-nominated *Night Cruise.*

In other words, if you can't find a Texas author's book to suit your taste, you just aren't trying hard enough.

THE FLORIDA MYSTERY SCENE

Harrison Arnston

FLORIDA.
Sometime in midwinter, their minds numbed by gray skies, leafless trees, dirty snow, and bitter cold, people from northern climes start thinking of Florida in almost worshipful terms. Men and women sit at cluttered desks, staring at dirty windows, their minds conjuring up images of sunshine, theme parks, deep-sea fishing, golf courses, swimming pools, beaches, alligators, tan bodies, fresh oranges, green grass, romantic candlelight dinners under gently swaying palms, and a hundred other reasons to get away from the snow and cold. Those who spend their time sitting around a pool or lying on a beach and watching their skin turn to leather would be well advised to wear a wide-brimmed hat and sample the work of some of the scores of Florida-based mystery authors. They'll return home refreshed, invigorated, and better informed, because mystery writers are putting out some of the best writing done anywhere, anytime.

First, a little reality.

Florida is famous for sun, sand, sea, condos, trailer parks, retirement villages, and—thanks to the successful TV show *Miami Vice*—crime. It's unfortunate, but though fourth in the nation in population, Florida is second only to Washington, D.C., in acts of violent crime according to crime statistics for 1991 (the latest available). In 1991 there were 1248 murders or nonnegligent manslaughters (a fancy term for murders pled down to a lesser charge) in the state. That's a whole lot of dying.

There's big crime here, and lots of it—the *boys* find winters as distasteful as the rest of the snowbirds—but because Florida is so close to the South American illegal drug factories and because the state has so many hundreds of miles of coastline, it's a natural port of entry for those engaged in the highly lucrative illegal drug business. The federal agencies, DEA, FBI, U.S. Coast Guard, to name but a few, understaffed and underbudgeted, manage to stop an estimated five percent of the cocaine entering Florida. Even so, hardly a week goes by without a press conference featuring grim-faced drug agents standing behind a table filled with tall stacks of confiscated hundred-dollar bills and five-kilo plastic bags of nose candy. The drug business is big here, but drugs and violent crime aren't the only problems.

Florida is known as America's scam capital, a dubious honor, and one due in part to the state's high percentage of older, retired Americans. Whirling minds are constantly at work devising ways to separate these citizens from their money. Once again, law enforcement agencies are hard pressed to keep up.

Like the rest of the country, our prisons are full. A thirty-year stretch isn't what it used to be—it's more like five. And with the courts as clogged as they are, anyone who wants to do away with plea-bargaining will be forced to confront the specter of indicted citizens waiting years for trial. Since the Constitution makes that a no-no, plea-bargains are here to stay. As well, the citizens of Florida hate to be nicked for the money needed to build more prisons, so the revolving doors spin faster and faster.

Violent crime gets most of the attention. The first five minutes of your average news broadcast is usually a body count. Something new—attacks on tourists—reached a zenith in late 1992 and early 1993, and things were so bad that the countries of Canada and Germany issued dire warnings, suggesting that their citizens choose somewhere else for a vacation. Since tourism is the lifeblood of the state, the politicians answered the Klaxon call and worked overtime to set things right. Extra police patrols were just one action taken to stem attacks on tourists. Car rental agencies were encouraged to change the license plates on rental cars (previously a tipoff to criminals), and pull off the bumper stickers that announced to the world that the driver was a tourist. The efforts paid off, and the warnings have since been rescinded.

The tourists may be better off, but crime marches on. And because it does, Florida is fertile ground for writers of crime fiction. More than a few Florida-based crime fiction writers who toiled in rel-

ative obscurity for many years have developed large—even worldwide—followings during the past few years. Crimewise, authors are putting Florida on the fiction map, giving it a status previously reserved for New York and Los Angeles. Even non-residents are getting into the act, with authors from all over the country giving their stories a Florida setting.

Enough of reality. With fiction, *you* pick the time and place for violent confrontation. And picking up any of the books mentioned here will be most rewarding.

The late John D. MacDonald lived here much of his life. He was a quiet, interesting man, and his name is still mentioned in reverent tones seven years after his death. His fictional hero, p.i. Travis McGee, is known and admired all over the world. The McGee novels—unique in many ways besides the use of a color word in every title—were set in Florida. McGee lived and worked out of a houseboat known as *The Busted Flush*. Ed Hirshberg, Professor of English at the University of South Florida, publishes an annual retrospective for John D. MacDonald bibliophiles. Professor Hirshberg also conducts an annual fall seminar in Fort Lauderdale, where writers and fans gather, swap stories, and visit the newly dedicated dock where the fictional boat was moored. Fiction becomes fact. Most of MacDonald's seventy or so novels are still in print, and thousands of new fans discover the pleasures of reading MacDonald every year. And in Sarasota, the Friday Liar's Poker Club that John D. helped found still meets every week. Precise records of wins and losses go back to the very first lunch. (Note: John D. was lousy at the game)

Charles Willeford is another venerated author who has left us. *Miami Blues, New Hope for the Dead, The Way We Die Now,* and *Sideswipe* are novels starring Hoke Moseley, a sleuth who knows the dark and seamy Miami as intimately as any movie star knows the lines in his face.

Among the living, there are hundreds of Florida-based authors who have made Florida the locale for their novels. What follows is, given the twin constraints of time and resources, a very incomplete list, but it's a start, and the names are given in no particular order, shape, or form. For those excluded, my sincere apologies.

James W. Hall: Hall's newest highly regarded novel is *Hard Aground* (Delacorte), the story of an unfocused man's sudden ascension from torpor when his brother is murdered. As usual, Hall brings in many other elements to give his novel a solid, rich texture. Hall's other titles include *Under Cover of Daylight, Squall Line, Tropical Freeze,* and *Bones of Coral.*

T. J. MacGregor: T.J.'s new novel (featuring the crime-fighting team of Quin St. James and Mike McClear) is *Storm Surge* (Hyperion). Set in Miami Beach, this is the eighth in the St. James-McClear series. Other titles (from Ballantine) include *Spree* (set in Gainesville), *Death Flats* (with a South Florida locale) and *Kin Dread* (set in the Everglades). T.J.'s books written under the pen name Alison Drake are also set in Florida. Titles are *High Strangeness* and *Black Moon.* Husband Rob MacGregor is the author of several very successful Indiana Jones novels, and his *The Crystal Skull* (Ballantine) features p.i. Nick Pierce, who uses New Age mysticism to solve Miami Beach murders.

Carl Hiaasen: A writer with a Miami newspaper, Carl has seen his Florida-based novels gain world fame in a few short years. Carl's newest is *Striptease* (Knopf), set in the Florida Keys. Many expect this book to make it to the top of the best seller lists. All of Carl's other titles are still in print, including *Native Tongue* and *Skin Tight.*

Edna Buchanan: Edna is a former crime reporter for the *Miami Herald.* Her newest novel is *Miami, It's Murder* (Hyperion), featuring a crime reporter named Britt Montero. Buchanan's protagonist first appeared in *Contents Under Pressure.* Another earlier Buchanan title, *Nobody Lives Forever* (Zebra), features homicide detective Rick Barrish.

Lawrence Sanders: Lawrence is one of America's most enduring authors and his novels have used many cities for locales. *McNally's Risk* (Putman) is the most recent novel featuring the popular Palm Beach–based p.i. Archy McNally. McNally is also seen in action in *McNally's Luck* and *McNally's Secret.*

Harrison Arnston: Of his eight novels, two are set in Florida. *Act of Passion,* a courtroom drama that tells the tale of a betrayed woman falsely accused of murdering her husband and his mistress, takes place in Clearwater, while *Trade-Off,* with lawyer Laura Scott defending a vicious killer much to the indignation of her friends and neighbors, is set in a fictional town near Orlando. Both are from HarperPaperbacks.

David A. Kaufelt: David is the author of eleven novels. His newest is *The Fat Boy Murders* (Pocket), his first pure mystery. He's been writing about Florida since 1979, when *Late Bloomer* was published. Other novels include *Silver Rose* and *American Tropic.*

Paul Patti: Two novels set in West Palm Beach feature top homicide investigator Andy Amato. Both stories involve serial killers. *Death Mate* and *Silhouettes* are from St. Martin's Press.

Randy Wayne White: Randy's *Heat Islands* (St. Martin's) features protagonist Doc Ford, up to his ears in murder and drug-running, and uses Florida's West Coast as a setting. Randy's protagonist was also featured in the earlier much-heralded *Sanibel Flats.*

Jerome Sanford: A hardworking assistant U.S. attorney, Jerry's first novel, *Miami Heat* (St. Martin's), is a thriller filled with murder and mayhem and features former FBI agent, now p.i. David Knight, who has good reason to think the world is against him.

Michael McKinney: *A Thousand Bridges* (Walker) is a critically acclaimed story of murder in the Florida Panhandle. It's the first in a series starring p.i. MacDonald Clay, a character hailed by critics as one of the most interesting to come along in some time.

Linda Grey Crockett's latest, *Carousel* (Tor), is set in Florida, as is Alice Hoffman's *Turtle Moon* (Berkley). And Charlotte Douglas's *Jacaranda Bend* (HarperPaperbacks) is a pure mystery with an 1885 Florida setting. Because the book is cleverly disguised as something else, you'll never find it in the mystery section. All three fine writers are building large followings.

Authors living outside the state who have chosen Florida as a setting include, to name but a very few:

Elmore Leonard, whose newest is *Pronto* (Delacorte). Other Leonard titles set in Florida include *Rum Punch* and *Maximum Bob.* In these books (as with all his books) the master of crime fiction (and 1993 president of Mystery Writers of America) never disappoints, serving up a tasty menu of oddball characters and plot twists to satisfy the most jaded mystery reader. John Lutz (a former president of MWA) has a new book out called *Spark* (Holt), staring p.i. Fred Carver of the invented town of "Del Moray." Carver can also be seen in *Bloodfire*

(Avon). John Katzanbach's *Just Cause* (Ballantine) features reporter Matt Coward trying to save a man from the electric chair.

There is another group of prominent Florida mystery writers whose novels use locales other than Florida. It's impossible to name all of these fine people, but a partial list includes: Alan Trustman, Stuart Kaminsky, John Leslie, Frank Strunk, James Neal Harvey, Dick Francis, Paul Levine, Jonellen Heckler, Daniel Keyes, Brian D'Amato, Margaret Clark, and Carol Cope.

Florida is unquestionably a searing, screaming, bloody, seething core of crime and crime fiction.

It must be the heat.

The Ten Most Underrated Mystery Writers
Selected by Douglas G. Greene

Clyde B. Clason
B. L. Farjeon
Milward Kennedy
Rufus King
Katherine Moore Knight
Paul McGuire
Rupert Penny
Jonathan Stagge
(though the same author's books as Patrick Quentin and Q. Patrick are well known)
Darwin L. Teilheit
Clifford Witting

Notable Northern California Novels
Selected by The Editors

Janet Dawson
Kindred Crimes

Sue Dunlap
Death and Taxes

Joe Gores
32 Cadillacs

Lia Matera
Prior Convictions

Janet LaPierre
The Cruel Mother

Bill Pronzini
Shackles

Margaret Lucke
A Relative Stranger

Marcia Muller
Wolf In The Shadows

Shelly Singer
Suicide King

Julie Smith
New Orleans Mourning

Collin Wilcox
Silent Witness

Bruce Zimmerman
Blood Under the Bridge

TRADITIONAL MYSTERIES

INTRODUCTION

Jon L. Breen

WHAT EXACTLY IS A traditional mystery? It depends on what tradition you come from. In one categorization of a few years ago, the hard-boiled private eye novel was identified as the traditional mystery, a designation that was greeted with appropriate cries of objection from proponents of the *real* traditional mystery, which is the form that Poe invented, Conan Doyle popularized, and writers like Dorothy L. Sayers, Agatha Christie, Ellery Queen, and John Dickson Carr brought to fullest flower in the so-called "Golden Age of Detection" between the World Wars.

The traditional mystery involves a criminal problem, usually a murder and usually with a perpetrator unknown to the reader, that is solved by a detective, who may be an amateur or a professional. The emphasis is on real detection from clues (physical, verbal, or psychological) that have been placed before the reader: though Conan Doyle did not practice this kind of fair play in the Sherlock Holmes stories, by the twenties, putting the evidence on the table and giving the reader a chance to beat the sleuth to the solution was a well-established requirement. Some writers, notably Father Ronald A. Knox in his "Detective Story Decalogue" (1929) and S. S. Van Dine (Willard Huntington Wright) in his "Twenty Rules for Writing Detective Stories" (1928)[1], promulgated lists of rules for the proper construction of detective novels.

Unfriendly critics have sometimes claimed that these books, in their stress on the cerebral, threw all considerations of good prose, characterization, and atmosphere out the window. This was never true of the best traditional practitioners, even those whose firmly laid rules gave ammunition to the critics. (Van Dine: "3. There must be no love interest. . . .16. A detective novel should contain no long descriptive passages, no literary dallying with side-issues, no subtly worked out character analysis, no 'atmospheric' preoccupations." Knox: "No Chinaman must figure in the story.")

The classical detective story has been a dominant form through most of mystery fiction history, and it is still practiced widely today, enjoying something of a renaissance in the increased vogue for so-called "cozy" mysteries in the eighties and nineties. But it need not be cozy, often existing in combination with tougher forms. For example, the big three of private eye fiction, Dashiell Hammett, Raymond Chandler, and Ross Macdonald, all observed at least some of the conventions of the traditional mystery in their whodunit plots, and writers like Rex Stout, George Harmon Coxe, Erle Stanley Gardner, and Brett Halliday, though using some of the trappings of the hard-boiled mystery, were essentially traditionalists at heart.

The type started with Poe's short stories, was further developed in Conan Doyle's, and remained a predominately short-story form through the early years of the century. Conan Doyle and R. Austin Freeman both wrote novels, but their short stories are usually considered to contain their most important work. This was also true of significant contemporaries like Arthur Morrison, Melville Davisson Post, G. K. Chesterton, and Jacques Futrelle. The reputations of writers like Carolyn Wells, who concentrated on the longer form in the period before World War I, have not survived.

One of the first important modern detective novels was E. C. Bentley's *Trent's Last Case* (1913), often cited as the precursor of the Golden Age. The impact of the world war may have delayed Bentley's influence from being fully felt before the next

---

[1] Both these compilations appear in Howard Haycraft's essay anthology *The Art of the Mystery Story* (1946), recently reprinted in trade paperback by Carroll & Graf. They have also been reprinted in many other sources.

decade. In 1920, a key year, Agatha Christie, Freeman Wills Crofts, and H. C. Bailey all made their first appearances, with only Bailey specializing in shorter forms. Through the twenties the novel predominated, although most of the major writers also did short stories. Other important British writers to enter the field included Eden Phillpotts, G.D.H. and M. I. Cole, A. A. Milne (with a celebrated one-shot, *The Red House Mystery,* 1922), Philip MacDonald, John Rhode, Anthony Berkeley (A. B. Cox, later known as Francis Iles), Margery Allingham, Gladys Mitchell, and (most significantly) Dorothy L. Sayers with the first Lord Peter Wimsey book, *Whose Body?* (1923). Fooling the reader while still playing fair was the challenge of the day, and no writer played the game more cunningly than Christie, whose *The Murder of Roger Ackroyd* (1926) deployed a gimmick that is still debated today. (Did she play fair? Certainly.)

For the most part, Americans lagged behind their British cousins in the twenties, though Earl Derr Biggers introduced Honolulu policeman Charlie Chan in *The House Without a Key* (1925) and S. S. Van Dine made a major impact with the Philo Vance series, beginning with *The Benson Murder Case* (1926). Posterity has not been kind to either writer, with Biggers's reputation compromised by the controversy over whether Chan is an ethnic stereotype (at least partly fueled by the fact, no fault of Biggers's, that a succession of non-Asian actors played Chan on screen), and Van Dine as underrated by latter-day historians as he was overrated in his own time.

Popular wisdom holds that British women dominated the classical form throughout the Golden Age. In 1934, the New Zealand author Ngaio Marsh introduced Roderick Alleyn in *A Man Lay Dead,* joining Christie, Sayers, and Allingham in making a strong case for feminine ascendancy. But two masculine British writers also began long and distinguished careers in the thirties: Nicholas Blake (C. Day Lewis), who introduced Nigel Strangeways in *A Question of Proof* (1935), and Michael Innes (J.I.M. Stewart), who first featured John Appleby in *Death at the President's Lodging* (1936; American title *Seven Suspects,* 1937).

It should also be remembered that American men were among the greatest Golden Age puzzle spinners. The Ellery Queen team, Frederic Dannay

and Manfred B. Lee, began with *The Roman Hat Mystery* (1929) and created a string of dazzlingly complex puzzle edifices throughout the thirties, both under the Queen byline and, in four novels about retired actor Drury Lane, as Barnaby Ross. In subsequent decades they would determinedly move with the times, shaking off the Van Dine influence and extending their range in character, theme, and realism without deserting the formal puzzle. John Dickson Carr, who began with *It Walks by Night* (1930) and also wrote under the transparent pseudonym Carter Dickson, was equally prolific of ingenious puzzle plots throughout the thirties and later would pioneer the historical detective novel, while never discarding his allegiance to the locked room and impossible-crime problem.

The classical detective novel reached full fruition in the thirties: plots were at their most complex and dexterous; established writers like Sayers and Berkeley were extending their reach while newer writers like Blake, Marsh, Innes, and Allingham stepped up the form's level of literary quality, at least at the top end. By the end of the decade, any number of important new talents in the traditional form were on the scene: in Britain, Josephine Tey and Cyril Hare; in America, Anthony Boucher (William Anthony Parker White), later to be the genre's foremost critic, Clayton Rawson, C. Daly King, George Bagby (Aaron Marc Stein), and Helen McCloy, a writer who (despite being named a Mystery Writers of America Grand Master) I believe continues to be undervalued by scholars and historians.

Though the forties saw the tough school of private eyes and fiction *noir* plus a war-inspired fad for espionage somewhat overshadow the traditional school, most of the top Golden Age writers carried on and new names like Christianna Brand, Elizabeth (E. X.) Ferrars, Edmund Crispin, Michael Gilbert, Julian Symons, and Frances and Richard Lockridge came to the fore. Through the fifties, though the hardy bylines of Queen, Christie, Carr, Innes, and others continued strong, the traditional school was commonly seen to be fading, its eventual demise dourly predicted despite the development of writers like Ellis Peters (Edith Pargeter) and Patricia Moyes. But even in the low point of the sixties, with that decade's overabundance of spies threatening to take over the whole crime fiction genre, formidable new talents in the classical school continued to emerge, Emma Lathen, P. D. James, and Ruth Rendell among them.

Two trends of the seventies were previewed decades before by Queen and Carr. Queen's *The Finishing Stroke* (1958) was possibly the first "nostalgia 'tec," set in the late twenties and recapturing the Golden Age's delight in puzzle spinning. Kingsley Amis's *The Riverside Villas Murder* (1973) is a serious attempt to recapture the feel of the Golden Age in thirties period, while James Anderson does the same in a parodic vein in *The Affair of the Blood-Stained Egg Cosy* (1975) and *The Affair of the Mutilated Mink Coat* (1982). H.R.F. Keating's *The Murder of the Maharajah* (1980) falls somewhere between the Amis and Anderson approaches in straightness of face. Carr had been regularly producing historical detective novels set in more remote periods since the early fifties, but not until the seventies and eighties work of writers like Jean Stubbs, Elizabeth Peters, Anne Perry, Francis Selwyn, and Peter Lovesey did they become common.

As the classical school joined with the private eyes in a seventies nostalgia phase, so too did they join in an eighties reawakening. In many cases this is a renaissance with an asterisk, however. Certainly

the whodunit aspect has been strong, and certainly the backgrounds of tight little villages and other locales with closed-circle potential have been effectively exploited, along with the classical tradition of not being too graphic about the blood and gore. But some practitioners of the so-called "cozy" have formed a regrettable tendency to shun pure detection, which is what many read an English village mystery or a closed-circle whodunit for. Charming as Agatha Christie's settings and characters may be, it was her skill in construction and reader bamboozlement that made her a master, and even Sayers's vaunted social observation and feminist themes would be a good deal less effective had they not been buttressed by sound and careful plot carpentry.

Among those who have endeavored to keep the pure puzzle plot alive without neglecting the other factors necessary to good fiction are Herbert Resnicow, Colin Dexter, Aaron Elkins, Carolyn G. Hart, Jane Haddam (Orania Papazoglou), Barbara D'Amato, James Yaffe, Francis M. Nevins, Jr., Michael Bowen, June Thomson, William L. DeAndrea, Gaylord Larsen, Catherine Aird, and Edward D. Hoch. With the present writer also trying to do his bit, maybe that's a long enough list to reassure traditionalists that the spirit of the Golden Age lives.

INTERVIEW:
BARBARA MICHAELS
T. Liam McDonald

IN THE EARLY SIXTIES a doctor of Egyptology named Barbara Mertz was a married mother of two, unable to get work in her chosen field. With a mind raging to express itself in some form, she soon found herself writing the mystery stories that she loved so much.

No luck.

At her agent's prompting she wrote a popular book of Egyptology.

It sold.

She wrote another.

And then something strange happened.

She wrote a gothic.

And it sold—under the name of Barbara Michaels—and, as they say, a star was born.

"*Never* use a pseudonym," she says. But how do you take her seriously when she has two of the things? Worse yet, both pseudonyms (the other is

Elizabeth Peters, from the names of her two children) are best sellers.

Think about it: two independently developed careers with completely different styles, and both incredibly successful. If that's not a sure sign of true talent and not merely dumb luck, I don't know what is.

You might not have read Barbara Michaels (who writes dark horror, suspense, and neo-gothic novels) or Elizabeth Peters (who writes witty mysteries), but millions of readers (mostly women) *do* know her. They regularly catapult her books onto the best seller lists. Oddly enough, for a woman who writes stories that are often supernatural and always scary, she remains lamentably unread by many regular readers of horror fiction. Strange.

Stranger still considering she writes some of the creepiest books available.

Barbara (Michaels) Mertz, a transplant from the Midwest, currently lives with a clowder of cats in an old house in Maryland. Born in Illinois, she fell in love with Egypt at an early age. She received her Ph.D. at the Oriental Institute of Chicago, then got married and, as she recalls, "found out that married ladies are not sent out into the field unless they are assistants to their husbands. That was back in the fifties, and times have changed a lot. I married the wrong one I guess. He was starting out in Egyptology and we had all these great plans to go out. Field work was very hard to get in those days, even for guys, because there's not a lot of money and it's very expensive. Then he changed fields, the dirty dog, and there I was, high and dry and pregnant. The baby put the final kibosh on it."

It took a few years for her to get around to trying her hand at mysteries. She had always loved writing, and had always wanted to write. "I was brought up on everything from Conan Doyle to *Weird Tales,*" she says, "so I've been reading horror, mystery, and so on for years. Once I started writing I found it was fascinating and kept on plugging. The first thing I did was called *The Master of Blacktower,* which was probably derivative: a nice way of saying that I stole the idea. The big gothic revolution of the sixties was going on, and all these books—with covers of ladies in their nightgowns trotting away from a house—were selling. Hell, I'd been reading them since Anne Radcliffe and Jane Austen, so I whopped one off. That was the first of

the mysteries that sold. I tell young writers you *do* have to have some talent, you have to have a lot of perseverance, but it's also partly luck. It's being in the right place with the right book at the right time."

Her late impressions of *The Master of Blacktower*?

"You'll do me a favor and never look it up. I guess it's better than many of its kind. In fact, I got a nice review from Anthony Boucher. He gave me a very kind review for a first book. It's one of those things you don't forget."

Having done three nonfiction books under her own name, selling a mystery presented a bit of a problem. Her agent said, "You will need a pseudonym, of course. I told them Barbara Michaels, is that okay with you?"

And so was born a pseudonym.

"You know how it is when you sell your first book," she said, "and that *was* my first in that field. I was beside myself. I didn't care what he called me. Call me H. P. Lovecraft. Call me Attila the Hun. I don't care—giggle giggle, whoopie, I sold a book. The rationality is (and I really find this contemptible) that the reader is so dumb they don't know the difference: the readers of the nonfiction books don't realize that something called *The Master of Blacktower* is not a book about Egyptology."

Well, when she wrote a second one in quick suit, she hit another block: two books back to back meant you were prolific, and that's bad. So was born Elizabeth Peters. In the long run, though, it was probably a good choice. The two pseudonyms are radically different, almost schizoid. (Though Elizabeth Peters did write a parody of a Barbara Michaels book.)

"I need them both. I have one more ghost story in mind, which probably won't be the next one. It will return to the style of *Ammie, Come Home,* which is a mixture of ghost story, horror story, and traditional mystery. One of the things I enjoy about writing is the challenge of the craftsmanship, and I've learned something new with every book I've done. It's a wonderful occupation because you never learn to do it right. I can't imagine ever getting bored with it: there's always some new trick, some technique. And when I start getting bored I try something else. I may not always succeed, but by God I'm going to go on trying it and I will not stick to straight formula. I had an editor on the last few books who was a darling person, and who was trying to make me a huge financial success. Because I respected her judgment and liked her, I sort of weakly let her get me into a pattern there. And the books were very popular.

"I'm also having a good time with Peters now because, with the last few, I've gone back to Rider Haggard and that crowd, whom I adored. And Haggard, as you know, has a strong supernatural bent. He was a very firm believer in the occult, and I haven't leaned as heavily on that as he did. I like the lost civilization and the wandering around the hinterland, so I thought, 'The hell with it' and hauled them out to a lost civilization for *The Last Camel Died at Noon.* I had a wonderful time with it, because I stole everything from H. Rider Haggard. I made up my civilization, and I had fun doing that because I based it on what was known, and then extrapolated: What would happen fifteen hundred years later if this thing had survived out there? Everything is totally logical and sensibly based. It was wonderful. God, I had human sacrifices and this and that! And the latest, *The Snake, the Crocodile, and the Dog*, is even more melodramatic and pulpy."

The same argument can be made about pulp fiction (and has been by some) that is made about the classic ghost story, i.e., that we in our allegedly advanced times frown on the simpler forms of entertainment that the pulps provide. Obviously, it's an attitude shared by publishers, who generally don't publish much pulp.

By way of explanation, Barbara says simply, "I think publishers are losing their wits. At the last two conventions I have given an address: last time on Haggard, the time before on Wilkie Collins. I get fifty to sixty people, all of whom know more about these fellows than I do. Publishers are not publishing the kinds of books the dedicated reader wants to read. They're hitting the one-time reader, the best seller–type reader, and they're not the people who keep me in my bread and butter. I'm not writing for those people, and I'm not going to patronize them by writing down to them. I take this profession rather seriously, and I just don't think I could. The *Shattered Silk* bunch is as close as I've gotten, and I enjoy books like that occasionally, if they're well done. I enjoy Phyllis Whitney, who writes that sort of thing. I had a good time with

Into the Darkness, but the others are more of a challenge.''

How does Dr. Mertz characterize the Michaels books?

"They're much more solemn and sentimental and romantic. I used to say I believe all that twaddle three days a week, and when I don't believe it I write Elizabeth Peters. The Michaels books sell better than the Peters, and I make a lot more money from them than I do the Peters. Still, I've got a fairly dedicated bunch of Peters readers out there.''

While readers go to Elizabeth Peters for funny mysteries, they go to Barbara Michaels for scary gothics.

But what is a gothic? Certainly the gothic horror novels of Monk Lewis and Charles Maturin and Anne Radcliffe were nowhere near the bodice bursters being ground out for so-called ''gothic romance'' lines. The elements that defined the classic gothic in its broadest sense were, often, a dark, creepy house, a threatened heroine, a Byronic hero, and some hint of the supernatural. Books from *The Castle of Ontranto* to *Jane Eyre* to *Northanger Abby*, can all be considered gothic. But what the hell is a ''gothic romance''?

Michaels readily acknowledges the problem:

"I did a panel once on the gothic romance and we got an infuriated phone call from a member of the Dracula Society who said, 'You're stealing our term and it's not right.' And I said, 'You're absolutely right. These are not gothic novels.' Now, some of mine have been. And I do think the appearances and the supernatural suggestion qualify. It has to have a supernatural suggestion. It does not necessarily need to have a supernatural solution, but it needs at least the trappings. And you can do it in a modern setting. I've always wanted to do one in a boring split-level house, but I don't think I could get away with it. You need the setting. You need the old house, the creaking pines outside the windows.''

There's yet another category that some try to fit Barbara Michaels, and several other women writers, into: that of romantic suspense. Just the words are enough to rankle this usually implacable lady. ''That's a whole can of worms,'' she begins. ''I think there's suspense written by women and there's suspense written by men. Women are more inclined, I think (and it's a nasty generalization), to introduce a romantic element as part of the plot, because it's part of your character. People are usually one sex or the other, right? And for them not to have some kind of romantic interest in someone of the opposite sex is cutting off some side of the life that you need to create to make them seem like real people. To show you their relationship with someone of the other sex shows you an awful lot about their character. Does he sock her, does he bring her flowers, does she nag him, does she darn his socks? It's a very simple and easy way of showing the reader what kind of people you're writing about.

"I think women are more inclined to do this because I think they're more interested in relationships than they are in action. But there's some men who do that kind of book extremely well, some from a woman's point of view, and *their* books are not labeled romantic suspense. The ones that are labeled romantic suspense is a misnomer just like *gothic writer*. I don't read romances. It's the one category I can't read. I think they're badly written on the whole. There are a few exceptions, people who have made the transition. But even when they were writing romances the romances weren't that good because the editors had such strict guidelines, and you get edited so desperately that you can't write as an individual in those lines."

After writing the stock gothic romance, Michaels struck out rather quickly on her own. In short, she turned the modern gothic on its ear, going back to the feel of the true gothic and injecting it with a modern sensibility and feminist perspective. Starting with *Ammie, Come Home,* she began writing books that no longer fit the category romance slot.

Ammie, Come Home is easily one of the finest, and most underrated, classic ghost stories of the last twenty-five years. It is a timeless tale—the restless dead intruding on our world—retold in a modern setting, a creepy tale of a ghostly triangle of love and murder. The heavy gothic trappings (the house positively drips with dread) are offset by a thoroughly modern approach and sense of character. Michaels accomplished something quite wonderful: she maintained the heroic proportions and character "types" while injecting a real sense of common humanity. The plot rolls like waves breaking on a shore: elegant crests ending in shattering crashes.

Her perceptions of the book?

"I thought, rather pretentiously I guess, that I was beginning to find my own voice with *Ammie, Come Home.* I'm certainly not the first one who's done that sort of thing, nor will I be the last, but it's a trademark, I guess. It seems like the kind of book that my readers like best.

"I was writing the kind of book I liked to read. The first books I wrote were spy stories, and they were very genteel, in the style of John McGuinnis and Alistair MacLean. Though I enjoyed those, I did not do them well. I was also trying to do a male protagonist, because that was before women became an acceptable protagonist as anything except beleaguered heroine. I think it was when I finally realized that I should be doing things from a woman's point of view, and doing the kinds of things that I really enjoyed the most, that I began to do well."

With her strong female characters—as opposed to the fainting, languid women who waited for the hero to act for them—she tapped a strong need in female readers. This was, to some degree, *new.* These were women with modern sensibilities, women who got things done on their own and had all the real needs of the women who—well, of the women who *read* these books.

Does Michaels think she anticipated the trend toward strong female protagonists?

Sort of:

"I would *like* to think that. I *was* twenty years ahead of the current strong female protagonist. My heroines have always been tough ladies. I wrote the first liberated gothic thirty years ago, where the heroine digs out both the heroes, turns them down, and then blackmails someone into giving her a job at a museum. I'm rather proud of that book. I think the reason I was able to earn a living during those years was that many women *did* like it. And I'm not, obviously, a man hater, because I like romantic elements in books. I like to see a partnership, really, between the two. I'm not trying to get rid of the man, but I think having a woman who is a strong character and able to stand on her own feet appealed to a lot of women. I would like to think that my little humble example had some effect on others, but who knows?"

These strong women usually come in two loose categories in a Barbara Michaels book: the young woman just starting to experience the world and the recently "manless" woman (either through some tragedy, divorce, or the failure of a relationship).

This is by no means to imply that the characters are ''stock.'' Far from it. But to begin the romantic dynamics that will drive one of her books, Michaels usually depicts a woman in some stage of life transition. It's become a trademark. Like the cats. (There are probably more cats in the collected books of Michaels/Peters than T. S. Eliot ever dreamed of.)

There are other Michaels trademarks too, and they are the things that define her own unique style and sensibilities. No matter what the book—horror or straight suspense—there is always some hint of the paranormal or the supernatural. In books where such hints have little bearing on the plot—such as the reincarnation aspects of *The Sea King's Daughter*—Michaels can't resist popping them in. Whether it's ancient religions, modern witches, precognition, paganism, satanism, or mere haunting, she returns again and again to the strange and exotic. Why?

''I just like 'em,'' she responds. ''I own a full set of *The Golden Bough,* and I use that over and over again. I also like ancient, pre-Christian religion, like Margaret Murray's thesis about the witch cult in Europe—based on an agricultural religion. I kind of like to bring these things in. I really can't explain it, because I'm a very rational person in my conduct. I read the horoscopes and laugh over them, and I do not base any of my activities on anything of that sort. But one part of my mind just loves the imaginative interpretation. Plus, if anyone says that we have a rational explanation for everything, he's cuckoo. We're an awfully long way from understanding the universe.

''I've never had any *experience,* except for what I loosely call ESP, which I seem to do better with animals than people. I swear to God the cats can read my mind. They know when it's their day for the vet. You can find a logical explanation, in some school of scientific theory, for almost everything. But that wears a little thin at times. I don't know why there's that streak in what is otherwise a very logical mind, but I've always been drawn to it. I read fairy stories and the 398 [supernatural] section in the library before I was ten.''

But the influence runs even deeper. Horror and pulp adventure dominated her reading life even as a little girl. ''My dad started me on *Weird Tales:* that probably accounts for a lot. 'Give me a child before he's seven ...': well, my old man got his

hands on me.... He was giving me Burroughs's *John Carter, Prince of Mars* for my eighth birthday. I loved it.

''I was an omnivorous reader, and I *do* think omnivorous readers are born, not made: the kind of person who reads the back of the toothpaste tube. I grew up in a house with books, but I grew up during the Depression, when books were hard to buy. If I wanted to read, I'd have to read what was there, so I borrowed books from neighbors and read everything in the house, over my mother's howls of protest. She kept trying to keep these things from me, but you know they were so pure. I remember overhearing an argument between her and Dad over my reading Doc Savage at one point. She didn't think it was appropriate for a little girl, and of course Doc never did a thing that would embarrass even my aged great-grandmother. He blushed and retreated when a lady even approached him.

''The same was true of most of it, even *Weird Tales.* The Lovecraft got a little grisly. Things like 'The Rats in the Walls': I absolutely adored those stories. I *like* that kind of horror. I remember reading Stephen King's *Danse Macabre,* where he talks about the two different strains of horror (if, indeed, you can simplify it to that extent): the more subtle kind and the rats chewin' up the bones. I *like* the rats, but I don't do it. I find much more horrifying the suggestion rather than the graphic description.''

And this brings us to another Barbara Michaels trademark: creeping terror. There is a feeling of shuddering fear in even her straight suspense books. But when she turns it on for a full-blown modern ghost story–cum–horror novel, the result is always more whisper than scream, more suggestion and haunting fear than drop-dead horror. M. R. James and Algernon Blackwood and the tradition of the classic ghost story.

Indeed, she cites James as ''one of the people I most admire. I have great respect for that sort of academic ghost story. I like the slow, leisurely building up the horrific detail. Oh, definitely, yes: 'Casting the Ruins,' 'Oh, Whistle, and I'll Come to You My Lad.' ''

But many say that the contemporary ghost story is dead, their logic being that the ghostly horror of James and Blackwood flourished in a time when our imagination had not yet been tamed by science. How does Michaels respond to such attitudes?

Quite simply:

Barbara Michaels

"I think that's a bunch of crap. I think the frission of horror and of the primal terror is a deepseated part of the human psyche. I can't even explain it in logical terms, and neither can anyone else. If you go back to Jung and all the rest of that crowd, they've got ideas, but who knows? It's *there*. To deny that is just goofy.

"I think what we're being fed today as a substitute rather kills the sense of wonder instead of encouraging it. The special effects are so good today that I stopped going to horror movies. The special effects are *too* good: I don't want to see that. I have a scene in this new book where a particularly horrific specter appears. Well, I don't describe exactly what he looks like: there are one or two hints, but then the woman says, 'He looks the way you would if you'd been dead and buried for eight months.' Now, I think that's enough. A little bit about the ragged eye sockets, a couple of adjectives, and then the reader creates his or her picture, which is a hell of a lot scarier than anything I could describe. I do think that's more effective.

"I found that with characters too. The last Peters book had a drawing of the three main characters on the cover, and I happen to love it. But I had a lot of complaints from readers who really didn't picture them that way. They had their own image and they really didn't want to see anyone's else's image of them. I think for horror that's even more the case. Everyone's got his own horror too. Re-

member that room in *1984?* That's where they take the dissidents from that society, and in that room is the most horrible thing a person can imagine, and it's different for everybody. That's what I try to work with, and in a way it's sort of a challenge. I also think it's kind of a cheap shot to haul out the rotting corpse. Everyone admits that rotting corpses are horrible but to make something horrible out of a sheet, the way M. R. James did, or a red plush armchair, as I'm trying to: then that's a challenge. If you get away with it, even with a few readers, you can pat yourself on the back and feel real proud of yourself."

Evidently she's done more than get away with it for a few readers. People return again and again to the Michaels books (currently being reissued by Berkley in a series of buy-me covers), making them multimillion-copy best sellers. They don't just buy them because the women are strong. They buy them because they like the subtle chills that define even the straightest Michaels book.

The southern gothic atmosphere of *Be Buried in the Rain* looms heavily over its characters, casting long shadows that may or may not hide the supernatural. Like the best of Faulkner, some sexual crime in the past has caught up with the present. The book is so delightfully ambiguous that even its chilling last line suffices only to throw the reader another curve. Was there supposed to be a ghost or not?

Apparently yes, but, according to Barbara, "My bloody editor wouldn't let me. She decided the supernatural wasn't going very well. But the new one, *Vanish with the Rose,* is definitely supernatural. I said the hell with this, I want a ghost, I'm having a ghost this time. I really enjoy doing it when it's sort of ambiguous. It's not that I don't like a good honest-to-goodness ghost story, but I like the challenge of constructing something that can be interpreted two different ways. *Be Buried* is, as far as I am concerned, a ghost story. But I got an infuriated letter from a woman who said she and her husband had been arguing for a week over whether the bones dragged themselves out of the grave or whether someone put them there. My own interpretation is: them bones walked again. I did another one where the ambiguity is there, but I always like to leave one little disturbing thing that the rational can't account for."

But why? Does she see fear as a valuable emotion?

"Not so much fear as uneasiness: what's going to come after me? One of the obvious answers is catharsis: you can get it out of your system by expressing it and by experiencing it in fiction rather than in real life. One of the reasons I do the kind of books I do is that there's enough real-life horror, with muggers and murderers and riots and everything else, perhaps it's a relief to turn to something that you know is never really going to happen, or can't happen. The fear and the apprehension is up to the author. The author ought to be able to create that out of anything if he or she does it right. Maybe it's a release to be afraid of a red leather armchair than of someone breaking into your windows at night. Well, I sleep like a baby. I live out in the country and there's not a soul around for miles and I never worry about burglars, muggers, or rapists. Yet, some nights I don't turn out the lights. I scared myself into fits writing *Ammie, Come Home,* as a matter of fact. I was writing late at night because I had small children then, and the only time I could write was between nine and two A.M. I tell you, around one thirty, when the darkness closed in and there was nobody awake, I would jump right out of my socks at the slightest sound. I'm much more afraid of ghosts than burglars."

But why is an admittedly rational mind afraid of the dark?

"It's that deep-seated primal something in all of us. There's something pleasurable in it too. You'll have to talk to a shrink or a Freudian for this, because I've never understood it. It's pleasurable because you don't really think it's ever going to happen. But why is fear a pleasurable experience? You got me.

"I remember standing on the back lawn one time, staring out into the woods. It was at twilight under that lovely apple-green sky and the shadows were gathering. *Something* howled back in the woods, and I don't know what it was. It wasn't something I was familiar with. I have heard that porcupines, when they're engaged in certain activities, make very odd noises (and one would well understand they might). But it sounded like a child in torment. Ghastly noises. I swear to God I was convinced it was a werewolf. I headed for the house as fast I could.

"Another thing is: you're on the inside looking out. The dark's outside. Even though ghosts can get through doors and windows, you feel safe because you're in your nice warm house, reading ghost stories, wrapping yourself around in physical comfort, and so perhaps you *can* take a chance of letting your mind wander out to the dark."

It's a persistent theme, not just in Barbara Michaels's books, but in all horror fiction: the dark on the other side. She explored a rather brilliant symbol of this in a book called, strangely enough, *The Dark on the Other Side.* On the surface, the book is about the evil worship of Gordon and Briggs, and the dark things that haunt Gordon's wife, Linda. But as with most Michaels books, there's a lot goin' on.

The title, taken from Tolkien's *The Lord of the Rings* ("they'll eat your soul and throw it out into the dark on the other side."), is a reference to a complex symbol that does, in fact, apply to all horror fiction. In the book, she turns Plato's cave allegory on its ear to offer a rather terrifying notion. In this allegory from *The Republic,* Plato likens mankind to a primitive in a cave who can face only one way: toward a wall. All he knows of reality are the shadows cast on the wall by creatures parading before a blazing fire behind him.

Plato wanted to know what happened when that primitive man turned around and had to face true reality rather than just the "shadows" it cast.

Barbara Michaels is more concerned with a) what creatures were casting these shadows and, worse yet, b) *what was out there in the dark, behind these creatures.* These figures before the fire are supposed to be true knowledge and reality, but what lies beyond knowledge and reality and rationality? It is the region of dark madness from which diabolists draw their power, a place of consuming darkness, where entities reside which in fact control that which we know as reality.

She is justifiably pleased with this spin on an old philosophical standby:

"I thought that was rather clever of me. That just came to me while I was writing that book. I liked the analogy because that's sort of what reality does mean to me: shadows cast on the wall. Then I suddenly got to thinking: there's fire in the cave, it's dark out there: *what's out there?*"

P.D. JAMES:
A Taste for Death
H.R.F. Keating

WITH A BOOK WRITTEN AS recently as 1986 I am clearly deprived of the assistance of my colleague, O. F. Time, in making my judgment that this is something worthy of my hundred-strong Temple of the Criminous Muse. But I have no hesitation in including it.

First, it is by any standards a very good novel of detection with a mystery, clues, suspects—and suspects presented at a fascinatingly deep level—and a genuine surprise solution. Second, P. D. James has succeeded here, I believe, in widening the scope of the crime novel in a way that has hardly been done before. By entering the worlds and minds of all her main characters—suspects, investigators, bystanders—she has been able to say more about life than has hitherto been attempted in the crime form. But, third, and most important to my mind, she has succeeded in writing, in the form of the crime novel, a book that has let her express her most profound beliefs.

Never before has there been a crime novel about religious faith. Yes, we have had dozens set in monasteries and convents or with churches, vicars, and rabbis in them, but what P. D. James has done here is to achieve what Conan Doyle abandoned Sherlock Holmes in order to do: to write a book expressing his deepest beliefs. With Doyle it was historical novels that were intended to set a pattern of behavior for all Britain to follow, a mighty ambition to which he was unable to rise. I believe that P. D. James, aiming rather less high, has succeeded. She has convincingly, if at times a little obscurely, put into a book all her feelings, doubts, fears, and hopes concerning faith in God. This is something that may not be obvious at a first reading when, as P. D. James intended, one is caught up in the outward story of who killed Sir Paul Berowne, just-resigned Minister of the Crown, and the dilapidated tramp,

Harry Mack. But at a second reading, or a thoughtful look back, the theme can hardly help but emerge.

Consider first where Sir Paul and Harry Mack were murdered: in the vestry of a church. Consider why Sir Paul was there to be murdered: because, visiting the building out of a mere interest in architecture, he had been struck by a divine revelation. Consider where the clinching clue is found: in that same church—a tiny, simple thing like a button in the box meant for candle money. Turn then to the book's last pages, where an author is completing what he or she has to say. Are they concerned with Commander Dalgliesh? With the murderer? With any of the major characters? No, P. D. James chooses to end with the character she began with, the church-mouse spinster who discovered the bodies. And what do we find her doing? Praying. But not praying any easy prayers; she is praying that her fast-failing faith may return. And in doing so she makes us, the readers, ponder on precisely the mystery of faith.

Or look at what might seem quite an incidental passage in this long book (long because it has a great deal to say). Chapter Eight begins with a sketch of the pathologist coming to examine the bodies. A piece of necessary filling-out, you might say. But no; P. D. James gives us Doc Kynaston as a man who has ''a taste for death,'' one fascinated by ''each new piece of evidence which might, if rightly interpreted, bring him closer to the central mystery.'' Because the central mystery of death is surely what comes after, the sustaining key to religious faith.

Or consider what Lady Ursula, Sir Paul's aged, sharp-tongued mother, says to Dalgliesh when he comes to see if he can extract from her evidence which he needs. She puts him off by telling him she has been visited by the priest of the murder church: "He seemed to me a man who has long ago given up the expectation of influencing anyone. Perhaps he has lost his faith. Isn't that fashionable in the Church today? But why should that distress him? The world is full of people who have lost faith; politicians who have lost faith in politics . . .

for all I know, policemen who have lost faith in policing and poets who have lost faith in poetry." Home jabs these, for doubting Dalgliesh. But, even more, the expression of P. D. James's central preoccupation in a long, ideas-crowded, wonderfully powerful book.

WHY COZIES?

Carolyn G. Hart

TO THOSE WHO WEAR Dashiell Hammett blinders, the success of Agatha Christie is not only incomprehensible but infuriating, especially since their hero will never sell a tenth as many books as she did.

So what is this thing called a cozy and why do millions of readers love it?

Very simply, cozy is a term (originally pejorative) for the traditional mystery.

Why should the private-eye readers object to the traditional mystery?

Because the traditional mystery eschews graphic violence and impersonal crimes and the books gen-

erally are set in a noncriminal environment. To many critics, crime is somehow more "real" in the mean streets than on the hearth. Ask any cop about domestic violence. You're just as dead in a living room as in an alley. But criminal violence isn't the point of the cozy.

Agatha Christie described the (traditional) mystery as the equivalent of the medieval morality play.

In the medieval morality play, tradesfair audiences watched actors who represented the seven deadly sins. The point, of course, was that those who let their lives be ruled by sloth or jealousy or lust could expect dreadful consequences.

This is precisely what we do in today's traditional mystery. I see today's traditional mysteries serving readers as parables. If this is how you treat your wife or your customer or your next-door neighbor, here's what may happen to you.

The truth of the matter is, the traditional mystery doesn't have to do with crime, it has to do with relationships. In seeking the murderer, the amateur detective explores the lives of those surrounding the victim. In this exploration, the detective is trying to find out what went wrong in these relationships—what fractured the ties between these people? Why did murder occur? This is the primary discovery to be made and this is the point of the traditional mystery.

But this definition doesn't include much of what makes cozies delightful to its readers.

In addition to the crime and the detective's search for why it happened, the cozy offers humor, entertainment, satire, a contest, a chance for serious mystery readers to learn something new, and a world view.

Most important, the cozy is—well—cozy.

So here's my outline for a successful cozy:

Take a good murder, toss in an attractive sleuth, provide interesting suspects with believable motives, remember that death is never funny but people are hilarious, include trenchant observations of the social scene, make sure the clues are relevant and fair, be yourself, offer your readers a chance to learn something new, have a surprise ending, and set the book in a recognizable world.

The Murder of Roger Ackroyd meets and surpasses all those criteria. At the same time, it is a brilliant exposition on the destructiveness of greed.

I'd agree with the beer ads on this one. It doesn't get any better than *The Murder of Roger Ackroyd.*

I can't say I consciously set out to incorporate each of these elements when I wrote *Death on Demand,* the first in my Annie and Max series for Bantam. But when I decided to write that book, at the most depressing point in my career (seven unsold manuscripts on hand), I was determined to stop giving any consideration to that ephemeral quest— to write what New York editors were looking for— and to write the kind of mystery that I'd always wanted to write and that I hadn't tried because too many agents told me nobody wants that kind of mystery.

What kind of mystery?

I think in fairly specific terms. I wanted to write a Tommy and Tuppence, a Pam and Jerry North, a Mrs. Latham and Colonel Primrose.

I wanted to be true to my view of the mystery, and that view was formed by reading and loving Agatha Christie, Phoebe Atwood Taylor, and Mary Roberts Rinehart.

Those three authors provided wonderful stories and stories that were fun to read.

So how do you create fun against an essentially serious, even somber, backdrop of murder?

You remember that people laugh a lot, even between tears. You remember that death is serious, but life needn't be. You remember that what is fun for you may be fun for readers.

So, I set off on a new beginning. I wanted a young heroine who always tries to do her best and who is very serious about those efforts but who sees

how absurd life can be. So I came up with Annie Laurance.

And I decided (authors do have agendas) that I wanted to celebrate love. I've never been a big believer in romance, but I definitely believe in love. I know this world is filled with unhappy people, survivors of divorce and disillusionment and disappointment. There are plenty of books out there with heroines who have experienced every kind of angst. But I know that there are good marriages, there are happy relationships, and that's what I wanted to write about. Max Darling with the easy grin and low-key charm walked right onto the page, looking for Annie.

And then I decided to celebrate mysteries, the mysteries I grew up with and loved. Many are still easily found (check the Christie section) but many are probably gone from bookstores forever. I wanted to share with readers the pleasure I've had through the years with many wonderful writers who today are mostly memories—Manning Coles, Henry Cecil, Mabel Seeley, Mary Collins, Constance and Gwyneth Little, oh, the list goes on and on. So I decided to set my mystery in a mystery bookstore, the kind of mystery bookstore then beginning to pop up around the country. I made Death on Demand a gorgeous bookstore with a coffee bar, fireplace, resident cat, stuffed raven, and the best collection of mysteries east of Atlanta.

The suspects in *Death on Demand* are all mystery writers. I had a lot of fun with different kinds of writers and how they act and think.

As for the intellectual game that cozy readers like to play, I did my best to provide clues, telling clues, that would give an observant reader a good chance to logically deduce the murderer.

Clues are a fascinating exercise for cozy writers. You don't want to stand up and wave a red flag and shout, ''Clue.'' But you definitely, if you honestly fulfill the bargain with your readers, want to give clues that will reveal the plot to a savvy reader.

My favorite clue is in *Deadly Valentine,* the sixth in the series. The blunt-talking Texan Buck Burger is replying to a question from Annie:

> Buck nodded. ''He's [the general] got a bad heart. Has to take a handful of pills. Insists he's okay.'' He sighed heavily. ''Damn fool won't quit playing golf and sometimes you can't get out of a foursome with him. Rather play with a

goddam rattlesnake. Got a real mean streak. Spends half the time popping nitroglycerin under his tongue. Course, if I had to take the damn blood pressure pills *he* takes, I'd be a mean shit, too. Damn doctors don't care whether you can screw, but I'd just as soon hang it up if I couldn't get it up. There's plenty of medicines for high blood pressure besides that one. That's probably why the old buzzard's always in such a nasty humor.'' There was a fleeting glint of sympathy in his eyes. ''I'd bet the ranch that's why he was so goddam down on Sydney. But hell, just because you can't eat the ice cream doesn't mean you ought to want to close up the ice cream store.''

That's a clue I take out to pet every now and then.

Mystery readers are smart. You never have to explain anything to them. And they love to learn. Writing about mysteries I've read and enjoyed in the past is not only a pleasure for me, it gives the Death on Demand books a bonus for readers who are truly interested in the genre. Perhaps the book in which I provide the most information is *The Christie Caper,* which tells readers so much about Agatha Christie, both her life and her work. But all the books provided snippets of mystery lore and sometimes a great deal of information. In each book, Annie has the monthly contest featuring paintings of famous mysteries of particular kinds. I've had readers tell me this is their absolutely favorite passage and they work hard at identifying the authors and titles.

As for a world view, in essence that's the writer putting his or her own spin on everything from politics to love to morality. It is this quality that makes an editor buy a book. Not the plot. That can be fixed. Not the background. Ditto. Not the weapon or the locale or the characters. Editors call it *voice.* It is what makes a book distinctive. If you took five pages each from a new manuscript by Nancy Pickard, Lia Matera, D. R. Meredith, Sharyn McCrumb, Joan Hess, Dorothy Cannell, Margaret Maron, and Annette Meyers and put those unidentified pages facedown, then I picked them up, I could tell you who wrote which pile every time.

That is voice.

Cozies excel in voice.

Readers want to be in the mind of a protagonist, and only voice makes that possible.

I've had fun lately because I'm writing a new series. This protagonist is Henrie O (Henrietta O'Dwyer Collins), a retired newspaperwoman with a zest for life and a talent for trouble. She makes her debut in *Dead Man's Island* when she answers a call for help from a former lover. These books will celebrate age and experience as the Death on Demand books celebrate youth and hope.

Both series are firmly cozies because they pursue an understanding of why people do what they do, why hearts break, why murders occur, but they are very different in tone and style. Annie and Max are written in the third person, Henrie O in the first. Annie is young and never cynical; Henrie O is old and sardonic. Annie and Max have a continuing cast of characters, some of whom provide plenty of chances for satire; Henrie O's horizons are always changing and it's a fresh crew with every book.

And the two series are also firmly in the cozy camp because their backgrounds are directly evoked from the backgrounds of most readers. It is this quality, in my view, that accounts for the enormous success of Agatha Christie. A Finn in Helsinki, an Italian in Milan, an American in Savannah, or a Turk in Istanbul all can identify with Christie's characters because they reflect the reality of human personality—the resentful son, the sex-obsessed lawyer, the greedy villager, the lonely old maid.

So my backgrounds are a resort island where everyone comes to play and various cities that a retired newspaperwoman might visit. The characters are people we know—a woman hungry for love, a son resenting his stepmother, a woman who believes she has everyone's best interest at heart as she tries to manipulate lives, the nosy landlady, a man to whom power means more than life. And more.

But no matter what I write, my aim is always the same: to provide readers with parables.

If this is how you treat your lover, if this is how you treat your employee, if this is how you treat your brother . . .

THE TOPICAL MYSTERY

Dorothy Salisbury Davis

Peter Carr

I HAVE REACHED THAT TIME in life when my mind skips a beat now and then. So it was that right after I had said I would write a piece on the topical mystery I could not, on my soul, remember the word *topical*. The word that kept coming to mind in its place was *confrontational*. Curiously, confrontational describes better than topical what I have in mind when I think topical. The hero/detective confronts—or is confronted by an evil that is abroad in the author's world.

What mystery writer, plagued by the question, "Where do you get your ideas?" has not responded, "In the daily paper," always wanting to add, "It's not the idea that's important, it's what the writer does with it." Mystery writers who read newspapers to their advantage do not all, obviously, grab the headlines and run with them. Most of us scratch about in lost and found, bankruptcy notices, obituaries, and personal columns. In the topical mystery, the idea is what's important.

I think the writer of the topical mystery tends to be a crusader: Perceiving something that is wrong, he/she wants to set it right, and in the wonderful world of fiction, it can be done. There is an immediacy to the mystery with a message. It rings true. However fantastical the author's approach, the reader is an able believer. He has been there, or somewhere very like it recently. Whether or not he is on the side of the gallant knight depends on his own agenda. Either way, he is aware of the issue, be its focus the environment, terrorism, child molestation, spouse abuse, drugs, sadism, cannibalism. You name it.

Is it too extravagant to say mystery fiction in general may owe its longevity to the topical novel? The change that released the genre fifty or so years ago from its golden chains came from the need of both reader and writer to face up to the realities of a ravished world—the war, the Holocaust, nuclear devastation, and to try, whether in fact or fantasy, to do something about it. Many of us, particularly in America, became intent on turning an escape fiction into an involved one. The *why* became more important than the *who* or *how*. To say more along this line would diminish the truth. For nothing so characterizes the mystery or crime novel as its diversity in both content and technique. In 1929 Dashiell Hammett wrote *Red Harvest,* in which the Continental Op confronted small town corruption, a topic for all seasons. The blood has not dried yet.

I would like to say the writers of the topical mystery inherit most from Hammett, Hemingway, Cain, and Burnett. I believe the best ones do. But that may well be because the topics that attract them demand the fast, hard-driving prose that carries place and character within the action instead of interrupting the action while the reader looks around to see where he is and who is there to greet him. No. It's not the topic that makes the demand. It's the writer. The writer of the good topical novel takes advantage of the reader's savvy and he is dead certain he can get away with it.

When I was starting out in the late forties, the writer doing what I hoped I could one day do was Dorothy B. Hughes. Her social awareness, always integral to her plot, was the way I wanted to go. I'm pretty sure my own first book centered on the death of an antiwar toymaker, the second on a coal mine disaster. The vehicle for *A Town of Masks* was a civil defense drill. In 1951 the Cold War was well under way. I seem to remember, too, banging the drums in that one for a gubernatorial candidate who talked like Adlai Stevenson. All these books are distant relatives, you understand.

Having suggested the limitations of the pre-1945 mystery, I must now admit that I still read Sayers, Carr, Christie, and Allingham and their inheritors today in England and America with admiration and probably more pleasure than I do the earnest lot of us writing topical novels now. And until I rummaged through my own work for topical themes, I had quite forgotten that *A Town of Masks* centered on a civil defense practice evacuation. The worth of the book lies in the character of Hannah Blake, not in my stroke against "the pattern of the times." Two giants in the field, Ellery Queen and Rex Stout, took on, at least once, real mischief they perceived in the world around them. In *The Doorbell Rang,* Nero Wolfe left a caller we may assume was someone very like J. Edgar Hoover with his finger on the doorbell while Wolfe went up to his dinner. But to my mind, neither author was at home in the topical novel. Both Queen and Stout belonged to the Golden Age, and their fiction was meant to be pure and simple "murder for pleasure," to use Howard Haycraft's felicitous title.

Topical crime novels of the late forties that are among their authors' best work are W. R. Burnett's *The Asphalt Jungle* and William Faulkner's *Intruder in the Dust.* In the case of Burnett, the jewelry heist is so well paced and the characters so well integrated within the action, it's easy to forget that the topic, really, is "the city," corrupt to the core. Faulkner's inclusion here might be argued, even as we dispute calling Dostoevsky one of ours, but there is a murder, and an investigator, and other trappings of the detective story. The topic is the relationship between the white townsmen and the black man accused of murder. A long line of race-related crime

novels have followed in its wake. Among those I find most durable are James McClure's *The Artful Egg,* with its South African background, Dorothy B. Hughes's *The Expendable Man,* Stanley Ellin's *The Dark Fantastic,* Thomas H. Cook's *Fire in the Streets,* David Stout's *Carolina Skeletons.* Any novel of Tony Hillerman's must rate high on the list. And Paco Taibo is both the voice and the conscience of Mexico.

The crime novel generally, but more particularly the topical crime novel, even when it is not contemporary, reflects its own time, and is more confined within it, I think, than other kinds of fiction. It reinvents itself almost daily. It is responsive to politics local, national, and international. I'm inclined to include the espionage novel in the category even though it is in eclipse since the Cold War is no longer in the headlines. If I were less sanguine of human intent, I would be wary of tomorrow's frost. We are bound now, following the World Trade Center bombing, to see a resurgence of novels of terrorism. I would pray that history would no longer justify more of the murderously relevant I.R.A. novels of Gerald Seymour.

I am bound to miss notable examples of the topical novel in today's scene if I start plucking out titles, but I shall name a few I feel have touched a raw nerve in our society: Jonathan Kellerman's novels on child abuse; Andrew Vachss's on the same subject; Nancy Pickard's *Marriage Is Murder* on domestic violence; Sara Paretsky's *Bitter Medicine* on abortion; Joseph Hansen's *Nightwork* on hazardous waste; Amanda Cross's *Death in a Tenured Position* on women in academe; Erika Holzer's *Eye for an Eye* on vigilantism.

Durability must be factored into the worth of every fiction. The topical novel of the contemporary scene is born with a natural handicap, so to speak, the pressure of its timeliness. I think the best fiction profits from the writer's keeping at a certain distance from his/her subject. I'm not seeking to mute the passion with which a partisan novelist imbues his work. I just don't want the fire to go out too soon. The answer almost has to be in characterization, doesn't it? One wants to know the villain as though he were the hero and to recognize in the hero a plausible, potential victim or, even, a saved villain.

What I think I'm asking of the topical novelist

is that he not only know his reader (as being tuned in on the topic), but that he know and use himself. There are not many of the world's inhumanities to which we cannot relate in some usable measure from our own experience. Stretch anger to rage, re-sentment to reprisal, loss to vengeance. In the end the reward of such self-extension can be a better novel. The least it may yield is the sure discovery of why the writer was attracted to the topic in the first place.

MY FIRST BOOK?
Dorothy B. Hughes

FOR YEARS I HAVE been saying that *The So Blue Marble* was my first book. It wasn't. Long before *Marble, Dread Journey,* a book of my poetry, had been published by the Yale University Press, the 1931 selection of the Yale Series of Young Poets, under the editorship of William Percy Alexander.

I had also had published a nonfiction book, *Pueblo on the Mesa,* a history of the University of New Mexico. This was written by request of James Zimmerman, then the university president, to honor the university's bicentennial in 1939. This year, 1989, the university celebrated its centennial, and *Pueblo on the Mesa* was reissued by the University Press, then and now its publishers. Which means that it was fifty years ago this spring that I wrote the book. It seems like last week.

And of course I had written any number of novels which had not been published. Fortunately. I don't know how my agent, Blanche Gregory, had the audacity to submit them to any publisher. They must have been just plain awful.

There may have been one mystery novel among the lot. All young writers will try any and every type of writing just to see if they can do it. I wasn't interested in writing mystery. My role model was John Galsworthy. I wanted to write family sagas in fine civilized prose, as Galsworthy did. The young writers of today will conclude that I wanted to write stuffy. Few of them are aware that Galsworthy was a revolutionary in his day. He based an early novel of the Forsyte Saga on a husband's rape of his wife. He also wrote matter-of-factly of divorce. Divorce was a condemnatory situation in that day.

But ... "Why did you become a mystery writer?" Doubtless this is the most-asked question of any and all of us in an interview. This is how it happened for me:

I was at home resting up from a season of burning the candle at both ends in Manhattan. I had been working on a magazine by day, taking courses at Columbia University in early evening, returning to my lonely room to sit up until two or three A.M., writing. And right here and now let's get that adjectival *lonely* tossed into the wastepaper basket. Writers, that is, real writers, cherish being alone. That's when they do their own thing, no conversations, no telephone trivia, no interruptions—I knew one writer who was not even interrupted for meals—without words, his wife placed his dining tray outside his closed door. When in due time starvation loomed, he opened the door long enough to bring the tray inside his room, where he could be close to his typewriter and unfinished manuscript. Writing is not "lonely." It is being blissfully alone.

Of course my candle-burning included nonwriting fun. I was only a year or so out of college. Some of the boys and girls I'd known at college house parties were also in town, all of us trying to get started in whatever was our chosen career. New York City then, and I daresay now, was a fun place for the college crowd. Then it was dancing to Rudy Vallee or to Guy Lombardo, walking along Riverside Drive with dreams, and, of course, going to the theater. Manhattan is Theater.

Although I was attending writing classes, including a valuable one in the short story with Dorothy Scarborough, I had been selling short stories before going back east, and continued to sell them, at least one a week, to what must have been romantic pulps. Most of the magazines went out of business shortly after paying me. However, my first agent placed stories only with those magazines that paid on acceptance, not on publication. I usually received $75 a story, sometimes only $50. But this was what in my family we call "play money," used not for necessities but for enjoyment. My play money enabled me to see every play on Broadway, more often than not on the opening night. A ticket to second balcony cost fifty cents. To be sure, the actors were quite small-sized, but the acoustics were great; moreover, actors knew how to project their voices. Not like today, where the majority of young actors seemingly speak not for the paying customers but rather so that if some motion picture or television or video worthy is in the audience, he will realize said actor is ready for film, where you do not raise your voice.

The result of all my activity in New York City, carried on for a year with no more than three hours sleep per night, landed me back home with a required rest cure. But of course I could keep on writing. And did. It was in that same period that I read my first mystery.

Frank, Jr., my high school brother, would go weekly to the library, or biweekly more often than not (all of my family to the third generation are fast readers) and each time return with eight books at a time. You didn't jump into a car and whiz out to your destination in those days, you took the streetcar or you walked. (To give today's generation an idea of such deprivation, there was only one car in our neighborhood, and it was an electric, which Mrs. Smith, our next-door neighbor, a white-haired proper gentlewoman, drove.)

Our neighborhood branch library was only ten or twelve blocks from our home. It never seemed a long walk; I did it many times when I wasn't enforced into a rest cure. Through my brother, the house was well supplied with reading material. Unfortunately for me, my brother was hooked on mysteries. I, from my lofty lit'ry position, a university graduate, class poet, straight A in English literature, looked down my nose at his plebeian taste.

Until the day when, having nothing else to read, I sampled one of his store. It was by E. Phillips Oppenheim, not a whodunit but the progenitor of all modern foreign intrigue suspense novels. And I

was hooked. I read every Oppenheim on the library shelves. And I began sampling other sorts of mystery.

There are always those who influence a writer whether or not he or she recognizes it. I know that I was influenced, first of all by Louisa May Alcott, when I as a child read *Little Women,* and what might be called today the spinoffs of that classic. In mystery, after Oppenheim, important influences were Mary Roberts Rinehart (then as now one of our important writers whether of mystery or of "straight" novels); Dorothy L. Sayers, Agatha Christie, Erle Stanley Gardner. And, of course, Eric Ambler, who will presently be discussed at greater length. Many, many more. No, I don't write like any of them. I don't want to. I never did want to. I want to write like me. Influence is an ineffable quality.

I have not mentioned the two writers who mean more to me than any others, William Faulkner and Graham Greene. No one writes as they do. I did not expect ever to reach such heights, they were influences nonetheless. They wrote poetry in prose.

To return to that first year of reading mystery. Of course it set me to writing a mystery then and there, whenever what seemed like a good idea dangled. But I did not take mystery writing seriously until I discovered Eric Ambler and *The Mask of Dimitrios*, (U.S. title, *A Coffin for Dimitrios*). I read it once. Then I read it again. And I thought to myself, "If a mystery can be that good, I am going to write one."

As soon as I made that decision, the ideas sprang full blown, as Minerva from the brow of Zeus. And I wrote the greatest mystery novel ever written. It was sheer delight because it developed easily and well, page by page. When it was finished, I called together my reading circle. A word or two about this valuable group who listened to me read aloud each mystery I wrote in those early days. The personnel was my sister, Calla Hay, a newspaperwoman; my husband, Levi A. Hughes, Jr, a businessman; our friend and lawyer, Herbert Greer, and his wife, Charlotte, a professional dancer in the studios before her marriage. They did not come together to praise Caesar. Praise was not permitted. They listened for flaws, in words, in ideas. By reading aloud, a writer is able to hear what he has written, word repetitions, ideas that get lost unsolved, ideas that do not work—the ear reveals flaws which the eye does not see. After my reading circle had pointed out all the things wrong, they summed up their feelings on the whole book, was it bad or good, salable or forget it. With this one they agreed with me, this was a great book, a sure success.

So off it went to my agent. She submitted it. And submitted it. *And* submitted it. It went to every publisher in New York. Every one of them turned it down. Was I heartbroken? Did I go into a decline? Did I try to rewrite it? The answer to all these foolish questions is a loud *no*. I was already at work on another mystery novel, which I called *The So Blue Marble*. In due time this new book was completed. It was read to the reading circle. Flaws were discussed and eliminated. Verdict? The same as my own. This one was going to be the breakthrough. Off to my agent. Sent to publisher one and publisher two and so on through the entire list of established publishers. They all turned down *The So Blue Marble*.

What I did not know was that *fantasy* was a bad word in publishing circles at that time. Both the first book and this one had fantasy elements in them. In both, these were essential to the story.

And then a really fantastic thing happened. A new publishing company had been founded by three young men, all with sound publishing experience. Charles Duell was a former vice president at Morrow, Sam Sloane was of the esteemed Sloane publishing house, and Cap Pearce was an editor at *The New Yorker*. Duell had brought to the new house as mystery editor, Marie Rodell, also of Morrow. She had gone directly from Vassar to Morrow, where among other assignments she was one of the editors who handled the Erle Stanley Gardner novels.

Around Thanksgiving came the word. Duell, Sloane, and Pearce would publish *The So Blue Marble*. *If* . . . came a letter from Marie. *If* I would cut 25,000 words. *If* I would cut one important (to me) character, a district attorney, an older brother to the twins. *If* I would cut a few too fantastic (to Marie) bits, and have the book back to the publishers by January first.

Would I do it? Any writer who has made it knows that if you were asked to swing from a trapeze with the typewriter in your teeth as you typed the requested changes in a first book, you would be delighted to do so. I finished the rewrite by late December, typed the manuscript seated arm's length from the dining room table, where the typewriter sat (no offices in our house, we used what we had) as I was having a baby in early February and could get no closer to the table. The manuscript reached New York on time. And my first mystery was accepted.

No one said a word about the fantasy then or until long years after, when a new generation asked questions. The cuts toned down certain incidents. I had never thought of the book itself as fantasy. It was true that the twins could do things that most persons had long forgotten how to do. The book also was streamlined by the 25,000-word cut—I am wordy—so that it moved sharply, not slowly meandering along. When several of the leading mystery editors of New York at the time it was published asked me why the manuscript hadn't been sent to them first, I answered the truth, "It was." True, they did not see the same book that was published, they saw the uncut version. And I bless the day Marie nudged me into learning to cut.

And why didn't I return to writing straight novels? (As they were then called. I don't know what today's wordage for them is.) It was like this. In those days a contract called for two mysteries a year, as did each renewal of contract. This keeps a writer busy, out of sidelines. By the time you've finished the one, champing at the bit to start the next one which has been flooding you with its ideas from the wings. And so you become a mystery writer. And it's a lot of fun.

SEARCHING
FOR AGATHA CHRISTIE

Carolyn G. Hart

CAN WE EVER REALLY KNOW Agatha Christie?

This is a question I didn't directly address in *The Christie Caper,* my mystery that celebrates the centenary of the birth of the world's greatest mystery writer. Although I expect readers come away from the book with a warm impression of Christie, her personality isn't discussed in detail. *The Christie Caper* focuses primarily on Christie as a writer.

But what of the woman behind the books?

Agatha Christie.

What does her name conjure?

Wonderful mysteries with clever plots, believable characters, and quick, sure touches of humor.

But who was Agatha Christie? What was she like? What was she really like, this utterly British woman who wrote the world's most successful mysteries?

Many who knew her agree that she was—
exceedingly shy
a stalwart friend
disciplined
self-conscious about her lack of formal education
brave
well read in the Victorian sense, familiar with the classics, with Shakespeare, with the Bible
aloof
an accomplished musician.
The author saw herself as—
good-tempered
exuberant
scatty
forgetful
shy
affectionate
completely lacking in self-confidence
moderately unselfish.

Her second husband, Max Mallowan, said that she radiated love and happiness.

But looking beyond these one-line descriptions, what was this remarkable woman like as a person?

Some essayists have insisted that we can never know Christie, that this most elusive and reclusive of authors hid herself behind her books with the clear intention of remaining inscrutable, unfathomed.

Christie's autobiography concentrates upon her childhood, in which she recalls in loving detail a most protected youth.

Janet Morgan's excellent biography is based upon information provided by an adoring family, and Christie is portrayed with dignified restraint.

The most revealing of all the books about Christie is the recent biography by Dr. Gillian Gill, which focuses primarily upon Christie's books written as Mary Westmacott. These books are clearly autobiographical and tell us how Christie saw her own life.

But is this the nearest we can come to the essence of Christie?

Happily, the answer is no. The truth about Agatha Christie is easily found, just as the truth about any writer can easily be found. Read Christie's books once again. Read this time, not for plot or character, not for pleasure or intellectual stimulation, but read as an ornithologist watches for a rare, hard-to-sight quarry.

Read for the author's heart.

It's there, speaking to us through her characters, just as clearly and forthrightly as Christie would speak, could she walk into her drawing room today and greet a friend.

Every writer reveals in print the stamp of his soul. The qualities an author admires, the emotions that rule an author's heart, are there for the finding.

I'd like to share with you some of the comments made by characters in various Christie novels that have formed my picture of Dame Agatha:

Anne Beddingfield in *The Man in the Brown Suit:* ''I had the firm conviction that, if I went about looking for adventure, adventure would meet me halfway. It is a theory of mine that one always gets what one wants.''

This eagerness for adventure, this longing for the new and different and exciting would be one of Christie's most distinguishing characteristics throughout her life. She never hesitated a moment when she and her first husband, war-hero Archie Christie, had the opportunity in 1922 to travel around the world as part of a British Empire mission to help plan for an upcoming trade exhibition. In her autobiography she said, ''Going round the world was one of the most exciting things that ever happened to me.''

This willingness to seek out adventure changed the course of her life many years later. After her divorce from Archie, she planned a holiday in the West Indies. The tickets were purchased, the plans made. At a dinner party two days before her scheduled departure, Agatha fell into conversation with a naval couple who had recently returned from Bagh-

dad. She was so entranced by their stories that she canceled her trip to the West Indies and bought her first ticket on the Orient Express. During this journey she visited the excavations of Sir Leonard Woolley at Ur. She so charmed both Woolley and his autocratic wife, Katherine, that she was invited to return the next year. On that second trip, Christie met a young member of the Woolley expedition who had been absent the previous year—Max Mallowan. He would become her second husband.

Anne Beddingfield isn't Christie's only character to seek out adventure. There is Tuppence of Tommy and Tuppence and Lady Eileen (Bundle) Brent and Victoria Jones (*They Came to Baghdad*). Listen to what these characters say, it is the author's ever-eager heart speaking.

And listen to the young nurse in *Towards Zero,* speaking to the would-be suicide bitter at being saved: ''It may be just by being somewhere—not doing anything—oh, I can't say what I mean but you might just—just walk along a street someday and just by doing that accomplish something terribly important—perhaps without even knowing what it was.''

Christie understood duty. No matter what happened to her in life, no matter how heartbreaking or agonizing the circumstances, she was determined to finish the course. She was devastated when her husband, Archie, left her at the same time that she was grieving over her mother's death, but she kept on because, quite simply, it was her duty to do so.

In *The Secret of Chimneys,* Virginia Revel says: ''It's just as exciting to buy a new experience as it is to buy a new dress—more so, in fact.''

In *The Hollow,* John Christow says to his lover, Henrietta, a sculptor: ''If I were dead, the first thing you'd do, with tears streaming down your face, would be to start modeling some damned mourning woman or some figure of grief . . .'' In this passage Christie is revealing a secret known to all authors, that writing is not a product of discipline, as admirers believe, but that writing is essential; writing is the core of life; writers must write.

In *Mrs. McGinty's Dead,* Ariadne Oliver comments on the misery of having a book adapted to the stage: ''. . . you've no idea of the agony of having your characters taken and made to say things they never would have said, and do things they never would have done.'' Oliver is Christie's gently satiric portrait of herself, a scatty middle-aged

The great Agatha Christie through the years.

woman addicted to apples who sometimes finds her creation (for Sven Hjerson read Hercule Poirot) irritating beyond words. Christie also found many of the filmed versions of her books unsatisfying. Although she admired Margaret Rutherford as an actress, she saw Rutherford as a disastrous Miss Marple. Christie would have been delighted with Joan Hickson's Miss Marple.

Also in *Mrs. McGinty's Dead,* Maureen Summerhayes says: "I never think it matters what one eats—or what one wears—or what one does. I don't think things matter—not really." Christie enjoyed beautiful homes and fine furnishings, but she knew that it was the family that mattered, not the house.

In "The Blood–stained Pavement," a short story, Miss Marple comments: "There is a great deal of wickedness in village life. I hope you dear young people will never realize just how very wicked the world is." Christie was a firm believer in the reality of evil. She once described the mystery as the modern equivalent of the medieval morality play. She was convinced that human beings

choose—through their acts—their own destiny. The mystery provided her with a vehicle to point out just how those choices can twist and ruin relationships and lives.

In *Ordeal by Innocence,* Hester Argyle says: "It's not the guilty who matter. It is the innocent." Christie would today have been a staunch supporter of victims' rights. The suffering of those touched by crime continues far beyond the pain of the moment.

In *The Mirror Crack'd,* Miss Marple says: "Children feel things, you know. They feel things more than the people around them ever imagine." When Christie was a little girl, her family took a vacation in the French Alps. One day she and her father and brother and sister went on a donkey ride up in the hills. The guide, meaning well, captured a lovely butterfly and pinned it to Christie's hat. The butterfly fluttered and fluttered, its wings beating against her hat, struggling to be free until it died. From that point on during the outing, to the exasperation of her siblings and her father, she was struck dumb and began to cry. No one could figure out what had gone wrong. Finally, in bad spirits, the party returned to the hotel. Her mother awaited them. When Agatha got down from her donkey, her eyes red-rimmed, her face pale, her mother rushed forward and unpinned the butterfly. Agatha clung to her mother and cried. She couldn't bear the butterfly's struggles, but she hadn't been able to speak out and tell the guide and hurt his feelings.

In *The Hollow,* sick old Mrs. Crabtree speaks to Henrietta Savernake, who is mourning the death of her lover: "Don't fret, ducky—what's gorn's gorn. You can't have it back." This was a painful knowledge Christie had been forced to accept upon the collapse of her first marriage.

In "The Case of the Middle-aged Wife," Parker Pyne says: "A woman tears a passion to pieces and gets no good from it, but a romance can be laid up in lavender and looked at through all the long years to come." Christie was a very beautiful young woman who received at least six proposals of marriage. She knew whereof she spoke.

In *The Body in the Library,* Miss Marple says:

"The truth is, you see, that most people—and I don't exclude policemen—are far too trusting for this wicked world. They believe what is told them. I never do. I'm afraid I always like to prove a thing for myself." Christie knew that the world often isn't as it seems. She had thought that her marriage to Archie would never end, that his love for her would last forever. He became the living embodiment of a nightmare that had plagued her as a child, that of a familiar and loving face turning into a visage of horror. She would always fear the false face, and this fear became the basis of many of her books.

So many wonderful characters. These are just a handful of quotes, but they point the way toward knowing Agatha Christie. Read her books. She is there, in Miss Marple's clear-eyed view of life, in the insouciance of Tuppence, in Poirot's commitment to justice, in so many laughing quips and telling jibes. Read Christie's books once again. You will catch glimpses of that most-elusive, most-reclusive author. Read for Christie's heart—it is there to find.

MISTRESS OF MAYHEM:
The Best of Agatha Christie on Film
John McCarty

MYSTERY FANS IN GENERAL and Agatha Christie mystery fans in particular probably agree with the late Dame Agatha herself that, on the whole, the stage and television have been much kinder to her work than the medium of film. Very likely, they will also agree that of the hundred-odd adaptations of Christie's works that have appeared over the past sixty-five years, the most faithful have been the most recent.

Indeed, for most Christie fans and buffs, Joan Hickson's incarnation of the mistress of mayhem's octogenarian supersleuth Jane Marple in the BBC's meticulous period mountings (1984–1993) of a half

dozen of the Marple novels will forever remain definitive—like Raymond Massey's Lincoln, or Vivien Leigh's Scarlett O'Hara. As will David Suchet's mincing portrait of Hercule Poirot in Granada television's sumptuously produced and still-continuing series of Poirot novel and short-story adaptations. And James Warwick and Francesca Annis's Roaring Twenties amateur detectives in London Weekend Television's mid-eighties series *Partners in Crime* based on Christie's Tommy and Tuppence Beresford stories. Pity that Christie, who died in 1976, never lived to see them.

The record is clear that Christie never much cot-

Beth Gwinn

toned to most big-screen versions of her work. She was convinced that the intimate nature of television was much better suited to evoking the cozy qualities of her stories than the giant wall-to-wall screens of the cinema. In fact, she stated as much when she sold the rights to a number of her Marple and Poirot novels to MGM in the early sixties, saying that she hoped (but did not contractually stipulate) that the studio "would use them for television." Instead, MGM miscast the dotty, rambunctious Margaret Rutherford as Marple (who emerged a sort of female Nigel Bruce), marginally miscast Tony Randall as Poirot, updated the stories, and turned them into B movie features, the latter Poirot film (*The Alphabet Murders,* 1966) directed in slapstick, comic-book style by Frank Tashlin, who had cut his directorial teeth helming the early shenanigans of Bugs Bunny.

Christie was so aghast that she publicly expressed her desire that the films would be critical and commercial flops. On the whole, they were neither. Nevertheless, in the wake of the experience, Christie refused to sell the rights to any of her works not already filmed. And she stuck to her guns until 1972, when British producer John Brabourne, aided by his father-in-law, Lord Mountbatten (a Christie friend), argued that if she'd let him make a big-screen version of *Murder on the Orient Express,* he and his chosen director, Sidney Lumet, would do right by the book in every category, from script to costume to casting. Brabourne sweetened

the request with an offer of profit participation in addition to a generous fee for the rights. Christie was finally won over (who would not have been?), and she was generally pleased with the result, aesthetically and financially. The film was a huge critical and commercial success, and a multiple award-winner as well. Agreeably, she contracted with Brabourne to film several more of her books. But she never lived to see them, and went to her reward believing that *Murder on the Orient Express* (1974) was the best the cinema had done with her work, and the best it would probably ever do.

Is it? Or are there other Christie movies which, the authoress's understandably hypercritical personal opinions aside, deserve mention—perhaps even more honorable mention—as well?

I believe so. Let's take a look.

Love from a Stranger (1937). This virtually forgotten entry in the filmography of underrated director Rowland V. Lee (*The Count of Monte Cristo, The Three Musketeers, Son of Frankenstein, Tower of London*) was made in England and boasts a music score by no less a personage than Sir Benjamin Britten. It was based on a 1936 play adapted by actor-writer-director Frank Vosper from Christie's "Philomel Cottage," one of several short stories that had appeared in her 1934 anthology *The Listerdale Mystery.*

Vosper's suspenseful melodrama was overshadowed considerably by the critical acclaim heaped on Emlyn Williams's similiar-themed "wolf-in-the-fold" drama *Night Must Fall,* which made its debut on the London stage during the same theatrical season. The competition for reviewer plaudits and audience dollars continued in the fall, when the two plays made their American premieres. Again, *Night Must Fall* stole the critical and commercial thunder; Vosper's play closed in less than a month. Ironically, the same thing happened with the respective film version. The rights to Williams's play were scooped up by big-money MGM, the rights to Vosper's by Britain's small-time Trafalgar Studios, for distribution in the U.S. through United Artists. The films were released in America exactly eleven days apart. *Night Must Fall* was a hit that earned several Academy Award nominations. *Love from a Stranger* generated lukewarm reviews and identical box office. In subsequent years, *Night Must Fall* became a staple of community theater and high school drama groups everywhere, whereas *Love*

Peter Ustinov as Hercule Poirot in *Death on the Nile*. Ustinov is seen here with, from left, David Niven, George Kennedy, and Simon MacCorkindale.

from a Stranger remains one of the least produced of all the "Christie plays."

Vosper's fate was even bleaker. The year the film was released, he went overboard during a transatlantic crossing. His body was found, but the mystery surrounding his fate—was it suicide or murder?—has never been solved. Maybe Christie should have turned one of her august fictional detectives loose on the case.

One of the reasons *Night Must Fall* overshadowed *Love from a Stranger* may have been that its plot (loosely based on England's notorious Patrick Mahon "head-in-the-hatbox" case) about a boyish charmer with a psychosexual fondness for chopping ladies' heads off was a bit more daring and ghoulish (at the time) than Vosper's variation on the much overworked theme of the modern bluebeard who murders his women chiefly for their money. *New York Times* movie critic Frank S. Nugent noted as much when he called the picture a "throwback."

Director Lee, screenwriter Frances Marion, and, especially, star Basil Rathbone (who plays the part of the bluebeard acted onstage by Vosper himself) clearly realized this themselves. And rather than pretending otherwise, they transformed the film version into an initially subtle comedy of bad manners that goes wildly over the top during the last half hour when Rathbone reveals his murderous nature (and penchant for Dukas's *The Sorcerer's Apprentice* played "Faster! Faster!") to new bride Ann Harding in a sustained passage of deliciously unchecked scenery-chewing that makes his performances as the nerve-shredded title character in Lee's *Son of Frankenstein* and the cocaine-addicted Sherlock Holmes seem restrained by comparison. Harding almost matches his hyperactive, sharp-tongued, eye-rolling intensity during these scenes when, to save herself, she pretends to be an even shrewder killer of husbands, and verbally drives the cad into suffering a fatal heart attack. Christie was not pleased. But it's a sourpuss indeed who doesn't come up smiling when Rathbone finally cuts loose. Or when Joan Hickson pops up in a small role as a thoroughly brainless maid.

The film was nicely remade in 1947 under the same title with Sylvia Sidney as the put-upon wife and John Hodiak as the bluebeard, a Latin-American smoothie this time around who is not nearly as wonderfully looney as Rathbone.

And Then There Were None (1945). Who could possibly dislike a charmingly droll tale of mass murder that doesn't have a mean-spirited frame in its celluloid body? This René Clair film, the first (to date) of four filmed versions of Christie's classic 1939 novel *Ten Little Indians,* is just that.

Taking a cue from Christie herself, Dudley Nichols's witty screen adaptation followed Christie's 1943 stage version of the novel rather than the novel itself, which was published in England under the politically incorrect title *Ten Little Niggers* and ended on a rather sour note. In the book, no one is left alive at the conclusion. In play and film, hero and heroine survive the machinations of the killer and escape to get married, providing a very different, though perhaps no less acerbic, meaning to the final line of the nursery rhyme on which Christie's classic tale of murder is hung—and which Clair used as the title for the film.

Following the course she had charted with her groundbreaking Poirot novel *The Murder of Roger Ackroyd* (1926), which caused a stir among detective story buffs with its controversial narrator-as-murderer twist ending, Christie challenged herself with an even more daring bit of sleight-of-hand in *Ten Little Indians* by revealing the killer to be one of the victims—albeit a bogus victim, obviously. And she pulled it off. As does Clair in his delightful film version, which is even more of a comedy of bad manners than Lee's *Love from a Stranger.*

Ten strangers have been invited to a secluded

A scene from *And Then There Were None.*

island estate for an evening of murderous retribution for their "past crimes." As they find their ranks gradually whittled down in keeping with the portentous lines of the nursery rhyme, they grow understandably paranoid and suspicious of one another. To keep an eye out, they progress to stalking one another from room to room in perfect parody of one of the classic gags of silent film comedy, the genre in which Clair had made his reputation. And the film's sardonic verbal ripostes match its visual wit every step of the way. For example, the killer's closing line as he prematurely dispatches himself with poison is a killer in itself.

And Then There Were None proved cinematically influential as well, for in adapting Christie's stagebound piece to the screen, Clair and Nichols finally solved a problem that had plagued movie versions of this type of drawing room whodunit from day one. Rather than revealing who dun it and how with a static dialogue sequence in which the detective gathers the remaining suspects together to "explain it all," Clair flashes back at different points to *show* us who dun it and how the crimes were committed—occasionally repeating critical earlier scenes from different angles to show us what we missed or couldn't observe the first time around. This seemingly obvious device for keeping the story moving and the viewer's eye and mind engaged come solution time has since become a staple of virtually every filmed Christie whodunit, and many others as well.

The three remakes of *And Then There Were None,* all of them released under the play's original title *Ten Little Indians,* remain considerably less noteworthy, especially by comparison. All were produced by the same man—low-budget-filmmaker Harry Allan Towers, who apparently holds the rights to the tale in perpetuity and has decided to turn remaking it into a minor cottage industry. Towers wrote or cowrote the scripts as well, using his pseudonym Peter Welbeck.

Of them, the first, released in 1965, is arguably the best. Towers shot it in England, although he transposed the setting to a remote inn on the Swiss Alps, and employed George Pollock, the director of the concurrent Margaret Rutherford Miss Marple films on whose modest coattails Towers was clearly trying to ride, at the helm. Capitalizing on the success of *Murder on the Orient Express,* Towers took his second shot at the Christie warhorse in 1975,

this time setting the tale in a Byzantine palace in pre-Ayatollah Iran. One can only be thankful that Mr. Towers didn't hold off until the fall of the shah and the notorious events that followed, or the ever-exploitative fellow might have seen his way to retitling the film "Ten Little Hostages." Capitalizing on what concurrent success I've no idea for his most recent, and worst, go at the story, Towers was back at it in 1989—this time setting the story on safari in Africa.

Witness for the Prosecution (1957). Billy Wilder sandwiched this definitive screen version of the Christie stage classic in between two of his most sophisticated comedies: the Lubitsch-like *Love in the Afternoon* (1957) and the rambunctious *Some Like It Hot* (1958). *Witness* contains a fair degree of comedy as well—notably in the byplay between Charles Laughton's heart-patient/barrister with a craving for illicit cigars and brandy, Sir Wilfred Robards, and Elsa Lanchester's overly solicitous nurse, Miss Plimsoll, a part created expressly for the film so that the husband-and-wife team could work together. Recreating her Broadway role as the murder victim's irascible and slightly deaf maid, Una O'Connor added some laughs as well. But on the whole, *Witness* is not in the same comedy-of-bad-manners vein of *Love from a Stranger* and *And Then There Were None.* It's a straightforward murder yarn, straightforwardly presented.

One of the top hits of 1957, it earned several Academy Award nominations, including one for Best Picture, though it failed to win. Wilder, director of the lust-murder classic *Double Indemnity* (1944), and a fan of such fare, especially British murder mysteries, returned to the genre but once more with his ambitious *hommage, The Private Life of Sherlock Holmes* (1971). But that film was drastically cut by its distributor, United Artists, prior to release. And gem though it is even in its truncated form (Wilder's original cut was shorn of more than eighty minutes of never-replaced footage), it flopped at the box office. And the heartbroken Wilder stuck with acid comedies for the remainder of his career.

Christie adapted her play from a short story of the same name she'd written for her 1933 anthology *The Hound of Death and Other Stories.* In both short story and play, a likable young man, Leonard Vole, is arrested for murdering an elderly widow for her money. All the evidence is against him. Only his wife, Romaine, can support his alibi. But

Archive Photos

Margaret Rutherford as Agatha Christie's Miss Marple in *Murder Most Foul*.

she turns the tables on him and his barrister by claiming that she and Vole are not legally married, and serving as a surprise witness for the prosecution instead. But the barrister exposes her on the stand as a liar, and Vole is acquitted. In a twist ending, it is revealed that Romaine, a former actress, had acted the part of the deceitful wife, knowing she would be sentenced for perjury, in the belief that the jury would not have accepted the word of a loyal wife compelled by law to testify only on her husband's behalf. In a further twist she reveals why the charade had been necessary: Vole was guilty after all.

Christie embellished the ending of the play by having Romaine stab Vole to death following the verdict when she finds that despite all she's done for him he intends to jilt her for a younger woman. As the curtain falls, Vole's own barrister jumps to take on the remarkable woman's case. The play's

backers protested this violent ending. But Christie felt the play needed a kicker that would show up Vole for the heel he is, believed it to be "psychologically sound," and refused to let the play go on without it. She won, and the rest is theatrical history. *Witness* went on to become one of her most financially successful and oft-produced plays.

Wilder's screen version, which the director cowrote with Harry Kurnitz, retains the play's violent twist ending but goes Christie one better by slipping in numerous clues to Vole's (Tyrone Power) possible guilt along the way. These clues pop up in two flashbacks dealing with Vole and Romaine's (Marlene Dietrich) first encounter in Berlin after the war and Vole's relationship with the murder victim, which Wilder and Kurnitz added to the film. Blink and you'll miss them. But they're there—in Power's skillful alteration of tone and gesture as he occasionally lets his mask of likability slip and reveals what a manipulative (and surly) cad he truly is. Ironically, these flashbacks are told from Power's own point of view; in effect, the arrogant criminal exposes himself, believing everyone around him too stupid to notice.

Now, *that's* what you call psychologically sound.

The not bad made-for-TV remake (1982) starring Sir Ralph Richardson as the barrister, Diana Rigg as Romaine, and Beau Bridges as Vole follows the Wilder-Kurnitz original quite closely, but fails to include these intriguing clues.

Death on the Nile (1978) and *Evil Under the Sun* (1982). Attempts to launch a series of detective films featuring Christie's loquacious Belgian supersleuth, Hercule Poirot, began with the advent of the talkies themselves. *Alibi* (1931), based on a 1928 stage adaptation of Christie's celebrated novel *The Murder of Roger Ackroyd,* reached the screen first. The play had starred Charles Laughton as Poirot—ideal casting, it would seem, although Christie deemed the actor "too portly" for the role. The film version replaced Laughton with Austin Trevor, whose tall, dark, slim, and "veddy British" demeanor resembled Christie's character not at all. Trevor repeated the role in the next Poirot film, *Black Coffee* (1931), based on an original stage play by Christie herself. The poorly received series concluded with *Lord Edgware Dies* (1934), based on Christie's novel of the same name which is known in America under the title *Thirteen at Dinner,* and was remade as a television movie in 1985 starring Peter Ustinov (future Poirot David Suchet was featured in the cast as well).

The Trevor films found so little favor with Christie that she refused to sell the screen rights to any more of her Poirot novels and plays for years. But since audiences hadn't found much favor with the series either, studios in Britain and in America weren't exactly clamoring to scoop them up. More than a quarter of a century would roll by before Poirot returned to the screen in *The Alphabet Murders,* the first of a proposed series of Poirot films which MGM hoped would follow the moderate success of its Miss Marple films starring Margaret Rutherford. Initially, Zero Mostel was set to star as Poirot. But when Christie discovered that this adaptation of her novel *The ABC Murders* had been altered to include a racy bedroom scene involving her fastidious and sexually ambivalent detective, she

scuttled the project until it was taken over by different hands. The film that emerged, starring Tony Randall, omitted the bedroom scene but substituted a trendy post-*Hard Day's Night* style, replete with numerous sight gags. Christie hated it. Audiences did too. The series idea was scrapped. And almost a decade went by before a major studio (this time Paramount) and Christie took a chance on another Poirot film.

In many quarters, this film, *Murder on the Orient Express,* is still considered to be the best of the big screen Poirot adaptations. British actor Albert Finney's droll performance as Poirot—he is virtually unrecognizable in the part—captured an Academy Award nomination as Best Actor and even won the approval of Christie herself, although she is quoted as having disdained the style of mustache Finney wore for the role, which she considered not elegant enough. In addition to Finney, the film boasted an all-star cast of top-drawer talent. And producer John Brabourne delivered on the rest of his promise to Christie as well by giving the picture the most lavish, no-expense-spared treatment of any Christie adaptation so far. Paul Dehn's script follows the Christie original quite faithfully and keeps the audience guessing right to the end. But except for Finney's performance and some other amusing bits here and there from other cast members, the overall film lacks the lighthearted mood that is intrinsic to Christie's work and was captured so well by René Clair, Billy Wilder, and even Rowland V. Lee. This is especially apparent on repeated viewings when we are no longer caught up in the plot and concentrating our "little grey cells" on solving the mystery.

The fault lay in Brabourne's choice of director, Sidney Lumet, a filmmaker whose heavy-handed, even lugubrious style is more suited to intense dramas like *The Pawnbroker* (1965) and gritty, urban police thrillers like *Serpico* (1973), his previous film, than escapist fare such as this. The same problem plagued Lumet's overly solemn screen version of Ira Levin's comedy-of-murders, *Deathtrap* (1982), Lumet's woefully unfunny black comedy *Bye Bye Braverman* (1968), and, especially, his big-screen version of the Broadway hit *The Wiz* (1978), which, in Lumet's hands, emerged as one of the dreariest, most lead-footed movie musicals ever made, Michael Jackson's zesty dance numbers notwithstanding.

Archive Photos

Albert Finney as Agatha Christie's Hercule Poirot with Martin Balsam (*center*) in *Murder on the Orient Express.*

In the final analysis, I think the reason *Murder on the Orient Express* is so exalted among mystery fans is that the source material is one of Christie's most ingenious and credible concoctions (most Christie buffs consider it her best book), and Brabourne did indeed do right by it in terms of script, costume, and casting. And for general audiences and critics, the film's "glamorous journey into a mythical past" (in the words of the film's pressbook) served as a welcome respite to the ugly real-life mysteries of Watergate, which were still unraveling at the time.

Brabourne and partner Richard Goodwin's follow-up, *Death on the Nile,* was not as well reviewed or received by audiences, though in terms of capturing the lighthearted mood of the Christie oeuvre, it is, in many ways, the better of the two films. Christie's original novel, which she wrote in 1937 and adapted for the stage as *Murder on the*

Nile in 1946, remains almost as beloved by Christie buffs, although even they tend to agree with most critics that the twists and turns of her plot, which rely heavily on coincidence and split-second timing on the part of the killers, stretch credibility to the limit. The film version, faithfully adapted with tongue firmly in cheek by Anthony Shaffer, the author of *Sleuth,* follows suit. Befitting the film's spectacular Egyptian locale and larger-than-life scenery of the pyramids, the Sphinx and Valley of the Kings, John Guillermin directs—and his all-star cast acts—the material with an over-the-top sense of humor and gaiety so in keeping with the spirit of the piece that credibility matters not at all.

Albert Finney declined to reprise the part of Poirot. Peter Ustinov took his place, and although he doesn't match Christie's description of the character, he slipped into the role so comfortably, it seemed as if he'd been perfecting it for years. His performance is just as droll as Finney's, but much less mannered and "actorish." Ustinov is a champion scene-stealer, but in this entertaining, all-stops-out extravaganza in which even the bit players are given a chance to shine, he is upstaged on occasion by Indian actor I. S. Johar's delightful turn as the unflappable manager of the Nile steamer on which the murders are committed. Filmgoers best remember Johar as the Arab Peter O'Toole rescues from the "sun's anvil," then, ironically, must execute to avoid a tribal bloodbath in *Lawrence of Arabia* (1962). The worst Johar has to deal with here is a lethal king cobra which the killers place in Poirot's stateroom to prevent his "little grey cells" from smoking them out. David Niven dispatches the snake with aplomb, but Johar's response to the suspenseful scene ("Never have I seen such a reptile in a first-class cabin!") brings down the house.

Ustinov played Poirot again in the next Brabourne/Goodwin outing, *Evil Under the Sun,* which in terms of style, atmosphere (the film is set on a lush Mediterranean island), and charm is almost as good, although it drew equally lukewarm reviews from the critics. Anthony Shaffer delivered another witty screenplay (adapted from Christie's 1941 novel), and the man at the helm this time was Guy Hamilton, the director of *Goldfinger* (1964), arguably the best, and snappiest, entry in the long-running James Bond series. Once again the scene-stealing Ustinov had his work cut out for him—this time in the form of Diana Rigg's hilariously bitchy victim whose seaside murder is the springboard for this lavishly mounted, baffling-to-the-end, and thoroughly engaging whodunit. This film did not repeat the huge box-office success of *Murder on the Orient Express* or the moderate success of *Death on the Nile,* however, and so Brabourne and Goodwin concluded their series of class-act Poirot films with it. But they went out on a very high note indeed.

By this time the actor most associated with the role of Poirot (at least until David Suchet came along), Ustinov was coaxed back by other producers to repeat it on four more occasions. But the films were fairly dreary and by no means up to the standard set by the Brabourne/Goodwin series. Three of these films—*Thirteen at Dinner* (1985), *Dead Man's Folly* (1986) and *Murder in Three Acts* (1986)—were made for television and updated the character to the present day, ignoring the fact that

the venerable detective's "little grey cells" would probably not be working as well in the mid-1980s since the character would be more than a hundred years old.

Set credibly in period but just as dreary was Ustinov's last big-screen brush with the role in *Appointment with Death* (1988), a failed attempt by hack director Michael Winner to recapture the extravagant flavor of the Brabourne/Goodwin films. Shot in Israel with an all-star cast that included Lauren Bacall and Sir John Gielgud, the film was based on Christie's 1938 novel of the same name, which she adapted for the stage in 1945 (the ubiquitous Joan Hickson had a small role in the play, as she did in 1962's *Murder, She Said,* the first of Rutherford/Marple films). The book is considered by critics and buffs to be one of Christie's best. The film version, co-scripted by Anthony Shaffer, director Winner, and Peter Buckman, is the pits. Boasting a notable lack of atmosphere, style (the production even *looks* cheap) and charm, it also flops at the basics—for the filmmakers fail to interest the viewer in even finding out who dun it.

Agatha (1979). Rounding out this series of the best of Agatha Christie on the big screen is this very unusual entry drawn not from one of Christie's novels, short stories, or plays but from an event in her life, which the filmmakers recreate in the style of one of her own cozy period mysteries.

In 1926, Christie's roadster was found in a ditch not far from her manor house, called Styles. Some of her belongings were found on the seat, but the authoress herself had vanished into thin air. Headlines around the country and the world rang with news of her mysterious disappearance. Rewards were posted and a manhunt launched involving police and hundreds of private citizens equipped with bloodhounds and airplanes. A short time later she was recognized by an employee at a resort hotel, where she was living under a false name. Pressed for details as to what happened to her, Christie claimed total loss of memory, and never spoke publicly of the incident—her own personal "mysterious affair at Styles"—after that, nor did she write about it in her comprehensive and otherwise quite forthcoming autobiography, published a year after her death. In any case, the incident had a profound effect on her life. Already becoming well known at the time as the result of her novel *The Murder of Roger Ackroyd,* which had recently been published and hit the British best seller list, she emerged from the incident a household name—the first lady of mystery—and professionally and financially never had to look back again.

Was her disappearance a publicity stunt? The result of a nervous breakdown brought on by the breakup of her marriage? Or had she simply had an accident and been knocked out, losing her memory for a time? We still don't know. And neither do the filmmakers of this intriguing speculation as to what really did happen, and why, which even includes the possibility that a murder attempt was being made on the author's life by ... well, I won't spoil the film for you by revealing it. What I will say is that Vanessa Redgrave makes a wonderful damsel in distress as the vibrant, youthful Ms. Christie, and future James Bond Timothy Dalton is equally strong as her total rotter of a husband. Only Dustin Hoffman, giving one of his typical ''watch me act'' performances as the all-too-modern American newshound on her trail, seems out of step with the film's richly evocative Roaring Twenties atmosphere.

One can't help but think that the subject herself would have smiled approvingly at this one.

A Guide to Agatha Christie on the Big Screen

(The name in parentheses is that of the director)

1928: **Die Abenteuer G.m.b.H.** a.k.a. **Adventure Inc.** (Fred Sauer)
The Passing of Mr. Quinn (Julius Hagen)
1931: **Alibi** (Leslie Hiscott)
Black Coffee (Leslie Hiscott)
1934: **Lord Edgware Dies** (Henry Edwards)
1937: **Love from a Stranger** (Rowland V. Lee)
1945: **And Then There Were None** (René Clair)
1947: **Love from a Stranger** (Richard Whorf)
1957: **Witness for the Prosecution** (Billy Wilder)
1960: **The Spider's Web** (Godfrey Grayson)
1962: **Murder, She Said** (George Pollock)
1963: **Murder at the Gallop** (George Pollock)
1964: **Murder Most Foul** (George Pollock)
Murder Ahoy! (George Pollock)
1965: **Ten Little Indians** (George Pollock)
1966: **The Alphabet Murders** (Frank Tashlin)
1972: **Endless Night** (Sidney Gilliat)
1974: **Murder on the Orient Express** (Sidney Lumet)
1975: **Ten Little Indians** (Peter Collinson)
1978: **Death on the Nile** (John Guillermin)
1979: **Agatha** (Michael Apted)
1980: **The Mirror Crack'd** (Guy Hamilton)
1982: **Evil Under the Sun** (Guy Hamilton)
1984: **Ordeal by Innocence** (Desmond Davis)
1988: **Appointment with Death** (Michael Winner)
1989: **Ten Little Indians** (Alan Birkinshaw)

CATS IN MYSTERIES

Ellen Nehr

LILIAN JACKSON BRAUN'S two Siamese cats, Koko and Yum Yum, share their detective skills with ex-reporter Jim Qwilleran in eighteen adventures spanning twenty-six years. Koko came into Qwill's care after the murder of Koko's former owner, which he helped to solve in *The Cat Who Could Read Backwards* (1966). Yum Yum was a reward after Qwill's third adventure, *The Cat Who Turned On and Off* (1968). The pair reflects Braun's skill at attributing human perception to felines and is done so well that only the most pedantic reader can object. After all their adventures, the trio is still going strong.

D. B. Olsen featured a cat, Samantha, in her twelve-book series about the adventures of Miss Rachel Murdock, a little old lady amateur detective, who, from 1939 to 1956, found more bodies than half of the Los Angeles police force. Miss Rachel was an inveterate traveler and she took off with Samantha in a carrier basket at the least sign of alarm or "suspicious" activity among her far-flung relatives or acquaintances. Often accompanying the pair is Jennifer, Rachel's rigid, prim, and proper sister, who strongly and loudly disapproves of everything Rachel does. The first book, *The Cat Saw Murder* (1939), in which Samantha inherits a fortune, introduces the sisters and Rachel's police friend, Lieutenant Stephen Mayhew of the Los Angeles Police Department. Not only does Samantha have at least nine lives, but Miss Rachel doesn't age a bit even though the series lasted for seventeen years.

Sharon McCone has had several cats during her career as a private investigator. They seem to know she is a soft touch. In *Ask the Cards a Question* (1982), a white cat with both stripes and spots enters her life. In *Pennies on a Dead Woman's Eyes* (1992), a pair of kittens that Sharon has tried vainly to resist come home to stay.

Frances and Richard Lockridge used Pam and Jerry North's cats as background and conversational elements during the various "let's put all the pieces together" summary sessions. The cats were subjects to be discussed, but their names, Martini, Gin, and Sherry, were more a reflection of the Norths' favorite drinks than clues. Toward the end of the series other cats arrived but were not strongly featured.

Elizabeth Peters's most interesting cat is Bastet, an Egyptian animal who belongs to Ramses, the son of the archaeological pair, Professor and Mrs. Emerson, who are introduced in *The Curse of the Pharaohs* (1981). The Egyptian god Bast, who had the facial features of a cat or a lion, was believed to be responsible for the fertility of the land as well as the protector of pleasure. On several occasions Bastet uncovers missing papers or, by running away, leads the principal characters to clues, but in one instance in *Lion in the Valley* Bastet is seduced by the master criminal with a ration of cooked chicken who then enters a room at Shepherd's Hotel and lays a trap for Emerson. In *The Last Camel Dies at Noon* (1991), an unnamed cat acts as a messenger when Ramses sends a message to his parents, in Latin, on paper twisted around the cat's collar.

Professor Peter Shandy and his wife, Helen, have a cat, Jane Austen, who decorates their house on the campus at Balaclava Agricultural College. But it is Edmund, the cat who lives with their housekeeper, Mrs. Martha Lomax, who brings home the blood-soaked wig of her murdered boarder, Professor Herbert Ungley, in *Something the Cat Dragged In* (1983). Edmund hangs around the jail because Chief Fred Ottermole always has food to spare, and Edmund, by bringing facts to the police officer's attention, helps solve the murder.

Marian Babson's four-book series about London-based travel agent Douglas Perkins starts with *Murder at the Cat Show* (1972) with Pandora, a Siamese who entices Douglas to bring her home in between

Tony Mendozer/FPG International

episodes as the homicide rate escalates. The felines in the first book are working cats who are paid for their services in films, on TV, or as advertising symbols, as well as prime examples of blue ribbon breeds who provide the kittens available for sale at catteries. The two real stars of the show are Pyramus and Thisbe, Sumatran tigers. In the following three adventures with *Murder On a Mystery Tour* (1987), Douglas Perkins and Pandora take a coach ride along with a group of visiting Americans whose ranks have shrunk because death has tagged along on their vacation.

A perfect name for a cat is, of course, Macavity, and Gillian Roberts so named the pet who shares the brick town house of her leading character, Amanda Pepper, who appeared first in *Caught Dead in Philadelphia* (1987). T. S. Eliot deserves his place in mystery lovers' hearts for his creation of such a marvelous "mystery cat."

A new human detective, Catherine (Cat) Kaliban, created by D. B. Borton, is about to become a series character starting with *One for the Money* (1993). Cat, now a widow after a long marriage, is trying to set herself up as a private investigator. She buys a four-unit apartment house in Cincinnati and in what is supposed to be an empty apartment discovers the body of a bag lady who was, during the silent movies days, a film star. Cat becomes her own first client. Her menage contains three cats, one of whom, Sidney, is an attack cat with a predilection for biting ankles, and in one scene he actively holds on to a burglar until the police arrive.

Leopard Cat's Cradle by Jerome Barry (1942) features his soda-jerk character Chick Varney as the detective in a case in which a cheetah plays a murderous role.

Annie Laurance Darling, proprietress of Death on Demand, a mystery bookstore in Carolyn Hart's series, keeps bowls of cat food for Agatha, a black shorthair who was on the scene in the first book, *Death on Demand* (1987), that named the store and the newly introduced Dorothy L., a pure white, almost fully grown feline who arrived in *Deadly Valentine* (1990).

Louie, a large black male who considers Las Vegas his stalking grounds, was the chief detective in *Catnapped* (1991) by Carole Nelson Douglas. He led the heroine to the two Baker and Taylor mascots, who had been kidnapped from the exhibition hall at the beginning of the American Bookseller's Association convention. *Pussyfoot* (1993) continues his nocturnal investigative career.

M. K. Wren used the cat Meg as the basis for the title *Curiosity Didn't Kill the Cat* (1973) as she introduced her bookstore owner, private investigator Conan Flagg.

DOGS IN MYSTERIES

Ellen Nehr

ELIZABETH PETERS'S CHARACTER Professor Vicky Bliss breaks into an antique shop in Rome and finds a starving Doberman in *The Street of the Five Moons* (1978). She feeds him some exotic canned foods meant for people, and the next time she enters the shop, pretending to be an innocent tourist, the dog, recognizing a savior, slobbers all over her and identifies her as the burglar. At the end of the book she brings Caesar back to Germany, where he intimidates her visitors and keeps her company.

Former Army Captain Duncan Maclain, blinded in World War I, is Baynard Kendrick's detective. He was featured in twelve books and three novelettes from 1937 to 1961. Maclain has two dogs: Schnucke, a Seeing Eye dog, and Dreist, a police dog. Both animals assist him in his occupation as a detective and provide companionship at home.

Seeing Eye dogs were first trained in this country in the mid-thirties.

In an effort to do a friend a favor, Claire Malloy, owner of a bookstore in Arkansas, agrees to dog-sit two basset hounds in *Roll Over and Play Dead* (1990). She off-loads this chore for a fee onto her teenage daughter, Canon, and her friend Inez. When the girls report that the dogs are missing, Claire finds herself involved in a dog-napping case that is much larger than just the few missing pets in the neighborhood. Animals are being stolen and sold to laboratories. Claire has to convince authorities that this is actually happening, and her search for the head of the group puts her into major danger before the gripping final scene.

Bill Crider's Sheriff Dan Rhodes picked up a mutt now named Speedo at a crime scene in his first book *Too Late to Die* (1986). Being of an economical turn of wallet, Dan feeds Speedo Old Roy Dog Food from Wal-Mart. The dog doesn't detect but is a great audience as Rhodes verbally works out some of the complications of his cases.

John and Suzy Marshall, series characters in twelve books conceived by James M. Fox (1943 to 1955) about the private investigator and his brainy, beautiful wife, have a Great Dane named Kahn who assists in their adventures.

In Rex Stout's *Die Like a Dog* (1956), Archie finds a black Labrador near a murder scene and brings him home. The conflicts between Wolfe and Archie about what to call the animal are amusing, since the dog's kennel name is Champion Nero Charcoal. They settled on Jet. The dog had belonged to the murder victim, and Wolfe challenges himself to solve the case, which he does with some assistance from the dog. Nero Wolfe deduces the name of the killer by the behavior of the dog Nobby toward the killer *In the Best Families* (1950).

Michael Gilbert's series characters are espionage agents whose encounters were originally published in *Ellery Queen's Mystery Magazine*, after which they were collected into books titled *Game Without Rules* (1967) and *Mr. Calder and Mr. Behrens* by Harper & Row (1982). In "Emergency Exit," a dog originally called Sultan belonged to a spy that Mr. Calder was forced to kill. In the front of *Mr. Calder and Mr. Behrens* three biographies are presented in the format of *Who's Who* entries. One is for the renamed Rasselas, which reads: "Persian deerhound; by Shaw Jehan out of Galietta.

Height: 32 inches. Weight: 128 pounds. Color: Golden with darker patches. Eyes amber, nose blue-black. Hair rough, with distinctive coxcomb between ears. Neck, long. Quarters exceptional, head broad and flat. Blood group: (canine classification) A5.''

During the days of radio serials Sergeant Preston of the Yukon had a dog as a companion and partner, Yukon King.

The Captain Heimrich series written by Frances and Richard Lockridge introduced in *Burnt Offering* (1955) the bachelor State Police Inspector Heimrich to Susan Fayne, a widow with a small boy, Michael, and a large Great Dane, Colonel, who, over the series of books, protects the child from a kidnapping attempt as well as the natural hazards of boyhood in a rural atmosphere.

Susan Conant's canine-centered series includes such titles as *Paws Before Dying, A Bite of Death, Dead and Doggone, A New Leash on Death, Bloodlines*, and *Ruffly Speaking*. Holly Winter, over thirty, Cambridge, Massachusetts–based columnist for *Dog's Life*, is a canine aficionado. In *Gone to the Dogs*, which has a Christmas setting, she takes her two Alaskan malamutes, Rowdy and Kimi, and her veterinarian to the exclusive Cambridge Dog Training Club and, naturally, murder intervenes.

Norbert Davis had a light satiric touch when he presented the detective team of Doan and Carstairs. Doan is a plump private investigator who works with Carstairs, a fawn-colored Great Dane who occasionally eats the evidence and who is much in demand by owners of lady Great Danes to stand at stud. Their three titles are *The Mouse in the Mountain* (1943), *Sally's in the Alley* (1943), and *Oh, Murderer Mine* (1946).

Dogs are featured in short stories by such authors as Agatha Christie, whose Poirot story, "The Nemean Lion," concerns a stolen Pekingese, while Ellery Queen wrote "The Two-Headed Dog" that was the name of an inn. Oliver Quade, a creation of Frank Gruber, solved "The Dog Show Murderers." Raymond Chandler wrote "The Man Who Liked Dogs" for *Black Mask Magazine* and later incorporated it into *Farewell, My Lovely* (1940). The original story is in *Killer in the Rain*.

Best known now for the movie staring William Powell is *The Kennell Murder Case* by S. S. Van Dine.

The Hound of the Baskervilles by Sir Arthur

Conan Doyle is ninety-one years old and still being read and enjoyed. That is what makes it a classic.

There are two quotes concerning dogs that are better known than the stories from which they have been abstracted. "Yes," said Father Brown, "I always like a dog so long as he isn't spelt backwards." This was the opening line in "The Oracle of the Dog" by G. K. Chesterton (1915).

"Is there any point to which you wish to draw my attention?"

"To the curious incident of the dog in the night-time."

"The dog did nothing in the night-time."

"That was the curious incident," remarked Sherlock Holmes.

This famous conversational snippet is taken from the short story "Silver Blaze" contained in *The Memoirs of Sherlock Holmes* (1894) by Sir Arthur Conan Doyle.

A DOGGED LOOK AT LILIAN JACKSON BRAUN

Donna Huston Murray

nomenons are fascinating. Especially if they're in your chosen field.

I voluntarily moved on, and on and on—Scheherazade with knitting. Not because I wanted to know the ending, of course—I wanted to watch her hands.

My main lookout was for nauseatingly cute cat descriptions on every other page, at which point I planned to warm up my In-Sink-Erator. No surprise, Braun describes Koko and Yum Yum's activities with affection, but she staves off cat cringers with some refreshingly objective observation.

"At that moment Koko swaggered onto the porch with a show of authority and stared pointedly at Qwilleran.

" 'Excuse me while I feed the cats,' he said."

Perhaps they're looking regal and their owner would like to snap a picture. ". . . As soon as they saw him peer through the viewfinder, Yum Yum started scratching her ear with an idiot squint in her celestial blue eyes, while Koko rolled over and attended to the base of his tail with one leg pointing toward the firmament."

Often cat activities are small directional guides to steer the story. In *The Cat Who Sniffed Glue*

I'M A DOG PERSON. When somebody passed me a battle-weary copy of *The Cat Who Saw Red*, I thought, "Fat chance." But since I've been giving every Dashiell Hammett aspirant a chance for decades, I decided, "Why not?" Phe-

Qwilleran couldn't find the feline pair. A frantic search revealed signs of vandalism—an open desk drawer, scattered envelopes. Yum Yum, the drawer opener, was crouched on a shelf in her guilty position, "a compact bundle with elevated shoulders and haunches." Koko, who had licked all the envelopes, remained inscrutably silent.

"Qwilleran huffed into his moustache as the truth dawned upon him. Koko—with a glazed expression in his eyes and a peculiar splay-legged stance—was high on glue!"

The reporter than remembered that Koko "never did anything unusual without a good reason."

Speaking of cute, how about the eatery called Foo because the *D* fell off the sign? Or this exchange between Qwilleran and his best friend, Arch Riker.

RIKER: Don't forget I'm your boss.

QWILLERAN: Don't forget I'm your financial backer ... And if you don't start spelling my name right in my column, the interest rate is going up.

RIKER: I apologize. We gave the typesetter twenty lashes and an hour to get out of town.

On the scale of smiles, maybe a lopsided grin. But then, humor is indefensible, the most subjective ingredient of a highly subjective endeavor. The only option for an author is to amuse him or herself and leave the rest to luck.

Braun's characters also please readers by way of pleasing her. If Qwilleran and Polly Duncan and Arch Riker are caricatures, they're caricatures of our next-door neighbors; and each one benefits from unequivocal grandmotherly affection.

When Mrs. Cobb, an older woman with a penchant for pink, calls Qwill about noises in the night, Braun refrains from describing her as senile or silly. The woman "had a health problem, and the noises might very well be imaginary, the result of taking medication, but that made them no less terrifying." In other words, nobody's perfect.

Although some are less perfect than others. "Captain Phlogg never mixes, I'm glad to say. He's a stinker in more ways than one." That's as much nastiness as the author can manage.

Consequently, we don't just like the characters. We also like Lilian Jackson Braun.

Always the gracious hostess, Braun arranges for her readers to be comfortable. Tilt the light just right, fluff the cushions, draw the shades. She promises not to set off a frenzied rechecking of window

locks or make you worry about your blood pressure. Bad news will arrive with fair warning, but with so little fanfare that you may find yourself more preoccupied with whether Qwill will ever get his addition built than with what happened to the carpenter.

Meanwhile, if you step far enough into a Braun story, your disbelief will probably go the way of your wallet the time the pickpocket got it. A whole town that believes in UFOs? Sure, why not? "There was something in this north country—a kind of primeval force—that unsettled one's educated beliefs." In other words, hang in until she explains.

Naturally, the sticker, the butt of the jokes, the gimmick comes when Braun asks us to accept a cat who reads backwards and plays dictionary games. Quite a stretch, I admit—unless you've lived with a pet.

How does any animal lover defend the notion that Fido knows what he's thinking, or worse—vice versa? Probably it's just rapport developed over years, or maybe the pet is a medium for the owner's imagination. Either way, it's a safe bet that animal owners will have no problem believing Koko's contributions to Qwilleran's crime solutions. At the very least, Braun's readers want to allow the momentum to roll along undeterred.

And then there's the Effort Factor.

What with world news and everyday adult life, some days I'm simply too worn out to identify with a fictional superhero, male or female. Assuming the book I pick up has to be a mystery, which it does, a Cat Who offers a welcome departure. Jim Qwilleran is no white knight loner. He's an easygoing, undemanding, nice guy with loads of supportive friends and, of course, those inexplicable cats.

Maybe Braun's popularity says something about world news and everyday adult life.

Her detractors probably should be grateful that Qwill isn't meek.

THE STATUS OF WOMEN IN MYSTERY FICTION

K.K. Beck

LATELY, THE Mystery Writers of America have become embroiled in a controversy over the status of women mystery writers. Briefly, someone noticed that we don't win as many Edgars. Letters were written, a committee formed, a report emerged, it was analyzed and written about some more.

Far be it from me to criticize any of these ef-

forts. One of the chief advantages in being a writer is that it requires a minimum of meetings, reports, memos, and policy disputes. I am too grateful to those of us who can stand these activities to put down the fruits of their exhaustive labors.

The controversy did worry me some, however, because I am a member of the Edgar committee that is selecting the best paperback novel of 1986. (Okay, I did take on some committee work, but it mostly involves reading.) As I tackled the large carton full of paperbacks and the occasional smarmy letter from an editor (rather gratifying, as usually I have had to be the one writing smarmy letters to them), I found myself worried about being fair to my own sex. I also worried about being fair to men, who, no matter what we hear on the *Donahue* show, are a lot different than we are and can't help it.

Gender conscious is a term that came out of the MWA committee. Future judges were encouraged to be just that, but as this directive applied to the future, I felt justified in trying instead to become gender unconscious, and to try to judge each book on its own merits.

I soon discovered that it was impossible to become gender unconscious. While there are a lot of books that fall in the middle of the androgyny spectrum, it is a fact of life that many paperback books are marketed to one sex or the other. While I've read and admired Hammett, Chandler, Cain, and Ross Macdonald, I wasn't really very well read in recent hard-boiled detective fiction. When I started reading, I realized that the differences between men and women were even more profound than I had supposed. It was as if the authors of some of these works sat before their word processors with an IV drip full of testosterone next to them and the needle taped into their veins.

At the other end of the spectrum are, of course, intensely female books, including romantic suspense and another category which an editor has informed me is called "woman in danger" and is differentiated from romantic suspense by the fact that the heroine doesn't get a man at the end.

Differences between these two extremes became apparent at once. The hard-boiled hero is more likely to be Irish, Jewish, Italian, African American, or some combination of the above, allowing for a lot of good-natured ethnic slurs and racist badinage. The romantic heroines are all Anglo-Saxons with gray eyes and heart-shaped faces.

The hard-boiled heroes give themselves low marks in their personal lives, which are a shambles of broken dreams, too much booze, hangovers, and alimony, but are confident in their abilities to detect. The romantic heroines know they are nice people but the act of detecting makes them extremely nervous and they exhibit nervous symptoms while they work ... pounding hearts, dizzy spells, migraines, and every psychosomatic complaint short of a disfiguring skin condition.

Romantic heroines visit the ladies' room only to freshen up their light makeup, wash their hands, or bathe their wrists and temples in cool water when the rigors of detecting play hell with their nerves. Conversely, if a hard-boiled West Coast detective has to visit Tiajuana in hot pursuit and contracts a case of turista, we are likely to hear all about it.

But in no area is the differences in the subgenres more apparent than in relationships with the opposite sex. See if you can tell which of the following scenes I've put together is the male love scene and which is the female.

Number one:

When I got back to the apartment, there was a naked woman there. The face was vaguely familiar, as was the smell of formaldehyde, but it was that amazing body that tipped me off. It was old Doc Thorstensen's assistant down at the morgue. Debbie

had filled out that lab coat spectacularly, and I'd pretty much got the picture, but I didn't know that once released from the confines of starched linen, her lush, full breasts would stand out from her torso at a 45-degree angle. I don't know what kind of anti-grav device the little lady had going for her, but I liked the results.

"The manager let me in," she said. "I didn't think you'd mind."

"Okay by me," I leered, wondering if I should offer her a drink. Before I had a chance, she was all over me, tearing off my clothes and biting off the buttons of my shirt with her sharp little teeth.

Hey, I've had plenty of women in my time, but Debbie took me places I'd never been before. I taught her a few new tricks myself, if her incredible moans were to be believed. And I believed 'em.

Later, I popped open a can of Bud and switched on the basketball game. Debbie slipped behind the breakfast bar and cooked us a couple of steaks she'd thoughtfully brought along. This girl had class. She never even flinched as the sizzling grease spattered her naked chest. The Knicks won.

After we ate, we went at it again a few more times. She couldn't get enough, and she gave as good as she got. Then I got dressed and prepared to leave. After all, I was on a case. "Let yourself out," I said.

"Okay," she replied cheerfully. "I'll just take care of these dishes and sew the buttons back on your shirt before I go."

Occasionally, motivated no doubt by fear of a female editor, spouse, or lover, or by the need to consider himself a thoughtful, sensitive, emotionally mature and up-to-date kind of guy, the author will add a coda to this scene.

As I went out to the car, it occurred to me that Debbie was special. This could be it, the kind of caring, emotionally supportive relationship based on loving commitment that I'd been seeking since my ex-wife threw me over and out. And I knew Debbie understood my need for lots of space.

If this were real life we might say "Dream on, chump." While our protagonist is starting his car, Debbie would be sneering at his pathetic attempts at interior decoration, and measuring the windows in his apartment for new curtains. Later she'd get on the phone with her mother and/or best friend to talk about the new man in her life and what size wedding they should have.

Number two:

Sylvia felt dizzy and nervous, but she had to find out if Charles de Vere was as dangerous as she feared. The answer had to be in that exquisite Louis XVI desk. Trembling, she pulled open the drawer. There were the letters she knew he had hidden there.

"Aha!" She turned, startled, her heart churning at the sound of his low baritone, rich, like everything else about him. She noticed he was wearing a cream silk shirt, a tasteful pearl gray silk tie and an immaculately tailored Savile Row suit.

As he advanced toward her, she caught whiff of his cologne. At least forty dollars an ounce, she estimated. He seized her wrist, sending chills up and down her spine. Why, she wondered, did he have this strange effect on her? His mere touch made her weak and set the blood in her veins adance. This strange power he had over her was as mysterious as the true meaning of those letters.

"I—I," she stammered, but before she had a chance to come up with some plausible excuse for reading his mail, his lips sought hers in a lingering kiss. To her shame, her treacherous body began to respond then he pulled cruelly away.

"You could drive a man mad, Sylvia," he murmured huskily. "Go. Go before I . . ."

She ran from the room, leaving him staring moodily through the mullioned windows overlooking the immaculate gardens of his huge estate.

There were tears in her eyes . . . tears of frustration at her failed attempt to get a look at those letters and tears of anger at the strange emotions he dredged up from her soul. "I hate him, I hate him, I hate him," she said, stamping her foot. Deep down she wondered, if rich, powerful, handsome, brooding, rich, wealthy, rich Charles de Vere was ready for a serious commitment.

Here again, current sociological pressures may force the writer to add to this scene.

Of course, Sylvia didn't actually need Charles de Vere. After all, besides her career with the CIA, there was her well-established cover as the marketing VP of a Fortune 500 company. Not bad for a fresh-faced twenty-three-year-old from a small mining town in the West.

In real life, of course, Charles de Vere could be handsome or rich but definitely not both at the same time. Remember Aristotle Onassis? Even Jane Eyre didn't get her hands on Mr. Rochester until he was maimed.

In fact, brooding romantic heroes are about as scarce as cheerful, disease-free nymphomaniacs with cantilevered breasts. If men and women like them existed, they would very likely spend time with each other, and the rest of us would have to muddle on the way we always have. Which isn't all that badly considering, as proven by examples in modern detective fiction, men and women are members of distinctly separate species.

AMANDA CROSS:
Death in a Tenured Position
H.R.F. Keating

DEATH IN A TENURED POSITION (known in Britain, where tenure of an academic post is not such a fraught matter as in the States, as *A Death in the Faculty*) shows that in the 1980s the classic detective story still has life in it, though it is a life that needs more than mere nostalgic imitation to keep air flowing in and out of the lungs. It shows too—it is a notably well-written book—that the genre is, in these 1980s, attractive to the probingly intelligent, sensitive writer. "Amanda Cross" is the pseudonym of Carolyn Heilbron, Professor of English at Columbia University.

In the pages of this, her sixth detection work,

she brings together several strands of the genre into a well-woven and highly entertaining whole. Most obvious is the donnish school, with the Cross detective, Professor Kate Fansler, a worthy successor to Edmund Crispin's Professor Fen—if that is possible in a sleuth who in crossing the Atlantic has undergone a sex change and lost much of that fey British eccentricity (perhaps not such a bad thing).

Kate Fansler acts as a detective chiefly by applying the methods of literary criticism to puzzles of human behavior as particularly revealed by the advent of sudden death, in this case death by cyanide poisoning. Here she is explaining at last to a lawyer why the chief suspect is not guilty: "He didn't have the opportunity, or the means, to take your *sine qua non*, and he didn't even have mine: the motive." The motives of human beings are the stuff of the great novels that this professor of English spends her working life pondering, and they are equally the key to the murders she takes time off to solve. (She has that final necessary qualification for the amateur detective: private means).

Then, too, *Death in a Tenured Position* is a 1980s instance of the "backgrounder," popularized and established by Dorothy L. Sayers. Here the particular background is Harvard University with, behind it, academic life in general (described with knowledge and acuteness) and—an added important layer—what one might call the female status, as one is to avoid that equivocal word "feminism."

There is also, of course, the familiar contest between reader and writer which, however attenuated in form, cannot be omitted from any book in the detection mold. Here Amanda Cross sets a pretty puzzle indeed: who administered that cyanide to the newly appointed woman professor at stuffy Harvard, and why was her body found in the men's room, let alone why had she been found dead drunk in a bath in a woman's room together with an out-and-out libber sometime earlier? Without giving much away, I can say that the answer is the very least likely person.

Finally, our old friend that Great Detective here makes a ghostly appearance. Ghostly, I say, because Amanda Cross treats this mythic figure with a decidedly wry reverence. Three times in the course of the book is Kate Fansler given the attribute, but on each occasion it is implied that she both is and is not such a figure. She is, because that is the role she may be seen as inheriting; she is not, because in these 1980s no one, perhaps, can be. The age of the hero, even the female hero, has departed. Now we knowing readers think, possibly wrongly, that we have learnt too much to be able to believe in simple heroes.

The author's yet more knowing, yet cooler eye looks more positively, however, at everything her book encompasses, which is what makes it more than a mere imitation. The Harvard background is not offered simply as interesting in itself, but critically—very critically most of the time—as a still-active bastion of male prejudices.

The same cool, appraising, deliciously sharp eye is brought to the central subject, the female role in the world. A true academic is above partisanship so, finally, we hear Kate answering another out-and-out libber named Joan Theresa: 'Is Fansler your husband's name?' 'No. It's my father's name. Theresa, I take it, is your mother's.' Long live the assessing, balanced novelist in detection's pages.

JOHN DICKSON CARR:
The Magician of the Locked Room
Douglas G. Greene

JOHN DICKSON CARR was the greatest plot-magician detective fiction has ever produced. He was the unrivaled master of the locked-room mystery—a man is seen entering a room; no one else is in the room, and all the doors and windows are not only locked but watched by witnesses; yet, a short while later, his corpse is found stabbed or shot or poisoned. The solution to this situation was child's play for John Dickson Carr. During his writing career he devised more than fifty different ways of entering and exiting such a chamber, and (needless to say) Carr never used such ancient devices as secret passages to explain his locked-room murders.

Moreover, Carr wrought many changes on what has been called the Impossible Crime. A body is found alone in a building surrounded by snow or sand, with only the footprints of the victim leading to the door or windows. How could anyone have approached the victim without leaving a trace? In one of Carr's books, a young woman dashes through the front door of a house and totally disappears, leaving behind only her shoes, coat, and a mysterious bronze lamp from ancient Egypt. In another novel, a man dives, fully clothed, in a swimming pool, and onlookers see his clothes gradually drift to the surface. When the diver does not reappear, the authorities drain the pool and find no trace of him. In a radio play called "Cabin B-13," a newlywed goes on shipboard, and leaves her husband, and her luggage, in Cabin B-13. When she returns, husband, luggage, and even the cabin itself have vanished. Witnesses tell the captain that there never was a Cabin B-13 and that the panic-stricken bride was never accompanied by a husband. And yet, as Carr makes clear, the young woman was telling the truth. This situation was so terrifying—and Carr's explanation for the impossibility so convincing—that two feature-length movies have been based on his script.

Carr's plot fertility seemed limitless—he wrote stories about an apartment that disappears, about a murder in a nonexistent street, about the pistol fired by an empty pair of gloves, and about the man who receives a call from his dead wife over a telephone that is detached from the wall.

John Dickson Carr was a leading writer of the Golden Age of Detective Fiction which reached its height in the 1930s. He was always classified with Agatha Christie, Dorothy L. Sayers, and Ellery Queen among the most accomplished detective story writers. The Golden Age emphasized fair play to the reader. A detective story was fundamentally a puzzle in which the author tried to fool the reader by clues that were given to the reader and the detective at the same time.

The detective story (said John Dickson Carr) is a conflict between criminal and detective in which the criminal, by means of some ingenious device—alibi, novel murder method, or what

— 103 —

you like—remains unconvicted or even unsuspected until the detective reveals his identity by means of evidence which has also been conveyed to the reader.... [Besides fair play, the detective novel] will contain the quality of sound plot construction. And it will contain the quality of ingenuity.... But though this quality of ingenuity is not necessary to the detective story as such, you will never find the great masterpiece without it. Ingenuity lifts the thing up; it is triumphant; it blazes, like a diabolical lightning flash, from beginning to end.

Carr's ingenuity lay not only in the locked rooms and impossible disappearances, but also in the atmosphere of his books. Sayers and Christie as well as other luminaries like Ngaio Marsh, Margery Allingham, and Michael Innes wrote detective stories as comedies of manners often set in cozy country houses. Carr, on the other hand, wrote detective stories as gothic terror. Carr suggested throughout the first two thirds of the book that only a witch, a vampire, or a ghost could have committed the seemingly impossible crime—and he titled his books to hint at the supernatural: *It Walks by Night, He Who Whispers, The Hungry Goblin, Hag's Nook, In Spite of Thunder, Night at the Mocking Widow, The Witch of the Low-Tide, The Man Who Could Not Shudder*, and so on. "Let there be a spice of terror," he said, "of dark skies and evil things." He filled his stories with ancient lore—swords and occult playing cards, accounts of witchcraft and curses, crimes that repeat themselves generation after generation, eerie wax museums and a castle on the Rhine shaped like a skull.

Striding through his books, bringing order and reason to the world, are Carr's great detectives: Henri Bencolin, Dr. Gideon Fell, and Sir Henry Merrivale—the last appearing in books under Carr's nonsecret pseudonym of Carter Dickson. Carr's detectives act like exorcists. They bid the demons that infest the opening parts of his books to be off, and the order of the universe is restored.

John Dickson Carr was born in Uniontown, Pennsylvania, in 1906, the son of a lawyer who rose to be a Democratic congressman. The fact that his father was a Democrat is ironic, since John himself became a rock-ribbed reactionary, or (as he described himself) "a barnacle-covered Tory." As a boy he dreamed of swashbuckling adventures, of horsemen galloping by lone trees, of, indeed, almost anything that would remove him from small-town life. A precocious child, he had his own newspaper column at the age of fourteen, and among the most revealing remarks are his dreams of far-off romance:

> We thought of trips to Europe; of solitary rambles among the gaunt, crumbling ruins of ancient Rome; the cool, airy emptiness of a languorous Egyptian night; of glassy moonlit waters beneath the Southern Cross; of all the thousand scenes that bring with them the faint, musty breath of the past; suggestions of forgotten splendor and dynasties that are dust.

Carr's first stories were published in his high school newspaper—rather awkward combinations of Edgar Allan Poe and Sax Rohmer—but one of them, "The Ruby of Rameses" is important as his first attempt to place a corpse in a locked room. He continued writing when he attended the Hill School in Pottstown, Pennsylvania, and his stories were a little better. At Haverford College he edited the literary magazine and did much better indeed—writing whole issues himself, under his own name, anonymously, under pseudonyms, and sometimes even under the names of his unsuspecting classmates—a trick that can give bibliographers a headache. His Haverford stories were about evenly divided among ghost stories, detective stories, and historical romances (mainly about lost causes and dangerous women—whom he found amazingly attractive but destructive). Among these stories was a series about Monsieur Henri Bencolin of the Sureté, which included an impossible disappearance and more locked rooms, most notably one about murder in a locked railway carriage. Young Carr also wrote poetry during these years reflecting his youthful romanticism:

> In dim and dark Atlantis,
>   Where now the white shark gleams,
> A marble monster comes to life
>   Within a world of dreams;
> In brooding old Atlantis
>   The ghosts of temples rise,
> And, tipped with blood, the shattered sun
>   Along its roof-top dies.
>
> I loved in lost Atlantis;
>   I was a prince's son,

And all my courts were ringed with spears
    That spoke of battles won;
And loud my chariot wheels rang out
    Across the flaming day,
And all the glassy streets were bright
    With swords to clear the way.
I loved in that pale city,
    Whose boast was spent and done,
I loved in lost Atlantis
    A priestess of the sun!

Carr never graduated from Haverford. He consistently failed every mathematics course he took, and for the rest of his life he expressed his hatred of math—''the last refuge of the feeble-minded,'' he called it.

His father sent John to Paris in 1927 to study at the Sorbonne, but that's one thing he did not do there. Instead, he decided to become a novelist, writing and destroying a historical novel, which he later said was ''filled with gadzookses and sword-play.'' Either in Paris, or shortly after he returned to Uniontown, he decided to write a locked-room novel about Bencolin. This was published in 1930 under the title *It Walks by Night* and was an instant success. It began with a quotation from a fictitious manuscript:

And not least foul among these night-monsters ... is a certain shape of evil hue which by day may not be recognized, inasmuch as it may be a man favoured of looks, or a fair and smiling woman; but by night becomes a misshapen beast with blood-bedabbled claws. So I say to you, even you who live in the city of Paris, when your fire burns low by night, and you hear a gentle tapping of fingers at the window-pane, do not open your door to this supposed traveller.

Carr's early books all have this Poe-esque feeling of creepiness and madness, and even Bencolin is described as satanic in his appearance and his methods.

In 1930, on his way back from a holiday in France paid for by the advance on royalties from *It Walks by Night*, he met Clarice Cleaves, an Englishwoman from Bristol. They were married in 1932, and early in 1933 they moved to England—the country, John believed, where the true tradition of detective fiction could be found. His book called

Hag's Nook, published in 1933, begins with an atmospheric depiction of England:

There is something spectral about the drowsy beauty of the English countryside; in the lush dark grass, the evergreens, the grey church-spire, and the meandering white road. To an American, who remembers his own brisk concrete highways clogged with red filling-stations and the fumes of traffic, it is particularly pleasant.... [He] watched the sun through the latticed windows, and the dull red berries glistening in the yew tree, with a feeling which can haunt the traveller only in the British Isles. A feeling that the earth is old and enchanted.... For France changes, like a fashion, and seems no older than last season's hat. In Germany even the legends have a bustling clockwork freshness, like a walking toy from Nuremburg. But this English earth seems (incredibly) even older than its ivy-bearded towers. The bells at twilight seem to be bells across the centuries; there is a great stillness, through which ghosts step; and Robin Hood has not strayed from it even yet.

By this time Carr had tired of the mephistophelean Bencolin, and he introduced a new detective, the gargantuan Dr. Gideon Fell, with his jovial laughter, his scatterbrained approach to sleuthing, and his love of beer and pipes. Carr described Dr. Fell as resembling Old King Cole.

Carr had a regimen of writing between three and five books a year during the 1930s, and gradually he became recognized. The breakthrough came when Dorothy L. Sayers reviewed one of his books in the following words:

Mr. Carr can lead us away from the small, artificial, brightly-lit stage of the ordinary detective plot into the menace of outer darkness. He can create atmosphere with an adjective, and make a picture from a wet iron railing, a dusty table, a gas-lamp blurred by the fog. He can alarm with an illusion or delight with a rollicking absurdity.... In short he can write—not merely in the negative sense of observing the rules of syntax, but in the sense that every sentence gives a thrill of positive pleasure.

In 1936, Sayers sponsored him as the only American member of London's famed Detection Club, made up of the important British detective novelists. By this time, the creepiness of his earlier books had been replaced by a *New Arabian Nights* atmosphere. Robert Louis Stevenson in *New Arabian Nights* had described London as Baghdad-on-the-Thames in which (like Haroun al-Raschid in the original *Arabian Nights*) people could open any door and find adventure. Carr's characters seek what he called "adventure in the Grand Manner." They long to meet "an adventuress, sable and all, who slips into a railway compartment, whispers, 'Six of diamonds—north tower at midnight—beware of Orloff!' " And just as Carr was able to combine Poe-esque horror with straight detection in his Bencolin novels, he combined detection with adventure and a sense of wonder in his books of the later 1930s.

During this decade Carr began a series of comic detective novels about Sir Henry Merrivale. Wildly undignified, Sir Henry addresses a jury as "my fatheads"; he calls the prime minister "Horseface" and a member of the government "Squiffy." He enters a case, as Carr remarked in a letter, "with a rush and a crash, heels in the air." During his investigating career, H.M. drives a train and hits a cow, launches a ship by bopping a mayor on the head with a champagne bottle, disguises himself as a Muslim holy man, cheats at golf, and takes singing lessons with disastrous effects on the ears of everyone in the vicinity. In short, Sir Henry Merrivale is probably the funniest detective ever invented. But he has "a childlike, deadly brain," and like Bencolin and Dr. Fell, he specializes in Impossible Crimes. Probably his greatest case is *The Judas Window*, in which he proves that every room, no matter how carefully sealed, has a window to let a murderer enter.

Carr was visiting his parents in the United States in 1939 when Germany and Russia invaded Poland, and he hurried back to Britain to see the war out in the country that he had adopted. "A gallant and un-called for gesture," wrote Val Gielgud of the BBC. Gielgud, Sir John Gielgud's brother, got Carr a position writing propaganda plays for BBC radio—and occasional detective thrillers, including one in which the BBC announcer turned out to be the murderer.

In 1940 the Carrs had just purchased a new house in the Maida Vale section of the north London, when a German bomb took off the back of it. Clarice went back to her parents in Bristol and stored their surviving furniture there, but John, who was working for the BBC, moved into the London's Savage Club—where another bomb again took off a wall. He wrote to American correspondents that it was getting monotonous to live in places that resembled open dollhouses. He joined Clarice in Bristol, but the Germans seemed to be dogging them. This time a bomb destroyed their salvaged furniture. Carr remarked that "I can imagine the triumphant German airman hurrying back to Goering and saying, 'Ich habe busted der resten der furniture von Carr!' And Goering swelling under his medals and saying 'Gut! Sie wilst der iron cross getten! Heil Hitler!' "

In 1942 the American government called him home to sign up for military service, and while waiting for the government's decision, Carr wrote a number of classic radio plays for the famous CBS program *Suspense*. Finally, the government, in perhaps a predictably bureaucratic decision, decided to send him back to London to work for the BBC. During these years he also continued to write detective novels, though at a slower pace—only two a year. *He Who Whispers,* published shortly after the war, features impossible murder on a guarded tower; it is a marvelous combination of supernatural atmosphere with fair-play detection. Carr resigned from the BBC in 1946 to begin gathering material for his authorized biography of Sir Arthur Conan Doyle—a book which is still in many ways the classic study of the creator of Sherlock Holmes.

John Dickson Carr did not like the postwar world. It was too busy, too structured to supply the kind of romance, the sort of *New Arabian Nights* adventures that he valued. He was restless. He returned to the United States in 1948, but then moved every few years—to Tangier (on several occasions), to suburban New York, back to England—twice announcing that he was going to become a British subject, then complaining that taxes under Labour governments were too high.

As a writer, Carr also retreated from the modern world. He described the mid-twentieth century as bleak and gray. Because he had come to believe that adventure in the Grand Manner could be found only in the past, he began writing historical detective novels. Three of them are stories of time travel: a modern hero, like Carr himself, longs to return to the past. In 1950 he published the wonderfully titled *The Devil in Velvet,* set during the reign of Carr's favorite king, the Merry Monarch, Charles II. The next year he wrote another excellently titled book, *The Bride of Newgate,* this one set in Regency England. Carr was still fascinated by tricks and impossibilities, and his swordsmen and dandies were as adept at explaining locked rooms as Dr. Fell and Sir Henry Merrivale.

Beginning in the early 1960s, Carr suffered from various illnesses, and the quality of his books fell off. His enthusiasm was gone, and his writing became mechanical. Nevertheless, he was still an ingenious concoctor of mystifying plots, especially in *The House at Satan's Elbow,* which contains one

of his simplest (and most practical) explanations of crime in a locked room. In 1967 he left England for good and moved to Greenville, South Carolina, where he continued to write and became a local celebrity. He died there in 1977, at the age of seventy.

John Dickson Carr's career showed the power of ingenuity and imagination, of plot construction and atmosphere. Above all, he enriched the detective novel, which he called "The Great Game, the Grand Game, the Grandest Game in the World."

THE DOUBLEDAY CRIME CLUB
1928–1991

Ellen Nehr

DANIEL LONGWELL, production manager and advertising director of Doubleday, Doran, returned from a trip to England in 1927 with a suitcase full of British editions of Edgar Wallace, an author who was already on Doubleday's list. Longwell convinced Nelson Doubleday to start a subscription sales service of mystery stories that within a year evolved into the Crime Club. Although American publishers had been reprinting British "thriller" authors on an intermittent basis for some time, none had made a commitment to bring out hardcover editions of mysteries on a regular basis. Books by Edgar Wallace, who was billed as "king of the mystery writers," were best sellers even after his death in 1932, since several were finished by his secretary. In five years the Crime Club alone published thirty-four titles as well as his autobiography.

The first Crime Club book, published on April 1, 1928, was *The Desert Moon Mystery* by Kay Cleaver Strahan and was edited by Ogden Nash,

who had been a member of the editorial staff for six years.

In those early years Doubleday had eight salesmen whose job was to sell Crime Club books to bookstores. They were successful since bookstore owners were pleased to participate because they got a bonus for each subscription entered. One title a month was chosen as a Crime Club Selection by a group of judges that included a critic, an author, and a bookseller. They were bulk shipped to each store, which then sent them on to the customer about two weeks before they went on sale to the general public. In 1928 each subscriber received a copy of *Dramatic Crimes of 1927: A Study in Mystery and Detection.* This was an experiment with true crime, and after a couple of other attempts, the idea was dropped. Subscribers also received the *Crime Club News* monthly. All advertisements and end-paper notes were signed *The Mastermind.* At the end of each book was a warning: "Whether you were keen enough to solve this Crime Club mystery in its early stages, or whether the author succeeded in keeping you in suspense up to the last chapter, the Mastermind requests that you add to the next reader's enjoyment by remembering that—CRIME CLUB READERS NEVER TELL.''

The first two books by Leslie Charteris, *Meet the Tiger* and *Daredevil,* were both published in 1929. He was to become the author with the longest consecutive relationship with the Crime Club; his sixtieth book was published in 1973. The first and only book of poetry published by the Crime Club was *Hell in Harness* (1929), an oversize 9¼-by-6-inch tome that had a yellow-orange cloth cover with a pasted-on two-by-two label, and was dedicated to Ogden Nash.

Rufus King's first book, *The Fatal Kiss Mystery,* was published in 1928, but it was his *Murder by the Clock* the next year that Doubleday promoted heavily. Soon he was being referred to as the American Edgar Wallace and during the next decade was one of the Crime Club's most salable authors, with especially designed window display posters that were shipped to selected stores, who then shipped them on schedule to other establishments.

The publishing business was affected by a mild market elevation in 1931, which was the final flutter before the depths of the Depression. This led Doubleday to commission and announce fifty-two titles, mainly by British authors and almost all in the ''thriller'' category. Shortly thereafter, all Crime Club books were reduced to one dollar each, a price level that lasted about thirteen months. A beginning artist who had been hired by what was then Doubleday, Doran at a salary of twenty-five dollars a week in 1928 had been reduced, through two pay cuts, to eighteen dollars a week, but she, like all employees, kept her job.

The literary quality of the Crime Club books, now quite familiar with their gunman logo and the sometimes splashy jackets, was outstanding. Margery Allingham, Mignon G. Eberhart, Anthony Berkeley, David Frome, Nancy Barr Mavity, Sax Rohmer, Austin J. Small, John Stephen Strange, Van Wyck Mason, and Carolyn Wells were all on the list. As it grew, the Crime Club brought out something for everyone, with more American names and locales used as well as dust-jacket art. One of the artists, R. F. Schabelitz, later on, with his wife, Willetta Ann Barber, was to write and illustrate four Crime Club novels in which events as seen by the artist character provided the clues.

Crime Club books were not only well made, with sewn signatures and quality cloth covers, but artists including Frederic Dorr Steele were commissioned to provide jackets, interior designs, and chapter headings. Floor plans of mansions as well as maps were frequently inserted, while illustrated end papers were an occasional bonus. In 1933 the first of many Boris Artzybasheff jackets was designed for John W. Vandercook's *Murder in Trinidad,* and with it the Crime Club entered a new era. It wasn't long before jacket art was superimposed on the cloth spines of the books and frequently used as decoration on the title page. Crime Club books became works of art.

Unfortunately, the era of using coated papers or even substantial paper stock for the jackets had not yet arrived, and now finding jackets in even good condition is a matter of luck. Those that were preserved often were books owned by the rental libraries which went to great efforts to protect their stock, so collecting jackets is a tradeoff for impeccable condition.

The Crime Club introduced Van Wyck Mason, who provided international intrigue with hints of a forthcoming war. Allingham's Albert Campion gave mysteries an aristocratic touch, and Georgette Heyer, even with her bigoted attitudes, provided an amusing mix of amateur and Scotland Yard sleuthing. Clyde Clason's professor Theocritus Lucius Westborough was as delightfully eccentric and erudite as any reader could ask for, while Kathleen Moore Knight's Elisha Macomber, the Harvard-educated island fisherman and selectman of Martha's Vineyard, gave Phoebe Atwood Taylor's Asey Mayo a nice bit of competition. Stuart Palmer, Helen Reilly, Todd Downing, Dorothy Gardiner, and Virginia Rath supplemented the list but never fully supplanted the affection mystery readers had for British-sited stories. A wacky, oddball detective who claimed a certain audience was Baron Van Kaz, a creation of Darwin L. Teilhet, while Frank Packard's Jimmy Dale, a pseudo-crook, had his own audience. Jonathan Latimer was an immediate hit with the books as well as several films with his hard-boiled detective Bill Crane.

During the early years editors served the Crime Club for only short periods before they went on to more literary assignments. But in 1935 Isabelle Taylor, who had been a clerk in the Doubleday Book Shops during the Christmas season, was hired as secretary to Jim Poling, then the Crime Club editor.

She became his assistant, and when he was promoted a few years later, she took his place and held the job for over thirty years. It was her astute flair for recognizing talent in new authors that found Margaret Millar, Melba Marlett, Doris Miles Disney, Constance and Gwenyth Little, Aaron Marc Stein, Mabel Seeley, Hilea Bailey, Christopher Hale, and Charlotte Murray Russell.

In 1943 the Crime Club introduced Crime Club Bullseyes. These designs indicated the kind of stories being presented. They were printed on the spine and dust-jacket flaps as well as the bound-in internal blurbs. Some examples were a black owl: character and atmosphere; a grinning skull: humor and homicide; a black automatic with rays from the muzzle indicating that a bullet had just been shot: fast action; and a man's face, holding a cigarette in his mouth and wearing a soft felt hat on his head: some like them tough. With minor additions and deletions they were retained until 1969. In 1943, due to the paper shortage, all Crime Club books were printed on thinner paper, with narrow gutters and edges; both the height and width were reduced, and they were printed using smaller type and less substantial bindings.

After the war a disastrous purchase of highly acidic paper resulted in the production of books over a three-year period that are now browning and so brittle as to be almost unreadable. Doubleday did increase the height of the books but never came back to high quality paper, wide margins, or even larger type.

Emphasis on new authors seemed to be the order of the day in the fifties and sixties since many of the older ones had either stopped writing or had been lured away by other publishing houses with promises of larger print runs, more advertising, and the ultimate lure, more money. For the first time, authors were considering paperback reprints as part of the contract package, and Doubleday didn't have a reprint house. Between the American and British pool of new talent, the following names began to appear: Anthony Price, Ellis Peters, Ruth Rendell, John Ball, Leslie Egan, Joe L. Hensley, Catherine Aird, Alexandria Roudybush, and H.R.F. Keating.

For the first time, women artists were designing many of the dust jackets. Vera Bock produced the most amusing ones using multiple plot elements abstracted from the stories as well as tampering with the gunman logo in deliciously amusing ways. The Doubleday art department was flexible, so with artists on their staff such as Edward Gorey and freelance commissions given to Margot Tomes, Paul Galdone, Andy Warhol and Margo Herr, the jackets were as good as the books. The innovative use of the decorative symbols on the spine was an excellent selling point, as was the price of $2.50 since the Crime Club maintained a lower price structure long after competitors had raised theirs.

It was during the early fifties that thirty-six books per year became the norm. This count was continued until 1991, when the Crime Club published only twenty-seven books. Then, after sixty-three years and 2,486 books, the Crime Club ended.

TRADITIONALLY YOURS
(On the Face, Form, and Function of the Traditional Mystery)
Marilis Hornidge

ONCE THEY WERE ALL CALLED "detective stories." When you read about the genre, that's the phrase you run into most often. It's what Agatha Christie called them—so did Dorothy Sayers, so did Howard Haycraft, who wrote more on the subject (and better) than anyone else in the Golden Age and just after. So still does Julian Symons, who many think is a reincarnation of H.H. Then they were "murder mysteries" or "crime novels," and finally, my pick, just *mysteries,* a word that says it all.

Mysteries come in varied flavors for varying tastes, just like ice cream. There are many out there who prefer the classic, the traditional ... as the saying goes, "plain vanilla." Any true ice cream devotee knows, however, that perfect vanilla is the most elusive of all flavors as well as the all-time favorite—the hardest to define, the quested for, the basis of many arguments.

So is it with the traditional mystery and its followers: that's what this section is all about, the traditional mystery, where it came from, what it is, and how it got that way.

Any mystery reader can tell you what a traditional mystery *isn't.* First, traditional is not the professional detective. I know, that leaves out a whole bunch from Sherlock to Spenser in the hard to medium-boiled private investigator, and Amelia Butterworth (You never heard of her? The heroine of Anna Katharine Green's 1897 best seller *That Affair Next Door*? What kind of mystery buff are you, for Agatha's sake?) to Sue Grafton's Kinsey Milhone. It also drops all police procedurals (sorry, Dell Shannon) and, as long as I am licensed to be picky, all mysteries whose central character is a policeman, whether he's an Inspector Alleyn or Inspector Maigret. I am ambivalent about lawyers and judges as well.

Traditional is not the serial killer or the great courtroom drama (although both may play bit parts) or the big-city crime scene.

It is not the espionage tale or the political twister.

To quote experienced writer *and* reader Barbara Michaels, "I know it when I read it": all broadly read mystery buffs would agree. When you get to page six and your shoulders automatically settle back in your chair and you tuck your feet up comfortably under you and make sure whatever you are eating or drinking is directly at hand so that you won't even have to look up from the page, five will get you ten, it's a traditional. And if, like many of us, you tend to be a fast reader, when you find you are slowing down because it's so good and you don't want to hurry because then it will be over much too soon ... *then* you know it's the REAL THING.

If you enjoy separating things into ages or stages, the traditional mystery has played a big part in all three stages of the modern mystery, which I consider to be the Golden Age (1920 until the late 1940s), the Grand Plateau (the 1950s until the late 1970s) and the New Age (the 1980s and off into the future).

The Golden Age was exactly what it says, a time when the rules were just being set, when everything was bright and untried, when the sky seemed to be the limit and readership would burgeon forever.

The Grand Plateau refined the traditions and provided a firm foundation, hung a few ornaments here and there, and ignored the critics who frequently announced its demise.

The New Age tests the limits, experiments with combinations, tries out new disciplines, and gets the argumentative juices flowing within the form itself.

All mysteries experience these stages, of course, but the differences gradually building from one to another are perhaps easiest to see in the traditional mysteries, the canaries in the mine of trends and changes to come. Robin Winks, erudite and opinionated on this subject, emphatically does *not* call the reading of mystery fiction an escape, considering that the term denigrates both the form and the reader. It is, according to him, reading for engagement, reading to turn the engine on, not off, an active sport in which the brain takes part, trying to get there before the designated sleuth figure does rather than mere passive watching (as in the oft-accursed TV). Reader identification, that easy-to-say/hard-to-define quality that accounts for so much of the tremendous pull mysteries exert over their aficionados, runs deepest in the fabric of the traditional mystery. Imagination is one thing, involvement is another: traditional mysteries truly involve the reader.

The only bone of contention might be: do the Golden Age of the Mystery in general and that of the traditional mystery overlap? It depends on who is doing the looking and from what vantage point in the twentieth century.

Howard Haycraft in his *Murder for Pleasure* sets the overall date as 1918 to 1930: Ellery Queen in an introduction to a volume of short pieces called *The Golden Age: Part I* puts it from 1900 to the late 1930s: the modern compiling-duo of Muller/Pronzini in their introduction to *The Web She Weaves* sets the dates between 1925 and 1940. Before this, everyone agrees, the mystery was almost exclusively a problem in analytic analysis. Few of the mysteries from *that* Pleistocene era survive as anything except period pieces and curiosities. There would be no real argument as to who would be included as Golden Agers in both forms though—Agatha Christie, Dorothy Sayers, H. C. Bailey, Anthony Berkeley, Marie Belloc Lowndes, Mignon Eberhart.

During the Golden Age of the traditional mystery, the center of the plot—the crime—moved closer into the light of the everyday ... not everybody's everyday, mind you, but a lot of people's. Agatha Christie brought murder home to the village, the early Ellery Queen chased it all over New York—both city and state, and Mary Roberts Rinehart gave it a whole new look, the so-called Had-I-But-Known school—mocked by critics but adored by readers ... readers who toward the late part of

this Golden Age were more and more often female. Male writers, and presumably readers, continued to stick to the detective novel with its stalwart hero—and sometimes in the background, an adoring and oft-rescued damsel. Certainly women writers like Christie and Sayers and Josephine Tey wrote male detective heroes, but then, women have always read ''men's'' books even when there was no vice for their versa. Still, there flourished Christie's evergreen Miss Marple, Sayers's indomitable Miss Climpson with her detective bureau of elderly and underused ladies, not to mention Harriet Vane, and Tey's Miss Pym, that most disarming of sleuths-in-academe.

I stick to my guns—a professional detective as central character, no matter how charming, doth not a traditional make. The roots of the traditional mystery entwine with others of the Golden Age of the mystery in general, but the tree itself is only a sapling, overshadowed at this stage by its more robust neighbors.

With the last of the 1920s the playing field of the mystery as a whole began to shift, moving across the Atlantic with S. S. Van Dine's smarty-pants amateur sleuth Philo Vance, a translation from the Wimsey, as it were, and the early Ellery Queen, who was to prove a transitional figure between the age of gold and the next era, which I think of, for the traditional mystery especially, as a time of consolidation, cultivation, and culmination ... that mystery's equivalent of the Long Afternoon of Europe between the wars, the era I call the Grand Plateau.

From the 1930s to the late 1950s, the traditional mystery blossomed and burgeoned, was grafted on to other genres (sometimes successfully, sometimes not), and developed subgenres of its own. Mysteries, during the bombings of London in World War II, were the preferred reading of all who spent hours, sometimes nights in bomb shelters. The inexpensive paperback came into its own ... and the most purchased, requested, and read-to-shreds by the armed forces as well as those at home were mysteries of all kinds. In such an atmosphere, the traditional mystery—the puzzle-story involving real people—found an even broader audience and was never a stepchild again ... except to the critics, who persisted in not taking it seriously.

There were a number of mystery authors who came of age during this era. For example, Margery Allingham's Albert Campion, who might have been one of Peter Wimsey's younger cousins at first, grew up as she did . . . from a charming dilettante in *The Crime at Black Dudley* (1929) to a clever but more human figure in *The Tiger in the Smoke* (1952). Ellery Queen became not only less of a motor-mouthed wiseguy, he acquired a new respect for his police-inspector father . . . who wound up with a couple of faster-paced but equally intricate adventures of his own when he retired . . . just compare *The French Powder Mystery* (1930) to *The House of Brass* (1968). There were excursions into the world of mystery/comedy like the books of Craig Rice, and mystery set against a specialized background such as the adventures of Clayton Rawson's magician the Great Merlini. John Dickson Carr took the traditional locked-room puzzle to its furthest reaches and added the history-revisited mystery to the shelves, while Phoebe Atwood Taylor gave new style to the American regional and Edmund Crispin's Gervase Fen upheld the standard of Murder Most British—Traditional Style.

The New Age, a phrase which holds for many overtones of the offbeat, the nontraditional, the semi-occult, begins with the 1980s. The word itself begins to bite two ways—pro and con. "We need to see all things in a new light," say the rebels. "We need to get back to our basic roots," say the upholders of the standards. The reader sighs a little, tries a few, and then smiles. *Plus ça change, plus c'est la même chose*—the traditional mystery in its new clothes is the basis of the upswing in popularity which the mystery enjoys today (much to the amazement of critics who keep on saying that the mystery is on the way out).

Here come the new-old small towns all over the world where things happen in a strange and often deadly way; here are the people grounded in ordinary life to whom such things happen. Walk the streets of Rita Mae Brown or Sharyn McCrumb's small southern towns and feel the watching eyes. Go to exotic places with Aaron Elkins's anthropologist Gideon Oliver or to dog shows with Susan Conant's Holly Winter and look on while everyday things turn weird. Try an antiques hunt with Jonathan Gash's irrepressible Lovejoy, or go backward in time with Ellis Peters's Brother Cadfael. The very best vanilla, to return to my original metaphor, with rainbow stripes. And irresistible, as may be demonstrated by the fact that books thought of as

"just" mysteries have turned up on that marquee of marquees, the best seller list, a fact that is shrugged off by the Edmund Wilson wannabes.

Maybe it's just as well to note here that a great many books on that same best seller list are written by authors who are rarely slotted into the mystery category but who are writing in the mystery format . . . the *traditional* mystery format. Mary Higgins Clark comes to mind as does John Grisham and Stephen King and Robin Cook. The books are called by other names—romantic suspense, thrillers, courtroom novels, but you know what they say about roses by any other name.

The only exercise more delightful than setting up categories to fit ideas into is setting up rules for those same categories to conform to. Everyone has taken a shot at doing rules for a mystery. Dorothy Sayers did it, S. S. Van Dine did it, Howard Haycraft did it. As one who reads mysteries of all sorts for pleasure as well as for review, making a set of rules to define the traditional mystery has provided much soul-searching, hours of delightful reading and rereading cleverly disguised as research, and long discussions with similarly inclined friends. We mystery readers are at one and the same time a clannish and an enthusiastic lot. When we find an author we enjoy, we share the title and author, if not the actual book, with others of our ilk— knowing that the enthusiasm will be returned while the book may not. (We are also known to be opinionated and free with those opinions—"mouthy" this is known as in my neck of the woods.)

The following is a general consensus:

The traditional mystery has an amateur detective. That can be stretched to include an insurance investigator, possibly a researcher in a law office, but that's about as close as it gets to the minions of the law.

The traditional mystery is set firmly in its place, preferably not a big city, but possibly a neighborhood in one—not an exotic personal setting, someplace in which the reader just might feel comfortable . . . for a while at least.

The traditional mystery is about people, not stereotypes, but real people. The emphasis is on them rather than on some object or grand theory or atmosphere.

The traditional mystery is not a horror novel. The physical and emotional content is not overtly violent—although it may be even more disturbing when thought about later, and no blood-and-gore-all-over-the-floor descriptions either.

The traditional mystery plays fair in the old-fashioned sense of the term. All the central characters, murderer and murderee included, are introduced as soon as possible after the story opens, the method of murder is not some wildly arcane poison or outlandish weapon, and all clues are right there in black and white, every one of them shared with the reader.

And as a footnote, one friend stated with a gimlet eye firmly fixed on me; "There really should be a cat, my dear, possibly a dog . . . who is still there *in good shape* at the end." This is a lady who firmly and inexorably put down the latest book by a mutually favored author because the main character's dog was killed in mid-book, and would read no further. I tried to explain how necessary it was to the plot. She politely disagreed and has not trusted that author since.

But the ultimate and universal rules are the pair that cover all mysteries with any chance of lasting beyond current fads: the mystery must play fair and it must be enjoyably readable. In all my reading for this essay, it was not amazing to find that many classic traditional mysteries from the past had aged well . . . although it *was* occasionally surprising which ones did and which ones didn't.

It usually boiled down to that most elusive of reason, style. If I were asked to explain the differences in style between the three ages of the traditional mystery, I would simply ask the questioner to picture in the mind's eye the figures of three charmers—all considered knockouts in their day: Lillie Langtry, Marilyn Monroe, and Jane Fonda. The subject could be an essay on its own, had I but world enough and time—and about ten more pages.

As to content, the traditional mystery is the whodunit: it's also the whydunit and wheredunit and, very often whowuzit and whosawhat.

The defense rests.

But if you really want to liven up a cocktail party, a wedding reception, or a family gathering, and your hostess has outlawed sex, religion, and politics as topics for polite conversation, bring up the definition of the mystery and what makes a really good one.

The conversation will get livelier. the discussion will become brisk. In only a few minutes eyes will flash, the repartee will begin to bite, tempers will flare. Take notes (if only mental), because if you're really lucky, you will be able to do a bit of planning for a traditional mystery of your own. As long, of course, as you wind up playing the amateur sleuth—not the corpse.

Guaranteed.

BACKGROUNDERS

Marilis Hornidge

ANOTHER CATEGORY FOR the mystery? Who needs another category for the mystery?

We do.

We *readers* do.

Actually, it isn't "another," it's one that mystery readers will recognize right away. There isn't any special designation for the novels of James Michener either, but the fact that they zoom right to the top of the best seller lists should tell publishers (and critics) that something about a Michener novel says "read me" to a huge number of people.

That something is heavy duty *background*. Mysteries with such an emphasis are reader favorites; it's just that nobody has previously isolated that quality.

Well, *almost* nobody.

Never never never, my mother told me once,

think you have invented a brand-new story (in this instance, a smashing tale about someone or something else having invaded the cookie jar, *not* crumb-fingered me) and the same goes for a concept. The omnicognizant Howard Haycraft, in his *Murder for Pleasure*, wrote two pages on this very subject. He called it "the occupational or vocational story—the detective narrative with a specialized background" and pointed out that it was at its best when crime and solution were conclusively correlated with it. Dorothy Sayers, on the defensive for her *Gaudy Night,* said, "Readers seem to like books which tell them how other people live—any people . . . advertisers, bell-ringers, women dons, butchers, bakers or candlestick makers . . . so long as the detail is full and accurate and the object of the work is not overt propaganda." She wrote a couple of my favorites in *Murder Must Advertise* and *The Nine Tailors*, but, as did so many writers and readers or her era, she called them *all* detective stories.

I call that special brand of mystery Backgrounders. They are just about my favorite mystery reading, and I am by no means alone.

When, in July 1988, I wrote an offbeat article for that delight of the antiques trade *Maine Antique Digest* called "Life After Lovejoy," a survey of mysteries with a background in antiques and matters germaine to the trade, I had no idea that it was to grow into a yearly, and then a bi-yearly regular. Letters began to come in from people who enjoyed that sort of book (and read them with a gimlet eye out for mistakes, which was half the fun), suggesting new books, playing the mystery reader's eternal " . . . but have you read . . ." game.

Since then I have written enough specialized-interest mystery reviews to know that reader interest in Backgrounders goes across vocation and avocation as well, as long as the author has or has acquired a certain depth of expertise in the field used as background. I also speak to numbers of mystery-buff groups and they all agree—the Backgrounder is a surefire winner, a delight to find by accident in a new field of interest and a surefire winner in your own specialty.

Over the years I have set up a few criteria in order to clarify my own thinking on the subject and to answer the questions I have to field from the Mysterians to whom I give talk . . . and advice and lists. Perhaps the easiest question to answer is: When is a book just a mystery-with-background and

when does it qualify for Backgrounder status. The reliable H.H. was there before me and his rule still stands, the background must be an integral part of both mystery and solution. *The Godwulf Manuscript*, one of Robert Parker's popular Spenser series, is about a lost medieval manuscript. *The Manuscript Murders* by Roy Lewis is about a lost Shakespearean-era manuscript. *Godwulf* does not qualify—the lost manuscript is a mere plot device to hang the action on. *Manuscript,* in which the history and details concerning the lost item itself are very much part of the plot, and all the characters are involved with it are part of its history, qualifies in spades.

What is background and what isn't? I have my own theories on this one which are, I must admit, susceptible to the occasional exception. Strictly regional mysteries are not Backgrounders, nor are the wonderful mysteries of Martha Grimes which are set in and named for various British pubs. I do not include anything to do with the legal profession (which seems to be acquiring a cult status on its own as a mystery type) or politics (although I adore the mysteries of R.B. Dominic). I also give a skip to finance—high and low, even if the staid *Wall Street Journal did* print a small piece on its editorial page several years ago noting that mysteries starring economists (and they listed several) were up in the reader averages. (I must admit, however, that if Emma Lathen ever decides to give John Putnam Thatcher's Miss Corsa a book on her own, I'd consider starting a secretary-to-the-great category.) The same caveat goes for medicine, even forensic medicine. Mysteries that take place in hospitals should have a category of their own which you might call the Cook (as in Robin) category. Academe and religion are really too broad to fit, and I am iffy about the media as a category, although I make exceptions for the T.T. Baldwin series by Shannon O'Cork, the hard-to-find books starring Flash-gun Casey by George Harmon Coxe, and the adventures of Antonia Fraser's TV personality Jemima Shore. Computer-centered mysteries lose me too easily in their intricacies; either they have to be more user sensitive or I have to become more computer literate. Or both.

Finally, it isn't really a case of vocation over avocation or amusements over business either, as my top twenty list (over which I agonized, believe me) will attest. Under the heading antiques are ex-

The Top Twenty Backgrounders

(being a list made after much soul-searching and gnashing of teeth)

Antiques: *The Sleepers of Erin* by Jonathan Gash (WS)
Whistler in the Dark by John Malcolm (WS)

Cooking: *The Baked Bean Supper Murders* by Virginia Rich (WS)
The Body in the Bouillon by Katherine Hall Page (WS)

Magic: *Death from a Top Hat* by Clayton Rawson (WS)
Elephants in the Distance by Paul Galliard (S)
as a bonus: *The Hand of Mary Constable* by Paul Gallico (1-S)

Gardening: *Green Trigger Fingers* by John Sherwood (WS)
Green Grow the Dollars by Emma Lathen (1-S)

Theater: *Killer Dolphin* by Ngaio Marsh (1-S)
Murder Unrenovated by P. M. Carlson (1-S)

Cats and Dogs: *The Cat Who Turned On and Off* by Lilian Jackson Braun
A New Leash on Death by Susan Conant (WS)

Museums: *Murder by Reference* by D. R. Meredith (1-S)
Generous Death by Nancy Pickard (1-S)

Music: *The Philomel Foundation* by James Gollin (WS)
Ropedancer's Fall by M. K. Lorens (1-S)

Historic Recreations: *War Games* by Anthony Price (1-S)
Knight Fall by Mary Monica Pulver (S)

Mystery Games: *Design for Murder* by Carolyn Hart (1-S)
Murder at Madingley Grange by Carolyn Graham (S)

amples of two separate series in which the central character makes his living in the antiquities game. They are therefore vocational. On the other hand, Lilian Jackson Braun's The Cat Who ... series is not about the vocation of raising cats or even the vocation of being a cat (although there are those who would disagree). It is a great example of cats-integrated-to-the-plot and therefore qualifies, as does Susan Conant's wonderful series starring writer Holly Winter who both writes about and is part of the dog scene. These books are examples of the Whole Series (WS as I will abbreviate it on my list) in which the background continues over the author's entire output.

Emma Lathen's *Green Grow the Dollars* is a very different type of Backgrounder, one of a solid series of another subject, in this case a banker's look into the possibly dangerous mazes of the garden industry. Many of the books on my Top Twenty list belong in this subcategory. (I refer to it as 1-S), which is one of the toughest tricks going for a writer to pull off, a real double dipper. When it is done poorly, it is a real disappointment—like the Ellery Queen books featuring Drury Lane which tend to use the theater scene as a painted backdrop with the action going in front of it but never going in and out of it. When it is fully integrated, as in Ngaio Marsh's *Killer Dolphin* with its completely theatrical background into and through which its sleuth walks, it is a rereadable joy. In a bona fide Backgrounder, the main character/sleuth must understand the particular rules of the game in the arena in which the game is now playing (which may not be his or her own) and play by them.

And then there are the singletons, the one novel out of an entire output that centers on a particular background, carefully and craftily weaving it into the fabric of the plot, characters, and place, complete in itself. There are three of those on my list marked by the letters—I only wish I knew of more because any writer who can write a good Backgrounder gets my vote for reading anything else he/she writes. Perhaps some intelligent publisher of

mysteries will see the possibility of a series and contact the authors. Hope springs eternal.

I have made up a list of some of my favorite Backgrounders in their categories with symbols (explained in the text); limiting it to twenty was not easy. I picked them because they are one and all books I have reread at least once in the deeps of a Maine winter when split pea soup is dearer to the soul than boeuf daube, when settling back in the old wing chair with a favorite book appeals more than winging off to the Carib. Rereading is, to my mind, the acid test of a book—*any* book. These passed, one and all, with flying colors.

Got a list of your own? I have the biggest mailbox allowed by law and it's never been overworked.

THE CORNERSTONES OF CRIME

Angela and Barry T. Zeman

IN 1941 A LANDMARK BOOK was published in the field of detective fiction—*Murder for Pleasure: The Life and Times of the Detective Story* by Howard Haycraft, generally considered to be the first and standard definitive history of the detective story.

For mystery aficionados, the significance of Haycraft's work is twofold: first, he discussed key books in the development of the detective story, pinpointing many techniques used for the first time. Second, and of great significance to collectors, he systematically listed these key books in a chapter, "A Detective Story Bookshelf." A compendium of high spots published between 1845 and 1938, it was designed for the "plain reader ... detective story fans who may care to assemble for their own pleasure 'cornerstone' libraries of the best and most influential writings in the medium."

For the lover of detective fiction, the cornerstone list provides focus. This is especially true for those

to whom historical importance and literary form development are principal collecting elements.

In *Murder for Pleasure*, Haycraft used as a basis of definition the theory put forth by John Carter, editor of *New Paths in Book Collecting* (1934), that a detective story "must be mainly occupied with detection and must contain the proper detective (whether amateur or professional)." Haycraft restated this notion in his own work: "The essential theme of the detective story is professional detection of crime ... the distinguishing element that makes it a detective story and sets it apart from its 'cousins' in the puzzle (and purely mystery, spy, crime, or suspense) story."

For a few years this definition worked, but the inevitable growth and change within the genre eventually brought about a need for a new perspective.

In 1951, to celebrate *Ellery Queen's Mystery Magazine*'s tenth anniversary, Haycraft was asked to update his cornerstone selections to include books published within the decade following the first appearance of his list. This he did, but limited the additions to those published before 1948, feeling that the last few years' harvest needed the perspective of time to be judged fairly.

Two important features make the 1951 cornerstone list of greater interest to collectors: The first is that Haycraft gave up the strict definition of the pure detective story and agreed that the detective-mystery-crime story had "come of age" and was now the nature of the form.

However, even though Haycraft significantly loosened his own definition, he still couldn't yield to what many of us would consider an important part of the genre—fiction written with mysterious or criminal elements, and character studies that "employ crime as a catalyst."

This important development was left to the second important event: the additions to the cornerstone list by Ellery Queen, more specifically, Fred Dannay, who was half of the famous writing and editing partnership comprising Ellery Queen. Dannay took a much broader and more widely historical view of important books in the detective field and, with Haycraft's permission, added his choices to what became published as "The Haycraft-Queen Definitive Library of Detective-Crime-Mystery Fiction: Two Centuries of Cornerstones, 1748–1948." "Queen" also added commentary to selected books from the combined list, increasing interest in the choices for the dedicated collector.

The true first edition of "The Haycraft-Queen

Definitive Library of Detective-Crime-Mystery Fiction" was a pamphlet privately printed in an edition of five hundred copies by *EQMM* in 1951.

A final, newly revised version emerged in 1956 in the *Mystery Writers Handbook* written by members of the Mystery Writers of America, edited by Herbert Brean. This version extended the list to books published through 1952.

In reprinted editions, however, not only are the books from these latter four years often missed, but Howard Haycraft's selections of important anthologies are neglected.

Readers will find the final "The Haycraft-Queen Definitive Library of Detective-Crime-Mystery Fiction" and the updated accompanying "Selected List of Detective Story Anthologies" reprinted at the end of this article. Collectors and dealers will hopefully find it useful and of interest to have them available together. A more detailed version of this article, and the first ever reprinting of the updated H-Q cornerstone list *and* anthologies, originally appeared in *AB Bookman's Weekly*'s April 22, 1991, issue, celebrating the 150th anniversary of the detective story, with a second appearance in the 1992 winter issue of *The Armchair Detective* magazine.

The books on the H-Q cornerstone list illustrate the evolution of the genre. In terms of historical importance, developmental significance, and quality of writing, the cornerstone list provides a wealth of information and enjoyment for readers, writers, serious students, and collectors alike.

The Haycraft-Queen Definitive Library of Detective-Crime-Mystery Fiction

Two Centuries of Cornerstones (New and Revised List)

Asterisks denote titles added to the list by "Ellery Queen"

1748 Voltaire, *Zadig*. The great-great-grandfather of the detective story.

1794 William Godwin, *Things as They Are: or, The Adventures of Caleb Williams*. The great-grandfather of the detective story.

1828–9 François Eugène Vidocq, *Memoires de Vidocq*. The grandfather of the detective story.

1845 Edgar Allan Poe, *Tales*. The father of the modern detective story.

1852–3 Charles Dickens, *Bleak House*; 1870, *The Mystery of Edwin Drood*.

1856 "Waters" [William Russell], *Recollections of a Detective Police-Officer*. The first English detective yellow-back.

1860 Wilkie Collins, *The Woman in White*. An important "transitional" book.

The Haycraft-Queen Library

(Continued)

1862 Victor Hugo, *Les Misérables* (first edition in English, also 1862).

1866 Feodor Dostoevski, *Crime and Punishment* (first edition in English, 1886).

1866 Emile Gaboriau, *L'Affaire Lerouge; 1867, *Le Dossier N° 113;* 1868, *Le Crime D'Orcival;* 1869, *Monsieur Lecoq.* The father of the detective novel.

1866 Seeley Regester [Metta V. Victor], *The Dead Letter.* An example of the pioneer American detective novel—published twelve years before Anna Katharine Green's *The Leavenworth Case.* Detective: Mr. Burton.

1868 Wilkie Collins, *The Moonstone.* The father of the English detective novel.

1872 [Harlan Page Halsey], *Old Sleuth, The Detective,* 1885. The first dime novel detective.

1874 Allan Pinkerton, *The Expressman and the Detective.*

1878 Anna Katharine Green, *The Leavenworth Case.* Generally conceded to be the mother of the American detective novel.

1882 Robert Louis Stevenson. *New Arabian Nights;* 1866, *Strange Case of Dr. Jekyll And Mr. Hyde.*

1887 Fergus W. Hume, *The Mystery of a Hansom Cab.*

1887 A. Conan Doyle, *A Study in Scarlet;* 1890, *The Sign of Four;* 1892, *The Adventures of Sherlock Holmes;* 1894, *The Memoirs of Sherlock Holmes;* 1902, *The Hound of the Baskervilles;* 1905, *The Return of Sherlock Holmes;* 1915, *The Valley of Fear;* 1917, *His Last Bow;* 1927, *The Case-Book of Sherlock Holmes.*

1892 Israel Zangwill, *The Big Bow Mystery.*

1894 Mark Twain. *The Tragedy of Pudd'nhead Wilson.*

1894 Arthur Morrison, *Martin Hewitt, Investigator.*

1895 M.P. Shiel, *Prince Zaleski.*

1897 Bram Stoker, *Dracula.*

1899 E.W. Hornung, *The Amateur Cracksman.*

1903 [Erskine Childers], *The Riddle of the Sands.*

1905 Baroness Orczy, *The Scarlet Pimpernel;* 1909, *The Old Man in the Corner.*

1906 Godfrey R. Benson, *Tracks in the Snow.*

1906 Robert Barr, *The Triumphs of Eugène Valmont.*

1907 Jacques Futrelle, *The Thinking Machine.*

1907 Maurice Leblanc, *Arsène Lupin, Gentleman-Cambrioleur;* 1910, *"813."* The Leblanc-Lupin masterpiece. 1922, *Les Huits Coups de l'Horloge.*

1907 Gaston Leroux, *Le Mystère de la Chambre Jaune;* 1908–9, *Le Parfum de la Dame en Noir.*

1907 R. Austin Freeman, *The Red Thumb Mark.* The first Dr. Thorndyke book. 1909, *John Thorndyke's Cases;* 1911, *The Eye of Osiris;* 1912, *The Singing Bone.* The first "inverted" detective stories.

1907 Joseph Conrad, *The Secret Agent.* Said to be a favorite with both Eric Ambler and Graham Greene.

1908 Mary Roberts Rinehart, *The Circular Staircase.* The founding of the Had-I-But-Known school.

1908 O. Henry, *The Gentle Grafter.*

1908 G. K. Chesterton, *The Man Who Was Thursday;* 1916, *The Innocence of Father Brown.*

1909 Cleveland Moffett, *Through the Wall.* A neglected high spot.

1909 Carolyn Wells, *The Clue.* The first Fleming Stone book.

1910 A.E.W. Mason, *At the Villa Rose.* The first Hanaud book. 1924, *The House of the Arrow.*

1910 William MacHarg and Edwin Balmer, *The Achievements of Luther Trant.*

1912 Arthur B. Reeve, *The Silent Bullet.* The first Craig Kennedy book.

1913 Mrs. Belloc Lowndes, *The Lodger.*

1913 Sax Rohmer, *The Mystery of Dr. Fu-Manchu.*

1913 E. C. Bentley, *Trent's Last Case* (first U.S. title: *The Woman in Black*).

1914 Ernest Bramah, *Max Carrados.* The first blind detective.

1914 Louis Joseph Vance, *The Lone Wolf.*

1915 John Buchan, *The Thirty-nine Steps.*

1916 Thomas Burke, *Limehouse Nights.*

1918 Melville Davisson Post, *Uncle Abner.*

1919 J. S. Fletcher, *The Middle Temple Murder.*

1920 Agatha Christie, *The Mysterious Affair at Styles.* The first Hercule Poirot book. 1926, *The Murder of Roger Ackroyd.*

1920 Freeman Wills Croft, *The Cask;* 1924, *The Inspector French's Greatest Case.*

1920 H. C. Bailey, *Call Mr. Fortune;* 1932, *The Red Castle.*

1920 "Sapper" [Cyril McNeile], *Bull-Dog Drummond.*

1920 Arthur Train, *Tutt and Mr. Tutt.*

1920 E. Phillips Oppenheim, *The Great Impersonation.*

1921 Eden Phillpotts, *The Grey Room.*

1922 A. A. Milne, *The Red House Mystery.*

1923 G.D.H. Cole, *The Brooklyn Murders.*

1923 Dorothy L. Sayers, *Whose Body?* The first Lord Peter Wimsey book. 1934, *The Nine Tailors;* 1930, with Robert Eustace, *The Documents in the Case.*

1924 Philip MacDonald, *The Rasp.* The first Colonel Anthony Gethryn book. 1938, *Warrant For X* (English title: *The Nursemaid Who Disappeared*).

1925 Edgar Wallace, *The Mind of Mr. J. G. Reeder.*

1925 John Rhode, *The Paddington Mystery.* The first Dr. Priestley book. 1928, *The Murders in Praed Street.*

1925 Earl Derr Biggers, *The House Without a Key.* The first Charlie Chan book.

The Haycraft-Queen Library

(Continued)

1925 Theodore Dreiser, *An American Tragedy.

1925 Liam O'Flaherty, *The Informer.

1925 Ronald A. Knox, The Viaduct Murder.

1926 S. S. Van Dine, The Benson Murder Case. The first Philo Vance book. 1927, The "Canary" Murder Case.

1926 C. S. Forester, *Payment Deferred.

1927 Frances Noyes Hart, The Bellamy Trial.

1928 W. Somerset Maugham, *Ashenden.

1928 Leslie Charteris, *Meet the Tiger (U.S. title: Meet—The Tiger! 1929).

1929 Anthony Berkeley, The Poisoned Chocolates Case; 1937, Trial and Error; 1932 [Francis Iles], Before the Fact.

1929 Ellery Queen, The Roman Hat Mystery. The first Ellery Queen book. 1942, *Calamity Town; 1932 [Barnaby Ross], The Tragedy of X. The first Drury Lane book. 1932, *The Tragedy of Y.

1929 Rufus King, *Murder by the Clock.

1929 W. R. Burnett, *Little Caesar.

1929 T.S. Stribling, *Clues of the Caribbees. The only Professor Poggioli book.

1929 Harvey J. O'Higgins, *Detective Duff Unravels It. The first psychoanalyst detective.

1929 Mignon G. Eberhart, The Patient in Room 18.

1930 Frederick Irving Anderson, Book of Murder.

1930 Dashiell Hammett, The Maltese Falcon. *The Glass Key; 1944. *The Adventures of Sam Spade.

1930 David Frome. The Hammersmith Murders. The first Mr. Pinkerton book.

1931 Stuart Palmer, *The Penguin Pool Murder. The first Hildegarde Withers book.

1931 Francis Beeding, *Death Walks in Eastrepps.

1931 Glen Trevor (James Hilton) *Murder at School (U.S. title: Was it Murder?, 1933).

1931 Damon Runyon, *Guys and Dolls.

1931 Phoebe Atwood Taylor, The Cape Cod Mystery. The first Asey Mayo book.

1932 R.A.J. Walling, The Fatal Five Minutes.

1932 Clemence Dane and Helen Simpson, Re-Enter Sir John.

1933 Erle Stanley Gardner, *The Case of the Velvet Claws. The first Perry Mason book. 1933, The Case of the Sulky Girl.

1934 Margery Allingham, Death of a Ghost.

1934 James M. Cain, *The Postman Always Rings Twice.

1934 Rex Stout, Fer-De-Lance. The first Nero Wolfe book. 1935, *The League of Frightened Men.

1935 Richard Hull, The Murder of My Aunt.

1935 John P. Marquand, *No Hero. The first Mr. Moto book.

1938 John Dickson Carr [Carter Dickson], The Crooked Hinge; 1938, The Judas Window; 1945, *The Curse of the Bronze Lamp (English title: Lord of the Sorcerers, 1946).

In his original list, Mr. Haycraft chose The Arabian Nights Murder by Carr and The Plague Court Murders by Dickson; but on page 493 of his The Art of the Mystery Story Mr. Haycraft wrote: "After careful, and possibly maturer, re-reading I beg to change my vote" to The Crooked Hinge and The Judas Window.

1938 Nicholas Blake, The Beast Must Die.

1938 Michael Innes, Lament for a Maker.

1938 Clayton Rawson, *Death from a Top Hat. The first Great Merlini book.

1938 Graham Greene, *Brighton Rock.

1938 Daphne du Maurier, *Rebecca.

1938 Mabel Seeley, The Listening House.

1939 Ngaio Marsh, Overture to Death.

1939 Eric Ambler, A Coffin for Dimitrios (English title: The Mask of Dimitrios).

1939 Raymond Chandler, The Big Sleep. The first Philip Marlowe book. 1940, Farewell, My Lovely.

1939 Georges Simenon, The Patience of Maigret.

1939 Elliot Paul, *The Mysterious Mickey Finn. The first Homer Evans book.

1940 Raymond Postgate, Verdict of Twelve.

1940 Frances and Richard Lockridge, The Norths Meet Murder.

1940 Dorothy B. Hughes, The So Blue Marble (or In a Lonely Place, 1947).

1940 Cornell Woolrich [William Irish,] *The Bride Wore Black; 1942, Phantom Lady.

1940 Manning Coles, Drink to Yesterday; 1941, A Toast to Tomorrow (English title: Pray Silence, 1940). The first two Tommy Hambledon books.

1941 H. F. Heard, *A Taste for Honey.

1941 Craig Rice, Trial by Fury (or Home Sweet Homicide, 1944).

1942 H. H. Holmes [Anthony Boucher], *Rocket to the Morgue.

1942 James Gould Cozzens, *The Just and the Unjust.

1943 Vera Caspary, *Laura. A modern "psychothriller."

1944 Hilda Lawrence, Blood upon the Snow.

1946 Helen Eustis, The Horizontal Man.

1946 Charlotte Armstrong, *The Unsuspected.

1946 Lillian de la Torre, *Dr. Sam Johnson, Detector.

1946 Edmund Crispin, The Moving Toyshop (or Love Lies Bleeding, 1948).

1947 Edgar Lustgarten, One More Unfortunate (English title: A Case to Answer).

1947 Roy Vickers, *The Department of Dead Ends.

The Haycraft-Queen Library
(Continued)

1948 Josephine Tey, *The Franchise Affair*.

1948 William Faulkner, **Intruder in the Dust*.

1948 Robert M. Coates, *Wisteria Cottage*.

1948 Stanley Ellin, *Dreadful Summit*.

1949 John [Ross] Macdonald, *The Moving Target*.

1950 Eleazar Lipsky, *The People Against O'Hara*. Rated by Dorothy B. Hughes as the best detective novel of the year.

1950 Evelyn Piper, *The Motive*. Anthony Boucher considers this book a "major milestone" in the history of the whydunit, as opposed to the whodunit and the howdunit.

1950 Thomas Walsh, *Nightmare in Manhattan*.

1950 Helen McCloy, *Through a Glass, Darkly*.

1950 Bart Spicer, *Blues for the Prince*.

1950 Charlotte Armstrong, *Mischief*. Possibly to replace *The Unsuspected*, 1946.

1950 Raymond Chandler, *The Simple Art of Murder*. To replace an earlier choice or to be added.

1951 Dorothy Salisbury Davis, *A Gentle Murderer*.

1952 Lord Dunsany, *The Little Tales of Smethers*.

A Selected List of Detective Story Anthologies
Arranged alphabetically by compilers; U.S. dates, titles, publishers given

General

Macgowan, Kenneth, **Sleuths: Twenty-Three Great Detectives of Fiction and Their Best Stories** (New York, Harcourt, Brace, 1931).

Queen, Ellery, **Challenge to the Reader: An Anthology** (New York, Stokes, 1938).

Sayers, Dorothy, The **Omnibus of Crime** (New York, Payson & Clarke, 1929).

———— **The Second Omnibus of Crime** (New York, Coward-McCann, 1932).

————**The Third Omnibus of Crime** (New York, Coward-McCann, 1935).

————**Tales of Detection** (London, Dent [Everyman's Library], 1936).

Starrett, Vincent, **Fourteen Great Detective Stories** (New York, Modern Library, 1929).

Thwing, Eugene, **The World's Best 100 Detective Stories** (New York, Funk & Wagnalls, 1929).

Wright, Lee, **The Pocket Book of Great Detectives** (New York, Pocket Books, 1941)

Wright, Willard Huntington, **The Great Detective Stories** (New York, Scribner's, 1927).

Wrong, E.M., **Crime and Detection** (New York, Oxford University Press [World's Classics], 1926).

Juvenile

Haycraft, Howard, **The Boys' Book of Great Detective Stories** (New York, Harper, 1938).

————**The Boys' Second Book of Great Detective Stories** (New York, Harper, 1940).

"Specialties"

Allingham, Margery, and others, **Six Against Scotland Yard** (New York, Doubleday, Doran, 1936).

Detection Club of London, **The Floating Admiral** (New York, Doubleday, Doran, 1932).

———— **Ask a Policeman** (New York, Morrow, 1933).

Rhode, John [for the Detection Club], **Line-Up** (New York, Dodd, Mead, 1940).

SEX AND THE MYSTERY

Elaine Raco Chase

"I am still of (the) opinion that only two topics can be of the LEAST interest to a serious and studious mood—SEX and the DEAD."

HOW WRONG William Butler Yeats! Sex has long come with murderous intent and much enjoyment.

Those poor damsels in distress racing through the gothics in their sheer, cobweb-strewn nighties. Had-she-but-known: that the nice guy (handsome, polite, and attentive) was the villain of the piece; and the evil duke (dark, arrogant, and brooding) who made her heart skip a beat and whose lustful stares gave her the vapors would be her savior.

That pathetically unsuspecting heroine soon gave way to the ample-bosomed dowager. Umbrella and reticule in hand, she was looked upon with respect for her spunkiness and with great affection for her brains. Alas, that affection was well off the printed page.

It was always open season on brides. Most never made it to the honeymoon suite. Sexual bliss was the remembered kiss at the nuptials.

I'd be willing to bet the legendary Sherlock Holmes would have done so much more with The Woman, Irene Adler, had Conan Doyle written more action than memories and moodiness.

Bondian spy thrillers turned sex into names like Pussy Galore and Miss Goodthighs. And what was in a name? Not as much on the printed page as was on the movie screen.

When the sleuth had a mate, she was either terribly domesticated and spent her time listening to his great revelations. Or portrayed as the dizzy, accident-prone woman who always needed the "here comes the cavalry" rescue. Couples held hands, maybe even shared a quick hug. Romantic weekends did include bodies—but they were always very cold, very dead, and of significantly more interest to our hero than bundling with his wife. Even the inscrutable Charlie Chan, whose eleven children made reading the Kama Sutra unnecessary, never dallied with his wife while he was hot on the heels of a villain.

The Golden Age of the mystery brought in the lone-wolf detective. His version of sex walked in on million-dollar legs that never ended and large breasts that strained against a thin sweater. This was a woman who made grown men stammer like virginal schoolboys. Well, okay, maybe not our hero. They weren't called hard-boiled dicks for nothing!

But when a woman was packaged like that, the reader knew she would stop at nothing, not even murder, to keep her secrets. This dame was loaded with sin, she was trouble with a capital *T*. We are talking predatory lips, ruthless hairstyles, underwear left at home, and a body that could corrupt the Pope. *Or*, she was totally misunderstood, a virgin in disguise, spoiled for any other man by one night with our hero and—dead by chapter six.

The pulp market. Known for its sex, sadism, vulgarity, and violence. Was it *that* explicit and tawdry? I don't know, it took Mike Hammer till the

One of the great *noir* icons, Rita Hayworth.

last page to discover that Juno wasn't a woman!

But that didn't matter to me. Age fourteen. Just switching from Nancy Drew, girl detective, to Mickey Spillane's Mike Hammer. I read and reread each page, by flashlight, under the bedcovers. This was hot stuff. Wasn't it? Everybody was talking about *those* books.

Yes, the violence was there. Mike was the law. He was the jury. Certainly the vulgarities were there. I looked them all up in my Funk and Wagnall's just to make sure I knew what every word really meant.

About the sex. No monk he. However, it took Mike twenty years to take away Velda's virginity. (Twenty years! Velda, you were short-changed.) And the sex was more tell than show. Cigarettes and rebuttoning shirts. Blond hair tumbled against the pillowcase and sheets in a jumble on the floor. And that nice little symbolism about the size of his gun on the nightstand equaling the size of his—well, you know.

Despite the sexual attraction, our tough-guy detectives were all like Hammett's Sam Spade. They wouldn't "play the sap" for any dame. Who could blame them? If she'd killed her last love, he'd be checking for ice picks every night.

There were, of course, a handful of female crime fighters. Their male writers created every man's sexual fantasy. Women who were tough, talented, and untamable everyplace but between the sheets. Enter all those euphemisms where the *hero* of the piece settles into the saddle and gives our heroine the ride of her life.

What about our favorite partners in crime? The Charleses, Nick and Nora, played fast and fractious with wisecracks and martinis. Their affection was genuine, but with all that liquor, I'm positive Asta had a better sex life.

Lord Peter and the Vane, Harriet, were *wordy* lovers. He had "come home" to love; and she had found satisfaction in his heart. Harriet, you needed to look lower!

Erle Stanley Gardner writing as A. A. Fair made the big, beautiful Bertha Cool's G spot her dinner plate. When it came to America's favorite lawyer, Perry Mason, and his trusty secretary, Della Street—Gardner created a heroine who said *no* to five marriage proposals because it meant she'd have to give up her job.

That was Perry's stodgy idea. Della had a better one. She'd give up the gold ring to stay shoulder to shoulder with her man. Her rewards? Wonderful dinners, he was a great dancer, every so often a *buss* on the mouth, and those business trips for two. Nudge . . . nudge . . . did they share the same room?

Those thrilling days of yesteryear have given way to a new Golden Age of mysteries. Today the female of the species has become more deadlier than the male. Women writers have created ingenious female sleuths that rival their male counterparts both vertically and horizontally.

But has the sexual content of the mystery changed all that much now that women are on top? It all depends on the writer and how the book is written. If the book is plot-driven, the mystery is the main focus and the characters and their relationships are more illusionary. We are *told* they have feelings, often by the characters themselves, and have acted on them. The reader's imagination is called into play rather than the mechanics of inserting tab A into slot B.

Character-driven mysteries have been reformed. Today's heroes and heroines are not as *damaged* as they once were. There are still a few "super studs" in the genre, but most writers are creating real people, with baggage, who have real relationships.

Many crossover authors, like myself, started out in the romance genre. We were always taught to *show* not *tell* when it came to writing. This is what I've incorporated into my series. They have a mystery to unravel plus the ups and downs and ins and outs of their own relationship to deal with.

Sex is the next step in that partnership. I feel evocative word choices that show the characters' full range of emotions make a very strong book. A book where the mystery doesn't suffer and the action doesn't stop. And if a betrayal is in the works, how much more dramatic it becomes when the two characters have shared the most intimate of moments.

Sex has come full circle in the mystery novel. Someone will always be in distress, but today it's just as likely the man will be muttering "had I but known." In some cases, the misogynist has been replaced by the misandryst. Or it's the feminist eye that's appraising the masculine form and the gun shares space on the night table with a box of condoms.

When won't you find a sexual coupling? If the female sleuth is balancing a husband and kids—oh, wait a minute . . . this is fiction!

IT'S MURDER ON STAGE

Barbara Paul

IS THERE A MORE compatible setting for a whodunit than a theater? A cast of characters, a confined space, a restricted period of time, a deadly conflict . . . and an audience/readership ready to eat it all up. But theater overflows the building that contains it; all the world's, etc. Courtrooms are a form of theater. And religious rituals. And political ceremonies. Even the Rose Bowl parade. You want to know the ethos of a people? Look at their theater.

So it's no surprise that theater—and its myriad variations—should hold a lasting appeal to writers of mysteries as a perfect arena for the acting out of dark and dastardly doings. No one demonstrates this better than the late Ngaio Marsh, a former actor/producer whose love of theater never waned through her nearly fifty-year career as a mystery novelist. From the early *Vintage Murder* to her grand farewell performance in *Light Thickens,* she kept finding ways of reminding us that we are all actors in dramas we write ourselves.

Acting and sleuthing seem to go well together. Linda Barnes's Boston-based Michael Spraggue works at both professionally in *Bitter Finish* and *Dead Heat.* Acting comes first with Jane Dentinger's series character, Jocelyn O'Roarke, but "Josh" keeps finding herself involved in murder investigations (*First Hit of the Season; Dead Pan*). Stephanie Matteson's character, Charlotte Graham, who has retired from acting, also has a way of involving herself in the pursuit of killers in the cozies *Murder at the Spa* and *Murder on the Silk Road.*

Another accidental investigator is Charles Paris, Simon Brett's charming alcoholic actor who can never quite get either his career or his private life in gear (*Cast, in Order of Disappearance; Murder Unprompted*). And Simon Shaw writes about one Philip Fletcher, "the well-known actor and murderer." If wickedly dark British humor is your cup of tea, you won't do better than *Murder Out of*

Tune or *Bloody Instructions. Bloody Instructions* is also the title of a theater mystery Sara Woods wrote for her investigator, Anthony Maitland; another such is *Dearest Enemy.*

When she's not acting, Anne Morice's series character Tessa Crichton has an understandable interest in crime; she's married to a Scotland Yard detective (*Death in the Round; Dead on Cue*). For P.M. Carlson's amateur sleuth Maggie Ryan, it works just the other way around: she has an interest in theater because she's married to an actor (*Audition for Murder, Rehearsal for Murder*). Lydia Adamson's Alice Nestleton works as a cat-sitter between acting jobs (*A Cat in the Manger; A Cat in the Wings*). And Pauline Glen Winslow's Scotland Yard detective, Merlin Capricorn, is trying (not always successfully) to escape the influence of the theatrical family he was born into (*Death of an Angel; The Rockefeller Gift*).

Eileen Dewhurst's Inspector Neil Carter delves into backstage mayhem in *Curtain Fall* and *Playing Safe.* Marian Babson reveals a somewhat-less-than-awestruck slant on theater folk in the lighthearted *Murder, Murder, Little Star* and *Nine Lives to Murder.* And John Marston gives us nothing less than the granddaddy of the English-speaking stage: the public theater of vibrant and yeasty Elizabethan London. Series character Nick Bracewell sniffs out murderers while working as the stage manager of an acting company called Lord Westfield's Men (*The Nine Giants; The Mad Courtesan*).

"Lyric theater"—a fancy name for opera—provides a dramatic musical accompaniment to murder. Former diva Queena Mario turned her hand to writing mysteries when she retired from singing; *Murder Meets Mephisto* and *Death Drops Delilah* are campy and fast-moving. Paul Myers's sophisticated series character Mark Holland is a music promoter and agent; he deals with foul play at the concert hall in *Deadly Cadenza* and at the opera in

— 124 —

Deadly Crescendo. Chelsea Quinn Yarbro shows us the San Francisco lyric theater scene in *Music When Soft Voices Die* and *False Notes.*

Theater on film and tape has its share of profession-oriented mysteries. Jim Stinson writes of good-natured Stoney Winston, a filmmaker who wanders through low-budget Hollywood doing whatever he can to stay in the business—including investigating murders (*Truck Shot; TV Safe*). Stuart Kaminsky takes us back to the Hollywood of the thirties and forties; his private investigator Toby Peters meets the Munchkins in *Murder on the Yellow Brick Road* and Mae West in *He Done Her Wrong.*

Laurence Payne's unusual investigator is Mark Savage, a movie star turned p.i. in *Dead for a Ducat* and *Knight Fall.* Stan Cutler's slam-bang comic mysteries *Best Performance by a Patsy* and *The Face on the Cutting Room Floor* offer odd-couple detectives: a jaded macho p.i. is paired with a gay writer of as-told-to autobiographies. David Handler makes wisecracking ghostwriter Stewart "Hoagy" Hoag his investigator in *The Woman Who Fell from Grace* and *The Boy Who Never Grew Up.*

William DeAndrea's character Matt Cobb is a TV network troubleshooter; we see him at work in *Killed in the Ratings* and *Killed in the Act.* Charles Larson uses a TV producer, Nils Blixen, as his detective in *Matthew's Hand* and *Muir's Blood.* Antonia Fraser's character Jemima Shore is an investigative reporter on London TV; her job leads her to discover murderous plots in *A Splash of Red* and *Cool Repentance.* Eileen Fulton's investigator Nina McFall is a star in a soap opera, the set of which has seen more murders than Cabot Cove (*Take One for Murder, Fatal Flashback*).

A number of writers set their stories in a variety of show-biz backgrounds. Herb Resnicow sends his wonderful characters Norma and Alex Gold to the theater in *The Gold Gamble* and to the opera in *The Gold Curse*; they end up wishing they'd stayed at home. Ed Gorman puts one series character (Jack Dwyer) onstage at the local theater in *Murder in the Wings* and another (Tobin) on camera for a syndicated movie review show in *Murder on the Aisle.* The 1987 MWA anthology of short stories, edited by Mary Higgins Clark, is also titled *Murder on the Aisle;* the stories cover a variety of the aisle seats we cherish, from the bleachers to the movies to the concert hall.

Audrey Williamson's character, Superintendent Richard York, investigates crime at the opera in *Funeral March for Siegfried* and on the legitimate stage in *Death of a Theatre Filly.* Barbara Paul moves from modern-day Broadway in *The Fourth Wall* to the Metropolitan Opera of Caruso's time in *Prima Donna at Large.* Kay Nolte Smith writes of the New York theater scene in *Catching Fire* and of an enigmatic opera singer in the haunting *Death of a Soprano.* And George Baxt has created a gay African American private investigator named Pharoah Love who, like Sherlock Holmes, had to be resurrected from the grave to keep his fans happy (*The Alfred Hitchcock Murder Case; The Noel Coward Murder Case*).

And there are more; the number of mystery writers who have been drawn to some form of theater background for their books is impressive. Feast on these other show-biz mysteries . . . and be generous with your applause.

Show-Biz Mysteries
Selected by Barbara Paul

Margery Allingham
Dancers in Mourning

Elizabeth Anthony
Ballet of Death

Margot Arnold
Exit Actors, Dying

Richard M. Baker
Death Stops the Rehearsal

Robert Barnard
Death on the High C's

Phil Berger
Deadly Kisses

Andrew Bergman
Hollywood and LeVine

Carole Berry
Good Night, Sweet Prince

W. Edward Blain
Love Cools

Lionel Black
The Life and Death of Peter Wade

Anthony Boucher
The Case of the Baker Street Irregulars

Edgar Box (Gore Vidal)
Death in the Fifth Position

Caryl and S. J. Brahms
Murder à la Stroganoff

Christianna Brand
Death of a Jezebel

Lilian Jackson Braun
The Cat Who Knew a Cardinal

Gordon Bromley
Midsummer Night's Crime

John Bude
Death Steals the Show

R. Wright Campbell
Murder of Kings

Melissa Cleary
A Tail of Two Murders

Robin Close
The Boheme Combination

Laura Colburn
Death of a Prima Donna

Michelle Collins
Premiere at Willow Run

Bruce Cook
Death as a Career Move

Gordon Cotler
Shooting Script

Trella Crespi
The Trouble with Moonlighting

Edmund Crispin
The Case of the Gilded Fly

John Crozier
Murder in Public

E. V. Cunningham
The Case of the Angry Actress

Elizabeth Daly
Unexpected Night

Clemence Dane & Helen Simpson
Enter Sir John

Dorothy Daniels
Castle Morvant

Dorothy Salisbury Davis
Lullaby of Murder

Kenn Davis
The Forza Trap

Dexter Dayle
Death in the Theatre

Jeffery Wilds Deaver
Death of a Blue Movie Star

Michael DeLarrabeiti
The Hollywood Takes

Thomas B. Dewey
A Sad Song Singing

Roger Dooley
Flashback

Bernard Dougall
The Singing Corpse

Gillian B. Farrell
Alibi for an Actress

Evan Field
What Nigel Knew

David E. Fisher
Variations on a Theme

David Fletcher
Don't Whistle "Macbeth"

Leslie Ford
The Devil's Stronghold

Jonathan Gash
The Very Last Gambado

Rosemary Gatenby
The Nightmare Chrysalis

Anthony Gilbert
The Musical Comedy Crime

Michael Gilbert
The Night of the Twelfth

James Gollin
The Philomel Foundation

Caroline Graham
Death of a Hollow Man

Winston Graham
Take My Life

Richard Grayson
Death Off Stage

Kate Green
Shooting Star

Parnell Hall
Actor

Robert Lee Hall
Murder at Drury Lane

David Hanna
The Opera House Murders

Joyce Harrington
No One Knows My Name

Carolyn G. Hart
Something Wicked

Ellen Hart
Stage Fright

Roy Hart
Blood Kin

Rebecca Holland
Danger on Cue

Gavin Holt
Death Takes the Stage

Joe Hyams
Murder at the Academy Awards

P. D. James
The Skull Beneath the Skin

F. G. Jarvis
Murder at the Met

William Jefferies
Shallow Graves

Hazel Wynn Jones
Shot on Location

Marvin Kaye
The Soap Opera Slaughters

H. R. F. Keating
Death of a Fat God

Faye Kellerman
The Quality of Mercy

David Keith (Francis Steegmuller)
Blue Harpsichord

Sara Kemp
The Lure of Sweet Death

Show-Biz Mysteries
(Continued)

William X. Kienzle
Deadline for a Critic

Terence Kingsley-Smith
The Murder of an Old-time Movie Star

Perry Lafferty
Jablonski and the Erotomaniac

Maria Lang
Death Awaits Thee

Jane Langton
The Memorial Hall Murder

Janice Law
Time Lapse

Layne Littlepage
Murder by the Sea

Nancy Livingston
Death in Close-up

Richard Lockridge
The Old Die Young

Philip Loraine
Exit with Intent

Marc Lovell
The Spy Who Barked in the Night

Philip MacDonald
The Crime Conductor

Charlotte MacLeod
The Plain Old Man

Lee Martin
Murder at the Blue Owl

Helen McCloy
Cue for Murder

E. M. McDuff
Murder in the Theatre

Patricia McGerr
Murder Is Absurd

Jill McGown
Murder Movie

N. J. McIver
The Assassin Prepares

James Melville
Raven's Forge

Judi Miller
Phantom of the Soap Opera

Gladys Mitchell
Death in the Opera

Patricia Moyes
Falling Star

Hugh Munro
The Brain Robbers

Amy Myers
Murder in the Limelight

Richard Nehrbass
A Perfect Death for Hollywood

Lillian O'Donnell
Pushover

Sister Carol Anne O'Marie
Murder in Ordinary Time

Robert B. Parker
Stardust

Don Pendleton
Copp in the Dark

Max Perry
Final Cut

Ellis Peters
The Funeral of Figaro

T. Arthur Plummer
The Muse Theatre Murder

Paul Rawlings
Fade to Black

John Reeves
Murder by Microphone

John Reeves
Murder with Muskets

Ron Renauld
Fade to Black

Ruth Rendell
Death Notes

Simon Ritchie
Work for a Dead Man

Kelley Roos
Made Up To Kill

John Russo
Limb to Limb

Norma Schier
Demon of the Opera

Diane K. Shah
Dying Cheek to Cheek

Gerald Sinstadt
The Fidelio Score

Martha Smilgis
Fame's Peril

Susannah Stacey
A Knife at the Opera

Anita Stewart
Devil's Toy

L.A.G. Strong
Murder Plays an Ugly Scene

Betty Suyker
Death Scene

Julian Symons
A Three-Pipe Problem

Josephine Tey
The Man in the Queue

Tom Tolnay
The Big House

Robert Upton
Fade Out

Jonathan Valin
Natural Causes

Gerald Verner
The Show Must Go On

Donald Ward
Death Takes the Stage

Mignon Warner
Illusion

David Weiss
The Assassination of Mozart

Anna Mary Wells
Sin of Angels

Carolyn Wells
Prilligirl

Robert Westbrook
Rich Kids

Barbara Whitehead
Playing God

Kate Wilhelm
The Hamlet Trap

J. R. Wilmot
Death in the Theatre

Michael Wolk
The Big Picture

Sherryl Woods
Hot Secret

Eric Wright
Final Cut

James Yaffe
Mom Doth Murder Sleep

Dorian Yeager
Cancellation by Death

Margaret Yorke
Cast for Death

Ursula Zilinsky
A Happy English Child

DOES ANYBODY
LOVE A RESEARCHER?
Walter Albert

AUTHORS OF MYSTERY FICTION have their devoted readers queue up at conventions and bookshop signings for autographs and a fleeting smile of appreciation. The readers are also courted by publishers and booksellers, the booksellers by publishers and authors, and the publishers by printing houses and authors. But who—other than another researcher—sees a reference book as anything more than an overpriced, dourly bound volume usually shelved out of reach in the local bookstore or notable for its absence from the dealers' tables at the rapidly proliferating mystery conventions?

There was, of course, a time when mystery novels themselves were secret pleasures, not to be spoken of seriously in polite company. G. K. Chesterton's "A Defense of the Detective Story," first published in 1901, led the attack against the entrenched opposition to popular fiction almost a half-century later as the lead essay in Howard Haycraft's seminal collection of essays, *The Art of the Mystery Story* (Simon & Schuster, 1946). "The trouble . . . is that many people do not realize that there is such a thing as a good detective story; it is to them like speaking of a good devil . . . [However], not only is a detective story a perfectly legitimate form of art, but it has certain definite and real advantages as an agent of the public weal."

This anthology and Haycraft's *Murder for Pleasure* (Appleton-Century Crofts, 1941), the first book-length history of the detective story, are still cornerstone texts in any reference library devoted to the subject. Jon Breen recently recognized the significant contribution of Haycraft by dedicating to second edition of his annotated bibliography, *What About Murder* (Scarecrow, 1993). If Chesterton—himself a notable writer of detective stories—was one of the earliest and still the most eloquent defenders of the faith, Haycraft laid the foundation for studies of the subject. And *Murder for Pleasure*'s account of the first hundred years of the genre has yet to be displaced by a comparable study.

In the 1940s, Haycraft's work as an anthologist and historian was complemented by that of Ellery Queen, not only an influential writer of fiction but also a bibliophile and editor of *Ellery Queen's Mystery Magazine*, whose introductory notes to the stories are themselves a notable contribution to the critical literature. And it was also during this decade that Anthony Boucher began a quarter-century of reviewing, with the centerpiece of his work the "Criminals at Large" column published in the *New York Times Book Review* from 1951 to his death in 1968. Like Queen and Chesterton, Boucher was a superb writer of detective fiction and, like them, he had an acute critical sense that made of his still largely uncollected columns perhaps the best history we are likely to have of that period.

Boucher's successor on the *Times* was Allen J. Hubin, who was at that time the editor and publisher of *The Armchair Detective*, whose first issue was mailed in October 1967 to sixty subscribers who had responded to a prospectus letter that went out to a list of some 225 names.

It is difficult to overestimate the importance of that offset fanzine, which Hubin published for almost a decade before a painful transition period, recounted by him in an article in *TAD-Schrift: Twenty Years of Mystery Fandom in* The Armchair Detective (Brownstone, 1987). (This period was happily resolved by the transfer of the editing and production to Otto Penzler and Mysterious Press.) But it was, perhaps, somewhat mitigated by the special Edgar the Mystery Writers of America awarded Hubin in 1978 for the first ten years of *TAD*.

Hubin's contribution to the field is not limited

to the founding of *TAD*. In January 1971 he began to append to the magazine a supplement that contained a bibliographic listing of titles by author. That initial sixty-page listing eventually culminated in his monumental *Bibliography of Crime Fiction, 1749–1945*, published in 1979. This bible of primary sources, updated by a second edition in 1984 and a supplement in 1988 (both published by Garland), will be further updated in late 1993 by a comprehensive revised third edition. Hubin's work is truly definitive and would undoubtedly be a desert-island choice as long as the reclusive collector had access to a mail-order dealer.

Another essential compendium is the unfortunately long-out-of-print *Encyclopedia of Mystery and Detection* (McGraw Hill, 1976), edited by Chris Steinbrunner and Otto Penzler. It is chock-full of entertaining, informative essays on writers, books, films, and fictional characters—in short, a browser's delight as well as a one-volume source of information on almost all authors of note. This turns up with some frequency at book sales and should be acquired, whatever its condition, to be taken home and lovingly read and preserved.

The academic writer did not hesitate to enter the market, even though studies on popular literature were not favorably considered by members of tenure review committees. It remained to a librarian, Ordean Hagen, to compile and publish an 800-page guide, *Who Done It* (Bowker, 1969), ground-breaking but outclassed by the indispensable Hubin. This was followed in 1971 by *A Catalogue of Crime* (Harper & Row; second edition, revised, 1989), compiled by a formidable academician, Jacques Barzun, and a colleague, Wendell Hertig Taylor. Their tastes tended toward the British classical mystery (a fact somewhat grumpily noted by Ross Macdonald in a celebrated review in the *New York Times Book Review* on May 16, 1971), but their short appreciations of novels are always fun to read even if you disagree with their opinions.

Although *TAD* has dominated the field of specialized magazine publishing for over a quarter of a century, it was preceded by *The John D. MacDonald Bibliophile*, first published in 1965 by Len and June Moffatt and, by just a few months, by *The Mystery Lovers Newsletter* (Lianne Carlin; 1967–73). *The Rohmer Review*, published by Robert E. Briney and the most elegant of the amateur magazines, followed shortly in 1968 (and has been ''on

hiatus'' since 1981). The seventies saw the first publication of a number of fanzines, among them *The Mystery Fancier* (Guy M. Townsend; 1976–92), *The Poisoned Pen* (Jeff Meyerson; 1978–86), and *The Not So Private Eye* (Andy Jaysnovitch; 1978–80). A host of magazines followed in the 1980s, and today a wide array of publications stands ready to be served up to the hungry reader. The most prominent of these (see the list at the end of this article for publishing data) are *The Drood Review of Mystery, CADS, Mystery Scene, Clues,* and *The Mystery Readers' Journal.* And the still besieged academic, looking for viable outlets for research projects, is addressed by *Murder Is Academic,* a newsletter published by Professors B. J. Rahn and Sharon Villines.

The trickle of books on mystery fiction in the sixties and seventies became a spring freshet in the 1980s and is approaching flood stage in the early 1990s. I began tracking the articles and books in an annual column in *TAD* in 1973. In 1985 I published *Detective and Mystery Fiction: An International Bibliography of Secondary Sources* (Brownstone Books), which received a special Edgar in 1986. A second edition in 1993 will be twice the length of the first edition, and the original two-page compilation in *TAD* was, in the post-1985 issues, so extensive that annual updates were published in three parts.

Given this massive growth of studies on mystery fiction, the real difficulty now is in selecting a manageable number of books to fill out the shelf holding the Hubin, Barzun/Taylor, and the *Encyclopedia.* You will certainly find on the reference shelf of most specialists the three editions of *Twentieth Century Crime and Mystery Writers* (1980, 1985, 1991), edited by John Reilly (first two editions), and by Lesley Henderson (third edition). The author entries, which contain bibliographies of their books, biographies, and critical essays, are a handy if somewhat expensive guide to several hundred writers. Each successive edition has dropped some writers and added others, with the result that these are not disposable volumes. The reservation is that the choice of authors is sometimes questionable, and the quality of the essays varies. Other contenders for the *TCCMW* slot have been published in the last few years, including the well-edited three-volume *British Mystery Writers* (Gale, 1988–89), edited by Bernard Benstock, and the Magill four-volume *Crit-

ical Survey of Mystery and Detective Fiction (Salem Press, 1988).

These books, all of which cover a wide spectrum, are doors that open out onto hundreds of books and articles. The British Golden Age and the American hard-boiled writers have been the most heavily researched subjects, but the eighties were the decade of the ascendancy of the female mystery writer, and this topic bids fair to be a dominant one in the forseeable future. Hammett, Chandler, Christie, Ross Macdonald, Sax Rohmer, Georges Simenon, and Cornell Woolrich had substantial bibliographies, while dozens of other first-rate and important writers are virtually ignored. The nineteenth century awaits its definitive historian; the nonfiction writings and short stories of Hammett languish in limbo; the critical writings of Boucher and Queen should be published in definitive critical editions; and the juvenile mystery, pulp fiction, and dime novel are just beginning to be taken seriously and to receive some of the attention they deserve.

In addition, the files of the major publishers are a virtually untapped resource, and it can only be hoped that more researchers will follow the groundbreaking work of Ellen Nehr in her *Double-day Crime Club Compendium 1928–91* (Offspring Press, 1992), and chart the rich history of American detective fiction imprints.

The obvious answer to the question posed at the beginning of this article is that there are many people who love reference books. Just as there is fiction for every taste, there are reference books that will inform and enrich the appreciation of the writers and works that make of leisure reading such a profitable and pleasureful activity.

Periodicals

The Armchair Detective. Published by Mysterious Press, 129 West 56 Street, New York, NY 10019. Quarterly.

CADS [Crime and Detective Stories]. Editor/publisher Geoff Bradley, 9 Vicarage Hill, South Benfleet, Essex, SS7 1PA England. 3 issues annually.

Clues: A Journal of Detection. Biannual. Popular Press, Bowling Green University, Bowling Green, OH 43403

Drood Review of Mystery. Editor/publisher, Jim Huang (Kalamazoo, Michigan). Monthly. The Drood Review, Box 1292, Brookline, MA 02146.

JDMBibliophile. Editor, Ed Hirshberg, Biannual, Department of English, University of South Florida, Tampa, FL 33620.

Mean Streets. Editor/publisher, Stuart Coupe, 214 Hat Hill Road, Blackheath, NSDW 2785, Australia. Irregular publication.

Mystery & Detective Monthly. Editor/publisher, Cap'n Bob Napier. 11 issues annually. 5601 N. 40th St., Tacoma, WA 98407.

Mystery Readers Journal. Editor/publisher, Janet Rudolph. Quarterly. Mystery Readers International, P.O. Box 8116, Berkeley, CA 94707.

Mystery Scene. Every six weeks. Mystery Enterprises, P.O. Box 669, Cedar Rapids, IA 52406-0669.

Twenty-Five Great Reads
Selected by the Editors

Lawrence Block	*The Burglar in the Closet*
Fredric Brown	*The Fabulous Clipjoint*
Raymond Chandler	*The Lady in the Lake*
Loren D. Estleman	*Peeper*
Stanton Ford	*Grieve for the Past*
Richard Forrest	*A Child's Garden of Death*
Brian Garfield	*Recoil*
Dorothy Gilman	*The Tightrope Walker*
Carolyn G. Hart	*The Christie Caper*
Joan Hess	*Roll Over & Play Dead*
George V. Higgins	*The Friends of Eddie Coyle*
Chester Himes	*The Big Gold Dream*
Dean R. Koontz	*The Vision*
Francis & Richard Lockridge	*Murder Within Murder*
Marie Belloc Lowndes	*The Lodger*
Ross Macdonald	*The Far Side of the Dollar*
Charlotte MacLeod	*The Gladstone Bag*
Ed McBain	*Sadie When She Died*
Margaret Millar	*The Murder of Miranda*
David Morrell	*First Blood*
Barbara Paul	*Liars & Tyrants & People Who Turn Blue*
Elizabeth Peters	*The Last Camel Died at Noon*
Rex Stout	*Some Buried Caesar*
Donald E. Westlake	*Adios, Scheherazade*
Margaret Yorke	*The Come-On*

Twelve "Overlooked" Contemporary Writers
Selected by Jon L. Breen

(Note: "Overlooked" and "underrated" are highly relative terms. Though some of these writers are comparatively obscure and others quite well known, none of them in my opinion has been as highly valued as deserved.)

Harold Adams
James Anderson
Miriam Borgenicht
K. C. Constantine
Warwick Downing
Tony Fennelly

Richard Forrest
Joyce Harrington
William Harrington
Joe L. Hensley
James Sherburne
Tobias Wells (Stanton Forbes)

The Twelve Most Important Spy Novels and Short-Story Collections
Selected by Douglas G. Greene

Huan Mee	*A Diplomatic Woman,* 1900
William LeQueux	*Secrets of the Foreign Office,* 1903
Joseph Conrad	*The Secret Agent,* 1907
John Buchan	*The Thirty-Nine Steps,* 1915
E. Philips Oppenheim	*The Great Impersonation,* 1920
Somerset Maugham	*Ashenden,* 1928
Graham Greene	*The Confidential Agent,* 1939
Eric Ambler	*The Mask of Dimitrios,* 1939
Ian Fleming	*From Russia, With Love,* 1957
Len Deighton	*The Ipcress File,* 1962
John le Carré	*The Spy Who Came in from the Cold,* 1963
Patricia McGerr	*Legacy of Danger,* 1970

Fifteen Contemporary Traditional Mystery Novels

Selected by Jon L. Breen

(all by living writers and published in the last twenty years)

Barbara D'Amato	*Hard Tack*
William L. DeAndrea	*The Werewolf Murders*
Colin Dexter	*The Wench is Dead*
Peter Dickinson	*One Foot in the Grave*
Susan Dunlap	*A Dinner to Die For*
Aaron Elkins	*Old Bones*
Jane Haddam	*Precious Blood*
P. D. James	*The Black Tower*
Gaylord Larsen	*Atascadero Island*
Francis M. Nevins, Jr.	*Corrupt and Ensnare*
Elizabeth Peters	*The Murders of Richard III*
Herbert Resnicow	*The Hot Place*
John Sladek	*Black Aura*
Scott Turow	*Presumed Innocent*
James Yaffe	*Mom Meets Her Maker*

THE BLACK DETECTIVE

Chester Himes/Archive Photos

CHESTER HIMES AND THE BLACK EXPERIENCE

H. R. F. Keating

IN SELECTING my favorite books, I try to avoid basing my choices on anything other than the merits of the books themselves, but in the case of Chester Himes, another consideration has influenced me: his life, though the book I have chosen, can stand comparison with my other choices. But Chester Himes, who was born in 1909 and died in 1984, spent seven of those years in the Ohio State Penitentiary, and so had an experience of the authentic depths. It was while he was inside that he took to reading the books of Dashiell Hammett and decided, approaching the age of fifty, that he, too, might be able to produce something of the sort if he "told it like it is."

The other important fact about Chester Himes as a man is that he was black. His books are so firmly imbued with the experience of being black in America, and to a small extent in France, where he spent the last part of his life, that there is no getting away from the race question.

His notion of telling it like it is paid off, though not with the certainty it deserved to. His first book, written originally in French, as were all his books except this one, won for him the Grand Prix de la Littérature Policière. But subsequently, with the books going into paperback only in the English-speaking countries, he went through a bad patch. He did not deserve to. The books, especially this one, bring us a fundamentally tragic vision in terms that are often wildly funny.

And in Coffin Ed Johnson and Grave Digger Jones he created a duo of detectives fit to stand beside any in the roll of memorable sleuths. They embody, in an uncompromisingly black way, all that is best in the American private eye tradition, though they are in fact detectives of the New York Police Department. They contrive, however, to get themselves so loosely linked to the white police

high-ups of the world outside Harlem where they operate that, beyond just reporting by radio to Captain Anderson when they find a corpse, they are to all intents as much their own men as Philip Marlowe or Lew Archer. They didn't care, Himes writes, who became boss. "We just get pissed off with all the red tape," Grave Digger once said. "We want to get down to the nitty-gritty."

So they do, to the nitty-gritty of the horrifyingly violent and macabre world of black Harlem, where they war industriously against their soul brothers on the other side of the law, as tough and violent themselves on occasion as the criminals they aim to prevent from committing worse violence. They maintain a grand unconcern with such lesser crimes as prostitution and its feeder vices like bottle peddlers, short con, and steering, and as far as they are concerned "pansies could pansy all they pleased."

And they make jokes. The first thing to learn about whorechasing, Coffin Ed gravely observes, "is what to do with your money while screwing." Simple, Grave Digger answers, feeding him: you leave what you don't need at home. And Coffin Ed comes up with the punchline. "And let your old lady find it? What's the difference?"

But they also make comments on the sordid surroundings they work in, like the indoor walls of an apartment house they visit in the course of a night's duty, "covered with obscene graffiti, mammoth sexual organs, vulgar limericks, opened legs, telephone numbers, outright boasting, insidious suggestions, and impertinent or pertinent comments about the various tenants' love habits." Grave Digger takes it all in. "And people live here," he says, his eyes sad.

There is worse than this too. As the book's twin stories of grotesque and serious crime draw to an end, there is an extraordinary scene in a subway train beneath teeming Harlem when a blind man gets in, believes himself to be insulted, pulls out a big .45 revolver, and attempts to shoot a ''fat yellow preacher'' who has tried to calm him with ''Peace, man, God don't know no color.'' And pandemonium follows as the blind man looses off shot after shot.

It is a fearful symbol of how Chester Himes came to see life, in Harlem and elsewhere. He says in a preface that he was told this true story by a friend, and then thought ''that all unorganized violence is like a blind man with a pistol.''

Notable Novels About Black America
Selected by the Editors

Gar Haywood
Fear of the Dark

Chester Himes
The Crazy Kill

Chester Himes
All Shot Up

Chester Himes
The Big Gold Dream

Chester Himes
The Heat's On

Chester Himes
A Rage in Harlem

Ed Lacy
Room to Swing

Ed Lacy
Black and Whitie

Ed Lacy
Harlem Underground

Michael Kingsley
Black Man, White Man, Dead Man

Walter Mosley
White Butterfly

Percy Spurlark Parker
Good Girls Don't

RELIGIOUS MYSTERIES

INTRODUCTION

Jon L. Breen

ALTHOUGH THERE HAVE ALWAYS been close links between religion and detective fiction, only recently have religious controversies and the details of religious practice been a frequent subject of mysteries. While early detective fiction assumed a moral order and the existence of a higher power, usually based on the Judeo-Christian theology of the European and North American society that produced most of it, any deep consideration of religious teachings and values was generally off limits, as was the inclusion of any character or situation that might put the church in a bad light.

The most famous early example of a clerical detective was, of course, G. K. Chesterton's Father Brown, who appeared in no novels but five volumes of short stories, beginning with *The Innocence of Father Brown* (1911) and concluding with *The Scandal of Father Brown* (1935). Featuring many impossible crimes and inexplicable occurrences elucidated with a frequent use of Chestertonian paradox by the deceptively mild and inconspicuous priest, the stories reflected their author's attraction and eventual conversion to Roman Catholicism.

Though churchly backgrounds were sometimes employed in other detective fiction of the time— Agatha Christie's first Miss Marple novel, *The Murder at the Vicarage* (1930), and Dorothy L. Sayers's novel and bell-ringing handbook, *The Nine Tailors* (1934), are two famous examples—Chesterton and Father Brown had the religious detective series pretty much to themselves during the period between world wars. The other strongly religious detective character of the period, Melville Davisson Post's nineteenth-century Virginian, *Uncle Abner, Master of Mysteries* (1918), was a pious layman rather than preacher. Father Ronald Knox did not feature a clerical sleuth in his novels, and Canon Victor L. Whitechurch did not employ a member of the clergy in a detective *series*, though he did feature Vicar Westerham in a single book, *The Crime at Diana's Pool* (1927).

When more clerical detectives did appear, they were usually, like Father Brown, Catholic. Fiction's first nun-detective, Sister Ursula, appeared in two novels by H. H. Holmes (William A. P. White, best known as Anthony Boucher): *Nine Times Nine* (1940) and *Rocket to the Morgue* (1942). Edward D. Hoch, writing in the essay collection *Synod of Sleuths* (Scarecrow, 1990), notes that readers of the first Ursula novel will be reminded of Chesterton by such elements as "the paradox, the bogus cult at the Temple of Light, the locked-room murder, and the erudite conversation. . . . In fact, if Chesterton had ever written a Father Brown novel it probably would have been quite a bit like *Nine Times Nine*. The novel remains Anthony Boucher's best effort" (page 5).

Other Catholic clerical detectives to appear in a series include Jack (not-the-TV-star) Webb's Father Joseph Shanley, who teamed with Jewish police detective Sammy Golden in a series beginning with *The Big Sin* (1952); Henri Catalan's Soeur Angele in three French novels, the first translated as *Soeur Angele and the Embarrassed Ladies* (1955); and Leonard Holton's (Leonard Wibberley) Father Joseph Bredder in a series beginning with *The Saint Maker* (1959).

Were there no non-Catholic clergy sleuths in the decades before 1960? Not many, and the most prominent, Margaret Scherf's Reverend Martin Buell, who first appeared in *Always Murder a Friend* (1948), is not noted for his theology.

The first rabbi-detective did not appear until 1964, but when he did, he became one of the most commercially and artistically successful religious sleuths in detective fiction. When Harry Kemelman created Rabbi David Small in *Friday the Rabbi Slept Late* (1964), he had a considerable track record as a writer of detective short stories about college professor Nicky Welt, but his original intention was to write a straight novel about Jewish temple life, adding a detective to the mix only at the suggestion of an editor. Though the novels include sound formal puzzles, these are only an excuse for Kemelman's real intent. He writes in *Synod of Sleuths*, "The purpose of the books is to teach and explain Judaism to Jews and Gentiles" (page 130). In fact, in addition to the ten Rabbi Small mysteries to date (the full week plus three wild cards), he also wrote one seminovel (actually a series of essays in dialogue form) called *Conversations with Rabbi Small* (1981) that teaches about the Jewish faith with no mystery plot at all.

The seventies saw the number of mysteries with religious themes increase, and the trend continues to this day. Often ignored in discussions of religious mysteries are the Navajo Tribal Police novels of Tony Hillerman, beginning with *The Blessing Way* (1970), which have probably taught more people about Native American religion and culture than all the nonfiction works ever written. As with Kemelman, the aim is to explain, not to proselytize.

Catholics continue to be in the majority for whatever reason. Prominent priest-detectives to debut since 1970 include Ralph McInerny's Father Roger Dowling, in *Her Death of Cold* (1977); William X. Kienzle's Father Robert Koesler, in *The Rosary Murders* (1979); Andrew M. Greeley's Father Blackie Ryan, in *Virgin and Martyr* (1984), followed by a paperback series of mysteries based on the Beatitudes, beginning with *Happy Are the Meek* (1985); and, outranking the others, William T. Love's Bishop Francis Regan, in *The Chartreuse Clue* (1990). Of the four authors, only Greeley is a practicing priest, though Kienzle is a former priest. The first nun (to my knowledge) to pen a mystery series is Sister Carol Anne O'Marie, whose Sister Mary Helen solved her first case in *A Novena for Murder* (1984). Best-known of several other nun-sleuths currently active is Sister Mary Teresa, whom McInerny writes about under the brilliant punning pseudonym Monica Quill. The book titles, beginning with *Not a Blessed Thing* (1981), usually also feature puns.

Many have reasonably assumed Harry Kemelman is a rabbi, which he is not. But Joseph Telushkin, the creator of the second well-known rabbinical sleuth, Daniel Winter, is himself a rabbi. Winter makes his first appearance in *The Unorthodox Murder of Rabbi Wahl* (1987) and has appeared twice more to date. Like Kemelman, he has a knack for

classical puzzle plotting as well as a desire to educate about Judaism.

But what happened to the Protestants? Though they haven't really held up their end in the clerical detecting stakes, they do have Charles Merrill Smith's Con Randollph, who appeared in five novels beginning with *Reverend Randollph and the Wages of Sin* (1974). A Methodist minister and the author of such volumes of clerical humor as *How to Become a Bishop Without Being Religious* (1965), Smith's real calling was as an informal essayist rather than a fiction writer, and after the first couple of books their quality purely as detective fiction slid somewhat. But they never stopped being entertaining. After Smith's death, his son Terrence Lore Smith penned a sixth volume in the series, *Reverend Randollph and the Modern Miracles* (1988). Though I have reason to believe the book actually exists (I saw a review somewhere but don't remember where), I have never seen a copy. It is so scarce, some have suspected it is a "ghost" book.

With the passing of Smith, the most prominent Protestant series character is Isabelle Holland's Reverend Claire Aldington, who made her first appearance in *A Death at St. Anselm's* (1984).

Along with the religious detectives per se, more and more writers are including theological themes in books not concerning clerical sleuths. Conservative Christian publishers have brought out quite a few mysteries. Not surprisingly, the effort to evangelize has sometimes overshadowed the books' value as mysteries, but some are worth reading purely for entertainment. Gaylord Larsen, whose first two books, *The Kilbourne Connection* (1980) and *Trouble Crossing the Pyrenees* (1983), were from religious houses, has since moved to secular publishers. Many writers have featured televangelists in mysteries in recent years, mostly with satirical scorn—Larsen introduces one of the most interesting of the breed, because not one-sidedly villainous, in *Atascadero Island* (1989).

Numerous writers have used Jewish backgrounds to good effect. The Rina Lazarus series of Faye Kellerman, beginning with *The Ritual Bath* (1986), is set in an Orthodox Jewish community, as is Rochelle Krich's *Till Death Do Us Part* (1992). Kellerman also wrote a memorable novel about Jewish conversos in Elizabethan England in *The Quality of Mercy* (1989). Jewish life in Britain is explored in S. T. Haymon's series about detective Ben Jurnet, beginning with *Death and the Pregnant Virgin* (1980).

The Church of Jesus Christ of Latter-Day Saints, which figured (not too favorably) in Arthur Conan Doyle's first Sherlock Holmes story, *A Study in Scarlet* (1887), has returned strongly as a detective fiction subject in the 1980s, most notably in Cleo Jones's angry novel about the condition of Mormon women, *Prophet Motive* (1984), and Robert Irvine's continuing series about Salt Lake City private eye Moroni Traveler, beginning with *Baptism for the Dead* (1988).

Mention should also be made of Ellis Peters's (Edith Pargeter) long series about the medieval monk-detective Brother Cadfael. The herbalist of Shrewsbury's Abbey of Saint Peter and Saint Paul first appeared in *A Morbid Taste for Bones* (1977) and since has averaged more than one new case a year. A one-shot medieval mystery that achieved

surprising best seller status was Italian novelist Umberto Eco's long, difficult, and rewarding *The Name of the Rose* (English language edition 1983), about Brother William of Baskerville, a Sherlockian Franciscan.

In early 1993 I served on a panel at the Left Coast crime mystery convention that tackled, among other things, the question: what is a religious mystery? My definition, not necessarily shared by the other panelists, was that it is a mystery that attempts to convey some sort of religious feeling or religious message, that doesn't just use religion as a backdrop. Some of the books discussed above would qualify under this definition, and some would not. But such is the freedom enjoyed by mystery writers of the nineties that it is permissible for a novel to exude genuine religious faith without having a background or characters specifically concerned with the practice of religion. One such book is Kevin Robinson's *Mall Rats* (1992).

THE JEWISH MYSTERY

Serita Stevens and Fanny Zindel

Serita Stevens

So, YOU WANT TO WRITE a mystery? *Nu?* What's stopping you? Ah, you want to write not just a mystery but a Jewish mystery, something with a little *Yiddishkite* maybe? More power to you. It should only have a million printings and be a best seller a billion times over—at least.

So? What's the problem? You're not writing? A mystery is a mystery is a mystery. With only a few published mysteries to my credit—and a couple or four gothics—who am I to tell you what a mystery needs? Go. Learn that from experts.

But if you're doing a mystery with Jewish characters, you need to know a *shmeckle* (small bit) about Judaism. I can't say that I blame you for wanting to do a Jewish mystery. A boom there's been lately in that field, even a whole committee for awards now. So, if you're Jewish and you write a mystery, does that make it a Jewish mystery?

Let me think. No. I don't believe it does. You see Alex Delaware with a *keepa* on his head or *dovening* three times a day? No, sirree, and yet Jonathan Kellerman, a dearer man there should be, does. So, the Alex Delaware series is not Jewish mysteries. But his wife, Faye . . .? Now, she's horse radish of a different color. With her a mystery is a Jewish mystery because her character Rina (*Ritual Bath, Sacred and Profane, Day of Atonement, False Prophet*, etc.) is religious and Pete is becoming so.

Why are Jewish mysteries so popular?

You see, we Jews, we read a lot. After all, we're not called the ''People of the Book'' for nothing. (Of course the book they refer to is our Torah. Still, why do you think so many Jews wear glasses? Sorry, a small diversion.)

So, you need to decide just what a Jewish mystery is and then you need to decide if you want to be a Faye or a Jonathan. Believe me, I wouldn't mind the success of either of them. Still, you need to know about Judaism to decide how you want to structure this great best-selling mystery of yours.

Ach, Hillel (a great medieval Jewish sage) I'm not. Teaching you all about Judaism while you stand on one foot, I can't. But maybe a little *sechel* (common sense) you can get. Better still, you should learn a bit with the rabbi, maybe. Read a book. A few books even. Oh, I see you don't have time to read a few books. *Oy vey*, (tsk, tsk). Well, something I'll give you here, but not much. A few things for your characters to chew on. At least it will get you started writing the great Jewish mystery. So. I do what I can.

I'm not going to tell you the whole *megellah* about Judaism. That you have to find out yourself. But so you know, I'll tell you that we read the *Megellah* at Purim—the whole story of Queen Esther saving the Jewish people from doom.

As they say, here goes nothing.

Still teething on my nouns and pronouns I was, when my writing professor at Antioch, in London, saw that I was having trouble with my characters. ''Since you identify with your Judaism and your heritage so much, why don't you pretend all your characters are Jewish.''

''But they're not,'' I protested of the Irish saga I was then writing. (A Jew during the Battle of the Boyne? Well, I'm sure there were some since we're like grains of sand—everywhere. Sometimes you like us, and sometimes we rub raw on your nerves.

Even in China we were, during Genghis Kahn, no less. But again, I digress.)

So again, we come back to that question. What is a Jewish mystery?

I've heard it said that a religious mystery is one that has both evil and good in it. But what makes that different from any other mystery? Questioning further, I understood. Most religious communities— be they the Amish in *Witness*, Muslim, Episcopalian, Catholic, or Jewish—have a certain hierarchy, definite laws, and definite ways of doing things. People who come in from the outside are in conflict with the close society. It's the gefilte-fish-out-of-water concept. (Personally, I like the water rather than the jellied broth.)

For instance, those who are very Orthodox ask their *rebbe* (rabbi) questions on almost everything, since the Torah has finite answers for everything in our daily lives. (Some of this was seen in the movie *A Stranger Among Us*). The editors, and readers, like it when they learn about a life and a world they aren't privy to.

So, readers of Harry Kemelman learn not only about the character of David Small, but about some of the inner workings of the Torah, the Talmud, and the Conservative synagogue. And the readers of Joseph Telushkin learn about the rules of forgiveness both in *The Unorthodox Murder of Rabbi Wahl* and *An Eye for an Eye* as well as how the Orthodox and Reform movements mesh together. Faye Kellerman's *Ritual Bath* showed us some of the laws of purity that the religious women follow and also the importance of lineage, since Peter's natural mother was a Jew, that made him a Jew. Even though he hadn't been practicing, once a Jew, always a Jew. Therefore, he could marry Rina as long as he started to practice and study the traditions.

But I also learned that the Jewish mystery doesn't have to be a *Till Death Do Us Part, A Stranger Among Us, An Eye for an Eye,* a *Red Sea, Dead Sea,* a *Bagels for Tea,* or even a *Ritual Bath.* It can have the religion in the background too, almost like that *Unorthodox Practices* or where Judaism is a cultural thing, like *Crimes and Misdemeanors.* And the character, like Moses Wine, doesn't have to be a religious Jew to go *Raising the Dead.*

In *Red Sea, Dead Sea* and in *Bagels for Tea,* Fanny Zindel is both a Conservative Jew and a cultural Jew because she identifies fully with the history and heritage even though she may not keep all the laws as the Orthodox do.

So again, what makes a Jewish mystery?

Further questioning came up with character. Well, Fanny certainly is a character.

To quote my editor, Ruth Cavin (St. Martin's Press), "Character is everything. If you have a good character, you have a good mystery."

But the fact is, each person—character—is a direct result of what has gone before him and how his family adjusted to it.

So? What or who is a Jew? It depends on who you ask. Probably we should start at the beginning: the birth. They say if you talk with two Jews, you will get three opinions. Such a headache like you wouldn't believe that question causes.

If we're dealing with Orthodox, then we have to follow the *halacha* (Jewish law) which says that only those born of Jewish mothers are Jewish. Fathers? Not a chance. Did you know that fifty-two percent of American Jews have intermarried? And if it's a father who is Jewish, that's like eating sour cream and borscht with ham, something those who observe don't do. In other words, the kid is not a Jew if her mother isn't. As I said, a headache.

If you're Reform, however, they'll accept a child of a non-Jewish mother. But if the half-Jew kid from the father's side wants to marry a whole Jew, then chances are she/he would have to convert Orthodox. As I pointed out with Peter Decker, since his mother was a Jew, even though he wasn't practicing, he did not have to formally convert.

I know quite a few adults who have become bitter at not being accepted by the Jewish community, and yet they were considered Jewish enough to be murdered by rabid right wingers in Nazi Germany or in our great South by the Klan.

So lineage is important for your character. In fact, we used it as a partial motive in *Bagels for Tea*.

Then again, there are those who call themselves Jewish but are really of a Christian sect called Jews for Jesus. Some of them might have been born Jewish and converted out, but a good percentage of them are not. Now, that's conflict, especially when you put them up against the Jews for Judaism, who try to win the Jewish cult converts back into the fold.

It's important, therefore, to decide who your characters are and if they are following the laws

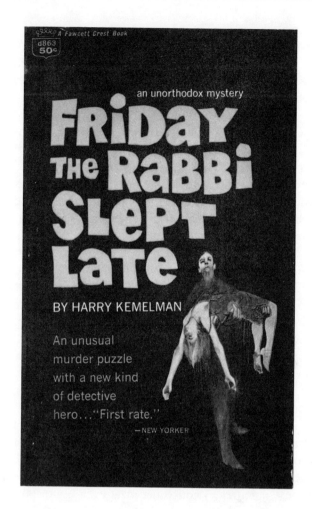

as Orthodox, traditional, Conservative, Reform, or marginal, cultural Jews who enjoy some of the ceremonies and the traditional foods as gefilte fish and beet borscht. Did they grow up this way? Did they give it up later? Did they keep it up? Because they "had to" or because they wanted to?

You can see Jewish characters are an endless variety from the Orthodox, who wear the traditional garb (black hats and fur strimels, but only a small number do this); to Orthodox who wear modern clothes; from women who cover their hair to women who don't; from egalitarian or traditional; to Conservative, reconstructionists; and congregations that have women rabbis; to the gay synagogues; to those who don't practice at all.

The fact is that of all those who identify themselves as Jewish, the Reform movement is the biggest. So chances are, unless you choose to have your character be Orthodox or Conservative, he'll probably be Reform or, sad to say, one of the many unaffiliated Jews, some who don't even want to recognize their religion and who don't want coworkers to know.

So, you need to get to know your characters and decide which of the many laws they will do and which they will ignore.

Of course, even these nonobservant Jews often can't help being affected by the major dictates of our religion—helping other people. The majority of us are liberal, Democratic do-gooders, except those few of us who murder, or arrange murders, as Meyer Lansky (Jewish Mafia head who was refused admittance into Israel) or even the guy in *Crimes and Misdemeanors*.

There's a saying "It's hard to be a Jew." If only you knew. We have 613 commandments—laws—that should be followed. For each one we do, we get blessings or points and it's considered a *mitzvah*. But with all those laws, you can see why Jewish guilt is a real thing.

The fact is, only a small percentage of us follow all the 613, but many of us try to obey the majority of them—especially the big ten. (Not schools, commandments.)

Even so, if your character keeps the Sabbath but drives to synagogue (*shul* for the Orthodox), or worse yet has to go in to work on Saturday, he'll feel guilty. If he keeps kosher at home, but maybe tastes some (*trayf*) nonkosher meat even by mistake (don't even think about bacon and ham), he feels guilty. If he wants to date a non-Jewish girl, he feels guilty. Worse yet, he'll feel the scorn of his mother. (Religious families sit *shiva*—mourning—for members who marry out.) Would a mother kill for her son? Maybe not, but you answer. I've heard of fathers paying off the prospective bride or groom to stay away.

Believe me, all of it, it's not easy.

So, just do me one favor. Be a *mensch*. If you're going to write about religious Jews or have items relating to Jewish traditions and culture in your story, then get it right. If you have a question, ask. No one will bite.

One example especially sticks out like a pork sausage (which you should know we don't eat) in the middle of the gefilte fish ball. In one book, a detective goes to the home of an ultra-Orthodox woman. The woman has her hair covered with a *tichel* (scarf), as prescribed by religious law. The man he is seeking is also supposedly religious. Yet the detective sees Oreo cookies on her counter. Since Oreo cookies are not kosher, she would not

have had them open on her counter, let alone even in her home.

In the book I'm working on now, the heroine is saved because she won't eat the unkosher meat—which she doesn't know, by the way, is poisoned.

Since there are too many laws to go into or even explain, as if I knew the half of them, I'll just give a couple more examples on how character affects what your story Jew does.

The Sabbath. Rules for this vary for where each person is on the religious scale. Fanny carries her purse and sometimes goes shopping on the Sabbath after *shul* since she was based on my grandmother who did this. But I leave work early on Friday to get my *Shabbos* (Sabbath) ready.

Since the Jewish calendar operates on a lunar cycle, the dates change each year. If your character observes the holidays, or your mystery takes place during the fall, check them out, as they may affect the story or provide a good alibi for him. Many of the holidays fall midweek. How do coworkers feel about Jews absent from the workplace for seven days (two for Rosh Hashanah, one Yom Kippur, two Sukkoth, two Simchath Torah) in the fall and four days in the spring for Passover? I had plenty of complaints from others about how they had to take up my slack during that time. Would it be a motive for murder? Who knows?

A Jewish character in a non-Jewish scene is always a good conflict, especially in a red-necked profession or a small biased southern town.

And, of course, with character comes voice. Most, I have to tell you, don't speak like me. *Oy gevalt!* The ones that do are usually *alta cockers* (old men and women). The true fact, *bubbe*, is that very few Jews speak with such exaggerated Yiddishisms, but since I'm a stereotype, who should care? But so you should know I do have an excuse. My mama and papa came from the Old Country—usually Eastern Europe—and being first-generation American, my folks spoke a lot of Yiddish in their English. So this is what I learned. So shoot me. But it's the producers in Hollywood from where I really learned my accent, that I will tell you. And from them, most of it is not quite kosher.

Characters have to have names. So, what's a Jewish name? Believe me, it can be just about anything. The Jews in your story don't have to be Cohens, Fischmans, Rosenbergs, Glassenbergs, or Mendelsons. Because many came from places where the names were not pronounceable to the

Ellis Island guards, everything was changed, short-ened, and Anglicized. True, there are some names that are still obviously Jewish but many more, espe-cially with intermarriage, that you'd never guess. Even a name like Stevens can be Jewish. So your characters can have just about any name you want to give them, as long as you know their history.

So, now you have the Jewish character, but you need more than character to make a good mystery. Believe me, Judaism itself, both religiously and cul-turally, has plenty of conflict and possibilities of themes if you want to stay within the folds. And even if you don't, that's okay too. But look, here are a few possible ideas that make a Jewish mystery an even Jewisher one.

Again, I ask, what can be a finer example than *Red Sea, Dead Sea* or *Bagels for Tea*? You should excuse my bragging. Or my friend's *Till Death Do Us Part*. (Rochelle, you can pay me later.)

In fact, as I write this, Passover (*Pesach*) is inching up. Cleaning the house to get rid of any *chumitz* (wheat products or any foods used during the year) is enough to make anyone crazy. An easy time it would be to "gaslight" someone, especially if they were already nuts from getting ready for the holiday.

It was during this time that the ritual murder accusations started and many a writer—including yours truly—has made use of this. (The first one started in England in 1140 when the Jews were ac-cused of using the blood of Christian children for their unleavened cakes [*matzas*]. A wonderful novel on this is *The Fixer* by Malamud.)

Again, everything is up to the character and his history. He could also be a *Bale-tchuvah* (newly righteous)—someone who has refound the reli-gion—our equivalent of a Born Again or he could be somewhat Sabbath observant, and somewhat ko-sher, or he could be someone who has given up everything because his father forced him to do things as a kid. If she got involved with someone who didn't want her to be observant, if maybe she was making that someone crazy by her newfound zeal, maybe that someone might decide to do away with her. (This actually happened in our community recently. They found the wife cut up into little bits in the husband's garage.)

Okay, so I ask you again, what makes a Jewish mystery?

Oh? You were asking me? So, how should I know? I only write them.

Information sources:

Orthodox:
Union of Orthodox Congregations
333 Seventh Ave
New York, NY 10001
(212) 563-4000

Conservative:
United Synagogue of America
155 Fifth Ave
New York, NY 10010
(212) 533-7800

Reform:
Union of American Hebrew Congregations
838 Fifth Ave
New York, NY 10003
(212) 249-0100

Council of Jewish Federations
730 Broadway
New York, NY 10003
(212) 598-3500

Jewish Community Centers Associations
15 East 26th St
New York, NY 10010
(212) 532-4949

Fox, Rabbi Karen and Phyllis Zimbler Miller, *Seasons for Celebration.* Perigee (Putnam), 1992.

Donin, Rabbi Hayim Halevy *To Be a Jew.* Basic Books, 1972.

Almost anything by Rabbi Ayeh Kapplan

Or any rabbi of the sector you want your character to be.

SAINTS PRESERVE US:
The Catholic Mystery
Ralph McInerny

ST. AUGUSTINE SAID he knew what time was until someone asked him for a definition. Of course he could easily tell you what time it was—if he was in the vicinity of a water clock. Similarly, most of us think we know what a Catholic novel is, and derivatively, a Catholic mystery novel, until we are pressed for a definition. Nonetheless, like knowing what time it is, as opposed to knowing what time is, we know one when we see it.

It is oddly true that writers pretty universally recognized as Catholic novelists—e.g., Graham Greene—vigorously denied being any such thing, whereas a writer like Flannery O'Connor, only one of whose short stories has Catholic characters, considered herself to be a Catholic novelist.

Here is a list of descriptions that will *not* do in identifying a Catholic novel or mystery novel:

1. It is written by a Catholic.
2. It deals with Catholic themes.
3. It has a priest in it.
4. It has an *imprimatur.*
5. It is on the Index of Prohibited Books.

Ad 1m. Joseph Conrad and Ford Madox Ford were Catholics, so was F. Scott Fitzgerald and, for a time, Ernest Hemingway. But surely it would be Pickwickian to call them Catholic novelists.

It would be difficult to find a French, Italian, or Spanish writer who wasn't baptized as a Catholic, so the problem might seem to be one of discovering who in those countries is a non-Catholic novelist. Among mystery writers (and Belgians) Georges Simenon was Catholic in this minimal sense. . . . Clearly this is not a helpful tack to take.

Ad 2m. Franz Werfel wrote *The Song of Bernadette* and he was Jewish.

Ad 3m. Was Shakespeare a Catholic? More or less, but the friar in *Romeo and Juliet* would not suffice to make the play Catholic.

Ad 4m. Novels do not receive ecclesiastical permission to be printed.

Ad 5m. The *Index librorum prohibitorum* has gone the way of Friday abstinence.

Doubtless there are other, and more serious, ways of trying to define the Catholic novel, but I suspect they would all fail by either excluding or including too much. I think it is more useful, though not very tidy, to take a novel as paradigmatic of the Catholic novel, work up a description from it, and then see what other works are like it. Call this the family-resemblance approach.

Dante's *Divine Comedy* is a massively Catholic work of the imagination. What is the literal sense of the poem, according to Dante? The way in which men and women, by the use of their free will, merit eternal reward or punishment. Seeing human action through the lens of the eternal stakes involved is the mark of the *Comedy* and provides a touchstone for Catholic literature.

In the case of mystery fiction, it is not adventurous to take Chesterton's Father Brown stories as paradigmatic. What are some of the marks of these stories?

First of all, like Dante, Chesterton puts before us human beings, acting in the fleeting contingent circumstances that define our lives, making decisions which are decisive for who they morally are.

Second, over and above the couplet crime and punishment, there is another: sin and forgiveness.

If we consider the first of these two marks, we will soon realize that it is not peculiar to Chesterton's mystery stories. Indeed, some version of it seems to show up all across the spectrum of fiction. Flannery O'Connor says somewhere that *all* literature has an anagogic sense. (The anagogic is one of the nonliteral senses of a text—this theory was developed to talk about how to read Scripture on several levels.) I think O'Connor meant something like what I stated as the first mark of Chesterton's Father Brown stories.

This sums up the problem: If O'Connor is right, what I give as the first mark of the Father Brown stories, as paradigmatic Catholic mysteries, is a mark of literature *tout court.* So let us make a virtue of necessity and agree with O'Connor. Perhaps anything we would recognize as fiction is the presentation of human agents engaged in making choices that have moral import such that the way they act reenforces or weakens their moral character. Doubtless this is why children and adults, the young and old, men and women, instinctively turn to imaginative reenactments of human action for some sense of what it all means.

Mystery fiction does this on a fairly superficial level. Will the criminal be caught and punished? Will the murderer be identified and put in the slammer? Such stories play out against the assumption that killing other people for fun and profit is wrong and ought to be punished, and the detective who discovers who dun it is performing an essential societal function.

It is the second mark of the Father Brown stories that indicates what sets them off as Catholic—perhaps generically as Christian, maybe even as religious (and, if you are Socrates or Plato, as philosophical). *The consequences of action reach beyond time and the span of earthly life.* This enhances the importance of fleeting deeds; it puts an enormous premium on what we do here and now. Religion

was once dismissed as pie in the sky, but the pie, or its withholding, is the just desert of what one does on earth. The moral dimension of human action is included in the religious, but not vice versa, and that is why the first mark is, as Flannery O'Connor suggests, universal to imaginative literature.

Heavy stuff. I suspect that by and large, readers are willing to use far more superficial criteria to separate Catholic fiction and Catholic mysteries from others. And the obvious note will be the presence of a priest or nun. When I began the Father Dowling stories, I wanted a priest to represent the contrast of sin and forgiveness and a cop, Captain Keegan, to represent that between crime and punishment. The novels exhibit the way these two overlap, interlock, and play off against each other. But it would be difficult for me to think of those stories without all the lore of a parish rectory, the liturgy, the various tasks of a pastor's day, etc.

So, too, when on a half-serious dare from my agent I began the Sister Mary Teresa series, writing

as Monica Quill, the distinctive religious garb of my main character and the orderly existence of my nuns and their outlook on life spurred me on and give the novels their particular flavor.

It is easy for me to see how those two series differ from my Andrew Broom series and the new series I have begun under the pen name Edward Mackin. But the differences are, I think, however essential to those series, in another sense superficial. Certainly *I* feel I am engaged in the same task whether I am writing a Father Dowling or one of my *hors de série* mysteries, like the recent *Infra Dig*.

When Graham Greene denied being a Catholic novelist, he did so out of fear that he would be regarded as somehow a spokesman for the Church. Most novels turn on actions that fall short of an ideal rather than exemplify it. Like most of us, Greene wrote mostly about sinners. He wasn't recommending sin, but he had a salutary sense that it is in our failures that most of us get such intimations of the good as we have. That is an Augustinian thought, or at least a thought inspired by Augustine's rocky road to conversion. He called the story of his life *Confessions*. Maybe that is a good way to think of Catholic novels—they put before us humans like ourselves whose lives are negatively measured by the ideal. That is, they fall short of it. Reading, we feel what Aristotle said we would—pity and fear. Pity, because they are so much like us; fear, because failure comes so easily to us as well.

At the base of all fiction, mystery or not, Catholic or not, there has to be plain good old story, engaging the reader, pulling him along to see how things come out. If that isn't there, nothing else will interest us.

Some Notable Religious Mysteries
Selected by the Editors

Umberto Eco
The Name of the Rose

Thomas Gifford
The Assassini

Andrew M. Greeley
Happy Are the Witches

Jane Haddam
Precious Blood

Isabelle Holland
A Fatal Advent

Harry Kemelman
Someday the Rabbi Will Leave

William X. Kienzle
Deathbed

Ralph McInerny
Basket Case

Thomas Monteleone
The Blood of the Lamb

Sister Carol Anne O'Marie
A Novena for Murder

Monica Quill
The Veil of Ignorance

PRIVATE EYE MYSTERIES

INTRODUCTION

Jon L. Breen

CARROLL JOHN DALY'S Race Williams, who made his first appearance in the *Black Mask* novelette "Knights of the Open Palm" (June 1, 1923), is usually accorded the distinction of being the first of the tough private eyes, beating to the post by an eyelash another *Black Mask* character, Dashiell Hammett's Continental Op, who first appeared in "Arson Plus" (October 1, 1923, as by Peter Collinson).

But it's not that simple. For after all, Sherlock Holmes was a private eye—he was not a part of an official police force and he performed his investigations for payment—and so was American dime-novel-hero Nick Carter. Many other consulting detectives, English and American, followed in the footsteps of Holmes: such once popular, now fairly obscure characters as Arthur Morrison's Martin Hewitt and Carolyn Wells's Fleming Stone were sleuths-for-hire. What distinguished them from Williams and the Op? For one thing, the *Black Mask* characters rose from a different tradition: not of the formal cerebral detective story that began with Poe but of the more action-oriented adventures of the dime novels.

Through most of the twenties, the tough private eye was a pulp magazine phenomenon, though by the end of the decade both Hammett and Daly had been published in book form. Daly's 1927 novel, *The Snarl of the Beast,* called his masterpiece by Charles Shibuk in the introduction to the 1981 Gregg Press reprint, contains as many of the conventions of private eye fiction to come as does Poe's "The Murders in the Rue Morgue" of classical detective fiction. Daly provides the urban atmosphere, the tough slang, the p.i. code of honor, the snappy repartee, the colorful villains, the contrast of low life and high society, plenty of physical action (with fist, car, and gat) and vivid violence, gallows humor, picturesque prose (including similes), a complicated plot, and even some literary allusions.

As Williams calls himself a halfway house between the cops and the crooks, the novel represents a halfway point between pre–World War I dime-novel melodrama and the more sophisticated hard-boiled sleuthing offered by Hammett, Chandler, and their successors. The novel is a museum piece to be sure, but it offers the same kind of fascination to a hard-boiled devotee that a very early talking picture offers a film buff.

Daly fell by the wayside as a hardcover author and spent the rest of his career back in the pages of pulps. Hammett is another matter entirely. The first two Continental Op novels, *Red Harvest* and *The Dain Curse* (both 1929), probably would have been enough to assure him a place in crime fiction history, but their three successors far surpassed them—in different respects. *The Maltese Falcon* (1930) is the only book-length case of San Francisco private eye Sam Spade, but largely because of movies and radio, Spade became a far more famous sleuth than the Op. The novel, combining the tough *Black Mask* prose with the fair-play plotting of the classical school, is one of the most influential in the history of the genre. The whodunit surprise has the dubious honor of being the most frequently imitated in later private eye novels. His last two novels—*The Glass Key* (1931) and *The Thin Man* (1934)—feature gambler Ned Beaumont and retired cop Nick Charles respectively, so neither is technically a private eye novel, but the one ranks among his finest artistic achievements while the other is the least of his novels artistically and, again thanks to the movie screen, his greatest commercial success. Though he produced no more novels and little substantial writing of any kind after 1934, Hammett remained a major and influential figure.

Private eyes grew in popularity through the thirties. Jonathan Latimer's alcoholic Chicago sleuth Bill Crane debuted in *Murder in the Madhouse* (1935). Rex Stout first unveiled an unbeatable combination, the breezy private eye narrative of Archie Goodwin with the eccentric supersleuth persona of Nero Wolfe, in *Fer-de-Lance* (1934) and continued to chronicle their adventures into the seventies. Stout also created one of the first female private eyes, Dol Bonner, in the 1937 novel *The Hand in the Glove,* but he never returned her to a starring role.

If 1923 was the most significant year in private eye history, 1939 can't be far behind. Not because Erle Stanley Gardner took on the pseudonym A. A. Fair and created the detecting team of Donald Lam and Bertha Cool in *The Bigger They Come.* Not even because Brett Halliday's Miami shamus Mike Shayne began his long and successful career in *Dividend on Death.* And certainly not because gentleman amateur sleuth Ellery Queen made his one tentative foray into private-eyedom in *The Dragon's Teeth.*

No, 1939 was the year Raymond Chandler, who had been serving a pulp apprenticeship for several years, published his first Philip Marlowe novel, *The Big Sleep,* and emerged as the greatest private eye writer of them all—or, some would argue, second only to Hammett. Chandler's colorful, picturesque, simile-strewn prose became the most imitated style in the genre and remains so today. Though, like Hammett, he didn't completely eschew the puzzle plotting of the classicists, he concentrated his efforts on creating dramatic scenes, sometimes to the disadvantage of plot clarity. Few readers minded. Also like Hammett, he owed much of his commercial success to successful film and radio adaptations of his novels and his continuing character.

The private eye was a stronger presence than ever through the forties, with such memorable characters as John Evans's (Howard Browne) Paul Pine, Frederic Brown's Ed and Am Hunter, and Wade Miller's (Robert Wade and Bill Miller) Max Thursday arriving on the scene. The last part of the decade saw the next major developments in private eye writing: the debuts of Mickey Spillane's Mike Hammer and of John (Ross) Macdonald's (Kenneth Millar) Lew Archer. Hammer, more a commercial than an artistic milestone, was a character who sold unprecedented numbers of copies while offending nearly everybody with equally unprecedented sadism and sexuality. His first case was *I, the Jury* (1947). (I admit I find little to admire in Spillane's work and believe the negative reactions of many

contemporary critics were right on the money; however, I have to say a number of writers and critics whose opinions are worthy of respect believe he is an important writer of crime fiction.) Archer, who gathered momentum more slowly from his first appearance in *The Moving Target* (1949), initially seemed one of many Marlowe clones (especially heavy on the similes) but gradually established his own style of plotting and social observation and brought new consideration from mainstream literary critics to the detective story form.

Through the fifties, the private eye reached his (not often her at that time) peak of popularity. Paperbacks became more and more important, in some respects taking the place of the pulp magazines as a fiction market. Though Spillane's work appeared first in hardcover, he was essentially a paperback phenomenon. Major writers and characters of the decade who debuted in hardcover included Thomas B. Dewey with Mac, William Campbell Gault with Brock Callahan, and Bart Spicer with Carney Wilde. Invented for paperback original (and for the most part staying there) were such sleuths as Richard S. Prather's Shell Scott, Stephen Marlowe's Chester Drum, Dewey's Pete Schofield, and Gault's Joe Puma. Some who had started in hardcover, like Henry Kane's Peter Chambers, Frank Kane's Johnny Liddell, and Michael Avallone's Ed Noon, continued their successful careers in paperback original.

The unprecedented spy boom of the sixties almost finished off the private eye. Despite the introduction of a few important new characters, notably John D. MacDonald's "salvage consultant" Travis McGee and Michael Collins's (Dennis Lynds) Dan Fortune and the continuation of the hardier existing series, the private eye was unquestionably an endangered species. Even Spillane opened a second front as a spy writer with his series about Tiger Mann.

The seventies saw some rejuvenation, though many of the new private eyes carried a note of nostalgia. Bill Pronzini's aging pulp magazine collector usually known as Nameless, one of the best new series characters of the last quarter century, made his first appearance in *The Snatch* (1971). Andrew Bergman's Jake LeVine and Stuart Kaminsky's Toby Peters operated in past decades that seemed to be more amicable to the tough loner detective. Robert B. Parker's Spenser made the biggest commercial and critical splash. *The Godwulf Manuscript*

(1973) was a notable first, and its successor *God Save the Child* (1974) even better, but Parker gradually deemphasized plot and seemed to rest on his laurels, while never losing the ability to come up with dazzling snatches of prose and dialogue.

Joe Gores invented a new hybrid, the private eye procedural, introducing the San Francisco firm of Daniel Kearny Associates in *Dead Skip* (1972). George Chesbro's Mongo Frederickson is a dwarf, and if you think *that's* unusual for a fictional p.i., it pales next to the wildly fantastic cases he investigates, beginning with *Shadow of a Broken Man* (1977). Other new series, more conventional but of high quality, included Lawrence Block's Matt Scudder and Arthur Lyons's Jacob Asch.

Through the decade of the seventies, the first relatively realistic female private eyes began to appear. (Earlier attempts like G. G. Fickling's Honey West and Carter Brown's Mavis Seidlitz, both of whom date back to the fifties, clearly don't count, though some commentators make a case for Will Oursler and Margaret Scott's forties creation, Gale Gallagher.) Fran Huston's Nichole Sweet, whose feminine-sounding author is really Ron S. Miller, made her one appearance in *The Rich Get It All* (1973). Maxine O'Callaghan's Delilah West was first to the post of the currently active group, appearing in the short story "A Change of Clients" (*Alfred Hitchcock's Mystery Magazine*, November 1974). In 1977, Marcia Muller's Sharon McCone made her debut in *Edwin of the Iron Shoes*.

The eighties brought a renaissance to the private eye form. Robert J. Randisi founded the Private Eye Writers of America, which began to give out its own annual award (the Shamus) for outstanding works in the form and found no shortage of viable candidates. Max Allan Collins's Chicago operative Nate Heller, who first appeared in *True Detective* (1983), is the best of the historical private eyes, encountering casts of characters almost entirely made up of real people. The rise of the regional p.i. was another salutary trend. At one time the fictional shamus almost always operated out of L.A., New York, San Francisco, or Chicago, with an occasional oddball like Miami's Mike Shayne, Philadelphia's Carney Wilde, San Diego's Max Thursday, or Boston's Spenser. A precursor of the new spate of regional private eyes was an early seventies creation, Michael Z. Lewin's Indianapolis op Albert Sampson, who also pioneered in not being all that hard-boiled. The eighties saw the introduction of private eyes from Detroit (Loren D. Estleman's Amos Walker), Salt Lake City (Robert Irvine's Moroni Traveler), Cedar Rapids (Ed Gorman's Jack Dwyer), Cincinnati (Jonathan Valin's Harry Stoner), Seattle (Earl Emerson's Thomas Black), Meriwether, Montana (James Crumley's Milodragovitch and C. W. Sughrue), and Grantham, Ontario (Howard Engel's Benny Cooperman). Others brought new blood to the form in more familiar backgrounds: Mark Schorr's frankly psychotic Red Diamond operates out of New York, for example; Frank McConnell's team of Bridget O'Toole and Harry Garnish call Chicago home; and Robert Campbell's Whistler and Robert Crais's Elvis Cole work in Los Angeles, as does the nineties', first sure bet for long-term success, Walter Mosley's Easy Rawlins.

The female private eye came into her own in a big way in the eighties, with Liza Cody's British operative Anna Lee making her first appearance in *Dupe* (1980), Sue Grafton's Kinsey Millhone starting her path through the alphabet in *A Is for Alibi* (1982), Sara Paretsky's V. I. Warshawski debuting in the same year's *Indemnity Only*, and Linda Barnes's Carlotta Carlyle making her novel-length bow in *A Trouble of Fools* (1988). Several promising successors have followed.

Even with all the new activity of the past couple of decades, some still find the private eye an anachronism, but that view may presuppose too limited a definition. There is no necessity that the private eye be male, have a bottle of rye in the bottom drawer, get hit over the head, recount his or her dreams, or get beaten up. Neither does the private eye have to follow the newer traditions: he or she need not jog, need not cook, need not have an extended family, and can even get along without a psychoanalyzing significant other. The private eye doesn't even have to be particularly tough, at least in the conventional physical sense. The private eye can take any form, have any gender or sexual preference, operate in any milieu. The fact remains that to have a detective with a profit motive but unencumbered by the technicalities or the workload of the official police provides an extremely effective and convenient way to tell a detective story. Thus, in whatever form, the private eye will be around as long as the detective story will.

IN THE TRADITION OF ... HERSELF

Marcia Muller

Bachrach Studios

WHILE BROWSING THROUGH my library this morning, I stopped to contemplate my "contemporary women's shelf." I originally set it up in the early 1980s, to keep separate the kind of realistic mystery novels I write and enjoy reading: those featuring modern American women who are independent, self-reliant, and damn good sleuths—be they professionals or talented amateurs. It was a very roomy shelf at first, but now the books spill over; familiar and well-established names jump out at me from their spines—Barnes, Dunlap, Grafton, O'Donnell, Paretsky, Pickard, Smith, Uhnak. And there are other new and promising names as well.

The special shelf, I've realized, has become obsolete. It's time to integrate the books among the general population of the library, where they'll mingle with those by American male authors, British and other foreign writers of both genders, contemporary American women who write novels of a "softer" or historical nature, and women of previous generations who blazed the trail for those of us who came later—under conditions far more difficult than we experience today.

These women writers of the thirties, forties, fifties and sixties are less well known than their British contemporaries. While Christie and Sayers became household names, American women labored in relative obscurity. One of the early training grounds for mystery novelists was the detective pulps, such as *Black Mask* and *Dime Detective*. Writers for these publications—and with few exceptions they were all male—learned their craft while working at it, essentials that stood them in good stead throughout their careers. But because of the detective pulps' strong male orientation, most women found writing for them uninteresting or off-putting; a number of our best early female suspense writers came to the genre not by way of them but by way of the love pulps, thus bringing a strong romantic slant to the mystery novel. *Ellery Queen's Mystery Magazine* began providing a less limiting short story market in the early 1940s, but not a large enough one for all the talented women who wanted to break into the genre.

The male orientation of the mystery market forced a narrowness of scope both in subject matter and characterization upon novels by women. Nearly all of the highly praised series prior to 1970 featured male protagonists, such as Phoebe Atwood Taylor's Asey Mayo (who is consistently touted as one of the best fictional detectives of the thirties and forties). Dorothy B. Hughes and Helen Nielsen produced some of the best novels of psychological suspense ever written, but more often than not, their viewpoint characters were men. Women also authored hard-boiled private eye novels with considerable success—notably Leigh Brackett and Dolores Hitchens—but again, their detectives were male.

And other women resorted to adopting male pseudonyms in an attempt to give their work more credibility in the marketplace: Francis Bonnamy (Audrey Boyers Waltz), Craig Rice/Michael Venning (Georgianna Ann Randolph).

What changed this unfortunate state of affairs? As with many other aspects of our lives, it was the women's movement of the late 1960s and '70s. Suddenly, females were moving into new spheres of activity: they were becoming cops, private detectives, attorneys, business executives, technical workers. They were shedding old conventions and restrictions, speaking their minds, experimenting with alternative ways of living. And with these changes, a host of interesting new situations and problems was just waiting to be explored fictionally.

The 1970s were a breakthrough period for the woman heroine in crime fiction. Slowly women, as they exist in the real world, began to emerge as series characters, most notably in police procedurals such as Lillian O'Donnell's Norah Mulcahaney novels and Dorothy Uhnak's trilogy about Christie Opara. A few truly bad female private eye novels authored by men (and emphasizing such unfortunate character flaws as bitchiness and sexism toward males) appeared and mercifully fell by the wayside. In the 1980s the pace picked up significantly, and we now have a rich and satisfying assortment of cops and private eyes, attorneys and reporters, and other amateurs of every description.

A phrase I've been hearing a lot lately is "humanistic crime fiction." Used to describe novels that incorporate in-depth characterization with plot, realism and social commentary with detection, the phrase is not confined solely to books authored by women. But this type of novel has become more visible because of the large influx of women into the field, and their proliferation has freed writers of both genders to cast off the restrictive trappings of an earlier era and experiment with the form.

The characters in the "humanistic" novels are feeling, thinking, caring people. The women are fully their own persons and detect independently. This does not necessarily mean they are loners; most have wide support systems of friends, coworkers, lovers, and families which lend the stories a diverting personal element and a further touch of realism. The range of characters, situations, and approaches represented by this collective body of work is enormous, and without a doubt its writers are revolutionizing the genre.

While women writers of today readily acknowledge their debt to their forebears both male and female ("In the tradition of Hammett/Chandler/Hughes/Nielsen" is, after all, a positive accolade), they are now taking advantage of the opportunity to simply do their own work. And that's an even more positive accolade: "In the tradition of . . . herself."

RALPH DENNIS–
The Science Fiction Writer?
David Everson

I GOT A SINKING FEELING when I saw the hand-lettered sign which said: RALPH DENNIS MEMORIAL BOOKRACK. The used books in the rack were a mix of mysteries—not all hard-boiled. But then, he had written me that along with Ross Thomas and James Crumley, he liked Jonathan

Gash and Charles McCarry. I shrugged. Maybe it's an inside joke, I told myself. I called my son, Chris, over and showed him the sign. He said: "What does it mean?"

"He may have died," I said, but I really could not believe he was gone.

We were in the Oxford Too—a used bookstore in Atlanta—hoping to finally meet Ralph Dennis. Chris and I had admired his Hardman series in the seventies and had corresponded with him. On a rainy Atlanta day in eighty-seven (on our way to Florida), we had missed him—it had been his day off.

I walked over to the counter with the books Chris and I had picked out. "When will Ralph Dennis be in?" I asked with some apprehension.

The female clerk looked puzzled. She turned to the male who was working at a computer. "He doesn't work here anymore, does he?"

The male clerk looked up at me and frowned. We were less than an underhand toss from the bookrack. "The science fiction writer?"

I didn't correct him. Somehow, the mistake seemed symbolic of Ralph's late career.

"He died about six months ago," the clerk said matter-of-factly.

I nodded. I had never even talked to him, but I felt the loss.

I had first read Ralph's p.i. novels set in Atlanta in about 1974. His work and Robert B. Parker's started at about the same time. Especially in the early books, you had to get past the lurid covers which suggested a men's adventure series. The books were tough, gritty, and funny. They dealt with racial tensions as well as any fiction I knew. I loved the titles: *The Deadly Cotton Heart, The One Dollar Rip-Off, The Last of the Armageddon Wars*. The Atlanta locale was sharply drawn. And

best of all—there were lots of Hardmans. They seemed to come out in bunches—none of this waiting for a year for a new one. I devoured them as quickly as they appeared—and often reread them. They were reviewed favorably in such diverse publications as *Mother Jones* and *The New York Times*.

Ralph also published two non-Hardman paperback originals and one hardcover, *MacTaggart's War*, a big caper novel—with a great firefight scene—set during WWII. Then suddenly the flow of his work ceased. Every so often Chris and I would say: "Wonder when Ralph Dennis will publish another Hardman?"

Never, it turned out.

Flash forward to the mid-eighties. I had taken tentative steps toward my own mystery writing career. I was eager to break into print. I had subscribed to Wayne Dundee's *Hardboiled*, but short story writing was not in me. Chris and I concocted the idea of writing a piece lauding Dennis. Dundee knew Dennis's work, liked it, and thought the idea was a good one. For some basic facts, Chris tracked down an article on Dennis that had appeared in an Atlanta newspaper. We wrote "A Hardman is good to find: A Hardman is hard to find." (*Hardboiled*, Summer 1986). We said that the Hardman series was "arguably the best 'tough guy' material of the '70s." I think we were being conservative. The Hardman novels stack up against the best p.i. fiction. Ever. Yet most readers, and even many p.i. writers, are unaware of Ralph Dennis's work.

Go read. If you can find one.

About that time I learned from a short piece in *Mystery Scene* that Dennis worked at Oxford Too in Atlanta. I looked up the address in the Atlanta phone book and I sent Dennis a copy of the piece.

I received a long letter in reply. It began; "Thanks for the magazine. The article about the Hardman books might have been a bit kinder than the books . . . written in two months each . . . deserved. As I remember I did ten pages a day for a month and I had a first draft and then a rewrite . . . ten pages a day . . . and then I shipped it off to New York. To paraphrase Fitzgerald, who wrote that there were no third acts in American lives . . . I guess I'd say there are no third drafts in paperback originals."

Ralph went on to say that he stopped doing the Hardmans because of "the special burnout that shows up in series writers."

He wrote about his recent frustrations. "You're

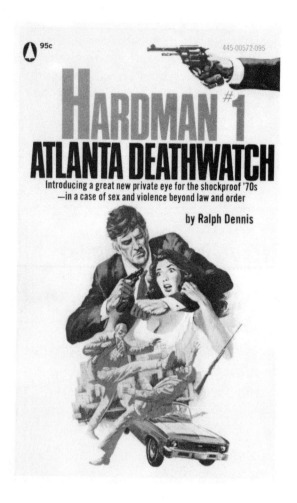

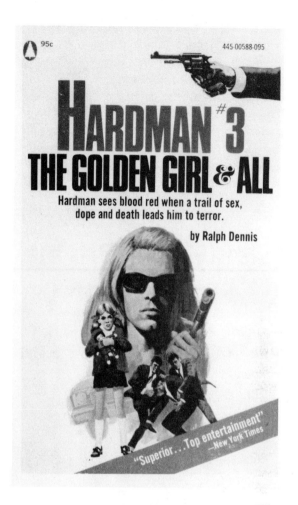

as bankable as your last book,'' he wrote, reporting that after *MacTaggart's War*—which sold eight or nine thousand—he had penned five books ''and nobody wanted any of them.'' He described each briefly. One was on college basketball. I happened to be writing a novel on the same theme at that time.

I would love to read them all.

He had finished a new book for which he had hopes. He wrote: ''It's titled *Dust in the Heart*. It's about a sheriff in a small town in the triangle area of North Carolina on the hunt for a child-molester murderer. I like the book. I've taken a lot of time over it. Now we'll see what the body-eaters up there in New York think.'' He promised to let me know what came of it.

One of the Hardman series had been reprinted by Pinnacle. He wrote: ''I thought the idea was to reprint four or five of the ones I liked best . . . then the editor moved . . . and the other people at Pinnacle weren't interested.'' He complained about ''literary slavery.'' Pinnacle had gone into bankruptcy.

''We asked for the rights back. The judge . . . has ruled that the contracts are part of the assets of Pinnacle. Hell, I could be sold off to the highest bidder with no say in the matter. Wasn't slavery outlawed?''

He said he was going to send our article to his agent.

I replied to his letter, telling him about my own writing.

Then came our failed attempt to see him in the spring of '87. In June I received another letter. It came to me indirectly because he had misplaced my address. His luck was still bad—*Dust* had *almost* sold. He was sorry we had missed connections. Thought someone at the store should have pointed us the direction of his ''watering hole.'' He wanted another copy of the *Hardboiled* article—a low-budget Hardman film was maybe in the works. ''Iffy,'' he said. I rushed the copy off to him, hoping it was not too late. He promised to send me copies of some of the Hardmans I lacked.

In August of '87 I nervously sent him a copy

of my first novel, a paperback original entitled *Recount*, which had a brief tribute to Hardman (and Hump, his black sidekick) buried in it.

I never heard from him again.

I don't know any of the details of his death, so I don't know if the weight of the rejections contributed somehow.

To me, Dennis was the Joe DiMaggio of private eye writers. It seemed he did it effortlessly. I do know that *no one*—and I include giants like Robert B. Parker and John D. MacDonald—has ever had a better run—a longer hit streak—than Ralph Dennis did in the Hardman series. There was no drop-off in quality as the series continued. It will be a crime if this series is not made available to contemporary p.i. readers.

Dust in my heart. Ashes in my throat.

Ralph Dennis—the science fiction writer?—he doesn't work here anymore.

Twenty-Five Private Eye Novels (all-time)
Selected by Jon L. Breen

Andrew Bergman	*The Big Kiss Off of 1944*
Lawrence Block	*When The Sacred Ginmill Closes*
Howard Browne	*The Taste of Ashes*
Robert Campbell	*In La-La Land We Trust*
Raymond Chandler	*Farewell, My Lovely*
Max Allan Collins	*Stolen Away*
Michael Collins	*Minnesota Strip*
Thomas B. Dewey	*The Mean Streets*
Loren D. Estleman	*The Glass Highway*
Erle S. Gardner (as A. A. Fair)	*The Bigger They Come*
William Campbell Gault	*The Convertible Hearse*
Joe Gores	*Interface*
Sue Grafton	*"I" Is for Innocent*
Dashiell Hammett	*The Maltese Falcon*
Joseph Hansen	*Death Claims*
Robert Irvine	*The Angels' Share*
Ed Lacy	*Room to Swing*
Jonathan Latimer	*The Lady in the Morgue*
Ross Macdonald	*Black Money*
L. A. Morse	*The Old Dick*
Walter Mosley	*White Butterfly*
Marcia Muller	*There's Something in a Sunday*
Robert B. Parker	*God Save the Child*
Bill Pronzini	*Shackles*
Paco Ignacio Taibo II	*An Easy Thing*

GAY
MYSTERIES

INTRODUCTION
Jon L. Breen

FOR MANY YEARS, homosexuality was virtually a taboo subject in mystery and detective fiction. When gay or lesbian characters appeared, it was subtly and nonexplicitly, and they were more often employed as evil agents of menace or comic relief than as real people. Agatha Christie sometimes introduced a proper (because discreet) lesbian couple among her cast of suspects. That the trio of villains in Dashiell Hammett's *The Maltese Falcon* (1930)—Caspar Gutman, Joel Cairo, and Wilmer Cook—were homosexuals is made clear even in John Huston's 1941 movie version, which could deliver the sly hints of their nature even under the constraints of Hollywood's Production Code. Other gays appearing in hard-boiled fiction were usually objects of scorn and derision by the macho private eye. Even William Campbell Gault, whose strong social conscience led him to preach against offensive epithets for ethnic groups, did not extend this tolerance to gays in his novels of the fifties. (After his comeback in the eighties, this changed.)

In an article about homosexuals in mysteries in the revised edition of Dilys Winn's *Murder Ink* (1984), Joseph Hansen finds Hammett, Chandler, and Ross Macdonald all homophobic. The latter's "handling of a pair of middle-aged little-theater type homosexuals in *The Drowning Pool* (1950) may pretend at sophisticated tolerance but adds up to a very thinly disguised disgust" (page 131). He finds the same contempt in Golden Age British writers Dorothy L. Sayers, Ngaio Marsh, and Agatha Christie. A negative treatment of homosexuality in Elmore Leonard's *Stick* (1983) causes him to doubt things have changed that much.

Some writers of the fifties dealt with homosexuality sensitively—see, for example, some of Aaron Marc Stein's early novels under the byline Hampton Stone, particularly *The Murder That Wouldn't Stay Solved* (1951). Vin Packer's paperback originals often had homosexual themes, notably *Whisper His Sin* (1954), which seems to be trying to acknowledge the reader's prejudices and depict the gay lifestyle sympathetically at the same time, a difficult balancing act.

Before the sixties, the idea of a homosexual sleuth would have been anathema. True, there have been rumors about the sexuality of some of the Golden Age great detectives—in the essay collection *Agatha Christie: First Lady of Crime* (1977), H.R.F. Keating makes a case for a gay Poirot—but they are unconfirmed. Probably the first acknowledged gay male sleuth in fiction, and certainly the first from a major publisher, appeared in George Baxt's *A Queer Kind of Death* (1966) and two subsequent novels. Pharoah Love is a black homosexual cop, thus a member of three oppressed minorities at once. But he is a wild, outrageous, and not entirely sympathetic character, certainly not one with whom the straight audience could be expected to identify. I haven't read any of Don Rico's spy spoofs about Buzz Cardigan, beginning with *The Man from Pansy* (1967), but the offensive title doesn't suggest a sensitive treatment.

The first realistic gay sleuth was Joseph Hansen's Dave Brandstetter, who made his first appearance in *Fadeout* (1970) and appeared in a dozen novels, ending with *A Country of Old Men* (1991). Insurance investigator Brandstetter is low key and likable, a businesslike professional and a responsible citizen, not at all flamboyant or colorful. He was a character all kinds of readers, straight and gay, could take to their hearts.

At the time the first Brandstetter novels appeared, at the close of a decade that symbolized liberation (or decadence, depending on your point of view), the gay sleuth seemed an idea whose time had come, but Hansen had great difficulty selling the idea to a major publisher. Not coincidentally, the editor who took a chance on Brandstetter was Harper & Row's Joan Kahn, the same editor who had published the first cases of pioneering black sleuths Touie Moore (in Ed Lacy's *Room to Swing* [1957]) and Virgil Tibbs (in John Ball's *In the Heat of the Night* [1965]).

For a time, Brandstetter was a one-of-a-kind phenomenon. Mainstream publishers' lists did not fill with gay sleuths in the seventies. In Michael Nava's anthology *Finale* (Alyson, 1989), he cites Richard Halls' *Butterscotch Prince* (1975), a Pyramid paperback original, as a pioneering gay detective novel, while recognizing *A Queer Kind of Death* but (oddly) making no mention of Hansen.

Nava's lawyer-sleuth Henry Rios, who first appeared in two novels from the specialist publisher Alyson before achieving mainstream publication with *How Town* (1990), and Richard Stevenson's Albany, New York, private eye Donald Strachey, who first appeared in *Death Trick* (1981), are likely the best gay male sleuths to follow in the wake of Hansen and Brandstetter. Mark Richard Zubro's novels about gay high school teacher Tom Mason, beginning with *A Simple Suburban Murder* (1989) are also worthy of mention. The eighties also saw more gay characters in important subsidiary roles: Jonathan Kellerman made psychologist-detective Alex Delaware's principal police contact a gay cop, Milo Sturgis, in the best-selling series beginning with *When the Bough Breaks* (1985). All of these writers essentially advanced Hansen's theme that aside from their sexual preference, gay people are not that different from everybody else, doing ordinary jobs, seeking monogamous relationships, and in some respects holding conventional attitudes.

Other writers mined the gay subculture for humor and an exotic and colorful background. Nathan Aldyne, the joint pseudonym of Michael McDowell and Dennis Schuetz, featured the gay/straight sleuthing team of Dan Valentine and Clarisse Lovelace in *Vermilion* (1980) and three subsequent novels. Gay sleuth Matt Sinclair figures in two funny and somewhat gross novels from Tony Fennelly, *The Glory Hole Murders* (1985) and *A Closet Hanging* (1987).

The lesbian detective has been slower to find a niche in the mainstream publishing world. This is paradoxical, since lesbianism was an acceptable topic for mainstream mass market fiction in the fifties—Gold Medal, for example, published a number of lesbian-themed novels by Vin Packer and others—when male homosexuality was not. Lesbian sleuths (and they are more numerous than their gay male counterparts) have mostly come from feminist publishers like Seal Press and Naiad rather than from mainstream houses. The reason for this discrepancy undoubtedly lies in sexual politics, both in the mystery field and in society at large.

The first clearly lesbian detective in fiction, though it isn't spelled out in so many words, is probably Joyce Porter's Honorable Constance Morrison Burke (the Hon. Con.), who first appeared in *Rather A Common Sort of Crime* (1970). As a comic stereotype of the lesbian, nearly as disgusting as the author's male sleuth Wilfred Dover, the Hon. Con. hardly makes any list of positive role models.

Perhaps the best of the more realistic lesbian sleuths (and the star of what may be the best series ever published by a small press) is Katherine V. Forrest's L.A.P.D. policewoman Kate Delafield, who first appeared in *Amateur City* (1984). The series illustrates the problems of a lesbian who must remain closeted for professional reasons. The most recent book in the series, *Murder by Tradition* (1991), makes an especially striking use of this theme. As an editor at Naiad Press, Forrest has helped in the development of numerous other lesbian detective series. Barbara Wilson, whose *Murder in the Collective* (1984) began her series about Pam Nilsen, is the best-known author for another feminist publisher of lesbian mysteries, Seal Press. The first realistic lesbian sleuth to be published by a mainstream publisher is probably Sandra Scoppettone's Lauren Laurano, who appears in *Everything You Have Is Mine* (Little, Brown, 1991). More can be expected to follow, including some of those nurtured by the specialist presses.

INTERVIEW: SANDRA SCOPPETTONE

Ed Gorman

Q: *Our generation seems to be reassessing the sixties, which is one of the themes of your new novel,* Everything You Have Is Mine *(Little, Brown). Why are you starting to look back now?*

A: I don't think I was reassessing the sixties, although I certainly make use of the decade in *Everything You Have Is Mine.* Perhaps the reason writers and others are harkening back is that, as unbelievable as it may seem sometimes, the sixties are now history. And if you're dealing with people in their forties and early fifties, their youth happened in the sixties.

I was in my twenties then and I missed most of it because I was drunk a lot of the time. I didn't get sober until 1973. So for me it's almost an arcane subject.

Q: *Many of your characters seem to be victims—of each other, of themselves, of society. Are you aware of this in your writing?*

A: Funny you should ask! I only recently became aware of it. Especially regarding the subject of incest. I've written about that in three novels. I had no idea why, at the time, but recently I discovered that I'm a survivor of incest. I'd kept it completely buried in my subconscious for fifty years (I know this sounds bogus, but it's true). The memories came back to me in analysis. My grandfather on my father's side was the perp. I can hear readers now: "Why is she telling us all this personal stuff?" I guess because there are so many others (one out of three women and one out of seven men by the time they're eighteen) who have the same experience and either feel alone or, like me, don't remember. Once it came back to me, I saw how it had affected my life. Also, it makes clear to me why I wrote about it . . . three out of twelve novels is a lot, I think.

Q. *You're able to create different voices for your different books.* Donato and Daughter *is rendered in modern American third person; the Jack Early books manage to be both tough and breezy; with* Razzmatazz *being almost bitchy in its social observations; and now, with* Lauren Laurano, *there's another voice—more considered, more consciously literary in the good sense. How do these different voices evolve?*

A: I don't consciously choose a voice be it third or first person. What I mean is that I don't say to myself, "Now I'm going to write a book from third person or first." The voice or voices come in my head and prescribe to me how and who. There is a kind of tyranny involved in this!

For instance, the first Jack Early book, *A Creative Kind of Killer,* was written because the voice of Fortune Fanelli spoke to me and this was first person male. I had no choice in the matter. It was one of the major reasons I decided to take a male pseudonym.

I'm not sure what you mean by "consciously literary." I don't think I write anything that would be considered literary. Lauren Laurano is just another voice that spoke to me, albeit the closest to my own voice I've ever written.

Q: *Were you apprehensive about making Lauren gay?*

A: Years ago I would have been because I don't think anyone would have published it. In fact, I remember someone suggesting that to me and my reply was, "Please, I have to make a living."

Q: *Was there any particular reason you chose to make her gay?*

A: I wanted to write under my own name again, and the voice that came to me this time was Lauren

Laurano. Because I'm a lesbian (this has nothing to do with the incest) I decided to make Lauren a lesbian. I wanted to be truer to myself. I honestly didn't know if any mainstream publisher would want the book because no mainstream house had yet published a lesbian private eye, even though there have been quite a few published by small presses. I had to write this book . . . for myself and for political reasons. There have been several gay male detectives published by mainstream houses and my feeling was that it was the same old thing: the men are accepted but the women are not.

Q: *What lies ahead for Lauren? Presumably, this is the start of a series*

A: Yes, this is the start of a series and I've begun the second book. But I'm not going to tell you more than that, except to say that I intend to carry over a number of the characters that are in the first book. William and Rick will figure prominently, for instance.

Q: *Are you continuing to work on mainstream novels or are you now devoting all your time to mysteries? Or do you see mysteries as becoming mainstream, given the permanent residency of so many mystery writers on the best seller lists?*

A: I have no interest in writing anything but crime novels at this point in my life. And if you think about it, it's all I've ever written for adults. My contract with Little, Brown dictates that in the next fourteen months I write the second Laurano and a second Fanelli. After that I'd like to do a nonseries book which I've had on my mind for over three years. This will be based on a real case that, unfortunately, affected me personally. But what are we talking about here . . . 1994?

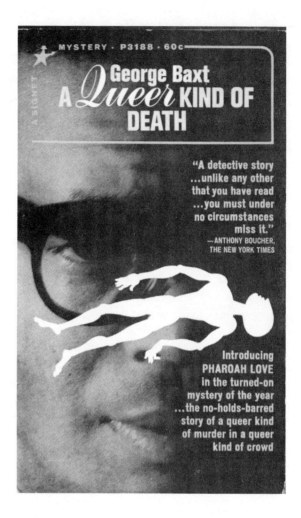

As to whether mysteries are mainstream or not? It's a mystery to me.

Note: Since this interview, Sandra Scoppettone has published I'll Be Leaving You Always, *the second in the Lauren Laurano series, and a CBS-TV film has been made of* Donato and Daughter, *starring Charles Bronson and Dana Delaney.*

THE GAY AND LESBIAN MYSTERY

Mark Richard Zubro

THERE IS NO DOUBT that the emergence of Joseph Hansen's David Brandstetter character introduced in 1970 was a major turning point in how gay men were portrayed in mystery stories.

David Brandstetter was no longer victim, fop, or screaming queen, but a guy with a job, and sometimes a love life, who came out of the hard-boiled mystery tradition set on the West Coast of the North American continent.

Beginning with *Fadeout* and ending with *A Country of Old Men*, Hansen set the trend and standard that continues today. His being published by mainstream publishers beginning with Harper & Row was an enormous achievement.

In Hansen's books, for the first time, probably in any literature, much less the mystery, the gay person is portrayed as not involved in the angst of coming out or being miserable because of his sexual orientation, or as some kind of pathetic pervert just killed or about to be murdered, but as a three-dimensional character involved in real life and real problems with his sexuality being the same part of his life as it is for his heterosexual counterparts. This was far more revolutionary than most suspected or were even aware of at the time and was light-years ahead of even nongenre fiction. This put the mystery field at the cutting edge of literary culture.

In the early eighties two more authors appeared with central characters who are gay. One was Richard Stevenson creating the Don Strachey mysteries set in Albany, New York. Starting in *Death Trick,* Don is your classic private eye with his own business, a smart mouth, and a penchant for danger. The second author, Nathan Aldyne, began in *Vermilion* a series using two amateur sleuths, a gay man, Daniel Valentine, and his straight woman friend, Clarisse Lovelace. He is a bartender and she is a real estate agent, although eventually in *Slate,* one of the later books in the series, they open a bar together. Again neither of these authors used plots specifically or particularly concerned with the concept of coming out. Both sometimes immersed themselves in the gay milieu, either railing against injustices done to gays, or making more overt political statements related to gays and society, but the plot was not driven by anxiety over their sexuality. Strachey and Valentine are shown as two sleuths who are comfortable with their gay identities. Strachey has a lover, but before AIDS he was willing to dally with other men. Daniel Valentine is given several dates and is allowed a love life. This made the characters in both books more well-rounded figures. Neither sacrificed his mystery plot to make political or sociological points, and the books were not always concerned with such, but it is often true the existence of such positive characters is a statement in and of itself and thus a bone in the throat of bigots and hate mongers.

In the late 1980s Mark Richard Zubro and Michael Nava emerged as major figures in the gay mystery world. Zubro has two series, the first of which begins with *A Simple Suburban Murder.* This set of mysteries features Tom Mason, a high school English teacher, as the main character/amateur sleuth, and his lover, Scott Carpenter, a professional baseball player. Zubro also has the first gay male police procedural published by a mainstream publishing house in the books *Sorry Now?* and *Political Poison.* These books feature the Chicago police detective Paul Turner. Nava, first published by the smaller gay press Alyson, came out with his main character, lawyer Henry Rios, proving that using members of a law firm as hero/leading man is not limited to books with heterosexual lawyers as main characters. Both of these writers involve politics, lovers, and the gay community to varying degrees, but again the focus is on the murder and following the path to the solution wherever it might lead, whether that involves a gay or straight milieu.

The situation of the gay male with the straight heterosexual male sidekick has been explored recently by Stan Cutler in his series that began with *Best Performance by a Patsy* and features the co-protagonists gay writer Mark Bradley and the heterosexual private investigator Rayford Goodman.

In the last few years a number of other writers have come to the fore in the field. While most of the above continue to be published, there are other newcomers such as Grant Michaels (*A Body to Dye For*) with his amateur sleuth Stan Kraychik, a hairdresser. Perhaps using such a gay-identified stereotype means the cliché world has come full cycle and it is now okay for a gay person to be a hairdresser as well as be in any other profession.

Other mysteries of recent vintage in this arena are *Final Atonement* by Steve Johnson which features a gay New York police detective. Jack Ricardo's gay character Archie Cain in *The Night G.A.A. Died* has set up his private investigator's business in Greenwich Village. *The Glory Hole Murders* by Tony Fennelly has Matt Sinclair as an antique dealer in New Orleans.

The lesbian mystery has also come more to the forefront in recent years. Numerous smaller presses have been publishing mysteries with lesbian protagonists for years, notably Naiad Press. One of the most popular of these writers has been Katherine V. Forrest with her lesbian L.A.P.D. Detective Kate Delafield who first appeared in *Amateur City.* Others in the field writing with lesbian main characters are Ellen Hart (*Hallowed Murder*), Mary Wings (*She Came in a Flash*), Nikki Baker (*Lavender House Murder*), Rose Beecham (*Introducing Amanda Valentine*), Lauren Wright Douglas (*A Tiger's Heart*), Claire McNab, now almost as popular as Katherine Forrest, with *Dead Certain*, Jaye Maiman (*Crazy for Loving*), Deborah Powell (*Houston Town*), Penny Sumner (*End of April*), Dorothy Tell (*The Hallelugah Murders*), and Pat Welch (*A Proper Burial*).

Sandra Scoppettone's private investigator Lauren Laurano in the recently published *Everything You Have Is Mine* is widely accepted as the first mystery with a lesbian main character published by a mainstream house.

While currently the gay secondary character has become more positive and, more numerous, by far the most successfully portrayed and most well-known is in Jonathan Kellerman's series featuring Alex Delaware. In these books Milo Sturgis is a gay Los Angeles police detective who is a fully realized person and, as Alex's best male friend and helper in mysteries, vital to the stories.

There were notable forays into the gay subculture in mysteries prior to Joseph Hansen. The more well-known ranged from lesbians in two Dorothy L. Sayers mysteries in the 1920s, to characters used by Gore Vidal writing as Edgar Box in *Death in the Fifth Position* in 1952.

Other pre-Hansen occurrences of gays being portrayed in mysteries are in James Quartermain's *The Man Who Walked on Diamonds*, and Tucker Coe's *A Jade in Aries.* Some of the best-known books in that era included gay characters. Examples are: Rex Stout's *Forest Fire*, Raymond Chandler's *The Big Sleep*, Ross Macdonald's *Dark Tunnel*, Margaret Millar's *Beast in View*, Meyer Levin's *Compulsion*, Mickey Spillane's *I, the Jury*, and Anne Hocking's *A Simple Way of Poison.* A number of these contain extremely negative portrayals of gay people and their lifestyles.

Even Agatha Christie in *A Murder Is Announced* included two women, Murgatroyd and Hinchliffe, who, while not stated to be lesbians, live together, raise ducks and chickens, and when one is killed, the other is devastated.

Patricia Highsmith in the fifties and sixties had gay main characters but their sexuality was very well hidden.

In the 1960s, characters and settings began to change. In Lou Rand's *Rough Trade* and George Baxt's *A Queer Kind of Death*, for the first time there were gay detectives as protagonists. Baxt's main character is Pharoah Love, who is a black male Manhattan cop. Love is generally regarded as the first American gay sleuth.

Negative depictions of gay people continued in the 1960s as evidenced in Ellery Queen's *The Last Woman in His Life* and Roderick Thorp's *The Detective*.

Other notable books with positive gay characters that appeared after Hansen were Richard Hall's *Butterscotch Prince* and John Paul Hudson's *Superstar Murder*.

Some negative portrayals of gay people continue to exist today. Authors do need to be careful and avoid the politically correct pitfall that gay characters cannot be villains, murderers, or victims, but this cannot be all that gay people are. Today any stereotypical depiction is unwelcome in any author's writing, and when such a view is based on hate, prejudice, or deliberate ignorance, it can easily be seen as malicious or irresponsible. The main character as amateur sleuth, detective, cop, hero, or heroine, and being incidentally gay, is entrenched and thriving in the world of mystery.

Some Notable Gay Mysteries
Selected by the Editors

Nathan Aldyne
Canary

George Baxt
A Queer Kind of Death

Tony Fennelly
The Glory Hole Murders

Joseph Hansen
Early Graves

Sandra Scoppettone
Everything You Have Is Mine

Richard Stevenson
Ice Blues

Mark Richard Zubro
A Simple Suburban Murder

BRITISH
MYSTERIES

Two or Three Things You Should Know About British Crime Fiction,

or, A Lightning, Uncritical Anatomy of the English Mystery Scene Today in Ten Easy Lessons

Maxim Jakubowski

It's Christie Whatdunit

SOME MIGHT ARGUE that the modern land-scape of British crime and mystery fiction still labors heavily under the awesome shadow cast by the heritage of Agatha Christie and those two other mighty ladies of tradition, Dorothy L. Sayers and Margery Allingham. I shall discreetly omit Ngaio Marsh, as she hailed from New Zealand, though historical accuracy would corral her among the other female culprits as a sister in crime.

The proponents of this theory are both right and wrong. On one hand, the conventions, guidelines, and dictates of our criminal holy trinity still influence many of today's genre practitioners heavily and many an archetype of the Golden Age still pervades the work of even younger writers. Even American authors like Martha Grimes and Elizabeth George are not immune. Recently, Michael Dibdin, a fluent and modern British author, even felt compelled to write a novel, *The Dying of the Light*, which fits snugly into the old traditions, possibly as an exercise in style, or as an exorcism to get the ghost of Christie and Co. out of his system. But even in Dibdin's book the irony was muted. The best parody of this particular type of writing remains a play, not a book, Tom Stoppard's delightfully witty *The Real Inspector Hound*.

On the other hand, the opposition to the heavy burden of detection traditions strives in many ways. Over the years, the country house model, where the

inspector calls, ponders, and solves, has metamorphosed into specific forms of British police procedurals, with an emphasis on the characterization of the investigating detective character and a deepening of the psychology of the criminal he faces. This subgenre, epitomized by Colin Dexter's Inspector Morse, in fact appears to have taken over the British televisual scene wholesale. In turn, these "intelligent" procedurals have bred grittier forms of procedural, where the rougher, inner life of British society is reflected with various degrees of accuracy, a formula well known to American practitioners. Further, younger contemporary authors strive toward all form of brutal reality, and in recent years we have seen a mild neonoir renaissance (spearheaded by the youngest sixty-year-old in the genre, the eccentric Derek Raymond).

Sleuthettes, psychological suspensers, historical mysteries, and other parallel categories all flower in the new modern British mystery scene, but the cutting edge remains at that mysterious frontier that we cannot find on a map but that all of us instinctively "feel" to various degrees: the opposition between the old traditions of the country house murder tale and the reality of the present-day world.

It has been argued that the cozy, traditional British mystery does not reflect the Britain of the 1930s, but an imaginary world that never really was, a mythical land of green fields, Britannia rules the foreign waves, and antiquated class system. Possibly. If this is the case, it is even more surprising that this artificial genre is still practiced with bravura by many current authors, who set their mysteries in a world that hasn't changed an iota since, and deliberately avoid all contact with reality, historical or social. This is the domain of the ultra-British cozy: the Miss Seeton stories of Heron Carvic, continued by, briefly, James Melville as Hampton Charles and currently Sarah J. Mason as Hamilton Crane, the epitome of the country house classical tale, *The Killings at Badger's Drift* and later Barnaby novels by Caroline Graham, the ironic adventures of the band of legal sleuths in the novels of Sarah Caudwell, much of the work of Robert Barnard.

Sometimes described as the Mayhem Parva school of writing, these are all highly talented mystery writers for whom plot is everything, as is wit and deliberately lightweight characterization. You feel the writer's ironic presence smiling at you between the lines and pages, playing chess with your own ingenuity as he or she weaves complicated webs of suspects, red herrings, and confusing alibis in an intellectual game of clues and false clues. Their books are often like a game; they haven't so much modernized the classical Christie/Sayers/Allingham formulas as they have dusted the mode with a strong veneer of humor and professional skill.

These classicists are the crowd pleasers who have no better ambition than to entertain the reader. Sometimes it can be enough.

The most popular in their midst are (in no particular order) the aforementioned Caroline Graham, Sarah Caudwell (both frustratingly unprolific) and a large gang of cozy storytellers including Ann Granger, C. F. Roe (Scottish medic Dr. Jean Montrose), Ann Quinton, Catherine Aird (cozy procedurals set in the imaginary county of Calleshire), Marian Babson (American, but has lived in London for ages), Janet Laurence (a specialist in entertaining and often mouth-watering gastronomic mysteries), M. C. Beaton (again Scottish-set), Pat Burden, June Thomson (who also doubles as an apocryphal Sherlock Holmes chronicler with enjoyable results), Kate Charles (another British-based American whose mysteries are all set in the Church of England), Ann Cleeves (bird-watching whodunits are her innovation), Ruth Dudley-Edwards, Anthea Fraser, Barbara Whitehead, John Buxton Hilton, Eliza-

beth Ferrars, Marjorie Eccles, Clare Curzon, Gwen Moffatt, Anna Clarke, etc. . . .

Of course, ghettoizing writers into specific categories is a dangerous generalization and should be avoided at all cost. Most authors are sufficiently perverse and recognize the restrictions that artificial categories and, often, commercial considerations, impose on them and will from time to time make incursions into other areas. Some of the writers mentioned in this chapter will be encountered in several different subgenres, so these groupings should not be taken as gospel. However, it is unlikely the reader will come across many of the above sneaking into the neonoir field. Possibly in the historical field, or outside crime and mystery, in romance. But surprises would always be welcome.

The Men Who Solve the Crime

And so we move from heroic amateur sleuths of the Golden Age kind to the heroes of today, the professional policemen who man the mysterious enquiries.

Whereas the American police procedural genre is very much a tale of place and setting, where the city almost acts as a character, this is less pronounced in the British novel of detection. On the other hand, the writers take much greater pride in rounded characterization and many of their fictional sleuths are gems of humanity, idiosyncrasies and all. If the ladies of the cozy worshipped at the shrine of Christie and cohorts, most of these proceduralists do so at that of Conan Doyle, creator of the archetypal sleuth Sherlock Holmes. Or, to a lesser extent, John Creasey's heroic cops of the hack jungle.

This is an area that is particularly rich in talent, a codified type of crime and mystery writing that suits the British practitioner well. It might well be argued that many of the books here represent modern British crime writing at its best.

A sketchy list of notables:

Peter Lovesey's Victorian policemen Cribb and Thackeray have now made way for his contemporary *Last Detective* series, but without losing humanity and pathos. He also writes a series featuring Bertie, Prince of Wales.

Both Bill James and Peter Turnbull feature gritty Scottish cops in procedurals most reminiscent of the American strand. Maybe it's something about the bleakness of Scotland?

Keith Wright has published only three novels so far, but is fast shaping up as a future talent. A serving detective in Nottingham, he is a rare British crime author with actual police experience.

Ian Rankin's Scottish Inspector Rebus is a traditional misfit who more often than not ignores the rules, but the verve of Rankin's (prolific) writing is ʻontagious and marks him as a future favorite.

What is it about Italy that three prominent English authors choose to feature Italian cops as protagonists in their series? Michael Dibdin highlights Inspector Aurelio Zen in alternate novels, while Magdalen Nabb follows the sweaty, plodding Marshall through the villainies of Florence, and Timothy Williams also involves his coppers in the land of spaghetti and chianti.

Although he lives in Canada, Peter Robinson cannot leave his native Yorkshire behind, and his series of local procedurals involving gruff but sensitive Inspector Banks is shaping up into a major mysterious opus.

Veteran Gwendoline Butler has two main characters. Under her own name she follows the exploits of Coffin, whileas under her Jennie Melville pseudonym she features woman police investigator Charmian Daniels.

Until his recent death, Mark Hebden's Inspector Pel of the Paris Sûreté was Britain's best solution for the lack of new Maigret novels. The series has now been continued by his daughter, Juliet.

Michael Pearce is another more at ease in other climes and times, with the sometimes farcical detections of the Mamur Zapt, an English policeman based in turn-of-the-century Cairo.

Nicholas Freeling is another criminal expatriate. Inspector Van der Valk (now deceased, but prequels allow some latitude) detects in Holland, and Inspector Castang in France.

Reginald Hill's Dalziel and Pascoe, a pair of ill-matched policemen, have now been associated for many years and novels, and are great popular favorites. Hill has recently also launched a p.i. series.

Robert Richardson's Maltravers is another urbane, dogged investigator in a classical mold.

Other creators of case-solving cops include Roy Hart, Alan Scholefield, John Brady, James McClure (the Kramer and Zondi South Africa based series), Peter Whalley, John Wainwright, Roger Ormerod, Jonathan Ross, Miles Tripp, Roy Lewis, Alan Hunter, Timothy Holme, Michael Kenyon, etc. . . .

Quite an impressive gallery of official sleuths ranging from a member of the royal family (Peter Lovesey) to a joking, doggerel poet (Kenyon's Peckover)! Although most of the authors in this elastic category obey the rules of realism, they lack the hardness to be called hard-boiled, but then there are other sleuths, professional or amateur, who distinctly veer to the soft-boiled. And we're not referring only to their taste in eggs. . . .

Amateurs and Professionals

Perhaps the finest species of gently boiled heroes is Colin Dexter's Inspector Morse, whose Oxford beat is statistically one of the most dangerous in England, what with the regular amount of bodies that keep on cropping up on his patch!

Beer lover and crossword-puzzle solver, morose and so often in the grip of unrequited affection for beautiful suspects, Morse has been perfectly immortalized on television and stands uncontested as the most popular British sleuth since Miss Marple (well, Poirot was a Belgian, wasn't he?).

Other softie sleuths include W. J. Burley's Cornish policeman Wycliffe, R. D. Wingfield's Inspector Frost, James Melville's Otani, Tim Heald's business investigator Simon Bognor, David Williams's banker Mark Treasure, H.R.F. Keating's Ghote, Dorothy Simpson's Detective-Inspector Luke Thanet with his rich panorama of family life, Robert Barnard's infrequent Perry Trethowan, Staynes & Storey's Bone, expatriate American Paula Gosling's various sleuths, soft-boiled all despite the image of Sylvester Stallone on the cinema screen. . . .

All these detectives, whether official or not, operate in a slightly stylized world that isn't quite Britain today (with a daughter at the university there, I can assure you Oxford is not as dangerous as the Morse novels and stories indicate), and this British generation of sleuths probably owe more to the cozy tradition rather than the police procedural. However, where many of its practitioners excel is in gently updating a tradition and taking it away from its village and hackneyed country house setting, without intruding too harshly into reality. There's a gentle veneer of gentility that surrounds all these crimes and low-gear chases and detections.

This is also a particularly British strand of crime writing where sleuthing in sporting milieus occurs as a subgenre in its own right.

Dick Francis and his highly popular horse-racing thrillers belong here. Rich in detail, seemingly modern but at heart exponents of Golden Age storytelling, Francis and his cohorts are splendid entertainers with a reassuring touch. If you want to read about murder, learn a lot about an interesting area of life, but don't wish the sordid details dwelled upon, this is for you.

Following the worldwide success of Dick Francis, ex-jockey John Francome is another horse-racing thriller specialist, as is Mark Daniel.

And if it's the sea or yachting you want to read about, with just the right amount of crime, mystery, and suspense, then Sam Llewelyn is your mate. Golf? Try Keith Miles (also Martin Inigo). Botany? John Sherwood.

Ladies of Suspense and One Lonely Man

But what of the undisputed queens of British crime fiction, P. D. James and Ruth Rendell? Where do they fit into the puzzling ten-part map I have been outlining?

Well, the lineage is school of Christie perverted by the right touch of psychology and a bleakish view of reality. Starting from straight detective stories, many of the school of British psychological suspense move on to a novel of characterization and atmosphere, which effectively blends aspects of the traditional cozy, the police procedural (in most cases professional police people are the main protagonists rather than talented amateur sleuths) and the tale of detection and suspense. It has indeed become a very British genre, in no way similar to most of the American companion genre, with its frequent emphasis on children and families in peril.

Even though she is American (but lives in Europe), Patricia Highsmith at her best is a perfect example of this hybrid, successful branch of crime fiction.

P. D. James, of course, has poetry-writing Adam Dalgliesh, and Ruth Rendell family man Wexford, but they do not restrict themselves to series and, often, their stand-alone novels are their most impressive. Rendell actually now divides her novels between the more traditional detective tales of Ruth Rendell and the murkier tales of manners and psychology of Barbara Vine.

A relative newcomer, but one who has fast established a reputation, is ex-barrister Frances Fyfield, who chronicles the bittersweet ongoing romance of her protagonists, lawyer Helen West and Detective Superintendent Geoffrey Bailey. Fyfield also explores darker seams in nonseries novels under her real name, Frances Hegarty.

Still much underappreciated, and a veteran of the genre who has been icily dissecting the ills of family life and genteel crime for many years, is Margaret Yorke, while writers like Celia Dale, Celia Fremlin, Sheila Radley, and Maureen Duffy all mine similar territory with chilling accuracy. These are not always exciting authors to read if you're looking for the thrill of detection and the intellectual pleasure of the solving of the puzzle, but they all offer fascinating insights into human nature. Even if the social background is thinly sketched, you do feel that they are telling it like it is, that they have the measure of the fallibility in human beings, in all of us.

Sitting on the borderline of psychological suspense and the traditional whodunit is the younger Jill McGown, a deft plotter with strong character empathy, possibly one of the most promising of this British female posse of suspensers and a writer still likely to make a major impact on the genre.

All ladies so far, so what of the men? Do they not enjoy the cruel dissection of characters and the twists of human nature on the edge? Few do, preferring the pastures of noir, where the quirks of the human soul are better analyzed under cover of violence and realism. But Michael Dibdin, with a foot in the whodunit and the procedural too, is the current master with novels like *A Rich Full Death,* *Dirty Tricks,* and *The Tryst,* which probe at the festering under the smooth surface of English life like a devious surgeon. Like Dexter, another Oxford crime writer. Is it the water they drink?

Fresh Blood

Toward the end of the 1980's, an increasing number of younger British crime writers began feeling that their contemporaries were just not delving far enough, and a healthy burst of strongly hard-boiled, neonoir texts started to appear.

The most interesting aspect of this phenomenon is that this trend evolved without being truly influenced by modern American counterparts (Leonard,

Willeford, Parker). Encouraged, yes; influenced, no.

The mainstream English novel has always had a strong social realist strand, and many of these newer writers (some of whom grouped together in the amorphous Fresh Blood group) were in fact following in this tradition, and leavening the realism in the process by an injection of mystery and crime plotting. In this respect, they are in the lineage of Dickens by way of precursors like Patrick Hamilton, John Lodwick, Gerald Kersh, and other dark London writers of the immediate postwar period.

After some isolated examples in the seventies and eighties by writers like G. F. Newman, Ted Lewis (the Carter novels), Julian Barnes's bisexual Duffy as Dan Kavanagh, the noir examples didn't truly flourish until Derek Raymond (better known in Europe under his real name, Robin Cook—which he had to abandon to the American medical chiller author to avoid confusion in England and the U.S.) began his Factory series.

With their ever-pessimistic unnamed narrator, the Factory series, now into five volumes (to which Raymond has added *The Hidden Files,* a fascinating exercise in autobiography and the study of the "black" novel), is a bleak panorama of hell on earth, suffused by empathy and morality, where London almost becomes a pit of despair, like a painting by Bosch. Cult material in France, the Factory series is crime writing at its hard-hitting best and is already proving a major influence on younger authors.

John Harvey's Resnick series blends the provincial procedural (the novels are set in Nottingham) with the hard-boiled to strong effect, while black British author Mike Phillips features a black amateur sleuth in his tales of London and Midlands underworld. Both authors display savvy street realism hitherto unseen in British mystery books.

Although he hasn't published a new book in some years, John Milne with his Jenner novels is another rare example of British hard-boiled realism, while Mark Timlin, a prolific but compulsive South London Spillane, offers pace and colloquial dialogue with his Nick Sharman novels.

Other Fresh Blooders of note include computer journalist Denise Danks, whose four Georgina Powers adventures provide a harder edge to the female investigator canon (her third novel, *Frame Grabber,* not content with innovative virtual reality sex, also

sees Georgina involved in an ambiguous sadomasochistic affair with the main culprit), Northerner Chaz Brenchley, sometimes on the horror borderline, Paul Buck, novelizer of *The Honeymoon Killers* and explorer of deviance, acclaimed Scottish author William McIlvanney, creator of the hard-edged Laidlaw, Russell James, who mixes a sense of despair à la David Goodis to his downbeat tales of small-time crooks.

Although many of these newer writers who pay obeisance to reality have little in common apart from the fact they all stand at an interesting cutting edge between the old traditions and a cyberpunklike renewal of the British crime novel, they form an interesting movement of sorts, one that could potentially contribute much different writing in times to come.

Among the Sleuthettes

Although popular in sales terms, the female private eye phenomenon which has single-handedly (well, hand in hand with the obligatory serial killers) overtaken the American marketplace, has not been too much of an inspiration to British writers.

Where Marcia Muller broke the ground for the best-selling Sue Grafton and Sara Paretsky, the British precursor, as early as 1980, was Liza Cody, who introduced her feisty ex-policewoman and p.i. Anna Lee in *Dupe.* This likeable series has now reached six volumes (and television), while Cody has also begun another, involving a female wrestler (*Bucketnut*).

Are we more sexist in Britain, or is it that British skies do not shine favorably upon the female investigator? Cody's contemporaries are few and far between, if all much talented.

A rapid survey would include Hannah Wolfe, created by TV presenter Sarah Dunant, some of Lesley Grant-Adamson's heroines, Susan Moody's black Penny Wanawake, Joan Smith's investigative academic Loretta Lawson, Janet Neel's Francesca Wilson, and Val McDermid's left-wing, Manchester-based Kate Brannigan.

Not strictly a p.i. but feet firmly entrenched in the feminist camp is also Helen Zahavi whose *Dirty Week-End,* featuring the savage revenge of a woman under pressure, created a minor sensation in Britain as our local answer to *American Psycho.*

History and Other Specialties

Another particularly popular strand of British mystery writing currently much in favor is the niche specialist area, where the Brits excel in the realm of historical and art crimes. After all, we have the past and the taste!

Prominent among the historical mystery writers is Ellis Peters and her chronicles of medieval monk-cum-sleuth Brother Cadfael. These are ultracozies with a difference, where the detection blends in seamlessly with a wealth of accumulated historical detail that succeeds in bringing the past and its often colorful characters to life.

Most periods of British and world history are gradually being mined with brio by current British authors. Edwardian, Victorian, Reformation days: Anne Perry (another resident American), the ever-prolific Paul Doherty as P. C. Doherty, Paul Harding, Michael Clynes and C. R. Grace, Edward Marston (a pseudonym of golf mystery specialist Keith Miles), Amy Myers, Keith Heller, Elizabeth Eyre (alias the earlier mentioned duo of Staynes and Storey), Alanna Knight and D. M. Greenwood, all contribute to this healthy genre strand.

Art mysteries also thrive elegantly in the novels of practitioners such as John Malcolm, Iain Pears, Anthony Oliver, and Peter Watson.

A recent variant of the historical mystery adds foreign places to past times: Lindsey Davis's love-lorn centurian Marcus Falco walks down the ironic mean streets of ancient Rome, while Anton Gill's old Egypt scribe Huy tackles the unusual crimes of the era of Akhenaten and after. Which inspired me with an idea I now contribute free to the greater good of the mystery novel: after Rome, Egypt, and Greece, where to next? I suggest adding a zest of mystery to those prehistoric days of yore. . . . Down these mean ice ages, a Neanderthal must go! But what then? All yours.

The Men Who Stay out in the Cold

Lest it be forgotten, John le Carré began his career (and the ineffable George Smiley's) with a couple of crime novels, fairly traditional at that. Which serves to remind us that British spy and thriller writers are without equal, and that the roots of their storytelling owe much to the tale of detection. Unlike, say, the majority of American techno-thriller

authors who offer an innovative blend of science journalism and retrograde science fiction.

Once again, if searching for sources of inspiration some might hark back to Conan Doyle and his Brigadier Gerard tales of spying, battle, and adventure in Europe, or later to Erskine Childers's *Riddle of the Sands* and John Buchan's Richard Hannay tales. Maybe deviousness and treachery come easily to the British mind, but with the exception of Charles McCarry and Robert Littell, I can think of no American practitioner who comes anywhere near the majority of British spy scribes.

Le Carré naturally still rules the roost, with the Everest of *The Quest for Karla* Smiley saga, which elevated the genre to major literary summit levels, and still prospers in the post–cold war era through the strength of his compassion and splendid characterization as demonstrated in his recent *The Night Manager*.

A step away from the throne sits Len Deighton, another cold war shenanigans chronicler and a master of plotting, although more recent titles away from the spy genre have been unconvincing.

Then we have a veritable legion of first-rate thriller experts such as Colin Forbes, Tim Sebastian, Craig Thomas, Ted Allbeury, Frederick Forsyth, John Gardner (when not in James Bond mode—his Herbie Kruger almost equals Smiley for spymaster stature), veteran Eric Ambler, Julian Rathbone, Gavin Lyall, Anthony Price (now retired from journalism and seemingly no longer interested in writing fiction either, to the great disappointment of hordes of fans), Brian Freemantle, and Adam Hall. And this is just the leading pack.

Associational to this field, we also have an impressive cohort of adventure thriller authors like Alastair MacLean, Hammond Innes, Desmond Bagley, Philip McCutchan, etc. . . . where the spying elements are muted or absent, but the storytelling skills are as abundant.

Not strictly crime, but a group of writers who should not be overlooked.

The Jokers in the Pack

Another British trademark, I am often assured, is our sense of humor. And this is often displayed to good effect in mystery fiction, where a sense of the ridiculous and of the understatement can prove an effective foil for the horrors that real crime often exhibits in illiberal doses.

This is a category that often crosses over with others, although many of the best British practitioners of the theatrical mystery appear to be humorous. Writers like Simon Brett and his buffoonish thespian Charles Paris, and actors-cum-authors Simon Williams and Simon Shaw are the best exemplars of these pratfalls on the boards.

Then you have the legal comedies of John Mortimer and the inestimable Rumpole of the Bailey, Sarah Caudwell's zany barristers; the antique capers of Jonathan Gash's lovable rogue Lovejoy; Mike Ripley's wisecracking cab-driver-cum-sleuth Angel (both Gash and Ripley live in the same small East Anglian village—once again, it must be the water); the cookery capers of Michael Bond's Monsieur Pamplemousse; the Sherlockian jollities of M. J. Trow's Inspector Lestrade; the lightweight romantic adventures of Dorothy Dunnett, etc. . . .

Odd Men Out and the Grand Old Men

Finally, you have the crime writers who don't fit in anywhere else really. Either because they're too innovative or individual or because they straddle so many demarcation lines that they defy any attempt at categorization.

In many cases, these are authors who operate as shooting stars with a single memorable book that makes a dent in the soft landscape of crime fiction before they move on to other fields, but I would like to highlight two recent such buccaneers, both, curiously enough, from the world of filmmaking, who I hope will linger in our criminal waters some more.

Paul Mayersberg established his reputation as a screenwriter for esteemed directors like Nicolas Roeg (*The Man Who Fell to Earth, Bad Timing, Eureka*) and Nagisa Oshima (*Merry Christmas, Mr. Lawrence*) and has also moved behind the camera to direct (*Captive, Nightfall*). Frustrated by the time it often takes to see scripts make it into actual production, he has penned two novels (with a third under contract), with strong crime elements: *Homme Fatale* and *Violent Silence*. Fascinating, strongly erotic tales of dark doings in an American setting that owes much to the movies, these are genuinely unsettling and provocative books.

Christopher Petit began his career as a film critic and later became an assistant to German director Wim Wenders before helming his own features (which include the distinct European road movies *Radio On* and *Flight to Berlin*). His first noir novel, *Robinson,* is a curious hybrid, at times reminiscent of Derek Raymond (whom Petit greatly admires) and J. G. Ballard, with a tale of shady doings in London's Soho.

Peter Dickinson, on the other hand, is one of Britain's most protean writers, moving elegantly from traditional mystery to grave whodunits, children's books, fantasy, and other genres with consummate ease. Although he enjoys an excellent reputation, by never sticking to one area he may have reduced his impact on the mystery scene.

Another odd man out, and a publishing phenomenon of 1992, is Victor Headley, a black London writer whose first novel of crime in South London's black community, *Yardie,* was a major best seller, although initially self-published and distributed. Starkly realistic to the extent that the language used often requires the equivalent of subtitles, this is the first genuine example of homegrown crime writing of a different type. His follow-up novel, *Excess,* confirms his striking new voice.

But pride of finishing place must go to the two remaining grand old men of British crime and mystery fiction: Michael Gilbert and Julian Symons.

Both are now in their eighties, but still eminently active, inheritors of the Golden Age mantle who have survived critically by sturdy plotting, characterization, and intelligence. Their crime world is a genteel one, miles removed from noir contemporary realities, urbane and elegant.

Michael Gilbert moves effortlessly from legal tales to whodunits and espionage, a master of storytelling whose charms never date and appears impervious to anachronisms.

Julian Symons, on the other hand, proudly upholds the traditions of detection (he is one of the founders of the highly conservative Detection Club), leavened most agreeably with shards of dark contemporary psychology that in no way betray his age.

Both are masters of the craft, whose shadow looms over our modern mystery landscape the way Christie and her ladies in waiting did up to the 1950s, and we are all none the worse for it, as the British Isles, for all their contradictions, remain a perfect compost heap for the growth and development of all things criminous, literary speaking of course.

Some Notable Modern British Mystery Novels
Selected by Maxim Jakubowski

Robert Barnard	*The Case of the Missing Brontë*
Sarah Caudwell	*The Sirens Sang of Murder*
Liza Cody	*Bucketnut*
Denise Danks	*Frame Grabber*
Lindsey Davis	*The Silver Pigs*
Len Deighton	**Hook, Line and Sinker trilogy**
Colin Dexter	*Last Seen Wearing*
Sarah Dunant	*Fatlands*
Frances Fyfield	*Deep Sleep*
Caroline Graham	*The Killings at Badger's Drift*
John Harvey	*Wasted Years*
Reginald Hill	*Bones and Silence*
P. D. James	*Devices and Desires*
Dan Kavanagh	*Duffy*
Philip Keer	**Berlin Noir trilogy**
John le Carré	**The Quest for Karla trilogy**
Peter Lovesey	*The Last Detective*
William McIlvanney	*Laidlaw*
Paul Mayersberg	*Homme Fatale*
Janet Neel	*Death Among the Dons*
Ellis Peters	*A Morbid Taste for Bones*
Derek Raymond	*I Was Dora Suarez*
Ruth Rendell (as Barbara Vine)	*Gallowglass*
Julian Symons	*The Three Pipe Problem*
Mark Timlin	*Take the A-Train*

An assortment of Edgar, Anthony, and Dagger winners and losers, a few trilogies (but they count as one), oddities, covering the spectrum from ultra-cozy to super-noir.

SOME OF MY CHARACTERS WHO HAUNT ME

Margaret Yorke

Berit Rhone

MAJOR JOHNSON HAD BEEN in my mind for several years before I wrote about him in *No Medals for the Major,* published in 1974. I had a clear image of a small, dapper man who felt young and sprightly, although he was "fifty-eight years old, a short man, stockily built, with wisps of grey hair around a bald dome, and a neatly trimmed moustache." On retirement, he went to live in the village of Wiveldown, where he set about becoming a pillar of the community. First, he refurbished his bungalow, named Tobruk because he had been in the siege there. Then, when planning the garden, he borrowed helpful books from the library, guided by the librarian, Celia Mainwaring. He met Celia, also, at evening classes, where both were learning cookery, and he was by no means the only male pupil. Celia's widowed mother had been the cook in their family, and after her death Celia felt a lack of confidence in the kitchen, so sought to repair the deficiency. While playing his role in the village, Major Johnson felt lonely; hitherto, he had had the company of his military colleagues and a structured life decreed by army rules. The thought of marriage came to him. It would offer him companionship. As a young man, he had once been in love, but the girl had married someone else and "then somehow, the years ran out. . . . He sank gradually into his bachelor role. . . . Now . . . he was adrift in an unfamiliar society." He began to court Celia Mainwaring, who, behind his back, ridiculed him. All the time there was, among his acquaintance, widowed Ruth Fortescue, who was eager to be his friend but who was so tall beside him that he never saw her as a possible partner.

Two tearaway boys spoiled Major Johnson's dream by stealing his car and running over a small girl whose body they stowed in the boot (trunk) of the major's car, then returned it to the place where they found it. When, after an anxious search, the body was found, the innocent major was blamed by the villagers for her death and was almost lynched. The police were sure that he was not responsible despite the weight of circumstantial evidence against him, but Major Johnson felt that his honor had been impugned and so he was destroyed.

As I wrote about the major, I became deeply involved with his fate, and I still think of him stepping out briskly along the village street, with his nemesis awaiting him. The book was exciting to write: the characters dictated the story and it all came together very quickly, needing very little revision. It was the first of my suspense novels and a breakthrough in my career. Major Johnson was a victim of his own vulnerability and there are many such people in the world.

Mrs. Anderson, however, the central figure in *The Scent of Fear,* published in 1980, was determined not to become one. Old and frail, missing her only surviving son who had emigrated to Australia years before, she lived alone in the huge house on a hill above Framingham, where she had raised her family. A new bypass had separated her house from the rest of the village, and she had to walk down the hill and through an underpass to reach the library and the shops. Unknown to her, Kevin, a youth who worked in a local garage, had made a refuge for himself in an attic in her house. He would enter by a downstairs window while she slept and would spend hours there, warm and snug with an electric fire he had found, and during the night he would wander around the house, helping himself to food. Mrs. Anderson began to wonder if she was losing her wits when food she expected to find in her larder was missing, or when the loaf was jaggedly cut. Then a murder was committed in Framingham; Kevin, the killer, hid in Mrs. Anderson's house, and when it was cut off by a blizzard, she discovered him.

She knew then that she had not gone senile; here was the explanation for the vanished food; but she knew, too, that he was a very dangerous individual. In the time she spent with him—not afraid to die, but fearing the manner of her death—she resolved that despite her physical weakness, she would not be vanquished by a young man who was an inadequate coward, and she succeeded.

She and Major Johnson linger in my memory, and I often think of them; I grew particularly fond of them, perhaps because both, in their different ways, were admirable people. Many of my villains are so evil or so twisted that I am glad to leave them at the end of the book in which they appear.

There is a little boy I remember too: Peter, in *Safely to the Grave*, published in 1986. He was another positive character. When planning the book, I thought first of him, a small boy who made a den in a clapped-out old car abandoned in a wood. He (like Kevin) cherished this secret place, where he kept comics and crisps; it was his haven when he visited his spunky aunt Marion with whom he spent a lot of time after his father remarried. Peter had friends in the village, among them the childless Laura, who treated him like a son, and when she was murdered, he was grief-stricken. But the man who killed her had a second victim in mind: Peter's aunt Marion. When he made his bid to kill her, Peter was able to escape from the cellar in which he had been locked by the murderer, and, showing matchless courage, he saved the day.

These three special characters share some qualities. All were brave, and they were solitary. Peter and Mrs. Anderson managed to triumph over more powerful antagonists, and Major Johnson was a winner, too, because he never lost his integrity. It is important to me to make this point in my work: I believe that many major crimes arise from small ones that escalate because of fear and cowardice on the part of the perpetrators. To write about potential victims who somehow overcome those who threaten them seems to me to be a positive action, and those of my characters who manage this stay in my memory.

Of course there is someone else I have created who haunts me: Dr. Patrick Grant, M.A., D. Phil., sometime dean of St. Mark's College, Oxford. He was my first sleuth, solving mysteries because, unlike the police, he had deduced that crime had been committed where, on the surface, all seemed straightforward. I grew very fond of Patrick, with whom I began my own criminal career after writing eleven earlier novels. At the time I had been working in Oxford college libraries and felt that a don would be an appropriate amateur detective, one with whom I could empathize. Patrick shared many of my own convictions and prejudices. Conversely, he had strengths I lacked, and erudition: he was a Shakespearean scholar, where I was merely an enthusiastic devotee always struggling to keep up with him. He featured in five novels and became my invisible companion because I would wonder, during any experience, how his reactions would differ from mine. Patrick always knew best, but he could not manage his personal life and was a lonely individual who longed for love but could not make a full emotional commitment. He seized any opportunity to solve puzzles created by the deeds of others because it meant he could avoid trying to unravel his own. He was loyal, a moralist, and stubborn; his persistence carried him to the resolution of mysteries encountered in places as disparate as Athens, the Austrian Alps, and Stratford-upon-Avon. Because Patrick was fluent in French, German, and Italian, he had to be unable to speak Greek, and that meant that he and I both had to learn that language. He maddened me, but I loved his company while I wrote about him. By ceasing to do so, I never destroyed our excellent cerebral relationship, unlike other writers, who have harnessed themselves for life to fictional sleuths of whom, eventually, they tire. Discovering Major Johnson freed me from writing about Patrick, and made me appreciate the liberty I now have, with a new cast for every book, to explore areas that would be closed to him.

A curious thing happened last September, when I went on a Mediterranean cruise. Our ship called at Mykonos, where I had been several times before. I was happy to be in Greece again after an interval of several years, and I remembered a particular taverna, high above the town, where one ate on a terrace under some vines. Could I find it again?

I did, and sat at a table to order an ouzo and Greek salad. There was only one other occupied table, some distance away. As I sat there, I suddenly felt, close to me, taking me over, the presence of Patrick Grant. I pulled some paper and a pen from my bag and began to write. All at once I knew just what had happened to Patrick from the time that we had parted, after his last adventure nearly twenty years ago, until that day when there he was, telling me about his rift with Liz and his subsequent career, and how he came to be here on the island now, part of me, guiding my pen.

I don't think he will ever completely leave me, my friendly academic ghost.

THE ORIGINS OF CHARLES PARIS

Simon Brett

IN A CAREER OF MANY unsuccessful auditions, it is surprising the ease with which Charles Paris got his first job. I don't mean his first job in the theater, because obviously that happened long before I knew him—I refer to his first job in one of my books. He sort of walked straight into it. Since he was the only actor who applied for the role, there was no contest. As soon as he came into my consciousness, I knew that no one else could play the part.

I'm not sure exactly how long the part had existed, but something of the sort had been floating around in my head for quite a while. The year was 1974. I was working for BBC radio as a producer of light entertainment. I enjoyed the job but felt a slight unease in it. I knew I was buzzing around the area where I wanted to be, but I still didn't feel that I'd found my perfect niche within that area. After each long day in the studio producing programs, I would leave feeling slightly unfulfilled. So I started to ask myself who in that studio had had a better time than I had as producer. Who, ultimately, was I jealous of?

It wasn't the technicians, I knew that. I maybe envied their skills and their easy camaraderie, but my ambition was not to be one of them.

For a long time I had wondered whether it was the actors. I was—and still am—hopelessly stage-struck. I had done a lot of amateur acting in my teens, played Richard II and Prospero at school, Edgar and Leontes ("callow and splenetic"— *Oxford Times*) at college. I had been president of the Oxford University Dramatic Society. I had watched actors in radio studios having enormous fun.

And yet, somehow I knew it wasn't they, either, whom I really envied. I doubt whether I would have had the talent to make it as a professional actor, but I know I wouldn't have had the temperament. All that waiting around, all that psyching oneself up for auditions, all that failure and psyching oneself up yet again, all that "resting," all that passivity—I couldn't have coped with it.

So, if I felt unfulfilled as a producer, yet wasn't jealous of either the technicians or the actors, who else was there around the studio setup who I reckoned was having a better time than I was? Could it possibly be the writers?

The more I thought about it, the more firmly I knew that I had the answer. Come the studio day, the writers had been through their worst agonies. They may have sweated blood in the weeks before, but by the day of recording, apart from tinkering with the occasional line, there was little more that they could do. They were free to just be around, relax in the congenial studio apartment, even have a couple of drinks at lunchtime, secure in the knowledge that they had already done their bit. Yes, that's who I was jealous of—the writers.

And it wasn't as if I didn't write already. I had scribbled away ever since I was capable of holding a pen. My teens were daubed over with an unrelenting graffiti of poems, plays and stories. I had finished my first full-length novel at the age of sixteen. It had been dreadful, but at least it showed me that I could go the distance. The challenge thereafter was to write sixty thousand words that might be of interest to someone other than their morbidly adolescent progenitor.

Four other full-length novels had followed over the next ten years. All of them were—very properly—unpublished. The time was undoubtedly approaching when I should take a new direction in my writing life. A revolutionary thought struck me. Suppose, rather than writing something that I wanted to get off my chest, I had a go at writing *something that someone else might want to read*?

The type of book that should be the first beneficiary of this mold-breaking new approach was not in doubt. Around that time, mysteries were bulking larger in my life than they ever had before. True, during my teens I had rattled through my share of Agatha Christies, a few Ngaio Marshes and the odd

limp Margery Allingham, but I was by no means an expert on crime fiction. And, as for the idea of writing the stuff, I thought: forget it, you have to have an amazing mathematical mind and the deductive powers of a computer even to contemplate the idea.

What changed my thinking on the subject was a job that was delegated to me at the BBC. Ian Carmichael had recently been a big success as Lord Peter Wimsey on television; my bosses were keen to have him star in the same role on radio. Because of the difference between the two media, new adaptations of the books would have to be commissioned, and I was appointed producer of the series.

It was working very closely with the adaptor, Chris Miller, on those Wimsey scripts that demystified the mystery for me. As we took the books apart, the clockwork plotting that had so frightened me seemed suddenly much less important than character and dialogue. The books broke down into a sequence of duologues—Lord Peter talks to the butler, Lord Peter talks to the head gardener, Bunter talks to the undergardener, etc., etc., etc. Well, even though I still wasn't too sure about my plotting skills, I did feel confident that I could write dialogue. I decided to have a go at writing a mystery.

It was not difficult to find my setting. As I mentioned, I had always been stagestruck. Show business, with its constant juxtapositions of glamour and tackiness, had appealed to me. And there was no problem about research. As a radio producer, every time I answered the phone, I was talking to an actor, an agent, a musician, or a writer. Yes, I would write a mystery with a show-biz background.

One of the incidental pleasures of the Lord Peter Wimsey series was that I was working with a lot of middle-aged actors. They intrigued me. I liked their humor, their camaraderie, their flamboyance, their fatalism, their vanity, their vulnerability. Suppose, I wondered, I were to write a mystery with an actor as detective . . . ?

It was at this point that Charles Paris appeared, demanding the part. I don't know where he came from. All I know is that suddenly on a page of my notebook was the name Charles Paris, together with a fairly detailed background and plot for what was to become *Cast, in Order of Disappearance*. It was all there straightaway. Apart from a change to his wife's name—"Veronica" I think it was in the notebook; subsequently, of course, Frances—the plot and detail was more or less worked out. All that remained to be done was the small matter of the writing—or in the delightful phrase of a writer-friend of mine, the "wording-in."

When I finished the first novel, I had no intention of making Charles Paris a series character. But Livia Gollancz bought the book and asked about my plans for a sequel. Charles himself was game for another excursion, and so I settled down and wrote *So Much Blood*. After that he became a kind of fixture. He makes his thirteenth outing in *A Series of Murders* and, though I am now involved in many other kinds of writing, I have no intention ever of giving up on him.

Charles Paris's got me in a cleft stick, you see. As he keeps reminding me, I can't abandon him. Nobody else ever gives him any work.

THE TRANSPLANTED BRIT
Dorothy Cannell

WILL THE GRASS ALWAYS have been greener for me on the other side of the ocean? Probably. I pine for the ivied walls of Oxford, even though I never went to Oxford, even on a day trip. I hunger to walk through a bluebell wood on a misty-eyed April morning and hear the cuckoo's magic call one more time. I long to sit by a coal fire on a winter afternoon, toasting bread for tea on a long-handled brass fork while I listen to *Woman's Hour* on the wireless.

What I want, of course, is the England of my girlhood; in memory I love it all. Our kitchen with the kettle singing to the boil and always cut-and-come-again cake in the tin with the thatched cottage on the lid. The stifled giggles of children playing hopscotch in a street otherwise so quiet someone might have turned the volume down. Lady Wentwhistle walking her Hungarian wolfhound in the mews. Elderly gentlemen pedaling their bicycles up-hill with no thoughts of keeping fit. Gray-haired ladies in dresses old enough to be accidentally fashionable again, who dream of glory in the annual flower show. The pub on the corner of Honeypot Lane with its home-brewed cider that glows like fruited amber. And, of course, the Spider Web tea shop—its interior dimly lit and cheerfully mysterious, like a friendly ghost inviting guests to join him in a break from the real world. Ah, teacakes! Dripping with buttery goodness. And a pot of tea fragrant enough to satisfy a maharajah's palate. Then, for formal occasions, the Manor House, a Regency residence turned restaurant, it's style reminiscent of a portentous old butler, very correct if a little bit superior. Such worldly pleasures! All within a stone's throw of the churchyard that is entered through an iron gate that groans like a rheumatic old pussycat as it creeps back into place. The dear old Frankenstein monster could not fail to enjoy picnicking among the tombstones that crane forward to glimpse the visitor. And within the Norman walls of St. Anselm's Church the air is centuries-old while stained glass filters sunlight onto brass name-plates. Who, pray tell, was Winifred Pottingsworth, 1643–1742? Did the hours spent on red velvet knee-pad insure her redemption?

And more to the point, is that the way it really was for me? Living among the hollyhocks, before I replanted myself in the United States? Silly question. For a fiction writer, fact is always an iffy thing.

It stretches my credulity to believe I left hearth, home, and family at the tender age of twenty to seek my fortune as a shorthand typist in Chicago. I brought with me one suitcase and sixty pounds on which to exist until I found a job, and I rented a room in a brownstone apartment building, hung with a sign advertising TRANSIENTS WELCOME, which seemed so fitting considering I had no intention of remaining permanently in the New World. Three months to the day after getting off the boat, someone broke into my bedsitter and committed the indelicacy of making off with all my worldly goods, but never fear! There are some items that can't be filched. I had brought with me two things of infinite value, whose hiding place was safe within myself.

My father, an avid reader, had inspired in me a great love of the written word. And my mother, who had a wonderful gift for anecdote, had been

my role model as a storyteller. From my early childhood I wanted to write books, or, rather, I wanted to be an author whose books lined themselves up proudly on row upon row of library shelves. The process of getting from plot to page one had always struck me as a task similar to scaling Mount Everest with only a toothpick for assistance. And in writing my letters home I did not realize I was embarking upon my apprenticeship, but looking back, I suspect that was when I found my avuncular muse. Feeling a moral obligation to keep the family abreast of my life experiences but not wishful to strike terror in the hearts of my nearest and dearest, I resorted to spoofing up the truth when recounting such occurrences as the burglary and the equally thrilling blind date. That never-to-be-forgotten night when I opened the door at the appointed time, asked, "Are you Bob?" and, receiving a bright nod, sallied forth to see *Lawrence of Arabia,* only to have my room-mate open the door three minutes after our backs were turned to find another Bob on the step, who looked quite nonplussed when she explained I had just left with him.

Having been blessed with a father who read so-called "women's books" without feeling his manhood was impaired, I had grown up steeped in romances from Victorian novels to serials in *Woman's Weekly.* I believed my destiny was happily fulfilled when a young man by the serendipitous name of Julian sought my hand in marriage. His being an American was a handicap bravely to be borne, and, if not quite so thrilling as a limp resulting from a hunting accident, or a dueling scar searing his manly cheek, I was not prepared to look a wedding ring in the mouth. Life with me would surely bring forth latent cynicism and a tendency to raise a dark, sardonic eyebrow. I did mention in a fit of wild abandon that I had yearnings to be a writer, and I seem to remember his suggesting I not use the checkbook for any flights of fancy.

Contentment is a curse; four children and numerous cats and dogs later, my writing was still limited to letters home; then one day lightning struck in the form of a question from my six-year-old son, Jason:

"Mommy, what are you going to be when you grow up?" The little darling had certainly mastered the haughty stare.

Talk about biting the hand that feeds the chocolate chip cookie. In one fell swoop I realized that a life of alphabetizing the towels in the linen closet, and making bread in flowerpots had its limitations. When Julian came home that night, I informed him I was at last ready to pick up my quill.

"Are you telling me," he said, "that you intend to write the great American novel?"

"No, silly!" I replied. "I am going to write the great British novel."

Being the hero he is, he appeared the next day with a secondhand manual typewriter tucked under his arm and set to work after dinner building me a desk (well, let's call a shelf a shelf) in the laundry room, within easy walking distance of the washing machine and dryer.

"You're too good," I said, sidestepping the box of cat litter to press an impassioned kiss upon his work-weary brow.

"You don't think you're tackling too big a job?" he asked with a throb in his voice that caused me to believe he was remembering my venture into macramé. What had started out as a dishcloth had taken on a reptilian life of its own, crawling up two flights of stairs and taking over the entire house before we called in the exterminator.

"How hard can it be to write a book?" It was my turn to raise a sardonic eyebrow. "It's just a matter of putting one word in front of the other." Motherhood makes the weak strong. After misplacing one child at Disney World and another at Glacier National Park, I had no doubt I could climb Everest without a toothpick and write my way up hill and down dale and plant my banner, emblazoned with the words THE END.

I wrote *Down the Garden Path* (originally as a Regency romance) and *The Thin Woman* on that fifty-dollar typewriter with numerous breaks to catch my youngest daughter as she came down the laundry shoot. Seven years later I hadn't sold a word, but what I had achieved was possession of a magic carpet that allowed me to travel home every time I sat down to work on either a novel or a short story. Later an editor would tell me that I had an advantage in being able to write about England as a true Brit but with an American viewpoint. I would put it this way—that I write with the abiding love of a native and the wide-eyed enthusiasm of a foreigner. And I wonder sometimes, had I not left, would it have been enough to walk through a bluebell wood on an April morning and never try to capture that dew-sweet enchantment on paper? If she had been ever-near, would I have strained to hear my mother's voice telling me stories of an eccentric family of cousins? They were all named after flowers, drove a Rolls-Royce, and sent Christmas cards they had received on some previous year and from which they had (not very successfully) erased the old signature. Those cousins became Hyacinth and Primrose Tramwell in *Down the Garden Path*. I haven't heard the cuckoo's call in a long time, and it has been almost as long since I heard my father's voice. But I can still hear the echo of his words—"You are what you read."

If we are also what we write, I am doubly blessed in having lived in the old world and the new. I love my adopted country and see the dogwood and magnolia bloom with a renewed sense of wonder and delight each spring. But given the opportunity, would I choose to go back and live in England? Perhaps, if I could set up house in a thatched cottage with Miss Marple living next door.

HUMOROUS CRIME
or, Dead Funny
Mike Ripley

IN TOM STOPPARD'S HYSTERICAL send-up of the country house murder mystery *The Real Inspector Hound,* one of the critics turned participant in the drama asks: "Is this some kind of joke?" The answer comes back: "If it is, Inspector, it's in very poor taste."

And it is in poor taste, for there is nothing to laugh at in a murder, or a mugging, or a burglary, or a random drive-by shooting. So why is humor such a long-standing part of the framework of mystery fiction? And not just a facet of mystery writing, but, in some cases, a fully fledged comedy crime subgenre?

To begin, it has to be recognized, as Alfred Hitchcock did so masterfully, that there is a thin line between a scream and a laugh. Under stress, people turn to humor, however nervously, and as mysteries revolve around stressful situations, humor becomes a legitimate tool of the crime writer.

The hero who can laugh in the face of danger and who doesn't know the meaning of the word *fear* must surely be an okay guy and the reader is safe in his hands. Or so we are led to believe. Only on reflection do we think that someone who laughs at danger and doesn't know the meaning of the word *fear* is in fact a hysterical illiterate.

But people are basically humorous beings. With few exceptions they like to laugh and they enjoy making other people laugh. Any writer aiming for realistic dialogue can do no worse than to hang around in a bar, listening to the regular customers, the source (I am convinced) for this description of a third party by an everyday Arkansas wit in Joan Hess's *Malice in Maggody:*

"The boy's a day late and a dollar short, and he doesn't have the sense to zip his fly in a tornado."

In less than two dozen words Hess provides a character sketch of the third party referred to, a good idea of the character of the person talking, and the setting of the book. There is no way that we are in St. Mary Mead, or Knightsbridge, or Harlem or Miami here. This is downstate Arkansas, and you have been warned!

One of the funniest female writers around, Sarah Caudwell, sets her scene in a different way in *The Shortest Way to Hades.* In a prologue, the androgynous Professor Hilary Tamar warns the reader that they may have bought the book under a misapprehension and urges them to return it to the bookseller:

I for my part (for publisher and bookseller I cannot speak) would rather forgo the modest sum which would accrue to me from a sale— very modest, meagre might be a better word, one might almost say paltry—would indefinitely rather forgo that sum than think it obtained by deception.

Apart from striking a chord with most mystery writers, this apologia immediately sets the tone of the book. Here we will meet erudite, slightly dotty, establishment characters in a world of their own (actually the London legal system), and unmistakably English.

So humor can be a useful tool in establishing character and setting. It also acts as a security blanket, for, after all, we are writing about crimes. It is a way in which the writer can reassure the reader that this is only a story. You don't really have to be frightened, or shocked, and you don't have to clean up the mess on the library carpet, because here's a joke to relieve the tension.

The distinguished English crime critic T. J. Binyon[1] maintains that facetiousness (à la Lord Peter Wimsey), wisecracks (Marlowe), and witty writing (such as that of Edmund Crispin) are all "tolerated" in the detective story. There seem, however, to be few examples of pure comedic writing.

Parodies of the genre there certainly are, and it is surprising that perhaps there aren't more. Leo Bruce, in *Case for Three Detectives* (1936), almost did for the whole genre in one fell swoop, having three guest detectives under the thin guises of Lord Simon Plimsoll, Amer Picon (probably Belgian), and Monsignor Smith.

Julian Symons could have finished it off a few years later (1945) with *The Immaterial Murder Case* and a detective called Teak Woode, and today the British writer M. J. Trow plays havoc with the reputation of Mr. Holmes and Dr. Watson in his own hellzapoppin style with his adventures of Inspector Lestrade.

But there is a long tradition of comedy in crime, not simply a tolerance of it.

In "the first and greatest" (T. S. Eliot) English detective novel, *The Moonstone* (1868), Wilkie Collins doesn't so much send in the clowns to relieve the tension as order a tactical comedy strike in the shape of the narrative of Miss Clack. One and a quarter centuries later, the activities of Miss Busybody Clack, handing out semireligious tracts faster than an Uzi on full auto, are still very funny. It is a consummate piece of comedy writing, though no one would describe *The Moonstone* as a comedy-thriller.

There are some authors on whom the critics agree when handing out the label "comedy." Almost all include George Bagby's Inspector Schmidt books, the Dover tales of Joyce Porter, the Irish thrillers of Michael Kenyon, the academic fripperies of Michael Innes, the criminal farces of Donald E. Westlake, and, the name mentioned above all others, the late Colin Watson.

Watson is perhaps best known in his native England for his critical work *Snobbery with Violence* and for coining the immortal phrase "Mayhem Parva" as the ubiquitous setting for the traditional cozy mystery. His novels, basically what became known as the Flaxborough Chronicles, set new standards of comedy crime in the 1960s by introducing a genuinely black edge to the proceedings. At the same time, John Gardner was spoofing the growing espionage fiction market with the Boysie Oakes tales, starting with *The Liquidator,* although with the growth of the Bond film industry, that particular genre went into self-parody in a big way.

The Watson books are worth rereading thirty years later, though few remain in print in the U.K. and Watson was one of the few writers to bridge the gap between what H.R.F. Keating calls the two models of crime writing: "the black face of violence and the spreading hips of cosiness."[2]

Keating, no slouch himself with a comic touch, maintains that it is in the "cozy" field where comedy will flourish. The wisecracking private eye is allowed to wisecrack to assert his or her independence of the normal procedures of law, order, and society. For examples go no further than the one-liners everyone can quote from Chandler and the exchanges of Archie Goodwin and Nero Wolfe. But the private eye, or "hard-boiled," novel is not a comedy.

Elmore Leonard creates wickedly funny dialogue (with the bad guy getting most of the good lines) and Reginald Hill has a supremely comic creation in Fat Andy Dalziel, but the ultimate aim is not a farce.

And Keating has astutely recognized that humor of the deflationary sort frees the writer from the confines of the whodunit? formula. Assuming the central character is realistic and sympathetic to the reader, the more bizarre the plot, the better. Almost invariably those become how-does-he-get-out-of-this plots (Or, in my case, how-the-hell-did-he-

---

[1] *Murder Will Out: The Detective in Fiction* by T. J. Binyon (Oxford University Press, 1989).

[2] *Writing Crime Fiction* by H.R.F. Keating (A & C Black, 1986).

get-into-this?) and the comedy element is allowed to dominate.

Today's comedy crime writers are crossing the boundary from comic cozy to black comic hard-boiled. In Britain, Michael Dibdin produced in *Dirty Tricks* the ultimate black comedy of sexual manners. R. D. Wingfield has done the same for the police procedural with his Inspector Frost trilogy, piling grisly incident on grisly incident.

But is is probably America that takes the comedy honors at the moment, if only for the outrageous torturing of the funny bone perpetrated by Kinky (''Find something you like and let it kill you'') Friedman and the gloriously over-the-top Carl Hiaasen. If Carl Hiaasen survives being sued by the Pit Bull Owners of America, the Bass Fish-ermen of Louisiana, Disneyland, the World Wildlife Fund, and the State of Florida, then he surely deserves the title King of Comedy Crime; for the time being anyway.

There is, however, a benchmark classic in the field of comedy crime without mention of which no résumé of the subject could be complete. In 1937 an established pair of comedy writers, Caryl Brahms and S. J. Simon, turned their heads to crime and produced *A Bullet in the Ballet,* not only a satire on the pretensions of the world of ballet, but a damned good whodunit and very funny to boot.

That, surely, is the one to beat. All crime writers should read it. Aspiring comedy crime writers should read it and weep.

DARK
SUSPENSE

INTRODUCTION

Jon L. Breen

WHAT EXACTLY DO WE MEAN by dark suspense? It is a term of fairly recent coinage—literary dictionaries don't define it—but its roots somewhat parallel those of the film noir of the forties. Dark suspense, though, must be interpreted somewhat more narrowly. There is some overlap with the hard-boiled school, but there are also major differences. Dark suspense plays against the essential optimism of most mystery and detective fiction: that the crime will be solved, the guilty punished, order restored. In dark suspense even more than in hard-boiled fiction, there is no order to restore. Life is capricious, fortune arbitrary. Existence is marked more by tragic irony and circumstantial traps than by any kind of plan or design. To the extent that it is a crime novel, Horace McCoy's *They Shoot Horses, Don't They?* (1935), with its sense of the hopelessness of life, could be considered a precursor of the form, as could James M. Cain's hard-boiled classic *The Postman Always Rings Twice* (1934).

Dark suspense has no mother. Few if any women writers have practiced it—and that's not necessarily to their discredit. If the category has a father, it is Cornell Woolrich, who began in the twenties as a jazz-age Fitzgerald acolyte, transformed himself into a versatile pulp writer through the thirties, and became a suspense specialist of unusual power in the forties and fifties. The adaptability of his novels and short stories to radio, television, and film was one key to his considerable financial success. *The Bride Wore Black* (1940), *Phantom Lady* (1942; as William Irish), and the short story "Rear Window" are examples that speak for themselves.

Woolrich had a sentimental streak, and his work has some surprisingly light and pleasant moments. For a haunted recluse who spent most of his life occupying a hotel room with his mother, Woolrich had a good grasp of all sorts of human relationships, including healthy ones. But what makes him fit the mold of dark suspense writer is the profoundly

bleak point of view embodied in the unused story title that Francis M. Nevins, Jr., appropriated as a subtitle for his definitive biography, *Cornell Woolrich: First You Dream, Then You Die* (Mysterious, 1988); or these lines of Woolrich's fragmentary autobiography *Blues of a Lifetime* (Bowling Green University Popular Press, 1991): "I was only trying to cheat death. I was only trying to surmount for a while the darkness that all my life I surely knew was going to come rolling in on me someday and obliterate me. I was only trying to stay alive a brief while longer, after I was already gone" (page 152).

Many, perhaps most, of Woolrich's stories, which had to conform to a degree with the demands of the market, had conventionally happy endings. But with this writer, you were never sure what was coming. As Nevins notes in *Twentieth-Century Crime and Mystery Writers,* "there are no series characters in his work, and the reader can never know in advance whether a particular story of his will be light or dark—which is one reason why his stories are so hauntingly suspenseful" (page 1108, third edition).

David Goodis, who like Woolrich was by all accounts a rather strange and tortured character, made a big impact in the suspense field with early novels like *Dark Passage* (1946), *Nightfall* (1947), and *Of Missing Persons* (1950), but through the fifties he switched to the paperback original market that was most receptive to dark suspense. Goodis carries the sense of hopelessness to a possibly reductive extreme. Quoting Nevins again in *TCCMW:* "In Goodis's paperbacks . . . there is no basis for even a moment's hope and thus no real suspense. His people are born losers and victims who try to cheat their fate by living as zombies, shunning all involvement with others and the world, sustained by booze, cigarettes, and mechanical sex. What they learn is that there is no way out of the trap they're in and that, whatever they do or don't do, life is going to get them" (page 447).

Jim Thompson, who seems by evidence of Michael J. McCauley's biography *Jim Thompson: Sleep with the Devil* (Mysterious, 1991) to have been a relatively normal person, at least in comparison with Woolrich and Goodis, may have had the darkest sensibility of all. His best-known (and brilliant) novel *The Killer Inside Me* (1952) is told from the point of view of a psychopathic killer, small-town sheriff's deputy Lou Ford. He somewhat reworked the same situation in *Pop. 1280* (1964), which Thompson scholar Max Allan Collins believes to be an even better book. Thompson had in common with Woolrich and Goodis the adaptability of his works to film, though in Thompson's case the recognition came too late to earn him much money. In 1990, thirteen years after his death, successful film adaptations of no less than three of his novels appeared: *After Dark, My Sweet, The Kill-Off,* and *The Grifters.*

The fantasist, critic, and essayist Harlan Ellison certainly belongs among the dark suspense masters for some of his short stories, notably the Edgar winners "The Whimper of Whipped Dogs" (1973), based on the notorious Kitty Genovese case, and

"Soft Monkey" (1987). James Ellroy's work borders both the private eye and police procedural, but the nightmarish vision of fifties Los Angeles found in his quartet of novels *The Black Dahlia* (1987), *The Big Nowhere* (1988), *L.A. Confidential* (1990), and *White Jazz* (1992) certainly qualifies him for the dark suspense club. Other contemporaries in the form include a number who overlap the horror genre, e.g., Joe R. Lansdale, Rex Miller, Thomas F. Monteleone, and Dan Simmons. Indeed nonsupernatural horror is a fairly close synonym for dark suspense. Writers like Stephen King (in a book like 1987's *Misery*), Peter Straub, and Dean R. Koontz occasionally at least border on this area, but generally their outlook is probably not quite pessimistic enough to qualify. However, a close associate who reads everything this trio writes tells me Koontz is moving more and more in the direction of darkness, particularly in his most recent novel, *Dragon Tears* (1993).

A critic's confession: much as I admire many of the writers discussed above, a little dark suspense goes a long way with me.

BUILDING THE BATES MOTEL
Robert Bloch

DO YOU BELIEVE IN COINCIDENCE? $750 is what a book dealer listed in a recent catalogue as the price of an autographed first edition copy of *Psycho.*

$750 is the advance a publisher paid me for *writing* the book.

Of course I didn't get that much money in one lump sum. It came in installments—half after the acceptance of my manuscript in final form, and the other half upon actual publication many months later. Nor did these payments add up to $750 for my share; after an agent took out his ten percent I finally ended up with a grand total of $675. So perhaps we can forget about the coincidence theory.

When the same agent sold the same book to Shamley Productions for a motion picture, he didn't

know the name of the company's owner, and a price was arrived at only after nerve-racking negotiations. From an initial offer of $5000 it eventually escalated to a colossal $9500. My agent took his ten percent off the top, my publishers took their fifteen percent off the top, the IRS and the state tax people got their cuts, and I ended up with something like $6250.

Unfortunately, in order to make such a magnificent deal I had to place myself entirely in my agent's hands. I'd never sold a book to the movies before, knew nothing about the film industry, lived two thousand miles away from Hollywood, and wisely left things like contractual matters to the good judgment of my agent. Combining his good judgment with my good faith, I duly signed away

all remake rights, all participation in film profits, all television, theatrical, radio and audio recording rights, all merchandising rights, and retained only literary usage. There was no guarantee of my name being listed in advertising credits, and in some cases it wasn't.

In retrospect it doesn't seem like the greatest deal in the world. No wonder we dumb writers need knowledgeable agents to protect us.

Still, when the novel proved to be a success on its own, my agent saw to it that for the next book they must continue to pay me my $750 advance.

So much for the story that *Psycho* made me a fortune.

But there are many stories about *Psycho,* most of them equally false.

The true story begins on November 16, 1957, when Edward Gein murdered Mrs. Bernice Worden in Plainfield, Wisconsin. Arrested for the crime, a search of his rundown rural residence yielded grisly evidence involving possible prior killings, grave-robbing, necrophilia, cannibalism, and other forms of occupational therapy. Hints gradually gave way to detailed accounts over the months and years ahead, by which time Mr. Gein had been committed to a mental institution, but what was leaked immediately to press and public proved enough to provoke horrified reactions nationwide.

Those reactions were particularly evident in Weyauwega, a town about forty miles away from Plainfield, where I happened to be living at the time.

Like my fellow citizens, I was shocked that a community similar to but even smaller than our own could harbor a monster in its midst for years without anyone being the wiser.

After all, this was 1957—squeaky-clean Dick Clark grinned at the teenagers on *American Bandstand,* Elvis Presley delighted crotch-watchers everywhere, Dad barbecued in the backyard, while Mom baked apple pies in the kitchen, and if there really were such things as serial killers somewhere, they certainly wouldn't be living in *our* neighborhood.

No way. Particularly in a rural area where everyone knows their neighbors and their neighbors' business, and what they don't know they speculate about. As a mystery-suspense writer, the idea of a mass murderer living undetected and unsuspected in a typical small town in middle America sparked my imagination.

That's what turned me on, and over the long years I've had to repeat this statement many times. It wasn't Ed Gein who "inspired" me to write *Psycho.* It was the situation itself, not the man involved in it. At the time I mulled over a storyline for the book I still knew very little about the killer over in Plainfield—a place which, by the way, I never visited, since I didn't own or drive a car, and forty miles seemed rather a long stroll. Nor did I know that much about the hobbies with which he brightened his bachelor existence.

Thus the real-life murderer was not the role model for my character Norman Bates. Ed Gein didn't own or operate a motel. Ed Gein didn't kill anyone in the shower. Ed Gein wasn't into taxidermy, Ed Gein didn't stuff his mother, keep her body in the house, dress in a drag outfit, or adapt an alternative personality. These were the functions and characteristics of Norman Bates, and Norman Bates didn't exist until I made him up. Out of my own imagination, I might add, which is probably the reason so few offer to take showers with me.

As long as we're on the subject, I must also inform you that Alfred Hitchcock never met Ed Gein either.

Though the film was billed as "Alfred Hitchcock's *Psycho,*" Hitch himself didn't deny its source. When interviewed for Charles Higham and Joel Greenberg's book *The Celluloid Muse,* he said: "*Psycho* all came from Robert Bloch's book. The scriptwriter, Joseph Stefano—he'd been recommended to me by my agents, MCA—contributed dialogue mostly, no ideas.''

Not everyone has been that frank. A while after the successful emergence of the film, Stefano wrote a guest column for a vacationing staffer of the *Los Angeles Times* and confided: ''For several years I have enjoyed the delicious distinction of being identified as the author of *Psycho*.''

It was a distinction he didn't bother to deny in the column—nor elsewhere in print at the time. And when he did another screenplay, *The Naked Edge,* also adapted from somebody else's novel, the advertisements for the film proclaimed: ''Only the man who wrote *Psycho* could jolt you like this.''

The ad itself jolted at least one person—my recently acquired film and television agent, Gordon Molson. He contacted the picture's producer, Arthur Hornblow, Jr., and demanded the ad be changed. Hornblow pleaded that it was impossible to do so; newspaper plates and mats had already been made and distributed nationwide at great expense. He offered a choice of a thousand dollars or an apology printed in the film industry's daily trade papers. My agent said we'd settle—for both. And that I must be allowed to word the public apology for them and they must sign.

It was a done deal. I promptly penned copy for the half-page ad, but instead of humiliating either Hornblow or Stefano, I chose to write the following:

> Mr. Robert Bloch—the only author of the novel *Psycho*—congratulates Mr. Joseph Stefano on his screenplay *The Naked Edge.*

I promptly received a letter of congratulation from the staff members of Hitchcock's TV show. There was no word from Stefano. Nor has there ever been.

Now we must skip forward for a moment to another TV show—*Hard Copy,* which for a half hour, five nights a week, offers startling in-depth reports that take viewers behind the scenes of news stories.

Several years ago I was asked if I'd consent to be interviewed about *Psycho* on the program. I agreed, and as is customary, the segment was taped in my home by a cinematographer, sound engineer, and director—in other words, a roundup of the usual suspects. All were professional and proficient, but I felt uncomfortable. The interviewer's questions

seemed designed to establish one salient point—that Norman Bates was modeled on real-life murderer Ed Gein.

I kept repeating that this was not the case; Norman Bates was my own creation; I'd been shocked when, long afterward, I learned that some of the traits I invented for my fictitious character were paralleled in the persona of the real-life killer. But as I emphasized that my concept for *Psycho* was in no way a roman à clef, the interviewer looked unhappy. I couldn't figure out what was bugging him and why he was using a questioning technique that went out of style with the old-fashioned third degree.

In days that followed I waited word on when the show would be aired. None was forthcoming, but in due time the program did appear. And it was then I discovered that the segment I'd been interviewed for was being advertised and promoted as the real inside story of ''how Alfred Hitchcock got the inspiration for *Psycho*.''

And, by golly, that's what they delivered. It seems, according to voice-over revelations, that there was this weirdo Ed Gein out in Wisconsin who did all these gross things, and Alfred Hitchcock learned about it (maybe by reading a newspaper in the john: they didn't say for sure) and he decided to make a movie about it and he did.

There were film clips of Hitch, shots of little old Ready Eddie himself, accounts of how the lawmen had taken a sort of Universal tour of his house, and souvenirs they'd found there. It was all very graphic and detailed, with only one thing missing—the interview with me.

Correction; something else was missing too. There was no mention of my name, or that I'd written a novel called *Psycho* from which Hitchcock made the film. A film which, incidentally, followed the plot of my book right down to the very last sentence.

I had become a nonperson. And *Psycho,* despite forty editions in twenty languages worldwide, was a nonbook. The fact that I was still alive and my novel was still in print apparently didn't prevent the fearless journalists of *Hard Copy* from revealing the startling truth about how Alfred Hitchcock got his inspiration for *Psycho*.

But does it really matter if I and my little would-be scary novel were ignored on a pseudodocumentary television show?

Perhaps not. But what *does* matter, profoundly,

is how clearly this petty incident demonstrates the power—and misuse of power—in the media. Minor it may be, but if supposed news sources can twist the truth, fabricate falsehood, pitch a predetermined story by arbitrary editing and omission and pass it off as fact, then what's to prevent them from using the same techniques to distort important information and news items?

Now, *that's* scary.

The history of *Psycho* is that of novel and film almost inextricably intertwined. Writing and selling the book to a publisher was not too difficult; compared to what Hitchcock confronted when making the film, I had no problems. A recount of his deals and ordeals would fill a book of its own, and has, in Stephen Rebello's meticulously researched *Alfred Hitchcock and the Making of* Psycho (Dembner Books, 1990). Meanwhile, take my word for it that he had to overcome obstacles, objections, and opposition before he managed to put this offbeat offering onscreen.

At one point he'd even inquired if I might be available to write the screenplay; MCA agents promptly assured him that wasn't possible. Truth to tell, I was still sitting at the typewriter in Weyauwega, two thousand miles and a million light-years away from a career in Hollywood.

And it wasn't the success of *Psycho* that got me there. I actually arrived almost nine months prior to the release of the film—a film which insiders in the movie industry predicted would be a disaster. Associating my name with such an enterprise was hardly a plus; I went out on the strength of a single script assignment on a low-budget TV syndication show, and stayed when television offers continued to come in.

When the film did appear, it became an instant hit with audiences. Critical response was another matter. *Time* derided it and Bosley Crowther (God's stand-in at *The New York Times*) offered a scathing review. So it wasn't much of a boost to my status, nor did it contribute to my receiving an offer to write my first screenplay. *Psycho* was profitable for Hitch; prestige was elusive.

But life is like a roller-coaster ride—alternately thrilling and nauseating. As the film's grosses rose to unprecedented heights, so did the esteem of the critics. And six months after he'd condemned *Psycho* as a blot on Hitchcock's career, Bosley Crowther placed it on his list of the Ten Best Films

of the Year. In another five years he—like many others—was referring to it as a "classic."

For my novel there were similar ups and downs. Its reception upon publication had been better than that of the picture; the same *New York Times* that frowned on the film had beamed on the book. In fact, it was its glowing review of the novel that brought *Psycho* to Hitchcock's attention. Still, when the time came for the Mystery Writers of America to bestow their annual Edgar award, my work wasn't even in the running. The prize for Best Novel went to Celia Fremlin for her unforgettable *The Hour Before the Dawn*.

Ups and downs, I said. Ten years later I was the president of the Mystery Writers of America. And there were a lot of people, who if they remembered *Psycho* as a book, assumed it must be a novelization of the movie that had been created by Alfred Hitchcock. Film historians embraced the *auteur* theory now, and in many of their disquisitions on *Psycho* the book isn't mentioned at all. It's the director who's lauded for daring to kill off his heroine so shockingly, unexpectedly, and early in the story. And how astute of him to set the murder in a shower stall, where a potential victim is naked, unprotected, unprepared for and vulnerable to danger! In a few instances I'm identified in a throw-away line as the author of an obscure pulp story Hitch utilized merely for his own creative inspiration. Apparently such authorities never read the book, for they don't note either major similarities or minor discrepancies between novel and film. Their omniscience rides on Hitchcock's work alone. How, for example, my unspecified midwest *locale* for the Bates Motel was shifted to California or some other southwestern site remains a mystery to these Hitch-hikers.

Hitchcock *did* make some changes, and his film benefits from them, just as my book benefits from its own original composition. What some critics don't realize is that what works best on film doesn't necessarily work best in print; there's a necessary distinction between the visual and the verbal. Hitchcock and I both kill off our hapless helpless heroine in the shower. But it takes Hitchcock forty-five seconds of repeated stabbings with a butcher knife to do what I accomplish in one short sentence.

Both methods are correct, within their context. If Hitch had used mine—decapitating the victim with a single sudden stroke—it would not have had the cinematic strength of his in-your-face (and in-her-body) impact. Conversely, if I'd lingered over a multiple-stabbing description on paper, I'd lose *my* shock effect in detailed and disgusting description. As it is, we both achieved the surprise we intended—but by using exactly opposite techniques.

Hitchcock's approach included use of detailed sketches and storyboards to work out exactly how he intended to shoot every bit of footage in his films. These methods were well publicized, along with his observation that by the time he'd finished preparations, he considered his work completed, and the actual filming bored him.

Nobody ever publicized my methods; suffice it to say that I prepare for a story, script, or novel with the care and foresight necessary in order to open a can of worms. But unlike Hitchcock, I don't get bored by the actual production of my work. It's then that I finally get to meet and know the characters. My advance planning can be considered the equivalent of directing, while writing is the equivalent of acting. It's then, in effect, that I *impersonate* my characters.

Does that make me a role model for Norman Bates?

If so, it also makes me a role model for Dan Morley, the serial killer of my first novel, and the kidnapper and arsonist protagonists of novels that followed. It means I'm also a mentally retarded ten-year-old boy, a simpleminded adult, a pedantic scholar, a gay, a flaming heterosexual, an innocent teenager of another era, a psychotic elderly woman, and hundreds of others whose deeds I've detailed, frequently in first-person narration. I'm no more Norman Bates than I am his mother.

But I *am* his father.

With due and great respect for Hitchcock's genius and for the talents of everyone connected with the film version, I think I'm entitled to claim paternity.

Hitchcock lopped a dozen years off Norman's age, Stefano gave him some arch double entendres to deliver, Anthony Perkins added a touch of epicenity. But in spite of face-lift and heel-lift, Norman Bates remains readily recognizable as my boy to anyone who has ever encountered him in the book. And if I hadn't written the book, there'd be no film. Conceivably Stefano may have remained in radio, Perkins could function as a low-budget Montgomery Clift, and Hitchcock might have gone on to glory by directing *Mary Poppins.*

But there *was* a film, and if imitation is the sincerest form of flattery, then both Hitchcock and I have had ample reason to feel praised, if not plagiarized. Mine was not the first book to deal with mental illness or serve as the basis for the first film on the subject. There'd been countless motion pictures featuring "mad" doctors, scientists, and proctologists, but in few instances were their disorders explained. Filmmakers avoided dealing with the reasons for unreason, from *The Cabinet of Dr. Caligari* on. Fritz Lang, with the assistance of Peter Lorre, presented a daring portrait of a tormented child-murderer, but without the slightest reference to cause or antecedents. Hitchcock himself had dabbled in psychotherapy with several previous films, but though some of his characters were walking time bombs, we didn't find out what made them tick.

Such matters were just not dealt with openly in our polite society. Almost everyone had heard about or had personal knowledge of an unfortunate relative locked up or hidden away in somebody's attic. Infrequently, in a few offerings like *The Old Dark House*—such a character might make a brief climactic appearance on film, or the printed page.

Then, with *Psycho,* I let the guilty secret—and the secretly guilty—out into the light of everyday life. The novel exemplified something I'd been expounding for over a decade; that supernatural horror pales in comparison to the dreads that dwell in the depths of the human mind and psyche.

Over the years many others have followed suit, but we still have more than our share of mad slashers who are seemingly mindless; gratuitous gore gloatingly described or pictured. Understandable characters like Norman Bates still remain comparatively rare.

But the bottom line regarding *Psycho* remains the same.

Timing is all.

In his prime, Lord Byron was the literary lion of an era. Today nobody would throw him a bone; we don't pay money or attention to romantic poets. If born fifty years later, Fred Astaire might still be the greatest tap dancer in the world, but the only career he'd enjoy today would be as an over-the-hill chorus boy. And what if Elvis Presley had been a young man in Victorian London? Talent is meaningless unless it's in the right place at the right time.

Psycho came along just as the public began to become aware of what prompted me to write it in the first place—that society was growing ever more dangerous, and violence no longer confined to "criminal elements" in "bad neighborhoods." In other words, what gave *Psycho* its initial—and enduring—strength is the disturbing element of *truth*. People have learned, many of them the hard way, that Norman Bates gets around these days.

Lock your doors.

Twenty-Five Notable Dark Suspense Novels
Selected by the Editors

Robert Bloch	*Psycho*
Fredric Brown	*The Screaming Mimi*
Max Allan Collins	*Quarry's Deal*
Dolores Hitchens	*Sleep with Slander*
Jonathan Katzenbach	*Day of Reckoning*
Stephen King	*Gerald's Game*
Stephen King	*Misery*
Dean Koontz	*Shattered*
Dean Koontz	*Whispers*
Joe R. Lansdale	*Savage Season*
John Lutz	*Bonegrinder*
John D. MacDonald	*Soft Touch*
Ed McBain	*He Who Hesitates*
Dan J. Marlowe	*The Name of the Game is Death*
Dan J. Marlowe	*One Endless Hour*
David Martin	*Lie to Me*
Barbara Paul	*First Gravedigger*
Bill Pronzini	*Masques*
Peter Rabe	*The Box*
Ruth Rendell	*The Lake of Darkness*
Ray Ring	*Arizonia Kiss*
Mickey Spillane	*Kiss Me, Deadly*
Mickey Spillane	*The Long Wait*
Theodore Sturgeon	*Some of Your Blood*
David Wiltse	*The Serpent*

WOMEN'S SUSPENSE

INTRODUCTION

Jon L. Breen

WOMEN HAVE CONTRIBUTED significantly to crime, mystery, and suspense fiction in all its permutations, but there is one type that has been a particular specialty of theirs, variously called romantic suspense or the modern gothic or "pure" suspense or "character and atmosphere" or (most slightingly) the "had-I-but-known" school. Characteristics include a strong thread of romance in the story, an emphasis on interrelationships of character, a domestic background, and a special strain of nail-biting suspense. Perhaps because it is so firmly associated with one sex, though its readers have certainly been drawn from both, the category has not always received the respect it deserves from scholars and historians of crime fiction.

Mary Roberts Rinehart, whose first novel in book form, *The Circular Staircase,* was published in 1908, remained a highly successful practitioner of mystery and other fiction through her final novel, *The Swimming Pool,* in 1952. Based on reading her autobiography, *My Story* (1932), and a sampling of her fiction, she seems to me formidable as a stylist and as a feminist. In the toughest test of an author's staying power, some of her novels remain in print today in paperback. But she has received nothing like the critical attention and respect afforded classical writers Agatha Christie and Dorothy L. Sayers, possibly because of her identification with the dreaded HIBK school. Michele Slung, writing in *The Sleuth and the Scholar* (Greenwood, 1988), can't resist topping off her spirited defense of Christie with the following body slam: "Agatha Christie may not be Shakespeare, but then, she's not Mary Roberts Rinehart or Judith Krantz either. She's a legend, not a mere phenomenon" (page 67). Rinehart deserves better than being compared with a contemporary schlockmeister like Krantz.

In his classic history *Murder for Pleasure* (1941), Howard Haycraft, a not entirely sympathetic observer of the Rinehart school, described the author's standard narrator as

> usually a woman, most often a romantic spinster engaged in protecting young love from unjust suspicion, who alternately complicates the plot and aids detection in unpremeditated fashion—a combination of participating (usually interfering!) Watson and detective-by-accident. This is the readily recognizable "Rinehart formula," still delightful when practiced by its originator, but becoming increasingly tedious in the hands of her far-too-numerous imitators among American women writers (page 89).

The best romantic suspense writers of a later time would also suffer by their imitators, many of whom by the sixties were men using female bylines.

The name most frequently bracketed with Rinehart's in the HIBK school is Mignon G. Eberhart, who has had one of the longest careers in crime fiction. First appearing in magazines in the mid-twenties, her first novel, *The Patient in Room 18,* coming in 1929, she is still living in her mid-nineties at this writing and published a new novel, *Three Days for Emeralds,* as recently as 1988. Though highly praised in the thirties and forties, her reputation has also eroded, for similar reasons. In common with Rinehart, Eberhart usually introduced a new heroine for each book and made little use of series characters. But each writer created a figure especially well suited to romantic suspense, the nurse-detective Sarah Keate in Eberhart's first novel and a few later ones, Hilda Adams in Rinehart's *Miss Pinkerton* (1932) and *Haunted Lady* (1942). After stating Eberhart "achieved something of a blend of the conventional American-feminine method with a type of tale slightly reminiscent of some of Mrs. Belloc Lowndes's psychological studies of murder" (page 215), Haycraft goes on to list several other writers in the Rinehart tradition, most little remembered today: Dorothy Cameron Disney, Charlotte Murray Russell, Constance and Gwenyth Little, and (most admiringly) Mabel Seeley, another writer highly valued in her day but long out of print. The same is true of Hilda Lawrence, who made a strong impression on readers and reviewers in the forties.

Humorists and parodists had a field day with the HIBK school. Early Doubleday Crime Club mystery editor Ogden Nash gave the type its name in his poem "Don't Guess, Let Me Tell You," one line of which reads,

> Had I But Known narrators are the ones who hear a stealthy creak at midnight in the tower where the body lies and, instead of locking their door or arousing the drowsy policemen posted outside their room, sneak off by themselves to the tower and suddenly they hear a breath exhaled behind them, ... (Haycraft's *Art of the Mystery Story*, page 319).

And Ben Hecht also had fun with the form in his parody, "The Whistling Corpse:"

> I shall never forget the bright summer afternoon when poor Stuffy found the green button under Grandma Marnoy's knitting bag—on the lawn out there, a stone's throw from Indian Creek that bisects the rolling Marpleton grounds where Toppet, Ruby, and I used to play pirate and chase butterflies. I have often wondered what would have happened if Stuffy had given me the button instead of swallowing it. For one thing, Consuela Marston would never have met the man with the pickax and I would never, of course, have gone to that dreadful carnival which was the beginning of everything (*Ellery Queen's Mystery Magazine*, September 1945, pages 84-85).

But drawing parodists is no reflection on the quality of the original. Quite the contrary. Look at Hemingway.

The forties also saw the rise to prominence of Charlotte Armstrong, whose name was once as synonymous with pure suspense as that of Cornell Woolrich's. After three relatively conventional detective novels about the little-remembered character MacDougal Duff, Armstrong made a major impact with *The Unsuspected* (1946), controversial because the murderer's identity was revealed early in the going. This raised the ire of traditionalist Haycraft, who believed the book would have been still more effective had the secret been maintained. Writing in *Twentieth-Century Crime and Mystery Writers*, Carol Cleveland says, "Armstrong was an expert at creating a situation in which an innocent is threatened, setting a rescue effort in motion, and then manipulating the world of ordinary events into a crescendo of perfectly maddening delays and mishaps" (3rd edition, page 31). Through the fifties and sixties, Armstrong continued as one of the most honored and admired writers of suspense fiction, winning an Edgar for *A Dram of Poison* (1956), but, continuing the pattern, her work has not received significant critical attention since her death. The same is true of Evelyn Piper, author of the pure suspense classics *Bunny Lake Is Missing* (1957) and *The Nanny* (1964), and of Vera Caspary, author of the famous *Laura* (1943).

A type of romantic suspense that was certainly not new but newly faddish took a big share of the crime fiction market in the sixties: the so-called modern gothic. Owing more of its pattern to Daphne du Maurier's classic *Rebecca* (1938) and Charlotte Brontë's *Jane Eyre* (1847) than to the eighteenth-century gothic novels of Ann Radcliffe and "Monk" Lewis, the novels centered on young women who encounter romance and danger, often but not always in old houses, sometimes but usually not while employed as governesses. Among the major writers of the sixties were Phyllis A. Whitney, Mary Stewart, and Victoria Holt; later they would be joined by Barbara Michaels (Barbara G. Mertz, who also writes as Elizabeth Peters), Velda Johnston, Anna Gilbert, and numerous others. The glut of books in the sixties and seventies, many in paperback original and most far from the high standard of these writers, caused the subgenre to shake out in the eighties and nineties, leaving only the most capable practitioners still in the field. But new writers continue to be attracted to the form, a recent example being Carolyn Llewelyn, whose 1988 debut novel, *The Masks of Rome*, is worthy of the best.

Present-day examples of romantic suspense are often called in the trade by the tag "woman in jeopardy." In the 1980s there developed a smaller but potent subgenre called "children in jeopardy," pioneered by Mary Higgins Clark's celebrated first novel, *Where Are the Children?* (1975).

While I believe that the perceived lack of attention and respect to female crime writers has often been overstated—certainly classicists like Sayers, Christie, Allingham, and Marsh have more than received their due, and the current crop of female detective fiction writers are getting at least their fair share of critical and scholarly note—proponents of romantic suspense have a legitimate beef. Suffering by the limitations of their less talented imitators, and perhaps by a degree of bias in the critical community, writers like Rinehart, Armstrong, Whitney, and even du Maurier have not received the extended consideration they merit.

MARY ROBERTS RINEHART

Charlotte MacLeod

HOW DOES A YOUNG HOUSEWIFE become a national monument? In Mary Roberts Rinehart's case, the catalyst appears to have been her uncle John from Cincinnati.

For five years or so, Dr. Rinehart's wife had been whiling away the evenings, after her three little boys were abed and the doctor was still out making house calls at two dollars a visit, writing poems, short stories, anything her fertile brain could produce to earn some extra housekeeping money. She'd already churned out a serial called *The Circular Staircase*.

Always ready for a bit of fun, she'd written her tale as a spoof of the pompous crime novels that had been the vogue since another woman, Anna Katharine Green, had captured America's attention with *The Leavenworth Case* in 1878, two years after Mary was born. Mary had sold her manuscript to *All-Story* magazine, they'd published it in installments from November 1907 to March 1908, she'd stuffed the carbon into the desk she'd bought secondhand for twenty dollars, and forgotten about it.

Then Uncle John came to visit. He'd heard his niece had a new hobby and was curious to read something she'd written. Mary rummaged around, came upon the bedraggled carbon of her serial, and diffidently suggested he might find it amusing. Uncle John read steadily all morning, gobbled his lunch, and went back to read some more. His final verdict was that he'd read lots worse and why didn't she get the book published.

Mary didn't think the story was good enough to be a book, but Uncle John argued her into giving it a try. So Mary took the carbon to a bindery and squandered three dollars getting the pages trimmed and bound inside a flexible cover with the title printed on it in gilt letters. Emboldened by seeing her work in this elegant form, she reached into her bookcase for an Anna Katharine Green mystery, copied out the publisher's name, and sent her three-dollar gamble off to Bobbs-Merrill of Indianapolis.

Mary was not hopeful. She got quite a surprise some days later when she was interrupted at the butcher shop, trying to decide between lamb chops and stew meat, by a telephone call from her husband. A letter from a Mr. Hewitt Howland of Bobbs-Merrill had arrived and he thought she'd like to know what it said.

"My dear Mrs. Rinehart," the letter began, "I have read *The Circular Staircase* not only with pleasure but with thrills and shivers."

Howland wanted her book. He wanted more books; he wanted to come and talk to her about them. He even wanted to pay for the publishing! Mary reacted as any normal housewife might; she wired Mr. Howland to come ahead, then rushed home to sew new curtains for the guest bedroom.

Howland came, saw, and was conquered by the Rinehart kids, the dogs, and perhaps even the new curtains. Mary had two other manuscripts to show him; he bought them both. After dinner she played the piano and they all sang, her new editor and the family collie included.

By the end of 1908, *The Circular Staircase* was in print as a book and selling like crazy. In 1915 it was made into a moving picture. By then Mary Roberts Rinehart had already become a genuine celebrity.

It must be remembered that she was no novice. She'd been writing ever since she was a child and she'd been selling her work since 1904. In its serial form *The Circular Staircase* had been her sixty-seventh recorded sale. Few of the early pieces she'd peddled for small sums had been in any way memorable, but she'd been learning her craft. She'd had more education than many girls of her time, having stayed on through high school and graduated at sixteen.

Far more important than her formal schooling, however, had been Mary Roberts's love for books and storytelling. She'd read her way through the Allegheny Free Library, not to mention a stash of dime novels she'd discovered inside a kitchen box bench while visiting relatives on a farm. At fifteen she'd entered an "Our Amateur Contributors" contest in the Pittsburgh Press. She didn't win, but she did get her first short story, "Lord Ainsley's Heir," published on March 27, 1892.

Omnivorous reader that she was, Mary Roberts Rinehart could hardly have missed becoming familiar with the sensationally popular works of Arthur Conan Doyle. His first Sherlock Holmes story had appeared in England in 1887 and found its way overseas very soon after. He'd tried to kill off or

at least retire the detective he'd come to regard as his incubus, but in 1908, while Mary was relishing her first triumph, he was still writing *Wisteria Lodge* and *The Bruce-Partington Plans*. One sees little of Doyle's influence in Rinehart's writing style, but it's interesting to note some of the parallels between their personal lives.

Both had rock-ribbed mothers who'd long outlived their cloud-walking husbands and remained strong influences in their children's lives. Both had started their careers in the field of medicine, Conan Doyle as a general practitioner, Mary Roberts as a nurse. She'd entered training at Pittsburgh Homeopathic Hospital right out of high school, having indulged in a spot of hyperbole with regard to her actual age. She'd stuck out the rugged three-year course and got her cap, which had already for some time been set firmly in the direction of Dr. Stanley M. Rinehart, then a member of the hospital staff. They'd become engaged in defiance of hospital rules and were married shortly after Mary's graduation, thus disqualifying her from practicing as a professional nurse according to the mores of the time.

Both Conan Doyle and Rinehart had started writing solely in the hope of easing the financial pinch; neither had expected anything to come of what they considered their hack work. They were equally dismayed at finding themselves famous, but both took advantage of their increased prestige to do constructive things for others. Both got caught up in wars. Conan Doyle volunteered as a doctor in the Boer War. Rinehart, a member of the American Red Cross Association, visited field hospitals in France during World War I. Both, of course, wrote up their experiences for publication. Both became involved in politics; he ran for office (and lost), she sat on various presidential committees.

In addition to their mysteries, both wrote "straight" novels, nonfiction, and long-running plays; both wrote funny stories in which he, disguised as Professor Challenger, and she, as Miss Letitia Carberry, better known as Tish, behaved as outrageously as they might have liked to do in real life. Of all their works, they both seem to have taken their mysteries least seriously. Yet these are the works that are still being most widely read and enjoyed to this day.

In the mystery field, as elsewhere, many new stars have flashed into public view over the decades, and many of them have turned out in the end to have been merely skyrockets. But here now, virtually a century since *The Circular Staircase* first appeared in print, Mary Roberts Rinehart, like Conan Doyle, still has the power to keep us reading, has that same unkillable spark Conan Doyle tried in vain to quench under the Reichenbach Falls, the spark that draws us back like moths to a gaslamp and kindles our imaginations over and over again. Here's the way she opened her first best seller, so many years ago:

"This is the story of how a middle-aged spinster lost her mind, deserted her domestic gods in the city, took a furnished home for the summer out of town, and found herself involved in one of those mysterious crimes that keeps our newspapers and detective agencies happy and prosperous." *The Circular Staircase* is also the story of a pretty little woman who would go on to charm a nation of readers throughout her long life, and far beyond. Had she but known!

Some Notable Women's Suspense Novels
Selected by the Editors

Mary Higgins Clark
Where Are the Children?

Anna Clarke
Soon She Must Die

S. K. Epperson
Borderland

Joy Fielding
Tell Me No Secrets

Judith Kelman
Someone's Watching

Patricia J. MacDonald
No Way Home

Barbara Michaels
Into the Darkness

Marlys Millhiser
Michael's Wife

D. F. Mills
Spellbound

POLICE
PROCEDURALS

INTRODUCTION

Jon L. Breen

READERS OF DETECTIVE fiction have always craved authentic details of police work, and authors have long endeavored (or at least pretended) to provide them—but that doesn't mean Dickens or any of the nineteenth-century writers of police fiction were writing procedurals in the sense we mean today.

The one principal factor dividing procedural from nonprocedural detective fiction is not the provision of a few details for the sake of verisimilitude but the serious attempt to present or at least to suggest the reality of police work. Classicists like Ngaio Marsh, Christianna Brand, and Michael Innes, though writing about police characters, made no pretense of doing this. More recently, Ruth Rendell has stated she intentionally ignores real police procedure in her Wexford novels because she is not interested in it. Almost all crime and mystery novels have police in them, but only a few can be called police procedurals.

The police procedural is the mystery subgenre for which it is hardest to pin down an origin. At least one thing is certain: Ed McBain, who has so defined and perfected the form with his long-running 87th Precinct series, did not invent it, though the popularity of his series has sometimes led superficial commentators to give him the credit. The form was already well established when *Cop Hater* appeared as a paperback original in 1956.

The consensus of knowledgeable sources is that there was no such thing as a real police procedural until the forties, but even that can be disputed. Phil and Karen McArdle, writing in *Fatal Fascination: Where Fact Meets Fiction in Police Work* (Houghton Mifflin, 1988), cheer fans of S. S. Van Dine by championing *The "Canary" Murder Case* (1927) as an early example of the type. The dust jackets of the Van Dine novels seem to back the claim: the authentic-looking police index cards clearly show that a realistic view of police procedure was one of the selling points of the series. Still, the stupidity of Sgt. Heath and the fact that an eccentric gifted amateur sleuth, Philo Vance, solves the cases combine to rule out Van Dine as a real procedural pioneer.

But what about an early work like Helen Reilly's *McKee of Centre Street* (1934)? Both the blurb and the design, which has a corpse's hand with identification tag on the endpapers and opposite the title page, certainly suggest that Doubleday's Crime Club believed there was such a thing as a police procedural in the early thirties and that this was it. The first chapter, set in the headquarters radio room, is full of authentic detail, as is the second, which shows various police specialists doing their jobs at a speakeasy crime scene. This sense of teamwork is certainly a procedural characteristic ("The effortless functioning of a perfect police machine relieves wear and tear on the individual and permits each man to work at the highest degree of efficiency" [page 64].) Ultimately, though, the character of Inspector Christopher ("The Scotsman") McKee gives the novel a closer resemblance to those of Van Dine, Ellery Queen, and Anthony Abbot than to what we now call a police procedural. McKee, with his many literary allusions and a philovancean store of esoteric knowledge, belongs to what George N. Dove, in his excellent book-length study, *The Police Procedural* (Bowling Green University Popular Press, 1982), calls the Great Policeman school, along with other thirties cops like Marsh's Roderick Alleyn, Innes's John Appleby, and Abbot's Thatcher Colt.

The real credit for creating the police procedural may not belong to print detection at all: Ellery Queen once argued that Chester Gould's comic strip sleuth Dick Tracy, who made his newspaper debut in 1931, was the first procedural hero. A more convincing candidate, though, is Sgt. Joe Friday in Jack Webb's *Dragnet,* which debuted on radio in 1949 and moved to television in 1952. Certainly the cases of L.A.P.D. cop Friday and his various partners did more than any book or series of books to popularize the form. However, at least one genuine procedural series was in print before *Dragnet*'s first broadcast.

Lawrence Treat is the writer deservedly credited with pioneering the police procedural as we know it today. His 1945 novel *V as in Victim* introduces cops Mitch Taylor and Jub Freeman, who would appear together or separately in several more novels, as well as in a long series of short stories in *Ellery Queen's Mystery Magazine*. In an essay in *Twentieth Century Crime and Mystery Writers*, George N. Dove identifies several procedural conventions introduced by Treat: "the cop with family problems . . . , the hostile public . . . , the inter- and intra-departmental rivalries (detectives versus patrolmen, conventional cops versus the police lab), and the perennially understaffed and overworked squad . . ." (page 1019, 3rd edition). These are matters the Great Policemen of earlier years seldom had to worry about. Probably Treat's greatest contribution is the sense of teamwork: the squad as a unit is the hero, with the focus shifting among old-style bulldog Taylor, scientific cop Freeman, and in later books commander Bill Decker. As Dove also points out, though, *V as in Victim* has at least as much in common with the Golden-Age fair-play detective novel as it does with latter-day procedurals.

While *V as in Victim* is a fine book that holds up well almost half a century after it was published, the first real classic of the police procedural form is Hillary Waugh's *Last Seen Wearing* (1952), a documentary-style account of the small-town investigation of a female college student's disappearance. Though Chief of Police Frank Ford does not reappear in future novels, Waugh produced a long series about the very similar Chief Fred Fellows of Stockford, Connecticut, many of whose cases have the same true-crime quality. *The Missing Man* (1964) is nearly as effective in this vein as *Last Seen Wearing*. Later Waugh would desert small-town police work for a New York City background in a series of three novels about Detective Frank Sessions, beginning with *"30" Manhattan East* (1968). After the appropriately titled *Finish Me Off* (1970), Waugh inexplicably abandoned the procedural entirely in favor of romantic suspense, private eye novels, courtroom drama, and even Golden-Age-style pure detection. His most recent novel, *A Death in a Town* (1989), proves he is still a master.

Jonathan Craig (Frank E. Smith), who featured Manhattan detective Pete Selby in several Gold Medal originals of the fifties, may not have received his full due as a pioneer of the procedural. The first Selby book, *The Dead Darling* (1955), beat the first 87th Precinct novel to the post by a year, and Craig was contributing procedural stories in the Police Files series to *Manhunt* before that. In the same period, Ed McBain, a *Manhunt* regular under his then-more-famous byline Evan Hunter, was also writing procedural short stories for the magazine under yet another pseudonyn, Richard Marsten. "Accident Report" (September 1953) and "Classification: Dead" (November 1953) even include that 87th Precinct staple, the reproduced police form. The back cover of the September 1953 issue uses the term "dragnet" in hyping the Marsten story and Richard Deming's "Bonus Cop," making it clear whence sprang the new vogue for police stories. Ironically, mystery novelist Jack Webb (*not* the *Dragnet* star) produced for *Manhunt* a series of stories about a specialized police unit, the Airport Detail, beginning with "Broken Doll" (May 1954). That the two Webbs were unrelated and separate was made clear on the biographical page of that issue, but somehow that didn't stop the confusion from persisting for years to come.

Two characteristics that are often used to differentiate police procedurals from other books in which police serve as detectives are certainly not hard-and-fast requirements as is sometimes suggested. (If they were, the bibliography of police procedurals would be rather short.)

1) Real police do not have the luxury of working on one mysterious case at a time but have several cases to juggle at any given point. In earlier detective novels there might *appear* to be separate cases, but convention demanded all threads be brought together at the end of the book. J. J. Marric's (John Creasey) *Gideon's Day* (1955), a landmark of the British police procedural, introduces the "modular" type of story, in which several unrelated cases are addressed—and stay unrelated. The various police series of Elizabeth Linington (a.k.a. Dell Shannon and Leslie Egan) always took the modular approach, beginning with Shannon's *Case Pending* (1960). McBain sometimes has done the modular mystery, but usually there is one central case at the book's core. John Ball, creator of African-American Pasadena cop Virgil Tibbs in the classic *In the Heat of the Night* (1965) and of small-town police chief

Jack Tallon, was another writer who sometimes went the modular route, but usually not. Today, as always, modular procedurals are in the minority, but not knowing for sure whether seemingly unrelated investigations will prove to be related can add to the reader's enjoyment—or exasperation if the reader is truly averse to the modular form.

2) In real-life police work, no one supersleuth dominates the detection. Police work is a team effort. Thus, early novels in which one cop dominates (e.g. Simenon's Maigret, Marsh's Roderick Alleyn, Freeman Wills Crofts's Inspector French, etc.) must be consigned to Dove's Great Policeman school rather than the procedural proper. This recognition of police teamwork, begun with Treat, probably reaches its fullest realization in the 87th Precinct novels, where a unit rather than an individual is the series character. Still, most procedurals, like most detective fiction of any variety, concentrate on one central investigator, and even in the 87th books, Steve Carella often proves "more equal" than his colleagues. The same is true of Martin Beck in the Stockholm-based novels of Maj Sjöwall and Per Wahlöö, one of the finest procedural series of the sixties and seventies.

Most police procedural writers—certainly including Linington, Creasey, McBain, Waugh, and Treat—are "civilians" who have done intensive research into police work. Early examples of real police who brought their expertise to bear in fiction include the British writers Sir Basil Thomson, who belongs to the preprocedural era, and Maurice Procter, whose first mystery appeared in 1949. The last few years have seen cops-turned-writers in almost as great demand as lawyers-turned-writers. One of the first successful American writers with real police experience was Dorothy Uhnak, who featured policewoman Christie Opara in a trilogy of novels: *The Bait* (1968), *The Witness* (1969), and *The Ledger* (1970). The L.A.P.D.'s Joseph Wambaugh, a

best-selling chronicler of police work since *The New Centurions* (1970), preceded several other literary talents from the same department, including Paul Bishop and Dallas Barnes. Britain's best cop writer may be the very prolific John Wainwright. Janwillem van de Wetering, a former Dutch policeman who now lives in the United States, writes his novels about the Amsterdam cops in English.

Lawrence Sanders's *The First Deadly Sin* (1973) pioneered a type of procedural that has become almost a cliché in recent years but that still provides some of the best books in the subgenre when done well: the big-city-cop-versus-crazy-serial-killer novel. These books tend to be longer than the average mystery and don't always concern series detectives. Among key practitioners are William Bayer and Thomas H. Cook.

Other prominent contemporaries in the procedural form include Collin Wilcox, with his long series about San Francisco's Frank Hastings; Peter Turnbull, whose P Division cops are a Glasgow equivalent of the 87th Precinct; William Marshall, who writes farcical modulars about Hong Kong's Yellowthread Street police; Reginald Hill, who features Yorkshire cops Dalziel and Pascoe in a archetype of the "odd couple" detecting team; Marilyn Wallace, who crosses the procedural with the woman-in-jeopardy novel in her series about Oakland's Cruz and Goldstein; Tony Hillerman, who has achieved bestsellerdom with his novels about the Navajo tribal police; Stuart Kaminsky and Martin Cruz Smith, both of whom have used the former Soviet Union as a procedural locale; Katherine V. Forrest, whose Kate Delafield is one of the most distinctive and complex series policewomen; and Susan Dunlap, whose series about Berkeley's Jill Smith exemplifies many series that have taken on some of the characteristics of the procedural but remain more in the tradition of the pure detective story.

EVAN HUNTER
ON WRITING MYSTERIES

John Pescatore

On Mysteries as a Reputable Art Form

"AFTER *KISS* CAME OUT, a friend sent me a postcard saying that out of twelve people in the first class section of US AIR out of Pittsburgh, four were reading *Kiss*—including two women. When I began the 87th Precinct series in the mid-fifties, not many people in first class were reading mysteries. That's why I began using the name Ed McBain—they thought it would be damaging to my career if Evan Hunter put his name on mystery novels. Mysteries weren't quite disreputable, you didn't have to carry them in brown paper wrappers. They weren't quite respectable, though.

"In fact, *New Yorker* magazine had an article saying reading mysteries is as witless an occupation as playing Mah-Jongg. It really colored Americans' perception of mysteries for a long time. Mysteries have always been popular in England, but it has taken a long time for American critics to recognize that you can say things in a mystery novel. I certainly use it as a sounding board.

"Although I don't like to analyze myself as a writer—I'm afraid it might jinx me—just recently I recognized something. I wrote *Blackboard Jungle* in 1954, and I must have been writing the first 87th Precinct book less than a year later. In retrospect, the styles are very similar: the ethnic breakdown of the school and the squad room; the teachers housed in a school and interacting in a lunchroom, while the police are in a police station and kibitz in the squad room. The gallows type humor was the same, with the same big, urban backdrop.

"So, because of the success of *Blackboard Jungle,* the Evan Hunter name was being jealously guarded as a serious writer who had to be seriously considered. Even though the style was very similar, with the 87th Precinct books I could just have fun with them, and for the first eight or nine books I

could have fun anonymously. I broke all the mystery writers' rules."

On Character Development

"I've been writing about the detectives of the 87th Precinct for over twenty-five years, but they constantly surprise me. I didn't know Steve Carella's father would be shot until he got shot. When he did get shot, it forced me to reexamine Carella's relationship with his father.

"I like that because of being able to find stuff about the characters that I didn't know. It's what happens in real life—you know someone for twenty years and out of the blue he'll tell you his father was killed in an air raid in Lyon. It suddenly casts that person in a new light—different and more intimate.

"For the Matthew Hope series, it has taken me ten books to get the repertory company in place. Now the players are set up and I have room to swing. It took me six books in and I switched to third person. In *Mary, Mary* I do an interesting stylistic trick. All of Matthew's scenes are in first person, everybody else's are in third person. I have the ability to go everywhere into people's heads, including the killer's head, without losing the intimacy of Matthew Hope. This goes against one of the rules of writing: never mix up viewpoints. So I mixed it up, and it was fun."

On the Eternal Youth Syndrome

"I think I am going to have to inch Carella's kids toward puberty. That was a conscious decision I had to make a while back, to freeze the ages of the characters. I used to read comics a lot when I was

a kid. You had the *Gasoline Alley* approach, where
the characters get old and become grandparents, or
Terry and the Pirates, where little Terry grows up
and has an affair with the dragon lady. Or you had
Little Orphan Annie, where no one ever aged.

"The detectives in my books were originally
veterans of World War II, or later the Korean War,
but that got awkward later on. I tried to put that all
to rest in one of the books by saying, 'Every male
of age in America is a veteran of one war or the
other.' Now I just say, 'He was in the war.' Maybe
soon people will think of that made-for-television
war—Desert Storm.''

On Writing Tightly

"The books are getting longer but I think they are
getting tighter. The only creative thing I got out of
my Hollywood years was an appreciation of cinematic style. When you're doing a screenplay, you
don't have to describe the actual clothing she's
wearing, you can simply say, 'She was elegantly
dressed,' and the costume designer takes care of the
rest. In a book you have to describe what she's
wearing; similarly, when you come into a room,
you have to describe the room. In a screenplay you
can say 'a penthouse suite on the Upper East Side,'
the set decorator designs the room with the Chagalls
and whatever. However, when you see that room
on the screen (except in rare artsy-fartsy instances)
the camera doesn't come in the room and start
going over every object in the room because you
don't have to do that. The viewer *bang* takes in the
room and the room says elegant or whatever the
hell, and the scene plays: 'How do you do, I'm here
to shoot you.'

"I try to do that in the novels now. I give it in
almost subliminal flashes: *bang*—black couch,
bang—red painting over it, *bang*—chrome furniture, *BOOM*—'How do you do, I'm here to shoot
you.' The book I won't read is: 'The car came down
the winding road past the steel mills on the left on
a gray, foggy afternoon. She could see the school-
house in the distance'—I feel like I'm getting a
travelogue.

"You can set the scene with listing the brand
name of every item. That's one of Stephen King's
flaws, he should get off it. He's too good to be
doing that kind of crap, that's a Judith Krantz trick.
I deliberately dressed Denker (a hired killer in *Kiss*)

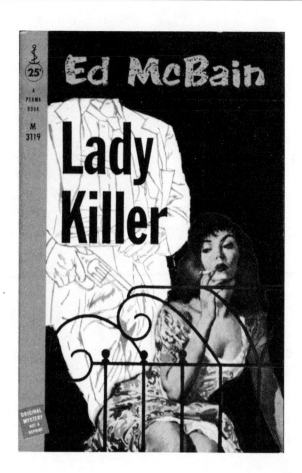

to the nines. I got the details from tailors. What
would he wear to go here, there—they taught me.
He prides himself on the way he dresses so you
can't just can't skip over that. This is part of his
character, he is an elegant dresser and he wants
people to know.''

On Organizing a Story

"I usually jump right in and see how far it will
take me and then start to seriously outline and consider the weight of each story line. Sometimes I
write each story line separately on the computer and
then combine them later. I did that with *Widows.*
In that book I wrote each story line separately and
laced them together in a checkerboard effect.

"My approach differs for each book. I know for
the next book I have to pick up certain threads. I
know I have to continue with Eileen Burke (a detective), who wasn't mentioned much in *Kiss.* I have
a nice man in mind for her.

"I wrote *Kiss* several times. I rewrote it more

than any other 87th Precinct book. I thought I was going to do something absolutely startling in the history of mystery fiction—I was going to catch the killer in the first chapter and hold the reader's interest in the rest of the book. There was no trial at all, I was saving for another book. Then I thought it would be interesting to juxtapose the trial and tell the murder mystery in the conventional fashion. *Kiss* ended up as three novels in one. It's a trial novel, a film *noir,* James M. Cain private eye novel, and it is a classic police novel. It was a juggling act, and it's fun to do that.''

On Working in Television and Movies

''I gave up doing television work five years or so ago. I was sixty or whatever it was, and I had just had a heart attack. I'm in meetings with twenty-year-olds who are explaining Motivation 101 to me. I really didn't need it, life is too short. You run a different risk—if you sell one of your books to TV or movies, they may assign another writer who may mess it up. But it's your choice. You could keep it on the shelf, pristine and safe, for the rest of your life.''

JOSEPH WAMBAUGH
The Glitter Dome
H. R. F. Keating

IN BRITAIN the police procedural novels written by former officers have given us accounts of police work and police life that ring true and, while not glossing over the bad, present us on the whole with pictures of policemen as heroes. In America a former detective sergeant in the Los Angeles Police Department, Joseph Wambaugh, has written police procedurals every bit as authentic-seeming, which to a large extent turn the British approach upside down. They show police work as often making of insufficient heroes debased men. They are police procedurals as comedy, black and cutting-edged.

Not that Wambaugh has a jaundiced view of the police. He left the L.A.P.D. only when he found that his celebrity as a writer—his books were tremendous best sellers—was interfering with the work he loved. One evening, called to the scene of an armed robbery, he asked the barman victim, who had blood streaming from his pistol-whipped face, which hand the gunman had used. Instead of answering, the man asked Wambaugh in his turn what George C. Scott (who starred in the films of his early books) was really like. Next day Wambaugh resigned.

The Glitter Dome is perhaps Wambaugh's finest work, especially if one regards *The Onion Field,* which Wambaugh calls a nonfiction novel, as falling outside the scope of this book. In *The Glitter Dome* Wambaugh depicts in a realistic way (though on occasion, one suspects, succumbing a little to the temptation to overegg the pudding) the life of pairs of police officers; two detectives, two narcotics men, two patrolmen. He shows us their humor, which is frequently extremely crude, their difficulties and degradations, and—in vividly splashed-on detail—the sex lives that are inextricably bound up with the police way of life in California, if nowhere else.

He tells us of their many woes and occasional semitriumphs, wandering around the murder of a Hollywood film mogul, in a strongly satirical manner and in short, chopped, juxtaposed fragments that have evoked comparisons with Joseph Heller.

This episodic way of telling a story not only makes the reader wonder time and again what is happening (and keep turning the pages in the hope of finding out) but, more important, it mirrors the chancy series of events Wambaugh sees as constituting the usual way a murder gets investigated. The two detective sergeants in the book, Al Mackey and Marty Welborn, by sticking to procedure in a mad, whirling world, get no more than near to the solution of the mystery.

Wambaugh shows us, with (I imagine) a good deal of justice, that the police approach to a major murder can be primarily concerned not with discovering the actual murderer but with providing the public at large with an acceptable account of the matter. Thus his two principal heroes, after much work and many difficulties, contrive an explanation for the finding of the body of Nigel St. Claire, the studio president, in the parking lot of a downtown bowling alley, and only afterward do the true facts come to light, by chance.

The work and the difficulties are presented to us in a fine flow of easy writing, with dialogue that smacks everywhere of the way actual policemen talk. Make no doubt of it, Wambaugh is another of the ex–police officers who are also natural writers of fiction. Look at his description of the life of the then-in-fashion roller skaters, a truly lyrical evocation. So the in-talk—the hints that are dropped and the digressions we get, or seem to get—swish by and we find ourselves at the end more or less clear about what has happened (and that's like much of life, after all), and certainly with a vivid idea of the way police action bites into the souls of the men who are foolish enough, or braggart enough, to take it up.

We are also left, perhaps above all, with the memory of the Glitter Dome; at once a garish, lights-swirling watering hole where tired and randy police officers of both sexes meet and mingle, and a symbol for the false world of Hollywood. And that is a symbol, too, of the falsities and hollow glamour of Southern California life (''Nothing was for free in the Glitter Dome''), and perhaps of much of life in the wider world.

A COP'S VIEW OF COP BOOKS
Hugh Holton

''COP'' BOOKS, or, as they are more formally called, police procedurals, have been around for quite a while. Sergeant Cuff, Wilkie Collins's detective in *The Moonstone,* was a policeman. But in more recent times the police procedural has become more standardized in nature. Within the pages of these cop ''yarns'' the reader can be exposed to the procedural aspects of working police officers solving a crime, or more than one crime. Often we will have them dealing with the emotional and social ramifications which the ''job'' of being a cop has on them in this contemporary, crime-riddled, cynical, fast-paced society.

There are a number of police procedurals that have been published over the years. Some have been quite good. In fact, I'd say a couple are bona-fide classics. Some have not been so good. Separating the good ones from the bad is more a matter of preference than anything else; however, my preference has been honed by my experiences as a cop over the past quarter of a century. I don't believe cop books have to be one hundred percent accurate as far as real procedures go, as they are works of fiction, but there must be some basis in real-life police operations in order for the work to be believable. In the beginning of each of his 87th Precinct mysteries Ed McBain writes:

> The city in these pages is imaginary. The people, the places are all fictitious. Only the police routine is based on established investigative techniques.

Well put, Ed. So with this in mind let's take a look at some of the cop books out there.

Actual police work is generally a team effort requiring a number of officers to interact to solve a crime or crimes. Although the loner cop has been lionized to a certain extent in the genre, the more believable books have a number of cops to the extent of entire detective squads of four, six, or even eight officers being involved. Each does something different and, probably, each will be working on more than one case simultaneously in addition to the main assignment around which the novel is constructed. I don't feel that having a number of characters in a police procedural is confusing, but rather, if the author properly identifies them along with giving them distinct personalities, such as Meyer Meyer in the McBain books, "Iron Balls" Delaney in the works of Lawrence Sanders, or the inimitable "Coffin Ed" Johnson and "Grave Digger" Jones created by Chester Himes, then the numbers won't confuse, but will rather enhance the authenticity of the work.

When we talk about actual procedurals, Joseph Wambaugh, a former Los Angeles police sergeant, has written some of the best novels in the genre that I have ever read. In classic works such as *The New Centurions, The Blue Knight,* and *The Choirboys,* Wambaugh took us inside the L.A.P.D. and gave us a close-up look at big-city cops. The reader was exposed to the warts, alcohol problems, cynicism, and that most unique attribute cops develop to keep from constantly crying or losing their minds in the face of encountering unbelievable daily tragedy, "cop" or "gallows" humor. With the trained eye of the veteran officer, Joseph Wambaugh has

also produced some fine nonfiction based on true police cases. Most notable are *The Onion Field* and recently *The Blooding,* which details the first murder case solved using DNA fingerprinting.

Another former police officer writing excellent police procedurals is William J. Caunitz, who is a retired New York City police lieutenant. In *One Police Plaza, Suspects, Black Sand,* and *Exceptional Clearance,* Bill approaches the solving of crimes by humanizing his police officers. In the pages of Caunitz's fiction the cops become real people who have the same wants, needs, and desires as do the readers and the general populace at large. Caunitz also imbues his police officers with pain and frustration, which further makes his books more real to his readers.

But it isn't necessary for an author to spend years as a cop on the streets of a major American city or even a rural town in order to write good or even excellent police procedurals. My personal all-time favorite police procedural novel is *The First Deadly Sin* by Lawrence Sanders. What Sanders did in *The First Deadly Sin* and in subsequent novels featuring Captain Edward X. "Iron Balls" Delaney was combine the commission of a crime (the novel's focus is on a number of crimes committed by a serial killer using a unique weapon), with in-depth profiles of the killer and Delaney. We see Captain Delaney as a somewhat rigid, inflexible human being in this first book, although he did make a brief appearance in Sanders's earlier novel *The Anderson Tapes.*

> Captain Edward X. Delaney, commanding officer of the 251st Precinct, New York Police Department, wearing civilian clothes . . . removed his Homburg (stiff as wood) . . . (and) planted himself solidly into an armchair, glanced swiftly around the room, then stared down at the hat balanced precisely on his knees.

Delaney then engages in the "observation game," which entails him recalling from memory the descriptions of everyone in the room with him.

As mentioned earlier, police procedurals generally have a cast of characters on the police end, because in reality police officers work in teams. In Sanders's books there are always support personnel to assist "Iron Balls" Delaney in his pursuit of the bad guys and, in keeping with the humanization factor, each of these officers must be more than just a body in a uniform. Let's take a look at one of Delaney's assistants.

> (Lieutenant) Marty Dorfman was an extraordinarily tall (6'4") Jew with light blue eyes and red hair that spiked up from a squeezed skull. He wore size 14 shoes and couldn't find gloves to fit. He seemed constantly to be dribbled with crumbs, and had never been known to swear.

I think we get a good picture of Lieutenant Dorfman from this brief description, but the author further individualizes him by telling us that he doesn't carry any bullets in his gun, he smokes, his socks don't match, his shoes are unshined, and he has been known to report for duty with shaving cream behind his ears. He is also a lawyer who cries at the funerals of police officers killed in the line of duty.

Another of my favorite authors of police procedural tales is Chester Himes, who created memorable but unorthodox N.Y.P.D. Harlem police detectives "Coffin Ed" Johnson and "Grave Digger" Jones. Originally, the Coffin Ed and Grave Digger tales were published in France; however, they found a wide readership when reprinted in America. Perhaps the two most popular novels in the series were *Cotton Comes to Harlem* and *For the Love of Imabelle,* both of which have been made into movies. *For the Love of Imabelle* became the recent movie *A Rage in Harlem.*

The Himes books were written in the 1950s before Miranda warnings and increased professionalism within law enforcement agencies. As a result, the exploits of Coffin Ed and Grave Digger are more in the hard-boiled tradition, as the two detectives brandish nickel-plated .44 Magnums to keep order on the wide open streets of Harlem.

Police procedural novels can be not only good mystery reads, but very rich and interesting because they tell some very real stories about the world in which we live. The flavor and rhythm of post–World War II Harlem is evident in the work of Chester Himes. The romance and intricacies of the Native American culture is showcased in the novels of Tony Hillerman, which feature Sgt. Jim Chee of the Navajo Tribal Police. As Hillerman explains in *The Dark Wind:*

> Navajo Tribal Policemen had absolutely no jurisdiction in a smuggling case or in a narcotics case, or anything involving the U. S. Drug Enforcement Agency. . . .

Yet Chee investigates cases that involve crimes indicative of the human condition, such as murder, and Hillerman's rich knowledge of Native American lore make all his Jim Chee books excellent reads.

As I stated earlier, I have selected the authors and their works because I have a personal preference for them. As a cop, they appeal to me most because they capture a flavor for what actual police work is like and what real cops do without letting the story get lost beneath an avalanche of detail. After all, I don't want to read a technical manual, which some police procedural authors produce. However, by the same token, if something in a police procedural is presented as a technical point or fact, then I suggest the author make sure that this item is indeed accurate. There are about a half million police officers in America who'll know instantly if a gross error has been made.

There's one other point I'd like to make from a purely cop standpoint. Police officers come in all different sizes, colors, and sexes. We're as different as are Captain Edward X. "Iron Balls" Delaney, Detectives "Coffin Ed" Johnson and "Grave Digger" Jones, and Sergeant Jim Chee. Stereotypes are as wrong for us as they are for any other group and each of us is an individual. That's one of the things I find so attractive about the police procedurals I've discussed; each of the police officers in them is different and approaches the job of crime fighting or crime solving from completely different perspectives.

Cop books will be around as long as people commit crimes requiring organized police forces to investigate. Of course, there are more police procedurals out there than I could ever mention in these brief pages. So, if you intend to write one, I would advise talking to a cop or two in the jurisdiction you are planning to write about, so you can get some of your facts straight. If you just want to read one, I'm sure you'll find a treasure trove of works in the genre at your local bookstore.

Goodreading.

Twenty-Five Police Procedurals
Selected by Jon L. Breen

John Ball	*In the Heat of the Night*
John Creasey (as J. J. Marric)	*Gideon's Fire*
James Ellroy	*The Black Dahlia*
Katherine V. Forrest	*The Beverly Malibu*
Michael Gilbert	*Blood and Judgment*
Reginald Hill	*A Pinch of Snuff*
Tony Hillerman	*The Dark Wind*
Stuart Kaminsky	*A Cold Red Sunrise*
Peter Lovesey	*The Last Detective*
Ed McBain	*Vespers*
James McClure	*The Steam Pig*
William McIlvanney	*Laidlaw*
William Marshall	*Thin Air*
Gerald Petievich	*To Live and Die in L.A.*
Lawrence Sanders	*The Third Deadly Sin*
Dell Shannon	*Case Pending*
Maj Sjöwall and Per Wahlöö	*The Locked Room*
Martin Cruz Smith	*Gorky Park*
Peter Turnbull	*Dead and Crisp and Even*
Dorothy Uhnak	*The Bait*
Janwillem van de Wetering	*The Japanese Corpse*
John Wainwright	*Blayde, R.I.P.*
Joseph Wambaugh	*The Blue Knight*
Hillary Waugh	*Last Seen Wearing*
Collin Wilcox	*A Death Before Dying*

HARD-BOILED
MYSTERIES

INTRODUCTION

Jon L. Breen

A NOT ENTIRELY FLATTERING definition of hard-boiled fiction is found in *Benét's Reader's Encyclopedia of American Literature* (HarperCollins, 1991): "a type of detective or crime story in which an air of realism is generated through laconic and often vulgar dialogue, depiction of cruelty and bloodshed at close range, and use of generally seamy environments" (page 416). The entry goes on to identify the category as a product of prohibition, as a reaction to "the attenuated prettification of the Conan Doyle School" and as an attempt to apply the "literary lessons" of writers like Ernest Hemingway and John Dos Passos to genre fiction. The definition invites argument, not only for its somewhat unfriendly tone. For one thing, there is a chicken-or-egg, who-influenced-whom question regarding the mainstream icon Hemingway and the pulp magazine pioneer of the hard-boiled story, Dashiell Hammett.

In introducing the essay collection *Tough Guy Writers of the Thirties* (Southern Illinois University Press, 1968), David Madden implies a somewhat more sympathetic and less mechanical definition in his description of the hard-boiled protagonist:

> An unusually tough era turns out the hard-boiled hero. A traumatic wrench like the Depression, its evils and despair touching all facets of human society, causes a violent reaction in these men as they find that they lay down in the great American dream-bed in the Twenties only to wake up screaming in the nightmare of the Thirties. Those hardest hit become the down-and-out, the disinherited, and soon develop a hard-boiled attitude that enables them to maintain a granite-like dignity against forces that chisel erratically at it. (page xvii)

Though it doesn't explain why the hard-boiled revolution, at least in detective fiction, started in the "dream-bed" before the stock-market crash, Madden's description suggests the subtle difference between hard-boiled fiction and the related field of dark suspense: the hard-boiled attitude is a response more to the conditions and circumstances of the time than to a pessimistic generalization about all existence. In most hard-boiled detective novels, the good guys win at least a partial victory.

The word *hard-boiled* is often followed by the phrase *private eye,* and indeed some of the most prominent examples of hard-boiled fiction—beginning with the works of Hammett and Carroll John Daly, who had much to do with inventing the form in the pages of *Black Mask*—concern p.i.'s. But much hard-boiled crime fiction projects an uncompromisingly tough world view while not including among its characters a private detective or, sometimes, any detective at all. Take Paul Cain's *Fast One* (1933), the account of gambler Gerry Kells, written in as close a stylistic approximation of the same period's Hammet as could be imagined. Or Hammett's own *The Glass Key* (1931), about gambler Ned Beaumont, considered by some his classic. Or W. R. Burnett's gangster saga, *Little Caesar* (1929), ancestor of all the accounts of organized crime to come, or the crime novels of James M. Cain, beginning with *The Postman Always Rings Twice* (1934).

On the other hand, while it is fair to call Raymond Chandler's Philip Marlowe, who was developed under other names in the pages of *Black Mask* before appearing in *The Big Sleep* (1939), a hard-boiled character despite his romantic and quixotic nature, it becomes more and more of a stretch to apply the label to his most prominent successor, Ross Macdonald's Lew Archer. To apply it to such latter-day private eyes as Michael Z. Lewin's Albert Samson or Howard Engel's Benny Cooperman is nearly absurd. Among the more prominent of the current female private eyes, only Sara Paretsky's

V. I. Warshawski might truly merit the label hard-boiled, and again it's a stretch. To say a first-person private eye must be hard-boiled is to commit a fallacy similar to that of a boyhood friend of mine who argued the following implied syllogism: All hit songs are rock and roll. "Love Is a Many Splendored Thing" is a hit song. Therefore, "Love Is a Many Splendored Thing" must be rock and roll.

Though enthusiastically embraced by the French, as are so many elements of American popular culture, the hard-boiled crime novel is essentially a North American art form. When British writers such as James Hadley Chase in the gangster novel *No Orchids for Miss Blandish* (1939) or Peter Cheyney in his novels about Lemmy Caution attempted it, they usually set the story in ersatz American backgrounds.

With some exceptions, among them Daly's literary descendant Mickey Spillane, the hard-boiled style probably exists in its purest form in the pulp magazines. When authors moved on to the slicks or to hardcover, there was often (not always) a certain mellowing of the style, with rough edges sanded down for a wider popular market. This can certainly be seen in the later work of tough *Black Mask* writers like Erle Stanley Gardner and George Harmon Coxe. While Gardner's Perry Mason could be deemed hard-boiled in his pulp-flavored earliest cases, he became much less so later in his career when his market influences shifted first to slick magazines, then to TV. Coxe's pulp character Flash Casey was replaced for hardcovers by the more polished and sophisticated Kent Murdock. In his 1946 anthology, *The Hard-Boiled Omnibus: Early Stories*

from Black Mask, the following were among the better-known authors Joseph T. Shaw selected to represent the style: Hammett, Raoul Whitfield (once as himself and once as Ramon Decolta), Chandler, Norbert Davis, Coxe, Paul Cain, Lester Dent, and Thomas Walsh. Notably omitted for whatever reason were Daly, Gardner, and Frederick Nebel.

When the pulps died out in the early 1950s, paperback originals became the prime source of hard-boiled fiction, purveyed by such skilled writers as Harry Whittington, Ed Lacy, Charles Williams, Peter Rabe, Gil Brewer, Lionel White, John D. MacDonald, and Chester Himes. In the decades to follow, many writers occupied or bordered the hard-boiled turf, among the most memorable Richard Stark (the straightfaced alter ego of Donald E. Westlake) with his novels about professional criminal Parker; Max Allan Collins, first with series crooks in the Parker mode, later with private eye Nate Heller and real-life crime-fighter Eliot Ness; and Andrew Vachss, a writer who has polarized readers of the mystery genre almost as much as Mickey Spillane forty years before. Elmore Leonard and Charles Willeford both toiled for years in relative obscurity before achieving recognition late in their careers for the excellence of their work, largely in the hard-boiled tradition.

At the risk of heresy, it may be time to retire the term hard-boiled, at least in reference to current crime fiction. Most books in the genre are too complex and ambivalent in their approach to be so handily labeled. The same is true of the polar opposite, cozy.

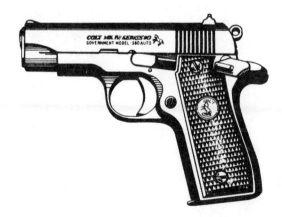

WARNING! WARNING!
Hitch-hikers May Be Escaped Lunatics!
Stephen King

WHEN A SIGN LIKE THIS appears by the side of the road in the nightmare world of Jim Thompson, no one even comments on it . . . which may be one of the reasons that Thompson's work is still worth reading some forty years after it first began to be published. When first released, his novels appeared almost exclusively as paperback originals, just a few more titles in a flood of fiction unleashed by the popular new "pocket-book" format. Most of the others published in the late forties and early fifties have long since been buried in the dust-heap of the years, but Thompson is still being read . . . more now than when he was alive and in his prime. We are, in fact, in the midst of a small Thompson revival: almost all his novels are in print in paperback, two collections of three novels each are available from Donald Fine under the title *HardCore,* and a book of his uncollected prose, *Fireworks,* has been issued.

Amazingly, almost all his books hold up as "good reads." More amazingly, two or three (*Pop. 1280, The Grifters,* and *The Getaway* would be my nominees) hold up as "good American novels of their time." And one, this one, remains as timeless and as important as it ever was. *The Killer Inside Me* is an American classic, no less, a novel that deserves space on the same shelf with *Moby-Dick, Huckleberry Finn, The Sun Also Rises,* and *As I Lay Dying.* Thompson's other books are either good or almost great, but all of them pale before the horrifying, mesmerizing story of Lou Ford, that smiling good ol' Texas boy who would rather beat you to death with clichés than shoot you with a .44 . . . but if the clichés don't do the job, he is not afraid to pick up the gun. And use it.

Before Kerouac, before Ginsberg, before Marlon Brando in *The Wild One* ("What are you boys rebelling against?" "What have you got?") or Yossarian in *Catch-22,* this anonymous and little-read Oklahoma novelist captured the spirit of his age, and the spirit of the twentieth century's latter half: emptiness, a feeling of loss in a land of plenty, of unease amid conformity, of alienation in what was meant, in the wake of World War II, to be a generation of brotherhood.

> *The subject suffers from strong feelings of guilt . . . combined with a sense of frustration and persecution . . . which increase as he grows older; yet there are rarely if ever any surface signs of . . . disturbance. On the contrary, his behavior appears to be entirely logical. He reasons soundly, even shrewdly. He is completely aware of what he does and why he does it . . .*

Lou Ford digs the above quote out of a psychology text by "a guy . . . name of Kraepelin" as his story winds toward its inevitable conclusion. I have no idea if Mr. Kraepelin is real or another product of Thompson's imagination, but I do know that the description fits a lot more people than one mentally disturbed deputy sheriff in a crossroads Texas town. It describes a generation of killers, from Caryl Chessman to Lee Harvey Oswald to John Wayne Gacey to Ted Bundy. Looking back at the record, one would have to say that it also describes a generation of politicians: Joe McCarthy, Richard Nixon, Oliver North, Alexander Haig, and a slew of others. In Lou Ford, Jim Thompson drew for the first time a picture of the Great American Sociopath.

It's not that Lou Ford is a killer without a conscience; it would be almost comforting if he were. But Lou Ford *likes* people. He goes out of his way to help Johnnie Pappas, son of the Central City restaurant owner and the local wild child. And when Lou breaks Johnnie's neck and hangs him in his jail cell to turn murder into something that looks like suicide, he does it with great and genuine sadness.

Yet when Lou leads Elmer Conway into the trap he has carefully constructed, and when Conway gets his first good look at the bait in that trap—the bludgeoned, grisly body of a prostitute named Joyce Lakeland—Lou begins to laugh, taking an extraordinary, vicious pleasure in both the battered woman and Conway's reaction to it.

> *I laughed—I had to laugh or do something worse—and his eyes squeezed shut and he bawled. I yelled with laughter, bending over and slapping my legs. I doubled up, laughing and farting and laughing some more. Until there wasn't a laugh in me or anyone. I'd used up all the laughter in the world.*

That Thompson was largely ignored by both the general reading public and the critics of his day can be taken as a foregone conclusion, I think, from the above sample of Thompson's nitro-and-battery-acid style. In a year (1952) when Ozzie and Harriet were America's favorite postwar couple and Herman Wouk's *The Caine Mutiny,* a novel about the ultimate victory of rationality over cowardice and insanity, was the winner of the Pulitzer Prize for Literature, no one really wanted to deal with this picture of a murderer so happy in his work that he laughs and farts before shooting the bewildered and drunken Elmer Conway to death with six bullets at point-blank range.

Nor does Thompson allow us the comfort of believing that Deputy Lou Ford is a mutant, a sport, an isolated aberration. In one of the classic passages from the novel, Thompson suggests just the opposite, in fact—that there are Lou Fords everywhere:

> *I've loafed around the streets sometimes, leaned against a store front with my hat pushed back and one boot hooked back around the other— hell, you've probably seen me if you've ever been out this way—I've stood like that, looking nice and friendly and stupid, like I wouldn't piss if my pants were on fire. And all the time I'm laughing myself sick inside. Just watching the people.*

The fact is, we've all seen guys who fit the description exactly, right down to the goofy smile and the CASE gimme cap tilted back on the head. The honest—if a little dopey—eyes, the sincere smile. We just know that the first thing out of this fellow's mouth is going to be "Howya doon?" and the last thing out is going to be "Have a nice day." Jim Thompson wants us to spend the rest of our lives wondering what's *behind* those smiles (and if you think the smiling villains don't exist, take a good close look at a picture of Ted Bundy or John Wayne Gacey, two real-life Lou Fords). In Jim Thompson's world, the signs warn of possible escaped lunatics instead of crossing wildlife, and Deputy Barney Phyfe is a raving psychotic.

There's nothing elegant in *The Killer Inside Me.* In fact, one of my chief amazements on rereading it was how much Thompson got away with (or how much Lion Books let him get away with) in an era when showing a woman in a bra was *verboten* in American movies and you could—theoretically, at least—go to jail for owning a copy of *Lady Chatterly's Lover.*

Thompson is not crude because he knows no other way to write; in fact, he twits more elegant writers who stretch their vocabularies more to say less:

> *In lots of books I read, the writer seems to go haywire every time he reaches a high point. He'll start leaving out punctuation and running his words together and babble about stars flashing and sinking into a deep dreamless sea. And you can't figure out whether the hero's laying his girl or a cornerstone. I guess that kind of crap is supposed to be pretty deep stuff—a lot of book reviewers eat it up, I notice. But the way I see it is, the writer is just too goddam lazy to do his job. And I'm not lazy, whatever else I am. I'll tell you everything.*

He does, too, including some things we're not sure we wanted to hear once we've heard them. And he tells us in amazingly blunt, no-holds-barred language.

For instance:

"The next son-of-a-bitch they send out here is going to get kicked so hard he'll be wearing his asshole for a collar."

"Well, whenever it gets too bad, I just step out and kill a few people. I frig them to death with a barbed-wire cob I have."

"[She's] One of those girls that makes you want to take off your shoes and wade around in her."

"Why, pardner that's . . . [as] easy as nailing your balls to a stump and falling off backwards."

And my own favorite among Thompson's assortment of picnic *crudités:* "There'd be all sorts of things to attend to, and discuss ... even the size of the douche bag to take along on our honeymoon!"

Some of these vulgarities are harsh enough to be startling even to readers who have become relatively inured to rough talk; they must have really "laid them by the heels," as Lou Ford likes to say, in 1952. Leslie Fiedler suggests in *Love and Death in the American Novel* that language itself is far less important than the *spirit* with which that language has been imbued, and even after all these years, the language Thompson employs to tell Deputy Ford's story has a kind of starey, socketed ugliness that rasps across our minds like stiff wire bristles. There is nothing pornographic in it, however; quite the opposite. In his introduction to Thompson's work (which is printed at the front of all the Black Lizard editions of Thompson's novels), Barry Gifford observes:

> He can be an excellent writer, capable of creating dialogue as crisp as Hammett's, descriptive prose as convincing as Chandler's. But then, all of a sudden, there will come two or three successive chapters of throwaway writing more typical of the paperback original Trash and Slash school of fiction.

This is a perfectly fair assessment of most of Thompson's books. The reason, I think, is the same one why even such good line-by-line writers as John D. MacDonald, David Goodis, and Donald E. Westlake (who spent that period writing under only God and Westlake himself know how many names) sometimes lapsed into fits of hackery: the big paperback machine was hungry, it needed to be fed, and the pay was so low you had to write a lot of prose to make a living wage. Books were often written in a month, sometimes in two weeks, and Thompson himself boasted that he had written two of his titles in forty-eight-hour stints (if one judges by quality, one of those two must have been the infamous *Cropper's Cabin*). There was little time to rewrite, and none at all to polish. The news that Joseph Heller would, two decades later, labor for seven years to produce a turkey like *Something Happened* would have caused these speed-writers to boggle with amazement.

But I would argue there is little or none of the salami writing of which Gifford speaks in *The Killer Inside Me*. In this one book, Thompson's muse seems to have led him perfectly. Every one of Lou Ford's casual country vulgarities is balanced—and outbalanced—by some pithy and unsettling comment on the human condition. Such comments run the risk of being of little use to the story ... of being, in fact, the negative image of the meaningless clichés with which the smiling Lou belabors the people he doesn't like ("It's not the heat, it's the humidity," "The man with the grin is the man who will win," etc., etc.). Instead, they have exactly the same startling, empty-socketed effect as Ford's vulgarities. Again, the language has been imbued with a tone that lifts it considerably above Thompson's rather pedestrian use of words.

"Why'd they all have to come to me to get killed?" Lou Ford complains suddenly in the midst of his tale. "Why couldn't they kill themselves?" Up to this point, Ford has been narrating, rationally and completely, the story of how the vagrant he ran out of town in the book's first chapter has returned to haunt him. Into this rational account, like a human skull rolling out of the darkness and into the lamplight, comes this paranoid, put-upon, Poe-esque shriek.

When this vagrant later sees the body of Amy, whom Lou has already murdered, he goes into a fit of horror that strikes Lou not as pitiful or frightening but as extremely funny ... and such is the power of his skewed vision that it strikes us funny as well.

> Did you ever see one of those two-bit jazz singers? You know, trying to put something across with their bodies that they haven't got the voice to do? They lean back from the waist a little with their heads hanging forward and their hands held up about even with their ribs and swinging limp. And they sort of wobble and roll on their hips.
> That's the way he looked, and he kept making that damned funny noise "Yeeeeee!", his lips quivering ninety to the minute and his eyes rolling all-white.
> I laughed and laughed, he looked and sounded so funny I couldn't help it.

I laughed too, God help me. Even as I was trying to imagine what Lou Ford must have looked like to a man on the edge of his own death at the hands of a maniac and *knowing* it, I laughed. It *did* look and sound funny.

In *The Killer Inside Me,* Jim Thompson sets himself one of the most difficult tasks a fiction writer can hope to perform: to create first a sense of catharsis with and then empathy (but not sympathy; never that; this is a strictly moral novel) for a lunatic. The passage above is one of the magical ways in which he achieves his end.

In a book that fairly bristles with painful ironies, we are not really surprised to discover that the motto of Central City, the Texas town where all this mayhem takes place, is *"Where the hand clasp's a little stronger."* It is a motto a fellow like Lou Ford can take to heart. Especially when it's *his* hands, around *your* neck.

Writing about the modern hard-boiled detective story, Raymond Chandler once said, "We've taken murder out of the parlor and given it back to the people who do it best." Thompson has gone that one better in *The Killer Inside Me*; Lou Ford is not only the sort of man who "does it best," but the kind of man who can do nothing else. He is the bogeyman of an entire civilization, a man who kills and kills and kills, and whose motives, which seemed so persuasive and rational at the time, blow away like smoke when the killing is done, leaving him—or us, if he happens to be the sort who kills himself and leaves the mess behind with no explanation—with no sound but a cold psychotic wind blowing between his ears.

At one point Lou tells us a story that seems to have no bearing at all on his own. It is the story of a jeweler with a fine business, a beautiful wife, and two lovely children. On a business trip he meets a girl, "a real honey," and makes her his mistress. She is as perfect in her way as his wife: married, and willing to keep it that way. Then the police find the jeweler and his mistress dead in a motel-room bed. A deputy goes to the jeweler's house to tell his wife, and finds her and both of the kids dead. The jeweler has shot them all, ending with himself. The point of the story is Lou Ford's judgment of the jeweler, chillingly brief and to the point: "He'd had everything, and somehow nothing was better."

Thompson, by the way, went on to write a very good novel called *The Nothing Man.*

Okay. Enough. It's time to get out of your way and let you experience this amazing piece of workmanship for yourself. I have explored the story in more depth than is my custom when writing introductory notes such as this, but only because the story is strong enough to do so without spoiling that experience. No amount of introductory material or post-morteming can prepare you for this work of fiction.

So it's time to let go of my hand and enter Central City, Jim Thompson's vision of hell. Time to meet Lou Ford, the nothing man with the strangled conscience and the strangely divided heart. Time to meet all of them:

> Our kind. Us people. All of us that started the game with a crooked cue, that wanted so much and got so little, that meant so good and did so bad. All us folks . . . all of us. All of us.

Amen, Jim. A-fucking-men.

THE STORY OF THE BIG LOVE
Lee Server

I N 1961 LANCER BOOKS released a nonfiction original paperback titled *The Big Love.* And there begins a thirty-year saga and one of the more curious tales in the history of softcover publishing. A fleetingly topical, sensationalized project from a second-rate house, *The Big Love* made little impact on release, but it would go on to become a talked-about cult item, a scarce, sought-after paperback collectable before anyone thought there were such things, and surely one of the few—

the only?—sleazy softcover originals to be turned into a major Broadway-produced play.

Not long before he died in 1959, that immortal swashbuckler Errol Flynn met his last and—one hopes—youngest mistress, fifteen-year-old Beverly Aadland, a stunning blonde, real-life Lolita to Flynn's dissipated rogue of a Humbert Humbert. The gossip pages of the day often offered shocked and disgusted items about this lascivious odd couple, along with the occasional paparazzi shot of the bloated, aged (only fifty but looking eighty) Errol leering at the lens as he balances the bikini-clad Beverly on his knee. *The Big Love* purported to tell the intimate details of the notorious relationship, "the behind-the-scenes story," as the book's cover lines had it, "told for the first time . . . all of their intimate secrets." An early example of the "kiss-and-tell" memoir (which Flynn pioneered with his raunchy autobiography *My Wicked, Wicked Ways*), *The Big Love* is not, however, what one might expect, the sordid confessions of Errol Flynn's jailbait mistress herself, it is the sordid confessions of Errol Flynn's jailbait mistress's mother, the one and—God help us—only Mrs. Florence Aadland.

Mrs. Aadland sets the book's tone of righteous prurience from the opening—and much-quoted—sentence: "There's one thing I want to make clear right off: my baby was a virgin the day she met Errol Flynn." Of course, we soon learn that "baby" was no longer a virgin the day *after* she met Flynn, and with far from a typical mom's see-no-evil view of events, Mrs. Aadland reassures us, and with a perverted enthusiasm, that she knows all her daughter's most intimate secrets: "When the time came she told me everything she did with Errol Flynn. And everything he did with her. Everything. And in detail, because she and I loved details and get a kick out of sharing things like that."

With the readers of this fifty-cent paperback, Mrs. Aadland shares all sorts of things about her daughter's and Errol Flynn's private life, from their nude swims and public makeout sessions to bathroom arguments about Flynn's need for an underarm deodorant. Not that it's all sordid tattling by any means. Throughout the book Florence holds Flynn in high esteem and continually defends him against gossip column slander such as the rumor that he was a chronic heroin and cocaine abuser. "I can state flatly and truthfully that Errol did *not* use drugs," says Mother Aadland in Chapter 16. "I

know how those dope addict stories get started. Errol himself started them . . . Being a great kidder, he often convinced his friends he was on dope." The old "act-like-a-dope-fiend" gag—well, maybe you had to be there.

Mrs. Aadland's fifth-wheel, backseat-driver p.o.v. is ludicrous on the face of it, an absurd extension of the pushy showbiz-mom stereotype. And yet, for all her considerable trashiness, this mother's tale is ultimately touching, a poignant glimpse of the delusions and disillusions of life in the alleyways of fame.

The idea for the book was Florence Aadland's own. Shortly after Flynn's death—his young mistress cut out of his will by a technicality—Beverly was caught up in another scandal. One night while Florence was in the hospital, a young man professing to be in love with Beverly raped her and then, holding her down, killed himself with a gunshot to the head. A furor erupted around "bad seed" Beverly and her mother. The girl was placed in a juvenile home and Mrs. Aadland was tossed in jail for "contributing to the delinquency of a minor." She lost custody of her daughter for good. Living alone in Hollywood in 1961, she contacted the Scott Meredith literary agency and said she had a juicy story to tell.

Meredith or his minions decided there was at least a quickie paperback sale in the second-hand Flynn story and they signed her on. But Mrs. Aadland was a drinking woman at this stage of her life and not likely to produce anything coherent by herself, so the agency assigned her a collaborator, a West Coast journalist and mystery writer named Tedd Thomey. "My first thought," says Thomey, "was the woman's a drunken bum and why does Meredith always give me these lousy assignments!"

In the 1940s Thomey was a reporter working the crime beat on the *San Francisco Chronicle*. "I was burning to try my hand at fiction writing," he told me. "I loved the idea of dreaming up dialogue and creating characters. I thought it would be much more creative than the newspaper business, and less dangerous. I remember one Christmas Eve in San Francisco I was covering a murder. A young woman killed her boyfriend in front of the Christmas tree. After a while the police officers and myself got into a police car and sat in there out of the cold while they decided what to do next. And one of the police officers had the murder weapon, a .32 caliber pistol, and he was playing with it while they were talking, and suddenly it went off. I was sitting in the backseat and the bullet went right through the seat and beside my head. It was just a coincidence, but I quit the *Chronicle* shortly after that and started writing pulp stories.''

A pulp writer friend of Thomey's named Richard Dermody gave him the name of an agent, August Lenninger. Thomey sent Lenninger a short story called ''$10,000 An Inch,'' about a six-foot heiress and a murderer, and it sold. ''I immediately quit my job on the paper to be a freelance writer. And my friend Dermody said, 'Don't do it, you'll starve.' And, of course, that's what happened.''

Thomey moved to a small beach town north of San Diego and wrote one detective story per week. ''I got $50 or $75 for these stories when we were lucky enough to sell one.'' Thomey's stories appeared in *Black Mask, FBI Detective Stories*, and other crime pulps operating in the late 1940s. ''I switched over from Lenninger to Scott Meredith around 1949 and he supplied me with a formula for writing these things. The most important part of the formula was that a dead body show up by page three of your story or forget about it. And I got so I could turn out these stories and they would sell. This was late in the game for the pulps, though, and most of the big names had gone somewhere else. They were still paying a penny a word. And then those magazines folded, one after the other. Scott Meredith was stuck with a backlog of my stories. Years go by and new magazines come out, *Manhunt*, magazines like that, and darned if they didn't buy those same old stories from the files for $800 and $900. And I would have been glad to get $75 for one a few years before!''

With the paperback boom on in the early 1950s, Thomey started writing novels. ''I sold to Gold Medal and Berkley and Avon. And I found it strikingly easy to write these novels. All I did was use everything that I learned from Meredith's formula for pulp stories, the dead body by page three and so on down the line. *And Dream of Evil* was the first one. Avon paid a $1,000 advance. And that book was quite successful. It sold all over the world and sold well, in all the best houses in France and Germany, and we got all kinds of money from all the foreign houses.

''In the opening chapter I've got a hero on a roof and he's handcuffed to a slot machine. He's going down a fire escape lugging this thing—if you've ever carried a slot machine, believe me, they're heavy—and then he makes love to a beautiful girl while still handcuffed to the slot machine. That's all in the first chapter! I thought it was a potboiler at the time, but I read it over a few years ago and heck, it was pretty good—it really moves. Gallimard brought it out in France, and in French they didn't have a word for slot machine, so whenever I used that term they put an asterisk and at the bottom of the page they explained what a slot machine was every time I used it.''

Thomey's *I Want Out*, about a tough bail bondsman, came out in an Ace Double edition, (Ace D401, PBO 1959, ed.). *Killer in White*, a Gold Medal Original (GM #546, PBO 1956, ed.), Thomey fashioned out of actual experiences with a female obscene phone caller and a gang of Long Beach chiropractor scam artists. Other novels followed. Thomey returned to newspaperwork in the 1950s and began a long tour of duty with the *Long Beach Press-Telegram*.

Which brings us back to 1961 and the writer's momentous first meeting with Mrs. Florence Aadland. ''She was drunk when I got to her place,'' he recalls. ''I thought she was just too trashy for me. Her place was a dump. I was afraid even to drink a glass of water there. I didn't like her and she didn't like me. But these stories she told about Errol Flynn—when I went home that night and thought about them I realized they were really very amusing. And she had an insight into Errol Flynn like no one else. Meanwhile, she was calling Scott Meredith in New York and trying to get me thrown off the book. But the office was closed in New York by then, three hours later. And I went back the next day and she was sober and we got along much better and we did the book. And it was one hell of a good book.

''Lancer Books gave us a $2,500 advance, which we split fifty-fifty, minus the agency commission. I taped her for about a week, and those tapes are just priceless. I still have them. She was very entertaining to listen to with this giggle of hers and I think I got a lot of that flavor into the book.''

Graced with a cover intended to resemble the front page of a sleazy tabloid newspaper, *The Big Love* hit the racks, sold poorly, and might have sunk without a trace. Then something unexpected occurred. An article appeared in *Esquire* magazine written by William Styron, already a distinguished name and the future author of *Confessions of Nat Turner* and *Sophie's Choice*. The article began: "It usually requires a certain arrogance to say of a new book that it is a masterpiece." And continued: "At certain rare moments . . . there will appear a work of such unusual and revealing luminosity of vision, of such striking originality, that its stature is almost indisputable; one feels that one may declare it a masterpiece without hesitation or fear that the passage of time might in any way alter one's conviction. . . . To Mrs. Aadland and her collaborator, Tedd Thomey, we own a debt of gratitude; both of them must feel a sense of pride and relief at having delivered themselves, after God alone knows how much labor, of a work of such wild comic genius."

And so on, for thousands of words. Styron's hyperbolic outburst was, to be sure, a mite tongue-in-cheek, but in those days before "camp" became an exhausted concept, his satiric review made *The Big Love* seem like uniquely delirious fun, at least to the sort of buttoned-down hipsters who read *Esquire* in that period. And indeed, all put-ons aside, it took a relatively sophisticated reader to appreciate the surrealism and absurdity in the book's wild mixture of sex, mother love, voyeurism, celebrity worship and self-pity. Thomey has fashioned a brilliant portrait of an American Gothic, Hollywood division. It was as if one of the characters from *The Day of the Locust* had come to life and decided to write a memoir in her declining years. "That was all her," said Thomey. "She was a fascinating woman, sad, funny, sweet, bad-tempered, foul-mouthed, sentimental."

The book became a minor sensation with the cognoscenti. It was the "in" thing to own a copy. MGM composer (at the time) Andre Previn, for instance, gave away a hundred copies as Christmas presents. Unfortunately, Lancer Books was unable to capitalize on the book's instant cult status. *The Big Love* had been released during a period of paperback "glutting," and most copies never made it out of the warehouse. "They put only 40,000 copies on sale, and the rest were all shredded," says Thomey. "People went around trying to find the book after the Styron review and they couldn't find it. They were all gone." A cult item and unavailable in stores, copies of *The Big Love* began to be traded

for unheard-of prices. "There were people offering $35, $50, and more for a copy," Thomey recalls. "But of course that didn't bring a cent to Florence or me—the book was out of print."

A few years later producer-director Robert Aldrich bought the film rights to *The Big Love*. He paid $20,000, half of which went to Florence's estranged daughter, Beverly, who would have otherwise blocked the sale. Aldrich planned to cast Bette Davis as Florence and brought the two women together for a meeting. Apparently, the pair got along like gangbusters. But the film fell through.

The book itself, remaining out of print, nevertheless continued to have a life of its own. It was named in a later issue of *Esquire* as part of the "Basic Library of Trash," along with *The Postman Always Rings Twice* and *The Big Sleep;* a Los Angeles radio station offered dramatic readings from the book; poet W. H. Auden included two excerpts from it in an anthology. And then, in the 1980s, William Styron reentered the picture with an idea for a stage adaption, turning the book's narrative into a series of one-woman monologues. Other adaptions followed. An off-Broadway production of the play starred Marsha Mason. In 1986, Warner Books reprinted *The Big Love,* along with William Styron's famous essay and a new afterword by Tedd Thomey. Stage versions continued to be planned, with various intriguing actresses named for the part. Finally, in the winter of 1991, a production opened on Broadway with a padded and peroxided Tracey Ullman playing Mrs. Florence Aadland. The production closed after a few weeks, but that's almost beside the point. How many other Broadway plays could boast the credit "adapted from a paperback original published by Lancer Books"?

Florence Aadland died in 1965 of acute alcoholic poisoning. "But really," says her collaborator, "she died of a broken heart. They took Beverly away from her and that killed her."

Beverly Aadland is now a wife and mother in Southern California. Her husband once tried to sock author Charles Higham for saying Errol Flynn was a gay Nazi.

And Tedd Thomey is still writing and working for a newspaper, and still amazed at the long, strange life of *The Big Love*.

jodie foster / anthony hopkins / scott glenn

the silence of the lambs

from the terrifying best seller

a jonathan demme picture / jodie foster / anthony hopkins / scott glenn / "the silence of the lambs" / ted levine / music by howard shore / production designer kristi zea / director of photography tak fujimoto / edited by craig mckay, a.c.e. / executive producer gary goetzman / based upon the novel by thomas harris / screenplay by ted tally / produced by kenneth utt edward saxon and ron bozman / directed by jonathan demme

R RESTRICTED

ORION

MCA

SERIAL KILLERS:
A Motive for Murder
Brian Harper

THE POPULARITY OF BOOKS, movies, and TV shows dealing with serial killers has left some people wondering what sort of sickness is spreading through our society to engender fascination with such a morbid subject.

Are serial-killer books a sexist backlash against successful career women, a means of allowing frustrated or intimidated males to vicariously work out their aggressions on the fictional killers' predominantly female victims? Or are they symptomatic of a society that, having lost its moral compass, now sees the perpetrators of heinous crimes as glamorous celebrities? Or are they yet another vehicle for glorifying the dehumanized violence and outright butchery that dominate so much of popular entertainment today—everything from rap videos to Saturday morning cartoons?

Even though I've written three novels about serial murders (one published, the other two forthcoming), I'll admit there is some truth in all of the above charges. I'm disturbed myself by some of the offerings in this genre—stories that strip the victims of moral stature and human dignity, reducing them to mere objects of mutilation and savagery, "pieces of meat," in effect. There may indeed be a vicious power trip at work in the minds of some writers—and movie directors and TV producers—in this field, along with a childishly perverse delight in throwing a spotlight on the most aberrant and abhorrent varieties of pathological behavior.

A desire to shock or revolt one's audience, or to strike out at those members of our society who are perceived to be most vulnerable, is hardly an uplifting motive for the act of artistic creation. If this were all there was to the genre, I would agree with those critics who view it in the most harshly negative terms.

But I think there is more to the popularity of the fictional serial killer than any of the above explanations would suggest. So, in defense of the genre, let me try to answer these criticisms while presenting some positive reasons to write and read these books, or to produce and watch the movies and TV shows based on them. Let me provide, if you will, a motive for murder.

For one thing, the serial killer affords the writer with a uniquely interesting villain. In conventional mysteries, the murderers may be divided into two basic types. There is the cunning, methodical plotter with a diabolically brilliant mind who stymies the police by leaving no clues. This character normally has a more-or-less rational motive for his crimes, such as gaining an inheritance or framing a business rival.

Alternatively, there is the "wild beast:" the deranged, subhuman monster who strikes at random, killing with the savage brutality of a feral animal. His murders are crimes of impulse, sloppy and pointless, and he has no motive other than insane hostility to all living things.

Well, wouldn't it be interesting if there were a way to combine the most striking attributes of both villains? To create a character who is simultaneously cunning and crazed—methodical and rational in his planning, but overwhelmed by an impulse toward unrestrained violence during the actual commission of his crimes? A killer who is frustratingly logical and efficient in his modus operandi . . . yet utterly irrational in his motive?

The serial killer, of course, permits precisely this integration of seemingly disparate personality traits. And whether the current archetypal figure is Jack the Ripper or Hannibal Lecter, people are invariably intrigued by the idea of a highly civilized, professional man—a medical doctor, a psychiatrist—engaging in wanton acts of slaughter for the sheer sadistic pleasure of the kill.

Besides making exceptionally good villains, serial killers are also topical. They have been in the news a good deal over the past decade, and anything that makes headlines will find its way into popular entertainment quickly enough. After the Watergate scandal, you may recall, there was a rash of thrillers about government conspiracies. The recent surfeit of TV movies about the "Long Island Lolita" case is perhaps a more obvious—and certainly more lurid—example of the same tendency.

But what about the moral implications of this type of escapism? There has been a lot of concern, some of it justified, about glamorizing serial killers. Certainly Dr. Lecter has become a cult fixture, though I doubt that his creator, Thomas Harris, ever wished him to be seen in a positive light. What is more bizarre, some misguided company recently marketed "serial-killer trading cards" to kids—a truly objectionable venture.

But criticizing books and movies for making a hero out of the killer generally misses the point. In many, probably most, of these stories, a clear distinction is drawn between good and evil, and the reader or viewer is strongly invited to side with good. In fact, serial-killer tales can be classified as modern examples of melodrama; and the essential ingredients of melodrama are a hero to root for, a victim to pray for, and a villain to hiss at. This formula has worked for a long time; you can trace it back at least as far as Shakespeare's *Richard III,* in which the title character is basically a serial killer who happens to wear a crown.

To the extent that a book or film depicts a mur-

derer in a sympathetic or even heroic light, it can certainly be criticized on moral grounds, though the work may still have merit when viewed from a strictly aesthetic standpoint. But if the story's sympathies lie clearly with the positive characters—if the villain is presented as evil, and his victims as good—and if the value of the victims as human beings is sharply and repeatedly stressed, not glossed over, then however grim the subject matter may be, the story is implicitly acknowledging a moral dimension to life.

Furthermore, most of these fictional killers are depicted in terms that are hardly flattering, let alone romanticized. Take Franklin Rood in my novel *Shiver.* Rood is neurotically insecure, terrified to the point of paralysis in the presence of any attractive woman, intelligent but an obvious underachiever. He lives a lonely, solitary life, and bases his precarious self-esteem on grandiose fantasies.

Would even the most confused or impressionable reader want to emulate this maladjusted and emotionally arrested basket case? I think it's much more likely the reader would empathize with the principled L.A.P.D. detective hunting Rood, or with the vulnerable but resilient woman who survives Rood's attacks and learns to fight back.

Mention of the woman in my story brings up the last objection frequently made about such books and films—that the whole genre is premised on victimizing women.

One common answer to this charge is that the overwhelming majority of real-life serial murderers are men, and most of their victims are women. Thrillers that depict a male killer in pursuit of a female victim are therefore merely reflecting the facts of most actual cases.

I don't find this line of defense compelling. There is some truth to it, of course; but fiction is not journalism, and there is no requirement that escapist entertainment mirror reality.

To me, a more persuasive argument is that, in most cases, the women in these stories ultimately are *not* victims. They triumph over their would-be destroyers, exacting the rough justice of revenge—precisely as any good melodrama demands.

It seems odd that when a Broadway play, *Extremities,* dramatizes the story of a rape victim who turns the tables on her assailant, critics praise the work for showing us a strong, resourceful woman who fights back against cruel abuse; but if a serial-killer novel or movie employs essentially the same formula, the same critics lambaste it as contributing to the degradation of women.

Strength of character can be demonstrated only under stress. A person who faces no threats or challenges is never tested, and can't be evaluated as either strong or weak. But put the same person in a life-or-death situation, pile up the dangers till they seem overwhelming, and then you will see what that individual is made of.

This is why I think that critics who find fault with the depiction of women in this genre are missing the point. These supposedly "weak" and "victimized" female characters are tested in ways that few of us, in real life, ever will be—or would want to be. And for the most part they emerge from the test as survivors—as victors, not victims. It is their adversaries who fail the test and perish, and who are shown, finally, to be weak, helpless, and pathetic.

There is another reason that women tend to be the focus of such stories. In our society, women are allowed to exhibit a wider range of emotional responses than men. This broader scope of emotions gives the author more to work with when presenting the reactions of a woman under stress, and tends, in general, to make female characters more vibrant, spontaneous, and alive than their male counterparts.

I might add that my impression is that the readership of psychological thrillers is tilted slightly toward women. From a strictly commercial standpoint, then, it makes sense to give a female character a prominent place in the story, if possible. The same marketing consideration probably holds true for TV shows, and perhaps even for feature films.

None of the above discussion is likely to allay the concerns of those who criticize the current popularity of serial killers in books and films. But such concerns, though no doubt sincere and well-intended, are nothing new. In every generation there has been some "shocking" trend in entertainment that caught on with the broad audience while alienating the would-be arbiters of public taste.

Critics and scholars sniffed at Shakespeare, and even tried to outlaw theater in his day; the author of *Macbeth* and *Hamlet* was a commercial hack, they said, whose bawdy humor and penchant for witches, ghosts, swordplay, and melodrama appealed to the worst instincts of the vulgar groundlings. The earliest motion pictures were dismissed by the intellectuals as mere novelties, pandering to sensationalistic appetites; the first screen kiss brought calls for censorship. Pulp magazines of the twenties and thirties were opposed by concerned parents, teachers, and preachers who sought to ban the periodicals out of fear that such lurid trash would rot young readers' minds; the "trash" included stories by Bradbury, Asimov, and Heinlein, whose imaginative visions, far from rotting minds, actually inspired some of these same young readers to become astronomers, rocket scientists, and astronauts.

No, there's nothing new here. Still, objections to the serial-killer genre will continue to be voiced. Violence—even safely fictional violence, set in the context of a moral universe, with the promise of eventual triumph by the supposed victim—is simply intolerable to some people, either because it threatens social stability or because it is "politically incorrect."

So perhaps the final word on this subject should go to a writer who, like Bradbury, Asimov, and Heinlein, got his start in the lurid pulps, and who went on to entertain millions with stories of good against evil, punctuated by acts of violence. His name is Louis L'Amour, and his words, taken from his memoir *Education of a Wandering Man,* seem peculiarly appropriate to the genre under discussion:

> We hear a lot of talk these days about violence, but we forget the many generations that have grown up on stories of violence. The bloodiest of all, perhaps, were the so-called fairy tales, but I would have missed none of them and doubt if I did.... If we were to eliminate violence from our reading, we would have to eliminate all history, much of the world's great drama, as well as the daily newspaper....
>
> It is always well to remember that many of us sleep safe at night because there are people out there cruising the streets and on call to keep it so. As many have discovered, violence is with us still, and no one is immune to a sudden strike in the night.

Some Notable Serial-Killer Novels
Selected by Jon L. Breen and Stephen J. Baines

William Bayer	*Switch*
William Bayer	*Wallflower*
Robert Bloch	*Psycho*
Thomas H. Cook	*Tabernacle*
Bill Crider	*Blood Marks*
Bradley Denton	*Blackburn*
Alison Drake	*Fevered*
Robert Duncan	*In the Blood*
Ed Gorman	*Night Kills*
Brian Harper	*Shiver*
Thomas Harris	*Red Dragon*
Thomas Harris	*The Silence of the Lambs*
William Heffernan	*Ritual*
Dean Koontz	*Whispers*
David Lindsay	*Mercy*
David Martin	*Lie to Me*
Billlie Sue Mosiman	*Night Cruise*
Richard Neely	*The Walter Syndrome*
Bill Pronzini and Barry Malzberg	*The Running of Beasts*
Ellery Queen	*Cat of Many Tails*
Lawrence Sanders	*The First Deadly Sin*
Lawrence Sanders	*The Third Deadly Sin*
Peter Straub	*Koko*
Shane Stevens	*By Reason of Insanity*
David Wiltse	*Prayer for the Dead*
Stuart Woods	*Chiefs*

FORMULA FOR THE PAST

Harold Adams

MY FIRST RECOMMENDATION for those who wish to write about the past is to be born early. Nothing else provides that rock-bottom background for the job. It adds that "old fart" edge you can't look up in a book or learn through interviews with super seniors.

Of course there are a few types who will write about periods preceding personal experience by decades, and that's fine for those who lack colorful families, lived dull lives, and have no bragging rights or grudges to settle without bloodshed. But that kind of writing calls for an inordinate amount of reading first, and sometimes even researching foreign areas and carrying on studies that cost too much in time and cash.

I write about the thirties mostly because my memories in youth are more precise than what I accumulate currently, and time has colored the scenery, expanded the characters, and made creativity overcome dull reality when necessary to keep the tales moving.

Another recommendation is, you make friends very early with exceptionally intelligent, imaginative, and perceptive people, and stay on good terms with what few relatives you have that share the same powers and talents as these selected friends.

What I did was, I got born in 1923, early in the year. And I was the second born in the family and had this bright, aggressive, and imaginative brother, named Dick, five years my senior, who knew everything by the time I showed up and has never been shy about keeping me informed.

(Let me note here that Dick was his christened name. My father's name was Lafayette Elihu and he made up his mind his kid would never have to go through life under a nickname.)

I made friends with Gail Myers when we were four and managed to keep track of him through luck, frequent visits back and forth, and a steady stream of mail. He even showed up in New Caledonia during World War II, so we had a chance to share occasional weekends and one three-day pass on that semitropical island.

Unfortunately I began my period pieces late in life, so I couldn't interview my father in midnovel, but he left some notes on family history and I remembered many of the stories he would spin during meals and occasional trips we took from Grand Forks, North Dakota, to Clark, South Dakota, where my grandparents lived. The grandparents were also a great reservoir of memories, because while a child, I lived with them through each summer. All of these people told stories of my uncle Sidney Dickey, Mother's notorious older brother, who became Carl Wilcox in my South Dakota mystery novels.

Along the way in the series published so far, Carl has become slightly washed up and buffed down, but his talent for getting into trouble, fighting men bigger than himself, and bedding cooperative women, remains faithful to the original.

The stories of his practical jokes are true, unless my relatives lied, and he did go to prison twice for crimes committed while under the influence of

Rural life during the Great Depression

Archive Photos/Jack Benton

widows and bootleg booze. Somehow his widows always needed more money than he had on hand, and unfortunately drinking made him more impulsive than skillful as either a holdup man or a rustler. And his gun was never loaded.

Besides brother Dick and friend Gail, I've resorted on occasion to history books and daily to Webster's Collegiate Dictionary, which provides dates for words—an invaluable tool for winning arguments with editors who think I slip in modern expressions on occasion. This research became routine after Bill Malloy, my smart and understanding editor at Mysterious Press, caught me on the word *hassle*. It was one used constantly by my boss when

I worked for the Better Business Bureau in Minneapolis. Since he was a man my father's age, I couldn't believe it didn't date from Carl's time until Webster's informed me it was born in 1945.

The Reader's Encyclopedia dates most of the writers I make references to, as well as their major works, in case we start to get more definitive, and I turn to my one-volume Columbia Encyclopedia on occasion. Sometimes I even borrow access to an Encyclopedia Britannica owned by friends. I resort to the public library only in desperation. I like to blame this laziness on the fact I wrote part-time for years while holding a full-time job and couldn't quite eke out energy for excessive research.

The true key to my period pieces is having the right forebears and friends, but most of all, one marvelous uncle.

Sidney Dickey, my mother's wastrel older brother, was born to be exploited by a writer. I have to confess that the last time I saw him I was five years old. He had been living with my parents for about a year in 1930 and left us when my father discovered he'd pried the diamond out of Mother's engagement ring and hocked it for booze. My dad was about the only guy in Sid's life with gall to match his, and when he told him to go, he went.

But I heard stories about him all my life.

I intend to share them with readers as long as I can write and publishers will cooperate.

Twenty-Five Notable *Noir* Novels
Selected by the Editors

Harold Adams	*The Barbed Wire Noose*
Lawrence Block	*After the First Death*
Fredric Brown	*The Wench is Dead*
Tucker Coe (D. Westlake)	*Don't Lie to Me*
Tucker Coe (D. Westlake)	*Murder Among Children*
James Crumley	*The Last Good Kiss*
James Ellroy	*Because the Night*
Thomas Hauser	*Agatha's Friends*
Dean Koontz (Owen West)	*The Fun House*
Dean Koontz	*The Voice of the Night*
Elmore Leonard	*Unknown Man #89*
John Lutz	*The Truth of the Matter*
Ed McBain	*Goldilocks*
Margaret Millar	*How Like an Angel*
Marcia Muller	*The Shape of Dread*
Marcia Muller	*Trophies and Dead Things*
Bill Pronzini	*Shackled*
Lawrence Sanders	*The Anderson Tapes*
Mickey Spillane	*Kiss Me Deadly*
Richard Stark (D. Westlake)	*The Seventh*
Ross Thomas	*Chinaman's Chance*
Teri White	*Triangle*
Charles Willeford	*New Hope for the Dead*
Cornell Woolrich	*The Black Curtain*
Cornell Woolrich	*The Black Path of Fear*

A scene from Orson Welles's *The Lady from Shanghai,* his contribution to *noir,* with Welles and Rita Hayworth.

THRILLERS
AND OTHER
MYSTERIES

HOW I CAME TO WRITE
THE SKIN OF RABINOWITZ
and Other Literary Milestones

Warren Murphy

I THOUGHT THAT TITLE would get your attention, and I promise to tell you all about it. But first . . . a word from my longtime sponsor.

Series Books:

When my partner, Dick Sapir, and I tried our first novel back between the First and Second Punic Wars, we never really believed we might be starting a book series.

Oh, yes, we thought it was pretty good and, sure, someone someday might even want us to write another about the same characters.

But a series? Forget it. In the first place, our adventure novel was very literary. Even the title— *Created the Destroyer*—came from the Bhagavad Gita. And besides, as one distinguished agent told us after pocketing our check for reading fees, *"Nobody* publishes series books." Would an agent lie?

Anyway, eight years later, in a roundabout route that involved a secretary, a dentist, a pervert, and like that, we finally got *Created the Destroyer* published; fifty thousand copies jumped off the shelves in two weeks, and our publisher called us to say congratulations and when can we have the next three books in the Destroyer series?

And Dick asked me, What the hell is the Destroyer series?

Since everybody I had been working for in the real world had just gone to jail and a grand jury was looking longingly at me, I took this as a sign that God wanted me to find a new line of work and the Destroyer series was it. So Dick moved into my attic, rolled a sheet of paper into his old Underwood, typed out "Destroyer Number Two" and we were series writers.

But Life, Folks, Is Not That Simple:

When we turned in the third book in the series, a publishing suit called us in and told us the book was totally unacceptable.

"What is all this humor?" he demanded. "Where are the bodies? Where is the blood?"

He raised himself to full height and shouted at our knees: "I need killing; I need sex."

Testy. Testy. We recessed the meeting for a while and Dick and I went around to the gin mill and tanked up with Dutch courage while we considered these latest events. We finally decided that the suit certainly did need killing and if he needed sex, he was just going to have to pay for it like everyone else, but we were not changing one word of our book.

"I'll go nuts if we have to write the same book over and over again," Dick said.

"You're already nuts," I said.

"Yeah, but *they* don't know that."

We won. Book three stood as written and Remo Williams and Chiun—the protagonists of the Destroyer—were free to go along the loony path we had chosen for them and we were free to write them anyway we wanted.

Eventually, Dick and I worked together on more than forty Destroyers. We sold umpteen million copies, made a lot of money, perpetrated what the *L.A. Times* called "flights of hilarious satire" and maybe had something to do with changing the rules forever about what writers could get away with in category books.

Even today, while my partner has died and I've become a golf bum, the Destroyer rolls on, in other hands than ours, with ninety-something titles, trans-

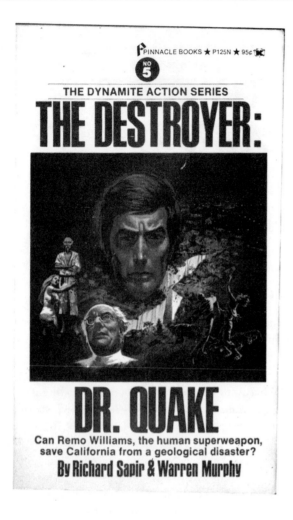

lations into a dozen different languages, a TV series, film, comic books, forty million sales. But uneasy lies the head . . .

Pinnacle's Terrible Idea:

Those early seventies were heady times in publishing. Anyone could be—and often was—published. Pinnacle Books (which still exists under different ownership) was squirting out series books like a pregnant frog dispensing eggs. At one time they had thirty-seven separate series, in almost every category imaginable, including the Destroyer.

And along the way, the mind-boggling idea: let's number the books in each series.

This was a throwback to the days of the pulp magazines and Street and Smith's savvy marketing of them. But these were *books* Pinnacle was publishing, not magazines, and with its one stroke, Pinnacle rendered the titles of the books secondary and less important than the number on the identical,

grimly predictable covers all the series seemed to share.

It was great for sales, but it destroyed any chance that the books might have been judged by their contents rather than by their covers. Books were now products like Oxydol and New Improved Oxydol Number II. Characters counted for less; stories for less; writing for less. The only thing that seemed to matter was the number of the beast.

In publishing, no truly bad idea goes uncopied. Other publishers climbed aboard. At times it seemed as if half the books on a drugstore rack were identified by number. (Even today, an unrepentant old Destroyer fan will accost me to let me know that he ''loved Number 16, hated Number 17.'') And *I* can't even remember the real titles anymore.

Hegel time. Thesis leads to antithesis. The market got oversaturated; series started to vanish. The Finisher and the Rubber-Outer and most of the rest of the junk bit the dust. The semiliterates got unhired. Only a few series survived. The new conventional wisdom was that ''series books are dead.''

As proprietors of one of the survivor series, Dick and I might have laughed with Liberace except . . .

I Am Cut to the Quick:

One night, a friend of mine asked me, ''How can I take you seriously when your books have numbers on them?''

The obligatory response was quick: ''I only worry about one number—thirty million. That's copies sold.''

But it got us to thinking. Had we traded in our reputations for a mess of pottage? Had we let ourselves be led along the road to literary leprosy? In the collective nonmind of publishers' row, was there a qualitative difference between books identified by title and those known best by number? Had we made a serious career mistake?

In a Word . . . Yes and No:

When Dick decided to write other, bigger books, he found so much resistance to his identity as co-creator of the Destroyer series that we wound up getting all the books reissued with his name taken off the covers.

But good work always outs. By the time of his tragic early death, Dick had finally reached the point in his career where he was poised for superstardom. (A *New York Times* review of his last book, published right after his death, said "Mr. Sapir is a brilliant professional.")

Just as he had been in all the years up until then too.

Meanwhile, I went a different way. Round-heeled by nature, I took the path of least resistance and kept writing new series, with only occasional forays into darker, more "serious" work. (It's time to share a secret with you. I write for a living; I have forty-six other things that I prefer to do for pleasure. Here I stand; I can do no other.)

What Goes Around, etc.:

After their kneejerky reaction to avoid being labeled series publishers, it took only a little while for most houses to realize that they had thrown out the baby with the bathwater.

And around that time came the resurgence of the mystery novel and the emergence of Sisters in Crime and other powerful forces, and publishers again began to actively court new series.

Which is where we are today. And, with the exception of a couple of dinosaurs—the Destroyer still being one—and a few sharply defined categories, there is not a number to be seen on any of these books. Plus, most of them are done first in hardcover, the original paperback mystery now being pretty much a dodo bird.

Some Words to Ignore:

And now the statement of the mystery grandmaster, the very excellent Julian Symons, a few years back:

"The series detective has limited many writers who would have fulfilled their talents more fully if he had been abandoned." Mr. Symons further said he gave up his only series character when he realized that "the crime novel could be used to investigate the psychology of relationships and to say ironic or angry things about the structure of society."

Thus implying that series books with continuing characters could not do the same thing.

Sorry, but I demur.

Dick Sapir and I managed to write forty volumes of American social satire under the guise of the Destroyer series. John D. MacDonald—who eschewed numbered titles in favor of colored titles, thus escaping opprobrium—was never shy about sounding off on society through the mouth of Travis McGee and Meyer. Larry Block, Sue Grafton, Michael Collins—all have ideas and all find a way to express them through the medium of the once-much-maligned series book.

Where Mr. Symons, I think, went wrong was in equating today's series with those of a half century or more ago. As wonderful as Sherlock Holmes is as a creation, he might as well have been on Mars for all that he noticed or commented on the misery in Whitechapel. Poirot could have worked on Venus. So, too, Sexton Blake and Ellery Queen and Nero Wolfe and so many others who appeared in earlier "Golden Ages" of mystery.

The series in which they appeared were written in a social vacuum, as devoid of subtext as a black hole.

No more, guys. For one thing, today's readers demand more. For another, today's writers are more numerous and—dare I say it—better. Holmes is of course *sui generis*. But we all know a half dozen series characters appearing today who are livelier, smarter, and better written than all those others I mentioned. (I caught some hell once for a statement which I've reconsidered but regard still as accurate: If Ellery Queen's first manuscript came over the transom in a publishing house tomorrow, it would be sent back with a form rejection notice. It's just not good enough anymore.)

And today's series characters aren't static. Immutability was the rule in the old days, but that's changed. Series leads today are more realistic. Like actual people, they molt. Spenser passes from yuppie to post-yuppie. With each book, Dan Fortune gets more biting. Remo Williams passes from patriotism, through smartass, to a Zen acceptance of his place in the scheme of things. D. C. Brod's creation, Sharyn McCrumb's . . . they not only change, they

grow, for God's sake . . . and can we accept any less from people with whom we choose to spend our evenings?

So what's this mean to a young writer?

Pons Asinorum. Or, Try It My Way:

It's this easy.

Series are always going to be with us. They always have been. You don't think the writers stopped at First Kings and First Samuel, do you? Unh-uh. Then came Second Kings and Second Samuel. And don't forget blind Homer. When he saw what a hit *The Iliad* was, he had to keep going with *The Odyssey*.

Sometimes we'll have more, sometimes fewer, but always we'll have series.

So, write yourself a good book.

Write it about a character somebody will care about.

Give him something to say.

Then hope for the best, keeping in mind the constantly daunting reality that writers don't create series . . . readers do. If nobody had liked Kinsey Milhone, Sue Grafton could have gone right from *A Is for Alibi* straight to *X Is for Extinct* and no one would have cared.

In my own life I've done series like the Destroyer or Trace, which did pretty well because readers liked the characters, and I've done series like the Seventh Son and Professor Leonardo which both sank below the waters without even leaving an oil slick. I loved them all.

Go figure.

Oh, the Pain:

If you're really lucky, you might just wind up with a book series that goes on so long that you wind up hating your character(s) and wishing them dead.

As Miss Christie once said of Poirot: "They think I love him. If they only knew."

And of course, Conan Doyle tossed the great Sherlock off a waterfall, thus freeing up his time to create his new favorite character: Brigadier Étienne Gerard, who found instant and deserved oblivion.

Not too many years ago Dick Sapir and I decided we were going to kill off Remo and Chiun once and for all. Unfortunately, Dick died first and they got a reprieve.

But hating your characters comes with the territory. It might have something to do with our refusal to have ourselves defined by our relationship with somebody who isn't even, dammit, really alive.

Or maybe it's just that familiarity really *does* breed contempt, and who's more familiar with our creations than we are?

Still, like a beautiful wife, it's a nice problem to have.

Good luck.

Oh, yes. Rabinowitz.

One of the charming by-products of doing a successful series is the flood of books you get from all over. On my bookshelves and in my attic, I have literally hundreds of foreign edition Destroyers, and since I have not languages, I never know what a foreign translator might be doing with them.

I always look at the French editions though. First, the French still do sexy paperback art; second, I like the way the Destroyer translates to *L'Implacable.*

One slid into my hands recently and, puzzled at the title, I asked my wife what it was called.

When laughter ceased to delight the living, she informed me that *Qui Veut la Peau de Rabinowitz?* translates to *Who Wants the Skin of Rabinowitz?* She further informed me that she didn't know if she could ever be worthy of being wife to the author of such an illustrious tome.

You could look it up. It came between my other great French best sellers, *Tovaritch Cow-Boy* and *Azteque Tartare.*

What are these people up to? Don't they know no one—not even a *moyel*—is going to buy a book about Rabinowitz's skin?

Then I looked at the spine of the book. There, in 42-point type, is the number: 67. L'Implacable 67.

And so it goes. You can't ever escape. Man complains but only God ordains.

Some Notable Thrillers

Selected by the Editors

Campbell Armstrong
Agents of Darkness

Tom Clancy
Patriot Games

William DeAndrea
Azrael

Len Deighton
Funeral in Berlin

James Frey
Winter of the Wolves

Bill Granger
The Last Good German

Graham Greene
The Third Man

Thomas Gifford
The Wind Chill Factor

David Hagberg
Without Honor

Adam Hall
The Quiller Memorandum

Somerset Maugham
Ashenden

David Morrell
The Fifth Profession

Warren Murphy and Molly Cochran
The Temple Dogs

Trevanian
The Loo Sanction

YOUNG ADULT
MYSTERIES

WRITING THE YOUNG ADULT MYSTERY NOVEL

Joan Lowery Nixon

HE RULES FOR WRITING young adult mystery novels are not complicated. Any confusion comes from the category itself. What exactly *is* a young adult mystery? Who are young adult readers? Let's begin with a short, multiple-choice mini-quiz that should make the answers crystal clear.

1. *Who reads young adult mysteries?* (a) fifth and sixth graders in elementary school, (b) junior high and middle school students, (c) high school students, (d) teachers and librarians, (e) adults buying books for kids, (f) adults buying books for themselves, (g) avid readers, (h) reluctant readers.

2. *What is the target market for young adult mysteries?* (a) general bookstores, (b) children's bookstores, (c) murder-mystery bookstores, (d) schools, (e) libraries, (f) book fairs, (g) librarians' conventions, (h) booksellers' conventions.

3. *A young adult mystery is most effective when it's written in:* (a) first person, (b) third person, (c) present tense, (d) past tense, (e) single viewpoint.

4. *In order to appeal to readers, the main character in a young adult mystery might be:* (a) an eleven-year-old boy, (b) a sixteen-year-old girl, (c) a married woman in her early twenties, (d) a Scotland Yard inspector, close to retirement, (e) a ghost.

The answer? Easy. All of the above.

The young adult mystery has a wider range of readers than any other type of mystery, and it's offered for sale to these readers through many channels. While stories told in single viewpoint—that of the main characters—are preferred, stories using multiple viewpoint are occasionally published. The person and tense is strictly up to the author, as are the choice of age and sex of the main character in the novel.

Does this mean that readers of young adult mysteries are easy to please? Not at all. They tend to be highly demanding, knowing exactly what it is they want.

Give Them a Story Opening That Will Immediately Hook Their Interest. This means plunging readers directly into the mystery with a paragraph or two of action, intrigue, or suspense. Any necessary background information can be woven in later through short flashbacks or through dialogue. Here's an example, from *The Dark and Deadly Pool* (Dell):

> Moonlight drizzled down the wide glass wall that touched the surface of the hotel swimming pool, dividing it into two parts. The wind-flicked waters of the outer pool glittered with reflected pin-lights from the moon and stars, but the silent water in the indoor section had been sucked into the blackness of the room.
>
> I blinked, trying to adjust my eyes to the darkness, trying to see the edge of the pool that curved near my feet. I pressed my back against the wall and forced myself to breathe evenly. I whispered aloud, "Mary Elizabeth Rafferty, there is nothing to be afraid of here! Nothing!" But even the sound of my own wobbly words terrified me.

A main character's thoughts can open a story with suspense; and in the following example from *Whispers from the Dead* (Dell), there are buzz words—*strange, bizarre, nightmare, shapes,* and *dark*—to which readers immediately respond.

> Because the things that happened to me were so strange, I know that some people will find them hard to believe. It's like when your mind slides from sleeping to waking and something takes place that's so bizarre, you tell yourself, "I have to be dreaming. This couldn't be real." Or when you jolt awake from a nightmare, and

there are still unfamiliar shapes that move through your dark room, and you stare at them with wide-open eyes, knowing they can't exist and you must be awake.

Readers Demand Strong Characterization. Readers need to be able to identify with the main character, entering his or her mind in order to live the story along with the main character.

Characters need to be three-dimensional—real people with personal problems that need solving, with flaws, and with hopes, dreams, and desires. Is the character unhappy in her home life? Is she lonely and wishing she had a friend she could unburden herself to? Does she carry a secret too heavy for one person to have to bear? Is he insecure? Frightened? Trying to live a life his father has planned for him—a life he never choose for himself? Readers can relate. Many of them have been there.

Characters need to be well motivated, consistent in their actions, and sensible about solving the mysteries in which they find themselves. They can make mistakes, choosing the wrong course of action, and they're sensible enough not to inanely rush into a dark tunnel without a flashlight! Modern readers of young adult mysteries are too intelligent to accept stereotyped, one-dimensional sleuths.

I write through my emotions because even though problems differ from one decade to another, from generation to generation, emotions don't change. Fear, happiness, insecurity, excitement, embarrassment—external situations may be different, but the emotions they cause are always the same. Basic needs never vary, and those of us who write for young adults remember vividly our needs and the emotions we felt when we were young adults. Whether tears or smiles, we transfer them to our characters.

Essential for Young Adult Readers Are Strong, Gripping Plots. The plot of a young adult mystery should have two levels: the main character's personal problem, which must be solved, and the mystery, which also must be solved. Suspense is involved in both of these story lines, but it's in the mystery itself that writers can let loose and create scenes so suspenseful that readers must keep reading to find out what happens next.

There are many ways of creating suspense. Description of the setting—if it's important to the story—can be utilized, and the writing should be highly visual, using sensory perception and strong, action verbs. In *The Ghosts of Now* (Dell), an empty house holds an important place in the story, so I gave it a detailed description:

> The Andrews place squats alone at the end of an empty, quiet street. Maybe it's because of the overlarge lot that surrounds it; maybe it's because the house looks like an unkempt, yellowed old man who badly needs a barber, but I feel that the other houses on the block have cringed away from this place, tucking in their tidy porches and neat walkways and dropping filmy curtains over blank eyes. . . .
> Someone once lived in this house and loved it, and for a few moments I feel sad that it should be so neglected, left alone to die.
> But the house is not dead.
> There are small rustlings, creakings, and sounds barely loud enough to be heard as the house moves and breathes with the midday heat. I feel that it's watching me, waiting to see what I'll do. Or could someone be watching, listening, just as I listen?

Ghosts in a story can be horrifying, even if the tone of the story is humorous, such as *The Weekend Was Murder!* (Delacorte). During a murder-mystery weekend at a hotel, a ghost (who plays an important part in the solution of the mystery) confronts main character Liz, who—at first—thinks he's one of the participants in the mystery game:

> "You're not supposed to be in here, you know," I warned him. "And don't expect me to give you any special information, because I won't."
> He picked up the telephone, which seemed to detach itself from its cord, and stared right at me with eyes like dark, hollow tunnels. Even though I was terrified, I couldn't look away. A horrible, cold wind wrapped around me, shaking me violently, then freezing me into an ice cube that couldn't move.
> I knew without a doubt that this man was the ghost! Someone should have warned me that the ghost was not a woman wearing a flowing gown and carrying a candle, but a man in torment. I struggled to scream, but my voice twisted into a hard lump, blocking my throat, so I wasn't able to make a sound; and as the man stood and slowly moved toward me, the tunnels

in his eyes grew into a black, swirling pit. The pit stretched wider and deeper, and I knew I was going to be sucked inside.

His lips moved, and the whisper came, swirling around inside my head: "Don't leave me."

The main character should become so involved in the solution of the mystery that she herself is in danger. In *The Name of the Game Was Murder* (Delacorte), Samantha is suspected of holding the answer to a puzzle that must be solved. Off in a tower bedroom, away from the guests, Sam awakes to find that someone is trying to silently break into her room.

I climbed out of bed and ran barefoot to the door, just in time to catch the key as it tumbled from the lock. Someone had poked it out of the door!

As fast and quietly as I could manage, with my hands shaking so violently they could hardly aim the key, I shoved it back into the keyhole. . . .

Was someone still there? Had he left when the key trick hadn't worked? Or, with all the noise of the thunder and wind, had I just imagined what I thought I'd heard? Maybe no one had been outside my door at all.

I was scared to death, but still so curious I couldn't stand it. I slid out my key and bent down to peer through the empty keyhole. Lightning lit up the sky, and in that sudden white-bright flash, I saw the gleam of an eye looking back at me.

The main character can become aware of some information that is kept from the reader for a while. Although writers must play fair and give readers every single clue, there's no reason why the main character can't tantalize readers by letting them know she's discovered something she's not ready to divulge immediately. In *The Stalker* (Dell), Jennifer, still in shock with news of a murder, questions her grandmother.

"Where is Bobbie? Did they say?"

"Good question. Police don't know where she is. Looks like she up and run away. Nobody on God's earth knows where that girl's gone off to."

Jennifer clutched the (freshly ironed) shirts to her chest, ducking into the smell of starch and scorch so that Grannie couldn't see her face. "I'll start supper," she mumbled, and hurried from the room.

Where was Bobbie? Suddenly, surely, Jennifer knew.

Suspense can build when readers are given hints at other kinds of secrets that are up to them to uncover; suspicion can be thrown on someone whom the main character has trusted; the story can take a sudden unexpected turn, making good use of the element of surprise; and a peculiar character can add suspense whenever he or she appears.

Old, established tricks can still be used when given new settings and situations. The "time is running out" technique always creates tension, and so does the technique of allowing readers—but not the main character—to realize that someone is silently climbing the stairs or standing outside in the dark, studying the house.

Chapter endings should be so intriguing or suspenseful that they lead readers from one chapter into the next, nonstop. From *The Other Side of Dark* (Dell):

If I shot Jarrod, wouldn't it be self-defense? And wouldn't it end the trials and the questions and the badgering and the harassment and the nightmares and the worries and the years and years of fear?

Carefully I aim the gun.

Suspense can't be maintained on a steady, high level. The story must build and peak, drop, then build again, and in the valleys that ensue, readers can catch their breath, relax, and learn more about the relationships between the main character and the other characters in the novel. The valleys are needed for the main character's moments of introspection and for her attempts to deal with the personal, non-mystery problem she's trying to solve.

Titles are extremely important. The title and the jacket art offer the first impression of the novel. The author has no control over the art, but should do a first-rate job in developing a title that reaches out to grab readers' attention and gives a hint of the mystery story itself. *The Dark and Deadly Pool, The Seance, Whispers From the Dead, A Deadly Game of Magic* . . . each of these titles leads into its story and leaves no doubt that the reader is in for some hours of suspenseful, scary reading.

It's a great feeling when readers write, "I couldn't put your book down, even when I got into trouble in school!" or "I read your new mystery, and I've never been so scared in my life. I can't wait to read the next one," or "I've read everything you've ever written. When is your next mystery going to be published?" and this very special letter: "Mysteries are the only way to go. Thank you for the gift of reading."

MUCH ADO ABOUT NANCY DREW

Christina Mierau

FOR THE NOSTALGIC MYSTERY FAN, it was an opportunity not to be missed: a chance to reminisce about missing wills, hidden stairways, shifty-eyed scoundrels, and stouthearted chums. Those who attended ranged in age from nine to ninety. Fifteen percent were men. There were doctors, writers, scholars, and schoolchildren—a farmer, a plumber, a stockbroker, and a diplomat.

Nearly four hundred in all gathered in Iowa City on a weekend in April 1993 to attend the Nancy Drew Conference, sponsored by the University of Iowa School of Journalism and Mass Communication. Carolyn Stewart Dyer, associate director of the school and director of the Nancy Drew Project, was amazed by the interest the conference generated. "We were inundated with phone calls," she reports. "It made for a much richer and diverse program than we had initially imagined."

Professor Dyer described the conference's goals in her opening remarks. "Our main objectives are to explore the phenomenon of Nancy Drew—its impact on people and their lifelong reading habits—and to focus public attention on the role of Mildred Wirt Benson in creating Nancy Drew."

Native Iowan Mildred Wirt Benson was being officially inducted into the School of Journalism's Hall of Fame. In 1927 Benson was the first woman to earn a master's degree in journalism from the university. She is also the writer who, under the pseudonym Carolyn Keene, breathed life into a character named Nancy Drew, one of fiction's most beloved heroines. For fifty years this accomplishment went unacknowledged because Benson was prohibited from claiming the work as her own due to contractual agreements with the Stratemeyer Syndicate.

For many lifelong fans of Carolyn Keene, their first glimpse of the original writer behind the pseudonym came when she was named ABC's Person of the Week on the opening night of the conference. As scholars prepared to discuss Nancy Drew as a social, cultural, and psychological phenomenon, Mrs. Benson put things in perspective with refreshing midwestern candor. "I didn't analyze things," she said. "I just sat down at my typewriter and put a piece of paper in there and let 'er roll."

The impact of the Nancy Drew stories on three generations of readers belies Mrs. Benson's casual attitude about the significance of her work. Nearly every person attending the conference had a story about Nancy Drew's influence on his or her life. Prominent mystery writers Nancy Pickard and Linda Barnes shared with their audience how reading Nancy Drew as young girls influenced their reading and writing and the way they thought about what *girls* could accomplish. Carol Gorman, an Iowa writer, recalls ". . . wanting to be Nancy—or at least be her best friend. She taught me about courage and persistence and determination. They were the lessons of a lifetime."

In the conference's keynote speech, feminist scholar Carolyn G. Heilbrun, who as Amanda Cross writes the Kate Fansler mysteries, described Nancy Drew as "a moment in feminist history." That theme—Nancy Drew as a positive role model for girls and women—would be scrutinized in several discussions ranging from the scholarly "Nancy Drew in the 1990's: A Feminist Update," to the more lighthearted "Nancy and Ned—Can This Relationship Be Saved?"

The conference schedule offered something for everyone. For younger fans, Nancy Drew films of the late 1930s and early 40s were shown throughout the weekend in the university's Bijou Theater. A Nancy Drew Write-a-Mystery program was offered for young authors, along with sessions playing Nancy Drew board games and solving puzzles and quizzes.

The conference also served as a showcase for four Iowa schoolchildren who won top honors in a statewide writing contest conducted by the School of Journalism. Eleven-year-old Rachel Lyle, a sixth-grader from Cedar Falls, in her winning essay,

"Nancy Drew—the All-American Girl," describes ". . . being chided repeatedly at the dinner table to '*put the book down*,' right when Nancy hears a piercing scream." Fans of all ages could identify with that!

"Nancy Drew and the Collector" featured David Farah, compiler of *Farah's Guide*, a must-have handbook for anyone interested in collecting Nancy Drew books and memorabilia. A group of sixty collectors crammed into the Indiana Room to hear Farah discuss some of the finer points of locating, grading, and pricing Nancy Drew books.

Farah, whose personal collection includes 250 pre–World War II volumes, said that pricing Nancy Drews is an uncertain process. It all depends on who's buying and who's selling. "A volume selling at auction for one hundred twenty-five dollars one day," he said, "might very well turn up at a garage sale the next afternoon for fifty cents."

Which Nancy Drew book is the most valuable? A first edition of one of the first three titles, in mint condition, and with its dust jacket, Farah estimated, would be worth "somewhere between one and two thousand dollars . . . maybe more." The veteran collector was reluctant to name an exact figure since such a volume has never been offered for public sale. Where one of the valuable books might eventually turn up is a mystery worthy of Nancy Drew herself.

Representing a departure from the general nostalgia of the conference were Anne Greenberg, an executive editor at Simon & Schuster, and Ellen Steiber, who currently ghostwrites Nancy Drew books. Their presentation, "The New Nancy Drew Series," offered a revealing, behind-the-scenes look at the writing and editing of a juvenile mystery series by tracing the evolution of a book from story idea to printed volume. Of great interest to young writers was Greenberg's explanation of how an editor evaluates a potential manuscript for the series.

Greenberg also discussed how the books have been updated to meet the interests of today's readers. "Nancy Drew," said Greenberg, "needed hormones."

In another session, librarians, teachers, and readers debated the controversial issue "Is Series Reading Bad for Kids?" Led by library media specialist Joel Shoemaker, the discussion centered around the decades-long controversy about the suitability of mass-produced fiction for schoolage children.

Esther Bierbaum of the university's School of Library and Information Science illustrated the prejudices of earlier librarians against series fiction for children by telling how they kept serialized volumes on the shelves to satisfy reader demand, yet didn't list them in the library's card catalogue.

In recent years, reported Bierbaum, popular opinion seems to have shifted. Librarians and teachers now generally agree that any kind of reading is preferable to a child's not reading at all. As Charlotte S. Huck points out in *Children's Literature in the Elementary School,* published in 1976, "Slightly older children usually become the mystery buffs who delight in reading one Nancy Drew book after the other....Obviously, they must be doing something right!"

Will the Real Carolyn Keene ...
A Profile of Mildred Wirt Benson

Millions of mystery fans know her only as Carolyn Keene, the writer who provided them with countless hours of adventurous sleuthing with Nancy Drew. In truth, however, it was Mildred Augustine Wirt Benson who engendered in three generations of readers not only a love of mysteries, but a love of reading. This, perhaps, is the writer's greatest achievement.

She was born Mildred Augustine on July 10, 1905, in Ladora, Iowa. In her essay, "The Ghost of Ladora," (1973) she speculates that her style as a writer of children's books most likely evolved from her own childhood reading of the action-packed stories in *St. Nicholas Magazine.* It was in the same publication in which Benson would first see her name in print as a writer—she was twelve years old.

A 1925 graduate of the University of Iowa, Benson secured her first job as a cub reporter on the *Clinton Herald.* A year later a newspaper advertisement offering the opportunity to write children's books led her to New York City, where she would meet a man who would dramatically alter her life.

Edward Stratemeyer headed a publishing syndicate that produced numerous popular juvenile series of the day. Impressed by samples of Benson's work, he hired her to salvage his Ruth Fielding series which was declining in popularity. Like the other freelance ghostwriters in Stratemeyer's employ, Benson was provided a title and brief synopsis from

which she would develop a plot and characters. For each completed manuscript—after relinquishing all claims to her work and future royalties—she would be paid a flat fee, usually around $125.

Benson's clear narrative style and quick pace proved to be the antidote the series needed. Within three years, during which Benson says she was "brain-deep in graduate work at the University of Iowa," she had become the syndicate's most promising "ghost."

Benson was, therefore, the logical choice to launch a new series Stratemeyer had in mind: mystery stories for girls that would serve as a counterpart to the popular Hardy Boys. The heroine would be a sixteen-year-old amateur detective named Nancy Drew.

Once again Benson was provided a title, *The Secret of the Old Clock*, a new pseudonym, Carolyn Keene, and the standard one-page outline from which to work.

"Certain hackneyed names and situations could not be ignored," writes Benson, so she dutifully wrote them into the plot and turned her attention instead to Nancy.

"I wanted her to be a more modern girl," Benson recalls. "A departure from the stay-at-home type portrayed in the girls' series of the day." Benson's Nancy was feisty, fearless, strong-willed, loyal, trustworthy, and smart. Her adventures set a new tone for girls who were more accustomed to what Benson calls "namby-pamby type of books."

While Stratemeyer was disappointed with Benson's characterization of Nancy Drew—calling the teenager "flip" and "bossy"—the publishers, Grosset and Dunlap, were delighted with the new character and quickly ordered two more volumes. Benson set to work immediately on *The Hidden Staircase* and *The Bungalow Mystery.* The three volumes would be released in 1930 as a set.

Edward Stratemeyer died suddenly on May 10, 1930, shortly following the debut of Nancy Drew and was succeeded at the helm of the syndicate by his daughters, Harriet and Edna. Mildred Benson completed three more Nancy Drew volumes while continuing to write the Ruth Fielding books and several of the syndicate's other moneymakers.

A dispute with the Stratemeyer sisters, who wanted to cut Benson's compensation to $75 per book, resulted in the eighth, ninth, and tenth volumes of the series being written by another ghost,

Walter Karig. The brief leave of absence afforded Benson the opportunity to write books under her own name, Mildred A. Wirt.

Benson resumed writing for the Stratemeyers in 1934. In all, she would pen twenty-three Nancy Drew titles, her final one being *The Clue of the Velvet Mask* in 1953. As Carolyn Keene, Benson also wrote the first dozen books in another popular Stratemeyer mystery series, the Dana Girls.

While Benson's books for the syndicate are undoubtedly her most widely read work, fans say the seventeen Penny Parker mystery stories that she wrote between 1939 and 1947 under her own name are her best.

Mildred Wirt Benson's career as a writer of juvenile fiction spanned thirty-two years and produced a body of work in excess of 120 complete novels for young readers.

Her life outside the professional sphere was no less fruitful. Returning to journalism in 1944 as a reporter for the *Toledo Times*, Benson managed to balance two busy careers, marriage (to Asa Wirt of the Associated Press in 1927) and motherhood (daughter Margaret was born in 1936), long before such a juggling act was considered fashionable. Widowed in 1947, she was remarried three years later to George A. Benson, editor of the *Toledo Times*.

Mrs. Benson developed some adventurous avocations as well. An avid interest in pre-Columbian archaeology would lead her on nine expeditions to the Mayan ruins of Central America. And, Benson wrote in 1973, "At an age when wiser persons welcome Social Security, this misguided author took up flying." She earned private, commercial, and seaplane pilot licenses, and continued flying until last year, when she decided to give her wings a rest.

Mildred Benson continues to work as a full-time journalist. Not surprisingly, her "On the Go" column for the *Toledo Blade* profiles seniors involved in interesting adventures. "Kind of an older person's Nancy Drew," quips Benson.

The writer hesitates to theorize about the long-lived popularity of her most beloved character, Nancy Drew. "Analysis is not one of my accomplishments," she says. "However, it seems to me that Nancy was popular, and remains so, primarily because she . . . enjoyed great personal freedom . . . and was far smarter than the adults with whom she associated. Leisure time was spent living dangerously."

It was a combination guaranteed to turn books into best sellers and millions of young readers into devoted mystery fans.

The Clue in the Old Reference Book

Those at the conference who attended Geoffrey S. Lapin's session, "Mildred Wirt Benson, Nancy Drew, and Girls' Adventures," were treated to an imformative, eye-opening presentation of how Lapin "solved the mystery of Carolyn Keene."

Lapin, a cellist with the Indianapolis Symphony Orchestra and adjunct professor of music at Purdue, outlined the paper trail he doggedly followed that led him to Mildred Wirt Benson and identified her as the original writer behind the pseudonym.

As a teenager during the summer of 1963, Lapin served as a volunteer at the Atlantic City Public Library. While browsing through the card catalogue, he came across a reference to Carolyn Keene, author of the Nancy Drew mysteries, of which he was a fan. What puzzled him was the lack of information provided about Keene. Ordinarily, the catalogue card would list an author's true identity along with any pseudonym, but, in this case, none was given. Over the next few years Lapin continued his efforts to identify Carolyn Keene—making inquiries at libraries and checking reference books—all with no success.

His first substantial clue was a penciled notation in the margin of an outdated volume of the Cumulative Book Index. Next to a list of Carolyn Keene's books, someone had written "see Wirt, Mildred A." and cited another reference "Howe's *American Women 1939–1940*."

Checking there, Lapin discovered an extensive list of Mildred Wirt's publishing credits written under a variety of pseudonyms. He set about unearthing as many of the titles as he could.

"As I read Wirt's books," Lapin told his listeners, "I immediately detected a rhythm, a flow—the distinctly readable style of Carolyn Keene." It convinced him that Mildred A. Wirt and the author of the original Nancy Drew were one and the same person.

For years it had been widely accepted that Harriet S. Adams, Stratemeyer's daughter, was the sole author of the Nancy Drew books and had been since her father's death in 1930. This "myth," as Lapin calls it, was steadily perpetuated in the Stratemeyer Syndicate's press releases and publicity campaigns.

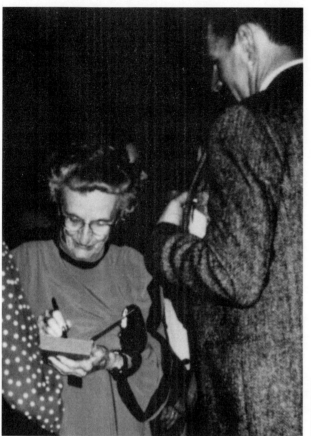

Christina Mierau

Mildred Wirt Benson autographing a book for a fan at the conference in Iowa City. Geoffrey S. Lapin is on the right.

Knowing what he did about Benson, he wondered how the syndicate could continue to justify its version of the truth.

In 1969 Lapin requested and was granted an interview with Mildred Wirt Benson. Although she was well aware of the public misconception about the origins of Nancy Drew, Benson had always abided by the legal releases she'd signed for the syndicate and kept silent. It was a contract she would continue to honor.

A 1980 court battle, Grosset & Dunlap v. Gulf & Western, would see Mildred Wirt Benson revealed as the original Carolyn Keene through testimony and documents, some of which Lapin was able to display to his fascinated audience at the Nancy Drew Conference. Still, despite evidence to the contrary, the myth about the book's authorship persisted, says Lapin.

In a 1986 *Publishers Weekly* article, "Nancy Drew: Then and Now," May 30, author Deborah

Felder wrote: "(Harriet) Adams ran the company in much the same way as her father. She wrote the plot outlines as well as some of the manuscripts, when time permitted. . . . But Nancy Drew was all hers."

In a letter to the editor of *Publishers Weekly* published in the September 26 issue that same year, Mildred Wirt Benson herself set the record straight:

Years ago when I tapped out the opening lines of the first Nancy Drew mystery ever written, I never dreamed I would spend most of my life defending authorship.

Edward Stratemeyer, although an author, did not write the first three volumes of the Nancy Drew series. Nor did Harriet Adams pen *Mystery at Lilac Inn* or any of the early stories that launched Nancy as a best seller. Stratemeyer originated the basic idea, provided titles, pen names, and a one-page plot. I turned out 50,000-word volumes that became instant best sellers. In 1930, without writing experience, Adams took over the business. But at the request of the publisher, I was kept on for many years as the sole writer of the Nancy Drews. . . .

Does authorship really matter? Probably not, but loyal Nancy fans, especially the earliest readers, deserve true information rather than slanted or incorrect publicity statements.

Lapin expressed hope that the recognition of Mildred Wirt Benson at the conference in Iowa City would finally put the authorship controversy to rest.

"It's the end to a long chapter," said Lapin, "It should have happened a long time ago."

The final chapter of every Nancy Drew adventure features a familiar aura of contentment. All swindlers, impostors, and ne'er-do-wells, having duly confessed their nefarious deeds to a triumphant Nancy, are carted off to jail. Any missing, stolen, or cleverly concealed heirlooms have been recovered, restored, and returned to their rightful owners. And loved ones, long separated by the fates or some form of underhanded collusion, are reunited—all thanks to Nancy's bravery and skillful detecting.

And so it was as the Nancy Drew Conference ended. Having witnessed firsthand the public acknowledgment of Mildred Wirt Benson's role in the creation of Nancy Drew, the participants headed home with the distinctly satisfied feeling that things were, at last, as they should be.

YOUNG ADULT MYSTERIES
A Few "Must-Read" Winners
Sharron L. McElmeel

THE STANDARD ELEMENTS in a young adult mystery novel include an interesting setting, characters readers care about, a personal problem for the main character, and a compelling mystery—all tied together with good writing that brings together the solution to the personal problem with the solution to the mystery. The trend these days is toward stronger (and more intelligent-acting) female protagonists and less cozy pivotal incidents. Murders are commonplace in many mysteries and the action is becoming more and more chilling. Mysteries for the younger reader were traditionally built around such incidents as lost lunch money, a stolen bike, and mysterious happenings—cozy events that provided a mystery but not a lot of heart-pounding suspense. Even the mysterious happenings were later explained away by natural events. But times have changed. Mysteries that once included "cozy" incidents are now laced with murders, drugs, and real villains. Young adult protago-

nists were once pitted most often against those of their own age; now they often find themselves confronting seasoned adult criminals. Themes once handled in a murderless mystery now often include a dead body or two. In 1954 Viking published Keith Robertson's *Three Stuffed Owls,* a page-turning mystery that resulted in two young boys discovering a jewel-smuggling operation. Thirty-six years later a smuggling theme is at the center of *The Dead Man in Indian Creek* by Mary Downing Hahn (Clarion, 1990). However, this time the smuggling involves cocaine and the book opens with twelve-year-old Matt and his best friend, Parker, discovering a body in Indian Creek. Hahn has moved with the changing society and has mirrored values and issues in the contemporary scene. Murders seem to be more commonplace in everyday life and certainly anyone who thinks of smuggling is more likely to think in terms of drugs than in jewels.

Young adult detective novels focus on the activities of the young adult in solving the crime. Adult police and detectives are tolerated as support personnel, but it is the young adult protagonist that is responsible for uncovering the important clues and weaving them together to uncover the villain. Carol Gorman's suspenseful detective tale in *Chelsey and the Green-Haired Kid* (Houghton, 1987; Pocket, 1992) has a wheelchair-bound seventh grader and Jack "the Green-Haired Kid" working together to uncover the truth about the boy who "fell" from the bleachers—in view of both Chelsey and Jack and the reading audience. The police feel the fall is an accident but Chelsey and Jack know better and they set out to prove it. Information Jack and Chelsey uncover pinpoints the murderers and the motive and puts both of their lives in jeopardy. Less than ten years earlier, in *Grave Doubts* by Scott Corbett (Atlantic/Little, Brown, 1982), sixteen-year-old Lester Cunningham and Wally Brenner teamed up in an attempt to solve the mysterious death of

Otis Canby, who died suddenly *just* as he is about to change his will. As in Gorman's title, the authorities do not think the death is murder but the young protagonists are determined that there is more to the death than natural causes or an unfortunate accident. Corbett's book features two male protagonists while Gorman's brings in a female character in an equal role. Greed for an inheritance precipitates the murder in Corbett's book, while efforts to keep information about high-stakes drug trafficking from leaking out brings about the murder in Gorman's books.

Personal problems are woven through the weft of the mystery novel. Carol Gorman's *Die for Me* (Avon, 1992) involves jealousy and the poor treatment of a classmate—treatment that goes back to second grade. Gorman's *Graveyard Moon* (Avon, 1993) deals with a teenage burglary ring and murders that are thought to be necessary in order to keep the burglaries from coming to the attention of the authorities. One of the characters, Miles, is an outcast among his peers and has a complicated home life, where he must deal with his father's alcoholism. Since the reader of this story knows the identity of the murderer long before the characters in the story do, suspense is built by placing the main character in situations where she is vulnerable.

Authors of mystery novels, as with mainstream novels, find themselves mirroring the changing society and drawing more and more on events that are occurring around them. In April 1990, when Alane Ferguson accepted the Edgar Allan Poe Award from the Mystery Writers of America for her 1989 title *Show Me the Evidence* (Avon) she did so in the name of her very best friend, Savannah, who had been brutally raped and murdered several years before. Her friend's murder and the subsequent investigation indelibly marked Ferguson's mystery writing for young adults. Through the experiences surrounding her friend's murder, Ferguson said that she "became both fascinated and repelled by the law. I had to testify at Savannah's murderer's trial and I remember staring at the hands of her killer, which at the time were folded harmlessly in his lap, and thinking how bizarrely civilized we'd all become . . . all of my mystery books have their genesis in the loss of my friend." The shadows of Ferguson's memories of that experience show up in *Overkill* (Bradbury, 1992). Lacey, a very smart, underachieving teenage girl, is the chief protagonist.

When Lacey has a dream that closely matches the murder of a friend, the police encourage her to reveal every detail of the nightmare to them, telling her that she may be psychic and that her dream could be the only chance they have to unmask the killer. Then she finds herself the prime suspect in the murder.

Ferguson's award-winning mystery, *Show Me the Evidence* (Avon, 1989), is a gripping and well-written tale of two seventeen-year-olds caught in the middle of the investigation into the deaths of three young children. The infants are first thought to have died of SIDS, but later, when the police link Janaan with all three babies' deaths, the authorities attempt to exhume the bodies and find the graves empty. Lauren, Janaan's friend, and Janaan prove themselves smarter than the police in a tightly drawn whodunit that touches on the exotic when the girls unravel the mystery and identify the culprit. The children had been drugged into a zombie state and retrieved only to be sold on the black market to unsuspecting couples. A chilling plot that came as Ferguson "watched Geraldo Rivera report a segment on zombies on *20/20*. [This was before Geraldo became *Geraldo!*] Four people had died and been buried in a tiny Haitian village, only to reappear years later among the living." Geraldo revealed that a poison extracted from Haiti's native puffer fish could cause the same "death sleep" Juliet experienced in Shakespeare's famous play. Ferguson almost abandoned the whole idea of the plot when she found out that virtually all SIDS babies in America are autopsied and then embalmed. But her plot was made plausible when she discovered that some religious denominations bury their dead by sundown.

Lois Duncan is a perennial favorite among young adult readers. Her novels *Summer of Fear* (Little, Brown, 1976), *Stranger with My Face* (Little, Brown, 1981), *Locked in Time* (Little, Brown, 1985), and *The Third Eye* (Little, Brown, 1984) continue her list of suspense novels. Duncan's books are dubbed "psychological thrillers." But the most chilling element of her novels came in the form of *Don't Look Behind You* (Dell, 1989). The heroine, April, was based on Duncan's eighteen-year-old daughter, Kait, who was murdered one month after the book's release. Many facts uncovered as part of the murder investigation coincided with bits and pieces previously written in some of

Duncan's novels. Both Kait and April were chased down by a hit man in a Camero. Mike Gallagher, a real-life investigative reporter, shared his name with a boyfriend of the heroine in *Summer of Fear*. All of the eerie coincidences were detailed in Duncan's *Who Killed My Daughter?* (Delacorte, 1992)—a book that became the ultimate mystery novel based on the real-life mystery surrounding the author's daughter's death. Duncan has not written another young adult mystery since the murder of her daughter.

Joan Lowery Nixon, a long-time standout in the field of mystery writing for young adults, often uses the technique of pushing a young adult into a sudden crisis that leads directly into involvement in a murder. In *The Dark and Deadly Pool* (Delacorte, 1987) Nixon's female protagonist discovers a body floating in the pool. Nixon's *The Séance* (Harcourt, 1980) is set in a small Texas town, in piney woods country, where a séance starts a chain of events that result in murder. *The Other Side of Dark* (Delacorte, 1986) grew from a newspaper item Nixon read about a young man in West Texas who after several years in a semicomatose state suddenly came out of it. Nixon used this incident to create a protagonist who awakens and finds herself four years older and the only witness to an unsolved murder. The discovery of a disfigured body of a classmate plays an important role in *Incident at Loring Groves* by Sonia Levitin (Dial, 1988). Bright and attractive, Ken and Cassidy fear that their involvement in the discovering may implicate them in the murder and unravel their thus far perfect world.

While murders do seem more prevalent, other events also provide the pivot for creating a novel filled with suspense. Writers often incorporate problems of society into their writing. *The Kidnapping of Christina Lattimore* (Harcourt, 1979) by Joan Lowery Nixon features a teenage heiress who is accused of masterminding her own kidnapping, and Norman Fox Mazer plays on the problem of parent kidnapping in her novel *Taking Terri Mueller* (Avon, 1981; Morrow, 1983). Thirteen-year-old Terri discovers evidence that shows her mother is still alive and that she had been kidnapped by her father. And the accidental uncovering of evidence also plays a major role in Cynthia Voigt's suspense novel *The Callendar Papers* (Atheneum, 1983) when Jean uncovers that the death of a man's wife was surrounded by mystery and that her own life is somehow part of the baffling events. Phyllis Reynolds Naylor used both suspicion and kidnapping as elements in the plot for *Night Cry* (Atheneum, 1984). When a child is kidnapped and held for ransom, Ellen fears that her often absent father is the culprit.

Another element that is frequently used in mystery/suspense novels for young readers are ghosts—an element used by Pam Conrad when she created *Stonewords: A Ghost Story* (Harper, 1990). Left by her mother to live with her grandparents, Zoe finds herself longing for her mother to return. It isn't long before Zoe finds a playmate—Zoe Louise. Years before, something dreadful happened to Zoe Louise and Zoe feels that she must discover what has caused her friend's death *before* it happens. The unexplained death of Zoe Louise, in her earlier life, provides the focal element often provided by a murder.

Today's young adult demands that the mystery include a crime—a significant crime. Often that crime is a murder or the threat of murder lurking in the background. Other crimes that are included in mysteries include high-stakes drug trafficking, kidnapping, or a mysterious family secret that threatens the well-being of the family or community. While the characters in the well-written mystery must be someone readers will care about, the clues and the puzzle are the significant elements of the novel. Readers care more about the plot's puzzle, which must be a complicated weaving of suspicion, clues, motives, and red herrings. The puzzle must be center stage at all times. Bits of background information must be woven throughout the novel as the story progresses. The first choice of most young adult readers are those novels that immediately grab their attention and keep it until the end of the book. Good mysteries do this from the very beginning to the very end.

SHORT
STORIES

INTRODUCTION

Jon L. Breen

THOUGH THE NOVEL has been the dominant length for mystery and detective fiction for many years, the genre was first developed and brought to major success in the short story form, beginning with Edgar Allan Poe's three Dupin tales, ''The Murders in the Rue Morgue,'' ''The Mystery of Marie Roget,'' and ''The Purloined Letter.'' While Sherlock Holmes was introduced at novella length in *A Study in Scarlet* (1887), it was with the series of short stories that would comprise *The Adventures of Sherlock Holmes* that Arthur Conan Doyle achieved a major mystery-writing splash. Throughout the rest of Holmes's career, short cases (fifty-six of them) dominated, while novel-length appearances totaled only four. Many of the best-known series sleuths to follow in the wake of Holmes appeared only in short stories—G. K. Chesterton's Father Brown, Arthur Morrison's Martin Hewitt, Melville Davisson Post's Uncle Abner—or primarily at that length—R. Austin Freeman's Dr. Thorndyke, Arthur B. Reeve's Craig Kennedy, Jacques Futrelle's The Thinking Machine.

The reason for the short story's one-time ascendancy and recently lessened role is largely economic. Because professional writers by definition write for money, the market determines what gets written. Late in the nineteenth century and in the early part of the present century, book publication was a prestige luxury while periodical publication put food on the authorial table. Among the best-known sleuths from the Golden Age of Detection, all best-known now for the novels in which they appeared, several had extensive short story careers as well, among them Dorothy L. Sayers's Lord Peter Wimsey, Agatha Christie's Hercule Poirot and Miss Marple, Margery Allingham's Albert Campion, Stuart Palmer's Hildegarde Withers, and Ellery Queen's Ellery Queen.

While the slick magazines paid the big money, the less pretentious pulps also provided a lucrative market for prolific mystery writers. Dashiell Hammett's Continental Op appeared in *Black Mask* stories before being immortalized between hard covers, while the same writer's Sam Spade cashed in on slick money in a series of short stories after becoming famous in the novel *The Maltese Falcon*.

The slicks continued to pay well for fiction through the forties and fifties, though television began to cut into the magazine fiction market: sitcoms and continuing dramas on the small screen appropriated the cultural role of long-running magazine series, and slicks came to emphasize abridged or serialized novels rather than short stories. Some of the biggest markets for slick mystery fiction—*American* and *Collier's*—folded in the mid-fifties. Even today, slicks like *Playboy* and *Redbook* pay big money for short fiction, but the market has shrunk.

As for the pulps, they died out in the forties and early fifties, the victim first of paper shortages and then of that familiar villain, TV. Their place as a beginning popular fiction market was taken over by paperback originals, inevitably a market for novels rather than short stories, and by the digest-size fiction magazines that flourished in the fifties.

Today, only two of those digests remain. The greatest of them, *Ellery Queen's Mystery Magazine*, began in 1941 under the editorship of Frederic Dannay (half of the Ellery Queen writing team). The magazine began as an all-reprint publication, but as the years went by it evolved to the almost-all-original magazine it is today. Dannay, who continued at the helm until his death in 1982, was probably the greatest short-fiction editor the genre has ever known, and his efforts at the helm of the magazine and in editing the long series of EQ anthologies were crucial in keeping the short form alive through the period. His achievement came in three categories: 1) getting top-name mystery writers, including those concentrating on novel length, to write short fiction; 2) discovering works of crime and mystery fiction by literary figures famed outside the genre; and 3) publishing the first stories of new writers. This last category was perhaps the most important. A very abbreviated list of writers who debuted with

EQMM short stories includes James Yaffe (who debuted in 1943 at age fifteen!), Harry Kemelman, Robert L. Fish, Jack Finney, Lillian de la Torre, Thomas Flanagan, Joyce Harrington, David Morrell, James Powell, Francis M. Nevins, Jr., R. R. (Robert) Irvine, and Stanley Ellin. Dannay's policies were continued by his successors, the late Eleanor Sullivan and the magazine's current editor, Janet Hutchings.

The other surviving mystery digest is *Alfred Hitchcock Mystery Magazine,* which began in 1955. It specialized from the first in the ironic, twist-in-the-tail shorts that could be adapted to the Hitchcock TV series of the same period. The famous director, of course, never had anything to do with the selection of stories or with the droll introductions ostensibly coming from him. The magazine's first editor was William Manners, while the longest-running and most influential were Ernest Hutter, Eleanor Sullivan, and the current editor, Cathleen Jordan. Writers like Henry Slesar, Lawrence Treat, James Holding, and Talmage Powell were long-time *AHMM* specialists.

Another important magazine market of the fifties was *Manhunt,* which specialized in tough, uncompromising crime fiction without the content taboos that existed in other markets. Beginning with a splash thanks to a Mickey Spillane serial, the magazine drew contributions from major mystery writers like Craig Rice, Ross Macdonald, and Raymond Chandler; writers with mainstream credentials like James M. Cain, Erskine Caldwell, and James T. Farrell; and a whole stable of developing short-story specialists: Jack Ritchie, Robert Turner, Bryce Walton, and others.

Though *EQMM* and *AHMM* remain as ready markets especially encouraging to new writers, the short story form has for years been subject to premature burial. Periodic efforts to start a third successful professional market, most recently the long-delayed but persistent *New Mystery,* have usually failed. Semipro magazines, designed to provide a beginner's market and sometimes to counter the perceived taboos of the regular markets, have come and gone, beginning with Michael L. Cook's *Skullduggery* (1980–81) and continuing with Wayne D. Dundee's *Hardboiled* and Gary Lovisi's *Detective Story Magazine,* the latter two currently combined as *Hardboiled Detective* under Lovisi's editorship.

But the main development in short mystery fiction in the eighties and nineties has undoubtedly been the rise of the original anthology. Though the original anthology has a long and distinguished history in the science fiction field, it was a rare bird in the mystery genre until the eighties. The existence of the original anthologies, many of them edited by Martin H. Greenberg either alone or with one or more collaborators, has insured (along with the efforts of the *EQMM* editors) that most well-known novelists in the mystery field write at least an occasional short story. Ironically, as the magazine market has shrunk, there are more anthologies being published than ever before, including several series of original collections (*Sisters in Crime,* the Canadian *Cold Blood,* the British *New Mystery, Cat Crimes, Malice Domestic,* and the Private Eye Writers of America anthologies), frequent reprint volumes (the annual Mystery Writers of America anthologies and the various compilations from the back files of *EQMM* and *AHMM*), and at least two best-of-the-year volumes: Edward D. Hoch's venerable *Year's Best Mystery and Suspense Stories* (Walker) and *Mystery Scene* magazine's *Year's 25 Finest Crime and Mystery Stories* (Carroll & Graf).

While the magazines—and only rarely the original anthologies—constitute a break-in market for new writers, the short story form often allows established writers to explore new areas. Some prominent series characters at novel length were originally characters in short stories, including Margaret Maron's Deborah Knott, Linda Barnes's Carlotta Carlyle, Maxine O'Callaghan's Delilah West, George C. Chesbro's Mongo Frederickson, and Wayne D. Dundee's Joe Hannibal. The last may be the most prominent character to emerge from the semipro mystery fiction magazines that have come and gone in the last twenty years.

Some of the best novelists in the mystery genre—Ruth Rendell, Robert Barnard, John Lutz, Celia Fremlin—regularly contribute in the shorter form. And a few notable writers still specialize in short lengths, though it is a truism that you can't make a living writing short stories. (The very prolific Edward D. Hoch, who keeps the tale of pure detection alive in his monthly contributions to *EQMM,* is invariably cited as the exception that proves the rule.) Among the writers who do outstanding work in the short form—and should be better known than they are—are Doug Allyn, William Bankier, Brendan Du Bois, Donald Olson, Stephen Wasylyk, and Barbara Owens.

ELLERY QUEEN'S MYSTERY MAGAZINE

Janet Hutchings

FOR FIVE DECADES, *Ellery Queen's Mystery Magazine* has played an important role worldwide in ensuring that the crime short story continues to flourish. It is not surprising, then, that we are so often asked where we are headed in the nineties. When Frederic Dannay launched the magazine in 1941, it was with an explicit manifesto: to "raise the sights of mystery writers generally to a genuine literary form," to "encourage good writing among our colleagues by offering a practical market not otherwise available," and to "develop new writers seeking expression in the genre."

The first of his goals is the most provocative for us now. Have the sights of mystery writers been raised to these heights in the intervening half century, or should *EQMM*'s editors continue to concentrate on this part of the manifesto? To some, the question may no longer seem valid, for certainly the crime genre has achieved a kind of respectability over the past couple of decades: courses in crime fiction have appeared on university syllabuses, Ph.D.'s may be taken on the works of the great writers in the field, readership has blossomed among the best educated and the most affluent. But while all of this was going on, the literary ambiance surrounding the mystery was changing.

In the forties, the task before those who wished to see the genre separate itself from hack writing and emerge as a genuine literary form was to encourage writers to produce the type of story in which enduring truths about the human condition could be expressed. The literary respectability the mystery now enjoys is not entirely the result of a larger number of mystery writers having reached that goal, although a great many writers now attempt more than the creation of a clever puzzle or suspense plot. Equally important to the mystery's acceptance in literary circles is a shift that has taken place in our society's thinking about literature. The distinction that was almost universally accepted in the forties between fiction intended purely for entertainment and fiction that also merits reading as literature has broken down. This cultural change has created greater acceptance for all genre fiction and, together with the boom in mystery readership that began in the seventies, has helped sustain the mystery by attracting many fine writers to the field. As a result, the overall standard of writing is high. But do we see more stories of depth and insight today; more writers in the field who not only write beautiful prose but have the moral and intellectual reach of the great writers Dannay published such as Stanley Ellin? In the short story arena, too few names come to mind. Despite the trend toward more realistic themes, the ability to distill from the sometime gritty reality depicted something significant about human relationships or society is relatively rare. As long as it remains so, *EQMM* will have an important role to play in encouraging serious writers to find expression in our genre.

At the same time, we believe that the crime writer's first obligation is to tell a satisfying story of crime or suspense. Many recent writers with aspirations to the mainstream seem to have forgotten this. Who has not read a crime novel or story recently in which the crime element is little more than an excuse for digressions on any number of other subjects that are clearly the author's central interest? The best writers of the past achieved something more meaningful through a successful development of the crime or suspense plot. In spite of their example, there has been a noticeable lack of attention to the art of the mystery on the part of many who now market their stories as mysteries.

Commercial considerations play a part in this: as the market for crime fiction grows, it creates a

The World's Leading Mystery Magazine

ELLERY QUEEN'S

Mystery Magaz

Charlotte Armstrong

Hugh Pentecost

Rufus King

P. G. Wodehouse

Craig Rice

Dashiell Hammett

Lord Dunsany

AUGUST 35¢

PDC

Courtesy of Dell Magazines

strong incentive for writers with other interests to tailor their stories to fit the genre. But we should not purchase our respectability as a genre at the cost of a lack of respect for the special arts of the crime story. Readers expect the focus of mystery publications to be crime and suspense, and this requires that authors do more than pay lip service to the mystery's conventions. As soon as we say this, however, we stumble onto one of those issues over which rivers of ink have already flowed: namely, how to define a crime story.

The complaint is often voiced to us, especially by readers who have followed the magazine for many years, that *EQMM* has moved away from the classic detective story that played such an important role in its early years to publish primarily shorter stories of suspense with little detection. While this is true, it has more than as not been solely the result of editorial choice. As even the most ardent fan must recognize, the closed circle detective story is an artificial construction that never came close to

mirroring any real segment of society. Nevertheless, its effectiveness as entertainment depends on our being able to suspend disbelief and take the world it depicts—a world of stable and understood social relations and motivated violence—as real for the duration of the story. Probably the biggest factor in the decline in this type of story is that it is no longer easy to find a natural setting in which to construct such a world. As one of our authors had his sleuth say only half facetiously in a recent *EQMM* story, the English village of mystery fiction is dead, populated as it now is with commuters and summer dwellers, most of whom exhibit a supreme indifference to their neighbors.

When the best writers in the field no longer find it natural to tell a certain type of story, a magazine that seeks to publish the best must change. This is not to say that one cannot find fine new examples of the classic detective story, but they are the exception, not the rule. In the short story form, only Edward D. Hoch continues to produce them regularly with the cleverness and skill of the early writers.

Even if there were an abundance of this type of story, however, we would hardly want them to constitute our entire diet. Long before the society in which the classic puzzle mystery found its home began to disappear, many writers were moving away from the restrictive rules and conventions of this subgenre in search of a form that would be more realistic. *EQMM* was very much in the forefront of this change in the forties, publishing writers such as Dashiell Hammett and expanding the conception of what could be considered a crime story. One critic commenting on the early years of editor Dannay's reign said, "He has made it seem as if every writer of note in history has produced at least one such (crime) story." And not, of course, because all these great figures had, as Faulkner did, a specific interest in the genre. It was rather that Dannay was willing to take as a broad criterion for inclusion in the magazine that the central focus of the story be on the motives, detection, consequences, or psychology of crime. *EQMM*'s success over five decades, and its importance not only as a mystery publication but as a fiction magazine, has much to do with this liberal understanding of what was within its scope.

Although we see every variety of crime fiction at *EQMM*, we would be very hard put to come up with a definition of what belongs to the genre, for it has less to do with rules and conventions than with the central interest of the story. Conventions must change if a form of fiction is to remain vital, and indeed they have changed even within the most rule-bound of the subgenres. The classic puzzle mystery seldom employs today the "great detective" sleuth of the past; its heroes resemble more often the fallible, less-than-brilliant protagonists of private eye stories. Our guess about the coming decade for the traditional mystery is that there will be more use made of historical settings and a greater attempt to treat themes of significance beyond the mystery.

The private eye story faces perhaps the greatest challenge in the nineties. During the eighties, few private eyes appeared in *EQMM*'s pages, an omission partly due to the difficulty many new writers have had in avoiding cliché in this form—perhaps nowhere else is it so easy to slip into unintentional parody of one's predecessors. Nevertheless, many unique voices have appeared on the scene recently, to say nothing of the excellent creations of leaders in the field such as Sue Grafton, Loren Estleman, Jeremiah Healy, and others.

Detective and private eye stories find a natural home between the covers of a mystery magazine. Yet such stories form only a small part of our fare. Nowadays most detective and private eye writers prefer the novel for the greater development it allows—not to mention the financial rewards. Mystery short stories have become shorter partly due to the space limitations of magazine editors, but mainly because the short story is no longer the primary means of expression for those writing tales with elaborate plotting or characterization. What we receive most often are stories that focus on a single idea or premise, an idea that probably would not serve for a novel. Such is the stuff of the great Hitchcock suspense thrillers, and *EQMM* excelled in this area under its last editor, Eleanor Sullivan. We want to maintain our preeminence in this area in the nineties, but we will also try to open our doors to other forms of crime fiction by accepting longer submissions. After all, the first published detective story, Poe's "The Murders in the Rue Morgue," was some thirty pages in length.

The nineties are bound to hold many changes for the crime genre as a whole, not just for *EQMM*. It was the boundary between mainstream fiction and crime fiction that began to give way in the eighties;

in the nineties perhaps the boundaries between crime and other forms of genre fiction will begin to fall. Some evidence of this can already be found in the importation of fantasy to the mystery story in novels such as Alice Hoffman's Hammett Award–winning *Turtle Moon*. And why not? Among the historical roots of the mystery are criminous tales of the fantastic and the supernatural.

EQMM was founded with the intention of being on the cutting edge of new developments in the field, and we intend to remain there in the coming decade. Yet an editor's job involves a delicate balancing of a sense of what the magazine ought to encompass and what its readers want to see. One of the magazine's hallmarks has always been a respect for the classic forms of the detective and crime story. Our most difficult task in the nineties will be to find the right balance between the traditional and the new as we try to ensure that *EQMM* remains a vital publication.

ALFRED HITCHCOCK MYSTERY MAGAZINE

Wendi Lee

THE "ALFRED HITCHCOCK PRESENTS" television show had been on the air for fifteen months before *Alfred Hitchcock Mystery Magazine* saw print. Published by HSD Publications in New York City, the first issue was released in December 1956 under editor William Manners's direction. Under the HSD flagship, two other editors later replaced Manners: G. S. Goster and Ernest Hutter. *AHMM* stayed pretty much the same for the first decade, only changing format from the small digest size to 8 ½ by 11 inches from May 1957 to January 1958, then going back to the digest format.

During the ten-year run of *Alfred Hitchcock Presents,* the goal of *AHMM* was to publish the same sort of black-humor mystery short stories as was seen on the TV show. In fact, many well-known writers saw their short stories adapted for

TV: Ray Bradbury, Roald Dahl, Robert Bloch, and John Cheever, to name a few.

In 1976, HSD had moved to Riviera, Florida, and the publisher was contemplating shutting down the magazine. Joel Davis of Davis Publications got wind of the rumor and, because there were so few mystery publications around, he bought the magazine and named Eleanor Sullivan editor. By 1981 Sullivan was concentrating on Hitchcock's companion mystery magazine, *Ellery Queen,* and Cathleen Jordan stepped in as the *AHMM* editor.

Over the years the focus of *AHMM* has changed, but the spirit and the quality has remained the same. "It's still mystery fiction, but in the broadest sort of term. We don't limit it to particular kinds of mystery fiction," Jordan says. "We do a little fantasy, a little science fiction, a fair amount of ghost stories. But by far, the majority are standard genre stories. Within that, we do private eye, espionage, suspense, and classic whodunits."

AHMM receives approximately 3600 manuscripts a year, of which only one hundred thirty are bought. "We have no commissioned stories," Jordan says. "We publish a number of new writers every year too."

The magazine always has a puzzle section called "Unsolved," book and film review columns, and "The Mysterious Photograph" contest, in which readers are shown a photograph and invited to make up a short (250 words or less) mystery story to go with it. The winner gets twenty-five dollars and the story printed in *AHMM.*

With thanks to Cathleen Jordan, Robert Weinberg, and Michael Cook's book, *Mystery, Detective and Espionage Magazines* (Greenwood Press, 1983).

GETTING STARTED

Edward D. Hoch

EACH WRITER'S BEGINNINGS are different. I first realized I wanted to be a writer early in 1947. I was seventeen years old, a high school senior who read books of all sorts, especially mysteries. *Ellery Queen's Mystery Magazine* had announced the winners of its first annual contest the previous year, and I had toyed with the idea of writing a mystery for its second contest.

I even had an idea for an unusual detective. He would be the president of the United States, secretly prowling Washington after dark to solve mysteries. (No doubt I imagined that with World War II at an end, things would be boring at the White House.) I never wrote the story, but early in 1947 the winner of the second contest was announced—"The President of the United States, Detective" by H. F. Heard. The story was more science fiction than mystery, and nothing at all like what I'd had in mind. Nevertheless, I imagined that if I'd written the story, I would have at least gotten a mention of some sort.

That was when I decided I would be a writer. Over the next few years I turned out a variety of stories—mystery, fantasy, and an occasional western. I even tried mainstream stories for the slick magazines, but all without success. My main interest was in mysteries, however, and in 1949 I joined Mystery Writers of America as an affiliate member.

Called into the army during the Korean War (I enlisted the day after receiving my draft notice), I found that I had less time for writing. Happily, however, I spent the entire two years of my enlistment in the New York City area, where I frequently attended meetings of MWA. I met and became friendly with writers like Fred Dannay, John Dickson Carr, Cornell Woolrich, Hugh Pentecost, Craig Rice, Brett Halliday, Helen McCloy, and Clayton Rawson. Editor Hans Stefan Santesson also attended the meetings, as did pulp writer Joseph Commings.

The short stories of Joe Commings usually concerned locked-room murders or other impossible crimes. When he announced around 1952 that he was editing a locked-room anthology for Joan Kahn at Harper, I submitted one of my own unpublished stories and he accepted it. For a time it appeared that I had made my first sale. Things weren't going to be that easy though. In the end Joan Kahn reluctantly decided against publishing the anthology, and by the beginning of 1955 I was still an unpublished author.

(The story which would have been my first was later rewritten and sold to *Argosy* as "The Magic Bullet," January 1969. It appeared in Hubin's *Best Detective Stories of the Year 1970* and in Greene & Adey's locked-room anthology *Death Locked In,* 1987. Many of the other stories Joe Commings had planned to use in his locked-room anthology appeared in Santesson's *The Locked Room Reader,* 1968. And Joan Kahn did publish a locked-room anthology, my own *All But Impossible!,* in 1981.)

Having finished my army duty in November 1952, I'd remained in New York and was working for Pocket Books, the paperback publisher. I tried to keep up with the new mystery magazines that came and went so quickly in those days. Early in 1953 I visited a loftlike building on lower Fifth Avenue, where Hans Stefan Santesson was editing a new magazine called *Private Eye,* under the pseudonym Stephen Bond. (Yes, editors used pseudonyms too!) It was coming on the heels of *Manhunt*'s successful launching, but had no name as big as Mickey Spillane for its cover. It lasted only two issues. A few years later I had an embarrassing experience. I received a rejection from *The Saint Detective Magazine* with a nice note from the new editor which started out "Dear Ed." He said he'd taken over as editor of *The Saint* and wanted to see more of my stories. This was every author's dream, to have a friend as editor of a leading magazine in the field, but I couldn't read the signature at the bottom of the note! I finally had to write him as "Editor," admitting I didn't know who he was. I received a reply with his name typed out. It was Hans Stefan Santesson.

But I was to publish twenty-two stories elsewhere before my first sale to Hans in 1957. The first several were to Robert A. W. Lowndes, the last of the pulp editors. In 1955 he had two bimonthly

mystery magazines, *Famous Detective Stories* and *Smashing Detective Stories,* as well as a pair of science fiction titles. A postcard from him dated July 6, 1955, stated simply, "Your story, 'Village of the Dead,' hit me just right, and I shall use it in a forthcoming issue of one of our detective magazines." I had made my first sale.

I was paid sixty-five dollars for that story, which was featured on the cover of *Famous Detective Stories* for December 1955. It went on sale on September 26, and I can still remember waiting impatiently while a local drugstore clerk opened the bundles of newly delivered magazines and revealed mine. It had a typical pulp cover of the period, with a gun-toting hero covering a girl's mouth with his hand as they view the body of a hanged man whose shadow is on the brick wall behind them. But my name and the title of my story were on it, which was all that mattered.

In those days I held a full-time job in public relations, so my writing was confined to evenings and weekends. Still, I managed to turn out stories for a variety of mystery, science fiction, and even western magazines whose names today are remembered only by the most avid students of these genres—*Famous Detective, Smashing Detective, Science Fiction Stories, Murder, Guilty, Crime & Justice, Crack Detective, Terror, Killers, Blazing Guns Western, Fast Action Detective, Double Action Detective, Future Science Fiction.* A brief story produced for an English composition class at the University of Rochester was recycled as "The Chippy" for *Guilty Detective Story Magazine.* I received a grade of B from the U of R and a payment of $33 from *Guilty.*

My first sale to *Manhunt* came early in 1957, and although the magazine was already past its glory days, it was the first important mystery publication in which I'd appeared. The story, a short-short titled "The Man Who Was Everywhere," was often reprinted during the 1960s and early 1970s. Another short-short written during this period for Hans Santesson's *Fantastic Universe* is still the most widely reprinted of any of my stories, "Zoo," a two-page science fiction tale with a moral, appeared in the magazine's June 1958 issue. Since then it has been reprinted more than fifty times in anthologies and textbooks, and has even been made into a short animated film.

Through 1959 and the early 1960s my stories

began to appear in better markets like *The Saint Mystery Magazine*. The year 1962 was a banner one, with my first *Alfred Hitchcock Mystery Magazine* appearance in their January issue, and my first *Ellery Queen's Mystery Magazine* appearance in that magazine's December issue. Still, most of my sales in that period continued to be to magazines with forgettable titles like *Real Western, Mystery Digest, Web Detective, Off Beat Detective, Tightrope, Two-Fisted Detective, Shock, Keyhole Detective, Magazine of Horror,* and *Startling Mystery Stories.*

I quickly discovered that mysteries were a better market for me than science fiction or westerns, so I concentrated on those. For a writer of short stories, however, it's sometimes important to take the money where you find it. Two of my early editors, Robert A. W. Lowndes and Hans Stefan Santesson, both became editors of nonfiction magazines concerned, oddly enough, with various aspects of the occult. I became a contributor of short articles to Lowndes's *Exploring the Unknown* from 1961 to 1970, and in 1970 I also contributed four articles to Santesson's short-lived *Sybil Leek's Astrology Journal.* In most cases these nonfiction pieces were outgrowths of occult lore and historical oddities previously mentioned in my Simon Ark mystery series. By that time I had won an MWA Edgar for one of my stories and published my first novel. I'd left my job to write fiction on a full-time basis.

When I look around at the possible short story markets today, I realize how much things have changed in the past thirty-five or forty years. Other than *Ellery Queen* and *Alfred Hitchcock,* there are no mystery magazines today with national distribution, and even these two are sold mainly by subscription. A few others are sold through mystery bookstores and by mail, but their circulation is negligible. It may be impossible today to make a living from writing short mysteries alone, as so many writ-

ers did during the pulp magazine days of the 1930s and beyond.

Then, too, editorial practices have changed. I still remember sitting in Hans Stefan Santesson's cluttered Fifth Avenue office after five o'clock one day in 1963 when a well-known writer appeared at the door with a manuscript. Hans skimmed it while the author waited, and immediately wrote out a check. Perhaps it helped buy the groceries that week. It was a scene that would not be repeated in any editorial office today. Editors able to issue their own checks usually have such small-scale operations that payment is slow. Larger operations require signed contracts, payment requests, check signings, and other red tape that can delay payment for weeks or months. When I first began writing, the speed with which an editor paid could occasionally be more important than the amount paid.

The demise of the pulp magazines and short-lived digest-size magazines that followed was not so much the result of television as it was the coming of the paperback book. People might go to fewer theatrical films because of the TV set available in their homes, but readers are readers. They found paperbound books handier and often handsomer than the magazines with their cheap paper and garish covers. It's not surprising that the few remaining mystery magazines today make a conscious effort to look more like paperbound books.

I sometimes wonder how I might have gotten started as a writer if all those minor mystery magazines hadn't existed. I wrote for eight years before I made a sale to one. It was to be another seven years before I broke into *Hitchcock and Queen.* Would I have lasted that long without a sale to encourage me? I think so. I think I would have kept on writing even if I'd never sold a thing to those nearly forgotten magazines.

Still, it was nice to have them around.

Ten Classic Mystery Anthologies
(historical)
Selected by Jon L. Breen

Anthony Boucher, ed., *Four-&-Twenty Bloodhounds* (1950)

Hugh Greene, ed., *The Rivals of Sherlock Holmes* (1970)

Kenneth MacGowan, ed., *Sleuths Twenty-Three Great Detectives of Fiction and Their Best Stories* (1931)

Mystery Writers of America, *Maiden Murders* (1952)

Bill Pronzini, ed., *Midnight Specials: An Anthology for Train Buffs and Mystery Aficionados* (1977)

Ellery Queen, ed., *101 Years' Entertainment* (1941)

James Sandoe, ed., *Murder Plain and Fanciful* (1948)

Dorothy L. Sayers, ed., *Great Short Stories of Detection, Mystery and Horror* (U.S. title *The Omnibus of Crime*) (1928)

Michele B. Slung, ed., *Crime on Her Mind: Fifteen Stories of Female Sleuths from the Victorian Era to the Forties* (1975)

Willard Huntington Wright, ed., *The Great Detective Stories: A Chronological Anthology* (1927)

Ten Reprint Mystery Anthologies
(since 1980)
Selected by Jon L. Breen

Jack Adrian and Robert Adey, eds., *Murder Impossible: An Extravaganza of Miraculous Murders, Fantastic Felonies & Incredible Criminals* (1990)

Jerome Charyn, ed., *The New Mystery* (1993)

Patricia Craig, ed., *The Oxford Book of English Detective Stories* (1990)

Thomas Godfrey, ed., *Murder for Christmas* (1982)

Ed Gorman, ed., *The Black Lizard Anthology of Crime Fiction* (1987)

Peter Lovesey, ed., *The Black Cabinet: Stories Based on Real Crimes* (1989)

William F. Nolan, ed., *The Black Mask Boys: Masters of the Hard-Boiled School of Detective Fiction* (1985)

Josh Pachter, ed., *Top Crime* (1984)

Bill Pronzini, Barry N. Malzberg, and Martin Greenberg, eds., *The Arbor House Treasury of Mystery and Suspense* (1982)

Eleanor Sullivan, ed., *Fifty Years of the Best from* Ellery Queen's Mystery Magazine (1991)

Ten Original Mystery Anthologies

(since 1980)
Selected by Jon L. Breen

Adam Round Table, *Murder in Manhattan* (1986)

Ed Gorman and Martin H. Greenberg, eds., *Solved* (1991)

Martin H. Greenberg and Ed Gorman, eds., *Cat Crimes* (1991)

Martin H. Greenberg and Francis M. Nevins, Jr., eds., *Mr. President, Private Eye* (1989)

Martin H. Greenberg and Carol-Lynn Rossel Waugh, eds., *The New Adventures of Sherlock Homes* (1986)

Tim Heald, ed., *A Classic English Crime* (1990)

Alice Laurence and Isaac Asimov, eds., *Who Done It?* (1980)

Sara Paretsky, ed., *A Woman's Eye* (1991)

Robert J. Randisi, ed., *The Eyes Have It* (1984)

Marilyn Wallace, ed., *Sisters in Crime* (1989)

Twenty Distinguished
Mystery Short Stories
(since 1980)
Selected by Jon L. Breen

Robert Barnard, **"The Woman in the Wardrobe"** (*EQMM,* December 1987)

Lawrence Block, **"By the Dawn's Early Light"** (*Playboy,* August 1984)

Liza Cody, **"Spasmo"** (*A Classic English Crime,* 1990)

Michael Collins, **"The Oldest Killer"** (*The Thieftaker Journals,* November 1983)

Harlan Ellison, **"Soft Monkey"** (*The Black Lizard Anthology of Crime Fiction,* 1987)

Ed Gorman, **"The Reason Why"** (*Criminal Elements,* 1988)

Linda Grant, **"Last Rites"** (*Sisters in Crime 4,* 1991)

Edward D. Hoch, **"The Problem of the Octagon Room"** (*EQMM,* October 7, 1981)

Wendy Hornsby, **"Nine Sons"** (*Sisters in Crime 4,* 1991)

Clark Howard, **"Horn Man"** (*EQMM,* June 2, 1980)

Peter Lovesey, **"The Crime of Miss Oyster Brown"** (*EQMM,* May 1991)

Susan Moody, **"All's Fair in Love"** (*A Classic English Crime,* 1990)

Elizabeth Peters, **"Liz Peters, P.I."** (*Christmas Stalkings,* 1991)

James Powell, **"A Dirge for Clowntown"** (*EQMM,* November 1989)

Bill Pronzini, **"Incident in a Neighborhood Tavern"** (*An Eye for Justice,* 1988)

Ruth Rendell, **"The Copper Peacock"** (*EQMM,* June 1989)

Jack Ritchie, **"The Absence of Emily"** (*EQMM,* January 1981)

Peter Robinson, **"Innocence"** (*Cold Blood III,* 1991)

Donald E. Westlake, **"Too Many Crooks"** (*Playboy,* August 1989)

Carolyn Wheat, **"Ghost Station"** (*A Woman's Eye,* 1991)

The Fifteen Greatest Detective Short Story Volumes Since Poe
Selected by Douglas G. Greene

Arthur Conan Doyle, 1892
The Adventures of Sherlock Holmes
G. K. Chesterton, 1911
The Innocence of Father Brown
Melville Davisson Post, 1918
Uncle Abner Master of Mysteries
Will Scott, 1924
Giglamps
Dorothy L. Sayers, 1928
Lord Peter Views the Body
Ellery Queen, 1934
The Adventures of Ellery Queen
Carter Dickson, 1940
The Department of Queer Complaints
Dashiell Hammett, 1945
The Continental Op
Lillian de la Torre, 1946
Dr. Sam Johnson, Detector
Agatha Christie, 1947
The Labôurs of Hercules
Ross Macdonald, 1955
The Name is Archer
Robert van Gulik, 1967
Judge Dee at Work
Edward D. Hoch, 1971
The Spy and the Thief
Randall Garrett, 1979
Murder and Magic
Bill Pronzini, 1983
Casefile

The Thirteen Greatest Mystery Anthologies
Selected by Douglas G. Greene

Dorothy L. Sayers, ed, 1928
The Omnibus of Crime
introd. G. K. Chesterton, 1935
A Century of Detective Stories
E. C. Bentley, ed, 1938
The Second Century of Detective Stories
Dennis Wheatley, ed, 1938
A Century of Spy Stories
1938
Fifty Famous Detectives of Fiction
John Rhode, ed, 1939
Detective Medley
Ellery Queen, ed, 1941
101 Years' Entertainment
Joseph T. Shaw, ed, 1946
The Hard-Boiled Omnibus
(1st & 2nd series) 1950, 1951
The Evening Standard Detective Book
Michele Slung, ed, 1975
Crime on Her Mind
Edward D. Hoch, ed, 1981
All But Impossible!
Bill Pronzini, ed, 1988
The Mammoth Book of Private Eye Stories
Jack Adrian, ed, 1988
Crime at Christmas

TRUE CRIME MYSTERIES

INTERVIEW:
ANNE WINGATE

Charles L. P. Silet

ANNE WINGATE IS THE AUTHOR of the Mark Shigata mysteries, featuring a fourth generation Japanese-American chief of police from Bayport, Texas. She is also the author of the Deb Ralston books under the pseudonym Lee Martin. For seven years Wingate was in police work in both Albany, Georgia, and Plano, Texas, where she was in charge of the crime scene unit. She is also a qualified fingerprint expert for both state and federal courts. A Writer's Digest School instructor, she recently published *Scene of the Crime: A Writer's Guide to Crime-Scene Investigations* for the popular Howdunit series published by Writer's Digest Books.

cs: *Obviously, the importance of science and of scientific investigation is playing a larger and larger part in mystery and suspense novels. What do you make of that; why is that, do you think?*

AW: Because people are becoming more and more informed. There are so many shows on TV that explain these things and also because the use of science in crime detection is changing. For example, if you wanted to write a book now about a fellow who shows up and claims to be the long-lost son of the family, you don't have a story anymore because it will take about two weeks to do a DNA test—to prove that he is or he ain't. If you want to do that kind of book, you have to put it in the past now. There're just so many ways scientific methods of detection can be done now that couldn't be done before and people know it.

cs: *Does this mean that crime books are going to become techno-novels?*

AW: Oh, no, not necessarily. For example, you can't do DNA testing if you don't have any DNA; you can't do fingerprint checks if you don't have any

fingerprints. So the writer by manipulating the story can do just about anything; it's just that, well, for example, if you really wanted to do the long-lost heir, you'd have to have every known member of the family die in an accident at sea or something. But how often do you have that type of story? Many, many crimes of all types in real life don't leave physical evidence. So, no, there's no reason why every writer needs to be a crime scene technician.

cs: *Does this somehow give an advantage to the police procedural over the individual p.i., who doesn't have all of this scientific apparatus at his or her command?*

AW: I very much doubt it. It's just that the person writing the p.i. novel will have to manipulate the story to where the physical evidence isn't available either to the p.i. or to the police; or, as more and more people who are writing p.i. stories are doing, the p.i. will have to have a friend who works at a lab, or have to have a lab under contract.

cs: *In* Scene of the Crime, *you talk about investigative procedures changing so quickly that I got a sense that the minute the book hit the stands it was already out-of-date.*

AW: Well, I can tell you that it's heading into its third printing and I have made minor changes in the second printing and I have made minor changes in the third printing and I anticipate that I will continue to make minor changes for every printing because so much is happening so *very* fast. For example, when I wrote the book, I had said something to the general effect that probably in the future there would be a DNA register of sex criminals and then just a few months ago I read that the FBI is in the process of setting one up and hopes to have it up and running within two years. During the time that I wrote the book, they began storing DNA samples from everybody in the U.S. Armed Forces so there will be no more unknown soldiers. It's just an incredibly volatile field. If you're not going to totally avoid technical stuff in your crime fiction, you've really got to try to stay on top of it. But that's not hard to do because all of the news magazines follow this kind of stuff avidly.

CS: *But can you envision crime fiction that basically avoids such technical material?*

AW: Oh, yes, there's always going to be room for the brilliant amateur and, as I said, in real life there are always crimes in which there is no usable physical evidence. It's always going to involve the writer manipulating the story, and the writer has to manipulate the story anyway. That's what writing is.

CS: *How much technology is too much in crime fiction?*

AW: It varies according to the writer. Too much is when you have enough to bore the reader. For example, in that Martin Cruz Smith book *Gorky Park,* which is a wonderful, wonderful book, he has one beautiful scene in which the New York cop and the Moscow cop are fingerprinting a laboratory in which fake Russian chests and icons have been made. The scene, I don't think it runs over seven pages, just knocked me over as a fingerprint expert. I've talked to other people who didn't know anything about fingerprints and it impressed them too. I had the occasion to meet Martin Cruz Smith and I asked him about it and he told me he had spent two weeks riding with a New York City crime scene unit in order to write that seven-page scene. Now, obviously he didn't put in there everything he knew. So it's a matter that some writers can get totally technical and keep the reader enthralled and other writers can put two sentences of technical stuff in there and the reader goes to sleep. So it just varies from writer to writer.

CS: *Now, in your own fiction, there doesn't seem to be a great deal of the technical material.*

AW: No, I don't hit it too hard. It doesn't interest other people as much as it does me, and my editors tend to cut it out because I try to go into the very technical mode when I'm writing. But also I'm writing about the Fort Worth Police Department which, I'm sorry to say, when I was there ten years ago, really did not have a good crime scene unit and I'm writing about a made-up, very, very small town which would not have a good crime scene unit. So I don't do a whole lot with it. More could be done and eventually I probably will write a book in which I do more. But from my own point of view, I've worked so much in the technical end of it that it is not the end that really lights up my galaxy as far as writing fiction.

CS: *Do you envision putting more of this in because of the availability of the information and the expectations of the reader?*

AW: Probably not. For instance, in the book that I just got through with—a Deb Ralston book which I write under the pseudonym of Lee Martin—I've got DNA evidence and fingerprint evidence but the guy is actually identified on the basis of a detective putting the pieces together and then suggesting that the fingerprints be checked. When the fingerprints match up, there's no need to run the DNA, although in real life they certainly would run the DNA, but I don't want the book to wait two weeks with nothing happening while they run the DNA. That's one of the problems with using DNA in fiction—it takes anywhere from two to four weeks to run the test.

CS: *Would you just talk for a minute about your own background that allowed you to write the* Scene of the Crime *book?*

AW: I actually don't have any college degrees in anything to do with forensics, crime scene work, or police work. I started out to be a high school English teacher. Nobody told me that there were three hundred applicants for every vacancy. Then I went to work as a reporter for a scandal sheet in Albany, Georgia, and they assigned me to the police beat and every time my editor threw a temper tantrum (which was two or three times a day) I'd go over to the police department and hide out until he was through. At that time Albany had one fingerprint person, and one day I was looking over his shoulder and he was charting a fingerprint and I said, "You know, I could do that." He kind of got that sort of "Yeah, right" look on his face and said, "Okay, well, tell me what I'm doing." So I pointed out the next three points and he was flabbergasted. I wound up parting company with the newspaper and at that time the department had no policewomen, so I went to work as Detective Bureau secretary, which was a job that the department formed specifically for me. They created the job requirements around me and I worked there for a year and left because my husband was transferred to Atlanta and I was pregnant. So I went to Atlanta and while I was there I was taking a correspondence course in fingerprints and then I went to work for the DeKalb County Police Department as an identification clerk, which was classifying fingerprints. They sent me to the FBI Basic and Advanced School but they had promised me they would hire me as a policewoman when they began hiring policewomen, and then they backed out on it because of my vision which didn't quite meet their requirements. They hired a woman who didn't have a high school diploma, but they couldn't stand someone with 20/90 vision. Anyway, we moved back to Albany and I immediately went to work for the Albany Police Department.

CS: *How did you develop your expertise with fingerprints?*

AW: Well, by that time I'd had three fingerprint courses and they were trying to form an identification section, so I was immediately put in it. I worked there for about five and a half years and left there because my husband was transferred to Texas. When I got to Texas, after I'd been there a couple of years, I got a job as the head of the identification section for the police department for Plano, Texas, and worked there for a year. Now I have been out of police work ever since, but all the time I was in police work, all the time I was between police jobs, I just read everything I could lay my hands on, trying to learn and learn. I have since then, of course, gone on reading to keep my fiction as good as possible.

CS: *What about the "crime scene" background?*

AW: I'll give you a little anecdote that might or might not be of any use to you but it helped me understand how a knowledge of how crime scenes work can benefit you. Right after I left Albany, before going back into police work, I went to work as a computer tape librarian for a department at Texas Christian University in Fort Worth. At that time they were having a series of fires on the TCU campus, clearly arson, and apparently nothing was happening and I finally went in and talked to the assistant chief of the campus police department. I said, "Look, you may feel I'm interfering in your business but I do have this experience, and just

about the last thing before I left Albany I took a course in arson investigation and if there's anything I can do to help you, I'd be very glad to." The guy was delighted and said, "The next one, before anybody touches anything, I'm going to call you to come out and look at the scene. Right now I want you to sit down and look through our files." So I spent about two hours sitting in his office, reading through all of his files relating to all of the previous arsons, and then I said, "Well, I'll be very glad to come out and look at your scene, but I can tell you right now, this guy's your arsonist." He said, "Huh? That's impossible, this guy has been helping us; he's reported some of the fires, he's been running around helping us to put out the fires." I said, "I understand all that. This guy's your arsonist." The chief said, "This is impossible, but since you seem so sure, we'll go and talk to him." About a week later, the chief hailed me in the parking lot and he said, "I want you to know we talked to the guy and he acted so funny that we asked him to take a polygraph, and he agreed, and in the car on the way to the polygraph he confessed." To anybody who knew anything at all about arsons and about crime scenes, it just jumped off the page. It was so obvious. One time in Plano we had a case and I really can't say much about it because the guy we know did it was never charged. There was never anything we could take to the grand jury. I was out of town when the case went down and one of my subordinates went to the crime scene. He was also an experienced crime scene person and when I got into town (I had my radio with me and they were hailing me), I headed right on over to this crime scene. I walked into the front room and looked around and said, "Oh, shit!" My assistant said, "Oh, you see it too?" I said, "Yes, isn't it a little bit obvious?" The senior officers were all standing around just snarling and the rookies were all asking "What are you talking about? What are you talking about?" Because the way the scene was set up, it was totally obvious to every experienced officer who saw it: I know who did it, I know how he did it, I know why he did it, I know we will never be able to prove it.

CS: *What was it, just the layout?*

AW: The way the scene was staged. It didn't happen the way it was supposed to have happened. But I can't go into any details because it would be slander. But crime scenes are so interesting, and you can read about them until hell freezes over. But you have to start going to them before you can really get a feel for them. It takes about two years, and all of a sudden after about two years of seeing it over and over and over, all of a sudden it clicks and you can walk into a crime scene and you know whether this happened the way it was reported, you know if somebody is staging it to make you think something else.

CS: *How many crimes are really solved through a scientific investigation? Are we talking about a fairly small number out of all the crimes?*

AW: It varies very, very sharply from department to department. A department with a bad crime scene unit could very easily solve absolutely none of its crimes scientifically. A department with a good one could solve as many as twenty-five percent. This is growing rapidly. For instance, the AFIS [Automated Fingerprint Identification System] which I mention to some degree in my book is just solving crimes right and left that couldn't have been solved before. In Albany, a city of 100,000 people, we could manually search fingerprints, we could make nonsuspect IDs. But New York, Chicago, hang it up, there's no way. But now with AFIS, you can do it. You will hear people all the time saying, ''Well, criminals are so smart now, they never leave fingerprints.'' That is bullshit! The FBI has determined that up to seventy percent of all crimes against property, probably a lower percentage of crimes against person, but even then, at a certain percentage even in crimes against persons there are fingerprints. All you have to do is look for them and find them and run them on AFIS.

CS: *You mention even with rubber gloves on, some people can leave fingerprints.*

AW: Right, now, this doesn't happen often, but it does happen. With a very very thin glove, the fingerprints will leak through. But my own feeling is that with the AFIS system, with computerized systems to test for DNA, especially in sex crimes 'cause sex crimes are where you're most likely to have DNA, I think that the number of crimes solved by scientific means is going to continue to grow. However, very often what happens is that a good detective will develop a suspect some other way

and then the evidence for court will be clinched with scientific means.

CS: *So it will be corroborating evidence.*

AW: Corroborating evidence, right. Because a good detective, a good experienced police officer, very often will know who committed a crime and there's nothing to take to court. You just get to where you know.

CS: *So intuition still plays a part in all this?*

AW: It's not intuition. It's not intuition at all. It's the small things that you can't take to court. You can't stand up in front of a jury and say, ''I happen to know this is the only person in town who likes to steal a car and also steals checks from the person that he stole the car from and also forges the check.'' Knowledge of m.o., knowledge of criminal habits, knowledge of the way things look. But no, it's not intuition, it's a kind of knowledge that you can't explain. That's why very often police will stop somebody who to them looks highly suspicious and you wind up with the screams of prejudice and so forth and it's impossible to explain prejudice is judging without facts. But a crime profile is judging with facts and yes, unfortunately, a lot of perfectly innocent people fit criminal profiles. Sometimes you have to have a look at somebody because that person fits a profile. Now, obviously you don't arrest somebody for fitting a profile, but it's the same type of thing. It's not intuition—it's going on the basis of knowledge you can't explain to somebody who doesn't already understand it. It's something you have to learn on the gut level.

CS: *You mentioned in your book that the size of a department will obviously determine how much scientific information is available. Is it the case that scientific methods of investigation are becoming more available even to smaller departments now?*

AW: Oh, yes, most states have at least one state crime lab and many states have regional crime labs, so that even the two- or three-person department can take evidence to a crime lab. Now the problem tends to be training. If you've got only three people in the department, how are you going to spare somebody to go to a two-week school to learn how to collect this evidence? So, obviously, the larger the department, the more likely you are to have well-trained people who will think of these things.

TRUE CRIME:
Stranger Than Fiction
Wendi Lee

IN 1974 I BOUGHT MY first true crime book, *Helter Skelter*. Although I hadn't been following the Manson family trials, I was aware of the murders of Sharon Tate and the LaBiancas. But it wasn't the lurid cover of *Helter Skelter* that made me want to buy it; rather, it was the back cover copy that hooked me: a beautiful pregnant actress and her houseguests murdered by hippie intruders.

The killers were part of a small cult that centered around one man, Charles Manson. He had a Rasputin-like hold over his disciples. Manson was at once both fascinating and repulsive. How could anyone willingly and blindly follow orders to kill anyone, let alone a pregnant woman?

Even twenty years ago, Truman Capote's colossal best seller *In Cold Blood* was considered a masterpiece that today has become a true crime classic. Still, when I bought *Helter Skelter,* true crime books were considered to be on a level just above *The National Enquirer* and *True Confessions*. Nevertheless, *Helter Skelter* went home with me and I avidly read it under the bedcovers with a flashlight.

Since those dark, early days, true crime has matured in many ways. Today it is quite acceptable to be seen on the bus or subway, reading a book about the Waco massacre or Amy Fisher. And the genre has grown in the past five years, particularly in paperback and "instant" books.

What is an instant book and how is it put together? "It's kind of 'book as magazine,' " says St. Martin's Press's true crime editor, Charles Spicer. "Basically, you have to have a writer who is able to work very quickly but who can also write."

Those who write true crime are a rare and hardy breed. The instant book writer must get the information fast and must work against a ferocious deadline. He has to compress a normal paperback production schedule of nine to ten months into, sometimes, just two or three weeks.

"Essentially, the writer is signed on to write a book in, say, one month," Spicer explains. "Then the writer spends the first two weeks putting together a list of people to interview and talking to as many of them as he can. The last two weeks would be spent writing the book."

Many true crime writers come from either a journalistic or law enforcement background. "I've used journalists more often. Don Davis, who did *The Milwaukee Murders* about Jeffrey Dahmer, and Ken Englade, whose big one was *Deadly Lessons,* which is about Pam Smart—the New Hampshire case—and Maria Eftimiades, who did *Lethal Lolita,* are all journalists. Maria works for *People* magazine, and Ken Englade and Don Davis are former UPI reporters. They have the ability to write and research very quickly on deadline."

Not only must the facts be accurately reported, but a good true crime writer must use his perception, giving the reader fresh insight and new angles into a case that may have already been overexposed in the media. He must have a bit of the novelist in him as well. Being a good reporter who has a capacity for writing pages and pages of information isn't good enough: the true crime writer must be able to assimilate the facts and the interviews into a compelling story that will carry the reader through 360 or so pages.

Aside from a good writer with the skills of a journalist and the talent of a novelist, what other elements make up a good true crime book? "It's a great read, for one thing. It has all the elements of a terrific crime novel. You have great characters, you have a trial, you have drama, you have heroes, you have villains," says Spicer. "But it's all real, so I think it adds that little extra excitement."

Sensational tabloid cases that have been turned into books tend to sell more copies than the smaller, less visible murder cases, according to Spicer. Big-name murder cases tend to sell especially well in paperback, although cases with less exposure are also sometimes published. "I always look for cases that perhaps haven't been widely reported but have fascinating characters involved, or intriguing people," Spicer says, although he adds that the market tends to be more open to paperback books. "But if you really have something that stands on its own, that is so fabulous and hasn't been reported one hundred ways to Sunday, you can sometimes do it as a hardcover as well."

Not all true crime books have satisfying endings—take the book about the Green River Killer, for instance. "I tend not to do those types of books," Spicer says. "I think people want an answer when they read a true crime book."

Lawsuits are always a big worry for publishers and true crime writers alike. "All the true crime books have to be gone over very carefully by a lawyer," says Spicer, "so the writer has to be someone who knows how to record and keep track of where the information came from, how'd he get it, what's the proof, et cetera, et cetera."

Before the book is accepted for publication, the writer goes through the very long, difficult, and tedious process of proving his claims to the publishing house's lawyers. If a lawsuit does come to light, this enables the publisher to stand behind the writer and his work.

American true crime is also beginning to sell abroad. "My Waco book has just been sold to England for a lot of money," says Spicer. "All my true crime books have basically been sold in England."

Like the category western novel, true crime seems to be a homegrown product. Europe and Asia don't appear to have enough interesting cases that can be turned into books. Although Russia did catch a serial killer last year, the news faded fast from the AP and UPI wire services.

"We do seem to supply the more sensational, better cases. The true crime genre is also helped enormously over here by the tabloid television shows," says Spicer. "I think that essentially, it has spurred an interest in awareness of crime and criminals. But the trend is starting to level off. It's become almost a category, particularly in paperback. Some people have been predicting that true crime will go away, but I don't think it will. True crime has been around since the Bible. In a sense, the story of Cain and Abel was an original true crime story."

Some Notable True Crime Books
Selected by the Editors

Truman Capote
In Cold Blood

Ronald Kessler
Inside the CIA

Anne Rule
The Stranger Beside Me

Ed Sanders
The Family

Josiah Thompson
Gumshoe

Joseph Wambaugh
The Onion Field

THE WRITING
LIFE

WHO REVIEWS?

Carole Nelson Douglas

Sam Douglas

ANY AUTHOR WHO HAS NEVER had a book victimized by an outrageously unfair, gratuitously cruel reviewer can stop reading right here. What follows is for gored oxen of the literary sort.

My first great awakening to publishing-world realities was the appallingly mediocre quality of reviews. I say this as a one-time theater reviewer who knows what it's like to sit on the aisle and pass judgment, not as a novelist presumably so blinded by love of my work that I can't tell a fair review from the wholesale praise supposedly expected. And mediocrity is nothing compared to the deliberately denigrating tirades that pass for reviews in some quarters.

After years of undergoing the review process—that double bind in which the author wails at not getting reviewed, then wails louder when he/she becomes well known enough to get reviewed regularly, but poorly—I've concluded that the surviving writer's sensibilities must be encased in an invisible bell jar.

There the author shelters while any passing ignoramus so inclined hurls mud and stones at the inhabitant. Once in a blue moon the author slips out from under the bell jar and roots in the muck to pluck up the occasional pearl of a review that seriously measures the work against a standard the author can respect. I exaggerate. I and most published novelists probably get far more even-handed, good, or rave reviews than incompetent ones, but it's the mud that sticks.

For these stinker reviews don't always rot around discarded fish and vanish in a decent three days. A 1991 newspaper feature on me quoted a 1985 review of one of my novels, an unsigned review I consider an outright lie masquerading as opinion. The feature writer's point was that my latest novels had "won over" that publication's reviewers. In fact, I simply had changed genres and finally got a new reviewer, one who was more geared to appreciate my work.

Newspaper work gave me a jaded view of reviewers, one reason I quit doing it myself. So many reviewers review because they get the book/record/CD free, and become an instant expert on a subject: you, the hapless author, and your creation. Some reviewers are would-be fiction writers and poets, and then beware, because you are published and they are not. Don't think they don't notice that.

Others review because they love books and love to read. These are amateurs in the noblest sense of the word: often librarians and readers whose motive is to share enthusiasm rather than establish authority.

A rare few are professional reviewers—writers or academics who enjoy analyzing the worth and workings of fiction. They may be paid or not, and may review in venues that sign reviews or not. Such reviewers find little reward in the glib surface sneer adopted by pseudo-reviewers. They usually ignore books they find inferior and concentrate on those that show promise or that achieve excellence. Their criticisms are balanced, the kind the author may not agree with fully, but can't complain about, or may take to heart.

Bless the even-handed reviewer who has the background to appreciate the context of a novel, who can spot the subtle metaphor, who rejects no book simply because of its genre designation or cover excesses. Bless him or her, and prepare to have your work too often dealt with by the rest.

So what makes reviewers arbiters beside their hunger to be experts, their need to go after such jobs—all too easy to get when the renumeration is nothing but a byline (or not) and a small fee? Where are their credentials listed when they pan a work by a long-published writer?

Why are their reviews too often inaccurate, dense, or wrong-headed—and worse, jeering and disdainful? Even if sixty or seventy percent of reviewers are fair and competent, the remainder can—and do—inflict a lot of damage. How do these bum-rap artists acquire the chutzpah to seek a public platform for their prejudices?

They start young, with incredible confidence in their own ignorance.

My introduction to fan reviewers came when a young man approached me at a science fiction convention signing with a crude, photocopied offering that he said contained a review of my tenth novel. Some instinct told me to keep on signing and glance at his publication later.

Its front-page motto was "no living writer will ever be safe." In my book's three-star review, rife with spelling and grammatical errors and serial insults, the major gripe was that he *enjoyed* the book despite its having no redeeming social value. Of course he totally missed the novel's subtext and feminist theme. Years later he turned up doing fan comics; according to a bio, he had been *seventeen* years old when he waltzed up to me with his poison-pen letter disguised as a review, hoping for a big reaction. Luckily, I disappointed him and consigned his review rag to my fat Atrocity File.

Seventeen, untried and uncriticized himself, and eager to cut down all living authors.

(A gender issue underlies this topic. Too few women review books, or review anything at all; this often results in "women's" issues and approaches in fiction being ignored or getting harsh treatment. Culturally, women are not rewarded for sticking their fists or their opinions in other people's faces, more a culturally approved form of male territory-

establishing. The American Association of University Women's recent report of classroom socialization showed that teachers rewarded boys for giving answers, *even when they were wrong*. Girls, on the other hand, were discouraged from expressing opinions and risking being wrong. Still, I don't know any male authors who take wrong-headed criticism any better than women.)

Here's another Atrocity File item courtesy of fandom extremes, which are particularly noxious: I received a copy of a foreign review pamphlet, gratified to see one of my books reviewed—until I read the review. The reviewer stopped reading the book on page twenty-three (of 383), yet still wrote a condemnatory "review."

Besides the fact that no self-respecting professional would pretend to review a book on the basis of eight percent, the reasons for disliking the first twenty-three pages were evidence of the reviewer's ignorance, not the writer's flaws. The objection: citations of bad writing, based on a) ignorance of the American expression "Milwaukee goiter" for a beer belly, and b) generic ignorance of theatrical crepe hair ("what does it feel like—a pancake, fabric, or wrapping paper?"). The reviewer ended, "My child, life is too short to waste on subliterate crap."

Life is too short to waste in replying to immature rabble-rousers like this, so they get away with it. This grossly unfair attack was carefully sent to me (never before, and never again, thank God) to rattle my cage. What else can you expect from self-appointed reviewers who take such pen names as "Lucifer," "the Accuser," and "the Mouth of the South."

So, who reviews, or, at least, who produces the inaccurate, sneering reviews that put good writers and books down? Brats. The egocentric personality that commits bad reviewing, that is capable of declaring works and writers worthless with no qualms of conscience, is the same arrested adolescent mentality that provokes the fan excesses. Such a person will never pause to ask if he or she might be wrong, or ignorant, or irresponsible.

And rarely do two such reviewers carp about the same supposed "faults" in the same work. It's all just a matter of opinion, some will say; don't take it so seriously. Unfortunately, most people *believe* what they read in print. Writers must go on the defensive to rebut reviewers and are seldom allowed to respond at similar length, if at all, in print. Many reviewers are moonlighters who never learned the professional journalist's responsibility in using a power that can harm careers, not to mention the creative artist's self-esteem and will to persevere in the face of such casually cruel, careless—and wrong—criticism.

Bad reviews, in the sense that they do the work a disservice, irk me particularly because I took responsibility for the accuracy of every word of journalism I wrote. More than once I sat in the office of the newspaper's lawyers with only that accuracy to defend me—successfully, I might add. To me, brutal and bad book reviewers have been granted a license to lie about a writer's work in public, with no sporting chance for rebuttal. At least nineteenth-century authors could challenge the lying hound to a duel. (Lady authors did not have that privilege unless they could cross-dress.)

Just how bad can reviews get? How about actionable? Example: a professional-level genre magazine review that caught up to me well over a year after publication. The reviewer hated the book and said so, then added that it owed much to a particular writer's particular trilogy. I had never read either that writer or that trilogy. The assertion was either mind-reading or libel. No evidence backed up the claim, and even then would have been questionable, given the synchronicity of creative ideas. Unless he had seen me reading those particular books, to make such a charge in print was utter fiction.

A letter of protest to the editor at that late date would have been meaningless. I intended to confront this individual if I ran into him at a convention. Instead, I recently confronted in a writers' publication, his article on the "art" of reviewing which begins and ends with boasts of the many outraged letters his reviews have drawn. He concludes that he must be doing something right since his magazine editor lets him keep going. This same gentleman confessed in another publication recently that it took him a long time to learn how to write novels, which he is now publishing. Too bad that didn't stop him from writing the 160 four-thousand-word columns (as he trumpets) critiquing the words of those who had learned to write novels well enough to get them published long before he did.

Unspoken assumption says that the author who objects to inadequate or scathing reviews is a whining, self-deluded incompetent unable to "take" the punishment of the real world, not a proven professional with pride in his or her work and reputation. The problem is that writing successfully, i.e., getting work published, earns some admiration and more jealousy. Everybody's a writer. Everybody's a judge. In a sense that's true. Each reader has an individual reaction to a book and decides whether it was good reading or not. The trouble comes when this very personal reaction goes public in print under the auspices of literary criticism.

So writers watch knee-jerk reviewers spout irresponsible claptrap, and usually say nothing, but grit their teeth and pull the bell jar over themselves more tightly, all the while trying to preserve the confidence and sensitivity so necessary for their work.

Recently, one of my novels was reviewed in my local newspaper (a coup for a "genre" writer) by an administrative assistant who'd never reviewed anything before. She blithely dismissed this novel as not one of my better books. So much for one's hometown reputation. Another writer, and the director of a university press, who had read the book under review called to express outrage. Did I even want her copy or should she burn it? I said I was tempted to send the book editor the novel's many overwhelmingly favorable reviews. No, she advised, forget it. It's just the luck of the draw.

But it isn't just the luck of the draw. It's the fact that newspaper book pages save money by letting staff members, even nonwriting ones, review fiction for the prize of a free book. It's the fact that newspaper book pages, long bastions of literary snobbery, seldom review popular fiction; when it is reviewed, it's a scornful concession.

While movie reviewers display a passion for the form that encompasses popular and art films equally, many newspaper critics, whether of books and even music, regard themselves as writers who, if they finally got around to writing that novel, would have a Pulitzer Prize piece of literary fiction, of course. In the meantime, the published popular author is dead meat for their razor-sharp prose. Magazine reviewers can be just as frustrated and just as bad. Unfortunately, letters from the outraged author are viewed as self-biased, and the outrage is almost never viewed as justified. The reviewer is somehow seen as free of error, self-aggrandizement, and outright mischief.

Luck of the draw is a feeble factor for careers,

livelihoods, and the well-being of one's artistic soul to depend upon. It's apparently the best the review establishment can offer most writers as long as editors of such sections automatically assume that protesting authors are too self-serving to have a legitimate gripe.

So who critiques the critics? Perhaps authors should. (Some have, and while we admire their fire, we also watch such protesters dismissed as irrational cranks.) It's time that we desert en masse the role of suffering in silence that is urged upon us. Write the letter that points out the error, send the contrasting reviews to the editor in charge. Holler and scream. Of course, we may just be adding polish to some sadistic reviewer's brass.

Better yet, one or more of our writers' organizations could serve as a clearinghouse for complaints from members on publications and particular reviewers, and publish periodic evaluations. That might get our protests taken more seriously. At least it helps to hear that a writer you respect has been burned by the same source. By the way, the director of a professional review journal, responding to the American Crime Writers League call for signed reviews because of perceived "book-bashing" by that journal, responded that a long-time reviewer reminded her that "———bashing is, as he put it, 'a time-honored sport.' " Sounds exactly like the protest of an aggrieved writer who feels unjustly criticized, doesn't it? Why does the journal's editor find the same argument valid when it is made by the critic rather than by the writer? In any event, united or alone, writers should challenge inadequate reviewers on their bad calls.

Here's a last, and I hope motivating, Atrocity File anecdote: Garrison Keillor and I have something in common; I'm sorry to say it isn't fame, fortune, or print runs. We both left St. Paul, Minnesota, after beginning our publishing careers.

I left town and the newspaper's staff after having "written" my way out of a career cul-de-sac via fiction.

Keillor left because he was outraged by the paper's columnists, who aggressively publicized his real estate and romantic relocations after he became a best-selling national figure. (It might have helped

if he'd gotten more local coverage and recognition before he became a household name. I wanted to profile him when his first Lake Wobegon book came out and was told that "he's had enough attention." Little did that squelching editor know . . .) Keillor's writing often jabbed at the newspaper's foibles and provincialism from afar. After some years, in 1992, he moved back to St. Paul and the local columnists girded their literary loins for his return.

One, Brian Lambert, offered a self-described olive branch.

Lambert discussed Keillor's "personalized poison dart aimed back here" on the issue of privacy invasion: "It wasn't pretty, it wasn't particularly dignified, and it certainly was beneath him. Keillor should have flicked off media criticism and the supposed invasion of his privacy like a water buffalo flicking at flies. Some may land and bite, but the wounds are insignificant, and from more than ten feet away, he's the only one anyone is paying any attention to."

Not unlike my analogy of the author and the bell jar and the mud-flinging swine.

Lambert went on to say that "most of us" assume that the famous "have a mechanism the rest of us lack for ignoring and shedding insults, real or imagined." They assume that people like Keillor "have a special immunity to our puny bites," that people like him understand another of the basic maxims of show biz, namely, "Never respond to your critics."

There you have the callous rationale of the unempathetic critic: You have more than I (fame, money, a book out), therefore you won't feel my retaliatory blows.

To paraphrase one of those impregnable writers so unlike "the rest of us" who's been libeled for centuries as a possible fraud: "Hath not a Big-Name Author (or even a puny one) eyes? Hath not an author ears, honor, pride, sensibilities? If you prick us, do we not bleed? . . . And if you wrong us, shall we not revenge?"

Now. Is it any wonder that so many mystery stories feature the murder of an obnoxious critic?

WHINE AND KVETCH, ANYONE?

Bill Pronzini

CRITICS ARE, among other things, harsh masters and mistresses.

Not only is it difficult to please them, they are forever slicing deep and with surgical precision into a writer's work and discovering all sorts of things the writer himself didn't even know were there. Take, for instance, my "Nameless Detective" series. Over the years critics have revealed in their reviews some astonishing facts that subsequently had a profound influence on me and on "Nameless." I'd like to share them with you here, as examples of the epiphanic nature of fiction writing. Live and learn.

Viz.: According to V. Kirkus, I am the "founder of the whine and kvetch school of mystery fiction."

When I first read this, I was pretty excited. It is every writer's dream to be the founder of *something,* and here a well-known reviewing service was bestowing on me the mantle of inventor of an entire "school" of crime writing. I considered the honor.

Kvetch is a Yiddish word meaning, in loose translation, to bitch and grumble. Whine, bitch, and grumble. Okay. But the more I thought about this, the more uneasy I felt. To be the inventor of the whine, bitch, and grumble school of mystery fiction placed a terrible burden of responsibility on my shoulders. In the past I was unaware of whining and kvetching when I wrote a "Nameless" novel or story. Now that I had been enlightened, I could no longer write in blissful ignorance. I had been proclaimed a standard bearer. I must bear the standard proudly and in full and faithful awareness.

I reread everything in the series, long and short, in an attempt to analyze just how and in what context I whined and kvetched. In some cases I could see it clearly; in others . . . no, nary a whimper nor a tiny fuss. I could only conclude that I had failed in some of my early work, had been inconsistent, too often untrue to my innovative vision. Henceforth I had to take great pains to include at least some sharp whining and spirited kvetching in every "Nameless" adventure, even those I intended to be light and amusing.

This has not been an easy task, friends. It requires constant vigilance and concentration to come up with suitable topics about which to bitch, and then bitch about them in an appropriately whiny fashion. Have I succeeded? V. Kirkus thinks so. In all their subsequent reviews of "Nameless" material, they have taken great pains to compliment me, in one fashion or another, on my whining and kvetching. And who am I, after all, to spit in the eye of the bestower?

Viz.: *Publishers Weekly* opined that I have "an unabashedly retro prose style."

This one threw me at first. Unabashedly retro? Nineties new-speak, I decided, for "shamelessly old-fashioned." But was this a compliment or a knock? Did *PW* mean I *should* be ashamed of having an old-fashioned prose style, or did they mean that my old-fashioned prose style was well enough rendered so that I could get away with it without feeling shame? And did they mean to say that my style was a reflection of my personality, that not only Pronzini's writing style but Pronzini himself was retro?

Well, I had to admit that I am not in fact a nineties kind of guy. Old-fashioned, all right, and proud of it. So *PW* must be right: retro guy, retro prose style. I also concluded that they felt it was okay with them that I was one and had one and that I could continue feeling unabashed about being one and having one as long as I was true to my old-fashionedness.

Fine. But I live in the nineties and am therefore constantly subjected to nineties influences. What if I allowed some aspect of the nineties to infect my retro prose style? This would not be so bad if it were an aspect about which I could whine and kvetch, but in all other cases I must guard against such taint. And just how retro *was* my prose style? Not eighties, surely. And probably not seventies. Sixties? Fifties, forties, thirties? Again I reread my early work. Then I reread Hammett, Chandler, Ross Macdonald, Spillane, some of my contemporaries. None of the reading was instructive. My style didn't really sound like any other p.i. writer's style, at least not to me, nor did it seem to fit into any of the periods in which others wrote. A touch of paranoia made me wonder if *PW* meant to place me in some sort of retro limbo. Then I danced over to the opposite end of the speculative spectrum and wondered if perhaps they were obliquely bestowing upon me yet another foundership, that of the school of neo-retro p.i. prose stylists. Finally I decided I was fretting too much about matters beyond my ken and that the only thing I could do was to continue to write as I always have, in my naturally retro prose style, and leave the critical analyses to those who were paid to concoct them.

Nevertheless, I now take considerable pains to keep any and all modernisms from creeping into my work, in particular new-speak terms like *retro*. The only exception is modernisms that lend themselves to whining and kvetching, which must, of course, take precedence above all else in the Pronzini Literary Schematic.

Viz.: The "Nameless" series, again in *PW*'s estimation, is "unrelentingly grim."

Another revelatory burden. Here I'd thought I was injecting humor into the series, wry comments and snappy patter, an occasional joke, some bawdy byplay; here I'd thought that now and then I had even written a funny story such as "Here Comes Santa Claus," or at least not too serious fare such as "Twenty Miles to Paradise" and "Bedeviled." Which just goes to show how wrong one can be about his own retro prose. Once more I reassessed the "Nameless" canon, paying particular attention to the stories mentioned above and to scenes in novels I had believed to be funny. And by golly, *PW* was right again. Funny wasn't funny and light wasn't light; it was all unrelentingly grim *under the surface*. An undercurrent of hopelessness. A wellspring of despair. Who was I to think I could be humorous once in a while? Who was I to think I could be any less or any more than I was? *PW*'s review was like a dark cloud pointing the way through the light.

Now everything I write is unrelentingly grim. In and out of the "Nameless" series. Fiction and nonfiction alike. Afterwords to short story collections not excluded.

Viz.: A reviewer for a tiny newspaper in the Midwest (I'd never even heard of the *town* before) said that "Pronzini piles layer upon layer of meaning into his stories, some of which work and some don't."

I studied this comment carefully. Did the reviewer think I consciously piled layer upon layer of meaning into my stories, or that I accomplished this tricky feat by accident? Just how many layers of meaning did she mean to imply by the phrase "layer upon layer"? Was it her contention that some of the alleged layers worked and some didn't, or that some of the stories worked and some didn't? Was there any profound significance in the fact that a book reviewer, even one for a small-town newspaper, had been allowed to publish a critical opinion that was both unclear *and* ungrammatical?

Again I determined that I was trying to ponder the imponderable. The important thing was that her comment, garbled though it was, was praise of the highest form. Layer upon layer of meaning. Shakespeare territory, by God: I remembered my college English professor using an almost identical phrase—"layers of meaning"—in his discussion of *Hamlet*.

But the glow such an implied parallel produced

in me soon faded. There was a burden here too, and it was doubly heavy. No longer could I write a story on a single level; it could not simply be what it was, a story meant to provide the reader with a few minutes or a few hours of entertainment. No, it must be more than what it was—much more. The more layers the better, one assumes. Four, five, six layers, like a fictional cake frosted with unrelentingly grim retro prose and served with whine and kvetch. And not only that, but I had to make absolutely certain each layer was properly whipped up, or else risk disappointing the midwestern lady and any other critical maven who might also be avidly gulping down my confections.

Now, every time I sit at this infernal machine I am forced into Machiavellian and/or Byzantine, not to mention Shakespearean, contortions in order to produce even a single page of fiction. I no longer plot a story; I layer it. Each scene, each bit of business, must be constructed to enhance and fit harmoniously into one or more layers. This is damned hard work, as you can well imagine. My production pace has fallen off radically. Last week I wrote but a single sentence on the next ''Nameless'' novel: ''The phone rang and I answered it.'' I've got this sentence's secondary and tertiary levels of meaning mapped out, and I'm pretty sure they're perfectly integrated into the whole, but I'm damned if I can come up with a viable quaternary layer.

Viz.: *The New Yorker* stated that ''what really distinguishes [the series] is the feeble state of the detective's health.''

Feeble? ''Nameless''? I'd always considered him rather robust for a man in his late fifties who had led a hard and rugged life. But *The New Yorker* cited a surprising number of narrative complaints of bronchial trouble, headaches, coughing fits, bitter phlegm, nausea, gas, and other physiological ills—

and all in a single novel! Once more I delved into previous titles. He wasn't quite so troubled in those, but ... yes, his health *did* seem to be leaning toward the feeble side. Must in fact *be* feeble: nobody who had so many afflictions could possibly be said to be in tiptop shape.

I was in a quandary. If I continued to have him suffer as I had in the past, how could he and I both go on? He would be ready for a nursing home, if not the boneyard, before he reached retirement age. And yet this tendency toward infirmity was part of his character, even though I had built it in all too unwittingly. I couldn't very well just ignore it from then on. Should I have him somehow miraculously regain his youthful vim and vigor, never to suffer even a pang or a twinge?

Compromise. Keep him hacking and wheezing, belching and farting, but not as often and not to the point where he can no longer function and requires hospitalization. Aches and pains, yes, but a sprinkling rather than a deluge. Days when he feels pretty good, when his temples don't throb, his chest isn't tight, and his bowels aren't inflamed. Whole stories, even, in which he is stricken with nothing more serious than stopped-up sinuses. Vigilant moderation, that was the ticket—in all things including feeble health.

I could go on and on, giving you numerous other examples culled from various reviews and critical commentaries—all burdens I've had to bear and am still bearing. But you get the idea and the point. We writers must not only please our editors and our readers, we must faithfully do our damnedest to scale the lofty pinnacles critics lay before us.

Is it any wonder some of us fail?

Is it any wonder many of us turn to strong drink?

CRITICAL CONTRASTS

Walter and Jean Shine

WE HAVE READ OVER eight-hundred reviews of John D. MacDonald's books in preparing a new edition of our MacDonald bibliography. A fascinating view of critical reaction for thirty-five years. What particularly intrigued us were the amazing contradictions in the responses to the very same book. Hard to believe they were reading the same book. Here are gathered a few that resulted from the publication of *One More Sunday,* perhaps the most critically reviewed (in terms of numbers) of all his works. [Each quotation is from a separate review.]

"**. . . one piece of preaching MacDonald should never have attempted . . .**"

". . . He's never been better than in *One More Sunday.*"

"**. . . MacDonald's obsession for describing people in physical detail doesn't carry over into character . . .**"

". . . he makes his characters human beings . . ."

"**. . . pretty much ho-hum . . .**"

". . . an engrossing tale told with insight and verve . . ."

"**. . . excruciatingly boring lump of a book . . .**"

"There isn't a boring bone in the body of the book."

"**. . . the shallowest sort of writing and with cartoons instead of characters . . .**"

". . . He uses words to create images, themes and characters so powerful they become real in the mind of the reader . . ."

"**. . . the characters lack depth . . .**"

". . . a full cast of the type of quirky characters that John D. MacDonald always seem to make human . . ."

"**. . . Inventing realistic is not MacDonald's forté. The characters . . . are flat, two-dimensional characters—crudely drawn stereotypes, actually . . .**"

"MacDonald has created marvelously distinctive characters to people this book . . ."

"**. . . he has several plot lines, and they all are diluted so that the reader does not have the chance to identify with any thread . . .**"

". . . the new novel is much better than *Condominium* for the simple reason that it has a stronger central story line . . ."

"**Readers should be warned that any likeness to ordinary life in the novel is only superficial.**"

". . . His descriptions of the church's organization . . . are brilliantly done, and the questions of conscience come vividly to life . . ."

"... there is not much to be learned from this author ..."

"... You learn a lot reading the book."

"... a sensitive portrayal of how religion can revitalize the lives of society's dispossessed."

"His polished descriptions of [place] and his thorough knowledge of business [are] fascinating to read ..."

"... loaded with information, which he passes along to you without putting you to sleep ..."

"... a minor melodrama ..."

"... This is an outstanding novel."

"... this book piffs into ineffectiveness ..."

"It is a long and devastating exposé that deserves a place alongside Elmer Gantry."

"... a timely novel lacking impact and focus."

"MacDonald's voice is just as true when singing a hymn as it is for jazz ..."

"... a very ordinary and uninspiring novel ..."

"... A big exciting story by a superb story teller ..."

BEGINNING A NEW SERIES
Margaret Maron

I'D READ PERRY MASON AND RUMPOLE and seen most episodes of *L.A. Law*, but when I contemplated creating a woman lawyer who wants to run for district court judge in a largely rural southern county, I suspected that her concerns were going to be closer to Judge Wapner's than Roz Shays's.

Armed with a notebook, I drove over to the county seat, found an occupied courtroom, and sat down behind some people in the middle section of benches a few minutes before the judge was due to enter. This new addition grafted onto our WWI courthouse is nondescript modern: blond wood; industrial-strength navy and gray carpeting; solid oak tables in front of the judge's high bench, one for defense, one for prosecution; jury box on the right. Almost immediately a bailiff came over to say that the central benches were reserved for the jury pool and we'd have to move to the side benches.

The judge came in, we all rose, we all sat, and not much happened. The young assistant D.A., the judge, an assistant clerk, and a couple of the lawyers exchanged pleasantries among themselves. Others lawyers wandered in and out. Eventually, a deputy sheriff brought in some prisoners and sat them down in the jury box to wait till called. Witnesses and family members came and went as cases were disposed of with lackadaisical ceremony and not much fanfare. Every time any civilians sat down in the middle section, the bailiff chased them. If they were white and well dressed, he came over and spoke nicely. If they were black or poorly dressed whites, he merely stood up at his chair between the jury box and witness stand and made peremptory shooing motions with his hands.

None of the accused asked for a jury trial that day. The judge alone heard both sides, then ruled on guilt or innocence and set whatever penance he wanted within his legal guidelines. (In fact, no jury pool was called for the next two days, but the bailiff was vigilant and kept those benches vacant just in case.)

In the meantime, I'd filled two legal pads with detailed descriptions of the courtroom, the uniforms worn by sworn law officers, the flowery print dresses of the young parole officers, the interaction between the female A.D.A. and the mostly male attorneys. I soon discovered that most of what's said is said in low conversational tones; so when a seat became vacant on the front row, I took it.

Audiences turn over quickly when an efficient judge is snapping out routine decisions. By midafternoon I was the only one left from the morning and I began to get surreptitious glances from the very people I was watching. A lawyer on the attorney's bench just in front of me turned around in his seat. "You waiting for a case to get called?" he asked.

"No." I smiled.

In one of the short recesses a candidate for D.A. with an eye toward my notebook offered a politician's handshake. "You a reporter from Raleigh or something?"

"No."

Another from the good ol' boy school of lawyering paused in the aisle. "Ma'am, you look familiar but I don't believe we've met. Your people from around here?"

"Yes," I admitted. "Pleasant Grove Township over in the western part of the county."

He waited for more. I smiled pleasantly and began asking *him* questions till court reconvened.

I'm not sure if it was the judge who sent him or whether he couldn't stand the curiosity any longer, but the bailiff finally came over and flat-out asked me what I was doing there. "I'm researching a book," I said. "I'm just here to learn how the court system operates."

By the time I took my seat the next morning, it was clear that everyone in court knew why I was

there. Self-consciousness stiffened the air. The bailiff moved a little more snappily and officiously, the candidate for D.A. made it clear that the only reason he was defending such an unsavory client was that it was a pro bono case, and the judge suddenly started explaining to each dazed defendant the specific law upon which judgment was based. All I had to do was cock my head and look puzzled and he'd immediately elaborate—all for the defendant's benefit, of course.

Fortunately, as the week wore on, I became a familiar (and ignorable) fixture, and everyone gradually reverted to normal. I signed up for some paralegal courses at the local community college and began to correlate what I was seeing in the courtroom with what's on the law books.

Ours is not a particularly criminous area, but our superior courts certainly hear their share of armed robbery, assault with a deadly weapon, possession with intent to sell. And every Monday morning when the weekly calendar is called in district court, it's the same long litany of larceny, B and E, D.W.I., uttering a forged instrument (legalese for signing someone else's check), statutory rape. Over and over and over again come the same charges. The faces may change—though not as often as one would hope—and for every scared kid facing the full impact of the legal system for the first time, there are a dozen recidivists who've been in court almost as often as the judge and lawyers.

I'm still a neophyte in the courtroom, but already I can see that boredom and a sense of futility are going to give my new character problems if she gets elected. Anyone can be judicious and conscientious in a spectacular murder trial, but how do you keep your humanity and concentration focused when the A.D.A. calls for the nineteenth worthless-check case of the week and it's only Wednesday? You sent this very same crack dealer to prison last January and here he is back again, same court, same reason for being here. How do you keep his flinty-eyed face from blurring into the face of the first-time teenager who has hardened his own eyes so you won't see how terrified he is?

Justice Learned Hand likened administering justice to shoveling smoke. I don't yet know what Judge Deborah Knott is going to call it.

ON THE ROAD WITH THELMA AND LOUISE

Joan Hess

FOR THOSE OF YOU who haven't been paying attention, I was busy this fall. In a two-month period I promoted my books in Atlanta, Colorado Springs, Boulder, Denver, Bellingham, Bellevue, Seattle, Portland, Beverly Hills, L.A., Pasadena, Orange, Sherman Oaks, Long Beach, Sacramento, S.F., Berkeley, Menlo Park, N.Y.C., Boston, D.C., Bethesda, Baltimore, Kansas City, Overland Park, Lawrence, Independence, Bartlesville, Tulsa, and Broken Arrow.

Yes, there will be a quiz over the material, and spelling counts.

I did panels and signings with such notables as Sharyn McCrumb, Wendy Hornsby, A. and E. Maxwell, Conrad Haynes, Carolyn Hart, Margaret Maron, Jean Hager, Eve Sandstrom, and Susan Rogers Cooper. I did a television gig with Sue Dunlap and Faye Kellerman. I chatted with fifteen hundred folks at the B'con. I had lunch with Rosemary Herbert and Susan Kelly, and dinner with Daniel Stashower. I had a wonderful time in Atlanta one Sunday evening at Agatha's, a participatory dinner-theater that dished up a delicious five-course meal with wine . . . and murder.

And then there were those cities where I sat alone in hotel rooms, bemoaning the fact that I'd worked my way through the Spectre-Vision flicks and was reduced to network television.

The Glamorous Author Tour was an experience I would wish only to those writers who make a helluva lot more money than I do and deserve whatever else they get. However, in an insincere display of camaraderie, I will share a few insights (and, if asked nicely, will show my scar tissue).

1) Take food. One memorable night, long about midnight, I arrived in a Sacramento hotel after seven relentless hours of GAT activity. I weakly inquired if there was room service and was told there most certainly was—until ten o'clock. Picture, if you will, the subject of the GAT sitting on the bed, eating Chee-tos and damn glad to have 'em.

2) Take books, magazines, crossword puzzles. But don't take a manuscript that, after a week or two of exhaustion, frustration, and bleak Chee-to nights, you'll be inclined to savage. Uncle Aaron warned me about this, and he was right. I may have sparkled in the bookstores, but when I hit the hotel room, often I was not in what one would describe as a charitable mood (many hotel clerks across this great land of ours will attest to this). I hate to think about the revisions I might have made on a perfectly decent manuscript. In blood, and not necessarily my own.

3) Take care. One night I was almost gunned down in the hallway of the Beverly Hills Hilton by a security guard with absolutely no sense of humor. This is not to say mine was in great shape, but this guy was downright grim. Do I have your attention? Okay, it seemed that the first eight rooms on both sides of the corridor were being used by an Arab emir and his extensive entourage (the bellman swore they were slaves). All doors were kept open, including the one with a desk, an array of communications equipment, and the above-mentioned guard. I was coming back from the bar (hey, there might have been movie stars) and happened to spot a closed-circuit camera hidden in a potted plant. I found this highly amusing, and proceeded to speak to it in the dippy voice one uses with babies and dumb animals. Apparently, this is precisely the same voice used by bomb-wielding maniacs intent on blowing up an Arab emir, his wives, his slaves, and his security guard.

4) Take a nap. This is done when one discovers the loquacious escort with whom one will spend many, many hours is of a radically different political persuasion. In truth, I was lucky as long as we avoided certain topics. Escorts were the only reason

I survived with what few remaining marbles I had. All I was required to do was appear—at the airport, the lobby, the bookstore—and some gentle soul would handle the rest.

5) Take advantage of the escorts. Most of them charge a flat fee for some number of hours. I never sent one to run errands on my behalf, but I did request detours so that I could shop for gifts for my children and . . . well, Chee-tos and other necessities of life. Whenever time allowed, I asked to stop by bookstores not on the schedule (in Boston we did five additional ones). And then there's gossip to be had from them. "So whom else have you driven?" I'd murmur sweetly. "Oh, really? What was he/she like?" I heard some good dirt.

6) Take advantage of the publisher. Yeah, yeah, they're footing the bill and presumably springing for swanky hotels (by the way, the escorts know your status based on where you stay). But the GAT cost me some bucks, not only for clothes and such, but also for the college student who stayed with my children and the outrageous gifts I bought to appease my maternal conscience and quiet their vocalized displeasure over my absence. Aunt Nancy told me that the first thing she did while on the GAT was to have a manicure and charge it to the room. I tried it, but the manicurist had to be paid at the time and I didn't have the nerve to turn in the receipt to my publicist. Then again, in Boston the concierge arranged for a theater ticket to *Shear Madness* and put it on the room bill.

7) Take a break. Go to the theater. After all, it doesn't cost anything if you call the concierge and . . .

8) Take shoes. Sure, it was sandal weather in Southern California the first week in October. Two weeks later in Boston, it wasn't.

Hmm, I seem to be out of truisms (although more may strike). The obvious question is whether I thought all this did any good. I really don't know. The booksellers and customers purported to be pleased to see me, but it's hard to determine how many books were sold simply because I waltzed across the threshold. The author who's been dominating all the best seller lists (as of late January, for sixteen weeks) calculated that she signed twenty thousand copies. Over two million copies have been sold, which means she signed less than one percent of them, and only in the last week has she been allowed to take the sling off her arm.

My figures are a bit smaller, I must admit, but

they don't have to be if all of you will get out there and—never mind. There's no way to know if drivers who listen to their radios during rush hour, instead of paying attention to potentially lethal concerns like city buses, will rush out to buy a book because the author explained on the air (for the zillionth time) where she got her ideas. At a signing in Kansas City, three people told me they'd come because they saw me on a local cable show. The particular show had been taped at ten-thirty at night—after a day that encompassed a seven A.M. flight, two other shows, a library talk, and a bookstore signing. Two minutes into the interview I lapsed into random neural activity. There I was, lights glaring, cameras glowing, and this nice young woman was talking away merrily. And I couldn't understand a word of what she was saying. But it sold books, apparently.

One of the escorts told me he estimated it cost $2000 per city on the GAT, including air fare (I certainly didn't run up any room service bills like that). It's a strong indication of a publisher's support to shell out that kind of money to send a bleary-eyed author reeling across the country. But there are other possibilities that might be more cost effective. Sisters in Crime sponsored a booth at the American Library Association convention in Atlanta in June, and we were received with great enthusiasm. Librarians are lovely, just lovely. In September several of us attended the Southeastern Booksellers Association, a mini-ABA of sorts, did a panel, and signed books. In that one weekend I felt as if I'd visited two hundred bookstores. I've already asked my publicist about the Southern Bookseller's show in New Orleans next September. For you novices, the trick is to whine for an extended GAT, the ABA, SEBA, ALA, Rio, Bologna, Frankfurt, the *Today* show, a full-page ad in *The New York Times,* and anything else you can think of—the more ludicrous, the better. They may toss you a few scraps to shut you up. No, I am not going to say which of you booksellers was a scrap. I love every one of you.

Back to Thelma and Louise, briefly. If you arrange to do a bookstore with someone else, it can be publicized as a panel rather than a signing. This lures in people who had no intention of buying a book and would have stayed away, and also people who like your compatriot and have never read your books.

There are other obvious perks. Being lost by

yourself in, say, Boulder, after having been lost for three gawdawful hours in Colorado Springs and Denver (out by the airport, for pity's sake; to this day I have no idea how I got out there to begin with), is not an occasion for levity. In contrast, being lost with a compatriot in, say, Seattle, can be the cause of much merriment, especially if you have the sense to ask directions from a clerk in a liquor store. If the two of you are signing in, say, a mall bookstore in Bellingham, you'll have someone to talk to when you are not busy explaining that you aren't an employee and therefore have no clue where the latest Stephen King novel is shelved.

As I was driving away from the last panel (dur-ing which, while gripped by exuberance, I accused Eve of alphabetizing her clothes; I'd like to take this opportunity to admit I was only speculating), I solemnly swore off any more promotion until the end of this summer. I shared this with the toll booth attendant an hour later.

Yeah, right. Guess who was on the phone the other day, setting up panels/signings for March in Florida (Tampa and Tallahassee), and in New Mex-ico (Albuquerque, Santa Fe, and Taos)? I seem to recall recent conversations with booksellers in St. Louis, Midlothian, Va., and Pittsburgh. And as long as I'm doing Pittsburgh, how far can it be to Akron?

A MODEST PROPOSAL FOR THE CATEGORIZATION OF MYSTERIES

Lawrence Block

SEVERAL TIMES IN RECENT YEARS there has been agitation for the establishment of of-ficial categories within the overall field of mystery fiction, especially in respect to awards. The argument has been advanced that a system that sim-ply recognized a "best" annual novel for the entire field is apt to lean toward books of a certain strip and slight others which, while every bit as worthy, are horses of another color. Judges, one is given to understand, consistently favor the realistic over the romantic, the dark over the light, the serious over the frivolous, the hard-boiled over the cozy, the yang over the yin.

There have been various attempts to rectify this situation. New organizations have sprung into being, each handing out an annual award for the best book in a particular category. *Mystery Scene* has established a whole slate of awards which di-vide the field into a host of subgenres. (I myself was greatly honored this past year when my book,

Out on the Cutting Edge, was nominated for an award in the category of Best Private Eye Novel with a New York Setting by a Male Writer Over 40; I only wish I'd walked off with the prize, but, with so much great work being done in that sub-genre, the nomination was honor enough.)

Mystery Writers of America has steadfastly re-sisted the pressure to establish categories of mystery fiction. The prevailing sentiment has always been that to do so would be to dilute the considerable prestige of the Edgar Allan Poe awards, which were established to honor the best work in the field with-out qualification. To establish a special award, say, for the year's best work of romantic suspense, would be to say in effect that the book in question would not merit recognition save in its particular category. To give such awards for the best juvenile mystery, the best paperback original, the best first novel, would not so demean the recipients, but to do so with subgenres would.

More recently, there has been increasing opinion favoring two categories—and a great deal of difficulty in determining just how those categories are to be defined. The best classic puzzle and the best realistic novel, the best hard-boiled book and the best cozy, the best dark book and the best light book, the best serious book and the best comic novel. The best yin, that is to say, and the best yang.

The problem here, it seems to me, is how to decide what book belongs in what category. Hardly a month goes by that I don't read a classic puzzle which is also a hard-edged look at crime in modern times, or a tough book which is also humorous, or a fine piece of crime fiction which is at once dark and light, and all shades of gray in between. To require of an Edgar awards committee or chairperson that he or she or they decide which nominated book is eligible for which award would place an impossible burden on a person or persons already overtaxed. To assign this chore to the various publishers who nominate the books would require such persons to be more familiar with the works they've published than they very often are. Even assuming the publishers have read the books, how good are they going to be in determining their place in categories we ourselves are hard put to define?

Yet another suggestion, that an Edgar be given annually for Best Book by a Male Author and Best Book by a Female Author, hardly deserves comment.

It occurs to me that there may be an easy way to manage a fair solution. I would propose two categories, so composed that one may determine instantly and without argument into which category any given book ought to be consigned.

To wit: Books with Cats and Books Without Cats.

The boundaries of these two subgenres are, it seems to me, quite perfectly defined. A book either has a cat in it or it does not. The role the cat plays—i.e., whether it solves the crime or merely crossed the hero's path—is immaterial. If there's a cat in the book, in any capacity whatsoever, the book is eligible for the Best Mystery with Cats award. If there's not, it's not.

At the same time, the distinction is not purely arbitrary. Books with Persian Rugs and Books Without Persian Rugs is every bit as clear cut, but serves no purpose. The cat, though, is a good litmus test for the mystery. It is true, to be sure, that there are cozies without cats, even as there are hard-boiled books with them, but that's no problem. Imagine the fun when a novel by James Ellroy, say, wins Best Mystery with Cats.

I won't pursue this any further. It is, to be sure, very much a modest proposal, with a great deal to be modest about. My intent is merely to launch it among you and let it go where it will—to run it up a tree, as it were, and see if it can get down by itself. Meanwhile, I've got a book of my own to write.

Don't ask.

ON THIS SIDE

with Michael Seidman

"Where have you gone, Joe DiMaggio?"

AMERICA TODAY IS A LAND STARVED for mythology, a people looking for a hero (or heroine, but the former has fewer letters, types more quickly; therefore, it is the word we will use, but in its most generic sense).

And when we have one, when we find one, then we begin to tear it down. Or place blame, become accusatory when our expectations cannot be fulfilled because the hero we have chosen, when the mythological figure we create from living flesh and blood, proves to be nothing more or less than that flesh and blood, *human,* we say they are at fault.

We've done it with John F. Kennedy. We've done it with Pete Rose. We've done it again and again. We've done it with Davy Crockett, establishing that he didn't die in the [vain]glorious way we learned on Walt Disney, as portrayed variously by Fess Parker or John Wayne, but that he surrendered and was executed, along with others in that small sandstone building next to a meandering stream.

Mythology? What are the American myths? There was Paul Bunyan and his great blue ox, Babe. Once upon a time, we learned of them. No more, though; the lumberman is not part of the curriculum. Maybe it is ecologically unsound.

John Henry, that steel-driving man. He's there in song (which is the proper place for the origins of myth, so many of the world's began that way. Or in epic poems, which are closely enough related that the difference is moot).

Pecos—Pecos, who? Was it Bill? Or Pete? I don't remember, remembering only that he rode the whirlwind, saddled the tornado, and crossed that same meandering stream that flows by the Alamo.

Joseph Campbell has talked of the hero of a thousand faces, of the impact of mythology on our lives. Psychologists (I spit on their race, even as I now use their words) have found a new classification for human behavior, positing that we model our lives—unconsciously or subconsciously—on the mythological figures. People have Promethean personalties, or Dianic . . . whatever. (Undoubtedly, parallel figures can and are found among the mythic characters of every race, every nation. Except America as we know her today, sadly.) So, be Loki or Siva or Spider or Raven or White Buffalo Calf Woman or Monkey. The archetype is there, part of the Jungian unconscious.

Except America, I said. Here, having become homogenized, melting-potted, we pay lip service in private to the myths of the culture we bore before assimilation. Which is fine. Which must never be lost . . . because we have nothing with which to replace it.

Yes, we hunger for it. Where do we find those to emulate? Separately or together we worship Madonna or Cher; Michael Jackson or Billy Ray Cyrus, or, or, or. Swoon for an actor, argue on behalf of an athlete. Rather than ranks of gods and demigods battling across the heavens, we pit the Los Angeles Raiders against the Phoenix Cardinals (both of which started out in different places; our gods are no less or more caring than any in the myths of man). Oliver North had his fifteen minutes under the laurel leaves; some still call him hero. Some. Who is there for all of us, woman and man, inno-

cent child or jaded adult? Where have you gone, Joe Di?

It is not right (forget "fair," forget "just." Neither of those is promised, guaranteed) for us to put the mantle on the living. With the possible exception of Mother Teresa, there are no saints. We do not have the *right* to ask someone to stand for us that way. We blame Pete Rose of letting us down . . . because he is human. We blame JFK. We look askance at the ways in which Michael Jordan does what he does with his money on the golf course or at the craps tables. We say that they have a responsibility to us . . . to the children . . . to be without sin. (And, finally, Charles Barkley performs in a commercial for Nike, making it clear that just because he does what he does with a basketball, it doesn't give us the right to ask anything else of him. He is not, he says, responsible for our children. Yes! And it counts.)

The writer is the shaman of the tribe. That's been said here before, but it bears repeating now. Imagine that day when humankind learned to communicate. In the beginning, yet even before the Word, there was the Question. Who? What? Why? And the first communications were the answers. The beginning of myth. The beginning of storytelling. Among the Arapaho, the story of the creation takes four nights to tell, four nights sheltered in lodges against the cold of the Plains. The story must be told the same way, word for word, every time. Else, the world will end. Then and now, such is the tradition, such is the myth of the myth. It is what makes storytelling, that ability to relate a tale in such a way that it can be remembered and repeated. Such is the importance of myth, of the hero, that the story is, indeed, repeated.

And we, us, repeat the tales whose origins are lost (but whose meaning is not; Cronus as parable). But where are the myths we are leaving for those who come next? Where are our heroes?

Once upon a time, the late Irving Stone wrote a novel titled *Men to Match My Mountains*. Where are the people, today, to match our mountains? Why aren't they in our fiction?

It is, of course, from our fiction that the hero must come, just as the mythological heroes, Hercules and his myriad cousins, sprang from stories created to explain the world. That is myth. And we still need myth, because we still don't understand what it is that is going on around us, why really, a young black boy is shot dead on a Bensonhurst street or a five-year-old child is shoved down the chute of a trash compactor. We need someone to fight for us because most of us are too weak to fight effectively. We need someone to represent us—positively, to be the things we lack. We need a hero, we need someone larger than life, we need a Batman or Superman (now, commercially, deceased) or Wonder Woman scaled down but still bigger than me and thee.

To a certain degree our readers have indicated that need. The straightforward antihero does not garner the overwhelming attention of the book-buying audience. Make them big enough, the Corleone Family perhaps, and we are fascinated. But some of the figures of myth were very, very bad. Not mildly; they were evil, a threat. Do you want your child to grow up a made man, get his bones? Yeah, the money's nice. But the *angst!*

We are fascinated by evil; there is a prurient interest and quite possibly a release in reading about an Edward Gein or a Charles Starkweather; true crime sells. Today. The grimier, the uglier, the more wicked and sordid, the better. We can wipe our brows and thank the gods that the characters are not ourselves, either victim or perpetrator. But someone catches the bad guy in the end, someone big enough to stand up against the horror walking among us in the guise of man. And a hero must have something large enough to fight, something worthy of the war. Elephant guns and flies just don't do it, after all. Our heroic figures—the ones we set up only to knock down, the stars—are not fighting anything, the cosmic battle has been reduced to one against himself. It is interesting for a short time. Perhaps that is one of the reasons we take such glee in discovering the feet of clay, why we search for it so willingly. (Or is it possible that *that* is the reality of the cosmos, that life is a deep well, as the guru said? Is it all so meaningless? Nah.)

We don't need heroes with warts in our fiction, they are too much with us day by day. We need strength—of mind and body. Abilities to envy, powers that are not out of reach, but just too far away to make chasing them viable for Everyman. It is the reason, the overriding reason, that Louis L'Amour was so successful in an area of writing marked by a notable lack of success today. His characters were men to match the nation's mountains. Horatio Alger with balls.

The situations they find themselves in, these he-roes I want—the ones we need—have to be real. That's why Jessica Fletcher just doesn't qualify. (Even acknowledging that there is a macho aspect to all of this. Strength, courage . . . things in disrepute in this age of technoporn and crystals and mantras . . . they still count. Deep down inside us, they still very much count.)

If writers interpret that which they see, and if what we are being offered to read is a valid representation of that which is seen (and not simply a game between author and reader) what more indication do we need of the sorry state we find ourselves in? There is evil around us—always has been, always will be; *Brave New World* is purely dystopic—but not everyone has been beaten. Those who are fighting the evil in the myths we read from our contemporary sayers and seers do not have to share Everyman's world-weariness. Alo Nudger has to get off Tums.

Those who watch the figures—sales, returns, advances, royalties, all the day-to-day minutiae which makes publishing so questionable an enterprise—wonder why certain books don't do better. After all, doesn't the book go right to the heart of what ails us, doesn't it describe, in brutal, bleeding color, the world we live in?

Isn't that the problem? The solution is not in the comic books, in the caricature of the heroic figure, but in the depiction of a real *goodness,* of honor, of strength. Our culture, because of our writing (which did come first, the chicken or the egg; it is all a Mobius strip), has accepted warts as all. But there are people who exist around us who fulfill all the criteria. We just don't seem to find them interesting as subjects because we can't identify with them as creators. We are not big enough ourselves and our work mirrors us. We don't see them because we refuse to look; we're too busy looking for the mugger.

Create a hero. Create A Hero. A HERO. Write large and bold. Create a myth worth telling over and over for a period of four nights, memorable so that it can be repeated, so that is has meaning for *all* who hear it, so that misstating it will bring permanent night.

Heroes should be legend, and legend should be legion.

It is all myth, and when myth ends, so do we.

America needs a myth. Where have you gone, Joe DiMaggio?

FANDOM

AN OVERVIEW
OF MYSTERY FANDOM

Robert Napier

FANZINES ARE THE GLUE that holds mystery fandom together.

A fanzine is a small magazine published by a fan for fans of a genre/character/author/whatever. They are generally supported by subscriptions and available only by mail from the publisher. A fanzine is a labor of love produced for the dedicated, knowledgeable reader or interested newcomer. Through them, people from around the world can meet, correspond with, and befriend other mystery lovers.

While it may be impossible to say with certainty when the first mystery fanzine was released, it is undeniable that 1967 was a watershed year for this phenomenon. That year saw the debuts of *The Mystery Lover's Newsletter* in August and Allen J. Hubin's *The Armchair Detective* in October. Lianne Carlin, editor of *The Mystery Lover's Newsletter* (which would later be called *The Mystery Reader's Newsletter*) opened her simple five-page prospectus

issue thusly: "This publication is being introduced in the hope that it will prove to both entertain and inform those who cherish the art of the mystery story." Under that banner a movement was born.

Not that the mystery had been entirely ignored to that point, but most journals had been geared toward specific authors and/or characters; i.e., Sherlock Holmes, Ellery Queen, Edgar Wallace, to name a few. Single-author publications tend to concentrate on their subjects exclusively. They pursue any avenue, mention any minutia, that relates to their area of focus. With *MLN* and *TAD,* the net was cast over a wider realm. Indeed, the entire world of the mystery story became the province of these magazines, and others that followed the path blazed by pioneers like Carlin and Hubin.

Rather than concentrating on the achievements of a single writer or series, fanzines presented material on anyone or anything relating to the field, whether private eye, amateur sleuth, police procedural, English manor house mysteries, village cozies, thrillers, espionage, etc. In addition, movie, radio, theater, and television were discussed, dissected, and reviewed.

Through word of mouth, notices in obscure journals, and blind chance, people who had read, collected, and studied mysteries were drawn to these publications. Many were eager to share their knowledge with the growing number of kindred spirits who subscribed to fanzines. Other fanzines sprung up, with titles such as *The Age of the Unicorn, The Mystery Nook, Xenophile, The Mystery Trader, Cloak and Dagger, The Poisoned Pen, The Mystery Fancier, The Short Sheet,* and *Sleuth Journal* (all now defunct, as is *Mystery Reader's Newsletter*).

Today, *TAD* is a slick, quality showcase of mystery appreciation, though Hubin has long since relinquished the reins. Two publications, *Mystery News* and *The Criminal Record,* devote themselves to reviews. *The Drood Review of Mystery* combines reviews with social and political commentary about the genre. *The Magnifying Glass* attempts to catalogue book-signing dates, transitions, and gossip. England gives us *CADS* (*Crime and Detective Stories*), a general-interest fanzine, and Australia offers *Mean Streets* for friends of the tough guy/girl school. *Mystery Readers Journal* turns out thematic issues. Yours truly publishes *Mystery & Detective Monthly,* which is devoted to discussion via letters to the editor and a listing of new releases. There are others, and each attempts to fill a niche in its own way.

In tandem with the proliferation of mystery fanzines was the yearly Bouchercon, named for author/critic Anthony Boucher, now subtitled the World Mystery Convention. Since it was launched in 1970, fans, authors, editors, booksellers, and other mystery aficionados gathered for a yearly celebration of the genre. This provided a channel for distribution of fanzines and a chance to increase the subscriber base, not to mention develop friendships, meet authors, and get involved with fannish pursuits.

With organization came expansion, and fanzines provided a stable base for this increase. Through the 1970s and into the 80s, the number of people intimately involved with mystery fandom grew.

The Bouchercon was a movable feast, celebrated in venues such as New York, Boston, Los Angeles, Washington, Chicago, Milwaukee, Baltimore, Minneapolis, Philadelphia, San Francisco and San Diego. Bouchercons went from small gatherings to SRO affairs, and have been held in England and Canada in recent years, giving them a truly international patina. Whereas there used to be no guarantee that someone would deign to host the following year's Bouchercon, today two or three committees vie for the honor of bringing the affair to their city and the bids are taken three years in advance.

While Bouchercon mushroomed, smaller regional U.S. conventions developed, such as Malice Domestic (the Baltimore/Washington, D.C., area), Left Coast Crime (California), and the Midwest Mystery and Suspense Convention (Omaha and Austin). Most conventions have added a Fan Guest of Honor to their dais. People like Marvin Lachman, William F. Deeck, Ellen Nehr, Linda Toole, Don Sandstrom, and Art Scott have been tapped to represent the important contributions made by fans to the

genre over the past quarter century. In fact, every mystery convention has been organized and staffed by fans who have volunteered their time and energy selflessly.

Bouchercon and Malice Domestic have also instituted literary awards à la the Edgar (the Anthony and Agatha, respectively), and the recipients proudly add these to their résumés and cover blurbs. These awards are voted upon by the convention's attendees, the majority of whom are fans. The American Mystery Awards, sponsored by *Mystery Scene* magazine, include a category for Best Fan Publication.

Fandom's influence is felt in the publishing field too. A number of fans have turned their efforts on behalf of fanzines into critical/biographical books. Witness Jon Breen's *Novel Verdicts* or Walter Albert's *Mystery & Detective Fiction: A Bibliography of Secondary Sources.* Monumental efforts such as Allen J. Hubin's *The Bibliography of Crime Fiction* boasts contributions by a Who's Who of mystery fans, many of whom wet their feet in fanzine waters. *Hardboiled,* a short story quarterly, represents a springboard for fledgling writers. Perhaps the most incestuous of fan publications is *The Big Jacuzzi,* a collection of short stories all titled "The Big Jacuzzi" based on an incident in a hotel lobby during a convention. Amazingly, this modest effort sold out and a second volume, *Farewell, My Lobby,* is in the works.

Perhaps the best indication that a fandom has reached its majority is when it is seen as more than a ragtag collection of enthusiasts, when it gains the noble distinction of being considered a consumer group. In this wise, mystery fandom has a ways to go. There are no big publishers turning out limited-edition, high-ticket works with an eye to hard-core mystery enthusiasts. However, a small publisher, Mystery Scene Press (Pulphouse Publishing), has given us paperbacks containing a single short story each by luminaries like Edward D. Hoch, Loren D. Estleman, Bill Pronzini, Marcia Muller, John Lutz, and Margaret Maron. *Drood Review* publishes an annual mystery update. Copperfield Press offers pocket-size checklists of selected authors' works for collectors. Experiments like this may not create wealth, but they demonstrate someone is willing to market unorthodox material for a specific audience, an audience best reached via fan gatherings and publications.

That the number of people who actively participate in mystery fandom is such a puny fraction of the mystery readers worldwide—and mysteries are an enormously popular genre—is a puzzlement in itself. I have been asked why this seeming disparity exists, why many millions of people read mysteries yet the number who participate in fandom, no matter how peripherally, is under ten thousand. Well under, no doubt.

I can only speculate, but my observation is that it is simply the nature of the beast. The average mystery reader is middle-aged, conservative (not necessarily politically, but behaviorally), and has an abundance of family, business, and/or social responsibilities. The majority are female. These people simply don't have the time or inclination to get involved with mysteries beyond reading them. Admittedly this is a broad generalization, but I think the foundation is solid. Having attended science fiction, comic book, and mystery conventions over the past twenty-five years, this reporter can tell you the differences between mystery fans and other genre fans are legion.

While the growth of mystery fandom has been steady but slow, the potential for new blood remains ever hopeful. The meteoric rise in the number of mystery specialty bookstores during the past decade, along with the burgeoning number of mystery conventions, conferences, and murder-mystery events, assures us that some of these people will discover the enjoyment and enlightenment that await anyone who joins mystery fandom. And it is, after all, the pleasure of the experience that keeps people in fandom. There is the joy of shared interests, the availability of a great reservoir of knowledge, and the friendships that develop both face-to-face and across the miles.

Mystery fandom is a loose coalition of enthusiasts, not all of whom share a widespread appreciation of the genre. Some people like gritty crime novels, others the restrained snooping of a little old lady. Whatever their interests, however, there is a fanzine somewhere that will appeal to their tastes.

The Armchair Detective, which recently celebrated its silver anniversary, would be my choice for gaining entry into the world of mystery fandom. It has been around a long time, and by all appearances will stay around. Such steadfastness is important when one considers that fanzines can come and go abruptly. *TAD* can be reached at 129 West 56 Street, New York, NY 10019. From there one can discover other periodicals, whether general-interest or single-author.

And if you decide to get involved with mystery fandom, remember this: Relax and enjoy yourself; you're among friends.

CONVENTIONS
Malice and Mayhem in Numbers
Janet A. Rudolph

ALTHOUGH MANY PEOPLE confine their interest in mysteries to reading by themselves in the privacy of their own living room, there are others who enjoy the camaraderie, the excitement, and the stimulation of gathering with other readers, writers, and fans at mystery conventions. Mystery conventions have been proliferating over the last ten years, and the globe is fast becoming "riddled" with these gatherings.

There are many reasons fans and writers choose to attend conventions. I asked a cross-section of attendees why they go to mystery conventions, and here are some of the responses I got.

"To get together with other fans and aficionados and talk and drink and socialize!"

"To find good books, to talk to other people about books, to find treasures."

"It's an opportunity to take a vacation built around an event."

"To rub elbows with famous writers I read and discover they're real people."

"To meet with and listen to other writers and hear about their successes and failures both in writing and getting published or produced."

"To listen to panels and find out what's new."

Another reason some people go to conventions is to sell a book. Agents and editors attend conventions, and even if they don't want to meet you at this time (after all, they're fans too), at least you have a chance to listen to them and find out what they're looking for. And you can meet other pre-published writers who can give you some pointers based on their experiences. Another reason for attending conventions is to become "inspired." Many people who would like to write but who haven't yet go to conventions, and as a result begin to write. Listening to writers often has that effect.

A major part of any mystery convention is the book room. Dealers from all over the world bring their specialty books and the books of the attending authors. This is important to fans and writers alike. I've met people at conventions who only visit the book room. They never attend panels. To each his own.

Whatever your reasons for attending, there are many conventions to attend. For the purpose of this article, I am addressing fan conventions. (Writers conventions for and by writers is another topic.) Mystery conventions take many forms. **Bouchercon,** the World Mystery Convention, is the largest convention. First held in 1969, it was composed of fans who got together to discuss mysteries and honor the memory of Anthony Boucher, writer, reviewer, and fan. What was originally a gathering of one-hundred fans has now grown into a huge convention of eighteen-hundred fans, writers, editors, and publishers. There is triple-track programming (three panels offered at the same time throughout the convention), a film program, a huge dealer's room, a banquet, other social functions, autograph signings, readings, and more. Panel topics can include anything from "Murder on the Menu: Culinary Crimes" to "Breaking into the Mystery

World." Topics are limited only by the committee's or participants' imaginations. Most panels are composed of a good mixture of fans, writers, and editors. Most mystery conventions have a guest of honor, and Bouchercon is no exception. Past guests of honor at B'con have included P. D. James, Ed Hoch, Charlotte MacLeod, Lawrence Block, Donald Westlake, Tony Hillerman, Simon Brett, Robert Parker, and Helen McCloy. Since the Bouchercon is a fan convention (organized and produced by fans) there is usually a fan guest of honor. Past fan guests of honor have included John Nieminski, Marvin Lachman, Len and June Moffatt, Bob Adey, Linda Toole, and William F. Deeck. Many conventions also include awards. The Bouchercon has the Anthony awards. These are best novel, short story, first novel, etc., awards nominated by and voted on by membership. Awards are a topic for another chapter of this book, but it should be noted that awards are a very important part of Bouchercon and some of the other conventions. And as if panels, banquets, book rooms, and the bar social scene isn't enough activity, many mystery groups, both professional and fan, such as Sisters in Crime, Mystery Readers International, Private Eye Writers of America, International Association of Crime Writers, and the American Crime Writers League hold functions at Bouchercon since so many of their members are in attendance. The Bouchercon convenes in the fall with the site rotating from the East to the Midwest to the West in the U.S. and with

Canada and England taking the eastern slot a few times.

But Bouchercon is too far away, you say? Or too big? There are now several regional conventions. The original intent of regional conventions was to accommodate local writers and fans who couldn't travel to Bouchercon or to emphasize the uniqueness of the region, but many of the same writers and fans attend regional conventions outside their own region. The reasons for this are many and varied. First, many writers and fans are just not content with gathering together only once a year. Another reason is that a convention is always a good place to promote a book. **Left Coast Crime** is the annual West Coast convention held President's Day weekend (three days of events). This convention is limited to four-hundred attendees, a third of whom are writers. Besides dual track paneling, this convention has added "fireside" chats, police lab visits, and forensic lectures. The small nature of this convention creates a relaxed atmosphere that gives fans ample time to get together and chat about favorite books, meet new friends, and visit with old ones. The **Midwest Mystery and Suspense Convention** is usually held in Omaha on Memorial Day weekend. It's also been known as the **Southwest Mystery and Suspense Convention** which was held in Austin the year Bouchercon was held in Omaha. This is another small convention, but it packs a wallop. It seems to emphasize the hard-boiled mystery, but all are welcome. The Private Eye Writers of America have an annual meeting at this time, where they nominate for the Shamus awards. The number of fans who attend and the focus on fans as well as writers is in the true spirit of conventions. The **Mid-Atlantic Mystery Book Fair and Convention** is held in Philadelphia in November. Centrally located, this convention draws people from all over the eastern seaboard. All of these regional conventions have panels, book rooms, banquets, signings, and more. By the time you read this, there will probably be many more of these smaller regional conventions.

There are also conventions that focus on a particular theme or single author or have grown out of the interest of a particular group. **Malice Domestic** is an annual convention dedicated to "cozy" crime. It is held the last weekend in April in Bethesda, Maryland. Since it's limited to 450 participants, there's plenty of time to meet other fans/writers in this very well run convention. Requirement: You must enjoy "comfortable domestic crime." One of the truly nice things about Malice Domestic is that since it's held in the same location every year, it's like coming home. Besides panels, a book room, and a banquet, there is a high tea held on the final day. Malice Domestic members nominate and vote on the Agatha awards. **Phantom Friends,** an organization of people who read and collect juvenile mystery series, holds an annual convention for its membership in June. Separate from this group, the University of Iowa held a three-day conference (convention) devoted to **Nancy Drew.** The **Dorothy L. Sayers Society** holds an annual convention in England every summer. Speakers, bell-ringing, dinner, and services are often part of the program. There are, of course, many Sherlock Holmes conventions, too numerous to mention here.

Some more general mystery conventions held in other countries have included the Symposium in Blockhus, North Jutland, Denmark, on Nordic crime fiction in 1992. And every spring **Shots on the Page** runs in conjunction with **Shots in the Dark,** an international film, television, and arts festival with a crime and mystery theme. **Semana Negra** is another international film and writers convention that is open to the public. It is held during the summer and consists of a week of meetings, talks, and films.

In addition, there are many libraries and universities that sponsor small conventions and conferences. The Friends of the Stockton (California) Library sponsored an annual Mystery Readers and Writers Conference. This one-day conference included a keynote speaker, small sessions, a rare mystery movie, dealer's tables, wine-tasting, and lunch all revolving around a single theme like the Ethnic Detective, Gumshoes Galore, or Religious Mysteries.

This is a brief summary of some of the conventions in the mystery world. Two more things about mystery conventions need to be mentioned. First, most of these conventions are organized by fans. Often there is a different committee each year. The committees organize these conventions at great expense of time and energy and with no monetary gain. Consequently, each convention is run differently and some are run better than others. The second thing to consider is how to find out about these conventions and how to sign up. Since the committees that handle these conventions are volunteer and always changing, there is no standard place to write for information. One place to find out about conventions is in mystery magazines or fanzines. *The Mystery Reader's Journal, Drood Review of Mystery, Mystery and Detective Monthly, Mystery News,* and *Mystery Scene* all have listings of upcoming mystery conventions. In addition, many of the mystery bookstores list mystery happenings (many of the bookstores have their own newsletters, as well). Local libraries, teachers associations, literary associations, and university literature departments often have listings of or flyers for mystery conventions.

One thing is certain, if you like getting together with other people who enjoy what you enjoy—mysteries—you'll love these conventions. Jump right in! Sometimes the sheer numbers attending a Bouchercon can be daunting, but remember you all have something in common. You love mysteries. Mystery conventions are a terrific place to meet other fans, learn about new writers and books, and begin lifetime friendships with other mystery readers. Remember that the worst thing that could happen if you attend a convention is that you could meet a bunch of people who like mysteries and the best thing is that you will have a great time.

A DINNER TO DIE FOR

Janet A. Rudolph

PICTURE YOURSELF at a pleasant dinner. A shot rings out. The woman you've been chatting with runs screaming from the room, dripping blood on the restaurant carpet. Should you call the police, or should you take on the role of amateur sleuth? You choose the latter because you plunked down hard cash to participate in a mystery event of overwhelming fun and farce. The murder-mystery craze has been sweeping the country, springing up in big cities, invading the suburbs, and spreading crime and wreaking havoc all over the countryside.

Murder-mystery weekends and evenings are not a new invention. They are derived from the old house-party parlor ''murder'' game of the 1920s. This unique form of mystery entertainment has evolved into many forms and has its own following of fans. There are games, books, interactive videos, and large-scale events that give participants the opportunity to become involved in ''real'' murders and mysteries. But the ones that are the most fun are theatrical events that take place on trains and ships, at ranches, restaurants, resorts, and hotels. These can occur over cocktails and dinner or extend over a weekend or even a week.

The fact that murder can be fun is not new to mystery readers, but it is to the uninitiated (or the unread). Murder that is violent and disturbing in real life is intriguing in the context of a mystery novel, movie, play, or event. There's a detached quality, however, in reading a novel or watching a film. There are many fans who think that even the most suspenseful book cannot compare with the real thing, and at murder-mystery events, guests are intricately involved in the plot as they become sleuths and suspects. Mystery events are a form of participatory theater where the guest matches wits with the detective.

In the United States the mystery-event craze as we know it today traces its origins to the first Mohonk Mystery Weekend, which was held in 1977. Originally organized by the owner of the first mystery bookstore in the United States and held at the Mohonk resort hotel in upstate New York, this was a very elaborate three-day event where the presentation of the team solution of the mystery was as important as the solution itself. The murder-mystery weekend/event received a big push when the 1984 Neiman-Marcus Christmas catalogue included the Mohonk Mystery Weekend. By 1986 there were over thirty companies in the United States alone who were actively writing and performing mystery events. I became involved in writing mystery events around 1984, and in 1986 I was quoted as saying that the mystery-event craze had six months to run. Boy was I wrong!

Okay, so why are people drawn to this kind of entertainment? First, one gets to play another persona, and lots of people enjoy being someone else. Many people want to be more than a passive receiver of adventure. Surely the popularity of Dungeons and Dragons and war games has proven this. People get the chance to leave their real-life self at home while they pretend to be someone else. And since many events are period pieces, costuming can enhance the experience. For many people, being involved in the process is more fun than solving the mystery.

There are several different types of mystery events. Some events involve actors (some more obviously than others); some have guests play all the roles. The more analytical events involve the guests in a lot of legwork with deductions and intuition becoming more important than viewing theatrical scenes. Many events have clues that simulate authentic police memos, autopsy reports, and crime scenes. And there is usually time for personal interrogation. Whatever the format, sufficient information should be given so that guests are able to solve the crime. Good mystery events should challenge amateur gumshoes without being so difficult to solve or so unlikely a plot that a guest feels cheated. The mystery should be satisfying, unique, able to be solved, and fun.

I have written many mystery weekends and fund-raisers that are open to the public (where individuals pay and plan to attend). Since my mystery events are participatory, I get the people involved in the action in many ways. I usually create some kind of hook for the guests (for example: attending the reading of a will, winning a radio contest circa 1947, sailing to Treasure Island for the 1939 World's Fair, attending an engagement party). As much fun as these public events are, most of my events are written for specific corporate clients, and I write each script to complement the interests and occupations of the corporation or association. This is what I love to do best. I really enjoy researching different companies.

A good fair-play script and good professional actors who are good at both script acting and improvisation are the most important elements of a successful event. I want my guests to be drawn into the mystery by the actors, the script, and the clues. That's what makes an event work. My own mystery events are custom designed to be startling, revealing, a lot of fun, and great team-building activities. It's a truly unique way of unifying a group.

Let me give you a scenario of a typical evening event for one-hundred people, which lasts about three hours (over cocktails and dinner).

When a guest enters the room, he is given a program that tells him about the scenario (what period it is set in—1920s, 1930s, the present, or whenever), the cast of characters, the rules, and a few other tidbits of information, possibly an obituary. In addition, each guest receives an individual clue. A clue might read "During the second course at dinner, go to a microphone and accuse John of lying about his whereabouts on the day of the crime" or "You heard that John pushed Susan at the office. Tell three people." Now, you can toss that or you can jump right in and search out someone with a name tag that reads John. These and similar (more difficult, perhaps) clues are worked into the story in various ways and at various times. Collectively, the clues will lead to the solution of any mysteries that might arise.

During the first hour an actor may get up and welcome everyone. He might say something like "My brother drowned in San Francisco Bay last month. Thank you, his dearest and closest friends, for coming here this evening at my invitation. I know that you believe like I do that it was no accident. It was *murder*. I know you'll help me solve this mystery tonight. Now, it's a long time since we've all been together, so you might not recognize his widow, his secretary, his partner, etc." The characters (and some of the suspects) are introduced. The reason I introduce all these characters early on is that with one-hundred people and a three-hour program, I believe one needs to know who is who quickly. And besides, in a company event, the guests know there are interlopers. They just want to know who they are. Cocktail chitchat continues for an hour. If you think the actors are just mingling, you're wrong. What they're doing is meeting a very tight schedule of rehearsed scenes (interspersed with improvisation with the guests). The actors are dropping hints and intriguing the participants. The guests don't hear everything? Right. Would you in "real" life? Every word at a cocktail party? Hardly.

The scene is set. The guests now have individual clues, programs, and a newspaper clipping or two about the past murder.

A shot rings out!!

Someone (an actor) is killed. Who did it and why? Is it connected to the past murder? Will the police come to investigate?

You betcha.

The police arrive and begin taking statements, questioning suspects, and more.

Meanwhile the guests go in to dinner. There are two to three scenes every five minutes, guest participation, and a lot of arguments over the meal. In addition, more clues like obits, photos, and memos are worked into the story and distributed. Guests will have quite a collection of material by the end of the evening. And remember, during dinner and cocktails, guests can question all suspects.

Guests must depend on teammates to fill in some of the clues and help with the solution; after all, at the same time the mystery is taking place, guests are eating, drinking, making small talk, or discussing the day's meetings. Working together, they have the opportunity to do some team-building and problem-solving, because by the end of the evening, the cop will ask who dunit! And who knows how many murders will have taken place by then? In my mysteries, usually about four more. Not only must the guests find out who dunit, they must come up with the motive for each nefarious deed. And guests certainly have an advantage over the regular police force, for all the suspects are assembled in one place. All the action takes place around and within the group.

My events are definitely participatory theater, and guests can get as involved as they'd like. Although there is a tightly scripted story, things can change as participants get more involved, but there is only one correct solution, since my events are fair-play mysteries. Guests work in teams, which is not only more efficient but gives everyone a chance to meet new people or see the executives in a new light.

In order to personalize these events, I find out information about my clients—what they do, why they do it, why they're getting together for the meeting, what their goals and objectives are, the agenda for the conference, the theme of the convention, etc., and information on at least ten people who most people will know. I then weave all of this into the mystery.

I have written events for groups as small as seven and as large as four thousand, and I have written events for all kinds of industries, corporations, associations, and private parties. My events have been performed at sales meetings, fund-raisers, product introductions, award dinners, and project completions. I've even written a mystery wedding! My actors can perform in Japanese, French, and Spanish. Some events tend to be more presentational than others, but that depends on the size of the group and the location. Speaking of location, since I live in the San Francisco Bay area, my theater troupe, Murder on the Menu, has performed at wineries, in caves, on yachts, aboard trains, in the splendor of Victorian mansions—just about everywhere.

Of course there are many strange things that happen at mystery events that can never happen in a novel. This is sometimes daunting to me as a writer, not to mention my actors. One time I wrote a clue that said a guest had inherited $50,000 in the will. When questioned by another guest, the heir answered, "How did you know?" In reality he had just inherited $50,000 from his mother's will. And then there was the time the owner of a winery arrived at the event late with a real countess in tow. No one believed her. Or the time someone had been shot and the supporting actors ringed the victim so that the guests would not see the "victim" breathing. A guest broke through shouting, "Let me through, I'm a nurse."

There are also some pitfalls to directing mystery events. One is that each performance is on a new "stage." An exit door that was unlocked an hour earlier was bolted when an actor tried to make an exit. An overzealous hotelier had locked the door. Or a gun didn't go off. Solution: hit the victim over the head with it. And, since most of my performances take place during meals, one has to take the catering staff into consideration at all times. Again, this is the difference between a novel or a stage play and participatory theater. Actors and directors must think on their feet.

Even with these pitfalls I think it's great fun. I have been creating murder, mystery, and mayhem for corporate, association, and private groups for over ten years. I've killed over two-thousand people, and I haven't gone to jail yet!

Some of the people in the mystery world who have been writing and producing events for the past ten years and whom I highly recommend are Karen and Bill Palmer of Bogie's Murderous Mystery Tours (New York) and Harriet and Larry Stay of Murder by Invitation (Bellingham, Washington). My own company is called Murder on the Menu (San Francisco Bay area). There are other companies that are performing at dinner theaters, special hotel weekends, and mystery fund-raisers. The quality varies, but I'm sure there are many other good mystery event companies.

This chapter should give you some idea of how mystery events work. And if you attend a good fair-play mystery event, you'll be "party" to a dinner to die for.

INTERVIEW
ALLEN J. HUBIN
Steven A. Stilwell

SAS: *In what year did you start* **The Armchair Detective***?*

AJH: In what year did I publish the first issue or what year did I start thinking about it?

SAS: *That's the next question, how long before the first issue did you start thinking about it?*

AJH: Well, the first issue was, ah, I have to think about this, 1967.

SAS: *And I believe the month was October.*

AJH: And I believe you're right.

SAS: *How long before October 1967 did you think about the possibility of doing this thing?*

AJH: I suppose it must have been sometime in 1966 that the notion surfaced. It seems that it came up in a conversation with Elmore Mundell [early crime fiction collector].

SAS: *How had you gotten in touch with Mundell?*

AJH: There was a bookstore in Chicago, Arthur Lovell's I believe, and I was there one time and I think Mundell was a regular customer and we got together that way. He was the other mystery collector I knew. I knew him before anybody, even Randy Cox [another Minnesota collector].

Anyway, we corresponded and agreed that a publication would be reasonable and I wondered why no one had ever done this. There were mystery fans all over, or so it seemed. Certainly there were readers all over. I couldn't be the only one who was buying from the catalogues I was receiving. Science fiction fans had been creating fanzines since the thirties, why not mystery fans. Certainly the example had been set. But mystery fans weren't connected. There were no conventions, no events, no publications to connect fans. There was MWA, but that was all. There were also only about five books on the field and none of them were bibliographic in nature. There had been no checklists formally published.

SAS: *How much of the original impetus for* TAD *came from your bibliographic and collecting bent?*

AJH: I think not much. It was just that having enjoyed the contact with Mundell, I thought it would be fun to have a means of communication. I thought it would be fun to share our enthusiasm. So I looked around for somebody to do it, but there was no network available to find somebody, so it ended up being me.

SAS: *It's hard to believe sometimes that twenty-five years ago nobody knew anybody else. There was Shibuk and Lachman and Penzler and Nevins all living in New York and you and Randy Cox living in*

Minnesota, not an hour apart, and nobody knowing anybody else. Amazing! Though you are loathe to take credit for it, I at least feel that TAD *is responsible for a number of the great books that have appeared about the field in the last twenty years.* The Encyclopedia of Mystery and Detection, What About Murder?, Locked Room Murders, The International Bibliography of Secondary Sources *and* Gun In Cheek. *If you hadn't started* TAD, *would any of these books have appeared? How would the field have been different? Was this going to happen anyway? Was there something magical about 1967?*

AJH: Maybe if I hadn't started *TAD The Mystery Reader's/Lover's Newsletter* might have continued and flourished[1] and all those books would have had their beginnings in that magazine rather than in *TAD.* I certainly think so and I'm loathe to take too much credit. If there was something right about 1967, and there seems to have been, from TAD's point of view anyway, certainly Anthony Boucher

still living and giving TAD space in his New York Times column was maybe the most important thing. He was extremely supportive both before the first issue and after, when he gave it maybe more praise than it deserved in his column. He wouldn't have been available a year later. Something else that suggests that the time was right was the rapid rate of growth of the magazine. Also Ordean Hagen was working on his bibliography at the same time, again independently.

SAS: *What role did your family play in the early years?*

AJH: Cheap labor. Actually in 1967 their ages were seven, five, three and just born. At that point they played no role at all. At least no helpful role. Except my wife, Marilyn, of course, whose contributions made all of it possible. And I certainly didn't think I was starting an empire that would end up contributing to their college educations. But that was more the sale of the books. *TAD,* at least in my tenure, was never a money-making proposition. Later, of course, they helped with the collating and mailing.

SAS: *Do they remember this fondly?*

AJH: They remember it. I think it's one of the quaintnesses of their childhoods.

SAS: *Without TAD would your book collection have grown as it did, peaking at around thirty-thousand volumes?*

AJH: Not to the degree it did. *The Times* [Al became the book reviewer for *The New York Times* after Boucher's death] job got me both free books—review copies—and the extra money to buy more books.

SAS: *The publishing end of things moved to California in 1976. If that hadn't happened, would you have continued the magazine? You were, by then, heavily into the bibliographic end of things.*

AJH: I was publishing it [the bibliography] in the magazine to solicit additions and corrections, so I would have continued to need the magazine at least until the bibliography was done, probably a year or more. But I was up to one-thousand subscribers and it had gotten fat. It was a lot of work, though I was getting some typing help. I did give the mechanical part to California with no qualms at all.

SAS: *After a relatively short time in California the magazine was in danger of dying from neglect by*

---

[1] *The Mystery Reader's/Lovers Newsletter* was a fanzine very similar to *TAD* that was started independently and almost simultaneously by Lianne Carlin of Massachusetts.

the publisher, and if Otto Penzler hadn't taken on publication, it would have died because you weren't prepared to take it back. Correct?

AJH: Certainly it is correct that I wasn't in a position to take the magazine back and fortunately, though that's a strange choice of words given how close the magazine came to dying, all the California problems came to a head about the time Otto was revving up Mysterious Press and The Mysterious Bookshop, so it fit in nicely with what he was going to do. Except that it was a drain financially and the business end of things had gotten severely messed up while in California. But, yes, we owe Otto a debt of gratitude for rescuing the magazine from oblivion.

SAS: *When did you stop doing the actual editing, and was it your choice to give it up?*

AJH: Yes, it was my choice to give it up. After it had been in New York a couple of years I felt it was time. Enough. And it made sense for Otto to have everything in house.

SAS: *Other than the actual physical look, how has the magazine changed since the early years and since you stopped being the editor?*

AJH: It kept changing even when I had it. It started out being a sharing by fans and then it was more than that. Ph.D. theses and popular culture papers and the like. Its personality has always been more a reflection of the correspondents than the editors. It was more folksy, informal, nonacademic in the earliest years. My objective was never to look pretty, to make money, or to be commercially successful. My objective was to get as many words on a page as I could to get as much information out there as possible. Now the objective is to be commercial, professional, slick, and polished. And those are very reasonable objectives. They just weren't mine.

SAS: *How much of the change has come because so much of the information in the early years was new information?*

AJH: You're right and that's a good point. By 1977 many things had appeared—books, bibliographic and otherwise, and other fan publications. There was less to share.

SAS: *There was more analysis than information.*

AJH: Yes, more analysis than discovery. So that had to change it.

SAS: *We've talked about how* TAD *has changed and what effect it had on the biographical, bibliographical, critical end of things. Now as an omnivorous reader, how do you feel the crime/detective/mystery novel has changed in the last quarter century?*

AJH: As Julian Symons says, there are more novels of crime than crime novels. There is more of an attempt to use the crime story framework for what some would see as a more serious purpose, a novelistic purpose, rather than for entertainment or pure whodunits.

There have been some cycles in the last twenty-five years. We've cycled through gothics. There was a cycle triggered by John le Carré of spy stories and the Cold War and I think they've peaked and not just because of the end of the Cold War. Also, what sleazy paperback publishers were publishing in the sixties is now being published in hardcover.

SAS: *Do giants walk among us today?*

AJH: I think you detect giants after they're gone.

SAS: *But did anybody start writing in the late sixties or early seventies that you think will last? I think a quarter of a century is nearly enough time to tell.*

AJH: Dick Francis. John le Carré. I want to say Emma Lathen, but can't. I don't know why. I guess she's a little frothy and hasn't enough intensity. Donald Westlake. A short list and by no means exhaustive.

It's almost unfair to make a comparison between earlier writers and writers of today.

SAS: *How so?*

AJH: Partly it's the number of years that they have been active. Partly it's that the earlier writers played a role in the forming of a literature. I don't know that the more recent writers are playing that same role. They're playing a role in the development and continuation of the literature.

SAS: *Is the field changing and growing? Is what is said about private eye fiction true? Have all the changes been rung and it's all ersatz Hammett and Chandler?*

AJH: Yes, I believe that. I still like to read it, but until one comes up with a happily married family-man private detective, there isn't anything new.

The earlier writers were creating a literature

more than the current writers except that those who have written the novel of crime have, since World War Two, done more creating. For example, Julian Symons and Ruth Rendell. Maybe James Lee Burke.

SAS: *You keep naming mostly Britishers. You have been accused of favoring the Brits over the Americans over the years. Care to respond?*

AJH: It may be true that I lean in that direction, but my excuse is the language. Americans use the language, the British caress the language.

SAS: *Do you think the recent activism of women writers has had an effect on the field and how do you think women writers of today compare to women writers of the earlier days?*

AJH: Each group is partly a product of their times.

Nobody writes in a vacuum and Helen McCloy, Margaret Millar and Dorothy B. Hughes, for example, were as much a product of their time as Paretsky, Grafton, and Muller are of theirs. Would the public of forty years ago have been as receptive to a female private detective as the public of today? Nobody really knows. There is also the issue of writing for the marketplace. The marketplace was ready for the activist women of today.

SAS: *One final question: Knowing what you know now, would you do it again?*

AJH: Sure. It was sort of an adventure, it was fun to see what would happen next. The *New York Times* job, editing the Best Detective Stories of the year series, The Mystery Library, two Edgar awards, all the friendships—who wouldn't do it again?

TELEVISION MYSTERIES

Fifteen Best Private Eye Movies
Selected by Max Allan Collins

1. ***Chinatown*** (1974)—smart, melancholy Roman Polanski/Robert Towne masterpiece, only true rival to Hammett's novel ***The Maltese Falcon***.

2. ***Kiss Me Deadly*** (1955)—dizzingly surreal portrait of the paranoid fifties, with Ralph Meeker's nasty zombie Mike Hammer the single most memorable p.i. performance ever.

3. ***The Maltese Falcon*** (1941)—director/screenwriter John Huston filmed the book with a perfect cast. What a concept!

4. ***Murder, My Sweet*** (1944)—Chandler's poetic prose deftly translated by director Edward Dmytryk and the smart-ass side of Philip captured by the screen's best Marlowe, Dick Powell.

5. ***The Big Sleep*** (1946)—Howard Hawks's direction, great dialogue, chaotic plot; screen's best Bogart as Marlowe.

6. ***I, the Jury*** (1953)—the look and feel of early Spillane; will we ever see John Alton's cinematography in 3-D again? Franz Waxman's score: best p.i. music ever.

7. ***The Girl Hunters*** (1963)—a charismatic central performance by nonactor Mickey Spillane as his own hero. Not a movie, a pop cultural event!

8. ***The Thin Man*** (1934)—the early entries are all entertaining, but this faithful rendering of Hammett's novel is still the best; will William Powell *always* seem modern?

9. ***The Two Jakes*** (1990)—low-key, somber *Chinatown* sequel; bittersweet, loving coda to the best p.i. movie of all time.

10. ***The Yakuza*** (1975)—Sydney Pollack directs Paul and Leonard Schrader/Robert Towne's blood-spattered tale; Robert Mitchum, in Japan, learns about honor from Takakura Ken.

11. ***Hickey and Boggs*** (1972)—early Walter Hill script directed by Robert Culp who joins *I, Spy* star Bill Cosby in *The Wild Bunch* of p.i. movies.

12. ***I, The Jury*** (1982)—Armand Assante, a brooding Hammer in Larry Cohen's violent, sexy updating, respectful to the spirit of Spillane, superior to Stacy Keach TV series.

13. ***Marlowe*** (1969)—violent, already dated version of ***The Little Sister.*** James Garner's Marlowe (an outline for his *Rockford Files*) is good company, as is the rest of fine cast.

14. ***Farewell, My Lovely*** (1975)—Robert Mitchum's world-weary Marlowe transcends overproduced would-be *Chinatown*.

15. ***Gunn*** (1967)—garish, violent, sexy, entertaining; Craig Stevens re-creates TV role to pulsing Henry Mancini theme.

SOLVING THE MYSTERY OF *MURDER, SHE WROTE*

Marlys Millhiser

Henning Droeger

THE FIRST TIME I SAW Jessica Fletcher solve a murder, I couldn't figure out what there was about the television show *Murder, She Wrote* that I found so tantalizing. Other than that my husband scoffed at her recognizing clues the sheriff of Cabot Cove did not. (He wasn't bothered by Matlock, Poirot, or Campion doing the same thing.) Or my children's indifference to a story line featuring someone Jessica's age. (Like the sneer I wear when my parents watch Lawrence Welk reruns.)

I have a life. I did not lose sleep over what made the show a hit. Still, it was a mystery and I'm a mystery writer. So someplace in the nether regions of my muse-drugged brain, it niggled.

What are we talking here—ageism, sexism, feminism? I don't know. I had no problem sitting through *60 Minutes* first—four old guys and a series of token blondes. Jessica had nothing on Miss Marple for age. I enjoyed Hercule and Albert and all

the rest on PBS's imported *Mystery*. I'm not Jessica's age yet, but if Angela continues to avail herself of nips and tucks and lifts, I'm soon going to look it. And it certainly wasn't the challenge of figuring out who was going to be a dead body or who would likely make it so.

Maybe it was as simple as Sunday night and popcorn. We have a tradition in this house that the cook makes Sunday breakfast and you're on your own the rest of the day. This was instituted by the cook who makes the big Sunday dinner on Monday night, when somebody might be around to eat it. And anything, especially a cozy, is going to seem special with popcorn and a flickering fire in the hearth.

It wasn't until they began messing around with the show that I began to solve the mystery of *Murder, She Wrote*.

What did we have here anyway? We had something different, always a problem with the power brokers of entertainment. We had an American woman who was a writer who did not write romances. She wasn't blond (well, not really—I don't know what they call that color) she wasn't young, and the sheriff didn't have to rescue her all the time. And if that wasn't bad enough, she could go for weeks solving murders without even being in danger! (For some reason, it's called *jeopardy* now.)

Add to that, she didn't really have a male sidekick. The sheriff and the doctor stood around asking dumb questions, but Jessica is the who one did the work. And she didn't even have the excuse of history—Jessica is now. *Now*—without excuses. Hell, even without *sex*! And the worst part is the show was successful.

Well, obviously something had to be done.

There were a hodgepodge of fixes for this disruption in the natural order of things. A series of potential sidekicks was introduced—hey, we've got the women's market, let's go after the men. (My husband continues to watch Jessica with me, but he keeps his smirks to himself so I won't pick on Captain Picard of the starship *Enterprise*.)

But the old-guy sidekicks were overpowered by a talented actress in a beloved role. And the young nephews (let's go after a more youthful market) were soon merely excuses to get Jessica out of Cabot Cove so she could detect in some fresh scenery. Then the old guys began appearing in their own pilots right after *Murder, She Wrote*. They tended to be more hard-boiled and you could get that on any channel any other night of the week.

So then we get a bunch of these old guys in Jessica's time spot and we are led to believe she is in the shows, but as it turns out she's only introducing them and it's their show. Not even popcorn could save that technique. I turned off after *60 Minutes*, crawled into bed with a good book, and ignored that time slot for the rest of the season.

Oh, and somewhere back in there they experimented, very briefly, with younger female detectives—which was cool—but the stories tended to saddle her with a sidekick. And, let's face it, Angela Lansburys do not grow on trees at any age.

So then whoever dreams up these disasters decided on mystery movies, hard-hitting two-parters to follow *Murder, She Wrote*—hey, maybe the little woman will sit still for these if the old man comes in to share the popcorn.

Apparently that wasn't the answer, so we tried something new. (Right, sure.) We'll have thriller movies where some old guy has to save some young blonde whose child has been kidnapped (women's issues, you know, but her man will like the thriller-hero part).

Jessica was back by now, so I turned off after her. But I followed what was to follow her through the full color covers on my newspaper's Sunday TV guide and the advertising before and during *Murder, She Wrote*, which is an indication of the amount of money being put behind these things.

As of this writing, the latest wrinkle is the

The First Lady of Television Suspense, Angela Lansbury.

''weep-o-rama'' combining women's issues, women in jeopardy (danger), women molested, women mistreated, women misunderstood, women overcoming all to gain control of their lives. Hell, it's eight o'clock on Sunday night. I've got my own week to face. Think I'll crawl in bed with a good book, preferably a mystery about a woman in control of her story and with a murder to solve. I don't care how old she is or if she uses tea leaves or handguns. And if there's a cute guy in her life, all the better.

Just as long as she doesn't have to stop and rescue him when she's going after the perp.

JESSICA IS NANCY DREW GROWN UP

Margaret C. Albert

TO THOSE OF US WHO SPENT the 1930s and 40s vicariously discovering the secret of the old clock and the moss-covered mansion, finding the password to Larkspur Lane and the clue in the broken locket, Jessica Fletcher is a natural heroine for the nineties. She is, in fact, Nancy Drew grown up.

We are in our fifties now—our children grown, our husbands looking to retirement, our own careers winding down. Our bridge between the weekend and Monday morning—once Jack Benny and Fred Allen—is now *Murder, She Wrote,* and its star, Angela Lansbury (a.k.a. Jessica Fletcher), has become our role model. For women who discovered their independence in the heroine of the fifty-cent mysteries and realized it under the tutelage of Betty Friedan, Jessica offers the assurance of continued vitality.

In the safe harbor of middle America forty years ago, we spent our summers with Nancy, tooling around River Heights in her maroon roadster. (Who among us dared to hope for a car of our own? Who, indeed, was even old enough to drive one when we identified with attorney Carson Drew's gracious, brilliant young daughter who passed through adolescence without acne, without sneaking a beer or a cigarette, and certainly without getting pregnant?)

It was a comforting world, where doctors saw patients in their homes and the local police chief sent out a special patrol car to keep an eye on the Drew house when things got sticky. Servants were devoted, friends never quarreled, and handsome Ned Nickerson had eyes only for Nancy but never, never made untoward advances.

But Nancy was more than a good little girl. She had guts. She survived what was the worst of our own innermost fears—the loss of her mother—and plowed ahead without an ounce of self-pity. Her youth and gender notwithstanding, she cracked mysteries that befuddled the police, mature and male though they were. She confronted dark passages and bad guys (although never murderers) with courage, and she triumphed not because she was beautiful or nice but because she was smart.

Long after the blue-bound books were consigned to the attic, Nancy stayed silently with us. We fought McCarthyism on college campuses and pursued careers that would make a difference. We worked to integrate schools and neighborhoods, and we lived the women's movement, proving—mainly to ourselves—that we could manage careers, children, and marriage. We reared daughters who played with Barbie dolls, read Judy Blume instead of Carolyn Keene, and explored territory that Nancy would never have touched.

At fifty-something, we're a few (or more than a few) pounds heavier, cutting down on cholesterol, and rinsing out the gray. After years of being too young to be listened to, we will soon be too old to be taken seriously. Role models are hard to find. Cagney and Lacey were too young, too absorbed in their personal problems. The Golden Girls are too old, too frivolous.

Jessica, however, is Nancy Drew reincarnate.

Cabot Cove is our own safe harbor, returned to us after all those years, where country doctors still practice and sheriffs pay attention to smart amateurs. Murder replaces the lesser crimes of our childhood, but it is good, clean murder, unsullied by perversity or raucous violence. Villains are nailed not by car chases and gunfire but by close observation and shrewd deduction.

Jessica is the nice person we see in ourselves— warm, gracious, sensitive. She is attractive but not impossibly svelte, not intimidatingly chic. Men find her attractive, but she doesn't sidetrack the story by becoming involved. Like Nancy, she has dealt with personal loss (her husband), and has gone on reassuringly about the business of living.

Jessica is not an old lady. She moves comfortably through a house of prostitution, parades as a frumpy hypochondriac out to expose a phony doctor, and adroitly (and politely) upstages big-city cops who underestimate her skills.

Most important, Jessica is a working pro, a skillful writer who continues to turn out a prodigious number of books, until recently on an old portable typewriter instead of a PC, and enjoys a national reputation.

Neither Nancy's world nor Jessica's is unflawed from a critical standpoint. Even good little girls in the real world of the 1930s were rarely given to exclaiming, "Why, Father! And leave that poor woman in the clutches of those unscrupulous rascals?" Nor did all "colored" people, even in those days, run elevators and speak in dialect ("Lady in a powerful big hurry. Reckon she tryin' to get to de bargain sale. . ."). Jessica's circle is only slightly less circumscribed than Nancy's. If blacks or gays, the mentally or physically disabled, the poor or the homeless reside in either River Heights or Cabot

Cove, they rarely if ever intrude upon the scene—or our heroines' private lives (which is their loss, and ours).

Few books—and fewer heroes—can, however, be all things to all people. In some ways, we really don't know either Nancy or Jessica. In lives uncomplicated, on the one hand, by siblings and on the other, by children, their patience is to an extent untried. Did Nancy ever rebel against her father and the fishbowl life of River Heights? Did Jessica's success threaten her marriage? Did the pressure of deadlines interfere with the housework?

No matter. Nancy and Jessica have modeled well the role of woman. They taught us, at opposite ends of our lives, to be what we wanted to be, to use our heads, to expect to be listened to and heard. They taught us not to be afraid of the dark.

The Eleven Greatest Mystery Films
Selected by Douglas G. Greene

Bulldog Drummond (1929)
The Kennel Murder Case (1933)
The 39 Steps (1935)
The Maltese Falcon (1941)
Murder, My Sweet (1944)
Green for Danger (1946)
The Lady in the Lake (1946)
The Third Man (1949)
Rear Window (1954)
North by Northwest (1959)
The List of Adrian Messenger (1963)

The Twelve Greatest Television Detective Series
Selected by Douglas G. Greene

Colonel March of Scotland Yard
Columbo
The Eddie Capra Mysteries
Ellery Queen (Jim Hutton)
Harry O
Inspector Morse (PBS's *Mystery*)
Murder, She Wrote
Perry Mason
Richard Diamond
The Rockford Files
Sherlock Holmes (PBS's *Mystery*; Jeremy Brett)

COMIC BOOKS

DEATH OF
AUTUMN MEWS

by Will Eisner

To the north of Central City, on a
hill overlooking the bustling metropolis,
lies abandoned Wildwood Cemetery.
Here, hidden in the tangled weedy growth,
is the hideaway of the Spirit. Accepted
by the police as a friendly 'outlaw' and
feared by the underworld, his true
identity is still a mystery.
Who is really the man behind the mask?
Every so often,
someone tries to find out...

ORIGINALLY PUBLISHED OCTOBER 9, 1949

THE FINE COMIC ART OF MURDER

Max Allan Collins

WHILE CRIME COMIC BOOKS were briefly popular in the early 1950s, the detective himself—but for those rare exceptions, *Dick Tracy* and *Batman*—has never been a four-color superstar. Periodically, spin-off syndicated strips and/or comic books featuring such established literary detectives as Perry Mason, the Saint, Nero Wolfe, and Ellery Queen have appeared, only to quickly disappear. TV "tie-in" comic books of such series as *77 Sunset Strip* and *The Untouchables* have lived similarly brief lives.

Even Sherlock Holmes has had little luck in the comics pages, though his Classic Comics adaptations stayed in print for years; and Gus Magers's satirical *Sherlocko the Monk* was a funny-page staple, but hardly a superstar.

Cops in Comics

Chester Gould's *Dick Tracy,* created in 1931, kicked open the door for comic-strip detectives. Though a plainclothes policeman skilled in the latest police procedures, Tracy displayed a two-fisted brand of lone-wolf sleuthing; in one early story, Tracy tells recurring villain Stooge Viller, "Next time I run into you, I'm going to shoot first, and investigate later." Tracy's trench coat with snap-brim fedora became the virtual uniform of the tough American detective.

In 1934, influential mystery novelist Dashiell Hammett teamed with rising comic-strip star Alex Raymond (of *Flash Gordon* fame) to present the hard-boiled adventures of a nameless government undercover operative, *Secret Agent X-9.* Designed to be King Features' "answer" to *Tracy,* the strip never really caught on, and both Hammett and Raymond left after about a year; but *X-9* carved

out a small niche for itself under subsequent writers, including *Saint* creator Leslie Charteris, and various Raymond imitators, notably Austin Briggs and Charles Flanders.

The lead character, and the strip itself, were eventually rechristened *Secret Agent Corrigan* for a long run under Mel Graff, a Milton Caniff wannabe who presented in the early fifties an anticommunist tale that branded a Hammett-like writer a "traitor." Having his own comic strip attack him probably only amused Hammett. In the 1960s and 70s, *Corrigan* featured sharp writing by Archie Goodwin and excellent Raymond-style artwork from Al Williamson.

Red Barry, another 1930s King Features "answer" to *Tracy,* was the work of sports cartoonist Will Gould (no relation to Chester), a vital but undisciplined creator whose missed deadlines cost him his strip; but its popularity, however brief, generated a Buster Crabbe serial and several Big Little Books. Today, this *other* Gould is highly regarded by comics aficionados, who consider the short-lived strip—with its *noir*-ish flavor, undercover hero, and urchin sidekicks—a forerunner to Will Eisner's classic, *The Spirit.*

Another King Features mid-thirties detective strip, *Radio Patrol* by writer Eddie Sullivan and artist Charlie Schmidt, enjoyed modest success, sparking a radio series and movie serial; but by the late forties, it was already a corny relic; the novelty of its patrol car gimmick long since passed.

Like X-9, Norman Marsh's *Dan Dunn* was a G-man, but the strip was a close carbon of *Tracy* down to the larger-than-life villains, pudgy sidekick, flying bullets, and cross-hatch art style. Largely forgotten today, *Dunn* spawned a long, popular run of Big Little Books, and was easily the most successful

HERE'S THE WILD MAN FROM CHICAGO

TONITE ONLY

JOHNNY DYNAMITE

I WAS OUT FOR BLOOD... AND I'D FIND IT. THE BOYS IN THIS DEAL WERE PLAYING IT FOR KEEPS. I GOT SUCKERED INTO THE SLIME AND FILTH THAT THRIVED ON THE SALE OF HUMAN FLESH... AND THERE'D BE THE DEVIL TO PAY WHEN I BLASTED OUT! IT WAS BIG AND ORGANIZED, BUT I'D MAKE MY DENT IN THE...

BIG RACKET

of the early *Tracy* imitators. When Marsh joined the service during World War II, the strip fell into other hands, eventually those of the controversial Alfred Andriola.

Andriola, who had written and drawn a Charlie Chan strip in the thirties, became Gould's only real competition in the late forties and beyond, when he phased out *Dunn* to introduce his own police detective Kerry Drake, who took on larger-than-life villains in a more soap-operaish continuity than Gould's. This is understandable, as *Drake* was ghostwritten by Allen Saunders, of *Mary Worth* fame. Andriola did not like to give Saunders any credit, and strongly substantiated rumor has it that Andriola—once the great Milton Caniff's assistant—farmed out virtually all of his work to ghost artists.

Among the comics-page detectives of the forties and early fifties, the most unique may be Invisible Scarlet O'Neill, a lovely redheaded amateur sleuth turned invisible by her scientist pop—fortunately, she could render herself visible again by touching a nerve in her wrist. The *Tracy*ish art and spoofy writing were both courtesy of former Gould assistant Russell Stamm.

A more straightforward spoof of the *Tracy* style came by way of Al Capp's wonderfully imbecilic hillbilly Li'l Abner worshipping his "ideel," dimwitted comic-strip flatfoot Fearless Fosdick. From the early forties until the very last Abner continuity in 1978, *Fosdick* appeared, occasionally, as a strip-within-the-strip. Even more square-jawed (and underpaid) than Tracy himself, Fosdick encountered such beyond-Gould villains as Anyface and the Atomic Bum, blasting enormous holes in his adversaries and dying numerous deaths.

After the war, private eyes were all over the comics sections—*Vic Flint, Rip Kirby, Peter Scratch,* even *Mike Hammer*—but none made any particular mark, though *Kirby* has lived a long and moderately popular comics-page life despite the premature death of its creator, Alex Raymond. *Peter Scratch*—a shameless imitation of the popular TV series *Peter Gunn*—was drawn by Lou Fine, one of the best artists of the "Golden Age" of comic books.

Fine also drew a series of single-page *Sam Spade* strips for newspaper and comic-book publication in the 1950s. These slickly drawn one-pagers were hair-tonic ads, tying in the sponsor of the

long-running *Spade* radio show starring Howard Duff. When Spade creator Dashiell Hammett became a victim of McCarthy-era witch-hunting, the radio show was renamed *The Adventures of Charlie Wilde,* and so were the comic-strip ads.

Spillane and the Comics

Of all the comic strips that sought to spin off from the success of a major mystery-novel series, the short-lived Mike Hammer strip is perhaps the most interesting. While Leslie Charteris's Saint strip ran longer, the Hammer strip takes on added significance due to the Hammer character's own pedigree in the world of comics.

As a young man, Spillane made a name for himself in the comic book world as a top scripter and sometime editor; he worked on such famous characters as the Human Torch, Captain America, Captain Marvel, and Batman. Returning from wartime service, Spillane created a new comic book character—Mike Danger, a rugged private eye—but before the new book could appear, a slump hit the postwar comics market, prompting Spillane to transform comics character Danger into mystery fiction's Hammer in the novel *I, the Jury* (1947).

Spillane's brief return to comics in the form of the Mike Hammer strip (which ran from 1953 into 1954) was hardly a famous writer slumming; it was more like going home, particularly since he would again work with Golden Age artist Ed Robbins. And detective Mike Hammer was finally appearing in the medium he'd originally been intended for.

Spillane wrote the Sunday page and coplotted the daily strip, with (initially) his friend, comic-book writer Joe Gill; later Robbins pitched in on the writing. That Spillane has never written Mike Hammer short stories per se (his Private Eye Writers of America Shamus Award–winning short story, "The Killing Man," was a condensation of his 1989 novel of the same name) gives weight and significance to his Mike Hammer strip writing. The voice-over narration, the rough-and-tumble violence, the sexy "dolls," were pure Spillane; and Robbins's deftly scratchy art style provided the properly *noir*ish flavor.

Unfortunately, the strip was canceled when editors objected to a typical Spillane torture sequence—a premature death for perhaps the liveliest, most faithful translation of a classic fictional detective from prose to comics.

Batman and Spirit

Surprisingly, no major private eye character emerged from the comic-book field in the thirties or forties, with the minor exception of *Superman* cocreators Joe Shuster and Jerome Siegel's *Slam Bradley* in the seminal *Detective Comics,* which was soon dominated by a *costumed* tough detective: *Batman.*

Batman was, essentially, Dick Tracy in super-hero drag (creator Bob Kane has admitted as much). Like Tracy, he was a firm-jawed hero who swore to battle crime over the corpse of a fallen loved one (in Batman's case, there were two loved ones, parents, whereas Tracy lost his father-in-law-to-be).

Like Tracy, he fought an array of grotesque villains whose physiognomies mirrored their colorful monikers. Like Tracy, he often fought side by side with a youthful ward (in Tracy's case, it was an adopted son, Junior). Like Tracy, he relied on crime-lab science to aid his already keen abilities as a detective. And, like Tracy, he never failed to track down and bring a rough sort of justice to lawbreakers.

Like Alfred Andriola, Kane is notorious for having done little of the material to which his name has been signed; his early work, however, is responsible for establishing the off-kilter German-expressionist tone to which subsequent *Batman* artists, from Jerry Robinson to Frank Miller, have aspired. The somber approach of Kane's early work was also invoked by scriptwriter Denny O'Neill in the late sixties through the 1970s, often with dynamic artist Neal Adams, in an attempt to banish the campy image of the popular mid-sixties TV series.

Of all Kane's ghost artists, the prime performer is the superbly stylish Dick Sprang. From the forties into the sixties, Sprang went to town with Batman's fiendish foes—his often-nameless square-shouldered fedora-topped zoot-suited thugs were Caligari-like caricatures of Warner Bros. heavies; and his Joker was a character charged with both menace and mirth.

Kane and writer Bill Finger, however, must be credited with the creation of the Joker, that most famous and memorable of Batman's opponents. The Joker and other recurring villains—the Penguin, Two-Face, Catwoman—have become almost as famous as Batman himself. Like the grotesque gallery of Gould ghouls, Batman's rogues' gallery has threatened to overshadow the very hero of the strip.

In 1940, comic-book impresario Will Eisner began a syndicated comic-book style supplement for Sunday comics sections, starring his own masked crimefighter, The Spirit. Batman's elaborate costume and gimmickry was not a part of the Spirit's world; ''deceased'' cop Denny Colt was closer to Sam Spade or Philip Marlowe in tone and temperament, and Eisner combined a grimly *noir*ish urban landscape with a wryly bittersweet, decidedly Jewish world view.

Few storytellers in the medium could match Eisner in his seven-page modern O. Henry–style vignettes; the Spirit is not the household word that Tracy and Batman are, but his creator, Will Eisner, is regarded as one of the medium's few true geniuses. A pioneer in educational comics, Eisner has, in recent years, produced a first-rate cycle of modern-day graphic novels for Kitchen Sink Press, usually with crime/mystery themes (but minus the Spirit).

Comic-Book Dicks

No private eye has ever really made a major mark in the comic-book field, with the possible exception of Ms. Tree, the female private eye created by myself and artist Terry Beatty in 1980.

Ms. Tree is the longest running comic-book p.i. strip, enduring over sixty issues of comic-book mayhem for various publishers, including DC Comics, where her appearances are currently limited to annual ones. Michael Tree—her mannish first name is the same as her late private eye husband's—is a female Mike Hammer with modern, even feminist touches; now a working mother, she has interrupted her feud with the mob to tackle such socially volatile issues as abortion, satanism, gay bashing, and date rape.

The outstanding comic-book private eye of the fifties was Pete Morisi's Johnny Dynamite. Johnny Dynamite was a Mike Hammer pastiche, and rivals the Spillane/Robbins official version. Dynamite wears an eye patch, closely resembles Warner Bros.' tough guy John Garfield, blasts bad guys with a .45 and

has a surprisingly sexy good time (for a comic-book character) with bevies of beauties, at least in the issues published before the Comics Code came in.

Somewhat similar to *Dynamite* was Dick Giordano's entertaining *Sarge Steel,* the longest running private eye comic-book prior to *Ms. Tree.* Steel was the first comic-book p.i. to be a Vietnam vet; in fact, he lost a hand there, replacing it with a steel mitt and lending the feature a faint superhero resonance.

This tough, well-written, well-drawn mid-sixties book—often scripted by Spillane crony Joe Gill—paved the way for Charlton Comics' later series of wry Mike Mauser stories written by Nicola Cuti and drawn by Joe Staton. Seedy, diminutive, bespectacled Mauser (not seen since the seventies) teamed with Ms. Tree for the First Comics three-issue miniseries, *The P.I.'s.,* in 1985.

Private eyes have made a modest comeback in recent decades: in the seventies, Jim Steranko presented an exquisitely drawn graphic novel, *Chandler;* another Collins/Beatty private-eye, Mike Mist, has starred in "Minute Mist-eries" since 1979, in both comic book and strip form; and DC (the letters stand for "Detective Comics," after all) has published a number of private eyes—writer Len Wein, creator of *Swamp Thing*, has come up with two: Johnny Double and the Human Target. Writer Mike Barr's Ellery Queen-influenced *Maze Agency* has enjoyed a modest success, and deserves more.

Crime Comics

The premier practitioner of crime comics in the 1950s was writer/artist Johnny Craig, particularly in the EC title *Crime Suspenstories.* Despite the bold *Crime* lettering on its covers, the book was not part of (though sought to cash in on) the supposedly "true crime" format of writer/artist Charles Biro's wildly successful *Crime Does Not Pay,* which spawned many imitators.

In stories taking up fewer pages than most modern comic-book *auteurs* would need to set the stage for some overblown "opus," Craig would spin vivid, compelling James M. Cain-inspired tales of human greed and lust. The characters in a Craig story, like a Cain story, are small, ordinary folks caught up in webs of their own devising, with some help by a nasty fate. They scheme, they sweat, they kill, they die.

Most of the crime comics of the postwar period pretend to be based on fact, possibly due to the popularity of Jack Webb's seminal *Dragnet* TV series, which made elaborate on-air pronouncements about each story's veracity. The *Dragnet* influence did not, however, extend into a wave of popular cop comics; there was, to my knowledge, no *Dragnet* comic book, although a short-lived comic strip surfaced, and a rip-off comic book called *I'm a Cop* briefly appeared.

Despite fifties pop shrink Frederic Wertham and various concerned congressmen of that era singling them out as a convenient bogeyman, the crime comic books of the fifties were read by adults more often than by kids. During the war, thanks to PXs and the portability of comics and a low literacy rate, comic books became a medium whose audience included many adults—specifically GIs. The grown-up concerns of fifties crime comics seem more in tune with semiliterate World War II vets than Howdy Doody–generation preteens.

Rarely do any of the *Crime Does Not Pay* school of comics, despite elaborate claims, seem pulled from actual case files, other than the occasional Baby Face Nelson or Dillinger docudrama. Some of the liveliest, and most outrageous, "true crime" comics from the Charles Biro/Lev Gleason stable were drawn, and possibly written, by the genius behind the *Plastic Man* superhero comics: Jack Cole, who later (before his tragic, early suicide) became one of Hugh Hefner's star cartoonists at the newly formed *Playboy.*

When the Comics Code Authority came in, in the late fifties, the words *crime* and *horror* were banned from the titles of Code-approved comics, killing off the form until an often perverted parodistic return in the form of late sixties "underground" comics by such masters of that medium as Robert Crumb, Greg Irons, Spain Rodriguez, and S. Clay Wilson.

The Future Mr. Gittes

At present, few detective comic strips exist—*Dick Tracy,* which I wrote from 1977 until 1993, and John Prentice's continuation of *Rip Kirby* are about it.

But the comic-book world is more promising. Kitchen Sink continues to publish wonderful Will Eisner graphic novels; *Ms. Tree* and *The Maze*

Agency keep popping up in one form or another; various publishers foist the delightfully demented post-underground pulp of Charles Burns and Kim Deitch on an unsuspecting public; and the controversial popularity of true-crime trading cards (which, if pressed, I'll admit to being one of the initial instigators thereof) has spawned new *Crime Does Not Pay*–style comic books.

Most heartening are plans from several major publishers in the comics field—including DC Comics—to create lines of *noir*-slanted mystery/crime graphic novels. Whether or not the greater American public—convinced that comics are inherently ''kids stuff''—will take to adult crime fare in comics form is a mystery that remains, at press time, unsolved.

Recommended Reading List
Selected by Max Allan Collins

The Dick Tracy Casebook, edited by Max Allan Collins and Dick Locher (St. Martin's Press, 1990), $15.95. Limited supply available from MAC Productions, 301 Fairview Avenue, Muscatine, Iowa 52761. (Enclose $2.00 postage/handling.)

Secret Agent X-9, Dashiell Hammett and Alex Raymond (Kitchen Sink Press, 1990), $13.95. Out of print; check mystery bookstores and/or comics shops; complete run of both Hammett and Raymond, including Leslie Charteris-scripted episodes.

Will Gould's Red Barry edited by Rick Marschall (1989), $9.95. Four 1930s episodes. Order from Fantagraphics Books; call toll free, 1-800-657-1100.

Fearless Fosdick by Al Capp (1990), $11.95. Order from Kitchen Sink Press; call toll free 1-800-365-SINK.

Mickey Spillane's Mike Hammer: The Comic Strip Vol. One (1982) and Vol. Two (1985), published by Ken Pierce, Inc., PO Box 332, Park Forest, Illinois 60466. $5.95 each, postpaid.

Batman: The Sunday Classics 1943–46, Bob Kane (1992), $19.95. Also: three volumes of '40s daily strips. Order from Kitchen Sink Press; call toll free 1-800-365-SINK.

Spirit Casebook, Will Eisner (1990). Also available: full line of Eisner's brilliant graphic novels. Order from Kitchen Sink Press; call toll free 1-800-365-SINK.

The Files of Ms. Tree, Collins & Beatty, Vol. One (1984), Vol. Two (1985), Vol. Three (1986); published by Renegade Press. $7.50 each postpaid, limited supply available from MAC Productions, 301 Fairview Avenue, Muscatine, Iowa 52761.

Crime Suspenstories Vols. 1–5, hardcover boxed set (1983). The essential Johnny Craig. $110 postpaid. Order from Russ Cochran, Publisher; call toll free 1-800-EC CRYPT.

NOSTALGIA

George Sander's droll interpretation of "The Saint."

NORBERT DAVIS
An Appreciation
John D. MacDonald

THE TIME FRAME IS IMPORTANT. The hard-boiled detective stories began to surface in the early 1920s in *Black Mask.* Carroll John Daly and Dashiell Hammett were leaders of a very small pack. Their stories were realistic—tough, sudden, and wry.

Through the 1920s, that kind of work, in that magazine, began to attract more readers and create a small surprise among the reviewers of more celebrated fiction, who were surprised to find a departure, a new kind of creative energy, in a pulp-paper magazine. By the late 1920s, the list of practitioners included Erle Stanley Gardner, Frederick Nebel, Tod Ballard, and Raoul Whitfield.

I remember well the opening sentence of one story by Whitfield. It moves the reader into the action more quickly than any other opening I have ever seen. "I dropped to one knee and fired twice."

I used that line, indirectly, years later, when Knox Burger, then editing the Gold Medal line at Fawcett Publications, told me that he thought my manuscript of *Darker Than Amber* began too slowly. So I accelerated the opening this way: "We were about to give up and call it a night when somebody dropped the girl off the bridge." It isn't as crisp as the Whitfield opening, but it is a lineal descendent.

In the 1930s, new names began to appear with some regularity. Norbert Davis, George Harmon Coxe, Lester Dent (who used to do the Doc Savage novels for Street and Smith), Raymond Chandler, and Paul Cain. The editor was Joseph Thompson "Cap" Shaw. He knew that he had control of an exciting new school, and he worked very hard on selection for quality, balanced makeup, and promotion.

Cap Shaw left *Black Mask* in 1936, when the magazine was at its creative peak. He went to work for the Sydney Sanders Literary Agency. In the late 1940s, after my first agent, Marian Ives, retired, I

went with the Sanders agency on the recommendation of MacKinlay Kantor, who had also served his time in the pulps. Cap Shaw handled my output and did very well with it, placing me in a full range of pulps as well as in *Colliers, American, Liberty, Esquire, Cosmopolitan, Redbook* and other slick-paper magazines. In the early fifties, when Syd Sanders died, Cap Shaw was seventy-eight years old. When he had differences with Mrs. Sanders, who took over the agency, he left and started his own agency, and I went with him.

Cap Shaw was a wise and gentle man. He had very strong opinions, and a lot of persistence. He had won a medal for swordsmanship with the épée in the 1922 Olympics, and as a consequence was the only man in New York City licensed by the authorities to carry a sword cane. He was a very thoughtful and considerate man. His office was in an eight-story building on, if memory serves, West Forty-Seventh Street. He died of a heart attack one winter midmorning, in the only elevator in the building. The police came when summoned, but the body could not be moved until it had been looked at by someone from the medical examiner's office. They did not arrive until midafternoon. It would have appalled Cap Shaw to know that he had inadvertently forced all the occupants of his building to use the stairwell to go to and from lunch. But it would have pleased him to realize that such an untidy demise could have appeared in a story by Hammett or Chandler or Norbert Davis, who all celebrated the ironic.

At the time Shaw left *Black Mask,* the magazine's only serious competition came from *Dime Detective,* owned by Popular Publications. It began publication in November 1931, with five stories by J. Allan Dunn, Frederick Nebel, T. T. Flynn, Edward Parish Ware, and Erle Stanley Gardner. It was edited by Kenneth S. White. After Shaw left, many of the *Black Mask* contributors switched their allegiance to *Dime Detective.*

After *Black Mask* was purchased by Popular Publications in the early 1940s, Ken White became editor in chief of both magazines. He featured the regulars like Roger Torrey, T. T. Flynn, Norbert Davis, and Tod Ballard in both magazines. By 1945–46, when I began writing for Popular Publications, the editors on the firing line were Harry Widmer, Mike Tilden, Alden Norton, and several others. It gave them an opportunity to trade off acceptable stories in order to give more effective balance to the magazines. Many times I would expect a story to appear in *Black Mask,* and it would appear in *Detective Tales, Fifteen-Story Detective,* or *Dime Detective.*

Between 1935 and 1943, Norbert Davis published nineteen stories in *Dime Detective.* My first one was published in 1946, three years after his last one, and my last one, of thirty-nine, was published in 1952. The magazine lasted for but six more issues.

It is difficult to assess the career of a writer who almost made it. Bill Pronzini, in his introduction to a Norbert Davis story collected in *The Arbor House Treasury of Detective and Mystery Stories from the Great Pulps* (Arbor House, 1983), says, "Norbert Davis (1909–1949) was among the most talented of all the writers who specialized in pulp fiction. He sold his first story, 'Reform Racket,' to Cap Shaw and *Black Mask* in 1932, while studying law at Stanford University, and followed it with hundreds more sold to a wide range of . . . publications. His fiction was fast-paced, occasionally lyrical in a hard-edged way, and often quite funny."

The story reprinted in *The Arbor House Treasury* is "Holocaust House," featuring the detective team, surely one of the most unusual teams in private eye history, of Doan and Carstairs. Doan was a short, chunky, smiling, amiable alcoholic with a taste for violence. Carstairs was a Great Dane, a dog Doan had won in a poker game. The dog believed he had come down in the world, being owned by a drunken detective. Once in a while, in the most dire extremity, he would help save Doan from disaster.

Norbert Davis wrote one other pulp novelette about this pair, and then wrote three novels about them, two published in 1943 and one in 1946. Davis came along just as the idea of a continuing series of stories featuring the same private eye lead was gaining momentum. Of course the precedents go back to Sherlock Holmes and Ulysses, but in the pulp magazines it did not begin to be endemic until the 1930s. Of Norbert Davis's nineteen stories in *Dime Detective,* eight featured a hero named Bail Bond Dodd, and five were about a "brilliantly screwball" detective named Max Latin.

It is intriguing to go through the list of people who contributed to *Dime Detective* during its span of twenty-two years and 273 issues. Two hundred and ninety-eight writers were involved, with but sixty-five of them contributing five or more stories. These names all stir memory to a greater or lesser extent: Wyatt Blassingame, Max Brand, Fredric Brown, Raymond Chandler, Donald Barr Chidsey, William R. Cox, George Harmon Coxe, Carroll John Daly, Bruno Fischer, T. T. Flynn, William Campbell Gault, Erle Stanley Gardner, Richard E. Glendinning, Larry Holden, Don James, MacKinlay Kantor, Day Keene, Baynard Kendrick, Murray Leinster, William P. McGivern, Robert Martin, Harold Q. Masur, Sam Merwin, Jr., Frederick Nebel, Talmage Powell, Oscar Schisgall, Luke Short, Theodore Sturgeon, Lawrence Treat, Robert Turner, Edgar Wallace, Thomas Walsh, Cornell Woolrich and Richard Wormser. Thirty-five (counting me) of 298. Of the names that ring a bell, loud or faint, some of them, such as Luke Short and Theodore Sturgeon, achieved their standing in other fields of fiction. Most of the others achieved that resonance through writing books. Some became known for their stories in more expensive magazines.

I knew a baker's dozen of these writers. None of them that I knew could have posed as a bond salesman. Take Dick Wormser, as an example. A very tall, thin, slightly stooped fellow, some kind of a nephew of Albert Einstein. He lived in the Southwest, and his personal stationery had a column list down the left margin of the things he could write. Instant Indian legends. Plausible excuses. B movies. Collection letters. That sort of thing. The list went all the way down the page. We were both clients of Littauer and Wilkinson, Literary Representatives, at that time. We met in the Fifth Avenue offices of Max Wilkinson one day by accident. It was in the early 1960s, when *Dime Detective* had been dead for eight or nine years.

We left at the same time and went and had a drink together. We talked about the old days, about

Ken White, Alden Norton, Mike Tilden, Harry Widmer, Bob Lowndes, Babette Rosmond—about all the pulp editors we had dealt with. The relationship between writer and editor was often a strange one. Both professions were underpaid. So sometimes money was lent. If it went from editor to writer, it was called an advance. If it went the other way, it was called a loan. We came upon an eerie coincidence. In 1932 Dick Wormser had lent an editor three hundred dollars to bail his wife and newborn son out of the hospital. In 1952, twenty years later, I had lent the same editor four hundred dollars to help get the same kid buried, after he had killed himself. Neither of us had been repaid, nor had we expected to be.

I never met Norbert Davis, but I have no reason to suspect that he was any less eccentric, or less anxious, in that penny-a-word environment than any of the rest of us.

But to get back to that small shock of recognition, Norbert Davis rings no bell with most of us. He wrote reasonably well, and he wrote and sold a lot. That is supposed to do it. What happened to Norbert Davis? I believe that luck is a factor too often overlooked.

In *Cheap Thrills, an Informal History of the Pulp Magazine,* by Ron Goulart (Arlington House, 1972), Goulart tells of a story called "Red Goose," written by Norbert Davis while he was still in a rooming house at Stanford University, working toward his law degree. A close friend of Davis's told Goulart: "Bert became so successful that he never bothered to take the bar exam."

"Red Goose" was published in the February 1934 issue of *Black Mask,* and Raymond Chandler referred to it in a letter written years later, saying, "It must be very good because I have never forgotten it."

Goulart goes on to say:

> Davis . . . specialized in tough, fast, and often whimsical private eye stories. This is what Raymond Chandler was attempting in his own stories and is one of the reasons he was fond of Norbert Davis's work. Davis wrote a great quantity of pulp material in the '30s and '40s, appearing eventually in most of the pulp detective magazines as well as *Argosy.* He also had some luck in slicks like *The Saturday Evening Post* before his early death in 1949.

Luck can result from good timing, from good decisions. I have a picture of Norbert Davis here, taken at a *Black Mask* dinner in January 1936. It is a group picture. Eleven writers, among them Dashiell Hammett, Raymond Chandler, and Horace McCoy. Davis is seated at the far right. Obviously tall, black hair, prominent dark eyebrows, a long, solid-looking jaw, an open smile as he looks into the camera. An attractive man.

Bill Pronzini tells us: "Davis abandoned the pulps in 1943–1944 when he began to have success with humorous stories for such magazines as *The Saturday Evening Post.*"

As one who has been there, I call this a bad decision. It tells me that Norbert Davis had some sort of counterproductive disdain for the market that had been feeding and housing him for eleven years. I suppose that in some sense it was socially more acceptable to write for the slick-paper magazines than for the pulps. Certainly it paid better. But writing is writing is writing. Pulp fiction was not some sort of whoredom. What you do, as a craftsman, is recognize the stipulations and the limits and the requirements of a specific market, and then, within those limits, you write just as damn well as you can. You write to please yourself and you write to learn, and you write to earn a living. Believe me, the stipulations and restrictions and boundaries set by the slick-paper magazines were at that time far more oppressive and restrictive than anything imposed by the pulps.

His decision to abandon the pulps says, in effect, that he could not learn anything more in that medium. Wrong. You will see what I mean as you read his stories. There are splendid patches, and there are awkward patches, and in between there is competence.

I do not want to hold myself up as some sort of walking miracle of good judgment, but I stayed with the pulp markets until the mid-fifties, when the last of them were shot out from under me. I enjoyed the freedom they gave me—to write about almost any damned thing that came into my mind, whether it was crime, science fiction, western, fantasy, or sports. And today people are still buying the rights to those old stories and putting them into anthologies. I did not devise a private eye to inhabit a series of stories because I did not want to get stuck with one. I wanted all the range I could get because I was still in a learning environment. I stayed with the pulps long after I had my first novels published. They were fun. If they were around today, I would write stories for them again. The slick-paper magazines are no fun. They are too self-conscious and have too limited a notion of what constitutes a solid piece of fiction.

I am dead-certain positive that somewhere in the back of his mind, Bert Davis sensed that it might be a mistake to give up the market that had nurtured him. Did someone influence him? A wife? A girl-friend? Well-meaning friends who told him he was ''too good'' for those dingy little magazines? An inept agent motivated by a desire for bigger pay-days? I believe that had he stayed with the pulps while continuing to place stories with the slick magazines, had he continued the learning process, he would have become one of those names today that ring lots of bells.

In this life when you guess wrong, a lot of things go wrong and keep going more wrong. Bert Davis had a string of marital failures. His agent died suddenly and unexpectedly. The slick magazines began to reject his work. So one day he got into his car, in his garage, and put a flexible hose from the tailpipe through a car window, and sat there and died, at age forty. His luck had run out.

GOLD MEDAL DAYS

Vin Packer

Zoë Kamitses

I DIDN'T EVEN HAVE a telephone the afternoon I got my first call from Dick Carroll, an editor with Gold Medal Books. It was 1951, and New York City was still feeling the effects of World War II's aftermath. I *had* found an apartment I could afford, so long as I shared it with three sorority sisters, all of us fresh from the University of Missouri. We had a two-bedroom up in Washington Heights, but we took our phone calls in the basement, on the super's line.

''One of your roommates has been telling me about you,'' said Dick. ''I hear you want to be a writer. How do you feel about being a reader in the meantime?''

Missouri grads were held in high esteem at Fawcett Publications. Ralph Daigh, the editorial director, had graduated from the Journalism School there.

I hoped I'd fare better on West 44th Street, in the Fawcett Building, than I had other places. Beginning at Dutton Publishing, and ending finally with *The Proctological Review* and *The Journal of Gaestroenterology,* I'd been fired from eight jobs in a little over a year . . . employers did not fancy my habit of writing on the side, while the filing piled up, and the letters I'd typed were filled with errors.

I reported to Fawcett on a Monday, where I was introduced to a tall, blue-eyed man with brown hair and a thick Irish accent. You'd have imagined Dick was right off the boat from Ireland instead of right off the train from Greenwich, Connecticut. He was filled with the old blarney, too, and would in a few

years be featured in Rona Jaffe's first novel, *The Best of Everything*. She was one of his assistants then, one of the regulars at the little table in the restaurant in the Fawcett Building, where a gang gathered every night after work to drink and talk, most of the drinks landing up on Dick's bill.

He was forever ordering another round when no one was finished with the first drink, then at the end of the month complaining bitterly that the bar padded his check.

Ah, but he was a happy fellow, mostly. He'd been dug up from the depths of despair out in Hollywood, to come east and help Bill Lengel "revolutionize the publishing industry."

At last, the writer was getting a good break. No longer would hardcover publishers rake off the huge shares of paperback royalties; Gold Medal was publishing paperback originals, and paying very nice advances . . . a typical paperback printing was 400,000 copies. As a new Gold Medal writer, you might get $2000 down and $2000 on delivery of your manuscript. . . . You were paid on print order, a penny a copy . . . it was a very sweet deal.

So I became a reader for a very short time. Bill Lengel received a complaint from a major writer of the day who'd had his book rejected by me. I'd said in the letter the plot was "tired," thus angering

a brand name Gold Medal would have liked including on its list.

Lengel fired me as proof to the writer I had no judgment or tact (true, true) and the writer was treated to a long dinner at the Algonquin next door, the result of which was a contract.

In those beginning days, Lengel was the chief; Dick was under him.

I decided to freelance full-time, because I'd sold a short story to *Ladies Home Journal* for $750. That was three months' salary in those days. The story I'd sold was set in a boarding school, and when it came out, Dick called and said to meet him for drinks immediately.

"How about a boarding school novel?" said Dick. "We are having tremendous luck with a novel called *Women's Barracks* by Tereska Torres."

Fawcett was getting their first hint of how well a theme of lesbianism sold.

I said I'd rather try fiction set in a sorority, since that experience was newer to me.

I outlined and wrote a chapter of a book called *Sorority Girl*. Dick advanced me two thousand against thirty-five hundred, and I was in business.

Dick changed the title to *Spring Fire* because James Michner had a best seller called *Fires of Spring*.

A year later, Roger Fawcett, the seldom-seen CEO, appeared in his office long enough to shake my hand and announce that I'd outsold *God's Little Acre* on the paperback best seller list.

Vin Packer was launched.

I'd chosen the pseudonym because I'd had a dinner one night with a man whose first name was Vincent and a woman whose last was Packer.

I had a lot of pseudonyms because I was my own agent, handling a dozen clients, all me.

The other pseudonyms began to slip away as Packer took over. I switched to homicide, solely because I'd heard that Anthony Boucher reviewed paperbacks in the Sunday *Times,* as did James Sandoe in the Sunday *Tribune.* I wanted to be reviewed.

Thanks to both Sandoe's and Boucher's encouragement, I stayed in the field around twelve years, producing some twenty books, ten of them suspense novels.

What I most liked writing were fictionalized versions of real crime.

I started in that direction at the suggestion of Boucher, who called my attention to a case in Australia, two girls killing the mother of one.

I sent for all the trial papers, and felt my hair rise as I read the diary of one: *Thousands die every day. Why not Mother?*

There was the title leaping out at me. *Why Not Mother?*

But of course I didn't reckon with Dick Carroll's passionate sense of the commercial.

"What you put inside the book is your business," he would tell me, "but the outside is mine."

By then he was the editor in charge, and Lengel was in retirement.

Dick was doing well. Writers like Cornell Woolrich, Richard Prather, and John MacDonald were aboard. Sales were good. Spirits high. "Spirits" were always high when Dick was on the scene, tossing back his scotch, telling his bawdy Irish jokes, thinking up titles to replace yours.

Why Not Mother? became *The Evil Friendship.*

Then when I made a novel of the Fraden/Wepman matricide some years later, my title *One to Destroy* (... is murder by the law), was changed to *Whisper His Sin.*

Now and then Dick would give in to me. I did the Emmett Till Mississippi Wolf Whistle case, and he let me keep my title *Dark Don't Catch Me.* (Dark don't catch me in this town...).

But more than often I was in tears as I caught a cab, on 44th and Sixth, certain weekday evenings after Dick took the 7:45 to suburbia. I would have just learned the new title of my book ... and read the cover copy.

Favorite phrases having little to do with the inside of my books, really, were: "sexual awakening," "sexual passions," "sexual guilt," "this startling novel," "terrible secrets revealed," "secrets that shattered," and "another tempestuous tale by the author of *Spring Fire.*"

One Christmas I made spaghetti sauce (my recipe) with a friend, for sorority Christmas gifts. We put a label on the jar: "Another tempestuous dish by the author of *Spring Fire.*"

Those years were good ones despite the lack of autonomy when it came to covers. I was able to launch myself as a full-time freelancer only because of Gold Medal. I could not have afforded the career of writing if I had had to depend on the average hardcover advance.

When I finally did go on to hardcover, I abandoned Packer, for the most part. I was myself for a while ... and then in the seventies I had a complete sex change and became M. E. Kerr, a young adult writer.

Although I do have a new suspense series launched featuring a detective's son, John Fell (*Fell, Fell Back, Fell Down, Fell in Love,* etc.) Ms. Kerr does not usually wander onto Ms. Packer's old turf.

I have to compete now with the likes of V. C. Andrews and Judy Blume, no simple task.

But Black Lizard claims to be bringing Packer back soon, and with it, for me, there will be many memories of the fifties in New York City, when Alfred Hitchcock's profile was just appearing on TV to the jaunty theme music, Rod Serling was inviting you to come to *The Twilight Zone,* and a lot of us were thinking we ought to go to the coast if we wanted to stay freelancers: television was the coming thing, wasn't it?

"In the sixties," Dick would say, "hardcover books will start to fade away, as they have in Europe. In the seventies, there'll just be paper ... you're in at the beginning of a revolution!"

And then he'd say what he always said, "Waiter? All the way around again! Make mine a double!"

THE GOLDEN ERA OF GOLD MEDAL BOOKS

George Tuttle

IN MAY 1950, FAWCETT'S Gold Medal Books changed the way the publishing industry did business. Up to that point, paperback publishers relied almost exclusively on reprints. They would buy the rights to a hardcover edition, with fifty percent of the royalties from the reprint going to the book's hardcover publisher and the other half going to the book's author. Since, in many cases, most of the profits from a book came from paperback sales, many authors found themselves sharing a large percentage of a book's profits with a hardcover publisher who seemingly did little to earn its share. Gold Medal Books were paperback originals and not reprints of clothbound editions; the author got one hundred percent of the book's royalties and didn't share any of the money with a hardcover publisher. Gold Medal's existence changed publishing forever, because it was the first line of paperback originals and the first serious attempt by a paperback publisher to challenge the hardcover publishers' domination of the paperback industry.

May 1950 is when the Gold Medal line became fully operational. Though Gold Medal released some test runs prior to this date, it was with the release in May of four novels—*The Persian Cat* by John Flagg, *I'll Find You* by Richard Himmel, *Nude in Mink* by Sax Rohmer, and *Stretch Dawson* by W. R. Burnett—that hardcover publishers realized that the serpent had entered their Garden of Eden and that they would no longer have complete control over paperback publishing.

May 1950 also marks the beginning of Gold Medal's Golden Era. It was a period when success came easily and many Gold Medal titles sold close to or over a million, at a time when million sellers were rare. This period lasted almost a decade. After it, the book publishing market changed and paperback originals became less popular. Gold Medal's

luck seemed to turn on March 11, 1959, the day Richard A. Carroll, Gold Medal's editor in chief, died. Dick Carroll was the man who guided this paperback publisher through the lion's share of its glory years. When he died, Gold Medal's magic died. Though it continued to be the leading publisher of paperback originals and went on to publish John D. MacDonald's Travis McGee series and other popular works, it was soon after Carroll's death that the market began to change, and times got tougher. Though the market didn't change because of Carroll's departure, his death seems to mark the beginning of leaner, less prosperous times.

Writing a history of this era isn't easy. Most of the key people who established the Gold Medal line are gone. Ralph Daigh, Jim Bishop, Dick Carroll, and Bill Lengel are all dead. Also gone is Fawcett Publications. The Fawcett family sold the company to CBS, who later sold it to Random House. Fawcett and Gold Medal Books are no longer distinct entities, just imprints of a large publishing conglomerate. Because of these factors, a large amount of the historical data about this paperback publisher is lost, including back issues of Fawcett's in-house newsletter, *The Fawcett Flame*.

Despite these barriers, a dedicated effort has been made to collect what information there is. The following Gold Medal editors were interviewed: Daniel Talbot, assistant editor 1950–52; Inez Salinger, associate editor 1952–55; executive editor 1955–1957; Hal Cantor, assistant editor 1952–54, managing editor 1954–55; and Robin Little, associate editor 1955–56, managing editor 1956–57, executive editor 1957–59. Also interviewed were Gold Medal author Mike Avallone and former Fawcett editors Arthur Orrmont, the first executive editor of the Crest line, and Leona Nevler, who succeeded Arthur at Crest and later replaced Ralph Daigh as the person in charge of Fawcett's editorial operations. Numerous articles were also read, including ones by Gold Medal writers Robert Colby and Vin Packer, plus other sources were used like Donald McCampbell's book *Don't Step on It—It Might Be a Writer* and correspondences provided by Piet Schreuders. (A partial bibliography is listed at the end of this article. Special thanks to all of the above, especially Hal Cantor, who was particularly generous with his time.)

Fawcett had been late breaking into paperback publishing. Throughout the 1940s it prospered, coupling its magazine empire with a highly successful comic-book line. But by 1949 the comic-book market had begun to wane. Meanwhile, the paperback market was growing by leaps and bounds. Rival magazine publishers Dell and Popular Library had cracked this market in the early 1940s and were enjoying the benefits. Fawcett realized that if it wanted to grow, it had to make the switch from comic books to paperbacks.

Since paperbacks used a newsstand distribution system, Fawcett was in a position to take advantage of the booming paperback market. The only problem that stood in its way was that the established firms like Pocket Books, Bantam, and N.A.L. (Signet), and to a lesser degree Dell, Popular Library, and Avon, were already well known to hardcover publishers. A new paperback house would have a tough time getting the trust of hardcover publishers and obtaining the reprint rights to major titles. If Fawcett was to become a major publisher of paperbacks, it would have to circumvent this problem.

Fawcett conceived a two-step approach to tackling the paperback market, an approach that was a combination of luck and genius. The luck involved N.A.L., and its need for a distributor, and the genius was how Fawcett exploited this opportunity to its advantage.

In September 1949, Fawcett signed a contract with N.A.L. to handle the distribution of Signet and Mentor books. The contract prohibited Fawcett from publishing reprints of hardcover books, but allowed it to produce paperback originals if it chose. When N.A.L. allowed this clause, it probably believed that the extent of Fawcett's originals would be limited to how-to books and other nonfiction titles similar to the magazine yearbooks it was already producing. It's doubtful that N.A.L. suspected that Fawcett would use this clause as a springboard for a major paperback operation. This contract was the first step

in Fawcett becoming a force in paperback publishing. Thanks to this contract, Fawcett was able to share in the success of Signet and didn't have to attempt to crash the paperback reprint market that was already dominated by more established firms.

The second step followed soon after, in the fall of 1949, when Fawcett exercised their right to publish paperback originals and released two collections of articles from *True* and *Today's Woman* magazines. The anthologies were entitled *The Best from True* and *Marriage and Sex*. Due to the success of these test runs, Fawcett Publications created Gold Medal Books. Roscoe Fawcett, Fawcett's circulation director, and Allan Adams, circulation manager, were the men responsible for thinking up this two-step approach and in realizing that a line that published only paperback originals could be profitable.

The next several months were spent organizing the line. Jim Bishop was hired as editor. He came to Fawcett from the Music Corporation of America, where he was director of its literary department. Prior to that, he had been executive editor at *Liberty* magazine and the war editor at *Collier's* magazine. He was a very gifted man who later became a successful writer and went on to write the best-selling books *The Day Christ Died* and *The Day Lincoln Was Shot*.

Another man brought in to assist Jim was Bill Lengel. He was kind of a senior statesman of publishing who was placed at Gold Medal to offer guidance. Former executive editor Robin Little described Lengel's position at Fawcett by saying, "Lengel, by that time, was an old man. The Fawcett brothers had him there because he had been very good and still had some interesting, workable, and commercial ideas, but for the run-of-the-mill day, he wasn't much help." Lengel had had a distinguished career that included working with Theodore Dreiser and with a number of noted publishers. He had been with Fawcett since 1942. His main contribution to Gold Medal was recruiting a number of name authors. He was responsible for the presence of Theodore Pratt, Octavus Roy Cohen, Eric Hatch, MacKinlay Kantor, Cornell Woolrich, Sax Rohmer, W. R. Burnett, James Warner Bellah, and Will Jenkins. Gold Medal planned to intersperse titles by these authors among titles by new and lesser-known writers. The intent was to give the line an impressive send-off.

Early in 1950, Gold Medal released its first two

books. Once again these were primarily marketing tests, but in May 1950, the line became fully operational when it released its first four novels. These titles sold well, well enough to scare hardcover publishers and paperback reprint houses, who wanted to maintain the status quo.

When these first four novels hit the newsstands, Gold Medal was the subject of a large amount of criticism by hardcover and paperback companies. Though paperback originals had been published previously, Gold Medal was the first serious attempt to mass-produce originals. Le Baron R. Barker of Doubleday said that the continued publication of originals would ''undermine the whole structure of publishing.'' He continued: ''If you carry that idea to its ultimate conclusion, it would mean that publishers would lose book club and reprint rights. . . . That would put three-quarters of the firms into bankruptcy.'' This never happened. But this was the belief held by many publishers, and it fueled more criticism, like claims that originals would lower the quality of paperback literature. Critics theorized that originals could not attract quality authors and that after Lengel had used up all of his contacts (Pratt, Kantor, Woolrich, . . .) the line would have to resort to hacks and second-raters. But this never happened either. Gold Medal's generous royalty plan attracted many talented authors and resulted in many novels with lasting appeal. The quality is reflected by the fact that many of these books are still being written about, reprinted, and made into movies.

Fawcett Publications maintained offices at two locations. The sales and distribution offices were located in Greenwich, Connecticut. The editorial offices were located at 67 West 44 Street, New York, New York. The Fawcett brothers (Wilford, Roger, Roscoe, and Gordon), who made up the board of directors, concerned themselves chiefly with the Connecticut side of the operation. Ralph Daigh, who held the title of editorial director, was in charge of the editorial offices. Daigh, next to the Fawcetts, was the most powerful man in the company. His offices were on the top floor of the Fawcett Building, which was symbolic of his importance.

In 1950 Fawcett Publications consisted of the following magazines: *Daring Detective, Mechanix Illustrated, Motion Picture, Movie Story, Startling Detective, Today's Woman, True* (the company's most profitable title, at the time), *True Confessions,* and *True Police Cases.* It also included a line of thirty-two comic-book titles that included *Captain Marvel, Hopalong Cassidy,* and *Negro Romances,* and a line of magazine yearbooks that consisted of titles like *Aviation Yearbook, 40 Homes & Plans for Building,* and *Handy Man's Home Manual.* Ralph Daigh supervised the production of all of these publications. He was also the one who named the new paperback line Gold Medal Books and thought up its incredible royalty plan.

For many writers, particularly writers of westerns and detective fiction, Gold Medal's royalty plan was the sweetest deal they had ever seen. In an era where a writer would sell a novel to a hardcover publisher for as low as $250, Gold Medal's $2000 minimum was fantastic. Also, unlike other book publishers who paid royalties to authors based on the number of copies sold, Gold Medal paid its authors on the number of copies printed, and the author received the payment due him, over the advance, as soon as the book was printed or ''within thirty days thereafter,'' as the contract stated. They paid the authors one cent for each copy up to 200,000 and a cent and a half for each copy over 200,000. Since each Gold Medal Book had a minimum printing of 200,000, the author was guaranteed a minimum payment of $2000. By January 1953 it started with minimum printings of 300,000.

Bishop was only editor at Gold Medal for a short time. He was hired late in 1949, announced his intent to resign about a year later, and departed a couple months after that. The official reason for his leaving was that he planned to work on a biography of noted Broadway columnist Mark Hellinger. But it should be noted that just before his departure, Lengel was given the title of editor in chief. This might have been a coincidence, but one can't help but wonder if there was friction between Bishop and Lengel involving who was in charge of the line. Bishop was editor, and Lengel was a titleless senior adviser. If there had been a dispute between Bishop and Lengel on who was in charge, and Ralph Daigh had sided with Lengel, it seems logical that the dispute would have been concluded by giving Lengel a title that stated his authority. If this did occur, it would not have been the only incident of this type to have happened at Fawcett. Six years later, after Lengel had been moved to the Crest line, the executive editor of the line, Arthur Orrmont, left due to a dispute with Lengel over who had the final say over book selection.

So in December 1950, Bishop announced his

retirement, Lengel was given the title editor in chief, and a new editor, Richard Carroll was brought in to replace Bishop. Carroll was an old friend of Bill Lengel's and had worked with him at *Liberty* magazine twenty years before. Carroll knew him and understood how to work with him.

Bishop left Gold Medal in February 1951, and Carroll was given the newly created title of executive editor (Bishop's title had just been "editor"). As executive editor, Carroll handled the day-to-day operation of Gold Medal. Lengel, as editor in chief, supervised the operation, a job which didn't involve much, since Carroll was very capable and didn't require supervision. During the first year of Gold Medal's operation, Lengel did do editing and did work with some writers (no doubt writers he brought to the line), but ironically, by the time he was given the title of editor in chief, he was doing no editing at all, and as far as it is known, he didn't do any editing during the rest of his tenure. He would work with Carroll on title changes and would contribute marketing ideas. He would also represent Gold Medal at meetings, but he was more of a figurehead than a man in charge.

Daniel Talbot, who worked under both Jim Bishop and Dick Carroll, described them both as writer's editors—in other words, editors who were sympathetic to the problems faced by a writer and who writers liked working with. But he contrasted the two by saying that Carroll was more worldly. In Talbot's words: "Dick just seemed to have a wider view of things. He just knocked around more than Jim."

Carroll had knocked around more. He was a veteran of World War I. He had worked as a newspaper reporter and editor with the *Boston Globe* and *New York Daily News*. He later wrote for slick magazines and was aviation and fiction editor for *Liberty* magazine. After *Liberty,* Carroll went to Hollywood, where he worked as a story editor for several different studios and earned a reputation as a story doctor. He received credit for a number of screenplays, including *Three Girls about Town* and *The Ape*. He was also a poker-playing buddy of John Wayne's and John Ford's. During World War II he enlisted, was given the rank of major, and worked on a number of film projects for the Defense Department. After the war he returned to Hollywood, until he was contracted by Bill Lengel for the job at Gold Medal.

Carroll's Hollywood experience contributed greatly to his more worldly point of view. He lacked the traditional book publisher's view of genre fiction. Under Carroll's tenure the distinction between genres was less obvious. A thriller would often have elements usually associated with a mainstream novel, and vice versa. Only the westerns were easy to distinguish, and that was because of their settings. It was because of its nonconventional atmosphere that Gold Medal became a chief exponent of the "*roman noir,*" or black novel. Carroll seemed to be open to almost any kind of experimentation. His only limits were that he would insist that a story be concise and not cluttered with unnecessary elements. As he told author Robert Colby: "Never explain too much. You may wind up explaining even the explanation" and also "never open a can of peas unless you intend to eat them," or, as Colby paraphrased, "If you introduce a gun on page one, you had better fire it by the time you reach page five."

Literary agent Donald McCampbell, who handled writers like Edward Aarons, John McPartland, and Day Keene to name a few, wrote a fine piece on Carroll in his book *Don't Step on It—It Might be a Writer*. The chapter is entitled "A Man for All Seasons," and in it McCampbell refers to this man as "the shrewdest editor I have ever known . . ." and also calls him a "roughneck," explaining, "His waterfront language . . . his gruff, unpolished manner was in such direct contrast to Old Bill [Lengel]'s suave demeanor that a good many professionals shied away at first, only to be won over in the end by the discovery that Dick Carroll knew his business."

Like Talbot, McCampbell describes Carroll as a writer's editor, stating, "Whereas most editors came in time to hate writers, he was their unfailing champion. He liked to discover them, start them selling, and keep them running." McCampbell also says that Dick had an ability for developing young talent. "He had a faculty for creating writers out of mailmen, bank clerks, Western Union operators, even bartenders—I think he could have trained a Neanderthal to write books for him."

The people who worked under Carroll echo McCampbell's affection for him. Daniel Talbot says Carroll was "very enchanting." Robin Little states he was "quite a remarkable man." Inez Salinger calls him an "Irish beguiler." Hal Cantor says, "He was a Black Irishman . . . and marvelous wit. The staff would go down at the end of the day and kind of sit at his feet, at a little bar, and we would listen to him talk . . . about his life. It was fascinating to just listen to him.''

Carroll was famous for taking his editors down to Leon's, a little bar in the Fawcett Building, after a hard day's work. There he would mesmerize them with stories of his past, of Hollywood, or of the publishing business. He liked to drink, but he never indulged during working hours. He'd have a bottle of stout during lunch, but that was his limit. After hours, though, he would live up to his Irish heritage. Though Carroll was known as a heavy drinker, it never interfered with his work. He always showed up on time and was usually the first one in the office.

Carroll organized the staff to work as a team, with the editors under him having the authority to reject submissions. When a manuscript came to Gold Medal, it was first given to one of the assistant editors or readers. The readers tended to get the unsolicited submissions. After reading the manuscript or reading as much as needed, the assistant editor or reader would write comments on a comment sheet and pass the manuscript to the associate or managing editor. They in turn would read the manuscript and add their own comment sheet and pass the would-be book on to Carroll, who would add his own comments and make the final decision if the work was to be published. Bill Lengel would then okay the book, which was a formality since he never rejected anything Carroll wanted to publish.

Hal Cantor describes Carroll as ''an extraordinarily astute editor with a very concise way of getting at a book. What's good about it. What problems it might have had. He never, never went on at great length in his written comments. In fact, I always got a kick out of that. On the assistant editor's level, we started out with lengthy and often quite detailed comments and suggestions about a book before we decided whether to recommend it or not. Then the next man up on the totem would write maybe a sentence or two. Dick would write a single sentence or phrase on the report, and Lengel would write, 'O.K. to publish.' ''

Cantor goes on to say, ''If we thought a novel was good enough to publish, we'd write lengthy reports on the assistant level . . . and then Carroll would read it and sort of recapitulate everything

that was suggested to the writer. Often those letters were extraordinarily well put, because he could take some of our more pompous phrases and turn them into more compatible lingo for a writer. Dick was never pompous.''

Cantor tells a story that reflects Carroll's lack of pretension. As an alumnus of New York's City College, Hal thought it might be a good idea to have Editor in Chief Bill Lengel give a talk about the operation at Gold Medal to a group in the English Department and give the members of the group an insider's view of book publishing. Bill agreed to attend, but at the last minute backed out and sent Dick Carroll to go in his place. So Carroll went, and when Hal introduced Dick to the chairman of the English Department, Carroll stated in a slight brogue, ''I really don't like education. It makes men complacent.''

As a rule, writers liked Carroll. He was down-to-earth and filled with Irish charm. They also liked working for Gold Medal because it was one of the top-paying markets and paid promptly. If there was any facet of Gold Medal's operations that tended not to be popular with writers, it was the fact that the author had no control over the title used for a book. In the book contract Gold Medal reserved the right to change the title. The reason this was done was that Fawcett realized that there was little one could do to promote a paperback original and that the chief means to convince the reader to buy was at the point of contact, the paperback rack. The cover was the best way of promoting a paperback. Covers and titles had to grab the readers' attention. It was for this reason that title changes were common practice. A book Bruno Fischer originally titled *The Golden Boy* was retitled *Run for Your Life.* Vin Packer's *Why Not Mother?* became *The Evil Friendship,* and Peter Rabe's *The Ticker* was changed to *Stop This Man!* Books were rarely published with the same title they were submitted with. Carroll and Lengel would often sit around, dreaming up new titles, cooking up blurbs, or thinking up anything that would make a book more marketable.

A noteworthy example: Elliott Chaze's book *Black Wings Has My Angel* had the original title of *Red Wings Has My Angel.* The title was changed to give the book a darker feel. As a matter of fact, Carroll not only changed the title, but also wanted to change the author's name. Carroll wrote Chaze and said that the book should be published under an earthier-sounding pseudonym, citing the sales success that Brett Halliday and Ryerson Johnson had had with the Matthew Blood pen name. Chaze wrote back, furious about the suggestion, and stated that his book would sell based on its content, and if they wanted to change his name, to send the manuscript back. Carroll quickly responded with a profusely apologetic letter, stating that the suggestion of a name change had resulted from Bill Lengel and himself having a few too many martinis. The matter was resolved with typical Carroll finesse.

Gold Medal's covers may have at times seemed crass, but they did the job. The books sold exceedingly well, and much of the credit must go to Fawcett's executive art director, Al Allard. Al's offices were on the same floor as Ralph Daigh's, and though Al was in charge of the cover art for Gold Medal, he actually answered to Daigh and not to Gold Medal. Despite this, he was always agreeable to ideas suggested by the Gold Medal staff. Both Inez Salinger and Robin Little worked closely with Al and describe him as a nice guy who was easy to work with and very capable.

Al described himself as a graphic designer and not an artist. He supervised the art and did the layouts. As artists went, Al's key resource was Barye Phillips. Al says of Barye in a letter to paperback historian Piet Schreuders: "When Gold Medal Books were started in 1950, I had to build a stable of artists. One of the first persons I contacted was Barye, who was ideal for this field. He was good. He was a fast producer. He had imagination. He was always in a position to meet deadlines. . . . He also had that rare ability of being able to change styles. He did so much work for me the first five years we were producing paperbacks, that it was a blessing he could change styles. I would have been severely criticized by the organization if this had not been the case."

By August 1951 it was obvious to all that Gold Medal was a success. A *Newsweek* article reported that Gold Medal had total sales around 29,000,000 for their first seventy-eight titles. Much of the success was attributed to "unknowns," new, talented writers Charles Williams, Gil Brewer, and Richard Prather. Gold Medal had a large editorial staff capable of sifting through the three hundred plus manuscripts received monthly and discovering this young talent. Dick Carroll was in charge of the staff, and like any good leader, motivated the people who

worked for him to realize they were part of a great operation. Webster Briggs was managing editor. Richard Roberts, and Karon Kehoe were associate editors, and Daniel Talbot, Roslyn Glick, and Louis Collins were assistant editors. (A *Writer's Digest* article from August 1951 provides a list of the staff.) Gold Medal also employed numerous in-house readers who helped handle the volume. Plus it hired outside readers who once or twice a week would go through a stack of manuscripts.

Briggs and Kehoe had been with Gold Medal since its conception. Roberts was hired in July 1951 to replace an editor named Del Webb. Changes are common in publishing, and Gold Medal was no exception. Kehoe left in 1952 to be replaced by Inez Salinger. Roberts left in 1953 to work at Bantam, but his position was left vacant. Assistant editors were always coming and going. One who joined the staff in January 1952 was Rona Jaffe.

Today Rona is known as a best-selling novelist. In 1952 she was a young woman fresh out of Radcliffe College. Her first book, *The Best of Everything,* was loosely based on her experiences at Gold Medal. As an assistant editor, she had a small partitioned space near the other assistant editors, which included Hal Cantor, who joined the staff in July 1952. Hal tells a rather humorous story about how young Jaffe met famous author Mickey Spillane. He used to visit the offices of Gold Medal on occasion. On one of these visits, Jaffe heard that he was in the outer office and exclaimed, "I must meet him." She ran out of the office and up to this guy who was sitting in the lobby and yelled, "Mickey, Mickey, if I unbutton my blouse, will you drill me full of holes?"

Antics like this were not totally uncommon conduct for editors who worked at Gold Medal. The offices had an informal nature. With Carroll supervising, there wasn't the pretentious quality often associated with book publishing. Carroll's background was Hollywood, and in many ways the offices had more of the atmosphere of a Hollywood script department than a New York publishing house.

In April 1954, Webster Briggs left Gold Medal to join his friend Richard Roberts at Bantam, and Hal Cantor became the new managing editor. The managing editor's duties also included the job of sending out the contracts for signing and mailing royalty checks and seeing that manuscripts went into production. There were five managing editors who worked under Carroll. They were Webster Briggs, Hal Cantor, Arthur Fields, Robin Little, and Don Preston.

In May 1954, Bill Lengel was moved to the editor's position at *True Confessions,* one of Fawcett's magazine titles, and Dick Carroll was given the long-deserved title of editor in chief. From the beginning Lengel had always been a little more than a figurehead, and Carroll had been the true man in charge. Hal Cantor states the prevailing opinion the staff had about Lengel, saying, "We all had the feeling that he [Lengel] was leaning on everybody for support. . . . He relied on the opinions and advice of everybody else and on particularly Dick Carroll. He really leaned on Dick Carroll."

When Lengel left, it did little to change the operation. It was almost as if he had never been there. The essential difference was in job titles. A little over a year after Carroll had his title changed to editor in chief, many of the other titles were adjusted. The associate editor became the executive editor and the assistant editors were now called associate editors. For Inez Salinger it was a reward for all of her hard work. She was, in a manner of speaking, Carroll's "right-hand man." She stayed in the position of executive editor until 1957. Robin Little succeeded her on May 1 of that year.

During its first six years, Gold Medal had twelve books that had documented sales of over a million copies. The twelve were:

Women's Barracks by Tereska Torres (2,036,048)
House of Flesh by Bruno Fischer (1,800,212)
Spring Fire by Vin Packer (1,463,917)
The Tormented by Theodore Pratt (1,344,912)
The Damned by John D. MacDonald (1,335,768)
Cocotte by Theodore Pratt (1,237,773)
Hill Girl by Charles Williams (1,226,890)
13 French Street by Gil Brewer (1,200,365)
Cartoon Laffs. True Magazine. (1,162,375)
Darling, It's Death by Richard Prather (1,125,112)
I Have Gloria Kirby by Richard Himmel (1,100,617)
Cassidy's Girl by David Goodis (1,036,497)

Over these years, Fawcett Publications had prospered. The success had been so great that it discontinued its comic-book line. This success also spawned rivals,

paperback publishers who wanted a part of the booming market in originals. Of these, Dell's First Edition line, which was initiated in 1952, provided the stiffest competition both for readers and in the bidding war for authors. Throughout the fifties Dell had a running battle over some of Gold Medal's top writers, particularly John D. MacDonald. Donald McCampbell states: "If perchance I showed up for lunch at the Lamb's Club [which was across the street from the Fawcett Building] and found Carroll sulking over his soup, I knew the reason without asking: Dell had snatched up MacDonald again! If Dick was usually boisterous, I knew he had somehow managed to get MacDonald back."

Gold Medal did not limit its success to twenty-five cent novels. The thirty-five cent paperback was an important facet of the operation. By 1952, Gold Medal was second to Pocket Books in the number of thirty-five cent titles released. This was ironic since two years previous, Ian Ballantine had warned that originals could bring down the average length of fiction and confuse the public as to what a novel really is. But this proved to be far from true. The super-size novel was a standard feature of the line, first with the Gold Medal Giants and then with Red Seal Books, which ran from 1952 to 1953. Red Seal Books, unlike the Crest and Premier lines, was a product of the same editorial staff that produced Gold Medal. The cover of the Red Seal book would state, "an original novel by Gold Medal Books." Red Seal was just an alternate way of marketing the Gold Medal Giants. When Red Seal was discontinued, the Gold Medal Giants returned.

The best remembered of these super-size novels was the *noir* classic *Driven* by Richard Gehmen. Dick Carroll thought so much of this book that he made arrangements to have the book published simultaneously by the hardcover publisher David McKay. For publicity, Gold Medal and David McKay jointly gave a cocktail party on April 1, 1954, to celebrate the simultaneous publication. Eighty guests from the book trade, newspapers, magazines, and broadcasting attended, and Gehmen autographed nearly one hundred Gold Medal editions and a dozen of the hardcover version.

In 1953 Fawcett added to the income of some Gold Medal writers when its new men's magazine, *Cavalier,* started reprinting Gold Medal novels. The practice began in its December issue with John D. MacDonald's *The Damned. Black Wings Has My*

Angel by Elliott Chaze, *The Tiger's Wife* by Wade Miller, and *The Snatchers* by Lionel White were among other titles featured in subsequent issues.

In 1955 Gold Medal won its first Edgar award when *The Girl with the Scarlet Brand,* the seventh book in its classic murder trial series, received honors for best nonfiction crime novel. Awards and honors were rare for paperback originals during the 1950s. It wasn't until the 1970s that literary scholars started to treat them with respect.

The year 1955 was also when N.A.L. tried to get even with Fawcett for creating Gold Medal. Gold Medal had always been a thorn in N.A.L.'s side because it was a successful publisher of paperback originals. So in retaliation N.A.L. did not renew its distribution contract with Fawcett, and Fawcett had to scramble to fill paperback rack space that had been on reserve for Signet and Mentor. Crest and Premier were created to fill that void.

Because Crest was new to the reprint field, it had a difficult time obtaining the rights to quality books and had to depend partially on originals itself. Though it would occasionally use manuscripts first submitted to Gold Medal, Crest originals were selected by editors of the Crest line.

For Richard Prather, 1956 was a big year, as his Gold Medal titles sold over five million copies. It wasn't surprising that Gold Medal's number-one and number-two sellers were Prather's *Strip for Murder* followed by his book *The Wailing Frail.* The next three in sales were *The Young and Violent* by Vin Packer, *City of Women* by Nancy Morgan, and *Little Sister* by Lee Roberts.

This year also revealed an increased interest by the film industry in Gold Medal. In the April 21, 1956, issue of *Publishers Weekly,* Fawcett Publications placed an ad which stated, ''18 Gold Medal Books currently being made into motion pictures.'' A month later, Managing Editor Arthur Fields told *Publishers Weekly,* ''Since our ad appeared in *PW,* five more of our original novels have been sold to the movies for a total of 23 Gold Medal Books currently being made into pictures.'' Though only a fraction of these pictures saw completion, the added revenues from motion picture rights were always welcomed by writers, even when a film version was never released. Some of those that were released as films include *The Incredible Shrinking Man, The Young Don't Cry,* and *Outlaw's Son.*

In 1957 overall sales of Gold Medal Books went up about nine percent over the previous year. *Women Without Men* by P. J. Reed-Marr, *Odd Girl Out* by A. Bannon, and *Three's a Shroud* by Richard Prather were the top sellers. *High Gun* by Leslie Ernenwein won a Spur award from Western Writers of America for Best Western Novel. The year 1957 was also big for Fawcett's Crest line, as it paid $101,000 for James Gould Cozzens's *By Love Possessed.* This move helped to make Crest a major player in the bidding wars for important hardcover titles. Despite the new respect Crest was earning as a reprint publisher, it still had to rely on paperback originals. The original *Little Tramp* by Gil Brewer was one of Crest's biggest sellers that year.

Gold Medal showed a ten percent increase in overall sales in 1958. The Shell Scott series was the big money-maker as Prather's *The Scrambled Yeggs* and *Slab Happy* topped Gold Medal's sales list. But 1958 is primarily remembered as a year that saw the beginning of some major staff changes. In October, Managing Editor Don Preston left for the job of executive editor at Avon. Later that year Dick Carroll became ill with lung cancer. He would never recover. Executive Editor Robin Little, who had recently married and was planning to have a child, filled in for Carroll, but she was making plans to leave soon too.

On March 11, 1959, Dick Carroll died. With his death, an era was ended. Gold Medal saw almost a completely new staff. Though Carroll's position was offered to Little, she turned it down, sticking to her plan to leave. As an alternative, Knox Burger, the man in charge at Dell First Edition, was hired as the new editor in chief. Walter Fultz, the former head of Lion Books, was brought in to fill the vacancy left by Little. Shelah Hillman was promoted from associate editor to managing editor. The staff was so new that Little had to return for a short time to help Burger locate contracts and get him acquainted with the office's layout.

Donald McCampbell states: ''Editors are plentiful in New York. But there was only one Carroll, and I doubt if we shall ever again see his equal.'' Carroll was an incredible man, larger than life. He was, as McCampbell described him, ''a roughneck,'' yet he had an underlying charm that always seemed to make him the center of attention. He was a Black Irishman who had a persona like that of a protagonist from a Gold Medal novel. He also was a gifted editor who had an eye for talent and a keen ability to work with writers. He made Gold Medal what it was.

SELECTED BIBLIOGRAPHY

Daigh, Ralph. *Maybe You Should Write a Book*. Englewood Cliffs, N.J.: Prentice-Hall, 1977.

"Debate about Original Fiction in 25-Cent Paper Editions." *Publishers Weekly,* October 21, 1950, pp. 1840–1842.

"Debate Continues as to the Merits of Paper-Covered Originals." *Publishers Weekly,* July 12, 1952, pp. 99–101.

Colby, Robert. "Fawcett On, Fawcett Off." *Mystery Scene,* October/November 1989, pp. 17–18.

"Gold Medal Now Buying 7 Books a Month—$2,000 Minimum Guarantee." *Writer's Digest,* October 1951, pp. 15–20 and 73–75.

Hackett, Alice Payne. *60 Years of Best Sellers. 1895–1955.* New York: R. R. Bowker, 1956.

McCampbell, Donald. *Don't Step on It—It Might Be a Writer.* Los Angeles: Sherbourne Press, 1972.

Neely, Mildred Sola. "25 Years of Fawcett: A Line that Began with Paperback Originals and Went on from There." *Publishers Weekly,* April 14, 1975, pp. 32–33.

"Original Paperback Publishing Grow; Its Merits and Effects Are Debated." *Publishers Weekly,* May 3, 1952, pp. 1831–1833.

Packer, Vin. "Gold Medal Days." *Mystery Scene,* May/June 1989, pp. 21–22.

"Richard Carroll, a Book Editor, 60: Gold Medal Executive Dies—Former Newsman Was Author of Short Stories." *The New York Times,* p. 158.

"25-Cent Originals." *Newsweek,* August 20, 1951, pp. 92–93.

THE GOLDEN HARVEST:
25 Cent Paperbacks
Ed Gorman

I STILL REMEMBER BUYING IT.
I could hardly forget. It packed the same charge of anxiety as purchasing one's first teen-age beer.

The woman behind the counter of the place—then called Horak's, now called the Neighborhood Tavern—peered down at me and said, "Pretty racy stuff, ain't it?"

Or at least that's what I think she said. Whatever formulation of syllables she used, the point was this: I was a fourteen-year-old Catholic-school boy in a working-class Irish-Czech neighborhood and this just wasn't the sort of thing kids my age were supposed to be buying.

But I would not be dissuaded. I put down my quarter and a penny for tax and she took it.

Outside, shut of the woman, I got my first good glimpse of it there in the new spring sunshine.

Gold Medal book number 663 was *Death Takes the Bus* by Lionel White.

This was the first of probably twenty novels I read by White. While nobody would accuse him of being a great stylist, he was a great, deft plotter (I think Donald Westlake made the same point somewhere) and his "bus" ride certainly proved it.

I can't define exactly what drew me to the book. The sex, such as it was, was great; so was the violence. It seemed, unlike the books I'd read up till then, real. More like the street-gang violence I'd come to know personally, and less like the heroic stuff of cowboy movies.

But ultimately it was White's people that made me start roaming the second-hand stores for more of the man's books. None of his innocents were quite innocent and none of his hoods were entirely bad. And none of them had many answers. Life was

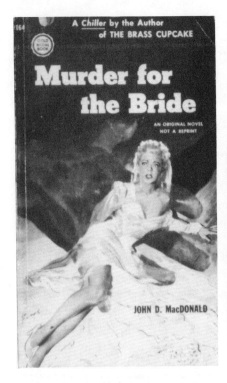

a curse, White seemed to be saying, and no matter what you did, you never got out with much of anything resembling dignity or meaning. A year later, when I discovered Hemingway, I found some of the same themes, and while Hemingway was the greater artist, of course, it was easier for me to identify with White's people. They hung out in grubby bus stations and prowled gray streets, much as I did. Not even the romance of war saved them.

That was my first Gold Medal Book.

Within a month I probably owned fifty of the things, mostly bought used for a nickel each. I lined them up along my bedroom window. They all had yellow spines with black type and the Gold Medal medallion at the bottom. I even got my cousin, Terry Butler, to read them. On the basis of their wisdom, and a few other suspicions, we came to the early conclusion that life was a sinkhole and that these guys knew it. They didn't pretty-up that fact and could even, once in a nasty while, rub your face in it. Marcus Aurelius and Celine had nothing on these guys in the despair department.

What I didn't know at the time was that much of these men's work derived from Hammett, Chandler, and James M. Cain—or some complex combination thereof. But it's too easy to dismiss the best

of the GM writers as simply derivative. And wrong too.

They filled in the details about life in the fifties the way no other group of writers did. For the most part—and again I make reference here to the best of them—they wrote about the people and places I knew. The taverns. The barbershops. The whores. The pathetic, scared little men. The predators.

Only recently have I realized that people such as Vin Packer came not from crime fiction but from the realists and naturalists such as the vastly under-valued John O'Hara.

But now let's take a look at some of the writers I read back in those days, at least a few of whom you might want to search the used bookstores for.

Note that I pretend to no special wisdom; what follows is merely my opinion as to who were the primary players in the Gold Medal fifties, and how their work has fared over the past three decades.

Peter Rabe

Probably the most original of the GM writers. This is not to say that he was the "best" necessarily, or even that he was always even very good. But there is great hard sorrow and real ingenuity in his

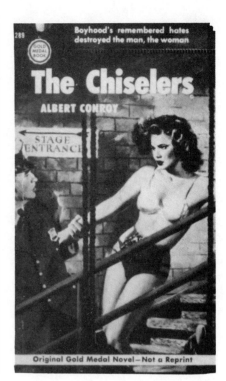

best work. Someday he will be recognized as being at least as important a crime writer as Jim Thompson or David Goodis. He could even handle black comedy, as he demonstrated in *Murder Me for Nickels.*

Mandatory reads: *Kill the Boss Good-by, Anatomy of a Killer,* and *The Box.*

John D. MacDonald

Where most GM writers set their stories in the working class, John D. generally dealt with the middle class. His heroes tended to be engineers, businessmen, construction managers, and civil servants rather than the drifters and ex-cons of most *noir.* He was a thundering moralist, a seductive stylist, and a very sly observer of our shortcomings, both as individuals and as a citizenry. Despite writing millions of early mediocre words to support a young family, he was the best crime writer of his generation. Sure Travis McGee was a Rotarian version of a hippie, but the later books, informed as they were with John D.'s own health problems, are moving and occasionally profound utterances about a man facing his own extinction.

Mandatory reads: *Slam the Big Door, The End*

of the Night, One Monday We Killed Them All, Soft Touch, and *Dead Low Tide.*

Malcolm Braly

Braly spent a good deal of his rather short life in prison and wrote, as his fifth novel, the classic *On the Yard.* Earlier he wrote three Gold Medal originals which were among the best things the company ever published. There was an almost numbing sadness in all Braly's work, and a hopelessness redeemed only by a certain nutty laughter. Read anything you can get by him. *It's Cold Out There* is probably my favorite, however, with its cast of crazed losers and grinding air of desperation.

Charles Williams

Line by line Williams was the best of all the Gold Medal writers. He has not found an audience the way Thompson and Goodis have because they are more appropriate to our era—splashy in their effects, titanic in their feelings. Williams was quiet and possessed of a melancholy that imbued each of his tales with a kind of glum decorum. John D. always claimed that Williams was one of the two or

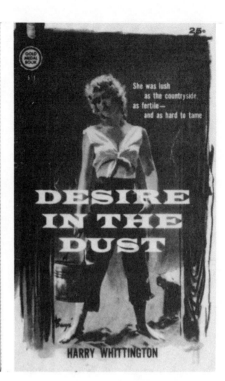

three best storytellers on the planet and I certainly wouldn't disagree. He was probably at his best in his books set at sea.

Mandatory reads: *Hell Hath No Fury, The Big Bite, Aground, Dead Calm,* and *Scorpion Reef.*

Dan Marlowe

Another writer who hasn't gotten his due. He probably did more with the pure hard-boiled story than anyone since Rabe, giving his tough guys true interior lives. Health problems interrupted his career at midpoint. He may have been the most exciting of all the Gold Medal writers. His best stuff just explodes every thirty pages or so. I always thought of Marlowe as an uncle of mine, always in a working-class shirt with Camels in the pocket, tavern whiskey on his breath, and a weary, knowing gleam in his eyes. He's a nice, cold treat.

Mandatory reads: *The Name of the Game Is Death, Strongarm,* and *One Endless Hour.*

Jim Thompson

Yes, I agree, he was upon occasion a genius; but he was also a stupendously lousy craftsman. It

is a credit to his vision (and I'm serious) that he was able to convey his particular truth despite some of the most sloppy, incoherent writing I've ever stumbled across. That said, I think that Thompson deserves most if not all the adulation he's getting today. He was a thoroughgoing original, a kind of Okie version of Graham Greene, all shifting ironic morality and honky-tonk remorse. And just as most of Greene's darkest books had unexpected comic moments, so, too, do Thompson's. A couple of his books break my heart every time I read them, his operative moods seeming to be pity and despair. Your education as a writer, reader, or would-be human is incomplete until you've read the basic Thompson library.

Mandatory reads: *The Killer Inside Me, Texas by the Tail* (I'm well aware, thank you, that everybody thinks this book stinks; I happen to love the damned thing), *Savage Night* (his best organized and most nimbly rendered novel) and *Pop. 1280* (his masterpiece).

David Goodis

Goodis didn't write novels, he wrote suicide notes. Like Thompson, he didn't always take a lot

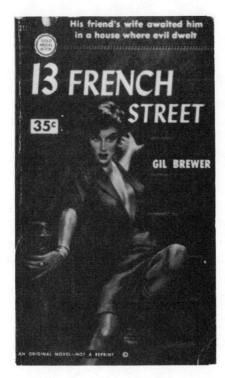

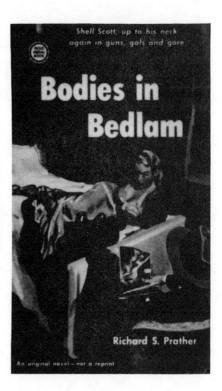

of care with his books either. He's the only writer I know who can make Cornell Woolrich's yarns seem sane and logical by comparison. But, like Woolrich, he was a sad, suffering guy and he was able to get that sadness and suffering down on paper. And that's why he survived. For a writer as introspective as he was, he had a nice reportorial knack. He gave us hellish glimpses of the inner-city ghettoes of the forties and fifties. He was the poet of vacant lots and abandoned buildings and bars where guys take turns going outside to puke. Just thinking about him bums me out and I'm not kidding. He seemed to be one of those guys who never knew a moment's peace or joy and that's never much fun to contemplate.

Mandatory reads: *Nightfall, Cassidy's Girl, The Burglar,* and *Dark Passage.*

Wade Miller

Some feel that Bob Wade and Bill Miller did their best work for publishers other than GM; others feel that four or five of their GMs are the strongest of their entire careers. Who cares. These two were past masters at mood, pace, and people. HarperCollins recently reissued four of their Max Thursday

private eye novels in beautiful trade paperbacks, and after rereading them all, I realize that they've been in the front ranks all the time . . . just nobody ever gave them proper credit. As for their GMs, I'd say my favorites are *South of the Sun, Devil May Care* (which reads in places like a collaboration between early Ray Bradbury and Cornell Woolrich—maybe it's all the great Mexican stuff) and *The Girl from Midnight.* But don't just read their GM books. Read virtually everything.

Mandatory reads: *Kiss Her Goodbye* (a powerful straight novel); *Badge of Evil* (which was the basis for Orson Welles's *Touch of Evil*); and *Pop Goes the Queen,* which is a screwball murder mystery about a hapless couple that wins a radio quiz show back in 1947. This book works a lot better for me than those antidepressants I've been known to take.

Donald Hamilton

I had always suspected that Jack Kennedy was a wienie and when I read that he preferred Ian Fleming to Donald Hamilton, I was sure of it. For me, Hamilton's first six Matt Helm novels are the best espionage books written in this half of the century. Le Carré may be better, but you couldn't prove

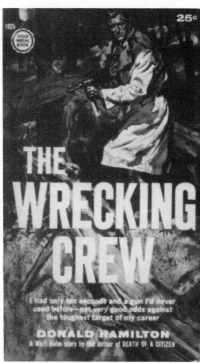

it by me. I've never been able to slog past page 27 in any of his lugubrious and fatally pretentious tomes. Hamilton has never been given his due for the psychological tension of his books (masterly, dark, and constantly surprising), nor the wry rococo language of their telling. He is a pure storyteller of the first rank. Just by carefully reading the first pages of *Assassins Have Starry Eyes,* you'll see what I'm talking about.

Mandatory reads: *Death of a Citizen, The Wrecking Crew, Line of Fire,* and *Assassins Have Starry Eyes.*

Vin Packer (Marijane Meaker)

Like John D. MacDonald, Vin Packer was obviously fond of John O'Hara. Her novels—early on, rather dark fables about the small-town South of the WWII era; later, hipper but no less dark fables about New York City—are novels of manners as much as they are crime tales. She was always reliable and many times brilliant in a nervous kind of way. Her major characters usually had secrets they desperately wanted to keep from those closest to them, and these secrets frequently became the basis for the books. In the late fifties Gold Medal began

packaging her as a mainstream writer whose books just happened to include crime. And that was fair. She was one hell of a writer. *Something in the Shadows* is one of the most breathtakingly cunning crime tales I've ever come across.

Mandatory reads: *Alone at Night, Intimate Victims,* and *The Damnation of Adam Blessing.*

Gil Brewer

Certainly the most uneven of all the primary GM players. In his memorable remembrance of Brewer, Bill Pronzini draws a portrait of an alcoholic who hastened both the end of his career and the end of his life. Brewer's early specialty was the "jailbait" novel—nice ordinary guy who starts bopping his baby-sitter and then ends up robbing a bank with her. Charles Starkweather *redux* but with a sexy, sixteen-year-old babe playing Charlie. John D. once said that most crime stories are really "folktales" and when you read Brewer, you know just what MacDonald meant. At his best, he hooked you in the first paragraph and never let you go. For me, his one true masterpiece was *A Killer Is Loose,* a strange, nightmarish story about a guy who goes out for a drink one sunny morning and winds up

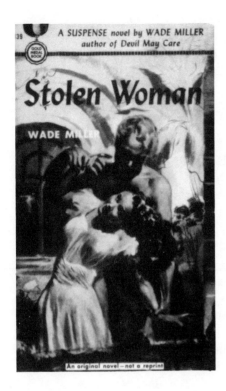  

being a hostage of sorts to a man who is shooting people at random. Fine piece of work, with the pith and punch of a barroom anecdote well told. A genuinely scary book.

Mandatory reads: *The Red Scarf, The Three-Way Split,* and *A Killer Is Loose.*

> "There's a difference between those earlier pulp writers and (myself). It deals directly with the difference between the novels of plot and the novels of character."
> —Warren Murphy

Murphy's right. After coming back from World War II and wanting a more realistic kind of popular fiction that spoke to veterans, a new generation of writers decided to bring some of the qualities of mainstream into pulp fiction.

This was evident almost from the start with Gold Medal. Such early John D.'s as *The Damned, Dead Low Tide,* and *Murder for the Bride* quietly announced that here was a new kind of fiction. No big revolution, you understand, but certainly a more realistic portrayal of life and people in the United States.

Not all writers took this path, of course. Some still tilled the older fields, but not without distinction. This is the next group we'll look at—writers more generally concerned with plot than people.

Day Keene

This guy almost always gets bad press in pulp circles. Yes, he wrote too fast; yes, he wrote too much, but he managed to do some first-rate work. His biggest writing problem was that the faster he wrote, the more flamboyant and unlikely his plots became, to the point that you sometimes wondered if he wasn't spoofing some of his own work. But when he was good. . . . He had a mean true feel for fallen men and women, even a sympathy for them, and in his best books he told compelling stories about working-class people trying to make some sense of existence, a slant that the best of his hundreds of early pulp stories also took. One of his last novels was *The Carnival of Death* which, despite the title and despite its throwaway publisher, was a reasonably fresh look at carnival life. At the end of his career he made the transition to mainstream and wrote four modest bestsellers, all fashioned more or less on the model of *Peyton Place.*

Mandatory reads: *Framed in Guilt, Home Is the Sailor,* and *Murder on the Side.*

Harry Whittington

It pains me not to put Harry up in the first tier, but I can't because most of his people were types rather than individuals. Several exceptions come to mind, notably the folks in *Rampage* and *Saturday Night Town,* but overall Harry was much better with plotting than psychology. But let us not be unappreciative—you could make the same claim about Saki and DeMaupassant and (everybody get his gun out now and point it at Ed), Roald Dahl. Harry was one of the wonderful campfire storytellers who came out of the pulp era and survived several decades after because he'd learned how to adapt to changing audience demands. He was always readable and on occasion of the very first rank. He was also, as a guy, one of the great charmers of all time. Early in life he got the notion that he was F. Scott Fitzgerald reincarnated and the notion never quite left him. But he was the good Fitzgerald not the bad Fitzgerald—garrulous, charitable, witty.

Let me note here that I frequently change my mind about Whittington. Most likely, he really does belong in the first rank.

Mandatory reads: *Brute in Brass, Strip the Town Naked* (as Whit Harrison), *A Night for Screaming,* and *Desire in the Dust.*

Edward S. Aarons

Pure, old-fashioned pulpster, true, but a very sleek, cunning writing machine. I loved the Sam Durrell spy books. Sure they were long on Cold War paranoia and self-righteousness, but they were also damned good adventure novels. Aarons was capable of writing place description just about as well as anybody, except maybe Donald Hamilton or John D., when he was really cooking. A writing student of mine once asked me what I really really thought of her work, and I said, "It's really really well written but it really really doesn't go anywhere." I gave her a couple of Sam Durrell novels and she said, "God, are you kidding?" and I said, "Huh-uh." A week later she had had a religious conversion, called me up, and said, "These books are really trash, but I see what you're talking about." Trash to her maybe; great lurid fun to me.

Mandatory reads: *Assignment–Suicide, Assign-ment–Treason,* and *The Art Studio Murders* (a very winsome fair-clue traditional mystery circa 1950, originally published under the pseudonym "Edward Ronns").

Bruno Fischer

Time has not been generous to much of what Fischer wrote. He came out of the old "spicy" pulps and some of that showed up in his style a couple decades later. But at his best, in maybe half a dozen books, he showed a true mastery of the suspense novel that combined a James M. Cain-ian sexual tension with a very good eye for the every-day setting. His people were invariably ordinary suddenly set upon by dark forces. Like Whittington, he probably belongs in the first tier, especially considering the fact that his last novel, *The Evil Days,* was one of the truly important books of the seventies. Well into his sixties, he helped reshape the contemporary mystery novel.

Mandatory reads: *The Bleeding Scissors, Murder in the Raw,* and *The Lady Kills.*

Lionel White

While White's people were interesting, it was usually their situations rather than their personalities that drew you in. What White could really do was plot caper novels that rivaled those of W. R. Burnett himself. The first GM novel I ever read, as I mentioned earlier, was White's *Death Takes the Bus.* I stayed up on a seventh-grade school night to maybe two, three A.M., mesmerized. White always grabbed me that way. He knew just when to wrap a scene fast, just when to wrap a scene slow. And he knew just when to put the twist in. If only he'd done a little more with some of his people . . . Stanley Kubrick filmed his books, as did several other notable directors. His most nail-biting book of all is *The Money Trap,* which seemed to have an enormous impact on the generation just before mine. I've seen several famous writers rewrite *The Money Trap* several times. It is one dazzling sumbitch of a book.

Mandatory reads: *The Snatchers, Flight into Terror,* and *Hostage for a Hood.*

Marvin Albert

Here's another guy who wrote too much too soon but who could sometimes work on a very high

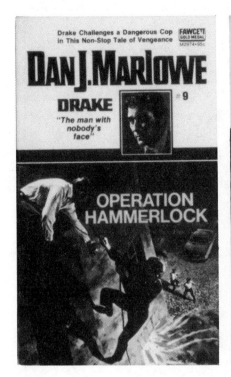

level indeed. His Tony Rome books are wonderful old-fashioned pulp, and his caper novel, *The Looters,* is right up there on the level of Lionel White. He did everything—men's adventure, westerns, even the "jailbait" novel, his *Devil in Dungarees* (as by Albert Conroy, 1960) coming just as the cycle was (you should forgive the expression) petering out. But, God, I haven't praised him enough. Go out and find yourself a copy of a GM book called *Driscoll's Diamonds* (1973). It's one kickass adventure novel, let me tell you, and shows Albert at his absolute best (oh, yeah: he published it under the name Ian MacAlister). He was also the then-king of the novelizations. He did a lot of them. He also had five or six international best sellers under his own name, and while they were eminently readable, I sort of prefer a lot of the stuff he did while cranking at top speed. He did some of the moodiest pulp stuff in GM history.

Mandatory reads: *My Kind of Game* (Tony Rome); and under the name Albert Conroy, *Nice Guys Finish Dead* and *The Chiselers.*

Robert Colby

Another guy who probably belongs on the first list. He wrote one of the great GM novels, *The Captain Must Die,* and several other good ones. In some ways he seemed too aware of market trends and as a consequence wrote a few books where nobody's home. He also wrote one of the all-time-great crime novelettes, "Paint the Town Green." He's a real writer, a sturdy psychologist, an excellent plotter.

Mandatory reads: *The Star Trap, Murder Times Five,* and *The Captain Must Die.*

This list could go on for several more pages, but it's got to stop somewhere, so I guess I'll pull the plug right here.

There are a number of other GM writers worth reading—Bernard Mara (the pen name of literary writer Brian Moore); Stephen Marlowe (one of my favorites, even if his last GM editor didn't like his stuff); John Trinian, who wrote mostly about ex-cons (because, it was said, he was one himself); Richard S. Prather, who, page for page, probably gave me as much enjoyment as any writer of my youth; Michael Avallone and his alternate-universe take on private eye conventions, another man who was a favorite of my misspent youth; John McPartland, who wrote anxious little books about anxious failed men and their anxious failed lives, and who, despite a tragically early death, left us one true minor masterpiece, *No Down Payment,* which also became the truest movie about the fifties I've ever seen (including *Rebel Without a Cause*); William Campbell Gault who, while not a GM writer as such, did several fine Joe Puma adventures for Fawcett; and people such as Gardner F. Fox and his eerie take on Jack the Ripper, *Terror Over London;* and James O. Causey, whose three novels curiously anticipated the direction crime fiction would take in the seventies, especially *The Baby Doll Murders,* which also had the single most erotic GM cover of all time (I guess I like sullen, pouty babes in white silk slips).

Little of GM was art of any kind, though some of it was, I think, minor art. A lot of it was slapdash and completely predictable; and some of it was even laughable.

But the best of it, the books I've discussed here, represent a very important period in the development of the contemporary crime novel. Such modern stars as Lawrence Block published with GM even before the fifties were quite over. Donald Westlake came along a few years later with his Stark books (he said somewhere that he intended the early Starks for GM, but that they turned him down and the books were published by Pocket). Harlan Ellison, Kurt Vonnegut, W. R. Burnett, and Jim Thompson were included in the next wave of sixties GM writers.

GM is gone now, fit company mostly for an old man's reveries, and yet I think the best of it is worth your time and trouble in looking up.

I had a ball with a lot of it; and you will too.

Two reputable dealers with extensive GM catalogs are:

Pandora's Books, Box 54, Neche, North Dakota, 58265.

R. C. Holland, 302 Martin Drive, Richmond, Kentucky 40478.

Fifteen Greatest Crooks and Rogues

(in no order)

Selected by Douglas G. Greene

A. J. Raffles
E.W. Hornung

The Saint
Leslie Charteris

Jimmie Dale
Frank W. Packard

Norman Conquest
Berkeley Gray

Nick Velvet
Edward D. Hoch

The Lone Wolf
Louis Joseph Vance

Dr. Nikola
Guy Boothby

Fu-Manchu
Sax Rohmer

Arsene Lupin
Maurice LeBlanc

Blackshirt
Bruce Graeme

Bernie Rhodenbarr
Lawrence Block

The Toff
John Creasey

Smiler Bunn
Bertram Atkey

Simon Carne
Guy Boothby

Colonel Clay
Grant Allen

Fifty Favorite Great
Gold Medal Crime Classics
Selected by Bernie Nalaboff

John D. MacDonald	*The Only Girl in the Game*
Wade Miller	*The Killer*
John D. MacDonald	*Murder for the Bride*
Wade Miller	*The Tiger's Wife*
John D. MacDonald	*Dead Low Tide*
Charles Williams	*Hell Hath No Fury*
Charles Williams	*Nothing in Her Way*
Charles Williams	*Man on the Run*
Gordon Davis	*I Came to Kill*
Lionel White	*The Snatchers*
Lee Roberts	*Little Sister*
Cornell Woolrich	*Savage Bride*
Richard Jessup	*Wolf Cop*
Charles Williams	*Go Home, Stranger*
Steve Frazee	*Running Target*
Lionel White	*Coffin for a Hood*
Harry Whittington	*Web of Murder*
Harry Whittington	*Fires That Destroy*
Harry Whittington	*Brute in Brass*
Gil Brewer	*13 French Street*
Wade Miller	*Stolen Woman*
Wade Miller	*Devil May Care*
Marvin H. Albert	*The Don Is Dead*
Gardner F. Fox	*Terror Over London*
Peter Rabe	*Benny Muscles In*
Jeff Jacks	*Murder on the Wild Side*
Jeff Jacks	*Find the Don's Daughter*
Clifton Adams	*Whom Gods Destroy*
John D. MacDonald	*The Brass Cupcake*
Charles Williams	*A Touch of Death*
Bruno Fischer	*The Fast Buck*

Gold Medal Crime Classics
(Continued)

Marvin H. Albert	*Nice Guys Finish Dead*
Wade Miller	*South of the Sun*
John D. MacDonald	*Girl in the Plain Brown Wrapper*
John D. MacDonald	*One Fearful Yellow Eye*
Marvin H. Albert	*Long Teeth*
Gil Brewer	*Hell's Our Destination*
John D. MacDonald	*Bright Orange for the Shroud*
Marvin H. Albert	*Driscoll's Diamonds*
Harry Longbaugh	*No Way to Treat a Lady*
James Marcott	*Hard to Kill*
John D. MacDonald	*Who Has Janice Gantry?*
John D. MacDonald	*Soft Touch*
Lawrence Block	*The Thief Who Couldn't Sleep*
John D. MacDonald	*Weep for Me*
Wade Miller	*The Big Guy*
Lee Richards	*Hell Strip*
Ross MacRoss	*The Beautiful and Dead*
John D. MacDonald	*One Monday We Killed Them All*
Donald Hamilton	*Death of a Citizen*

ORGANIZATIONS

Mystery Writers of America, Inc.

... a historical story

Angela and Barry T. Zeman

A FEW YEARS AGO, Lawrence Treat, former President of **Mystery Writers of America** and one of its founders, discussed MWA's beginnings: "Once upon a time, a writer, an editor, and a writer-editor had lunch together (Treat, Marie Rodell, and Clayton Rawson).

"Clayt told about the British crime writers who met irregularly and had a ritual involving a pledge always to play fair with their readers, and to make various other promises for the good of their craft. He suggested that we do something of the sort here, in America."

They invited a few writer friends to meet and discuss the idea. "The meeting was at Baynard Kendricks's apartment. Present, besides Baynard and the three of us, were Brett Halliday (Dave Dresser), Helen McCloy, Ed Radin, Ken Crossen, Dick Burke, and Kurt Steele. Ten in all. We decided to invite a larger group in a week or two...."

Baynard Kendrick recalled that fifty-four people attended that meeting. Erle Stanley Gardner furnished the drinks, and the precepts and principles of the organization were formulated that night. Among others who attended were Dorothy B. Hughes, Anthony Boucher, Rex Stout, Stuart Palmer, the Q. Patrick team, Fred Dannay and Manfred Lee (Ellery Queen), Helen Reilly, Octavus Roy Cohen, Leo Zagat, Roger Torrey, Kurt Steele, Edward D. Radin, the Lockridges, and Howard Haycraft. He also recalled that the first four officers were elected—himself as president, Ken Crossen as executive vice president, Clayton Rawson as treasurer, and Marie Rodell as secretary.

At length—on February 28, 1945— the articles of incorporation were filed.

Howard Haycraft wrote later, "The name of the organization was a cooperative effort. The slogan 'Crime Does Not Pay—Enough,' was pure Clayton Rawson." It echoed the founders' resolution to address their profession's economic problems. "... but I must take the 'punishment' for the doggerel latin—*qui fecit*? (Who done it?)—on the early letterheads."

The Third Degree, **MWA**'s newsletter, was born then too. Rawson both named it and served as its first editor. The first mailing list of prospective members was taken from Haycraft's landmark book, *Murder for Pleasure*.

For the first issue of *The Third Degree*— Volume 1, Number 1—Haycraft wrote an article outlining the concept of **MYSTERY WRITERS OF AMERICA** to prospective members:

> The **London Detection Club** was founded in 1928 by a group of English detective story writers headed by Anthony Berkeley....
>
> The London Club maintained ... membership headquarters and a professional reference library, supporting same (while keeping dues and fees at a nominal level) by the occasional publication of anthologies, to which the members were called upon to contribute their writings with royalties going to the club's treasury. **Mystery Writers of America, Inc.,** has similar plans and, also like its London counterpart, will hold periodic social, lecture, and instructional meetings and issue bulletins and professional manuals....
>
> The principal difference between the two organizations lies in the respective conceptions of membership. The London Club ... limits its membership to a chosen few. The founders of **Mystery Writers of America, Inc.,** on the other hand, and after due consideration, decided to open active membership to all writers of good repute in the mystery field, including fiction, fact, books, magazines, moving pictures, and the

radio. . . . In addition, associate membership is available to interested editors, critics, publishers, actors, directors—even accredited fans who have demonstrated their loyalty as "friends of the mystery."

Then, said Dorothy B. Hughes: ". . . a new idea was conceived by **MWA**. An award for the Best Mystery of the Year."

Although written mystery stories have been traced to as far back as 1211, and Fred Dannay (Ellery Queen) argued that stories with overtones of detection had origins in biblical times, Edgar Allan Poe has long been called the "Father of the Detective Story." Calling an award for mystery writing an "Edgar" seemed a natural thing to do.

Hughes continued: "Our award was to honor the mystery writer who didn't have a chance at the Pulitzer or National Book; our award was one to which all in our field might aspire. . . . It was yet another step in dignifying the mystery writer, in enhancing his work. . . ."

Lawrence Treat told about **MWA**'s early development: "Mystery writers all over the country were enthusiastic and we set up chapters in Chicago (the Midwest chapter) and California. Leslie Charteris was (southern) California's first president. Shortly afterward San Francisco set up a second (northern) California chapter. . . ."

In 1971 the New England chapter was started by Helen McCloy and Elizabeth Pratt. As writers across the country heard about **MWA**, more chapters were formed. At present, **MWA** is comprised of nine regional chapters: New York, SoCal, NoCal, Midwest, New England, Rocky Mountain, Southwest, Northwest, with the most recently organized chapter in Florida.

Ultimately, **MWA** created three types of membership. Members published in the mystery genre within any media were classified as "active." An "associate" membership was formed for nonwriting persons in a related field, such as editor, agent, publisher, bookseller, and so on. An "affiliate" section was created in order to allow fans or unpublished mystery writers to join.

Helen McCloy later wrote that "among members of **MWA**'s first board of directors were Mignon G. Eberhart, Anthony Boucher, Mabel Seeley, and Brett Halliday. . . .

"Ellery Queen was our second president, followed by Hugh Pentecost, Judson Phillips, Law-rence G. Blochman, John Dickson Carr, and then myself as the first woman president."

The presidents are a virtual Who's Who of the genre and include, among many others, Dorothy Salisbury Davis, Mary Higgins Clark, Georges Simenon, Anthony Boucher, John D. MacDonald, Raymond Chandler, Rex Stout, Kenneth Millar, Hillary Waugh, Ed Hoch, John Lutz, Thomas Chastain, the Lockridges, Ross Thomas, and in 1993—Elmore Leonard. These individuals are only a handful of the forty-five outstanding writers who have served as president.

To bolster the treasury, the founders set up the **MWA** anthology, a custom that continues to this day. For this volume, as well as those following, the proceeds went to **MWA**. The authors and editors traditionally donate their time and work. The profits from these anthologies and also from the *Mystery Writers Handbook* enabled **MWA** to keep the dues down to a minimum, a matter of importance to struggling writers.

It was Clayton Rawson's idea to have an annual banquet in which they would give the Edgar to the best first novel, but in those early days, not to the best novel. They worried that writers who felt slighted would resign.

Dorothy Salisbury Davis, former Grand Master and a member since 1951, recalls that there was a long ongoing fight within **MWA** about giving a Best Mystery Award, "because it was believed you could not, or should not, choose one book for such a distinction. In the early years, many felt we were not competent to judge this award. But, suddenly . . . they felt it was time." In 1953 Charlotte Jay won the first Best Novel Award for *Beat Not the Bones*.

In the first year, Edgar winners were presented with a special leather-bound edition of Poe made for the occasion by Viking Press. In the second year, the award was a special limited edition of twelve copies of Howard Haycraft's *Art of the Mystery Story*. The small ceramic statuettes of Poe appeared in the third year and are still used today.

Of all the awards **MWA** bestows at the Edgar awards banquet, none is more prestigious and coveted than the Grand Master. This award was established in 1954 to recognize not only important contributions to the mystery over time, but a significant output of consistently high quality as well. The first recipient was Dame Agatha Christie.

Thirty-four Grand Masters have been named

(through 1992), each meticulously chosen by their peers as the best of the best. Raymond Chandler, Erle Stanley Gardner, John Dickson Carr, Ellery Queen, Margaret Millar, Georges Simenon, Ross Macdonald, James M. Cain, Rex Stout, Mignon Eberhart, Stanley Ellin, Graham Greene, John D. MacDonald, Dorothy B. Hughes, Dame Ngaio Marsh, Daphne du Maurier, John le Carré, Julian Symons, Hillary Waugh, Ed McBain, Elmore Leonard, Phyllis Whitney, Tony Hillerman, Dorothy Salisbury Davis . . . and more . . . mystery's Hall of Fame.

The vigilance in the publishing world, the awards, the dinners, the meetings, the annual, the newsletter, the anthologies, and also the regional chapters that began forming all over the country— these functions of **MWA** were run by legions of member volunteers.

According to Lawrence Treat: "We were growing, we were stabilizing. We moved from our patch of wall space on 57th Street to the majesty of our own cubicle on Butcher's Row, Reade Street, where we had to run the gauntlet of great sides of beef and climb a narrow staircase to the *sanctum sanctorum*."

Wherever the headquarters have moved, they were ruled by a series of hardworking women entitled until recently: executive secretary. After original part-timer Catherine Mason, **MWA** member Dorothy Gardiner laid the foundation of the job. Today's Priscilla Ridgeway, who has been with **MWA** since 1987, was recently re-dubbed "executive director" in an acknowledgment of the vast range of her activities.

Since the president of **MWA** has been a largely honorary title bestowed in recognition of writing achievement and leadership, the chief executive of the organization has been, from its inception, the executive vice president. He or she, along with the executive director, runs all of the day-to-day operations, overseeing the needs of the two thousand plus members.

Many "household names" have put in their time (some more than once) of servitude as executive vice president, for example: Larry Blochman, Wm. S. Ballinger, Richard Martin Stern, Herbert Brean, Will Ousler, Lewis Thompson, Henry Klinger, Dorothy Salisbury Davis, Hillary Waugh, and Bruce Cassiday. The current chief is George Chesbro, creator of the Dr. Robert Frederickson ("Mongo") series.

All policy development and decision making is done by the board of directors, elected from regional chapters and through national at-large elections.

Most **MWA** chapters concentrate on monthly dinner meetings with speakers providing information helpful to writers, such as background ideas and details about police and FBI work, criminal defense or prosecution, forensics, and private investigation.

Market discussions have always been popular at meetings. John Creasey, the famous British mystery novelist who had by 1951 already published 273 mystery titles using nine pseudonyms and sometimes wrote two full-length books a month . . . comforted less successful writers at a meeting by reminding them of the seven hundred rejections that preceded his first sale.

MWA's skills in watching over the membership's well-being sharpened with use. Presidents over the years have issued calls to monitor situations important to writers, such as proposed revisions to copyright laws, Capitol Hill's subpoenaing privileged information documentation from the press, and monitoring opportunities brought about by the growth of pay TV.

TTD often carries articles spotlighting the state of the industry, keeping the membership knowledgeable of the prevailing winds of publishing.

"**MWA** didn't change [things] overnight, but, right from scratch, **MWA** did what it particularly set out to do. It dignified the mystery author. It gave him pride in his work, in his very name 'mystery author,' and naturally that pride rubbed off on all connected with the medium," said Dorothy B. Hughes.

MWA has served as historian for the genre at large—at least in reference to American contributions—procuring and storing in its library the important documents and markers of the passing years and the changes within the profession.

By 1968 the **MWA** library was reputed to be one of the most extensive collections of mystery fiction and the repository of much reference information useful to mystery writers. The sheer volume of books outgrew the limited space at each of **MWA**'s headquarters over time. Today the bulk of this collection, as well as **MWA** archives from its first thirty years, is housed as part of the 20th Century Special Collection at the Mugar Library, Boston University.

The headquarters library still contains thousands of novels and reference books, and is used extensively by its members, editors, publishers, and movie people.

Member Lucy Freeman wrote in a *TTD* column in '78 about a party given during a particularly steamy Manhattan August that was attended by Ken Follett and some other **MWA** members. Chris Steinbrunner walked into the room carrying a bag of peanuts. Stanley Ellin looked at the peanuts, paused, then said, ''Publisher's royalties?''

... Which is where **MWA** came in ...

The Grand Masters
Mystery's Hall of Fame

MWA members have named thirty-five Grand Masters up to 1993. Each was meticulously chosen by their peers as the best of the best.

1992	Donald E. Westlake	1975	Eric Ambler
1991	Elmore Leonard	1974	No Award
1990	Tony Hillerman	1973	Ross Macdonald
1989	Helen McCloy	1972	Judson Philips
1988	Hillary Waugh	1971	John D. MacDonald
1987	Phyllis A. Whitney	1970	Mignon G. Eberhart
1986	Michael Gilbert	1969	James M. Cain
1985	Ed McBain (Evan Hunter)	1968	John Creasey
1984	Dorothy Salisbury Davis	1967	No Award
1983	John le Carré	1966	Baynard Kendrick
1982	Margaret Millar	1965	Georges Simenon
1981	Julian Symons	1964	No Award
1980	Stanley Ellin	1963	George Harmon Coxe
1979	W. R. Burnett	1962	John Dickson Carr
1978	Aaron Marc Stein	1961	Erle Stanley Gardner
1977	Daphne du Maurier	1960	Ellery Queen
	Dorothy B. Hughes	1958	Rex Stout
	Ngaio Marsh	1957	Vincent Starrett
1976	Graham Greene	1954	Agatha Christie

WHO ARE ALL OF THESE SISTERS IN CRIME?

Elaine Raco Chase

AT LAST COUNT, we are 2200 writers, readers, booksellers, editors, agents, screenwriters, and librarians in the United States, Canada, and twelve foreign countries. What we are not is a union, a critic, a publisher, nor do we give prizes or have any connection to any of the major mystery awards.

And, yes, most of us are women, but we have some talented gentlemen who have joined our ranks. We are a group with one goal in mind: "to combat discrimination against women in the mystery field, educate publishers and the general public as to inequalities in the treatment of female authors, and raise the level of awareness of their contribution to the mystery field."

Why was an organization like Sisters in Crime even necessary? Because women authors were getting little respect on many fronts. Sisters in Crime began in October 1986 at the Baltimore Bouchercon (world mystery convention), when a number of women who read, write, buy, or sell mysteries met for an impromptu breakfast to discuss their mutual concerns. At the very least, we hoped to develop a camaraderie and to learn what women in the mystery field really wanted. There was a perception that women writers were reviewed less frequently, and that their books were taken less seriously than those written by men.

Sara Paretsky was the driving force in galvanizing and organizing the group. In May 1987 the first steering committee was elected and consisted of writers Charlotte MacLeod, Dorothy Salisbury Davis, Sara Paretsky, Nancy Pickard, and Susan Dunlap. Also joining in was mystery bookseller Kate Mattes and mystery enthusiast Betty Francis.

A letter was sent to *The New York Times* that pointed out that in 1985, of the eighty-eight mysteries which the *Times* had reviewed, only fourteen (sixteen percent) were written by women. We also began counting reviews in other major publications, hoping to collect enough data to chart whether or not our perception of inequality was correct.

This study is ongoing. The 1992 Book Review Monitoring Project showed definite progress over previous years. Of the twenty publications monitored, reviews of women's mysteries reached the thirty percent level. The very important *New York Times* made enormous strides with thirty percent (Sunday) and forty-four percent (daily) coverage, while other major newspapers and trade publications hovered at the thirty percent level as well.

A handful of well-known writers received the majority of the reviews, with newcomers and local writers being given some attention. The proportion of British writers seemed to be declining in favor of Americans.

Sisters in Crime does more than just monitor reviews. We keep our members alert to the treatment of women in mystery awards and at conventions, we share information through local chapters, national newsletters, and we have a wonderful Speaker's Bureau. We also cooperate in an ongoing study of images of women in crime fiction directed by Dr. Karl Pillemer, now of Cornell University, a well-regarded sociologist and expert in family violence. In 1991, in cooperation with the National Women's History Project, we surveyed women mystery writers and their protagonists. The survey found an emphasis on wits rather than violence, and on family connections and friendships of the independent, self-reliant protagonists.

Sisters in Crime members produce a wide range of books, gritty to genteel, and the organization favors full freedom of expression. We are *educational* rather than political. And our membership has a wide variety of views on books containing violent or sadistic scenes. We don't favor censorship, nor do we favor pornography. We recognize that opinions differ as to what (if anything) should be done about those issues.

With mysteries as a whole commanding nearly twenty-two percent of the bookselling market, we are delighted to note that mysteries by women and featuring women are selling at a furious pace. Mysteries by men, which have always sold well, still do. Every time a reader learns about a book by a member of Sisters in Crime, buys that book, and enjoys it, that reader is drawn back to the bookstore shelves that contain mysteries by *everyone*.

How do we get our message about women mystery writers and protagonists to the public? Our *Books in Print* catalog is published twice a year to educate booksellers, librarians, wholesalers, distributors, and critics to the availability of a wide range of mysteries.

A mailing list is maintained of these booksellers, librarians, wholesalers, distributors, and critics which our member authors may use to distribute their promotional material.

Press releases announce member nomination and award winners (although Sisters in Crime gives no awards themselves), plus we have a national press kit that has garnered impressive publicity in over a dozen major cities, articles in Delta Airlines' as well as other in-flight magazines, segment on *Working Woman* the TV show (syndicated), and articles in various major industry publications like *Publishers Weekly* and *Library Journal*.

Our full-color poster, "Solving Mysteries Coast to Coast," is available and highly visible at many mystery bookstores and libraries. Over seventy authors are featured in a unique display that promotes reading, literacy, and the mystery!

A national newsletter comes out four times a year and is sent to the membership, telling the who, what, when, where, and why of mystery interests.

The Speaker's Bureau has some of the most talented authors around the country who make themselves available to libraries, bookstores, conferences, etc., with the "women of mystery" panel.

We currently have eighteen chapters in the U.S., Canada, Australia, the U.K.—everywhere! The national board helps the formations along and promotes newsletter swaps and various efforts by chapters to assist their local communities through library fund-raisers for literacy, workshops, autographings, and other regional events. There is also an "outreach" liaison, so that wherever a Sisters in Crime member lives, she has a connection.

We have joined the electronic age by becoming a part of GEnie, the home computing service from General Electric. With GEnie we have an electronic chapter and a private as well as public Sisters in Crime category.

Yes—we still do so much more. Our publications include:

* *Breaking and Entering*—A guide to selling your manuscript, finding an agent, and other mysteries of publishing
* *Shameless Promotion for Brazen Hussies*—the best in publicity and self-promotion tips
* *So You're Going to Do an Author Signing*—suggestions for authors and booksellers on arranging successful book signings.

We have a clipping service so that authors can get their reviews from one place. Plus ongoing committees that deal with women of color who write mysteries, local publicity contacts for traveling authors, radio project for broadcasting pretaped programs, a booksellers directory, a mystery magazine and newsletter directory, and we always update our mailing lists.

Sisters in Crime has become a popular presence at the American Library Association (ALA) Convention each year and many authors attend the regional ALA conventions by request. We've also been a part of the American Booksellers Association (ABA) Convention, headed overseas for the Frankfurt Bookfair, been visible at Malice Domestic, Edgar Weeks, Bouchercon, and the Miami Bookfair.

And to honor the nation's number-one mystery fan, President Bill Clinton, Sisters in Crime created and donated the first ever White House Mystery Library that curator Rex Scoutin is making a permanent fixture.

With each passing year, Sisters in Crime has become *the* force to educate and promote the mystery. Our presidents have been strong women and strong writers who have left their own stamp on the organization. From 1987 to '88 Sara Paretsky; 1988 to '89, Nancy Pickard; 1989 to '90, Margaret Maron; 1990 to '91, Susan Dunlap; 1991 to '92, Carolyn G. Hart; 1992 to '93, P. M. Carlson; 1993 to '94, Linda Grant.

If you would like further information on Sisters in Crime, contact us at P.O. Box 442121, Lawrence, KS 66044–8933.

The Private Eye Writers of America
Jan Grape

Dateline: 1982
Place: Bogie's Restaurant, N.Y.C.
Purpose: PWA's first meeting

I WAS TENDING BAR at Bogie's when the gorgeous leggy blonde walked inside. She was wearing red—blood red. The clingy dress accented each curve and set off her blond hair to perfection. She wore a white wide-brimmed hat and white high-heeled pumps and a red purse dangled from her left shoulder.

"Okay," she asked, "where is he?" She flashed a badge in my face, too quickly for me to read but long enough for me to tell it was official-looking. "The man. Where's the man?"

"Who're you talking about, lady?" I shrugged. "What man?"

"Miles Jacoby. I was told he's always at Bogie's."

"Usually, but he got called out on a case, lady. He'll be back—he always comes back."

She handed me an envelope. "Give that to him as soon as he walks in. It's very important." She left and I could only wonder where Miles had met her. I looked at the envelope. It was sealed. On the outside in large black letters read *Nominees for the Shamus*.

Okay, it didn't exactly happen that way, but the Private Eye Writers of America, a.k.a. PWA, did meet for the first time in 1982 in Bogie's Restaurant. The organization, which began four months earlier, was a brainstorming idea by founder and current executive director, Robert J. Randisi. Charter members, besides Bob, were Michael Collins, John Lutz, Max Allan Collins, Loren Estleman, Bill Pronzini, Marcia Muller, Arthur Lyons, and Michael Z. Lewin. PWA's purpose was officially defined from the beginning as: to identify, promote, recognize, and honor these writers who were writing books and stories featuring a private eye as the main character. PWA wanted to make publishers and the reading public aware of the fine work being done

in the genre. PWA's first president was Bill Pronzini and vice president was Bob Randisi.

Randisi also came up with the idea of presenting awards to the best in the field each year, and after some discussion the name Shamus was chosen. The first nominations were announced at that luncheon at Bogie's and the first Shamus awards were given at Bouchercon in San Francisco in the fall of 1982. PWA also decided to give a Life Achievement Award, The Eye, to p.i. writers who have made a lifelong contribution to the genre.

The first Shamus winners for works published in 1981 were as follows: Best Private Eye Novel—*Hoodwink* by Bill Pronzini; Best Private Eye Paperback Original—*California Thriller* by Max Byrd; and The Eye Life Achievement Award was given to Ross Macdonald. Other recipients of The Eye are Mickey Spillane, William Campbell Gault, Richard S. Prather, Bill Pronzini, Michael Collins & Robert Wade, Howard Browne, Roy Huggins, and Joseph Hansen.

In 1983, a new Shamus was added for the Best Private Eye Short Story and given to John Lutz for "What You Don't Know Can't Hurt You." In 1984 the awards added one other Shamus for Best First Private Eye Novel which was given to Jack Early (Sandra Scoppettone) for *A Creative Kind of Killer*.

Each year the Shamus nominees and winners are chosen by committees made up of PWA members who volunteer to read books or stories in the p.i. genre. In recent years the category of p.i. has been redefined for award eligibility and membership eligibility to include characters who are *not* employed by a unit of government and are *paid* for services rendered in their investigative work—news reporters, lawyers who did their own investigating, and others similarly employed. The awards are given annually in October at Bouchercon.

Randisi says even before PWA began he had wanted to sell a collection of original private eye short stories and after PWA was organized he sold and edited a collection which became *The Eyes Have It,* the first PWA anthology, published in 1984 by Mysterious Press. Subsequent PWA anthologies, also published by Mysterious Press: *Mean Streets* in 1986, *An Eye for Justice* in 1988, and *Justice for Hire* in 1990. In 1992 *Deadly Allies,* a joint anthology by PWA and Sisters in Crime, was edited by Bob Randisi and Marilyn Wallace and published by Doubleday Perfect Crime. *Deadly Allies II* will be published in 1994. Some stories from *Deadly Allies* have been nominees of both the Shamus award and the Edgar award.

History tells us that in 1850 Allan Pinkerton founded a detective agency and for more than a century Pinkerton's trademark was an eye that never sleeps, an eye which seems to follow wrongdoers wherever they might try to hide. The Eye came to represent Pinkerton's and the term ''private eye'' soon became part of the nation's vocabulary. Many years later a former Pinkerton agent named Dashiell Hammett began writing stories and novels featuring his Continental Op.

Today's PWA membership boasts at least two members who worked as Pinkerton agents, John Carlson and Dick Stodghill. The membership also includes members who are active private eyes or who have worked as private eyes.

The early private eyes were males—tough, hard-boiled, quick with their fists and their guns; trouble was their business. Mike Hammer once told his policeman friend: ''You're a cop, tied down by rules and regulations. I'm alone. I can slap someone around and they can't do a damn thing about it.'' In the fifties, the private eye story began to evolve and change. John D. MacDonald used the ''errant knight in shining armor'' theme for his Travis McGee books. Travis was tough, but he was also caring.

The first modern-day female private eye, Sharon McCone, was introduced by Marcia Muller in 1977. Max Allan Collins and Terry Beatty introduced the first female p.i. comic-book character and series, *Ms. Tree,* which began in 1980. The comic book from DC Comics continues on an irregular schedule today with Mac still writing the stories and Terry still drawing the pictures. But in 1980 change was on the way. In 1982 Sue Grafton wrote about Kinsey Millhone and Sara Paretsky came up with V. I. Warshawski, thus changing the image of the hard-drinking, skirt-chasing, lone-wolf p.i. forever.

Today's p.i. stories are about realistic characters with families and friends and problems of everyday life. Today's p.i.'s are both sexes, all ages, all nationalities, sexual persuasions, religious philosophies, and those who are physically challenged. This ''new'' p.i. story gives the reader three-dimensional characters, not the cardboard characters of old. It's not surprising that some of the best writing in the mystery field today is being done in this genre.

In 1986 PWA and St. Martin's Press launched a contest for a First Private Eye Novel which has become an annual event. The entrants must not have previously published a private eye novel and the winner's book is published simultaneously in the U.S. by St. Martin's Press and in England by Macmillan. Guidelines for entering the contest may be obtained by writing to St. Martin's Press. The first winner was Les Roberts for *An Infinite Number of Monkeys.* Other winners of the first p.i. novel contest are: Gar Anthony Haywood for *Fear of the Dark* (1987), Karen Kijewski for *Katwalk* (1988), Janet Dawson for *Kindred Crimes* (1989), Ken Kuhlken for *The Loud Adios* (1990), Winona Sullivan for *Murder at the Norfolk Cafe* (1991) and the most recent winner, E. C. Ayers, will have his book published later this year.

In January '93, Les Roberts, winner of the first PWA/SMP contest, was elected president of PWA. Past presidents include Bill Pronzini, Lawrence Block, Michael Collins, William Campbell Gault, John Lutz, Sue Grafton, and Jeremiah Healy.

PWA publishes a quarterly newsletter, *Reflections in a Private Eye,* with news and happenings of the organization; the current editor/publisher is Jan Grape. Terry Beatty drew the copyrighted Man in Trench Coat which is used as the PWA logo.

PWA luncheons and meetings are held twice yearly, spring and fall, usually at a mystery convention. PWA's current membership stands at 180 with eleven international members. Current dues are thirty dollars annually for active and international members and twenty-four dollars annually for associate members. Membership chair is David Masterton, 330 Surrey Road, Cherry Hill, NJ 08002.

Recommended Reading List (titles of first books only) **of Notable P.I.'s:** A random sampling of private eyes that are among the best known from the early years are : Ed Noon by **Michael Avallone,** introduced in *The Tall Dolores;* Philip Marlowe by **Raymond Chandler;** introduced in *The Big Sleep;* Brock Callahan by **William Campbell Gault,** introduced in *Ring Around Rosa*; Sam Spade by **Dashiell Hammett**, introduced in *The Maltese Falcon*; Lew Archer by **Ross Macdonald**, introduced in *The Moving Target*; Travis McGee by **John D. Mac-Donald**, introduced in *The Deep Blue Good-bye*; Mike Hammer by **Mickey Spillane**, introduced in *I, the Jury*; and Shell Scott by **Richard S. Prather**, introduced in *Case of the Vanishing Beauty*.

In recent years this random sample of p.i. series (titles of first books only) have become popular: Matthew Scudder by **Lawrence Block**, introduced in *The Sins of the Fathers*; Carlotta Carlyle by **Linda Barnes**, introduced in *A Trouble of Fools*; Dan Fortune by **Michael Collins**, introduced in *Act of Fear*; Amos Walker by **Loren Estleman**, introduced in *Motor City Blue*; Jack Dwyer by **Ed Gorman**, introduced in *New Improved Murder*; Kinsey Millhone by **Sue Grafton**, introduced in *"A" is for Alibi*; Catherine Sayler by **Linda Grant**, introduced in *Random Access Murder*; Stanley Hastings by **Parnell Hall**, introduced in *Detective*; John Francis Cuddy by **Jeremiah Healy**, introduced in *Blunt Darts*; Toby Peters by **Stuart Kaminsky**, introduced in *Bullet for a Star*; Ben Perkins by **Rob Kantner**, introduced in *The Back Door Man*; Kat Colorado by **Karen Kijewski**, introduced in *Katwalk*; Sharon McCone by **Marcia Muller**, introduced in *Edwin of the Iron Shoes*; Delilah West by **Maxine O'Callaghan**, introduced in *Death Is Forever*; V. I. Warshawski by **Sara Paretsky**, introduced in *Indemnity Only*; Spenser by **Robert B. Parker**, introduced in *The Godwulf Manuscript*; "Nameless" by **Bill Pronzini**, introduced in *The Snatch*; and Leo Haggerty by **Ben Schutz**, introduced in *Embrace the Wolf*.

Some authors currently have two p.i. series being published on a regular basis: Nick Delvecchio, introduced in *No Exit from Brooklyn* and Miles Jacoby, introduced in *Eye in the Ring*, are by **Robert J. Randisi**; Fred Carver, introduced in *Tropical Heat* and Alo Nudger, introduced in *Buyer Beware*, are by **John Lutz**; Saxon, introduced in *An Infinite Number of Monkeys* and Milan Jacovich, introduced in *Full Cleveland*, are by **Les Roberts**; Nate Heller, introduced in *True Detective* and Mallory, introduced in *The Baby Blue Rip-Off*, are by **Max Allan Collins.** The duo of Smith & Wetzon, introduced in *The Big Killing*, is by **Annette Meyers**, and Pieter Tonneman, introduced in *The Dutchman*, is written by Annette and husband, Marty, under **Mann Meyers.**

Notable new p.i. series: Easy Rawlins by **Walter Mosley**, introduced in *Devil in a Blue Dress;* Truman Smith by **Bill Crider**, introduced in *Dead on the Island;* Phoebe Siegel by **Sandra West Prowell**, introduced in *By Evil Means;* Aristotle Socarides by **Paul Kemprecos**, introduced in *Cool Blue Tomb;* Cat Caliban by **D. B. Borton,** introduced in *One for the Money;* Dave Strickland by **Thomas D. Davis**, introduced in *Suffer Little Children;* and Harry James Denton by **Steven Womack**, introduced in *Dead Folk's Blues.*

On the international scene: Anna Lee (England) by **Liza Cody**, first seen in *Dupe;* Cliff Hardy (Australia) by **Peter Corris**, first seen in *The Dying Trade*; Hector Belascoaran Shayne (Mexico) by **Paco Ignacio Taibo II**, introduced to the U.S. in *An Easy Thing.*

Many authors listed above are winners of both the Edgar and the Shamus—it looks like the p.i. genre is flourishing—may it continue to do so.

FOR PROFESSIONALS ONLY ...

The American Crime Writers League

Charlotte MacLeod

ACCORDING TO OLIN MILLER, writing is the hardest way of earning a living, with the possible exception of wrestling alligators. The American Crime Writers League was founded to serve those who earn their money the hard way.

How the American Crime Writers League got

started is no mystery. Ed Gorman, well-known novelist and publisher of *Mystery Scene* magazine, is, has been, and will no doubt continue to be a man of vision and enterprise. Picture him, then, in early 1988, envisioning a writers' organization that would extract no high dues, hold no glitzy social events, offer no awards, and admit no member who was not already a published writer in the field of true crime and/or mystery fiction. Its whole focus would be to provide a clearinghouse for practical ideas and information about the business of crime writing. Robert R. Randisi, *Mystery Scene*'s co-founder, helped Gorman set up this organization.

For Ed Gorman, to envision was to act, and thus ACWL came to be. An ad hoc steering committee was recruited by telephone and on March 23, 1988, a first newsletter, still unnamed, went out to a small group of professionals. By the time issue number four was in the mail, the steering committee had put together a set of bylaws, set dues at twenty-five dollars a year, and geared up for its first formal election.

It was determined that officers would serve not more than two consecutive two-year terms. In January 1989 Charlotte MacLeod, who had been active on the steering committee, was elected ACWL's first president. Michael Seidman was vice president, Barbara Paul treasurer, and Ed Gorman secretary. Since January 1991, Barbara Mertz, a.k.a. Elizabeth Peters/Barbara Michaels, has held the reins of office and will continue to do so until December 1994, with Allen Simpson/M. D. Lake as vice president, Joan Hess secretary, and James R. McCahery treasurer. The executive board also includes the heads of all standing committees: present incumbents are Charlotte MacLeod and Janet LaPierre, editorial; Carolyn Wheat, legal; William F. Love, research; Jay Brandon, membership; D. C. Brod, publicity; D. R. Meredith, liaison; Carole Nelson Douglas, nominating.

While meetings are held as opportunity offers, usually at one or another of the mystery conventions that reflect the reading public's ever-increasing interest in the mystery field, ACWL's primary vehicle is its *BULLETin,* published regularly six times a year in alternate months. The format is informal and often lively but the content is always pertinent to the organization's stated goal of providing a forum in which members can exchange views on topics of general interest, from marketing one's work to changing one's agent or coping with one's writing blahs.

To keep the pot boiling, the *BULLETin* publishes interesting articles by reliable experts. Subjects may range from copy editing to publicity tours and how to survive them, to the complexities of how to achieve leakproof contracts between writer and publisher. It also gives tips on how to handle the unreasonable requests and outrageous demands that come from certain outsiders who seem to envision authors as performing seals instead of worker bees toiling for their small meed of nectar under conditions that would scare off all but the brave, the persistent, and those strange creatures who write not only because they love their work but because they can't help it.

ACWL has taken militant stands on a number of controversial issues such as unsigned reviews that not only cheat the critic of deserved recognition but also open the way to hostile trashing of certain books under a veil of anonymity. Aware of the problems faced by volunteer organizers, ACWL drew up a Code for Conventions that spells out the relationships to be established among authors, committee members, and fans, offers important advice on setting up, and defines the many factors that need to be considered in running a smooth, enjoyable convention. This code, like other ACWL-initiated projects of interest to writers and conventioneers in general, has been circulated among a network of other writers' organizations both within and outside the mystery field.

A recent poll has made it plain that members want to keep ACWL strictly a crime writer's group, not even granting associate membership to our own agents and publishers. We are equally inflexible about money. Once having realized that twenty-five a year was simply not enough to run a program like ours on, we upped it to thirty-five dollars. There it has stayed, and there we intend to keep it, because, as has been mentioned previously, professional writers earn their money the hard way.

For information on the American Crime Writers League, write to Membership Chairman Jay Brandon, 219 Tuxedo, San Antonio, TX 78209.

MYSTERY
BOOKSTORES

THE CARE AND FEEDING OF A MYSTERY BOOKSTORE

Jan Grape

Western Sun

PICTURE YOURSELF SITTING in a huge, overstuffed chair, a black cat is curled in your lap, and a mug of coffee steams beside you on a small table. You are reading an exciting mystery novel while outside the wind howls and rattles the windows. The bell over the door tinkles and a customer comes in with a smile on his face.

Picture yourself owning a mystery bookstore? Well, you're not the first. Most readers dream of owning a bookstore and their dream includes one highly unrealistic factor—you will never live long enough to read all the mysteries in your store.

The first retail bookstore devoted exclusively to mysteries, Murder Ink., in N.Y.C., was opened on June 14, 1972, by Dilys Winn. The store is still in business and is now owned by Jay Pearsall.

Predating Murder Ink., with mail order, Enid and Tom Schantz, owners of The Rue Morgue in Boulder, Colorado, began selling mysteries from their home in 1970. They opened their retail store in 1980.

I think one the first mystery bookstores I became aware of was The Mysterious Bookshop in N.Y.C., opened by Otto Penzler in 1979. When I saw it the first time in 1988, I thought the store looked exactly like a mystery bookstore should with a spiral staircase leading to the second floor. Penzler also owns The Mysterious Bookshop-West in Los Angeles.

In 1983 there were approximately thirty mystery bookstores around the country. In 1993 there are about eighty with another twenty-five or thirty mail-order or by-appointment-only dealers. Several general bookstores also have good mystery sections (see store list below). Owning a mystery bookstore isn't for everyone, but for the folks who love mysteries and like people it can work. However, like any small retail business, there are ups and downs. The economy and market in your area is a big factor.

My partners in crime around the country who answered questions for this article about the care and feeding of a mystery bookstore are as follows: (Rue Morgue's Enid Schantz was mentioned earlier.) Once Upon a Crime, in Minneapolis, was opened by Mary Trone in 1987. Steven Stilwell bought the store in 1991. The Mystery Bookshop in Bethesda, Maryland, owned by Jean and Ron McMillen, opened in 1989. The Poisoned Pen, Scotsdale, Arizona, is owned by Barbara G. Peters and opened October 1989. Mysteries and More, Austin, Texas, owned by Elmer and Jan Grape, opened in July 1990. The Snoop Sisters in Belleair Bluffs, Florida, owned by Susan Rose and Linda Tharp, opened in 1991.

Q: *What one single thing is the most important factor in owning a successful mystery bookstore?*

Barbara Peters said: "You have to love books. Enthusiasm is contagious. You also have to have the right location and the kind of store you want to run. Mine is a small boutique store in an upscale area.''

Enid Schantz said: "You should have an extensive knowledge of the field. Not just the current best sellers, but also the history of the genre. Keep rotating your stock to keep it fresh.''

Susan Rose said: "Customer service is most important in our store.''

Jean McMillen said: "I can think of several: 1. Run your store as professionally as possible, it *is* a business. 2. Establish good public relations with publishers. 3. Be reliable for your customers. 4. Do lots of research before you open and be flexible to changes and innovative ideas. 5. Hire and keep good help.''

Steve Stilwell said he'd give the dull and boring answer on this one: "Location, location, location.''

Elmer Grape said: "Giving good customer service is the only way we can compete with the discount stores just down the Interstate. Have a store that's clean, well-lit, and comfortable.''

Q: *What is an important no-no to remember?*

Enid Schantz said: "If you don't like mysteries, you shouldn't open a mystery bookstore.''

Susan Rose said: "Be careful about overstocking on books that people can buy at K mart, grocery and drugstores at discounts.''

Elmer Grape said: "Don't go too deeply in debt.''

Barbara Peters said: "Not learning the business end of bookselling. If you don't, you'll go under no matter how enthusiastic you are.''

Steve Stilwell said: "Don't get publishers angry at you.''

Q: *Are author signings important?*

Barbara Peters says: "Author signings are important. To the bookseller, it brings in people, dollars, and builds customer loyalty. To independent bookstores, it's a way of competing with discount stores by offering a unique product. To authors, it helps build an audience. To the publisher, it helps sell more books.''

Steve Stilwell said: "It's good for your customers.''

Enid Schantz said: "It's extremely important for our store; we have around fifty signings per year and it's helped to develop our customer base.''

Jean McMillen said: "It's a mixed blessing. Having big authors is great, but I don't want to be in a position to rely on author signings only. It's a wonderful service for our customers and it does bring them in.''

Susan Rose said: "It's important to help your name get out there because you do a press release or an ad. Sometimes it doesn't bring the expected sales, but it helps in the long run by helping you gain recognition.''

Elmer Grape said: "We usually never make money on these because we advertise and/or do big mailouts, but it reminds people that we are here or brings us new customers. It pays off in the future.''

Q: *What about author readings or special reader's club events?*

Susan Rose said: "Our reader's club works well and if an author speaks it's a chance for them to shine and pick up new readers.''

Jean McMillen said: "One of the best things is our reader's club. Friends get together monthly and besides discussing books, they discuss new ideas for the store; they also write articles and reviews for our newsletter.''

Enid Schantz said: "We always have a panel discussion or program with our authors and this is important.''

Barbara Peters said: "Readings are fun and accomplish many of the same things as a signing, but they don't bring in the same dollars for the time and money involved for my store. A bookseller must be careful not to get invested in a less-productive activity.''

Q: *Is advertising or word-of-mouth best?*

Jean McMillen said: "It takes both.''

Barbara Peters said: "Word-of-mouth and self-promotion brings more dividends for fewer bucks than advertising, although it takes longer to build recognition. I invest *all* my advertising money in my own publication mailed to customers. I consider my high rent to be part of my marketing cost, since my location itself draws in people.''

Susan Rose said: ''Word-of-mouth works best for us. People will come or call who've heard about us from a customer.''

Steve Stilwell said: ''I would recommend advertising in *Mystery Scene* or in *The Armchair Detective* because people travel around the country and like to visit mystery bookstores while doing so and it can also add new mail-order customers.''

Q: *What advice would you give to someone interested in opening a bookstore?*

Steve Stilwell said: ''Follow Otto Penzler around for six months.'' (Penzler owns The Mysterious Bookshops in N.Y.C. and L.A.)

Susan Rose said: ''Don't rely on the store for your living income in the beginning. Keep your overhead low. Be prepared before you do it. It takes long hours.''

Barbara Peters said: ''1. Don't right now, unless you are prepared to work slave hours for slave wages. Wait and see how the big stores and the publishers reposition themselves (and what Congress does about the sales tax question), what kind of small business financing develops, and how the market develops in your area. 2. Work for a bookstore for a while to understand what lies behind the romantic image (you will *not* have plenty of time to read all the books). 3. Attend prospective booksellers school and some book conventions. Study your local demographics. Make sure you want to run a business, not a hobby. Or if you want it as a hobby, make sure you can afford it. 4. Be prepared to have adequate capitalization. 5. Read as much as you can in your genre. There is no substitute for firsthand knowledge if you plan to be specialized. You *never* get to recommend a *bad* book twice.''

Jean McMillen said: ''Do the research. Have fun, but be professional and practical.''

Enid Schantz said: ''I'd almost advise against it because too many people think of it as just a hobby. It's a lot of work. Be sure there's not another mystery bookstore around you. You need a fairly large metropolitan area to support it and try to find reliable staff to work. You can't work it by yourself forever.''

Elmer Grape said: ''Plan and research as much as you possibly can. Expect to work long hours for little reward until you're established. Expect not to ever get rich owning a bookstore. If you are bound and determined to do it, go ahead, but do it the very best you can.''

The advice was fairly consistent from everyone and I can only add: if you are an author or a fan, support your nearest independent mystery bookstores. You won't get personal service at the discount stores.

A Sampling of Mystery Bookstores:

20th Century Books
108 King Street
Madison WI 53703

A Clean Well-Lighted Place for Books
601 Van Ness Avenue
San Francisco CA 94117

Abra-Cadaver House of Mystery
110 Dunrovin Lane
Rochester NY 14618

Avenue Victor Hugo Bookshop
339 Newbury Street
Boston MA 02115

Baker Square Book Center
13455 W. Center Road
Omaha NB 68144

Big Sleep Books
239 N. Euclid
St. Louis MO 63108

Book Carnival
348 N. Tustin Avenue
Orange CA 92666

Book 'Em Mysteries
1118 Mission Street
South Pasadena CA 91030

Booked for Murder
2701 University Avenue
Madison WI 53705

Books & Co.
350 East Stroop Road
Dayton OH 45429

Book Tree
702 University Village
Richardson TX 75081

Centuries & Sleuths Bookstore
743 Garfield
Oak Park IL 60304

Cheshire Cat Books
110 Caledonia Street
Sausalito CA 94965

Classic Book Shop
4314 N. Woodward
Royal Oak MI 48073

Cloak & Dagger Books
868 Lincoln Way W. Booth 63
Chambersburg PA 17201

Criminal Proceedings
2526 E. Webster Place
Milwaukee WI 53211

Deadly Passions
157 S. Kalamazoo Mall
Kalamazoo MI 49007

Elsewhere Books
260 Judah Street
San Francisco CA 94122

Escape While There's Still Time
488 Willamette Street
Eugene OR 97401

Fahrenheit 451
540 South Coast Highway
Suite 100
Laguna Beach CA 92651

Fantasy, Etc.
808 Larkin
San Francisco CA 94109

Future Fantasy Books
3705 El Camino Real
Palo Alto CA 94306

Footprints of a Gigantic Hound
123 S. Eastbourne
Tucson AZ 85716

Foul Play Books
13 Eighth Avenue
New York NY 10014

Foul Play II
1465-B Second Avenue
New York NY 10021

Foul Play
6072 Busch Boulevard
Columbus OH 43229

Foul Play
780 Arlington Street
Cambria CA 93428

Fountain of Mystery Books
1119 Prospect Street
Indianapolis, IN 46203

Gene's Books
King of Prussia Place
King of Prussia PA 19406

Haven't Got a Clue
1823 Western Avenue
Albany NY 12203

Heartland Books
214 Main Street
Woodstock IL 60098

I Love a Mystery Bookstore
55 E. Washington Street #250
Chicago IL 60602

Kate's Mystery Books
2211 Massachusetts Avenue
Cambridge MA 02140

Kepler's Bookstore
1010 El Camino Real
Menlo Park CA 94025

Lone Wolf Mystery Bookshop
160 Pennsylvania Avenue
Mt. Vernon NY 10552

Maxwell's Bookmark
2103 Pacific Avenue
Stockton CA 95204

Metropolis Tearoom & Mystery Bookstore
31 Union Sq. W. Penthouse 2
New York NY 10003

Mike's Mystery Bookstore
1912 N. Berkley Court
Bloomington, IN 47401

Mitchell Books
1395 E. Washington Boulevard
Pasadena CA 91104

Murder and Mayhem
6412 Carrollton Avenue
Indianapolis IN 46220

Murder by the Book
1281 North Main Street
Providence RI 02904

Murder by the Book
2346 Bissonnet
Houston TX 77005

Murder by the Book
500 W. Exchange Street
Akron OH 44302

Murder by the Book
7828 S.W. Capitol Highway
Portland OR 97219

Murder for Fun
2006 Fairview Road
Raleigh NC 27608

Mystery Bookstores

(Continued)

Murder Ink.
2486 Broadway
New York NY 10025

Murder in Print
4203 W. Green Oaks, Suite E
Arlington TX 76016

Murder Unlimited
2510 San Mateo Place NE
Albuquerque NM 87110

Mysteries & More
11139 N. IH-35, #176
Austin TX 78753

Mysteries from the Yard
101 Cemetery Avenue
Yellow Springs OH 45387

Mystery Books
14 Rittenhouse Place
Ardmore PA 19003

Mystery Books
1715 Connecticut Avenue NW
Washington DC 20009

Mystery Bookshop of Long Island
173-A Woodfield Road
West Hempstead NY 11552

Mystery Bookstore/Oceanside Books
173A Woodfield Road
West Hempstead NY 11552

Mystery Hound, Inc.
13416 Sante Fe
Lenexa KS 66215

Mystery House
545 Main Street
Harwich Port MA 02646

Mystery Lovers Ink
8 Stiles Road
Salem NH 03079

Mystery Loves Company
1730 Fleet Street
Baltimore MD 21231

Mystery Loves Company
3338 N. Southport
Chicago IL 60657

Once Upon a Crime
604 West 26th Street
Minneapolis MN 55405

The Poisoned Pen
7100-B East Main Street
Scottsdale AZ 85251

Rogue's Gallery
4934 Elm Street
Bethesda MD 20814

San Francisco Mystery Bookstore
746 Diamond Street
San Francisco CA 94114

Saratoga SF & Mystery Bookshop
10 Phila Street
Saratoga Springs NY 12866

Scotland Yard Books
556 Green Bay Road
Winnetka IL 60093

Seattle Book Center
2231 2nd Avneue
Seattle WA 98121

Seattle Mystery Bookshop
117 Cherry Street
Seattle WA 98104

Second Story Books
12160 Parklawn Drive
Rockville MD 20852

SF & Mystery Bookshop
752½ N. Highland Avenue NE
Atlanta GA 30306

Sherlock's Home
5624 East 2nd Street
Long Beach CA 90803

Snoop Sisters Mystery Book Shop
566 N. Indian Rocks Road
Belleair Bluffs FL 34640

Spade & Archer Mystery Bookstore
810 Third Avenue #440
Seattle WA 98104

Spenser's Mystery Bookshop
314 Newbury Street
Boston MA 02115

Tattered Cover Book Store
2955 E. First Avenue
Denver CO 80206

The Book Baron
1235 S. Magnolia Avenue
Anaheim CA 92804

The Bookcellar Cafe
1971 Massachusetts Avenue
Cambridge MA 02140

The Book Stalker
4907 Yaple Avenue
Santa Barbara CA 93111

The Book Sleuth
2513 W. Colorado Avenue
Colorado Springs CO 80904

The Corner Shop
116 East Water
Portland IN 47371

The Haunted Bookshop
100 Elmwood Avenue
Buffalo NY 14201

The Mysterious Bookshop
129 West 56th Street
New York NY 10019

The Mysterious Bookshop
8763 Beverly Boulevard
West Hollywood CA 90069

The Mystery Annex
1407 Ocean Front Walk
Venice CA 90291

The Mystery Lover's Bookshop
314 Allegheny River Boulevard
Oakmont PA 15139

The Mystery Bookstore
6906 Snider Plaza
Dallas TX 75205

The Mystery Bookshop
7700 Old Georgetown Road
Bethesda MD 20814

The Raven Bookstore
8 East 7th Street
Lawrence KS 66044

The Rue Morgue
946 Pearl Street
Boulder CO 80302

The Subject Is Murder
1183 Garden Place
Norcross GA 30093

Tower Books
211 Main Street
Chico CA 95928

Uncle Buck's Mysteries
390 Oak Hill Drive
Belleville IL 62223

Uncle Edgar's Mystery Bookstore
2864 Chicago Avenue South
Minneapolis MN 55407

Vagabond Books
2076 Westwood Boulevard
Los Angeles CA 90025

Whodunit
1931 Chestnut
Philadelphia PA 19103

CONTRIBUTOR NOTES

Harold Adams has published ten mystery novels, including nine in the Carl Wilcox series, whose most recent addition, *The Man Who Was Taller Than God,* won the 1993 Minnesota Book Award for Best Mystery and is a Shamus Award nominee in the same category. Adams lives in Hopkins, Minnesota, a suburb of Minneapolis.

Margaret C. Albert is a public relations consultant with a special interest in western Pennsylvania history. She lives in Pittsburgh with her husband Walter, also a contributor to this volume, and two dogs and two cats.

Walter Albert is a retired Professor of French from the University of Pittsburgh. He is also the Edgar Award-winning author of *Detective and Mystery Fiction: An International Bibliography of Secondary Sources.* He lives in Pittsburgh with his wife, Peg, also a contributor to this volume. He has two dogs and two cats as well.

Harrison Arnston was the founder, chairman, and CEO of an automotive accessory manufacturing company. He retired in 1984 to pursue his dream of a writing career. He has published seven novels, including most recently *The Third Illusion.*

K. K. Beck is the author of nine mystery novels, her most recent, *Amateur Night,* is the second in the Hane DaSilva series. Beck has won acclaim for her articles, along with her fiction, which includes *The Body in the Cornflakes* and *The Body in the Volvo.* She lives in Seattle with her three children.

Mary Helen Becker owns and manages Booked For Murder in Madison, Wisconsin. She knows many of the midwestern authors of whom she writes.

Robert Bloch is best known for the novel *Psycho* which Alfred Hitchcock make into the great film, but Bloch has also written dozens of other novels, including *Night of the Ripper,* and hundreds of short stories. He is a past president of the Mystery Writers of America. His most recent work is the unauthorized autobiography, *Once Around the Bloch.*

Lawrence Block has written over 35 mysteries, several writing primers, and three short story collections. He is a two-time winner of the Edgar Allan Poe—including most recently *A Dance at the Slaughterhouse* for Best Novel—Shamus, and Maltese Falcon awards, and has also received the Nero Wolfe Award. He and his wife share a small Greenwich Village apartment.

Simon Brett, a former president of the British Crime Writers' Association, has written fourteen Charles Paris mysteries, four Mrs. Pargeter novels, a collection of short stories, and two novels of psychological suspense, including *A Shock to the System,* which was made into the film starring Michael Caine. He and his family live in England.

Dorothy Cannell is the author of the Ellie Haskell mysteries. The series debut, *The Thin Woman,* which won the Best Paperback Novel of the Year award from the Romance Writers of America, is considered by many to be one of the best cozy mysteries to be written in the last decade. *The Widows Club* was an Agatha Award nominee for Best Novel. She was born in Nottingham, England, and currently resides in Peoria, Illinois.

Elaine Raco Chase has published several novels in the mystery field and has been very active in Sisters in Crime. She is the editor of a forthcoming anthology entitled *Partners in Crime.*

Max Allan Collins is the Shamus Award-winning author of some thirty novels of mystery and suspense. For many years he has written the internationally syndicated comic strip "Dick Tracy."

Bill Crider is the author of several mystery and suspense novels, including six in the Sheriff Dan Rhodes series. He is the chairman of the Department of English at Alvin Community College in Alvin, Texas. He has contributed to most of the journals and critical works devoted to the crime fiction field.

Barbara D'Amato's four mystery novels have won a substantial following among readers, and a chorous of praise from critics. Barbara is very active with the Mystery Writers of America's Midwest chapter and helps organize the annual Dark and Stormy Night seminars held in Chicago.

Dorothy Salisbury Davis is a seven-time Edgar nominee and in 1985 she was recognized by the Mystery Writers of America as a Grand Master (for lifetime achievement).

William DeAndrea has twice won the Edgar. He has written in many fields—most notably, perhaps, the difficult genre of espionage, in which he manages to combine wit and terror, no small task.

Carole Nelson Douglas, a former journalist in St. Paul, Minnesota, is the author of several mystery (including the Irene Adler and Midnight Louie series), fantasy and romantic suspense novels. She currently lives in Fort

Worth, Texas, with her kaleidoscope-artist husband and an excess of cats.

David Everson has published six novels all involving Robert Miles, private detective. Two of them were nominated for Shamus awards. He is a professor of Political Studies and Public Affairs at Sangamon State University in Springfield, Illinois.

Jan Grape is a contributing editor to *Mystery Scene* magazine and is editor of the PWA newsletter. She has had short stories published and is currently working on a novel. She runs the only mystery bookstore in Austin, Texas, with her husband Elmer.

Douglas G. Greene is one of the acknowledged experts on the "locked room" or "impossible crime" story. He has edited, with Robert Adey, two anthologies devoted to these stories. He is the author of a forthcoming biography of John Dickson Carr.

Brian Harper is the pseudonym of a well-known horror writer, one whom Stephen King said is "very, very good."

Carolyn G. Hart is the author of the "Death on Demand" mysteries featuring Annie and Max Darling. She is the first writer to win all three major mystery awards (the Agatha, Anthony, and Macavity). Her most recent work debuted a new series, featuring sixty-ish sleuth Henrie O'Dwyer, in August of 1993. Hart lives with her husband Phil in Oklahoma City.

Joan Hess is the author of eight (and counting) Claire Malloy mysteries and seven (and counting) books in the Maggody series, which will soon be a prime-time television sit-com. She has received numerous awards and nominations for her mysteries, including the American Mystery Award, the *Drood Review* Reader's Award, the Agatha Award, and the Macavity Award.

Edward D. Hoch has compiled several mystery anthologies and is the author of several novels. But he is best known as one of the most prolific mystery/suspense short story writers in the field with over 800 to his credit. Hoch is the past president of Mystery Writers of America and lives in Rochester, New York, with his wife Patricia.

Hugh Holton is a twenty-three year veteran of the Chicago Police Department and the author of several novels. He is a frequent panelist at mystery conventions.

Marilis Hornidge is a book reviewer of esteem and stature, particularly in the area of traditional mysteries, about which she writes with grace and wisdom.

Allen J. Hubin is the founding editor of *The Armchair Detective* (TAD) and author of *The Bibliography of Crime Fiction* (1979), the revision *Crime Fiction 1749–1980: A Comprehensive Bibliography* (1984) and the supplement *1981–1985 Supplement to Crime Fiction 1749–1980* (1988). Hubin received a special Edgar Award from the Mystery Writers of America in 1977 for his work editing TAD, and another Edgar in 1980 for *The Bibliography of Crime Fiction.*

Dorothy B. Hughes was one of the foremost writers and critics of her generation. Her greatest novels include *Ride the Pink Horse* and *The Fallen Sparrow,* and *In a Lonely Place,* all of which were made into successful movies.

Janet Hutchings is the current editor of *Ellery Queen's Mystery Magazine.*

Maxim Jakubowski is the owner of London's crime bookstore, Murder One, the world's only mystery "superstore." Jakubowski is a frequent reviewer for several newspapers and journals in England, along with being an editor and publisher of several works about crime fiction, science fiction, fantasy, film, and music.

H. R. F. Keating is one of Britain's most esteemed mystery novelists and reviewers. Most of his crime novels are set in India and feature Inspector Ghote.

Stephen King is not only a world-famous author, he's also a phenomenon, being one of those extremely rare writers who is as well known as major rock stars or movie actors. He has written numerous bestsellers, including *The Shining* and *Gerald's Game.*

Marvin Lachman, coauthor and senior editor of the Edgar Award-winning *Encyclopedia of Mystery and Detection* (1976), is a frequent contributor and book reviewer for *The Armchair Detective.*

Wendi Lee is the author of *Rogue's Gold* and other highly acclaimed western novels under the name W. W. Lee as well as dozens of articles and short stories.

Ed McBain has written countless mystery novels, including the Eighty-Seventh Precinct and Matthew Hope series, under this name and several pseudonyms. McBain was the recipient of the MWA's Grand Master Award. *Newsweek* rated his novel *Ice* as one of the ten best crime novels of all time.

John McCarty has written more than a dozen books on films and filmmakers, notably *Thrillers: Seven Decades of Classic Film Suspense* and *Movie Psychos and Madmen,* both of which were awarded highest marks by *Mystery Scene* reviewers.

John D. MacDonald graduated from Syracuse University and received an MBA from the Harvard Business School. He authored over 70 novels and is best known for his Travis McGee series. He was a past president of the MWA and received the organization's Grand Master Award in 1972. Other honors included winning the Benjamin Franklin award for short story, 1955; Grand Prix de Littérature Policiè, 1964; and the American Book Award, 1980. He passed away at the age of 70 in December of 1986.

Ralph McInerney is both an educator and a highly acclaimed mystery novelist. His Father Dowling novels are popular both on television and in bookstores.

Charlotte MacLeod (a.k.a. Alisa Craig) is the author of almost thirty adult mysteries as well as numerous young adult books. She was the recipient of a Lifetime Achievement Award at the Toronto Bouchercon XXIII and has won five American Mystery Awards, a Nero Wolfe Award, and two Edgar nominations. She lives in Durham, Maine.

Sharron McElmeel has authored two dozen books about writers and the books they write for children and young adults. Her articles and book reviews have appeared in *Mystery Scene* and *Library Talk* among many other publications.

Margaret Maron is the author of *Bootlegger's Daughter,* the 1993 Edgar Award winner for Best Novel, and the first in a new series featuring Deborah Knott. Maron, a past president of Sisters in Crime, has also written several books in the Lieutenant Sigfrid Harald series and has been nominated for the Anthony, the Macavity, and the American Mystery awards. She lives with her artist husband near Raleigh, North Carolina.

Kate Mattes is owner of Kate's Mystery Books in Cambridge, Mass, and the book reviewer for the *Boston Observer.* Kate was recently named the "Bookseller Who Has Made a Difference" by the Women's National Booksellers' Association.

Barbara Michaels is Elizabeth Peters is Barbara Mertz. Under any name she is a well respected and widely read writer. Her most popular series may be Amelia Peabody Emerson, now seven books long.

Christina Mierau is a new writer who practices both fiction and nonfiction. Her experiences at the Nancy Drew convention were especially gratifying to her, as she related in her fine piece on Nancy Drew fans of all ages.

Marlys Millhiser has written seven novels of mystery and suspense, including two in the Charlie Greene series. She has served as regional vice president for the Rocky Mountain chapter of the Mystery Writers of America.

Marcia Muller created the first of the contemporary female private eyes in Sharon McCone. She is also an accomplished anthologist and along with Bill Pronzini compiled the great reference work *1001 Midnights.*

Warren Murphy perhaps protests too much when he labels himself just another series writer. In addition to his successful series, he was written several dozen mainstream books that have won him twelve national awards, including two Edgars and a Shamus. He's also a screenwriter, with such major films as "The Eiger Sanction" and "Lethal Weapon II" to his credit.

Donna Huston Murray is a regular contributor to *Mystery Scene* and other suspense publications. She is also a knowing observer of mystery conventions, which grow in number every year.

Robert Napier is editor of *Mystery and Detective Monthly,* the field's only "letterzine." He was an honored guest at the second Midwest Mystery Convention.

Ellen Nehr is a reviewer for *Columbus Dispatch* and *The Bloomsbury Review* and formerly a senior contributing editor to *Mystery Scene* magazine. She currently publishes the review, *Murder Ad Lib,* and is one of the mystery/suspense field's most respected and knowledgeable aficionados, collectors, and reviewers of crime fiction.

Joan Lowery Nixon is the only author to have three Edgar Awards in the juvenile/young adult category. She is one of the best loved and most respected writers in the YA field. She lives in Houston with her husband Nick.

Vin Packer is the pseudonym of a prominent Young Adult writer, a woman who distinguished herself first in the crime field and then in the demanding world of fiction for children and teenagers. She has won numerous national awards for her fiction.

Barbara Paul is the author of more than fifteen novels. One of her series involves New York City Police Sergeant Marian Larch. Her most recent book is *The Apostrophe Thief.*

Nancy Pickard is the author of the award-winning "Jenny Cain" mystery series, including *Say No to Murder,* winner of the first annual Anthony Award, *Marriage is Murder,* winner of the Macavity Award, *Bum Steer* and *I.O.U.,* winners of the 1990 and 1991 Agatha Award for Best Novels. She lives in Kansas.

Bill Pronzini is a five-time Edgar nominee. He is, among other things, the author of the highly acclaimed series about the Nameless Detective, and, with his wife Marcia Muller, co-authored the great reference work *1001 Midnights.*

Mike Ripley is the crime fiction critic of the *Daily Telegraph* in London and the author of the "Angel" series of comedy thrillers. He has twice won the Crime Writers' Association's "Last Laugh" Award for humorous crime writing.

Janet A. Rudolph is the founder of Mystery Readers International and a columnist for both *Mystery Scene* and *The Armchair Detective.* She is also writer/director of Murder on the Menu, an audience participation theater company.

Michael Seidman is mystery editor of Walker Books and the author of many short stories and two exceptionally good books on the subject of writing, *From Print-Out to Published* and *Living the Dream.*

Lee Server's *Danger is My Business* is possibly the best book ever published about the pulp magazines. Server has a great interest in the literature of the thirties, forties, and fifties, and a love for the "junk" culture that is fun to be part of.

Walter and Jean Shine are among the world's foremost experts on the work of John D. MacDonald. Among the other works devoted to him they have published the *John D. MacDonald Bio-Bibliography.*

Charles L. P. Silet is a professor and a writer. His non-fiction pieces appear in a variety of magazines.

Charles Spicer is a senior editor at St. Martin's Press and a noted expert on the subject of true crime books.

Serita Stevens authored *Deadly Doses: A Writer's Guide to Poisons* and co-authored *Red Sea, Dead Sea* and *Bagels for Tea* with Rayanne Moore. She lives in Mission Hills, California.

George Tuttle is a scholar of the hard-boiled, a man who is able to look at the entire span of the sub-genre from its origins in the pulps to its hey-day in the paperback fifties.

Anne Wingate is a former police officer who holds a Ph.D. in English. She has written five novels in the Mark Shigata series. She is also Lee Martin.

Margaret Yorke, who lives in a village in Buckinhamshire, England, has written more than thirty novels since 1957. She has also been the chairperson of the British Crime Writers' Association.

Angela and Barry T. Zeman: Barry Zeman is currently the Mystery Writers of America archivist, librarian and director of fund raising. He and his wife Angela are both on the Board of Directors of the National and New York Chapters of MWA, and are working together on a mystery novel.

Mark Richard Zubro is the author of several gay mysteries, including the Lambda Award-winning "Tom and Scott" series and the "Paul Turner" series. When not writing, he is a schoolteacher and union president in Mokena, Illinois, and is also the former president of the Midwest chapter of the MWA.

About the Editors

Ed Gorman is a suspense novelist whom *The Bloomsbury Review* called "the poet of dark suspense." His novels include *Shadow Games, The Autumn Dead,* and *The Night Remembers.* His story collection *Prisoners* has been widely praised.

Martin H. Greenberg has been called "the world's most respected anthologist." He has edited well over 400 books of various kinds and has been associated with some of the most prestigious writers of fiction alive, including Dean Koontz, Tom Clancy, and Robert Ludlum.

Larry Segriff is a young fiction writer whose work has appeared in more than two dozen anthologies and magazines, a number of which have been judged "remarkable" and praised by such writers as Roger Zelazny.

Jon L. Breen is the double Edgar Award-winning author of *What About Murder: A Guide to Books about Mystery and Detective Fiction* and *Novel Verdicts: A Guide to Courtroom Fiction* among many other works including three other critical works and six novels. He also writes the review column for *Ellery Queen's Mystery Magazine.*

INDEX